Innovations, Developments, and Applications of Semantic Web and Information Systems

Miltiadis D. Lytras
American College of Greece, Greece

Naif Aljohani
King Abdulaziz University, Saudi Arabia

Ernesto Damiani
University of Milan, Italy

Kwok Tai Chui
City University of Hong Kong, Hong Kong

A volume in the Advances in Web Technologies
and Engineering (AWTE) Book Series

Published in the United States of America by
    IGI Global
    Engineering Science Reference (an imprint of IGI Global)
    701 E. Chocolate Avenue
    Hershey PA, USA 17033
    Tel: 717-533-8845
    Fax: 717-533-8661
    E-mail: cust@igi-global.com
    Web site: http://www.igi-global.com

Library of Congress Cataloging-in-Publication Data

Names: Lytras, Miltiadis D., 1973- editor.
Title: Innovations, developments, and applications of semantic web and
  information systems / Miltiadis D. Lytras, Naif Aljohani, Ernesto Damiani,
  and Kwok Tai Chui, editors.
Description: Hershey, PA : Engineering Science Reference, [2018] | Includes
  bibliographical references.
Identifiers: LCCN 2017034170| ISBN 9781522550426 (hardcover) | ISBN
  9781522550433 (ebook)
Subjects: LCSH: Semantic Web. | Information storage and retrieval systems.
Classification: LCC TK5105.88815 .I55 2018 | DDC 025.042/7--dc23 LC record available at https://lccn.loc.
gov/2017034170

This book is published in the IGI Global book series Advances in Web Technologies and Engineering (AWTE) (ISSN: 2328-2762; eISSN: 2328-2754)

British Cataloguing in Publication Data
A Cataloguing in Publication record for this book is available from the British Library.

All work contributed to this book is new, previously-unpublished material. The views expressed in this book are those of the authors, but not necessarily of the publisher.

For electronic access to this publication, please contact: eresources@igi-global.com.

Advances in Web Technologies and Engineering (AWTE) Book Series

Ghazi I. Alkhatib
The Hashemite University, Jordan
David C. Rine
George Mason University, USA

ISSN:2328-2762
EISSN:2328-2754

MISSION

The **Advances in Web Technologies and Engineering (AWTE) Book Series** aims to provide a platform for research in the area of Information Technology (IT) concepts, tools, methodologies, and ethnography, in the contexts of global communication systems and Web engineered applications. Organizations are continuously overwhelmed by a variety of new information technologies, many are Web based. These new technologies are capitalizing on the widespread use of network and communication technologies for seamless integration of various issues in information and knowledge sharing within and among organizations. This emphasis on integrated approaches is unique to this book series and dictates cross platform and multidisciplinary strategy to research and practice.

The **Advances in Web Technologies and Engineering (AWTE) Book Series** seeks to create a stage where comprehensive publications are distributed for the objective of bettering and expanding the field of web systems, knowledge capture, and communication technologies. The series will provide researchers and practitioners with solutions for improving how technology is utilized for the purpose of a growing awareness of the importance of web applications and engineering.

COVERAGE

- IT Readiness and Technology Transfer Studies
- IT Education and Training
- Information Filtering and Display Adaptation Techniques for Wireless Devices
- Web Systems Performance Engineering Studies
- Software Agent-Based Applications
- Ontology And Semantic Web Studies
- Web User Interfaces Design, Development, and Usability Engineering Studies
- Security, Integrity, Privacy, and Policy Issues
- Case Studies Validating Web-Based IT Solutions
- Data and Knowledge Capture and Quality Issues

IGI Global is currently accepting manuscripts for publication within this series. To submit a proposal for a volume in this series, please contact our Acquisition Editors at Acquisitions@igi-global.com or visit: http://www.igi-global.com/publish/.

Titles in this Series

For a list of additional titles in this series, please visit: www.igi-global.com/book-series

701 East Chocolate Avenue, Hershey, PA 17033, USA
Tel: 717-533-8845 x100 • Fax: 717-533-8661
E-Mail: cust@igi-global.com • www.igi-global.com

To all the people all over the world that honor, value and contribute to the international research collaboration that is visioning a better world for all the people, based on peace, happiness, prosperity, education, mutual respect and social inclusive sustainable development. To all our students that inspire our minds and souls.

Table of Contents

Detailed Table of Contents

In many applications, one has to fetch and assemble pieces of information coming from more than one source for building a semantic warehouse offering more advanced query capabilities. This chapter describes the corresponding requirements and challenges, and focuses on the aspects of quality, value and evolution of the warehouse. It details various metrics (or measures) for quantifying the connectivity of a warehouse and consequently the warehouse's ability to answer complex queries. The proposed metrics allow someone to get an overview of the contribution (to the warehouse) of each source and to quantify the value of the entire warehouse. Moreover, the paper shows how the metrics can be used for monitoring a warehouse after a reconstruction, thereby reducing the cost of quality checking and understanding its evolution over time. The behaviour of these metrics is demonstrated in the context of a real and operational semantic warehouse for the marine domain. Finally, the chapter discusses novel ways to exploit such metrics in global scale and for visualization purposes.

#### Chapter 2

This chapter describes the KnowledgeStore, a scalable, fault-tolerant, and Semantic Web grounded open-source storage system to jointly store, manage, retrieve, and query interlinked structured and unstructured data, especially designed to manage all the data involved in Knowledge Extraction applications. The chapter presents the concept, design, function and implementation of the KnowledgeStore, and reports on its concrete usage in four application scenarios within the NewsReader EU project, where it has been successfully used to store and support the querying of millions of news articles interlinked with billions of RDF triples, both extracted from text and imported from Linked Open Data sources.

Chapter 3

Wei Shen, Nankai University, China
Jianyong Wang, Tsinghua University, China & Jiangsu Normal University, China
Ping Luo, Chinese Academy of Sciences, China
Min Wang, Visa Inc., USA

Relation extraction from the Web data has attracted a lot of attention recently. However, little work has been done when it comes to the enterprise data regardless of the urgent needs to such work in real applications (e.g., E-discovery). One distinct characteristic of the enterprise data (in comparison with the Web data) is its low redundancy. Previous work on relation extraction from the Web data largely relies on the data's high redundancy level and thus cannot be applied to the enterprise data effectively. This chapter reviews related work on relation extraction and introduces an unsupervised hybrid framework REACTOR for semantic relation extraction over enterprise data. REACTOR combines a statistical method, classification, and clustering to identify various types of relations among entities appearing in the enterprise data automatically. REACTOR was evaluated over a real-world enterprise data set from HP that contains over three million pages and the experimental results show its effectiveness.

Chapter 4

Zenun Kastrati, Norwegian University of Science and Technology (NTNU), Norway
Ali Shariq Imran, Norwegian University of Science and Technology (NTNU), Norway
Sule Yildirim Yayilgan, Norwegian University of Science and Technology (NTNU), Norway

The wide use of ontology in different applications has resulted in a plethora of automatic approaches for population and enrichment of an ontology. Ontology enrichment is an iterative process where the existing ontology is continuously updated with new concepts. A key aspect in ontology enrichment process is the concept learning approach. A learning approach can be a linguistic-based, statistical-based, or hybrid-based that employs both linguistic as well as statistical-based learning approaches. This chapter presents a concept enrichment model that combines contextual and semantic information of terms. The proposed model called SEMCON employs a hybrid concept learning approach utilizing functionalities from statistical and linguistic ontology learning techniques. The model introduced for the first time two statistical features that have shown to improve the overall score ranking of highly relevant terms for concept enrichment. The chapter also gives some recommendations and possible future research directions based on the discussion in following sections.

Chapter 5

María Poveda-Villalón, Universidad Politécnica de Madrid, Spain
Asunción Gómez-Pérez, Universidad Politécnica de Madrid, Spain
Mari Carmen Suárez-Figueroa, Universidad Politécnica de Madrid, Spain

The first contribution of this paper consists on a live catalogue of pitfalls that extends previous works on modeling errors with pitfalls resulting from an empirical analysis of numerous ontologies. Such a catalogue classifies pitfalls according to the Structural, Functional and Usability-Profiling dimensions. For each pitfall, we include the value of its importance level (critical, important and minor). The second contribution is the description of OntOlogy Pitfall Scanner (OOPS!), a widely used tool for detecting pitfalls in ontologies and targeted at newcomers and domain experts unfamiliar with description logics and ontology implementation languages. The tool operates independently of any ontology development platform and is available through a web application and a web service. The evaluation of the system is provided both through a survey of users' satisfaction and worldwide usage statistics. In addition, the system is also compared with existing ontology evaluation tools in terms of coverage of pitfalls detected.

Chapter 6

    Souheyl Mallat, Faculty of Science of Monastir, Tunisia
    Emna Hkiri, LATICE Laboratory, Tunisia
    Mounir Zrigui, Faculty of Science of Monastir, Tunisia

In the aim of natural language processing applications improvement, we focus on statistical approach to semantic indexing for multilingual text documents based on conceptual network formalism. We propose to use this formalism as an indexing language to represent the descriptive concepts and their weighting. Our contribution is based on two steps. In the first step, we propose the extraction of index terms using the multilingual lexical resource EuroWordNet (EWN). In the second step, we pass from the representation of index terms to the representation of index concepts through conceptual network formalism. This network is generated using the EWN resource and pass by a classification step based on association rules modelOur proposed indexing approach can be applied to text documents in various languages. Next, we apply the same statistical process regardless of the language in order to extract the significant concepts and their associated weights. We prove that the proposed indexing approach provides encouraging results.

Chapter 7

    Slobodan Beliga, University of Rijeka, Croatia
    Ana Meštrović, University of Rijeka, Croatia
    Sanda Martinčić-Ipšić, University of Rijeka, Croatia

This chapter presents a novel Selectivity-Based Keyword Extraction (SBKE) method, which extracts keywords from the source text represented as a network. The node selectivity value is calculated from a weighted network as the average weight distributed on the links of a single node and is used in the procedure of keyword candidate ranking and extraction. The selectivity slightly outperforms an extraction based on the standard centrality measures. Therefore, the selectivity and its modification – generalized selectivity as the node centrality measures are included in the SBKE method. Selectivity-based extraction does not require linguistic knowledge as it is derived purely from statistical and structural information of the network and it can be easily ported to new languages and used in a multilingual scenario. The true potential of the proposed SBKE method is in its generality, portability and low computation costs, which positions it as a strong candidate for preparing collections which lack human annotations for keyword extraction.

Brian Walshe, Barclays, UK
Rob Brennan, Trinity College Dublin, Ireland
Declan O'Sullivan, Trinity College Dublin, Ireland

Linked Data consists of many structured data knowledge bases that have been interlinked, often using equivalence statements. These equivalences usually take the form of owl:sameAs statements linking individuals, links between classes are far less common Often, the lack of class links is because their relationships cannot be described as one to one equivalences. Instead, complex correspondences referencing logical combinations of multiple entities are often needed to describe how the classes in an ontology are related to classes in a second ontology. This chapter introduces a novel Bayesian Restriction Class Correspondence Estimation (Bayes-ReCCE) algorithm, an extensional approach to detecting complex correspondences between classes. Bayes-ReCCE operates by analysing features of matched individuals in the knowledge bases, and uses Bayesian inference to search for complex correspondences between the classes these individuals belong to. Bayes-ReCCE is designed to be capable of providing meaningful results even when only small numbers of matched instances are available.

Balaji Jagan, Anna University, India
Ranjani Parthasarathi, Anna University, India
Geetha T. V., Anna University, India

Customization of information from web documents is an immense job that involves mainly the shortening of original texts. Extractive methods use surface level and statistical features for the selection of important sentences. In contrast, abstractive methods need a formal semantic representation, where the selection of important components and the rephrasing of the selected components are carried out using the semantic features associated with the words as well as the context. In this paper, we propose a semi-supervised bootstrapping approach for the identification of important components for abstractive summarization. The input to the proposed approach is a fully connected semantic graph of a document, where the semantic graphs are constructed for sentences, which are then connected by synonym concepts and co-referring entities to form a complete semantic graph. The direction of the traversal of nodes is determined by a modified spreading activation algorithm, where the importance of the nodes and edges are decided, based on the node and its connected edges under consideration.

Floriano Scioscia, Polytechnic University of Bari, Italy
Michele Ruta, Polytechnic University of Bari, Italy
Giuseppe Loseto, Polytechnic University of Bari, Italy
Filippo Gramegna, Polytechnic University of Bari, Italy
Saverio Ieva, Polytechnic University of Bari, Italy
Agnese Pinto, Polytechnic University of Bari, Italy
Eugenio Di Sciascio, Polytechnic University of Bari, Italy

The Semantic Web of Things (SWoT) aims to support smart semantics-enabled applications and services in pervasive contexts. Due to architectural and performance issues, most Semantic Web reasoners are often impractical to be ported: they are resource consuming and are basically designed for standard inference tasks on large ontologies. On the contrary, SWoT use cases generally require quick decision support through semantic matchmaking in resource-constrained environments. This paper describes Mini-ME (the Mini Matchmaking Engine), a mobile inference engine designed from the ground up for the SWoT. It supports Semantic Web technologies and implements both standard (subsumption, satisfiability, classification) and non-standard (abduction, contraction, covering, bonus, difference) inference services for moderately expressive knowledge bases. In addition to an architectural and functional description, usage scenarios and experimental performance evaluation are presented on PC (against other popular Semantic Web reasoners), smartphone and embedded single-board computer testbeds.

Chapter 11

Ali Hasnain, NUI Galway, Ireland
Qaiser Mehmood, NUI Galway, Ireland
Syeda Sana e Zainab, NUI Galway, Ireland
Aidan Hogan, DCC, University of Chile, Chile

Access to hundreds of knowledge bases has been made available on the Web through SPARQL endpoints. Unfortunately, few endpoints publish descriptions of their content. It is thus unclear how agents can learn about the content of a given endpoint. This research investigates the feasibility of a system that gathers information about public endpoints by querying directly about their own content. It would thus be feasible to build a centralised catalogue describing the content indexed by individual endpoints by issuing them SPARQL 1.1 queries; this catalogue could be searched and queried by agents looking for endpoints with content they are interested in. However, the coverage of the catalogue is bounded by the limitations of public endpoints themselves: some may not support SPARQL 1.1, some may return partial responses, some may throw exceptions for expensive aggregate queries, etc. The goal is twofold: 1) using VoID as a bar, to empirically investigate the extent to which endpoints can describe their own content, and 2) to build and analyse the capabilities of an online catalogue.

Chapter 12

Dora Melo, Coimbra Business School, Portugal & Laboratory of Informatics, Systems, and Parallelism (LISP), Portugal
Irene Pimenta Rodrigues, University of Évora, Portugal & Laboratory of Informatics, Systems, and Parallelism (LISP), Portugal
Vitor Beires Nogueira, University of Évora, Portugal & Laboratory of Informatics, Systems, and Parallelism (LISP), Portugal

The Semantic Web as a knowledge base gives to the Question Answering systems the capabilities needed to go well beyond the usual word matching in the documents and find a more accurate answer, without needing the user intervention to interpret the documents returned. In this chapter, the authors introduce a Dialogue Manager that, throughout the analysis of the question and the type of expected answer, provides accurate answers to the questions posed in Natural Language. The Dialogue Manager not only represents the semantics of the questions but also represents the structure of the discourse, including the user intentions and the questions' context, adding the ability to deal with multiple answers and providing justified answers. The system performance is evaluated by comparing with similar question answering systems. Although the test suite is of small dimension, the results obtained are very promising.

Chapter 13

Andrea Ko, Corvinus University of Budapest, Hungary
Saira Gillani, Saudi Electronic University, Saudi Arabia

Manual ontology population and enrichment is a complex task that require professional experience involving a lot of efforts. The authors' paper deals with the challenges and possible solutions for semi-automatic ontology enrichment and population. ProMine has two main contributions; one is the semantic-based text mining approach for automatically identifying domain-specific knowledge elements; the other is the automatic categorization of these extracted knowledge elements by using Wiktionary. ProMine ontology enrichment solution was applied in IT audit domain of an e-learning system. After seven cycles of the application ProMine, the number of automatically identified new concepts are significantly increased and ProMine categorized new concepts with high precision and recall.

Chapter 14

Imelda Escamilla, Instituto Politécnico Nacional, Mexico
Miguel Torres Ruíz, Instituto Politécnico Nacional, Mexico
Marco Moreno Ibarra, Instituto Politécnico Nacional, Mexico
Vladimir Luna Soto, Instituto Politécnico Nacional, Mexico
Rolando Quintero, Instituto Politécnico Nacional, Mexico
Giovanni Guzmán, Instituto Politécnico Nacional, Mexico

Human ability to understand approximate references to locations, disambiguated by means of context and reasoning about spatial relationships, is the key to describe spatial environments and to share information about them. In this paper, we propose an approach for geocoding that takes advantage of the spatial relationships contained in the text of tweets, using semantic web, ontologies and spatial analyses. Microblog text has special characteristics (e.g. slang, abbreviations, acronyms, etc.) and thus represents a special variation of natural language. The main objective of this work is to associate spatial relationships found in text with a spatial footprint, to determine the location of the event described in the tweet. The feasibility of the proposal is demonstrated using a corpus of 200,000 tweets posted in Spanish related with traffic events in Mexico City.

Chapter 15

Ying Zhang, North China Electric Power University, China
Chaopeng Li, North China Electric Power University, China
Na Chen, Hebei Vocational College of Rail Transportation, China
Shaowen Liu, North China Electric Power University, China
Liming Du, North China Electric Power University, China
Zhuxiao Wang, North China Electric Power University, China
Miaomiao Ma, North China Electric Power University, China

Since large amount of geospatial data are produced by various sources, geospatial data integration is difficult because of the shortage of semantics. Despite standardised data format and data access protocols, such as Web Feature Service (WFS), can enable end-users with access to heterogeneous data stored in different formats from various sources, it is still time-consuming and ineffective due to the lack of semantics. To solve this problem, a prototype to implement the geospatial data integration is proposed by addressing the following four problems, i.e., geospatial data retrieving, modeling, linking and integrating. We mainly adopt four kinds of geospatial data sources to evaluate the performance of the proposed approach. The experimental results illustrate that the proposed linking method can get high performance in generating the matched candidate record pairs in terms of Reduction Ratio(RR), Pairs Completeness(PC), Pairs Quality(PQ) and F-score. The integrating results denote that each data source can get much Complementary Completeness(CC) and Increased Completeness(IC).

Foreword

Our societies are facing nowadays several critical challenges. One of them is the cultivation of a peace and creativity focused culture all over the world. Information systems research should promote this humanistic vision at its full capacity, capitalizing on international research collaborations honoring the contributions of individuals, groups, societies and nations.

The evolution of several technologies—including semantic web research—in the last decade can be seen as one more opportunity for the humanity to build unique, effective, innovative ways for the exploitation of knowledge and wisdom for advanced decision making and a social inclusive sustainable development.

The achievements of the semantic web and information systems research are magnificent. An entire sociotechnical ecosystem, of algorithms, methods, languages, tools, and applications is available for utilization in the real world context. Almost every domain of human activity can be benefited from the sophisticates semantic web research.

It is our distinct pleasure to present a volume, which is the outcome of the most amazing collaboration spanning several continents, involving accomplished scholars and educators, all of whom thought it was worthwhile to engage in a debate on added value of semantic web research towards a better society for all.

We take this opportunity to express our gratitude and say 'thank you' to all of the contributing authors individually for embracing our idea, joining the project aimed at the development of this edited volume, and sharing the outcomes of their research with us and the readers of this volume.

We are grateful to the publisher for the opportunity to open the important debate and reach the broad audience. Last but not least, we would like to thank our families and friends who were the witnesses of our work on this project. Any likely mistakes in the text are our own.

Miltiadis D. Lytras
American College of Greece, Greece

Naif Aljohani
King Abdulaziz University, Saudi Arabia

Ernesto Damiani
University of Milan, Italy

Kwok Tai Chui
City University of Hong Kong, Hong Kong

Preface

The evolution of Semantic Web and Information Systems research the last few years is magnificent. The integration of integrated approached to Ontology Engineering, combined with sophisticated methods and algorithms for Open Linked Data extraction, utilization and advanced decision making, create new opportunities for a bright future in our research domain. Additionally, significant research contributions in Logic and Reasoning capabilities of Semantic Web-enabled information systems provide new contexts for business exploitation.

From the other side the evolution of Cognitive Computing and the advanced capacity of Artificial Intelligence through Neural Networks, Machine learning and various other approaches sets the new vision. The promotion of a Cognitive Era for Semantic Web and Information Systems research.

We are happy for delivering this editing volume which in fact is a manifestation of some of the most interesting aspects of theoretical and applied research covering complementary facets of the semantic web phenomenon including topics like:

- Contextualization of Connectivity, Value and Evolution of a Semantic Warehouse.
- Management of Large Volumes of Interlinked Text and Knowledge.
- Analysis of methods and innovations on Semantic Relation Extraction over Enterprise Data.
- Introduction of a Learning Approach to Ontology Enrichment.
- Discussion of a pitfall-based system for ontology diagnosis.
- Exploration of fuzzy association rules in semantic network enrichment Improvement of the semantic indexing process.
- Elaboration on Keyword Extraction Based on Selectivity and Generalized Selectivity.
- Algorithms and sophisticated approaches on Detecting Restriction Class Correspondences in Linked Data.
- Discussion of Graph Based Abstractive Summarization: Compression of Semantic Graphs.
- Justification and empirical testing of Mini-ME matchmaker and reasoner for the Semantic Web of Things.
- Understanding Cataloguing the Context of Public SPARQL Endpoints.
- Promotion of Semantic Web Search through Natural Language Dialogues.
- Advanced methods for Ontology Maintenance through Semantic Text Mining: An Application for IT Governance Domain.
- Setting up and processing of Geocoding Tweets based on semantic web and ontologies.
- Semantic Web and Geospatial Unique Features based Geospatial Data Integration.

This book covers the discussion on the innovations, developments and applications of semantic web and information systems via 15 chapters. The summary of each chapter is given as follows.

The first chapter discusses the connectivity, value, evolution, requirements and challenges of semantic warehouse which is a new trend to support complex query. Five metrics have been proposed to quantify the semantic warehouse. They are connectivity metrics, metrics for comparing two sources, metrics for comparing a set of lattice-based sources, metrics for evaluation a single source and metrics for evaluating the entire semantic warehouse. More efforts are required to find out the metrics for quantifying literals and triples.

In Chapter 2, authors describe the KnowledgeStore, a scalable, fault-tolerant, and semantic web grounded open-source storage system for interlinking structured and unstructured data, aiming at presenting applications with a unified view over all the data resulting from Knowledge Extraction. Various scenarios (from 18k to 2.3M news articles) have been analyzed to verify the capability of KnowledgeStore in managing billions of interlinked text and knowledge.

A framework for semantic relation extraction from enterprise data (e.g., emails, web pages, databases and word processing files) has been proposed in Chapter 3. Differed from web data, enterprise data is characterized by low redundancy. The framework is a method which combines statistical method, classification and clustering algorithms to extract semantic relation from enterprise data. Statistical method can extract a set of representative entity pairs containing both positive and negative examples for the classifier. The classifier extracts related entity pairs as domain-independent features. A clustering algorithm is used to further identify the semantic relation between entity pairs.

The fourth chapter focuses on ontology enrichment which is an iterative process where the existing ontology is continuously updated based on new concepts. A hybrid concept learning approach has been adopted using statistical and linguistic ontology learning. This model introduces two statistical features namely term font size and font type to determine the context of a term. In addition to contextual information, the proposed method also incorporates the semantic information of terms using the lexical database WordNet and finally aggregates both contextual and semantic information of this term.

In the next chapter, Poveda-Villalón, Gómez-Pérez and Suárez-Figueroa have devoted efforts in ontology diagnosis using checklist of common errors against which the ontology is compared. The contribution of this chapter is two-fold. First, it consists of a live catalogue of pitfalls that extends previous works on modeling errors with pitfalls resulting from an empirical analysis of numerous ontologies. Such a catalogue classifies pitfalls according to the Structural, Functional and Usability-Profiling dimensions. Second, Ontology Pitfall Scanner is discussed as a tool for detecting pitfalls in ontologies and targeted at newcomers and domain experts unfamiliar with description logics and ontology implementation languages.

In Chapter 6, a statistical approach of semantic indexing of multilingual documents based on the conceptual network formalism is presented. This formalism naturally supports concepts and semantic relations between them. The extraction of concepts is divided into three parts. The first part is to identify simple and composite terms. Secondly, a weighting formula is applied on each term of a given document. This weighting is based on statistical and semantic measure. Lastly, a disambiguation process is carried out to examine the ambiguous terms in the context in which they appear in the document

Keyword extraction algorithm has been proposed in Chapter 7 based on selectivity and generalized selectivity. The node selectivity value is measured from a weighted network as the average weight distributed on the links of a single node and is used in the procedure of keyword candidate ranking and extraction. The generalized selectivity as the node centrality measures is included in the proposed method. It is worth mentioning that selectivity-based extraction does not require linguistic knowledge as it is derived purely from statistical and structural information of the network. Thus, it can be easily ported to any new language and used in multilingual scenario.

Chapter 8 aims at detecting restriction class correspondences in linked data. Linked Data consists of many structured data knowledge bases that have been interlinked. Many complex correspondences can be described as commonly re-occurring patterns, containing a small number of features. The proposed algorithm automates the process of finding complex correspondences which fit these patterns by searching for these features in matched instance data. Also, it is capable of detecting complex correspondences between the DBpedia, LinkedMDB and GeoNames knowledge bases.

A first of its kind semi-supervised bootstrapping approach via spreading activation is proposed in Chapter 9 which identifies the important components for abstractive summarization. While performing the spreading activation, the defined patterns match with the components of the semantic graph and the graph operations are applied iteratively to the selection of the important nodes. The tuples for performing each graph operation are defined, and set to each component in the pattern. The original spreading activation algorithm has been modified, by including the link information along with the node information, while the activation starts spreading over the graph.

In Chapter 10, the semantic web of things aims to support smart semantics-enabled applications and services in pervasive contexts. Due to architectural and performance issues, most Semantic Web reasoners are often impractical to be ported because they are resource consuming and are basically designed for standard inference tasks on large ontology. A mini matchmaking engine, a mobile inference engine is designed from the ground up for the semantic web of things.

When it comes to Chapter 11, it investigates the feasibility of a system that gathers information about public SPARQL endpoints by querying them directly about their own content. With the advancement of SPARQL 1.1, it is now possible to specify queries whose results would form a detailed profile of the content of the endpoint, comparable with a large subset of VoID. The main theme of this chapter is (1) using VoID as a bar, to empirically examine the extent to which public endpoints can describe their own content; and (2) to build and analyse the capabilities of a best-effort online catalogue of current endpoints based on the results collected.

In Chapter 12, authors have presented a dialogue manager for semantic web search. Throughout the analysis of the question and the type of the expected answer, it provides accurate answers to questions in natural language. The manager not only represents the question semantics but also the structure of the discourse. This helps to generate an answer that is more objective and with the information desired by the user. Hence, the system is able to deal with multiple answers and to provide justified answers.

Ko and Gillani deal with the challenges and possible solutions for semi-automatic ontology enrichment and population in Chapter 13. Manual ontology population and enrichment is a complex task that requires professional experience. Ontologies require regular maintenance regarding the changing environment. Manual maintenance work is error-prone and time consuming; a possible even semi-automatic support has a high added value. A framework namely ProMine is proposed for ontology learning and enrichment that uses lexical resources such as WorldNet and Wiktionary in combination with a domain Corpus. In addition, this chapter provides a review of ontology learning related literature and discussed the deficiencies of the approaches in the context of ProMine.

In Chapter 14, a methodology is proposed for the detection of geospatial real-world traffic-related events via analyzing the Twitter streaming, the ontology and user features. Results reveal that it can detect accurately whether clusters of tweets issued spatially close to each other, describing a real-world traffic-related event. The proposed geocoding approach is fully automatic, from the collection of tweets to visualization of the geographic objects that represent the traffic events.

The last chapter implements a prototype for geospatial data integration to address the issues of geospatial data retrieving, modeling, linking and integrating. Compared to traditional methods, the proposed method considers the geospatial data that has specific geospatial relationships, which is significant for linking but cannot be solved by the Semantic Web techniques directly. Such unique features can be used as geospatial data to implement the linking process.

Miltiadis D. Lytras
American College of Greece, Greece

Naif Aljohani
King Abdulaziz University, Saudi Arabia

Ernesto Damiani
University of Milan, Italy

Kwok Tai Chui
City University of Hong Kong, Hong Kong

Chapter 1
Connectivity, Value, and Evolution of a Semantic Warehouse

Michalis Mountantonakis
FORTH-ICS, Greece & University of Crete, Greece

Nikos Minadakis
FORTH-ICS, Greece

Yannis Marketakis
FORTH-ICS, Greece

Pavlos Fafalios
FORTH-ICS, Greece & University of Crete, Greece

Yannis Tzitzikas
FORTH-ICS, Greece & University of Crete, Greece

ABSTRACT

In many applications, one has to fetch and assemble pieces of information coming from more than one source for building a semantic warehouse offering more advanced query capabilities. This chapter describes the corresponding requirements and challenges, and focuses on the aspects of quality, value and evolution of the warehouse. It details various metrics (or measures) for quantifying the connectivity of a warehouse and consequently the warehouse's ability to answer complex queries. The proposed metrics allow someone to get an overview of the contribution (to the warehouse) of each source and to quantify the value of the entire warehouse. Moreover, the paper shows how the metrics can be used for monitoring a warehouse after a reconstruction, thereby reducing the cost of quality checking and understanding its evolution over time. The behaviour of these metrics is demonstrated in the context of a real and operational semantic warehouse for the marine domain. Finally, the chapter discusses novel ways to exploit such metrics in global scale and for visualization purposes.

DOI: 10.4018/978-1-5225-5042-6.ch001

INTRODUCTION

An increasing number of datasets are already available as Linked Data. For exploiting this wealth of data, and building domain specific applications, in many cases there is the need for fetching and assembling pieces of information coming from more than one sources. These pieces are then used for constructing a *Semantic Warehouse*, offering thereby more complete and efficient browsing and query services (in comparison to those offered by the underlying sources). The term *Semantic Warehouse* (for short warehouse) refer to a read-only set of RDF triples fetched (and transformed) from different sources that aims at serving a particular set of query requirements. In general, there exists *domain independent* warehouses, like the Sindice (Oren, et al., 2008) and SWSE (Hogan, et al., 2011), but also *domain specific*, like TaxonConcept (n.d.) and the MarineTLO-based warehouse (Tzitzikas, et al., 2013, November). Domain specific warehouses aim to serve particular needs, for particular communities of users, consequently their "quality" requirements are stricter. It is therefore worth elaborating on the process that can be used for building such warehouses, and on the related difficulties and challenges.

In brief, for building such a warehouse one has to tackle various challenges and questions, e.g., how to define the objectives and its scope, how to *connect* the fetched pieces of information (common URIs or literals are not always there), how to tackle the various issues of provenance that arise, and how to keep the warehouse fresh (i.e., how to automate its reconstruction or refreshing). This chapter has focused on the following questions:

- How to measure the value and quality of the warehouse (since this is important for e-science)?
- How to monitor its quality after each reconstruction or refreshing (as the underlying sources change)?
- How to understand the evolution of the warehouse?
- How to measure the contribution of each source to the warehouse, and hence deciding which sources to keep or exclude?

These questions have been encountered in the context of a real semantic warehouse for the *marine* domain which harmonizes and connects information from different sources of marine information[1]. Most past approaches have focused on the notion of conflicts (Michelfeit & Knap, 2012), and have not paid attention to *connectivity*. The term *connectivity* express the degree up to which the contents of the warehouse form a connected graph that can serve, ideally in a correct and complete way, the query requirements of the warehouse, while making evident how each source contributes to this degree. Besides, connectivity is a notion which can be exploited in the task of dataset or endpoint selection.

To this end, this chapter summarizes the methods and metrics introduced in Tzitzikas et al. (2014, March) and Mountantonakis et al. (2016) for quantifying the connectivity of a warehouse, reports their implementation on real datasets, and discusses interesting and novel works that exploit them. What the authors call *metrics* could be also called *measures*, i.e. they should not be confused with distance functions. These metrics allow someone to get an overview of the contribution (to the warehouse) of each source (enabling the discrimination of the important from the non-important sources) and to quantify the value (benefit) of such a warehouse. In a nutshell, this chapter presents:

- An extensive report on related literature on *dataset quality* and *quality assessment frameworks*, as well as the placement of the presented work.
- A set of *connectivity metrics* for comparing pairs and sets (lattice-based) of sources.
- A set of *single-valued metrics* for evaluating the overall contribution and the value of each source as well as the quality of the entire warehouse. The former makes easier and faster the identification and inspection of pathological cases (redundant sources or sources that do not contribute new information).
- Methods that exploit the proposed metrics for *understanding* and *monitoring* the *evolution* of the warehouse.
- Novel ways for exploiting such metrics in *global scale* and for *visualization* purposes.

The rest of this chapter is organized as follows: The second section describes the main requirements, and provides the context by briefly describing the process used for constructing such warehouses. The third section describes related work and what distinguishes the current one. The fourth section introduces the quality metrics and demonstrates their use. The fifth section discusses how these metrics can be used for monitoring and understanding the evolution of the warehouse over time, while the sixth section describes novel ways for exploiting the metrics in global scale and for visualizing LOD datasets. Finally, the seventh section identifies future research directions, while the last section concludes the chapter and identifies directions for future research.

BACKGROUND

Context and Requirements

The spark for this work was the recently completed *iMarine* project (and the ongoing *BlueBRIDGE* project) that offers an operational distributed infrastructure that serves hundreds of scientists from the marine domain. As regards semantically structured information, the objective was to integrate information from various marine sources, specifically from:

- **WoRMS**[2]: Marine registry containing taxonomic information and lists of common names and synonyms for more than 200 thousand species in various languages.
- **Ecoscope**[3]: Knowledge base containing geographical data, pictures and information about marine ecosystems.
- **FishBase**[4]: Global database of fish species, containing information about the taxonomy, geographical distribution, biometrics, population, genetic data and many more.
- **FLOD**[5]: A network of marine linked data containing identification information using different code lists.
- **DBpedia (Bizer, et al., 2009):** Knowledge base containing content that has been converted from Wikipedia, that by the time of writing this chapter, the English version contained more than 4.5 million resources.

For integrating the sources, *MarineTLO* top-level ontology (Tzitzikas, et al., 2013, November) was used. The integrated warehouse[6] is operational and it is exploited in various applications, including the gCube infrastructure (Candela, et al., 2010), or for enabling exploratory search services, e.g., (Fafalios & Tzitzikas, 2013, July), (Fafalios & Tzitzikas, 2014) that offers semantic post-processing of search results.

Warehouse Construction Process

Figure 1 sketches the construction process. For this, the tool *MatWare* (Tzitzikas, et al., 2014, May) can be used which *automates* the entire process. The proposed metrics are used in steps 4 and 8, and are important for *monitoring* the warehouse after a reconstruction. For example by comparing the metrics in the past and new warehouse, one can understand whether a change in the underlying sources affected positively or negatively the quality (connectivity) of the warehouse. More information about these steps can be found in (Tzitzikas, et al., 2014, May) and (Mountantonakis, et al., 2016).

RELATED WORK

Data quality is commonly conceived as *fitness of use* for a certain application or use case ((Knight & Burn, 2005), (Wang & Strong, 1996)). The issue of data quality, especially for the case of a *data warehouse*, is older than the RDF world, e.g., the database community has studied it in the relational world ((Ballou & Tayi, 1999), (Shanks & Darke, 1998)). *Connectivity*, as defined in the Introduction, can be considered as a dimension of data quality in the context of a Semantic Warehouse.

Figure 1. Warehouse construction and monitoring

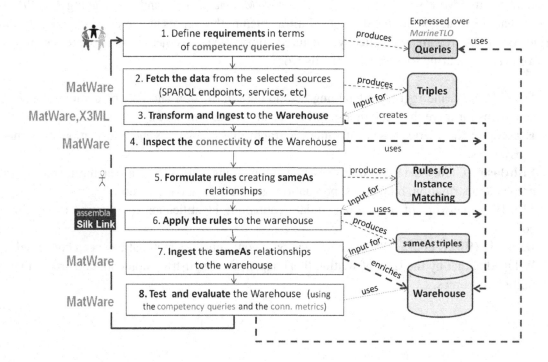

Fürber and Hepp (2010, May) investigated data quality problems for RDF data originating from relational databases, while a systematic review of approaches for assessing the data quality of Linked Data is presented by (Zaveri, et al., 2016). In that work, the authors surveyed 21 approaches and extracted 26 data quality dimensions (such as *completeness*, *provenance*, *interlinking*, *reputation*, *accessibility*, and others) along with the corresponding metrics.

Below, the authors first discuss some quality aspects that are especially useful for the case of a Semantic Warehouse, they report approaches that have tried to address them and they place their work in the literature. Then they compare (according to various perspectives) several frameworks and systems that automate quality assessment for the RDF world.

Quality Aspects

Completeness

Completeness refers to the degree up to which all required information is presented in a particular dataset. In the RDF world, completeness can be classified (according to (Zaveri, et al., 2016)) as: *schema completeness* (degree to which the classes and properties of an ontology are represented), *property completeness* (measure of the missing values for a specific property), *population completeness* (percentage of all real-world objects of a particular type that are represented in the datasets), and *interlinking completeness* (degree to which instances in the dataset are interlinked).

The problem of assessing completeness of Linked Data sources was discussed by Harth and Speiser (2012, July). Darari et al. (2013) introduce a formal framework for the declarative specification of *completeness statements* about RDF data sources and underline how the framework can complement existing initiatives like VoID (Keith Alexander, et al., 2011). They also show how to assess completeness of query answering over plain and RDF/S data sources augmented with completeness statements, and they present an extension of the completeness framework for federated data sources.

Provenance

Provenance focuses on how to represent, manage and use information about the origin of the source to enable trust, assess authenticity and allow reproducibility (Zaveri, et al., 2016). Hartig (2009) presents a provenance model for Web data which handles both data creation and data access. The author also describes options to obtain provenance information and analyzes vocabularies to express such information. Hartig and Zhao (2009) propose an approach of using provenance information about the data on the Web to assess their quality and trustworthiness. Specifically, the authors use the provenance model described by (Hartig, 2009) and propose an assessment method that can be adapted for specific quality criteria (such as accuracy and timeliness). This work also deals with missing provenance information by associating certainty values with calculated quality values. The same authors (Hartig & Zhao, 2010) introduce a vocabulary to describe provenance of Web data as metadata and discuss possibilities to make such provenance metadata accessible as part of the Web of Data. Furthermore, they describe how this metadata can be queried and consumed to identify outdated information. Given the need to address provenance, the W3C community has standardised the PROV Model (W3C, 2013a), a core provenance data model for building representations of the entities, people and processes involved in producing a piece of data or thing in the world. The PROV Family of Documents (W3C, 2013b), (Misser, et al., 2013, March) defines the model, corresponding serializations and other supporting definitions to enable the inter-operable interchange of provenance information in heterogeneous environments such as the Web.

Amount-of-Data

Amount-of-data is defined as the extent to which the volume of data is appropriate for the task at hand according to (Bizer, 2007) and (Zaveri, et al., 2016). This dimension can be measured in terms of general dataset statistics like number of triples, instances per class, internal and external links, but also coverage (scope and level of detail) and metadata "richness". Tsiflidou and Manouselis (2013) carried out an analysis of tools that can be used for the valid assessment of metadata records in a repository. More specifically, three different tools are studied and used for the assessment of metadata quality in terms of statistical analysis. However, such works do not consider the characteristics of RDF and Linked Data. Auer et al. (2012) describe LODStats, a statement-stream-based approach for gathering comprehensive statistics (like classes/properties usage, distinct entities and literals, class hierarchy depth, etc.) about RDF datasets. To represent the statistics, they use VoID and the RDF Data Cube Vocabulary. The RDF Data Cube Vocabulary (W3C, 2013c), (Cyganiak, et al., 2010) provides a means to publish multi-dimensional data (such as statistics of a repository) on the Web in such a way that it can be linked to related datasets and concepts. Hogan et al. (2012) performed analysis in order to quantify the conformance of Linked Data with respect to Linked Data guidelines (e.g., use external URIs, keep URIs stable). They found that in most datasets, publishers followed some specific guidelines, such as using HTTP URIs, whereas in other cases, such as providing human readable metadata, the result were disappointing since only a few publishers created metadata for their datasets.

Accuracy

Accuracy is defined as the extent to which data is correct, that is, the degree up to which it correctly represents the real world facts and is also free of errors (Zaveri, et al., 2016). Accuracy can be measured by detecting outliers, conflicts, semantically incorrect values or poor attributes that do not contain useful values for the data entries. Fürber and Hepp (2011) categorize accuracy into semantic and syntactic accuracy. Semantic accuracy checks whether the data value represents the correct state of an object, whereas syntactic accuracy checks if a specific value violates syntactical rules. For measuring accuracy, the authors used three rules and four formulas, whereas the results were evaluated by using precision and recall measures. They managed to detect syntactic and semantic errors such as invalid country combinations, rules for phone numbers and so forth. *ODCleanStore* (Knap, et al., 2012), (Michelfeit & Knap, 2012) names *conflicts* the cases where two different quads (e.g., triples from different sources) have different object values for a certain subject and predicate. To such cases conflict resolution rules are offered that either select one or more of these conflicting values (e.g., ANY, MAX, ALL), or compute a new value (e.g., AVG). Finally, Knap and Michelfeit (2012) describe various quality metrics for scoring each source based on conflicts, as well for assessing the overall outcome. In (Liu, et al., 2017), the authors computed the joint distribution of variables on a network called Source-Object network. This network captures three different types of correlations in order to trust data derived from reliable sources and it takes into account the sharing between different datasets.

Relevancy

Relevancy refers to the provision of information which is accordant with the task at hand and suitable to the users' query (Zaveri, et al., 2016). The existence of irrelevant data can have negative consequences for the query performance, while it will be difficult for the user to explore this data, since the user expects to receive the correct information. Zaveri et al. (2013, September) divide relevancy (for DBpedia) into the following sub-categories: (i) extraction of attributes containing layout information, (ii) image related information, (iii) redundant attribute values, and finally (iv) irrelevant information. The existence of a number of different properties for a specific subject-object pair is an example of redundant information.

Dynamics / Evolution

Dynamics quantifies the evolution of a dataset over a specific period of time and takes into consideration the changes occurring in this period. Dividino et al. (2014) lists probably all works related to the dynamics of LOD datasets. A related quality perspective, identified by Tzitzikas et al. (2014), is that of the *specificity* of the ontology-based descriptions under ontology evolution, an issue that is raised when ontologies and vocabularies evolve over time.

Interlinking

Interlinking refers to the degree to which entities that represent the same concept are linked to each other (Zaveri, et al., 2016). This can be evaluated by measuring the existence of sameAs links and chains, the interlinking degree, etc. Zaveri et al. (2013, September) classify interlinking into two different categories: (i) external websites (checking whether there are links among sources which are not available), and (ii) interlinks with other datasets (trying to detect incorrect mappings and links which do not provide useful information). The authors of (Nentwig, et al., 2014) created a portal for Link Discovery, called LinkLion, which contains mappings between pairs of 462 datasets. In that repository, one can find relationships between any pair of datasets. Furthermore, in (Gimenez-Garcia, et al., 2016) the authors computed the Pagerank for 319 datasets for providing a trust measure based on dataset interlinking.

Our Placement: Connectivity

The term *connectivity* express the degree up to which the contents of the semantic warehouse form a connected graph that can serve, ideally in a correct and complete way, the query requirements of the semantic warehouse, while making evident how each source contributes to that degree. The proposed connectivity metrics reflect the query capabilities of a warehouse as a whole (so they are important for evaluating its value), but also quantify the contribution of the underlying sources allowing evaluating the importance of each source for the warehouse at hand. Connectivity is important in warehouses whose schema is not small and consequently the queries contain paths. The longer such paths are, the more the query capabilities of the warehouse are determined by the connectivity.

In the related literature, the aspect of *connectivity* is not covered sufficiently and regards mainly the existence of sameAs links and chains (Zaveri, et al., 2013, September). Regarding the association of *connectivity* with existing quality dimensions, it is predominantly *interlinking* and secondly *relevancy* and *amount-of-data*. Of course, it can be exploited together with approaches that focus on *completeness*

(Darari, et al., 2013), *provenance* (Hartig & Zhao, 2009), *accuracy* (Knap & Michelfeit, 2012), etc. Regarding *relevancy*, a Semantic Warehouse as created by the proposed process (see Figure 1) does not contain irrelevant data since the data has been fetched based on the requirements defined in terms of competency queries. Furthermore, the proposed metrics can even detect redundant sources and sources containing data which are not connected with data found in the other sources. Compared to existing approaches on *amount-of-data* (like LODStats (Auer, et al., 2012)), the proposed connectivity metrics can be used to gather statistics that regard more than one source (like common URIs, common literals, etc.) Finally, as regards *dynamics/evolution*, existing works (Dividino, et al., 2014) concern atomic datasets, not warehouses comprising parts of many datasets.

Frameworks/Systems for Quality Assessment

Here, the authors discuss frameworks/systems that automate quality assessment. At first they give a brief description of each framework/system and what quality aspects it can handle, and then they compare them regarding several aspects.

ODCleanStore (Michelfeit & Knap, 2012) is a tool that can download content (RDF graphs) and offers various transformations for cleaning it (deduplication, conflict resolution), and linking it to existing resources, plus assessing the quality of the outcome in terms of *accuracy*, *consistency*, *conciseness* and *completeness*.

Sieve (Mendes, et al., 2012, March) is part of the Linked Data Integration Framework (LDIF) [7] and proposes metrics for assessing the dimensions in terms of *schema completeness*, *conciseness* and *consistency*. The role of this tool is to assess the quality by deciding which values to keep, discard or transform according to a number of metrics and functions which are configurable via a declarative specification language.

RDFUnit (Kontokostas, et al., 2014, April) measures the *accuracy* and the *consistency* of a dataset containing Linked Data. More specifically, it checks the correct usage of vocabularies according to a number of constraints (e.g., cardinality restriction on a property). One can use some custom SPARQL queries to quantify the quality of a specific dataset for the aforementioned aspects.

LinkQA (Guéret, et al., 2012) uses a number of metrics to assess the quality of Linked Data mappings regarding the dimensions of *interlinking* and *completeness*. This tool can be used for detected pathological cases, such as bad quality links, before they are published.

Luzzu (Debattista, et al., 2015) is a framework for assessing the quality of Linked data for 10 different dimensions, such as *availability*, *provenance*, *consistency* and so forth. In particular, by using this tool one can perform quality evaluation either by using some of the 25 available metrics or by defining his own metrics.

SWIQA (Fürber & Hepp, 2011) is a framework for the validation of the values of semantic resources based on a set of rules. This framework allows the calculation of quality scores for various dimensions, such as *completeness*, *timeliness* and *accuracy*, in order to identify possible problems with the data values. Moreover, it is also applicable on top of relational databases with the support of wrapping technologies (i.e., D2RQ).

SeaStar (Sarasua, et al., 2017) is a framework that analyzes the available links or a set of sources according to the set of principles of data interlinking. Its goal is to assess the quality and the accuracy of existing links, and to understand the gain of the connectivity for a source dataset when it is connected to a target dataset.

Finally, *MatWare* (Tzitzikas, et al., 2014, May) is a tool that automates the process of constructing semantic warehouses by fetching and transforming RDF triples from different sources. To this end MatWare exploits several external tools like SILK framework (Volz, Bizer, Gaedke, & Kobilarov, 2009), X3ML Engine (Marketakis, et al., 2016), and computes and visualizes the connectivity metrics described in this chapter.

Figure 2 illustrates the dimensions that the aforementioned approaches measure, while Table 1 provides a categorization according to several aspects.

Figure 2. Existing frameworks and the dimensions they measure

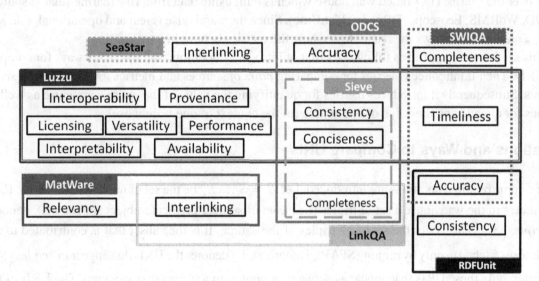

Table 1. Categorizing existing frameworks

	LinkQA	Luzzu	ODCleanStore	Sieve	SWIQA	RDFUnit	SeaStar	MatWare
Input	RDF/ XML	RDF/ XML	RDF/ XML	RDF/ XML	RDF/ XML	RDF/ XML	RDF/ XML	RDF/ XML
Number Of Sources	Set of Mappings	One Source	Collection of Quads	One (integrated) Source	One Source	One Source	One or Two Sources	Set of Sources
Output Kind	Numeric Values	Numeric Values	Numeric Values	Numeric Values	Numeric Values	Numeric Values	Numeric Values	Numeric Values, 3D
Output Format	HTML	RDF	RDF, HTML	Quads	HTML	RDF, HTML	HTML	RDF, 3D, HTML
Computability	JAVA	JAVA	JAVA	JAVA	SPARQL	SPARQL	JAVA	SPARQL, JAVA
Extensible	Yes	Yes	Yes	Yes	Yes	Yes	Yes	Yes

CONNECTIVITY METRICS

Def. 1. The term *connectivity metric* (or *connectivity measure*) refer to a measurable quantity that expresses the degree up to which the contents of the semantic warehouse form a connected graph that can serve, ideally in a correct and complete way, the query requirements of the semantic warehouse, while making evident how each constituent source contributes to that degree. ◊

They include measures of similarity between two sources in the form of percentages (e.g. regarding common URIs), natural numbers (e.g. cardinalities of intersections), matrices of measures, means of other measures, as well as relative measures (e.g. increase of average degrees, unique contribution and others). Such measures can assist humans on assessing in concrete terms the quality and the value offered by the warehouse. In addition they provide a summary of the contents of the warehouse which can be exploited by external applications in the context of distributed query answering.

To aid understanding, after defining each metric the authors show the values of these metrics as computed over the MarineTLO-based warehouse which is built using data from five marine-related sources (FLOD, WoRMS, Ecoscope, DBpedia, FishBase). Since the warehouse is real and operational, this way of presentation also allows the reader to see how the metrics behave in a real setting.

This section is organized as follows: At first, it introduces notations and discusses ways for comparing URIs. Then it introduces metrics for comparing *pairs of* sources and metrics for comparing a *set* of sources. Subsequently it introduces metrics for quantifying the value of the entire warehouse as well as metrics for quantifying the value of one source (in the context of one warehouse).

Notations and Ways to Compare URIs

At first some required notations are introduced. Let $S = S_1, \ldots S_k$ be the set of underlying sources. Each contributes to the warehouse a set of triples (i.e., a set of subject-predicate-object statements), denoted by $triples\left(S_i\right)$. This is not the set of all triples of the source. It is the subset that is contributed to the warehouse (fetched mainly by running SPARQL queries). U_i denotes the URIs that appear in $triples\left(S_i\right)$. Hereafter, only those URIs that appear as *subjects* or *objects* in a triple are considered. The URIs of the properties are not included because they concern the schema and this integration aspect is already tackled by the top level schema. Let W denote triples of all sources of the warehouse. In general, the set of all triples of the warehouse, say W_{All}, is superset of W (i.e., $W_{All} \supset W = \bigcup_{i=1}^{k} triples(S_i)$) because the warehouse apart from the triples from the sources, contains also the triples representing the top-level ontology, the schema mappings, the sameAs relationships, etc.

On Comparing URIs

For computing the metrics that are defined next, methods are needed to compare URIs coming from different sources. There are more than one method, or policy, for doing so. Below three main policies are distinguished:

1. **Exact String Equality:** Two URIs u_1 and u_2 are equal, denoted by $u_1 \equiv u_2$, if $u_1 = u_2$ (i.e., strings equality).

2. **Suffix Canonicalization:** $u_1 \equiv u_2$ if $last(u_1) = last(u_2)$ where $last(u)$ is the string obtained by a) getting the substring after the last "/" or "#", and b) turning the letters of the picked substring to lowercase and deleting the underscore letters as well as space and special characters that might exist. According to this policy:

http://www.dbpedia.com/Thunnus_Albacares≡http://www.ecoscope.com/thunnus_albacares since their canonical suffix is the same, i.e., thunnusalbacares. Another example of equivalent URIs:http://www. s1.com/entity#thunnus_albacares≡ http://www.s2.org/entity/thunnusAlbacares

3. **Entity Matching:** $u_1 \equiv u_2$ if u_1 sameAs u_2 according to the entity matching rules that are (or will be eventually) used for the warehouse. In general such rules create sameAs relationships between URIs. Here, SILK framework is used for formulating and applying such rules.

The presented metrics are defined and computed assuming policy [ii], i.e., whenever there exists a set operation, equivalence according to policy [ii] is assumed (e.g., $A \cap B$ means $\{ a \in A \mid \exists\, b \in B \text{ s.t. } a \equiv_{[ii]} b \}$). Then, after applying the entity matching rules, the metrics are computed according to policy [iii], which actually characterizes the query behaviour of the final and operational warehouse.

Metrics for Comparing Two Sources

Matrix of Percentages of Common URIs

The number of *common URIs* between two sources S_i and S_j, is given by $|U_i \cap U_j|$. The *percentage of common URIs* (a value ranging $[0,1]$) is defined as follows:

$$curi_{i,j} = \frac{|U_i \cap U_j|}{\min(|U_i|, |U_j|)} \tag{1}$$

In the denominator $\min(|U_i|, |U_j|)$ is used although one could use $|U_i \cap U_j|$ that is used in the Jaccard similarity. With Jaccard similarity the integration of a small triple set with a big one would always give small values, even if the small set contains many URIs that exist in the big set, while the Jaccard similarity reveals the overall contribution of a source. Now, the above metric is extended and consider *all pairs of* sources aiming at giving an overview of the warehouse. Specifically, a $k \times k$ matrix is computed where $c_{i,j} = curi_{i,j}$. The higher values this matrix contains, the more glued its "components" are.

For the warehouse at hand, Table 2 shows the matrix of the common URIs (together with the corresponding percentages). One can notice that the percentages range from 0.3% to 27.39%, while in some cases one can observe a significant percentage of common URIs between the different sources. The biggest intersection is between FishBase and DBpedia.

Measurements After Adding the Rule-Derived 'sameAs' Relationships and Applying the Transformation Rules

So far in the computation of the above metrics policy [ii] was used (suffix canonicalized URIs) when comparing URIs. Here the authors show the results from computing again these metrics using policy [iii] and after adding the triples as derived from the transformation rules described earlier. Moreover, extra URIs have been produced due to transformation rules (e.g., in order to assign a URI to a species name). As a result, now when comparing URIs, the authors consider the sameAs relationships that have been produced by the entity matching rules of the warehouse. In the current warehouse 11 SILK rules were used. An indicative SILK rule is the following: *"If the value of the attribute "preflabel" of an Ecoscope individual (e.g., Thunnus albacares) in lower case is the same with the attribute "label" in latin of a FLOD individual (e.g., 'thunnus albacares'@la), then these two individuals are the same (create a sameAs link between them)"*. It is worth noting that policy [ii] considers the triples as they are fetched from the sources. Computing the metrics using policy [iii], not only allows evaluating the gain achieved by these relationships, but it also reflects better the value of the warehouse since query answering considers the sameAs relationships.

Table 3 shows the matrix of the common URIs after the rule-derived relationships and the execution of the transformation rules (together with the corresponding percentages). One can see that, compared to the results of Table 2, after considering the sameAs relationships the number of common URIs between the different sources is significantly increased (more than 7 times in some cases).

Furthermore, Table 4 shows the Jaccard similarity between the pairs of sources. By comparing the results between these two tables, one can see that the percentages when using Jaccard similarity table have been reduced remarkably.

Table 2. Matrix of common URIs (with their percentages) using Policy [ii]

S_i \ S_j	FLOD	WoRMS	Ecoscope	DBpedia	FishBase
FLOD	173,929 (100%)	239 (0.3%)	523 (8.98%)	631 (0.9%)	887 (2.54%)
WoRMS		80,485 (100%)	200 (3.43%)	1,714 (2.44%)	3,596 (10.28%)
Ecoscope			5,824 (100%)	192 (3.3%)	225 (3.86%)
DBpedia				70,246 (100%)	9,578 (27.39%)
FishBase					34,974 (100%)

Table 3. Matrix of common URIs (and their percentages) using Policy [iii]

S_i \ S_j	FLOD	WoRMS	Ecoscope	DBpedia	FishBase
FLOD	190,749 (100%)	1,738 (2.64%)	869 (11.2%)	4,127 (5.46%)	6,053 (17.31%)
WoRMS		65,789 (100%)	809 (10.43%)	1,807 (2.75%)	4,373 (12.5%)
Ecoscope			7,759 (100%)	1,117 (14.4%)	2,171 (27.98%)
DBpedia				75,518 (100%)	10,388 (29.7%)
FishBase					34,973 (100%)

Table 4. Matrix of percentages of common URIs using Policy [iii] and Jaccard Similarity

S_i \ S_j	FLOD	WoRMS	Ecoscope	DBpedia	FishBase
FLOD	1	0.68%	0.44%	1.56%	2.69%
WoRMS		1	1.11%	1.29%	4.5%
Ecoscope			1	1.36%	5.35%
DBpedia				1	10.31%
FishBase					1

Matrix of Percentages of Common Literals Between Two Sources

The *percentage of common literals*, between two sources S_i and S_j can be computed by:

$$colit_{i,j} = \frac{\left| Lit_i \cap Lit_j \right|}{\min \left(\left| Lit_i \right|, \left| Lit_j \right| \right)} \tag{2}$$

To compare two literals coming from different sources, the authors convert them to lower case, to avoid cases like comparing "Thunnus" from one source and "thunnus" from another. Additionally, they ignore the language tags (e.g., *"salmon"@ en* ≡ *"salmon"@ de*). Table 5 shows the matrix of the common literals (together with the corresponding percentages). One can see that, as regards the literals, the percentages of similarity are even smaller than the ones regarding common URIs. The percentages range from 2.71% to 12.37%.

Table 5. Matrix of common literals (and their percentages)

S_i \ S_j	FLOD	WoRMS	Ecoscope	DBpedia	FishBase
FLOD	111,164 (100%)	3,624 (7.1%)	1,745 (12.37%)	5,668 (5.1%)	9,505 (8.55%)
WoRMS		51,076 (100%)	382 (2.71%)	2,429 (4.76%)	4,773 (9.34%)
Ecoscope			14,102 (100%)	389 (2.76%)	422 (2.99%)
DBpedia				123,887 (100%)	14,038 (11.33%)
FishBase					138,275 (100%)

Matrix of the Harmonic Mean of Common URIs and Literals

By combining the previous two metrics, a single metric is now defined which actually corresponds to their harmonic mean:

$$cUrisLit_{i,j} = \frac{2 * curi_{i,j} * colit_{i,j}}{curi_{i,j} + colit_{i,j}} \tag{3}$$

Table 6 presents the results of this metric.

Metrics for Comparing a Set of Sources (Lattice-Based)

The measurements described earlier are measurements between pairs of sources. However, one can generalize the present metrics between *any subset* of the sources of the warehouse, e.g., the number of common literals in 4 sources.

Table 6. Harmonic mean of common URIs and literals

S_i \ S_j	FLOD	WoRMS	Ecoscope	DBpedia	FishBase
FLOD	1	1.61%	10.44%	1.53%	3.93%
WoRMS		1	4.45%	11.02%	21.86%
Ecoscope			1	3.08%	3.82%
DBpedia				1	15.85%
FishBase					1

The idea is to provide measurements for each *subset* of the set of sources, i.e., for every element of $P(S)$ where $P(S)$ denotes the powerset of S. For visualizing (and understanding) these measurements, the authors propose a partial set-like visualization. Specifically, they propose constructing and showing the measurements in a way that resembles the *Hasse Diagram* of the *poset* (partially ordered set) $(S, \subseteq)$.

Let R be any nonempty subset of S (i.e., $R \subseteq S$). It is not hard to generalize the aforementioned metrics for every such subset. For example, consider the metric common triples. The nodes at the lower level of the Hasse Diagram (corresponding to the singletons of S), actually show the number of triples of each source in S, while the nodes in the level above correspond to pairs of sources, i.e., they correspond to what the matrices show. At the topmost level, one can see the intersection between all sources in S (i.e., the value $|U_1 \cap \ldots \cap U_k|$).

Figure 3 presents the lattice concerning the common URIs according to policy [ii]. One can see that the number of common URIs of DBpedia, FishBase, and Ecoscope are more than the number of common URIs among the subsets of the same level, while 74 common URIs are included in all sources.

This approach can be used for all metrics, e.g., for common URIs, for common literals, as well for the metrics that will be presented later for the entire warehouse. The diagram contains $2^{|S|}$ nodes.

Metrics for Evaluating the Entire Warehouse

Here the authors introduce metrics that measure the quality of the entire warehouse.

Figure 3. Common URIs lattice using policy [ii]

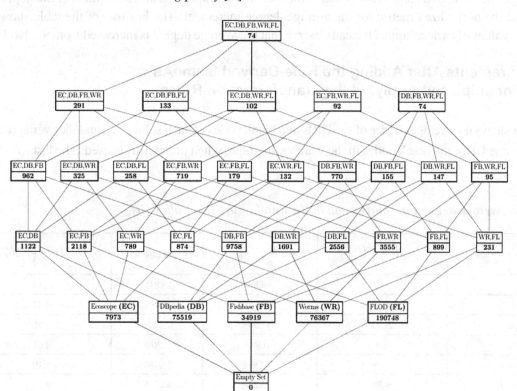

Increase in the Average Degree

Now, another metric for expressing the degree of a set of nodes is presented, where a node can be either a URI or a blank node (in our case the size of blanks nodes is much bigger (about twice) than the size of unique triples). Let E be the entities of interest (or the union of all URIs and blank nodes).

If T is a set of triples, then the *degree* of an entity e in T is defined as: $deg_T(e) = |\{(s,p,o) \in T \mid s = e \ or \ o = e\}|$ while for a set of entities E their average degree in T is defined as $deg_T(E) = avg_{e \in E}(deg_T(e))$. Now for each source S_i one can compute the average degree of the elements in E considering $triples(S_i)$. If the sources of the warehouse contain common elements of E, then if one compute the degrees in the graph of W (i.e., $deg_W(e)$ and $deg_W(E)$), they will get higher values. So the increase in the degree is a way to quantify the gain, in terms of connectivity, that the warehouse offers. Furthermore, a normalized metric for average degree increment can be defined i.e., a metric whose value approaches 1 in the best case, and 0 in the worst. To this end, the authors define:

$$DegIncr(S_i, W) = \frac{deg_W(U_i) - deg_{S_i}(U_i)}{deg_W(U_i)} \quad (4)$$

For each source S_i, Table 7 shows the average degree of its URIs and blank nodes, and the average degree of the same URIs and blank nodes in the warehouse graph. It also reports the increment percentage, and the normalized metric for the average degree increment. The last row of the table shows the average values of each column. One can observe that the average degree is increased from 9.39 to 15.29.

Measurements After Adding the Rule-Derived 'sameAs' Relationships and Applying the Transformation Rules

Table 8 shows the average degree of the URIs and blank nodes of each source S_i, and the average degree of the same URIs and blank nodes in the warehouse graph, when policy [iii] is used. The last row of the

Table 7. Average degrees in sources and in the warehouse using policy [ii]

S_i	avg $deg_{S_i}(U_i)$	avg $deg_W(U_i)$	Increase %	$DegIncr(S_i, W)$
FLOD	5.82	6.8	16.84%	0.14
WoRMS	4.14	4.24	2.46%	0.02
Ecoscope	21.37	47.56	122.52%	0.55
DBpedia	6.9	6.99	1.36%	0.01
FishBase	8.75	10.89	24.46%	0.19
AVERAGE	**9.39**	**15.29**	**62.89%**	**0.38**

Table 8. Average degrees in sources and in the warehouse using Policy [iii]

S_i	avg $deg_{S_i}(U_i)$	avg $deg_W(U_i)$	Increase %	$DegIncr(S_i, W)$
FLOD	5.82	52.01	739.64%	0.89
WoRMS	4.14	8.19	97.94%	0.49
Ecoscope	21.37	90.52	323.51%	0.76
DBpedia	6.9	42.97	523.23%	0.84
FishBase	8.71	18.99	117.19%	0.54
AVERAGE	**9.39**	**42.53**	**353%**	**0.78**

table shows the average values of each column. One can see that the average degree, of all sources, after the inclusion of the **sameAs** relationships is significantly bigger than before. In comparison to Table 7, the increase is from 2 to 9 times bigger. This means that a great increase was achieved in terms of the connectivity of the information in the warehouse.

Unique Triples Contribution

The authors now define metrics for quantifying the complementarity of the sources. The "contribution" of each source S_i can be quantified by counting the triples it has provided to the warehouse, i.e., by $\left| triples(S_i) \right|$. Moreover, its "unique contribution" can be computed by excluding from $\left| triples(S_i) \right|$ those belonging to the triples returned by the other sources. Formally, for the k sources of the warehouse, it is defined:

$$triplesUnique(S_i) = triples(S_i) \setminus \left(\cup_{1 \leq j \leq k, j \neq i} triples(S_j) \right) \tag{5}$$

It follows that if a source S_i provides triples which are also provided by other sources, then $triplesUnique(S_i) = \varnothing$. Consequently, and for quantifying the contribution of each source to the warehouse, one can compute and report the number of its triples $\left| triples(S_i) \right|$, the number of the unique triples $\left| triplesUnique(S_i) \right|$, the unique contribution of each source as:

$$UniqueTContrib(S_i) = \frac{\left| triplesUnique(S_i) \right|}{\left| triples(S_i) \right|} \tag{6}$$

Obviously, it becomes 0 in the worst value and 1 in the best value. To count the unique triples of each source, for each triple of that source the authors perform suffix canonicalization on its URIs, convert its literals to lower case, and then check if the resulting (canonical) triple exists in the canonical triples of a different source. If not, they count this triple as unique. Let $triplesUnique$ be the union of the unique triples of all sources, i.e., $triplesUnique = \cup_i triplesUnique(S_i)$. This set can be proper subset of W (i.e., $triplesUnique \subset W$), since it does not contain triples which have been contributed by two or more sources.

Table 9 shows for each source the number of its triples ($\left|triples(S_i)\right|$), the number of unique triples ($\left|triplesUnique(S_i)\right|$), and the unique triples contribution of that source ($UniqueTContrib(S_i)$). One can see that every source contains a very high ($> 99\%$) percentage of unique triples, so all sources are important.

Measurements After Adding the Rule-Derived 'sameAs' Relationships and Applying the Transformation Rules

As regards the unique contribution of each source using Policy [iii], the values in the first column are increased in comparison to Table 9. This is because of the execution of the transformation rules after the ingestion of the data to the warehouse, which results to the creation of new triples for the majority of sources. Finally one can observe that, in general, the unique triples contribution of each source is decreased. This happens because the transformation rules and the same-as relationships have turned previously different triples, the same.

Table 9. (Unique) triple contributions of the sources using policy [ii]

S_i	$\left|triples(S_i)\right|$	$\left|triplesUnique(S_i)\right|$	$UniqueTContrib(S_i)$
FLOD	665,456	664,703	99.89%
WoRMS	461,230	460,741	99.89%
Ecoscope	54,027	53,641	99.29%
DBpedia	450,429	449,851	99.87%
FishBase	1,425,283	1,424,713	99.96%

Table 10. (Unique) triple contributions of the sources using policy [iii]

S_i	$\left|triples(S_i)\right|$	$\left|triplesUnique(S_i)\right|$	$UniqueTContrib(S_i)$
FLOD	810,301	798,048	98.49%
WoRMS	528,009	527,358	99.88%
Ecoscope	138,324	52,936	38.27%
DBpedia	526,016	517,242	98.33%
FishBase	1,425,283	1,340,968	94.08%

Complementarity of Sources

The authors now define another metric for quantifying the value of the warehouse for the entities of interest. With the term "entity" they mean any literal or URI that contains a specific string representing a named entity, like the name of a fish or country. The set of triples containing information about the entity of interest can be defined as $triples_W(e) = |\{\langle s, p, o \rangle \in W \mid s = e \; or \; o = e\}|$. Specifically they define the *complementarity factor* for an entity e, denoted by $cf(e)$, as the percentage of sources that provide *unique* material about e. It can be defined declaratively as:

$$cf(e) = \frac{|\{i \mid triples_W(e) \cap triplesUnique(S_i) \neq \varnothing\}|}{|S|} \tag{7}$$

where S is the set of underlying sources.

Note that if $|S| = 1$ (i.e., there exists only one source), then for every entity e, $(e) = 1.0$. If $|S| = 2$, i.e., then there exists the following cases:

- $cf(e) = 0.0$, if both sources have provided the same triple (or triples) about e or no source has provided any triple about e,
- $cf(e) = 0.5$, if the triples provided by the one source (for e) are subset of the triples provided by the other, or if only one source provide triple(s) about e,
- $cf(e) = 1.0$, if each source has provided at least one different triple for e (of course they can also have contributed common triples). Consequently for the entities of interest one can compute and report the average *complementarity factor* as a way to quantify the value of the warehouse for these entities.

Table 11 shows (indicatively) the *complementarity factors* for a few entities which are important for the problem at hand. One can see that for the entities "Thunnus" and "Shark" each source provides unique information ($cf = 1.0$). For the entity "Greece" and "Astrapogon" unique information is obtained from three sources ($cf = 3 / 5 = 0.6$). The fact that the complementarity factor is big means that the warehouse provides unique information about each entity from many/all sources. Moreover, Table 12 shows the average complementarity factor of the species that are native to Greece. One can observe that there are no species with very small complementarity factor, which means that at least 2 sources provide

Table 11. Complementarity factor (cf) of some entities

Kind of Entity	$cf(\cdot)$
Thunnus	1.0 (5/5)
Greece	0.6 (3/5)
Shark	1.0 (5/5)
Astrapogon	0.6 (3/5)

Table 12. cf of species that are native to Greece

$cf(\cdot)$	No. of Species
0.2 (1/5)	0
0.4 (2/5)	116
0.6 (3/5)	180
0.8 (4/5))	113
1.0 (5/5)	35
Average: 0.63 (3.15/5)	Sum: 444

unique information for each species $cf(e) \geq 0.4$. Indeed, exactly 2 sources provide unique information for 116 species, while for 35 species unique data is returned from all the sources. In general the average complementarity factor for all species that are native in Greece is approximately 0.63 (3.15/5) (meaning that at least 3 sources contain unique information for such species).

Metrics for Evaluating a Single Source (in the Context of a Warehouse)

In this section the authors focus on metrics for quantifying the value that a source brings to the warehouse. Such metrics should also allow identifying pathological cases (e.g., redundant or irrelevant sources). In particular, at first they provide examples of such cases and introduce rules for identifying them. Finally they introduce a single-valued metric based on these rules for aiding their identification by a human.

Detecting Redundancies or other Pathological Cases

The metrics can be used also for detecting various pathological cases, e.g., sources that do not have any common URI or literal, or "redundant sources". To test this the authors created three artificial sources, let us call them *Airports*, *CloneSource* and *AstrapogonSource*. The *Airports* source contains triples about airports which were fetched from the DBpedia public SPARQL endpoint, the *CloneSource* is a subset of Ecoscope's and DBpedia's triples as they are stored in the warehouse, and the *AstrapogonSource* contains only 1 URI and 4 triples for the entity *Astrapogon*. In the sequel, the metrics were computed for 8 sources.

Table 13 shows in the first column the unique triples contribution and in the second column the degree increase. The metrics were calculated according to policy [iii]. As regards *Airports*, one can see that its unique contribution is 1 (all the contents of that source are unique). As regards *CloneSource*, its unique contributions is zero (as expected, since it was composed from triples of existing sources). Finally, concerning the *AstrapogonSource*, although the number of its triples contribution is very low, all its triples are unique.

Rules for Detecting Pathological Cases

It follows that one can detect pathological cases using two rules: (a) if the average increase of the degree of the entities of a source is low, then this means that its contents are not connected with the contents of the rest of the sources (this is the case of *Airports* where there was only 0.1% increase), (b) if the unique contribution of a source is very low (resp. zero), then this means that it does not contribute significantly (resp. at all) to the warehouse (this is the case of *CloneSource* where the unique contribution was zero).

A Single Metric for Quantifying the Value of a Source

To further ease the inspection of pathological cases (and the quantification of the contribution of each source), the authors define a single (and single-valued) measure. One method is to use the *harmonic mean* of the unique contribution, and the increment in the average degree (the harmonic mean takes a high value if both values are high). Therefore, one can measure the harmonic mean of the above two metrics and define the value of a source S_i, denoted by $value_0(S_i, W)$, as:

$$value_0\left(S_i,W\right) = \frac{2 * UniqueTContrib\left(S_i\right) * DegIncr\left(S_i,W\right)}{UniqueTContrib\left(S_i\right) + DegIncr\left(S_i,W\right)} \tag{8}$$

Table 13 shows these values for all sources of the warehouse, including the artificial ones, in decreasing order. One can see that the problematic sources have a value less than 0.04 while the good ones receive a value greater than 0.2. However, *AstrapogonSource* has the highest score although it contains only 4 triples. The two reasons why this source seems the best according to this metric are that all the triples are unique and the only instance that it contains has a lot of properties in other sources. Therefore, the degree increment of this source is almost 1. Consequently this metric makes evident the contribution of each source to the warehouse.

Although the above metric is good for discriminating the good from the not as good (or useless) sources, it ignores the number of triples that each source contributes. This is evident from Table 1 where AstrapogonSource gets the highest score. In general, a source with a small number of triples can have big values in the above two metrics.

For tackling this issue, there is a need of an analogous metric for the size of a specific source in the warehouse, specifically the authors define $S_iSizeInW\left(S_i,W\right) = \frac{\left|triples\left(S_i\right)\right|}{\left|triples\left(W\right)\right|}$. Then, they compute the harmonic mean of these three metrics and define the value of a source S_i, denoted by $value_1\left(S_i,W\right)$, as

$$value_1\left(S_i,W\right) = \frac{3}{\frac{1}{UniqueTContrib\left(S_i\right)} + \frac{1}{DegIncr\left(S_i,W\right)} + \frac{1}{S_iSizeInW\left(S_i,W\right)}} \tag{9}$$

Table 13. The value of a source in the Warehouse (using $value_0\left(S_i,W\right)$)

S_i	$UniqueTContrib\left(S_i\right)$	$DegIncr\left(S_i,W\right)$	$value_0\left(S_i,W\right)$
AstrapogonSource	1	0.93	**0.9637**
FLOD	0.9849	0.89	**0.935**
DBpedia	0.96	0.84	**0.896**
FishBase	0.9408	0.54	**0.686**
WoRMS	0.9988	0.49	**0.6575**
Ecoscope	0.129	0.76	**0.2206**
Airports	1	0.001	**0.02**
CloneSource	0	0.89	**0**

Table 14 shows these values for all sources of the warehouse, including the artificial one, in decreasing order. Now one can see that FishBase is the most useful source, and the score of AstrapogonSource is very low (almost 0).

Consequently, the first metric can be used for deciding whether to include or not a source in the warehouse, while second for inspecting the importance of source for the warehouse. In case of adding a huge out-of-domain source in our warehouse while there exist a lot of useful sources which are much smaller, the values of the useful sources will remain almost stable for the first metric. On the contrary, their values will be decreased for the second metric. Regarding, the value of the out-of-domain source, it will be low in both metrics, since the increase of the average degree for this source will be almost 0. Therefore, both metrics will show that the new source should be removed from the warehouse, however, the second metric will not show the real value for each of the remaining sources in this case.

WAREHOUSE EVOLUTION

The objective here is to investigate how one can understand the evolution of the warehouse and how can detect problematic cases (due to changes in the remote sources, mistakes in the equivalence rules, addition of a redundant or a "useless" source etc). Let v denote a version of the warehouse and v' denote a new version of the warehouse. A number of questions arise:

- Is the new version of the warehouse better than the previous one? From what aspects, the new warehouse is better than the previous one, and from what aspects it is worse?
- Can the comparison of the metrics of v and v', aid us in detecting problems in the new warehouse, e.g., a change in an underlying source that affected negatively the new warehouse?

It is also useful to compare a series of versions for:

- Understanding the evolution of the entire warehouse over time
- Understanding the evolution of the contribution of a source in the warehouse over time

Table 14. The value of a source in the warehouse (using $value_1(S_i, W)$)

S_i	$UniqueTContrib(S_i)$	$DegIncr(S_i, W)$	$S_iSizeInW(S_i, W)$	$value_1(S_i, W)$
FishBase	0.9408	0.54	0.405	**0.5572**
FLOD	0.9849	0.89	0.2304	**0.463**
DBpedia	0.96	0.84	0.1496	**0.3364**
WoRMS	0.9988	0.49	0.1501	**0.3091**
Ecoscope	0.129	0.76	0.0393	**0.0869**
Airports	1	0.001	0.0089	**0.0027**
AstrapogonSource	1	0.93	0.000001	**0.000001**
CloneSource	0	0.89	0.0089	**0**

To tackle these questions, the authors first describe the used datasets and then focus on how to inspect a *sequence* of versions.

Datasets Used

To understand the evolution several series of warehouse versions are needed. The authors used 3 real versions of the MarineTLO-based warehouse, specifically:

- MarineTLO-based warehouse version 2 (July 2013): 1,483,972 triples
- MarineTLO-based warehouse version 3 (December 2013): 3,785,249 triples
- MarineTLO-based warehouse version 4 (June 2014): 5,513,348 triples

Inspecting a Sequence of Versions

Suppose that there exists n versions, $v_1, v_2, ..., v_n$. One can get the big picture by various plots each having in the X axis one point for each warehouse version. Below there are described several useful plots.

1. For each v_i, $\left| triples\left(W_{vi}\right) \right|$ is computed. Figure 4 shows the resulting plot for the datasets.
2. For each v_i, $\left| U_{Wvi} \right|$ and $\left| Lit_{Wvi} \right|$ are plotted, where U_{Wvi} is the set of all URIs and Lit_{Wvi} is the set of all Literals in the warehouse of that version. Figure 5 shows the resulting plot for the datasets.
3. For each v_i, the average degree of the URIs of the warehouse $deg_W\left(U_{Wvi}\right)$ are plotted, as well as the average degree of the blank nodes and URIs of the warehouse $deg_W\left(U_{Wvi} \cup BN_{Wvi}\right)$. Figure 6 shows the resulting plot for the datasets.
4. For each v_i and for each source S_j, $value_1\left(S_i, W\right)$ is plotted (one diagram with k plots one for each of the k sources). Figure 7 shows how the contribution of the sources in the warehouse evolves, for the datasets.

The first three (i-iii) concern the warehouse per se, while (iv) shows how the contribution of the source in the warehouse evolves. Finally, Table 15 shows the average degree increment of the URIs and blank nodes of each source for the 3 different versions of the real datasets. In (Mountantonakis, et al., 2016) one can find more experiments for both real and synthetic datasets, where various aspects are tested, e.g., source enlargements, increased or reduced number of sameAs relationships, addition of new sources (either relevant or irrelevant to the domain), addition of erroneous data, etc.

EXPLOITATION OF METRICS AND NOVEL CONTRIBUTIONS

In (Mountantonakis, et al., 2016) one can find details about how the metrics can be implemented, how the results can be published by exploiting VoIDwh vocabulary, and how the results can be exploited for several real world tasks. The work presented in this chapter was the spark for extending the proposed

Figure 4. Triples of each version

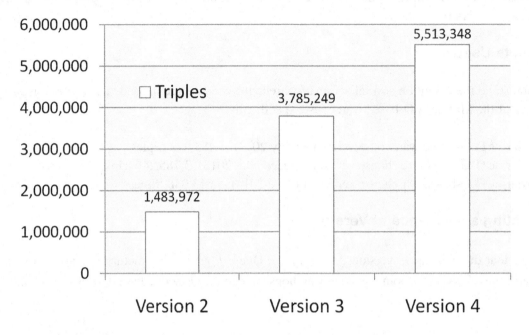

Figure 5. URIs and literals

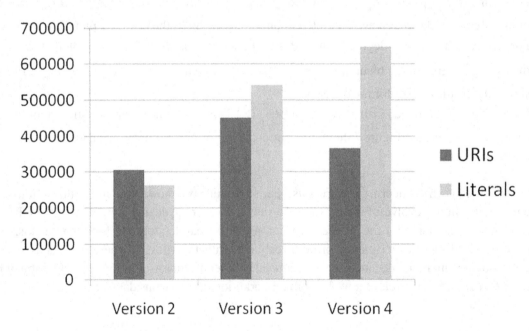

methods and services in order to apply them in LOD scale, i.e., for a large number of datasets of any domain and to create services that concern the whole LOD cloud. Below two state of the art approaches and services are described in brief: a) Lattice-based measurements, b) 3D visualization of LOD cloud datasets.

Figure 6. Average degree of warehouse

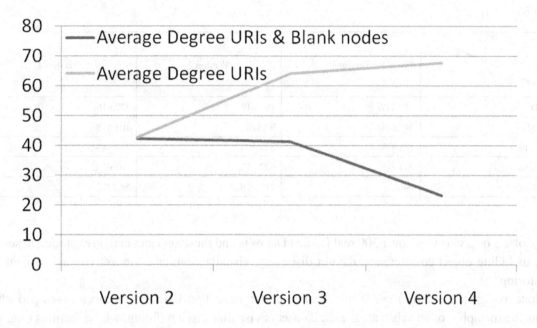

Figure 7. Value for each source in every version

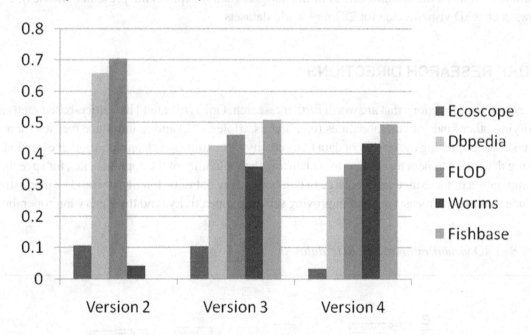

As regards a), in (Mountantonakis & Tzitzikas, 2016), the authors introduced indexes and measurements about the commonalities of a large number of Linked Datasets. In particular, they measured the number of common real world objects between any set of datasets, that is they computed the number of classes of equivalence of URIs after having computed the symmetric and transitive closure of the set of *owl:sameAs* relationships from all datasets. The corresponding research prototype, called LODsyndesis

Table 15. Average degree increment percentages for the URIs and blanks nodes of each source in every version

S_i $\diagdown$ v_i	Version2	Version 3	Version 4
FLOD	465.59%	793.64%	797.61%
WoRMS	548.67%	97.82%	103.61%
Ecoscope	108.97%	325.58%	396.84%
DBpedia	271.84%	522.75%	505.65%
FishBase	―	117.02%	58.43%

(n.d.), offers query services over 300 real Linked Datasets and these services can be exploited in several tasks including object co-reference, dataset discovery, visualization, and connectivity assessment and monitoring.

Concerning b), an *interactive 3D visualization* prototype, called 3DLOD[8], has been developed which adopts the metaphor of an urban area: each dataset is visualized as a building, whose features (e.g. volume) reflect various dataset's features (e.g. number of triples), while roads/bridges and the proximity of the buildings indicate the commonalities of the datasets (i.e., it exploits the presented metrics). Figure 8 shows such a 3D visualization for 287 real world datasets.

FUTURE RESEARCH DIRECTIONS

There are various directions that are worth further research. One is to extend the lattice-based metrics for quantifying other kinds of commonalities (e.g. literals, triples, etc.) and to introduce metrics for aiding other tasks for improving the quality of data like veracity estimation and cleaning. Another direction is to apply big data management techniques for enhancing the scalability of the approach, i.e., for speeding up the computation of these metrics over large in number and big datasets. Finally, it would be interesting to introduce methods for measuring and improving schema connectivity (and thus query interoperability).

Figure 8. A 3D visualization of 287 RDF datasets

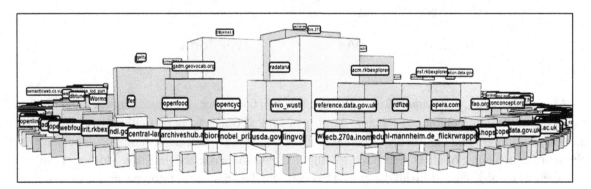

CONCLUSION

In many applications one has to fetch and assemble pieces of information coming from more than one source. This chapter describes the main requirements and challenges, based also on an experience in building an operational semantic warehouse for marine resources. The chapter first describes the process for constructing such warehouses and then presents metrics for quantifying the *connectivity* of the outcome.

By inspecting the proposed metrics-based matrices one can very quickly get an overview of the contribution of each source and the tangible benefits of the warehouse. The main metrics are: (a) the matrix of percentages of the common URIs and/or literals, (b) the complementarity factor of the entities of interest, (c) the table with the increments in the average degree of each source, (d) the unique triple contribution of each source, and (e) a single-valued metric for quantifying the value of a source. The values of (a), (b), and (c) allow valuating the warehouse, while (c), (d) and (e) mainly concern each particular source. For instance, by combining the unique triples contribution and the increment of the average degrees, one can understand that not only one get unique information from *all* sources, but also *how much* the average degree of the entities of the sources has been increased in the warehouse. Moreover, redundant sources can be spotted through their low unique contribution, while unconnected sources through their low average increase of the degree of their entities. In addition, the chapter presents metrics and plots suitable for monitoring the evolution of a warehouse. More specifically, these metrics are exploited for understanding how the warehouse evolves and how the contribution of each source changes over time. To this end, a set of plots that allow someone to quickly spot anomalies are provided, while novel ways for exploiting such metrics in global scale and for visualization purposes are briefly presented.

The ability to assess the quality of a semantic warehouse, using methods like those presented in this chapter and those in the literature, is very important also for dataset and endpoint selection, as well as judging whether the warehouse can be used in e-Science. In the long run the authors expect that datasets and warehouses will be peer-reviewed, evaluated and cited, and this in turn will justify actions for their future maintenance and preservation.

ACKNOWLEDGMENT

This work was partially supported by the projects: *iMarine* (FP7 Research Infrastructures, 2011-2014), BlueBRIDGE (H2020 Research Infrastructures, 2015-2018) and *LifeWatch Greece* (National Strategic Reference Framework, 2012-2015).

REFERENCES

W3C. (2013a). *PROV Model Primer.* W3C Working Group Note. Retrieved from: https://www.w3.org/TR/2013/NOTE-prov-primer-20130430/

W3C. (2013b). *PROV-Overview: An Overview of the PROV Family of Documents.* W3C Working Group Note. Retrieved from: https://www.w3.org/TR/prov-overview/

W3C. (2013c). *The RDF Data Cube Vocabulary: W3C Proposed Recommendation.* Retrieved from: https://www.w3.org/TR/2013/PR-vocab-data-cube-20131217/

Auer, S., Jan, D., Martin, M., & Lehmann, J. (2012). *LODStats - an Extensible Framework for High-Performance Dataset Analytics*. Berlin: Springer. doi:10.1007/978-3-642-33876-2_31

Ballou, D., & Tayi, G. (1999). Enhancing data quality in data warehouse environments. *Communications of the ACM, 42*(1), 73–78. doi:10.1145/291469.291471

Bizer, C. (2007). *Quality-Driven Information Filtering in the Context of Web-Based Information Systems*. Berlin: Freie Universität.

Bizer, C., Lehmann, J., Kobilarov, G., Auer, S., Becker, C. C., & Hellmann, S. (2009). DBpedia-A crystallization point for the Web of Data. *Web Semantics: Science, Services, and Agents on the World Wide Web, 7*(3), 154–165. doi:10.1016/j.websem.2009.07.002

Candela, L., Castelli, D., & Pagano, P. (2010). Making Virtual Research Environments in the Cloud a Reality: the gCube Approach. *ERCIM News, 2010*(83), 32.

Cyganiak, R., Field, S., Gregory, A., Halb, W., & Tennison, J. (2010). Semantic Statistics: Bringing Together SDMX and SCOVO. *WWW Workshop on Linked Data on the web*.

Darari, F., Nutt, W., Pirrò, G., & Razniewski, S. (2013). *Completeness statements about RDF data sources and their use for query answering. In The Semantic Web--ISWC 2013* (pp. 66–83). Berlin: Springer.

Debattista, J., Lange, C., & Auer, S. (2015). *Luzzu Quality Metric Language--A DSL for Linked Data Quality Assessment*. arXiv preprint arXiv:1412.3750

Dividino, R. Q., Gottron, T., Scherp, A., & Gröner, G. (2014). From Changes to Dynamics: Dynamics Analysis of Linked Open Data Sources. *1st International Workshop on Dataset Profiling & Federated Search for Linked Data (PROFILES'14)*.

Fafalios, P., & Tzitzikas, Y. (2013, July). X-ENS: semantic enrichment of web search results at real-time. In *Proceedings of the 36th international ACM SIGIR conference on Research and development in information retrieval* (pp. 1089-1090). ACM. doi:10.1145/2484028.2484200

Fafalios, P., & Tzitzikas, Y. (2014). Exploratory Professional Search through Semantic Post-Analysis of Search Results. In *Professional Search in the Modern World*. Lecture Notes in Computer Science. Springer. doi:10.1007/978-3-319-12511-4_9

Fürber, C., & Hepp, M. (2010, May). *Using sparql and spin for data quality management on the semantic web*. Berlin: Springer.

Fürber, C., & Hepp, M. (2011). *Swiqa-a semantic web information quality assessment framework* (Vol. 15). ECIS.

Gimenez-Garcia, J., Thakkar, H., & Zimmermann, A. (2016). Assessing trust with PageRank in the Web of Data. In *International Semantic Web Conference* (pp. 293-307). Springer. doi:10.1007/978-3-319-47602-5_45

Guéret, C., Groth, P., Stadler, C., & Lehmann, J. (2012). Assessing linked data mappings using network measures. In *The Semantic Web: Research and Applications* (pp. 87–102). Berlin: Springer. doi:10.1007/978-3-642-30284-8_13

Harth, A., & Speiser, S. (2012, July). *On Completeness Classes for Query Evaluation on Linked Data.* AAAI.

Hartig, O. (2009). Provenance Information in the Web of Data. *LDOW, 538.*

Hartig, O., & Zhao, J. (2009). Using web data provenance for quality assessment. *CEUR Workshop.*

Hartig, O., & Zhao, J. (2010). Publishing and consuming provenance metadata on the web of linked data. In *Provenance and annotation of data and processes* (pp. 78–90). Berlin: Springer. doi:10.1007/978-3-642-17819-1_10

Hogan, A., Harth, A., Umbrich, J., Kinsella, S., Polleres, A., & Decker, S. (2011). Searching and browsing linked data with swse: The semantic web search engine. *Web Semantics: Science, Services, and Agents on the World Wide Web, 9*(4), 365–401. doi:10.1016/j.websem.2011.06.004

Hogan, A., Umbrich, J., Harth, A., Cyganiak, R., Polleres, A., & Decker, S. (2012). An empirical survey of linked data conformance. *Web Semantics: Science, Services, and Agents on the World Wide Web, 14,* 14–44. doi:10.1016/j.websem.2012.02.001

Keith Alexander, M., Cyganiak, R., Hausenblas, M., & Zhao, J. (2011). *Describing linked datasets with the void vocabulary.* Academic Press.

Knap, T., & Michelfeit, J. (2012). *Linked Data Aggregation Algorithm: Increasing Completeness and Consistency of Data.* Charles University.

Knap, T., Michelfeit, J., Daniel, J., Jerman, P., Rychnovský, D., Soukup, T., & Nečaský, M. (2012). ODCleanStore: a framework for managing and providing integrated linked data on the web. In *Web Information Systems Engineering-WISE* (pp. 815–816). Berlin: Springer. doi:10.1007/978-3-642-35063-4_74

Knight, S. A., & Burn, J. M. (2005). Developing a framework for assessing information quality on the World Wide Web. *Informing Science: International Journal of an Emerging Transdiscipline, 8*(5), 159–172.

Kontokostas, D., Westphal, P., Auer, S., Hellmann, S., Lehmann, J., Cornelissen, R., & Zaveri, A. (2014, April). Test-driven evaluation of linked data quality. In *Proceedings of the 23rd international conference on World Wide Web* (pp. 747-758). ACM.

Liu, W., Liu, J., Duan, H., Hu, W., & Wei, B. (2017). *Exploiting Source-Object Networks to Resolve Object Conflicts in Linked Data.* Springer. doi:10.1007/978-3-319-58068-5_4

LODsyndesis. (n.d.). *LODsyndesis: Connectivity of LOD datasets.* Retrieved from: http://www.ics.forth.gr/isl/LODsyndesis

Marketakis, Y., Minadakis, N., Kondylakis, H., Konsolaki, K., Samaritakis, G., Theodoridou, M., & Doerr, M. et al. (2016). X3ML Mapping Framework for Information Integration in Cultural Heritage and beyond. *International Journal on Digital Libraries,* 1–19.

Mendes, P. N., Mühleisen, H., & Bizer, C. (2012, March). Sieve: linked data quality assessment and fusion. In *Proceedings of the 2012 Joint EDBT/ICDT Workshops* (pp. 116-123). ACM. doi:10.1145/2320765.2320803

Michelfeit, J., & Knap, T. (2012). Linked Data Fusion in ODCleanStore★. *11th International Semantic Web Conference ISWC,* 45.

Missier, P., Belhajjame, K., & Cheney, J. (2013, March). The W3C PROV family of specifications for modelling provenance metadata. In *Proceedings of the 16th International Conference on Extending Database Technology* (pp. 773-776). ACM. doi:10.1145/2452376.2452478

Mountantonakis, M., Minadakis, N., Marketakis, Y., Fafalios, P., & Tzitzikas, Y. (2016). Quantifying the connectivity of a semantic warehouse and understanding its evolution over time. *International Journal on Semantic Web and Information Systems*, *12*(3), 27–78. doi:10.4018/IJSWIS.2016070102

Mountantonakis, M., & Tzitzikas, Y. (2016). On measuring the lattice of commonalities among several linked datasets. *Proceedings of the VLDB Endowment*, 1101-1112. doi:10.14778/2994509.2994527

Nentwig, M., Soru, T., Ngomo, A.-C. N., & Rahm, E. (2014). Linklion: A link repository for the web of data. In *European Semantic Web Conference* (pp. 439-443). Springer. doi:10.1007/978-3-319-11955-7_63

Oren, E., Delbru, R., Catasta, M., Cyganiak, R., Stenzhorn, H., & Tummarello, G. (2008). Sindice. com: A document-oriented lookup index for open linked data. *International Journal of Metadata, Semantics and Ontologies*, *3*(1), 37–52. doi:10.1504/IJMSO.2008.021204

Sarasua, C., Staab, S., & Thimm, M. (n.d.). Methods for Intrinsic Evaluation of Links in the Web of Data. In *European Semantic Web Conference* (pp. 68-84). Springer.

Shanks, G. G., & Darke, P. (1998). Understanding Data Quality and Data Warehousing: A Semiotic Approach. In IQ (pp. 292-309). Academic Press.

TaxonConcept. (n.d.). Retrieved from: http://www.taxonconcept.org/

Tsiflidou, E., & Manouselis, N. (2013). Tools and Techniques for Assessing Metadata Quality. In *Metadata and Semantics Research* (pp. 99–110). Springer. doi:10.1007/978-3-319-03437-9_11

Tzitzikas, Y., Allocca, C., Bekiari, C., Marketakis, Y., Fafalios, P., Doerr, M., & Candela, L. (2013, November). Integrating heterogeneous and distributed information about marine species through a top level ontology. In *Metadata and Semantics Research* (pp. 289–301). Springer. doi:10.1007/978-3-319-03437-9_29

Tzitzikas, Y., Kampouraki, M., & Analyti, A. (2014). Curating the Specificity of Ontological. *Journal on Data Semantics, 3*(2), 75-106.

Tzitzikas, Y., Minadakis, N., Marketakis, Y., Fafalios, P., Allocca, C., & Mountantonakis, M. (2014, March). *Quantifying the Connectivity of a Semantic Warehouse*. EDBT/ICDT Workshops.

Tzitzikas, Y., Minadakis, N., Marketakis, Y., Fafalios, P., Allocca, C., Mountantonakis, M., & Zidianaki, I. (2014, May). Matware: Constructing and exploiting domain specific warehouses by aggregating semantic data. In The Semantic Web: Trends and Challenges (pp. 721-736). Springer.

Volz, J., Bizer, C., Gaedke, M., & Kobilarov, G. (2009). Silk-A Link Discovery Framework for the Web of Data. *Proceedings of the WWW'09 Workshop on Linked Data on the Web*.

Wang, R. Y., & Strong, D. M. (1996). Beyond accuracy: What data quality means to data. *Journal of Management Information Systems*, *12*(4), 5–33. doi:10.1080/07421222.1996.11518099

Zaveri, A., Kontokostas, D., Sherif, M. A., Bühmann, L., Morsey, M., Auer, S., & Lehmann, J. (2013, September). User-driven quality evaluation of dbpedia. In *Proceedings of the 9th International Conference on Semantic Systems* (pp. 97-104). ACM. doi:10.1145/2506182.2506195

Zaveri, A., Rula, A., Maurino, A., Pietrobon, R., Lehmann, J., Auer, S., & Hitzler, P. (2016). *Quality assessment for linked data: A survey*. Semantic Web.

KEY TERMS AND DEFINITIONS

Data Quality: Fitness of use for a certain application or use case.

Interlinking: The degree to which entities that represent the same concept are linked to each other.

Linked Data: A method of publishing structured data so that it can be interlinked and become more useful through semantic queries.

Semantic Integration: The process of interrelating information from diverse, heterogeneous data sources, which may conflict not only by structure but also context or value.

Semantic Warehouse: A read-only set of RDF triples fetched (and transformed) from different sources that aims at serving a particular set of query requirements.

Semantic Warehouse's Connectivity: The degree up to which the contents of the semantic warehouse form a connected graph that can serve, ideally in a correct and complete way, the query requirements of the semantic warehouse, while making evident how each source contributes to that degree.

Warehouse Evolution: The evolution of a warehouse over a specific period of time by taking into consideration the changes occurring in this period.

ENDNOTES

[1] Used in the context of the projects iMarine (FP7 Research Infrastructures, 2011-2014, http://www.i-marine.eu) and BlueBRIDGE (H2020 Research Infrastructures, 2015-2018, http://www.bluebridge-vres.eu).

[2] WoRMS - World Register of Marine Species (http://www.marinespecies.org).

[3] Ecoscope - Knowledge Base on Exploited Marine Ecosystems (http://www.ecoscopebc.ird.fr).

[4] FishBase (http://www.fishbase.org).

[5] FLOD - Fisheries Linked Open Data (http://www.fao.org/figis/flod/).

[6] The warehouse can be accessed from https://i-marine.d4science.org/.

[7] Linked Data Integration Framework (LDIF) - http://www4.wiwiss.fu-berlin.de/bizer/ldif/

[8] http://ww.ics.forth.gr/isl/3DLod/

Chapter 2
Managing Large Volumes of Interlinked Text and Knowledge With the KnowledgeStore

Francesco Corcoglioniti
Fondazione Bruno Kessler, Italy

Marco Rospocher
Fondazione Bruno Kessler, Italy

Roldano Cattoni
Fondazione Bruno Kessler, Italy

Bernardo Magnini
Fondazione Bruno Kessler, Italy

Luciano Serafini
Fondazione Bruno Kessler, Italy

ABSTRACT

This chapter describes the KnowledgeStore, a scalable, fault-tolerant, and Semantic Web grounded open-source storage system to jointly store, manage, retrieve, and query interlinked structured and unstructured data, especially designed to manage all the data involved in Knowledge Extraction applications. The chapter presents the concept, design, function and implementation of the KnowledgeStore, and reports on its concrete usage in four application scenarios within the NewsReader EU project, where it has been successfully used to store and support the querying of millions of news articles interlinked with billions of RDF triples, both extracted from text and imported from Linked Open Data sources.

DOI: 10.4018/978-1-5225-5042-6.ch002

INTRODUCTION

The last decades achievements in Natural Language Processing (NLP) and Knowledge Extraction (KE) have enabled the large-scale extraction of structured knowledge about world entities from unstructured text (Weikum & Theobald, 2010; Grishman, 2010; Vossen et al., 2016; Corcoglioniti, Rospocher, & Palmero Aprosio, 2016). As a result, new application scenarios are appearing where large amounts of information are available in different interlinked forms: text, the knowledge extracted from it, and the NLP annotations involved in the KE process. To support applications having to jointly store, access, and process all this information, there is an increasing need for scalable frameworks that seamlessly integrate structured and unstructured knowledge, providing the necessary scalability (e.g., up to millions of documents and billions of RDF triples) and data access and manipulation methods.

This chapter describes the latest achievements on the KnowledgeStore (http://knowledgestore.fbk. eu) extending the work previously reported by Corcoglioniti, Rospocher, Cattoni, Magnini, and Serafini (2015). The KnowledgeStore is a scalable, fault-tolerant, and Semantic Web (SW) grounded open-source (Apache License v2.0) storage system to jointly store, manage, retrieve, and query interlinked text and RDF knowledge extracted from it, e.g., using KE tools such as PIKES (Corcoglioniti, Rospocher, & Palmero Aprosio, 2016), or coming from Linked Open Data (LOD) resources. Conceptually, the KnowledgeStore acts as a data hub populated by KE systems and queried by end users and applications, whose contents are organized according to three representation layers: Resource, Mention, and Entity. To illustrate the interplay of these layers in the KnowledgeStore, and the capabilities it offers, consider the following scenario: among a collection of news articles, a user is interested in retrieving all 2014 news reporting statements of a 20th century US president where he is positively mentioned as "commander-in-chief." On one side, the KnowledgeStore supports storing resources – e.g., news articles – and their relevant metadata – e.g., the publishing date of a news article. On the other side, it enables storing structured knowledge about entities of the world – e.g., the fact of being a US president and the event of making a statement – either extracted from text or available in LOD/RDF datasets such as DBpedia (Lehmann et al., 2015) and YAGO (Hoffart, Suchanek, Berberich, & Weikum, 2013). And last, through the notion of mention, it enables linking an entity or fact of the world to each of its specific occurrences in documents – e.g., a US president to the documents mentioning him – allowing also the storage of additional mention attributes, typically extracted while processing the text, such as the explicit way the entity or fact occurs – e.g., "commander-in-chief" – and the sentiment of the article writer on that entity – e.g., positively mentioned. Besides supporting the scalable storage and management of this content, through an architecture compliant with the deployment in distributed hardware settings like clusters and cloud computing, the KnowledgeStore provides a ReST API and a user interface supplying query and retrieval mechanisms that enable accessing all its contents, and thus answering the example query presented above.

Thanks to the explicit representation and alignment of information at different levels, from unstructured to structured knowledge, the KnowledgeStore enables the development of enhanced applications, and favors the design and empirical investigation of information processing tasks otherwise difficult to experiment with. On the one hand, the possibility to semantically query the content of the KnowledgeStore with requests combining knowledge from structured sources and unstructured sources, similarly to the example previously discussed, allows a deeper exploration and analysis of stored data, a capability particularly useful in applications such as decision support. On the other hand, the joint storage of structured knowledge (both background and extracted knowledge), the resources it derives from, and mention information – all effectively accessible through a single API – provides an ideal scenario for developing, debugging, training, and evaluating tools for many NLP and knowledge processing tasks. NLP tasks can benefit from the availability of background knowledge and the textual grounding of mentions, exploiting them to improve their performance: an example is coreference resolution, i.e., identifying that two mentions refer to the same entity of the world, especially in cross-document settings (Zanoli, Corcoglioniti, & Girardi, 2011). Similarly, knowledge processors can exploit the linking of structured knowledge to mentions, and the linguistic features attached to them, to perform tasks such as knowledge fusion (i.e., the merging of possibly contradicting information extracted from different sources). Finally, by jointly storing the source documents and all the knowledge automatically extracted from them, the KnowledgeStore provides an ideal test-bed for the development of KE powered information retrieval systems, such as KE4IR (Corcoglioniti, Dragoni, Rospocher, & Palmero Aprosio, 2016).

Besides having its performances being evaluated through a number of experiments covering both data population and data retrieval, using different dataset sizes and numbers of concurrent clients, the KnowledgeStore has been concretely used in the NewsReader EU project (Vossen et al., 2016), where several KnowledgeStore instances were populated with millions of news articles and billions of RDF triples extracted from them, and a number of applications (mainly for decision support) were success-fully built on top of these instances. This experience is described and discussed in detail in this chapter, and demonstrates the capabilities of the KnowledgeStore.

The chapter is organized as follows. In the first section, an overview of the KnowledgeStore data model and architectural role is provided. The next section describes the KnowledgeStore system, focusing on its data model, architecture, API and user interface, while the following section discusses its concrete use in the NewsReader Project, showing how multiple KnowledgeStore instances have been configured, populated and their contents accessed in several application scenarios. Related state-of-the-art approaches are then surveyed, and some final remarks are reported in the conclusions.

THE KNOWLEDGESTORE: CONCEPTUAL OVERVIEW

To support the storage and alignment of knowledge of unstructured and structured information sources, the KnowledgeStore internally adopts a three-layer content organization (see also Figure 1):

- The *Resource layer,* similarly to a file system, stores unstructured content in the form of *resources* (e.g., news articles), each having a *representation* (e.g., a text file) and some descriptive metadata (e.g., title, actor, document creation date);
- The *Entity layer* is the home of structured content, which, following Knowledge Representation and Semantic Web best practices, consists of assertional (ABox) *axioms*, i.e., ⟨subject, predicate, object⟩ RDF *triples* (Beckett, 2004) describing the *entities* of the world (e.g., persons, locations, events), and for which additional metadata (e.g., the provenance and confidence attributes produced by KE systems) can be stored using the *named graphs* mechanism;
- The *Mention layer* sits between the aforementioned layers and consists of mentions, i.e., snippets of resources (e.g., fragments of text) that denote something of interest, such as an entity or a triple of the Entity layer; clearly, a resource may contain many mentions, and an entity or triple may be mentioned multiple times. Mentions are anchors where to attach attributes specific to the particu-

Figure 1. The three representation layers of the KnowledgeStore: Resource, Mention, and Entity

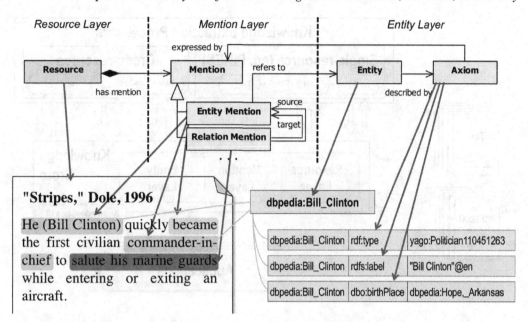

lar realization of an entity or triple in the text, including the NLP annotations produced by a KE tool and the attributes related to the particular way an entity is mentioned, i.e., to a sign-specific sense (e.g., writer attitude or sentiment, role or category the entity is described with).

Compared to related work, the explicit representation of mentions is a distinguishing feature of the KnowledgeStore, which has a conceptual grounding in the need for formally differentiating entities (aka, *referents*, *reference*) from their actual representations (aka, *signs*, *senses*), a topic extensively debated in philosophy of language (Frege, 2000). Furthermore, differently from the other state-of-the-art approaches that typically only highlight the key roles of documents and entities, and treat implicitly mentions as plain links between them (*2-layer approaches*), mentions can be extensively described in the KnowledgeStore by means of attributes that allow storing information that is specific to a mention, instead of the enclosing resource or the denoted entity. As it will be discussed in the next section, the KnowledgeStore adopts a flexible data model, enabling the representation of arbitrary mention attributes according to the specific requirements of the deployment context. As a limit case, a KnowledgeStore instance can be configured with no mention attributes besides the mention URI, thus making it analogous, in this configuration, to a 2-layer documents/entities framework (as storing mention attributes has an impact – e.g., in terms of disk space – the decision on which mention attributes to store should be carefully considered based on the requirements of the applications accessing the KnowledgeStore instance).

From an architectural point of view, the KnowledgeStore is a centralized service accessed by external clients for storing and retrieving the content they process and produce. These clients can be classified in three types, according to their main function (see Figure 2):

Figure 2. Interactions with external modules

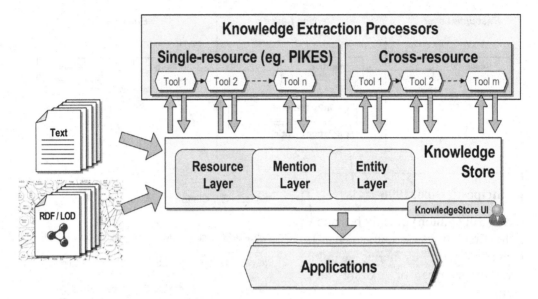

- **Knowledge Extraction Processors:** They produce the structured knowledge stored in the KnowledgeStore, extracting it from unstructured resources. Many NLP tools and suites can be used for this purpose, like PIKES (Corcoglioniti, Rospocher, & Palmero Aprosio, 2016) or the KE pipelines used in NewsReader (Vossen et al., 2016), both publicly available online. Knowledge extraction processors can be classified as either single-resource or cross-resource:
  - ◦ *Single-resource processors* perform tasks defined at the level of a resource or of a portion of it (e.g., a sentence), such as semantic role labeling, relation extraction, and opinion extraction (Palmero Aprosio, Corcoglioniti, Dragoni, & Rospocher, 2015); for these tasks, the processing of a resource is independent of the processing of other resources and thus multiple resources can be processed in parallel;
  - ◦ *Cross-resource processors*, on the other hand, perform tasks defined on whole collections of resources, such as cross-document coreference resolution; these tasks typically combine information from multiple resources, cannot be easily parallelized, and their cost may increase more than linearly with dataset size.
- **Applications:** They mainly read data from the KnowledgeStore offering services on top of its content, such as decision support systems or enhanced web-based applications.

Note that the KnowledgeStore does not enforce a particular client interaction paradigm for what concerns content access and population. Knowledge extraction processors and Applications may interact directly with the KnowledgeStore, possibly using it as a *data hub* and exchanging data through it. Alternatively, the interaction can be mediated by content *populators* and *exporter* tools: populators load the KnowledgeStore with files of unstructured or structured data, either coming from knowledge extraction processors or containing static data such as textual documents, web pages, or RDF/OWL *background knowledge*; exporters query the KnowledgeStore and generate dump files with the data requested by clients, in the formats they support. Moreover, content can be:

- Injected in one shot and then accessed by applications in a sort of "read-only" mode (*write once, read many*), or
- Continuously and incrementally added (as in case of a daily feed of news), where clients work more in a sort of "stream-oriented" mode (*write many, read many*).

SYSTEM DESCRIPTION

This section introduces the main features and components of the KnowledgeStore. Additional documentation, a demo video showcasing the navigation through the KnowledgeStore content, as well as binaries and source code of the system (released under Apache License v2.0), are available on the KnowledgeStore website (http://knowledgestore.fbk.eu/). A running KnowledgeStore instance is also publicly accessible online (http://knowledgestore2.fbk.eu/nwr/wikinews/).

The KnowledgeStore Data Model

The KnowledgeStore data model defines what information can be stored in the KnowledgeStore. As previously pointed out, it is centered on the resource, mention and entity layers. Resources and mentions are described using a configurable set of types, attributes and relations. Entities are described with an open set of annotated axioms consisting of RDF triples enriched with metadata attributes (e.g., for context and provenance). The KnowledgeStore data model is formalized as an OWL 2 (Motik, Parsia, & Patel-Schneider, 2009) ontology accessible online (https://knowledgestore.fbk.eu/ontologies/knowledgestore. html), with types, attributes, and relations identified via URIs. Terms from the Nepomuk Information Element vocabulary (Mylka, Sauermann, Sintek, & van Elst, 2013a), the Nepomuk File Ontology (Mylka, Sauermann, Sintek, & van Elst, 2013b), and the Grounded Annotation Framework ontology (Fokkens et al. 2014) are reused in the ontology. The UML class diagram of Figure 3 summarizes the main aspects of the KnowledgeStore data model.

Flexibility is a key requirement for the data model, as (i) different kinds of unstructured and structured content can be stored in different KnowledgeStore instances; and (ii) the kind of information stored in a KnowledgeStore instance may evolve in time. For this reason, the data model is divided in a *fixed part*, embodied in the implementation and kept as small as possible, and a *configurable part* that is specific to each KnowledgeStore instance and is used to organize and fine tune its storage layout. More in details, the fixed part is an OWL 2 ontology defining:

Figure 3. The KnowledgeStore data model, with its three layers and the configurable part

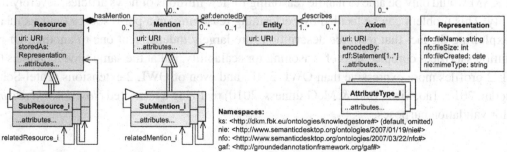

- The Resource, Mention and Entity classes;
- The Axiom class, whose instances are named graphs containing the RDF triples encoding the axiom, with the named graph URI being the subject of any metadata attribute about the axiom;
- The Representation of a resource, including its file and metadata managed by the system;
- The relation storedAs, linking a resource to its representation;
- The relation hasMention, linking a resource to the mentions it contains;
- The relation gaf:denotedBy (Fokkens et al., 2014), linking an entity or axiom to the mention(s) expressing it, used to track provenance of extracted knowledge and to debug information extraction pipelines used with the KnowledgeStore.

For a given specific application, the KnowledgeStore data model can be manually customized by defining another OWL 2 ontology – the configurable part – that is specific to that KnowledgeStore instance. This ontology imports and extends/refines the TBox definitions in the fixed part ontology, specifying:

- The subclass hierarchy of Resource and Mention (Entity refinement is done via axioms);
- Additional attributes of Resource, Mention, Axiom and their subclasses;
- Additional relations among resources or among mentions;
- Enumerations and classes used as attribute types (similarly to Representation);
- Restrictions on fixed part relations (not shown in Figure 3).

This modular approach enables accommodating very different configurations: from KnowledgeStore instances where mentions are just pointers for entities to the characters in the resources where they are referred (in this special case, the KnowledgeStore basically downgrades to a standard 2-layer resources/entities framework), to more enhanced instances where a very rich set of linguistic attributes is stored for each mention. A concrete example of application-specific customization of the KnowledgeStore data model is presented later when describing the use of the system in NewsReader.

It is worth noting that the choice of rooting the data model in OWL 2 and using an OWL 2 ontology for its configuration provides many benefits. First, it allows both the model definition and the instance data to be encoded in RDF, enabling the use of Semantic Web technologies for manipulating them and their publication on the Web according to LOD best practices. Second, to some extent, data validation can be performed using an OWL 2 reasoner. In this case, it must be noted that resource and mention instances form a huge ABox. Some rule-based reasoners, such as RDFox (Motik, Nenov, Piro, Horrocks, & Olteanu, 2014), support OWL 2 RL reasoning over large ABoxes, but their memory requirements would pose a limit on the scalability of the system. As an example, RDFox exhibits a RAM consumption of ~30-60 bytes per triple (Motik et al., 2014), which maps to 60-120 KB of RAM per news article considering an average of 2000 mentions per news. In this case, a powerful machine with hundreds of GBs of RAM would only be able to handle reasoning for few millions of news articles, severely limiting scalability. This problem can be tackled by performing reasoning on a per-resource (and its mentions) basis, exploiting the fact that resource descriptions are largely independent one to another. Of course, this solution sacrifices completeness of reasoning for scalability, but at the same time it enables the use of OWL 2 profiles more expressive than OWL 2 RL, and even of OWL 2 extensions (Patel-Schneider & Franconi, 2012; Tao, Sirin, Bao, & McGuinness, 2010) realizing a restricted *closed world assumption* useful for validation purposes.

The KnowledgeStore API

The KnowledgeStore provides several interfaces, offered as part of the KnowledgeStore API, through which external clients may access and manipulate stored data. These interfaces are available through three dedicated HTTP ReST endpoints: SPARQL Endpoint, CRUD Endpoint, and Custom Endpoint.

The *SPARQL Endpoint* allows querying of axioms in the entity layer using the SPARQL query language (Harris, & Seaborne, 2013), a W3C standard for retrieving and manipulating data in Semantic Web repositories. This endpoint provides a flexible and Semantic Web-compliant way to query for entity data, and leverages the grounding of the KnowledgeStore data model in Knowledge Representation and Semantic Web best practices.

The *CRUD Endpoint* provides the basic operations to access and manipulate any object stored in any of the layers of the KnowledgeStore (CRUD stands for Create, Retrieve, Update, and Delete); for instance, Figure 4 shows the HTTP invocation of a *retrieve* operation returning all the resources with dct:publisher being equal to dbpedia:TechCrunch. Several aspects (e.g., operation granularity, transactional properties, access control) have been considered in defining the operations provided by the CRUD endpoint (Corcoglioniti, Rospocher, Cattoni, Magnini, & Serafini, 2013). For efficiency reasons, the KnowledgeStore offers coarse-grained streaming operations that operate on multiple objects at once (e.g., the simultaneous update of all the mentions of a certain resource). As having fully transactional operations is unfeasible (as an operation can potentially affect all the KnowledgeStore content) and possibly unwanted (e.g., on an update operation on 1 million objects, failing on an object should not cause the rollback of the operation for the other objects), a coarse-grained API call behaves in a transactional way and satisfies the *ACID* properties – Atomicity, Consistency, Isolation, and Durability – only on each single object handled in the call (e.g., a single element in a set of mentions).

The *Custom Endpoint* supports the definition of custom ReST methods specific to a particular KnowledgeStore instance, which are instantiated by plugging custom request handlers (Java plugins) that map request parameters and data into a sequence of primitive KnowledgeStore API operations. This flexible endpoint enables more complex interaction patterns and content editing operations than CRUD, e.g., allowing users to interact live with data stored in the KnowledgeStore, reading and writing resources,

Figure 4. Invocation of Retrieve operation through the CRUD Endpoint of the KnowledgeStore

```
curl -request GET http://newsreader.fbk.eu/kstest/resources.rdf?$where=
    dct:publisher = dbpedia:TechCrunch (*)
```
                                        (*) URL encoding omitted
```
<rdf:RDF xmlns:nwr="http://dkm.fbk.eu/ontologies/newsreader#" ...>
  <nwr:News rdf:about="http://newsreader.fbk.eu/resources.rdf/r105">
    <dct:title>Salesforce Is A Platform Company. Period.</dct:title>
    <dct:publisher rdf:resource="http://dbpedia.org/resource/TechCrunch" />
    <dct:issued>2013-09-30</dct:issued>
    <nfo:fileURL>http://techcrunch.com/2013/09/30/...</nfo:fileURL>
    <nie:isStoredAs rdf:resource="http://newsreader.fbk.eu/resources.rdf/r105.txt">
      <nfo:fileName>r105.txt</nfo:fileName>
      <nfo:fileSize>15012</nfo:fileSize>
      <nfo:fileCreated>2013-09-30</nfo:fileCreated>
      <nie:mimeType>text/plain</nie:mimeType>
    </nie:isStoredAs>
  </nwr:News>
  ...
</rdf:RDF>
```

mentions, and triples. The implementation is based on RDF_{pro} (Corcoglioniti, Rospocher, Mostarda, & Amadori, 2015), and the custom request handlers are defined in terms of (combination of custom) RDF_{pro} processors. An instantiation of the custom endpoint was developed in NewsReader to support the incremental streaming-like population of the KnowledgeStore (more details later).

For all the endpoints, access control is employed to restrict usage of the KnowledgeStore API and contents only to authorized clients. Authentication is based on separate username/password credentials for each authorized client, while access may be limited to restricted parts of the KnowledgeStore content (e.g., only the mention layer, only resources from a certain provider). While the presented HTTP ReST endpoints are language- and platform-neutral and thus allow the integration of the KnowledgeStore in any computing environment, for clients developed in Java a specific client library is also offered to ease the interaction with the KnowledgeStore and take care of the optimal use of its endpoints.

The KnowledgeStore Architecture

The internal KnowledgeStore architecture is centered around the KnowledgeStore Server (Fig. 5), a specifically developed software component that implements the operations of the SPARQL, CRUD and Custom endpoints, handling global issues such as access control, data validation and operation transactionality; it also provides the KnowledgeStore UI.

Data storage is delegated by the KnowledgeStore Server to three software components that may run locally or can be distributed over a cluster of machines: Hadoop HDFS, HBase or Elasticsearch, and Virtuoso.

The *Hadoop HDFS* filesystem (http://hadoop.apache.org) provides a reliable and scalable storage for the files holding the representations of resources (e.g., texts and linguistic annotations of news articles), which are managed as binary objects. HDFS provides transparent data distribution and replication, and fault tolerance with respect to single node failures.

The *HBase* column-oriented store (http://hbase.apache.org) provides database services for storing and retrieving semi-structured information about resources and mentions. HBase builds on Hadoop HDFS and inherits its reliability and scalability characteristics, being particularly suited for random, real time

Figure 5. KnowledgeStore components: Hadoop and HBase/Elasticsearch comprise multiple, distributed processes, while the KnowledgeStore Server and Virtuoso are single processes

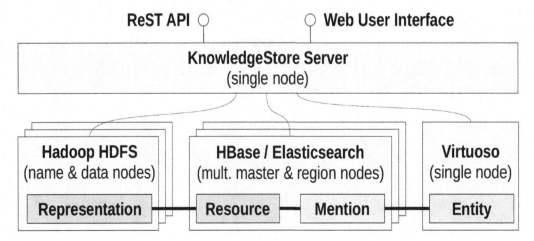

read/write access to huge quantities of data, when the nature of data does not require a relational model (like in the case of resource and mention data). In the current setup, each resource and mention is stored in HBase as a row indexed by its URI. This solution allows for optimal lookup performances, and is insensitive to the number of mentions per resource, i.e., it works equally well with very small and very large resources—what matters it the total number of objects stored (query performances may be however influenced by the distribution of mentions across resources, which affects the selectivity of relations such as gaf:denotedBy). On the other hand, retrieval by filter condition on one or more attributes often requires full table scans, a situation that is mitigated by the possibility to distribute and parallelize such scans over all the nodes forming the HBase cluster.

The *Elasticsearch* full-text search and analytics engine (http://www.elastic.co/products/elasticsearch) can be used in place of HBase for the storage of resources and mentions in the KnowledgeStore. Elasticsearch supports distribution over a cluster of machines, where it provides horizontal scalability, reliability, and easy management. While sharing similar distributed characteristics with HBase, Elasticsearch does not necessarily need a cluster to run, thus making it particularly suitable for small-to-medium size single machine installations of the KnowledgeStore.

The *Virtuoso* triplestore (http://virtuoso.openlinksw.com/dataspace/doc/dav/wiki/Main/) indexes the triples of axioms to provide services supporting reasoning and online SPARQL query answering. Virtuoso has been selected motivated by its excellent performances in recent benchmarks such as the April 2013 BSBM benchmark (Boncz, & Pham, 2013), further improved in the latest releases, as well as for its availability for both a single-machine and a cluster deployment configuration. Triples are stored in Virtuoso within named graphs, which can themselves be the subjects of metadata triples that specify properties applying to all the triples in a graph, such as the confidence and provenance metadata. Virtuoso supports a limited form of query-time RDFS reasoning but it is not used here, relying instead on forward-chaining RDFS reasoning with RDF_{pro} (Corcoglioniti, Rospocher, Mostarda, & Amadori, 2015) to materialize inferable axioms while keeping track of their provenance using named graphs.

Concerning the choice of the storage backend(s), it is worth noting that none of Hadoop HDFS, HBase or Elasticsearch, and Virtuoso can store all the data alone, and hence their combination is crucial to realize a hybrid storage system like the KnowledgeStore. In fact, the use of a triplestore for entity triples currently represents the state-of-the-art choice for providing efficient SPARQL access to this kind of data. At the same time, storing mention and resource data in a triplestore is problematic for large datasets, mainly due to the large amount of mentions data (in RDF terms, several thousands of triples may be necessary to store the mentions of a resource, limiting scalability to a few millions of documents as triplestore technology can hardly scale beyond a few billions of triples): hence an additional storage backend is needed (HBase or Elasticsearch). Finally, large textual content is poorly supported in triplestores and databases (both relational and NoSQL), and is best stored in a filesystem or similar structure (Hadoop HDFS).

The KnowledgeStore User Interface

While the KnowledgeStore can be programmatically accessed by clients through its API, human users can exploit the *KnowledgeStore User Interface* (UI) to easily interact with the KnowledgeStore (see demonstration video at http://youtu.be/YVOQaljLta4). The KnowledgeStore UI is a basic web-based application whose main purpose is to enable users to inspect and navigate the KnowledgeStore content without having to develop applications accessing the KnowledgeStore API. Two core operations are offered:

- The *lookup operation*, which, given the URI of an object (i.e., resource, mention, entity), retrieves all the KnowledgeStore content about that object; Figure 6a and Figure 6b show the output obtained by running a lookup operation for a resource and for a mention;
- The *SPARQL query* operations, with which arbitrary SPARQL queries can be run against the KnowledgeStore SPARQL endpoint, obtaining the results directly in the browser or as a downloadable file in various formats; Figure 6c shows an excerpt of the results obtained by running a query in the SPARQL tab of the KnowledgeStore UI.

Figure 6. KnowledgeStore UI: (a) Resource Lookup; (b) Mention lookup; (c) SPARQL query

These two operations are seamlessly integrated in the UI, to offer a smooth browsing experience to users. For instance, it is possible to directly invoke the lookup operation on any entity returned in the result set of a SPARQL query. Similarly, when performing the lookup operation on a resource, all mentions occurring in the resource are highlighted (see the "Resource text" box in Figure 6a) with a different color for the various mention types (e.g., person, organization, location, event), and by clicking on any of them the user can access all the details for that mention (see Figure 6b). Finally, the lookup of a mention (see Figure 6b) returns the attributes of the selected mention (box *Mention data*) as well as its occurrence in the containing resource (box *Mention resource*) and the structured description of the real-world entity it refers to (box *Mention referent*), capturing in a single page the three representation layers of the KnowledgeStore as well as the role of mentions as a bridge between unstructured and structured content.

In addition to the lookup and SPARQL operations, and integrated with them, the UI also allows generating informative reports that aggregate information from different layers of the KnowledgeStore. For instance, given an entity URI, the *entity mentions* (*aggregate*) report (exemplified in Figure 6.5a for instance dbpedia:General_Motors) produces a sortable and filterable table with all the distinct ⟨RDF property, RDF value⟩ attribute pairs describing the mentions of that instance, including the number of mentions each pair occurs in. This report makes easy spotting wrong attribute pairs (e.g., "Genetically

Figure 7. KnowledgeStore UI Reports: (a) Entity mentions aggregated; (b) Entity mentions details

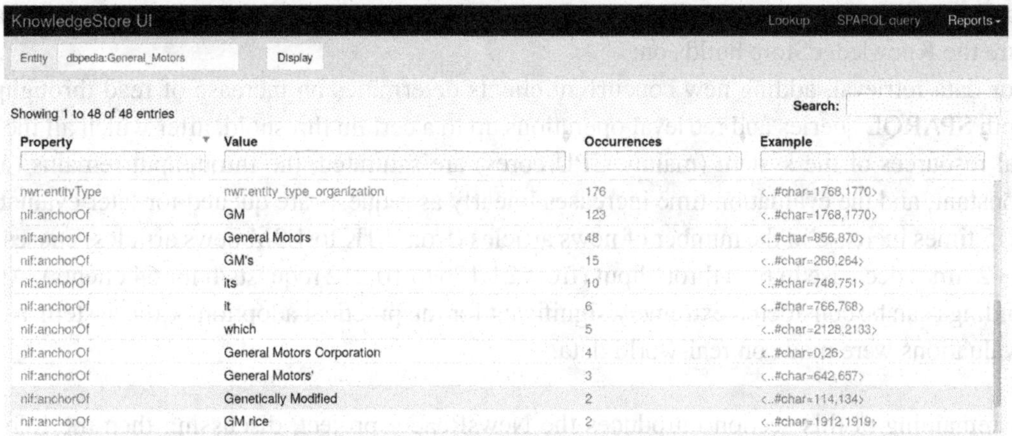

(a)

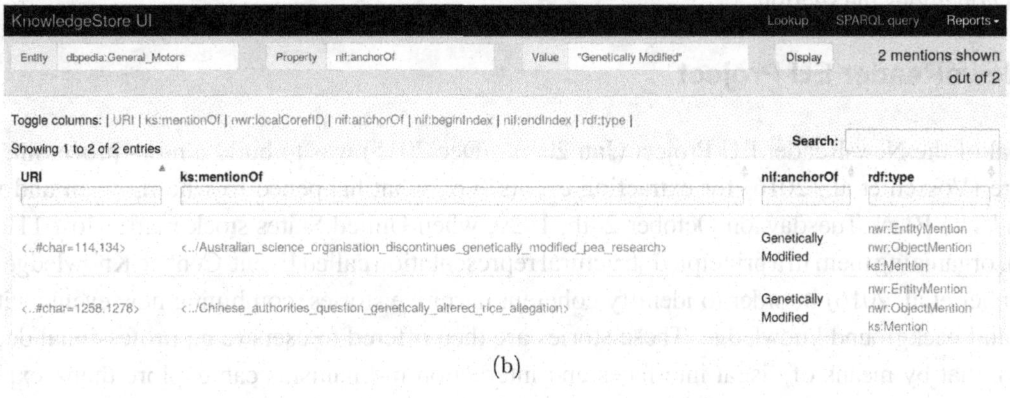

(b)

Modified" being a mention of dbpedia:General_Motors), which can be investigated by listing the corresponding mentions in another *entity mentions* report (Figure 6.5b). Additional reports are available and, altogether, provide concrete tools for spotting KE errors.

THE KNOWLEDGESTORE IN ACTION

In this section, we focus on the concrete use of the system, reporting on the successful deployment of the KnowledgeStore in different scenarios related to the NewsReader project, where it has managed real content extracted from news corpora varying in domain and size (from 18K to 2.3M news articles) and has supported enhanced applications for decision making and data journalism. The interested reader is recalled that a quantitative performance assessment of the KnowledgeStore is presented in a previous work (Corcoglioniti, Rospocher, Cattoni, Magnini, and Serafini 2015), where several experiments were conducted to evaluate the scalability of two core operations relevant for the practical adoption of the system: *data population* and *data retrieval* (evaluation tools available on KnowledgeStore website). Here, the main outcomes of these experiments are briefly summarized:

- For data population, resource and mention layers are populated around three orders of magnitude slower than the entity layer. Their population rate inversely correlates with the average number of mentions per news article, but remains roughly constant during the whole population process, thus suggesting that consistent population performances can be achieved given the software infrastructure the KnowledgeStore builds on;
- For data retrieval, adding new concurrent clients determines an increase of read throughput for both SPARQL queries and retrieval operations up to a certain threshold, after which all the physical resources of the system (mainly CPU cores) are saturated, the throughput remains (almost) constant, and the evaluation time increases linearly as requests are queued for later evaluation. A ~15 times increase in the number of news articles (from 81K to 1.3M news articles) causes 'only' a ~2 times decrease in read throughput (from 21,126 to 10,212 requests/h for 64 clients). All these findings can be considered extremely significant for the practical adoption of the system, as all the evaluations were made on real-world data.

The remaining of this section introduces the NewsReader project, discussing then the role of the KnowledgeStore, and presenting the four deployment scenarios considered; a discussion of lessons learned concludes the section.

The NewsReader EU Project

The goal of the NewsReader EU Project (Jan 2013 – Dec 2015) was to build a news processing infrastructure (Vossen et al., 2016) for extracting events (i.e., what happened to whom, when and where, such as "The Black Tuesday, on October 24th, 1929, when United States stock market lost 11% of its value"), organizing them in a principled structural representation called Event-Centric Knowledge Graph (Rospocher et al, 2016) in order to identify coherent narrative stories, combining new events with past events and background knowledge. These stories are then offered to users (e.g., professional decision-makers), that by means of visual interfaces and interaction mechanisms can explore them, exploiting

Figure 8. KnowledgeStore interaction with other NewsReader components

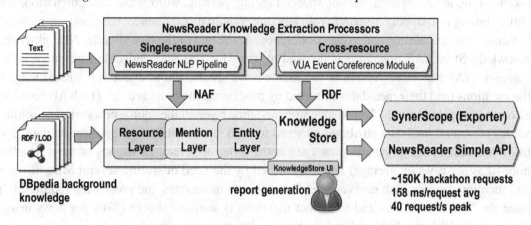

their explanatory power and their systematic structural implications, to make well-informed decisions. Achieving this challenging goal required NewsReader to address several objectives:

- To process document resources, detecting mentions of events, event participants (e.g., persons, organizations), locations, time expressions, and so on;
- To link extracted mentions with instances, either previously extracted or available in background knowledge resources such as DBpedia (Lehmann et al., 2015), and corefer mentions of the same instance;
- To complete instance descriptions by complementing extracted mention information with available structured background knowledge;
- to interrelate instances to support the construction of narrative stories;
- to store all this huge quantity of information (on resources, mentions, instances) in a scalable way, enabling efficient retrieval and intelligent queries;
- to effectively offer narrative stories to decision makers.

The KnowledgeStore in NewsReader

The KnowledgeStore has played a central role in addressing the objectives of the NewsReader project, acting as a sort of data hub populated with news articles and RDF knowledge extracted by the NewsReader knowledge extraction pipelines, and accessed by applications presenting the users with comprehensive views on the heterogeneous content stored in it (cf. Figure 8).

KnowledgeStore Population

The KnowledgeStore population in NewsReader has been performed starting from three sources, according to the way KE is performed in the project:

- **Resource and Mention Data:** A first single-resource KE processor – the *NewsReader NLP pipeline* (demo at http://ixa2.si.ehu.es/nrdemo/demo.php) – processes each news article provided in input, enriching it with NAF (NLP Annotation Format, Fokkens et al., 2014) annotations about:

tokenization, lemmatization, part-of-speech tagging, parsing, word sense disambiguation, named entity linking to DBpedia, semantic role labeling, nominal coreference, temporal expression recognition, opinion mining, and event coreference. At the end of the NewsReader NLP pipeline, the KnowledgeStore *NAF populator* is invoked to upload in the KnowledgeStore resource layer the complete NAF annotated version of the source news article, and to inject in the KnowledgeStore the mentions (and their metadata) extracted by processing the news article. The NAF populator is also used to upload into the KnowledgeStore resource layer all the source news articles, setting the values of several metadata attributes attached to each news article (e.g., publication date, author, title). Measured NAF population rates are in the order of several thousands of news articles per hour (0.5s per news on average) and are justified by the need of storing several MBs of resource and mention data for each news article. Compared to these rates, the processing required to produce the NLP annotations and to extract mentions is sensibly slower (170s per news using the NewsReader NLP pipeline) and makes this population cost negligible.

- **Entity Data From KE:** A second cross-resource processor – the *VUA Event Coreference Module* (demo at http://ic.vupr.nl/~ruben/vua-eventcoreference.ttl) – processes all the mentions extracted by the NewsReader NLP pipeline. Clusters of mentions referring to the same entity (e.g., event, person, organization) are identified using machine learning techniques and several features, including mention extents, links to DBpedia, and the event-actor links from semantic role labeling (more details in Cybulska and Vossen, 2014). An entity is created for each cluster of mentions, and axioms describing and linking these entities are asserted based on attributes and relations in the mention layer. These entities and axioms are injected into the KnowledgeStore via RDF_{pro}. In the injection, additional triples may be inferred and added to the KnowledgeStore according to the rules defined in the ESO (Event Situation Ontology, Segers et al., 2015) ontology. More precisely, given an event typed according to ESO, in many cases it is possible to materialize triples describing the situations holding before (*pre-situation*), during (*during-situation*), or after that event (*post-situation*). For example, for a "giving" event where a person gives an object to another person, in the pre-situation the first person owns the object, while in the post-situation it is the second person who owns the object. This reasoning is performed with a dedicated RDF_{pro} processor (*@esoreasoner*) which works independently, and hence efficiently, on each single event typed according to ESO.

- **Entity Data From Background Knowledge:** RDF_{pro} is also used to populate the KnowledgeStore with *background knowledge*, i.e., RDF content directly injected into the KnowledgeStore entity layer, that may (i) support some tasks performed by the information extraction processors, and (ii) complement the information automatically extracted from news with quality content available in structured resources such as DBpedia, Freebase, and GeoNames, to favor the exploitation of the KnowledgeStore content by applications built on top of it.

Given the nature of the textual resources considered (daily news), the NewsReader infrastructure was designed to handle a stream of news by processing them in small batches, incrementally updating the data in the KnowledgeStore based on the results of each batch. While data in the Resource and Mention layers are only monotonically added with this approach, for data in the Entity layer it may happen that new events are added but also that events previously asserted in the KnowledgeStore are merged together and enriched with new data, because of cross-document coreference. This situation is handled via the instantiation of a specific ReST method in the Custom Endpoint of the KnowledgeStore, called "*naf2sem*", which is invoked for each batch of RDF data produced by the VUA Event Coreference Module. The process implemented by the custom request handler is the following: first, it fetches (and removes) the RDF data in the KnowledgeStore affected by the operation; then, it merges and performs ESO reasoning on this data, together with some necessary post-processing; and, finally, it adds back the resulting triples to the Entity layer of the KnowledgeStore.

KnowledgeStore Clients

The contents loaded in the KnowledgeStore instances were accessed by users via the web UI, and by two applications via the SPARQL endpoint and ReST API:

- **NewsReader Simple API (Hopkinson, Maude, & Rospocher, 2014):** To support people not familiar with Semantic Web technologies such as RDF and SPARQL, the NewsReader Simple API was developed by ScraperWiki to act as a mediator between the KnowledgeStore and the end user or application. The NewsReader Simple API exposes an HTTP ReST API developed in Python that uses JSON and is easily accessible from JavaScript, where each method is implemented by evaluating a SPARQL query on the KnowledgeStore starting from a template that is instantiated at runtime with the actual parameters passed to the method. For instance, the method "*actors of a specified type*" implements a query that returns all entities having as RDF type the value of the parameter passed to the method.
- **SynerScope** (http://www.synerscope.com/)**:** SynerScope is a visual analytics application delivering real time interaction with network-centric data. SynerScope interacts with the KnowledgeStore through the *KnowledgeStore Exporter*, a tool that converts selected data stored in the KnowledgeStore to the format digested by SynerScope. SynerScope offers different views (e.g., table view, hierarchical view, map view) on the KnowledgeStore content, enabling users to navigate it through various interaction methods (e.g., selection/highlight, drill down/up, expansion). This way, it is possible to visually browse all events that involve a given person or company, or to build networks of persons/companies based on event co-participation.

KnowledgeStore Data Model

Figure 9 shows how the KnowledgeStore data model was manually configured for the NewsReader scenarios. The original news articles, together with their corresponding annotated versions obtained by processing them with NLP information extraction tools, are stored in the resource layer and described with metadata from the Dublin Core and Nepomuk vocabularies (hence, two resources are stored for each news article, with mentions attached only to the original news article). Several types of mentions are stored, which denote either an entity (e.g., person, organization, event), a relation among entities (e.g., participation links between event and participant mentions, as well as causal, temporal and subordinate links among event mentions and/or time expressions, derived from the TimeML standard by Pustejovsky, Lee, Bunt, & Romary, 2010), or a numerical quantity. The NLP Interchange Format (NIF) vocabulary (Hellmann, Lehmann, Auer, & Brümmer, 2013) has been used to define basic mention properties, thus enabling interoperability with tools consuming NIF data and vocabularies that are compatible and complementary with NIF, such as PreMOn (Corcoglioniti, Rospocher, Palmero Aprosio,

Figure 9. KnowledgeStore data model configured for the NewsReader scenarios

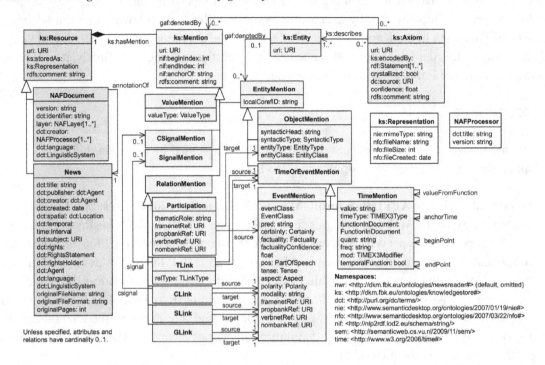

& Tonelli, 2016) for denoting linguistic predicates and their role. In addition, several specific attributes have been added to store information extracted from NLP processing. At the entity level, provenance, confidence, and contextual metadata have been associated to statements, exploiting also the Simple Event Model (SEM) vocabulary (van Hage, Malaisé, Segers, Hollink, & Schreiber, 2011). The ontology of the NewsReader KnowledgeStore data model is available online (https://knowledgestore.fbk.eu/ontologies/newsreader.html).

Deployment Scenarios

Table 1 summarizes the characteristics of the various KnowledgeStore instances that were deployed and populated in the different scenarios considered in NewsReader, focusing on population time and size (i.e., disk space occupation and number of objects in the three KnowledgeStore layers) with detailed breakdown for entities and axiom triples. Details on the domain, news article providers, and period when each instance was prepared are also reported.

To put the numbers in Table 1 in perspective, it is worth noticing that differences across the instances, especially in interpreting extracted information or population times, could be also due to different versions of the knowledge extraction processors, populators, and KnowledgeStore software used: the latest stable versions of these tools were used at the time of populating each KnowledgeStore instance. Also, note that different versions of background knowledge were injected in the various KnowledgeStore instances, to accommodate specific needs of the scenario considered or to use the latest official release of the original dataset. A collection of background knowledge datasets used for populating the KnowledgeStore (including additional datasets of possible practical interest) is available for download on the KnowledgeStore website.

Table 1. Overview of KnowledgeStore instances deployed in NewsReader; n/a means that the value was not recorded (data no more available); starred values for Wikinews (Ver. 2) refer to an alternative backend (ElasticSearch) instead

	Wikinews Ver. 1	Wikinews Ver. 2	FIFA World Cup	Cars Ver. 1	Cars Var. 2	Cars Ver. 3	Dutch Parliament
News	18,510	19,755	212,258	63,635	1,259,748	2,316,158	597,530
words/news	314	268	597	531	387	394	n/a
period	2003-2013	2003-2015	2004-2014	2003-2013	2003-2013	2003-2015	2008-2009
Mentions	2,629,176	5,206,202	76,165,114	9,110,683	205,114,711	842,639,827	9,231,113
per news	142	264	359	143	163	364	15
Entities	670,031	673,018	10,246,338	2,212,691	27,123,724	44,559,443	5,495,077
events	624,439	632,704	9,387,356	1,783,991	25,156,574	42,296,287	5,383,498
persons	19,677	17,617	403,021	199,999	729,797	895,541	43,546
in DBpedia	9,744	10,784	40,511	16,787	128,183	126,140	13,942
organizations	15,559	14,358	431,232	187,842	947,262	1,139,170	44,139
in DBpedia	6,317	4,940	15,984	8,695	60,547	44,458	12,907
locations	10,356	8,339	24,729	40,859	290,091	228,445	23,894
in DBpedia	7,773	7,369	16,372	11,364	88,695	76,341	11,167
Triples	105,675,519	110,861,823	240,731,408	316,034,616	535,035,576	1,240,774,944	188,296,316
from Mentions	9,700,585	16,688,833	136,135,841	46,359,300	439,060,642	1,146,601,954	65,631,222
from DBpedia	95,974,934	94,172,990	104,595,567	269,675,316	95,974,934	94,172,990	122,665,094
version	2014	2015	3.9	3.9	2014	2015	2014
Populated in	Feb 2015	Oct 2015	May 2014	Jan 2014	Dec 2014	Oct 2015	Jun 2015
time (hrs)	2	* n/a	56	30	160	n/a	42
rate (news/h)	9,300	* n/a	4,000	2,250	7,800	6,400	14,000
Disk space (GB)	17.64	16.33	82.48	30.67	260.20	967.99	n/a
resource layer	1.25	1.40	16.55	3.10	108.27	342.37	48.87
mention layer	1.49	1.64	41.72	4.77	112.00	558.74	4.84
entity layer	14.90	13.29	24.21	22.80	39.93	66.88	n/a

Scenario 1: Wikinews

Wikinews (http://en.wikinews.org/) is a source of general domain news in different languages, although only English news were considered in NewsReader. Two versions were processed at different times during the project: Wikinews (Ver. 1) and Wikinews (Ver. 2) (cf. corresponding columns). Differently from the other scenarios considered in NewsReader, Wikinews data are publicly available (Creative Commons Attribution 2.5 License). This allows publicly exposing the corresponding KnowledgeStore instances (accessible at http://knowledgestore2.fbk.eu/nwr/wikinews/) populated with a complete dataset consisting of structured content (mentions, entities, triples) linked to the source news from which it was extracted, this way favoring the dissemination of the project results and enabling other researchers and developers to exploit this content for various purposes, such as benchmarking their knowledge extraction pipelines, or building and testing new LOD applications. Given its controlled size, substantially smaller than the other scenarios here reported, Wikinews data – and in particular the MEANTIME (Minard et al., 2016) subset manually annotated by a team of linguists as part of the project – was used in NewsReader to support benchmarking of the knowledge extraction processors.

Scenario 2: FIFA 2014 World Cup

The second scenario is about revealing hidden facts and people networks behind the FIFA World Cup 2014, by building web-based applications on top of the KnowledgeStore.

A total of 212,258 football-related news articles, from various providers (including BBC and The Guardian) and distributed over a period of ten years (2005-2014), were processed and uploaded into the KnowledgeStore (cf. column "FIFA World Cup" in Table 1).

While data collection and preparation required significant time and effort, the development of applications on top of stored content was realized as part of a Hack Day event held in London, June 10th, 2014 (http://www.newsreader-project.eu/newsreader-world-cup-hack-day/). In this event, 40 people, a mixture of LOD enthusiasts and data journalists, gathered for one day to collaboratively develop web-based applications on top of the KnowledgeStore. Ten web-based applications, implemented in different programming languages, were developed in roughly 6 working hours. Each application was developed with a focused purpose: among them, to determine which teams some football player had played during his career (by looking at transfer events); to discover which football teams were most commonly associated with violence; to determine people and companies related to gambling; and, to establish the popularity of people, companies, and football teams in different locations.

During the Hack Day, the KnowledgeStore received 30,126 queries (on average, 1 query/second, with peaks of 20 queries/second), issued either directly through the SPARQL Endpoint or via the NewsReader Simple API, and successfully served them on average in 654ms (only 40 queries out of 30,126 took more than 60 seconds to complete).

Scenario 3: Global Automotive Industry Crisis Review

The third scenario is about analyzing the news related to the last decade's financial crisis, with a special focus on the global automotive industry sector, to mine its key events and to understand the role of major players (e.g., CEOs, companies) in it. The news articles were made available for project purposes by LexisNexis (http://www.lexisnexis.nl/), and three KnowledgeStore instances were prepared: Cars (Ver. 1), Cars (Ver. 2), and Cars (Ver. 3), with the number of news ranging from 63,635 to 2,316.158 (cf. corresponding columns in Table 1). Note that the Cars (Ver. 3) KnowledgeStore instance was populated with over 1.2 billion triples, most of them extracted from the news and only a small fraction coming from the background knowledge.

The main application in this scenario is SynerScope. In addition, the capability to query the KnowledgeStore content was exploited to deliver automatically generated reports (and plots) supporting decision makers. For instance, by retrieving the different events involving the ten major car companies, it was possible to generate a report showing the trend of the quantity of events per year in which these companies were involved in the considered period, and therefore to assess their popularity (according to the considered dataset) during the economic crisis. Similarly, by retrieving the different events with their locations and times, it was possible to produce maps (one per year) providing insights into how the localities of the global automotive industry changed during the crisis.

The Cars (Ver. 2) KnowledgeStore instance has been also exploited in two Hack Day events, held in Amsterdam, January 21st, 2015 (http://www.newsreader-project.eu/amsterdam-hackathon-recap/), and in London, January 30th, 2015 (http://www.newsreader-project.eu/london-hackathon/). In these events, enhanced applications were built to conduct exploratory investigations on top of the KnowledgeStore: among them, an in-depth analysis of the age of CEOs when they get hired or fired from companies, analysis of the most dangerous cars around, car companies with high cars recall rate, and so on. During the hackathons, the KnowledgeStore received 118,094 requests (3 requests/s avg., with peaks of 40 requests/s), issued directly through its endpoints or via the NewsReader Simple API, and successfully served them on average in 31 ms. The Cars (Ver. 3) instance was also used for an end-user evaluation in November 2015.

Scenario 4: The Dutch House of Representative

In this scenario, a KnowledgeStore instance (Dutch Parliament) was populated with content extracted from texts about an inquiry of the House of Representatives on the financial system, with the aim of making this information more insightful. The corpus consists of news and magazine articles, debate transcripts, and parliamentary papers provided by the Information Provision Department of the Dutch House of Representatives, and ~50K news articles about ABN-AMRO (one of the main financial players) by LexisNexis.

Differently from the previous scenarios, all the texts considered in this scenario are in Dutch and were processed with a version of the NewsReader knowledge extraction pipeline specifically tailored for this language. To account for this aspect, the KnowledgeStore instance was loaded with a multilingual version of the DBpedia background knowledge that contains textual attributes also in Dutch.

In June 2015, the navigation of the KnowledgeStore instance via SynerScope was presented to about 10 members of the Information Provision Department of the Dutch House of Representatives (including the head of the department), and to 3 members of De Nederlandsche Bank (The Dutch Bank) who had expressed their interest in this use case.

Discussion

The concrete usage of the KnowledgeStore in NewsReader has provided valuable insight on the practical issues and the user expectations encountered when deploying a system like the KnowledgeStore, permitting the validation of its design and the identification of its weaknesses. This section discusses the findings resulting from this experience, most of which are of general interest for any system addressing the same goals as the KnowledgeStore.

Unified Query Language

Concrete usage of the system shows that users appreciate the expressivity of SPARQL and ask for a unified, SPARQL-like language targeted at all the contents of the KnowledgeStore, including the ones currently accessed via the CRUD Endpoint. Providing such unified query facility is a challenging task due to the volume of data and the different storage backends involved.

Analytical Queries

Contrarily to expectations, the KnowledgeStore logs show the submission of many analytical SPARQL queries that match and/or extract a sensible amount of data stored in the KnowledgeStore. It turns out that users submit SPARQL queries to compute statistics, to analyze the loaded corpus and to assess the results and performance of knowledge extraction processors. While SPARQL can be used to a certain extent for these investigations, some analytical queries take long times to execute, in some cases due to improper query planning but most often due to their inherent complexity. While some of these queries were improved on an ad-hoc basis, e.g., via careful rewriting to help the query planner or by materializing some properties that help speed up queries (e.g., rdfs:isDefinedBy annotations linking vocabulary terms to the ontologies defining them), and although there are also many analytical queries whose evaluation times (few seconds) are compatible with the online use of the system, a more general and principled approach to handle analytical requests is clearly needed in the KnowledgeStore.

Flexible Access Control

Access control becomes a requirement in presence of copyrighted content whose provision and consumption involve different parties having different needs (e.g., researchers aiming at disseminating results vs. content providers aiming at protecting intellectual property). In general, different access control policies apply to resources from different sources and, within a resource, to its text and various metadata attributes (e.g., title and date can be publicly accessible whereas author and text may not). Access control policies also apply to mention and entity data derived from copyrighted resources, with the situation being more complex for entity data deriving from multiple resources, possibly with different distribution policies. While this need was anticipated in the KnowledgeStore, the solution had to be revised several times to adapt to changing requirements, thus showing the importance for systems like the KnowledgeStore of a flexible access control mechanism.

Built-In Knowledge Extraction Pipeline

Although integrating a KE pipeline is not an expensive activity and can benefit from many readily available NLP tools, it still requires a good knowledge of NLP concepts, tools and best practices. This hinders a wider usage of the KnowledgeStore by users that do not have this kind of background. For that reason, it is currently under investigation the possibility of defining an extension point in the KnowledgeStore where casual users may plug in standardized, possibly pre-packaged and pre-configured NLP pipelines to obtain a complete running system.

Scaling Down the System

While a system like the KnowledgeStore should be designed with massive scalability and deployment on a distributed infrastructure in mind, some usage scenarios do not require scalability and instead mandate for simple, lightweight single-machine deployments; these scenarios include the use of the system for evaluation or demonstration purposes and any other use case involving small datasets. The introduction of ElasticSearch described in this chapter, made possible by the plugin-based implementation of the

KnowledgeStore, serves exactly the goal of providing a self-contained, possibly scaled down (if distribution is not involved) version of the KnowledgeStore that can be used in those less demanding scenarios.

RELATED WORK

This section provides some background and further references concerning the development of the KnowledgeStore and presents an organized overview of related work in the broad area dealing with the storage and management of interlinked text and knowledge resulting from KE.

KnowledgeStore Development

The idea behind the KnowledgeStore was preliminarily investigated in the scope of the LiveMemories project (http://www.livememories.org/), where a preliminary version of the system, not yet using Semantic Web technologies, was developed to store texts and knowledge extracted from local Italian news sources (Cattoni et al., 2012; Cattoni et al., 2013).

The idea was reconsidered and further expanded in the scope of the NewsReader project, where the need arose for a storage system like the KnowledgeStore acting as a centralized data hub. In the work by Corcoglioniti, Rospocher, Cattoni, Magnini, & Serafini (2013), the initial KnowledgeStore design was thus greatly revised, introducing significant enhancements: (i) support for storing events and related information, such as event participants; (ii) a new architecture that favors scaling on a significantly larger collection of resources; (iii) a semantic querying mechanism over stored content, and (iv) a HTTP ReST API as well as a web user interface to seamlessly inspect contents. The solution was further extended in the work by Corcoglioniti, Rospocher, Cattoni, Magnini, & Serafini (2015), where a first complete, used in practice, and evaluated implementation of the KnowledgeStore was presented.

Further developments with respect to that work are documented in this chapter, and cover new deployment scenarios – Wikinews (Ver. 2), Cars (Ver. 3), Dutch Parliament – and KnowledgeStore features – ElasticSearch backend for mention and resource metadata, UI reports facilities, Custom Endpoint used for incremental population and ESO reasoning.

Domain-General Frameworks for Text and Knowledge

The development of frameworks able to store integrated and interlinked, unstructured and structured content has not been deeply explored in the literature, although some relevant works closely related to the KnowledgeStore contribution do exist that tackle the domain-general storage of interlinked text and knowledge: the KIM Platform, Apache Stanbol, and the Linked Media Framework.

The KIM Platform (Popov et al., 2003), now evolved into the Ontotext Semantic Platform (http://www.ontotext.com/products/ontotext-semantic/), aims at providing a platform for semantic annotations of documents, focusing on named entity recognition and linking to a knowledge base of known entities. The main components of the platform are a document index, a knowledge base and an annotation pipeline. The document index, based on Lucene (http://lucene.apache.org/), stores documents with their metadata and the entities recognized within them. The knowledge base contains the RDFS description of 80K entities of international relevance (background knowledge) as well as entities extracted from documents, based on a specifically-designed ontology (KIMO) defining ~150 top-level entity classes and associated properties. The annotation pipeline is based on the Gate NLP suite (https://gate.ac.uk/) extended to leverage information in the knowledge base, and allows the automatic annotation of documents with the entities they contain, typed with respect to KIMO and linked to known entities in the knowledge base. Several APIs and UIs are provided for document storage and annotation as well as for retrieving entities and documents using queries combining keywords and entities and allowing the navigation from documents to referenced entities and back. KIM has been used in production at several news providers such as BBC, and more recently has adopted the PROTON upper ontology (Damova, Kiryakov. Simov, & Petrov, 2010) in place of KIMO and selected LOD data as background knowledge. The methodology and the software architecture for these applications are described by Georgiev, Popov, Osenova, and Dimitrov (2013). Compared to the KnowledgeStore approach, the information extraction pipeline in KIM is fixed and closely tied to a specific ontological schema for entities (KIMO, then PROTON), whereas the KnowledgeStore is agnostic with respect to which pipeline, ontologies and background knowledge are used.

Apache Stanbol (Gönül & Sinaci, 2012), originated in the IKS Project (http://www.iks-project.eu/), is a modular server exposing a configurable set of ReST services for the enhancement of unstructured textual contents. The main goal of Stanbol is to complement existing CMSs with semantic annotation, indexing and retrieval functionalities. CMS documents and their metadata are fed to the Stanbol server, where a pipeline of content enhancers is applied to extract entities and additional metadata (e.g., language, topics). Extracted data are augmented with LOD data, and the result is indexed inside Stanbol in a triplestore (like the KnowledgeStore) as well as in a SOLR (http://lucene.apache.org/solr/) full-text index, supporting respectively SPARQL queries and keyword search. While the KnowledgeStore provides a scalable and reliable primary storage for resources, Stanbol is mainly focused on their indexing for search purposes, and thus their main storage remains in external CMSs.

The Linked Media Framework (LMF, Kurz et al., 2014) offers storage and retrieval functionalities for multimedia contents annotated with LOD data. Annotations are provided by external content enhancers such as Stanbol, while the focus of LMF is on storage and retrieval services as in the KnowledgeStore. Like Stanbol, the LMF data server is based on a triplestore (Sesame) storing annotations as RDF triples and on a SOLR full-text index storing document texts as well as selected metadata and annotation values chosen via XPath-like *LDPath* (http://code.google.com/p/ldpath/) expressions; the two storages enable respectively SPARQL queries and keyword-based document search. Like the KnowledgeStore, a ReST API extending the Linked Data HTTP publishing scheme allows read/write access to stored contents.

Compared to the KnowledgeStore, KIM, Stanbol and LMF all adopt a 'two-layer' model consisting only of resources (text and metadata indexed in a full-text index) and entities (triples indexed in a triplestore). Indeed, storing and querying mention attributes is not a goal of these frameworks. Although mention data could be stored as additional attributes of resources and/or entities, this is not the intended use of these layers and this expedient may lead to inefficiencies or it may be not feasible at all due to the huge amount of RDF triples required to represent mentions. On the other hand, using the KnowledgeStore as a two-layer system is possible too, but with a small overhead imposed by the unused Mention layer. Therefore, a fair quantitative comparison between the KnowledgeStore and these frameworks is not possible, as they provide different feature sets and they target different usage scenarios. Beyond the different number of layers, another distinctive feature of the KnowledgeStore compared to KIM, Stanbol and LMF is its use of named graph to track the provenance of entities and axioms and to qualify the context where an axiom holds.

Specialized Frameworks for Text and Knowledge

Apart the domain-general works mentioned above, some specialized solutions dealing with the management of text and related structured knowledge in specific domains do exist.

A first relevant work is the contribution presented by Croset, Grabmüller, Li, Kavaliauskas, and Rebholz-Schuhmann (2010). The authors present a framework, based on a RDF triplestore, that enables querying the bioinformatics scientific literature and structured resources at the same time, for evidence of genetic causes, such as drug targets and disease involvement. Differently from the KnowledgeStore approach, this work does not support storing unstructured content (triplestores currently provide only a limited support for integrating knowledge with unstructured resources, often consisting in simple full text search capabilities on RDF literals), and the framework is focused only on specific types of named entities appearing in the unstructured content, whereas a rich, unconstrained set of entities and mentions can be managed in the KnowledgeStore.

Another relevant work, in the biomedical domain, is Semantic Medline, a web application (available at http://skr3.nlm.nih.gov/SemMed/index.html) that summarizes MEDLINE citations returned by a PubMed search. Natural language processing is performed to extract semantic predications (the equivalent of entity axioms in KnowledgeStore terminology) from titles and abstracts. However, differently from the KnowledgeStore, Semantic Medline has a fixed domain-specific data model, built tailored on that application, and predications can be effectively navigated only on a reasonably small selection of citations (max 500 on the web site) with no possibility to perform structured queries on the whole corpus (to this respect, a global index of predications seems missing). Furthermore, while capable of handling large quantity of resources (21M Medline citations, see Jonnalagadda et al., 2012) the semantic content extracted and to be handled is proportionally rather small (~57.6M predications of 26 types, cf. with Cars (Ver. 2) KnowledgeStore instance, with 1.2B triples from 2.3M news articles).

A related line of works concerns document repositories based on semantics (e.g., Bang & Eriksson, 2006; Eriksson, 2007). In these approaches, ontologies encode the domain vocabulary and the document structure, and they are used for annotating documents and document parts. However, the repositories adopting these approaches: (i) emphasize the document structure (e.g., tables, title) rather than document content, (ii) they do not foresee an integrated framework for storing semantic content and unstructured documents together, and (iii) they are not meant to be applied in big data contexts.

Although exploited in a different specialized context, dealing with much smaller quantity of content, also semantic desktop applications such as MOSE (Xiao & Cruz, 2006) and Nepomuk (Groza et al., 2007) are partly related with the contribution here presented. Semantic desktop applications enrich documents archived on the personal PC of a user with annotations coming from ontologies. However, annotations are attached to the object associated to the document, and not to its content, thus not fully supporting the interlinking between unstructured and structured content.

Knowledge Extraction Systems for Populating a KnowledgeStore

Knowledge Extraction has become quite popular in the last decade, thanks to the spreading of LOD and Semantic Web technologies (for a review of state of the art up to 2011, see Petasis et al., 2011). In particular, in the last few years (2012 onward) several contributions were presented that explicitly account for mentions as the link between text and extracted knowledge, and can thus be used to populate systems like the KnowledgeStore. Among them, three publicly available, state-of-the-art open-source tools are FRED, the NewsReader pipeline, and PIKES.

FRED (Presutti et al., 2012) is a KE tool that builds on Discourse Representation Structures (DRS), mapping them to linguistic frames, which in turn are transformed in RDF/OWL via ontology design patterns; both ABox and TBox triples are emitted. Results are enriched based on the results of named entity recognition, entity linking, and word sense disambiguation.

PIKES (Corcoglioniti, Rospocher, Palmero Aprosio, 2016) is a KE tool extracting frames from English texts that leverages a combination of semantic role labeling and other NLP tasks (vs. DRS) and adopts a 2-phase KE approach where all extracted content, including the intermediate linguistic information, is exposed in RDF according to a comprehensive data model compatible with the one of the KnowledgeStore (i.e., based on resources, mentions, and entities). PIKES adopts NAF to encode text and NLP annotations, and thus is compatible with the NAF-based KnowledgeStore population tools described in this chapter.

The NewsReader pipeline (Vossen et al., 2016) was developed for extracting and coreferring events and entities from large (cross-lingual) news corpora, and was concretely used to populate the KnowledgeStore instances deployed within NewsReader. Like PIKES, the NewsReader pipeline combines several NLP tasks including semantic role labeling, and also covers cross-document concerns such as cross-document entity and event coreference. NLP annotations are collected in a single, layered annotation file based on the NAF format, and the conversion from NAF to RDF is performed according to a rule-based approach.

CONCLUSION

This chapter described the KnowledgeStore, a scalable, fault-tolerant, and Semantic Web grounded open-source storage system for interlinking structured and unstructured data, aiming at presenting applications with a unified view over all the data resulting from Knowledge Extraction.

Besides presenting the design, functionalities and implementation of the KnowledgeStore, including the latest development with respect to the version described by Corcoglioniti, Rospocher, Cattoni, Magnini, and Serafini (2015), the chapter focused on the concrete usage of the system within the NewsReader EU project in different scenarios (from 18K to 2.3M news articles), showing overall how the KnowledgeStore enables managing large volumes of interlinked text and knowledge in knowledge extraction applications.

Based on the reported usage experience, the chapter also discussed lessons learned and ideas for further development of the system, which provide insight and may be generalized to other systems addressing the same goals of the KnowledgeStore.

ACKNOWLEDGMENT

The research leading to this paper was supported by the European Union's 7th Framework Programme via the NewsReader Project (ICT-316404). The authors would like to thank all those who contributed to the implementation of the various versions of the KnowledgeStore, including Renato Marroquin Mogrovejo, Alessio Palmero Aprosio, Mohammad Qwaider, Marco Amadori, Michele Mostarda, Enrico Magnago, and Gianluca Apriceno.

REFERENCES

Bang, M., & Eriksson, H. (2006). Towards document repositories based on semantic documents. In *Proceedings of 6th International Conference on Knowledge Management and Knowledge Technologies (I-KNOW'06)*. Springer.

Beckett, D. (2004). *RDF/XML syntax specification (revised)* (Recommendation). W3C.

Boncz, P., & Pham, M. D. (2013). *BSBM V3.1 Results (April 2013)*. Retrieved on June 24, 2017 from http://wifo5-03.informatik.uni-mannheim.de/bizer/berlinsparqlbenchmark/results/V7/

Cattoni, R., Corcoglioniti, F., Girardi, C., Magnini, B., Serafini, L., & Zanoli, R. (2012). The KnowledgeStore: An entity-based storage system. In *Proceedings of the 8th International Conference on Language Resources and Evaluation (LREC'12)*. European Language Resources Association (ELRA).

Cattoni, R., Corcoglioniti, F., Girardi, C., Magnini, B., Serafini, L., & Zanoli, R. (2013). Anchoring Background Knowledge to Rich Multimedia Contexts in the KnowledgeStore. New Trends of Research in Ontologies and Lexical Resources, 91-112. doi:10.1007/978-3-642-31782-8_6

Corcoglioniti, F., Dragoni, M., Rospocher, M., & Palmero Aprosio, A. (2016). Knowledge Extraction for Information Retrieval. In H. Sack, E. Blomqvist, M. d'Aquin, C. Ghidini, S. Ponzetto, & C. Lange (Eds.), Lecture Notes in Computer Science: Vol. 9678. *The Semantic Web. Latest Advances and New Domains. ESWC 2016*. Springer.

Corcoglioniti, F., Rospocher, M., Cattoni, R., Magnini, B., & Serafini, L. (2013). Interlinking unstructured and structured knowledge in an integrated framework. In *IEEE 7th International Conference on Semantic Computing* (pp. 40–47). IEEE Computer Society. doi:10.1109/ICSC.2013.17

Corcoglioniti, F., Rospocher, M., Cattoni, R., Magnini, B., & Serafini, L. (2015). The KnowledgeStore: A Storage Framework for Interlinking Unstructured and Structured Knowledge. *International Journal on Semantic Web and Information Systems*, *11*(2), 1–35. doi:10.4018/IJSWIS.2015040101

Corcoglioniti, F., Rospocher, M., Mostarda, M., & Amadori, M. (2015). Processing billions of RDF triples on a single machine using streaming and sorting. In *Symposium on Applied Computing, SAC 2015*. ACM. Retrieved from http://rdfpro.fbk.eu

Corcoglioniti, F., Rospocher, M., & Palmero Aprosio, A. (2016, December 1). Frame-Based Ontology Population with PIKES. *IEEE Transactions on Knowledge and Data Engineering*, *28*(12), 3261–3275. doi:10.1109/TKDE.2016.2602206

Corcoglioniti, F., Rospocher, M., Palmero Aprosio, A., & Tonelli, S. (2016). PreMOn: a Lemon Extension for Exposing Predicate Models as Linked Data. In *Proceedings of Language Resources and Evaluation*. LREC.

Croset, S., Grabmüller, C., Li, C., Kavaliauskas, S., & Rebholz-Schuhmann, D. (2010). The CALBC RDF triple store: Retrieval over large literature content. In *Proceedings of the Workshop on Semantic Web Applications and Tools for Life Sciences (SWAT4LS), (Vol. 698)*. CEUR-WS.org. doi:10.1038/npre.2010.5383.1

Cybulska, A., & Vossen, P. (2014). Using a sledgehammer to crack a nut? Lexical diversity and event coreference resolution. In *Proceedings of the 9th International Conference on Language Resources and Evaluation (LREC'14)*. European Language Resources Association (ELRA).

Damova, M., Kiryakov, A., Simov, K., & Petrov, S. (2010). *Mapping the central LOD ontologies to PROTON upper-level ontology*. Ontology Mapping Workshop at ISWC 2010, Shanghai, China. Retrieved from http://proton.semanticweb.org/

Eriksson, H. (2007, July). The semantic-document approach to combining documents and ontologies. *International Journal of Human-Computer Studies, 65*(7), 624–639. doi:10.1016/j.ijhcs.2007.03.008

Fokkens, A., Soroa, A., Beloki, Z., Ockeloen, N., Rigau, G., van Hage, W. R., & Vossen, P. (2014). NAF and GAF: Linking linguistic annotations. In *Proceedings of 10th Joint ISO-ACL SIGSEM Workshop on Interoperable Semantic Annotation* (pp. 9–16). Association for Computational Linguistics. See also http://groundedannotationframework.org/

Frege, G. (2000). Ueber sinn und bedeutunq [On sense and reference]. *Perspectives in the Philosophy of Language: A Concise Anthology*, 45. Retrieved from http://en.wikipedia.org/wiki/Sense_and_reference

Gantz, J., & Reinsel, D. (2011). *Extracting Value from Chaos (Tech. Rep.)*. IDC Iview.

Georgiev, G., Popov, B., Osenova, P., & Dimitrov, M. (2013). Adaptive semantic publishing. In *Proceedings of the Workshop on Semantic Web Enterprise Adoption and Best Practice co-located with 12th International Semantic Web Conference (ISWC 2013), (Vol. 1106)*. CEUR-WS.org.

Gönül, S., & Sinaci, A. A. (2012). Semantic content management and integration with JCR/CMIS compliant content repositories. In *Proceedings of the 8th International Conference on Semantic Systems (I-SEMANTICS'12)* (pp. 181–184). ACM. Retrieved from http://stanbol.apache.org/

Grishman, R. (2010). Information Extraction. In The Handbook of Computational Linguistics and Natural Language Processing (pp. 515–530). Wiley-Blackwell. doi:10.1002/9781444324044.ch18

Groza, T., Handschuh, S., Möller, K., Grimnes, G., Sauermann, L., Minack, E., & Gudjónsdottir, R. et al. (2007). The NEPOMUK Project – On the way to the Social Semantic Desktop. In *Proceedings of I-SEMANTICS 2007*. Retrieved from http://nepomuk.semanticdesktop.org/

Harris, S., & Seaborne, A. (2013). *SPARQL 1.1 Query Language*. W3C Recommendation. Retrieved June 24, 2017 from http://www.w3.org/TR/2013/REC-sparql11-query-20130321/

Hellmann, S., Lehmann, J., Auer, S., & Brümmer, M. (2013). Integrating NLP using Linked Data. In *Proceedings of 12th International Semantic Web Conference (ISWC)* (pp. 98–113). Springer. Retrieved from http://persistence.uni-leipzig.org/nlp2rdf/

Hoffart, J., Suchanek, F. M., Berberich, K., & Weikum, G. (2013). YAGO2: A spatially and temporally enhanced knowledge base from Wikipedia. *Artificial Intelligence, 194*, 28–61. doi:10.1016/j.artint.2012.06.001

Hopkinson, I., Maude, S., & Rospocher, M. (2014). A simple API to the KnowledgeStore. In *Proceedings of the ISWC Developers Workshop 2014, co-located with the 13th International Semantic Web Conference (ISWC'2014) (Vol. 1268, pp. 7–12)*. CEUR-WS.org.

Jonnalagadda, S., Del Fiol, G., Medlin, R. R., Weir, C., Fiszman, M., Mostafa, J., & Liu, H. (2012). Automatically extracting sentences from Medline citations to support clinicians' information needs. In *IEEE 2nd International Conference on Healthcare Informatics, Imaging and Systems Biology, HISB 2012,* (pp. 72–72). IEEE Computer Society.

Kurz, T., Güntner, G., Damjanovic, V., Schaffert, S., & Fernandez, M. (2014). Semantic enhancement for media asset management systems. *Multimedia Tools and Applications, 70*(2), 949–975. doi:10.1007/s11042-012-1197-7

Lehmann, J., Isele, R., Jakob, M., Jentzsch, A., Kontokostas, D., Mendes, P. N., . . . Bizer, C. (2015). DBpedia - A large-scale, multilingual knowledge base extracted from Wikipedia. *Semantic Web, 6*(2), 167–195. Retrieved from http://dbpedia.org/

Minard, A.-L., Speranza, M., Urizar, R., Altuna, B., van Erp, M., Schoen, A., & van Son, C. (2016). MEANTIME, the NewsReader Multilingual Event and Time Corpus. In N. Calzolari, K. Choukri, T. Declerck, S. Goggi, M. Grobelnik, B. Maegaard, & S. Piperidis (Eds.), *LREC: European Language Resources Association*. ELRA.

Motik, B., Nenov, Y., Piro, R., Horrocks, I., & Olteanu, D. (2014). Parallel materialisation of Datalog programs in centralised, main-memory RDF systems. In *Proceedings of the 28th AAAI Conference on Artificial Intelligence,* (pp. 129–137). AAAI Press.

Motik, B., Parsia, B., & Patel-Schneider, P. F. (2009). *OWL 2 Web Ontology Language structural specification and functional-style syntax* (Recommendation). W3C.

Mylka, A., Sauermann, L., Sintek, M., & van Elst, L. (2013a). *NIE - Nepomuk Information Element Ontology*. Retrieved June 24, 2017, from http://oscaf.sourceforge.net/nie.html

Mylka, A., Sauermann, L., Sintek, M., & van Elst, L. (2013b). *NFO - Nepomuk File Ontology*. Retrieved June 24, 2017, from http://oscaf.sourceforge.net/nfo.html

Palmero Aprosio, A., Corcoglioniti, F., Dragoni, M., & Rospocher, M. (2015). Supervised Opinion Frames Detection with RAID. Semantic Web Evaluation Challenges, 251-263. doi:10.1007/978-3-319-25518-7_22

Patel-Schneider, P. F., & Franconi, E. (2012). Ontology constraints in incomplete and complete data. In *Proceedings of the 11th International Conference on the Semantic Web (ISWC'12)* (pp. 444–459). Springer-Verlag. doi:10.1007/978-3-642-35176-1_28

Petasis, G., Karkaletsis, V., Paliouras, G., Krithara, A., & Zavitsanos, E. (2011). Ontology population and enrichment: State of the art. In *Knowledge-driven Multimedia Information Extraction and Ontology Evolution* (pp. 134–166). Springer. doi:10.1007/978-3-642-20795-2_6

Popov, B., Kiryakov, A., Kirilov, A., Manov, D., & Goranov, M. (2003). Kim – Semantic Annotation Platform. In *Proceedings of the 2nd International Conference on the Semantic Web (ISWC'03)* (pp. 834–849). Springer Berlin Heidelberg.

Presutti, V., Draicchio, F., & Gangemi, A. (2012). Knowledge extraction based on discourse representation theory and linguistic frames. In *Proceedings of International Conference on Knowledge Engineering and Knowledge Management (EKAW)*, (pp. 114–129). Springer. doi:10.1007/978-3-642-33876-2_12

Pustejovsky, J., Lee, K., Bunt, H., & Romary, L. (2010). ISO-TimeML: An international standard for semantic annotation. In *Proceedings of the 7th International Conference on Language Resources and Evaluation (LREC'10)*. European Language Resources Association (ELRA).

Rospocher, M., van Erp, M., Vossen, P., Fokkens, A., Aldabe, I., Rigau, G., & Bogaard, T. et al. (2016). Building event-centric knowledge graphs from news. *Journal of Web Semantics, 37-38*, 132–151. doi:10.1016/j.websem.2015.12.004

Segers, R. H., Vossen, P. T. J. M., Rospocher, M., Serafini, L., Laparra, E. L., & Rigau, G. (2015). ESO: a Frame based Ontology for Events and Implied Situations. *Maplex 2015 Workshop*.

Tao, J., Sirin, E., Bao, J., & McGuinness, D. L. (2010). Integrity constraints in OWL. In *Proceedings of the 24th AAAI Conference on Artificial Intelligence, AAAI 2010*, (p. 1443-1448). AAAI Press.

van Hage, W. R., Malaisé, V., Segers, R., Hollink, L., & Schreiber, G. (2011). Design and use of the Simple Event Model (SEM). *Web Semantics: Science, Services, and Agents on the World Wide Web, 9*(2), 128–136. doi:10.1016/j.websem.2011.03.003

van Hage, W. R., & Ploeger, T. (2014). *Deliverable D7.3.1*. Retrieved from http://www.newsreader-project.eu/publications/deliverables/

Vossen, P., Agerri, R., Aldabe, I., Cybulska, A., van Erp, M., Fokkens, A., . . . Segers, R. (2016) News-Reader: Using knowledge resources in a cross-lingual reading machine to generate more knowledge from massive streams of news. *Knowledge-Based Systems, 110*. https://doi.org/10.1016/j.knosys.2016.07.013

Weikum, G., & Theobald, M. (2010). From information to knowledge: Harvesting entities and relationships from Web sources. In *Proceedings of the 29th ACM SIGMOD-SIGACT-SIGART Symposium on Principles of Database Systems (PODS'10)* (pp. 65–76). ACM. doi:10.1145/1807085.1807097

Xiao, H., & Cruz, I. F. (2006). Application design and interoperability for managing personal information in the Semantic Desktop. In *Proceedings of the Semantic Desktop and Social Semantic Collaboration Workshop (SemDesk'06) co-located at the 5th International Semantic Web Conference ISWC 2006, (Vol. 202)*. CEUR-WS.org.

Zanoli, R., Corcoglioniti, F., & Girardi, C. (2011). Exploiting Background Knowledge for Clustering Person Names. EVALITA 2011, 135-145.

KEY TERMS AND DEFINITIONS

API Endpoint: Any programmatic interface accessible via the network through which clients can invoke server functionalities through well specified and documented request/response operations. The KnowledgeStore exposes its storage and query services via three endpoints: SPARQL, CRUD (Create, Retrieve, Update, Delete methods), and Custom (instance-specific methods).

Data Model: A model that organizes elements of data specifying how they are described and how they relate to one another. The KnowledgeStore data model is based on RDF, is formalized by an OWL ontology, and allows representing and relating both unstructured content (textual resources) and the structured knowledge (entities and axioms) extracted from it.

Entity: Any person, organizations, location or other entity of the domain of discourse, treated as an ontological individual, described via logical axioms encoded with RDF triples. and denoted by mentions in textual resources.

Knowledge Extraction: The extraction of assertional (ABox, i.e., instances and facts) and/or terminological (TBox, i.e., classes and properties) formal knowledge from unstructured contents, anchoring it to existing ontologies and vocabularies.

KnowledgeStore: A scalable, fault-tolerant, and Semantic Web grounded open-source storage system to jointly store, manage, retrieve, and query interlinked structured and unstructured data especially tailored for Knowledge Extraction applications.

Mention: A fragment of a textual resource (e.g., characters from offset 1020 to 1040) that refers to some entity (its referent) or that expresses some axiom about an entity. In the KnowledgeStore context, mentions realize the link between unstructured textual content and structured knowledge expressed by that content.

Resource: A self-contained, globally identified, and immutable information object, described in terms of its content (e.g., the text of a textual resource) and the associated metadata. In the KnowledgeStore context, textual resources are the unstructured content from which knowledge is extracted.

Chapter 3
On Semantic Relation Extraction Over Enterprise Data

Wei Shen
Nankai University, China

Jianyong Wang
Tsinghua University, China & Jiangsu Normal University, China

Ping Luo
Chinese Academy of Sciences, China

Min Wang
Visa Inc., USA

ABSTRACT

Relation extraction from the Web data has attracted a lot of attention recently. However, little work has been done when it comes to the enterprise data regardless of the urgent needs to such work in real applications (e.g., E-discovery). One distinct characteristic of the enterprise data (in comparison with the Web data) is its low redundancy. Previous work on relation extraction from the Web data largely relies on the data's high redundancy level and thus cannot be applied to the enterprise data effectively. This chapter reviews related work on relation extraction and introduces an unsupervised hybrid framework REACTOR for semantic relation extraction over enterprise data. REACTOR combines a statistical method, classification, and clustering to identify various types of relations among entities appearing in the enterprise data automatically. REACTOR was evaluated over a real-world enterprise data set from HP that contains over three million pages and the experimental results show its effectiveness.

INTRODUCTION

Relation extraction is the process of discovering the relationship among two or more entities from a given unstructured data set. It is an important research area not only for information retrieval (Salton & McGill, 1986) but also for Web mining and knowledge base population (Shen, Wang, Luo, & Wang, 2012). The huge amount of valuable information contained in the unstructured text is recorded and

DOI: 10.4018/978-1-5225-5042-6.ch003

transmitted every day in the text form. Turning such information into the understandable and usable form is of high significance and has a lot of real applications.

Traditional relation extraction processes usually require significant human efforts: they need predefined relation names and hand-tagged examples of each named relation as input (Kambhatla, 2004 ; Zelenko, Aone, & Richardella, 2003 ; Giuliano, Lavelli, & Romano, 2006 ; Zhou, Zhang, Ji, & Zhu, 2007 ; Surdeanu & Ciaramita, 2007). Weakly supervised systems for relation extraction such as the bootstrapping systems require much less human involvements, but still require a small set of domain-specific seed instances or seed patterns that have a big impact on the system performance. Furthermore, the seed selection process requires substantial domain knowledge and is usually time consuming (Agichtein & Gravano, 2000 ; Zhu, Nie, Liu, Zhang, & Wen, 2009 ; Brin, 1998 ; Etzioni et al., 2005). Open IE is proposed as a new relation extraction paradigm that can identify various types of relations without predefinition. The goal of open IE systems is to gather a large set of relation facts that can be used for question answering (Banko, Cafarella, Soderl, Broadhead, & Etzioni, 2007 ; Banko & Etzioni, 2008 ; Etzioni et al., 2005 ; Shinyama & Sekine, 2006). Distant supervision approaches require existing knowledge bases (KBs) with which they align an unsupervised text corpus to generate training examples automatically (Hoffmann et al., 2011 ; Madaan et al., 2016 ; Mintz et al., 2009 ; Riedel, Yao, & McCallum, 2010 ; Ritter et al., 2013). Despite that, most relation extraction systems constrain the search for binary relations that are asserted within a single sentence (i.e., single-sentential relations) (Agichtein & Gravano, 2000 ; Hoffmann et al., 2011 ; Mintz et al., 2009 ; Zelenko et al., 2003 ; Brin, 1998 ; Zhu et al., 2009 ; Zhou et al., 2007 ; Hasegawa, Sekine, & Grishman, 2004), while relations between two entities can also be expressed across multiple sentences (i.e., inter-sentential relations). The analysis in Swampillai and Stevenson (2010) shows that inter-sentential relations constitute 28.5% and 9.4% of the total number of relations in MUC6 data set (Grishman & Sundheim, 1996) and ACE03 data set respectively. This places upper bounds on the recall of relation extraction systems that just consider single-sentential relations.

While most work on relation extraction focuses on the Web data, the amount of the enterprise data (including e-mails, internal Web pages, word processing files, and databases) has grown significantly during the past several years for all companies. Numerous real-world entities such as people, organizations, and products are contained in the enterprise data and these entities are connected by various types of relations. To make use of such rich information, it is desirable to build an entity relationship graph that can support efficient retrieval of entities and their relations. A key application of the entity relationship graph is in E-discovery, the process of collecting, preparing, reviewing and producing evidence in the form of Electronically Stored Information (ESI) during litigation (Crowley & Harris, 2007). In this process, lawyers need to find all the people and ESI that are relevant to a legal matter. For example, when a company is alleged to have infringed a patent related to a product, this company is required to disclose all the relevant information. The first question is which employees are closely related to this product. Furthermore, it will be more useful if the method could provide their specific roles to this product, such as product manager, product support, or sales manager. To answer these questions, semantic relation extraction from the enterprise data is an essential step.

However, the existing techniques on relation extraction cannot be applied to the enterprise data directly due to the differences in the data characteristics: the enterprise data has much lower redundancy than the Web data. Figure 1 shows the distribution for the occurrence frequency of entity pairs for the PEOPLE-ORGANIZATION (PEO-ORG) domain in the enterprise data set used in the experiments. It shows that more than 90% of the entity pairs occur less than four times, about two thirds of the entity pairs only occur once in the entire data set and the average occurrence frequency of all the entity pairs is

1.96. In this chapter, the occurrence of an entity pair means that the entities of that entity pair co-occur within the same sentence. Most existing techniques rely on the high redundancy nature of the Web data for an abundant supply of related entities to achieve reasonable recall. The recall will fall dramatically when applying such techniques to the low-redundancy enterprise data. Considering the sentence "… Bob, technology consultant for Software Division …" which just appears once in the data set, a good algorithm should be able to extract the following relation: "Bob" (PEOPLE) is a "technology consultant" of "Software Division" (ORGANIZATION). However, the existing techniques can hardly discover it since they consider the relation only appearing once is unreliable. On the other hand, some other characteristics of the enterprise data could be leveraged for more effective relation extraction. For example, the enterprise data is less noisy than the Web data, and people usually have some known knowledge or databases within an enterprise that can be leveraged to support the entity recognition process. Therefore, they could exploit the existing useful information to minimize the human involvement and improve the performance of relation extraction on the enterprise data.

This chapter introduces a novel unsupervised hybrid framework called REACTOR. It uses a statistical method in conjunction with the classification and clustering techniques to extract semantic relations and can label the extracted relations with representative tags over the enterprise data. It also applies the pronominal anaphora resolution techniques to extract inter-sentential relations. Specifically, given an enterprise data set where entities of interest have been identified already, REACTOR first adopts a statistical method to extract a set of representative entity pairs that contain both positive and negative examples for the classifier. Then some features are extracted from the positive and negative examples to train the classifier that is in turn used to classify all the other entity pairs each of which appears in the same sentence as related or not. For each entity pair classified as related, a context vector consisting of the words from all its occurring sentences is generated, and a clustering algorithm is used to identify the semantic relations of entity pairs. Furthermore, to describe the semantic relations for the entity pairs in each cluster, REACTOR employs a closed frequent sequence pattern mining algorithm to extract some representative tags. To extract inter-sentential relations, the authors apply an anaphora

Figure 1. The distribution for the occurrence frequency of entity pairs (in PEO-ORG domain)

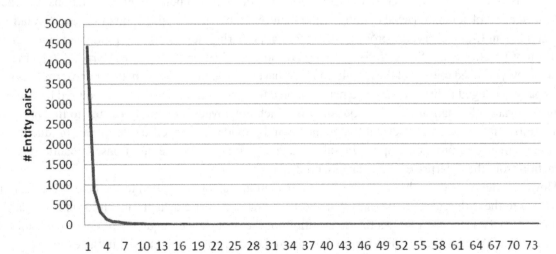

resolution algorithm to the original documents and get the substitution text where pronominal references are substituted by the noun phrases they refer to. Accordingly, they transform inter-sentential relations expressed by the pronominal anaphora to single-sentential relations that can be processed by REACTOR. Subsequently, REACTOR uses the methods introduced above to process the substitution text to extract the single-sentential and inter-sentential relations together. Note that a very preliminary version of the paper has been published as a poster in WWW'11 conference (Shen, Wang, Luo, Wang, & Yao, 2011).

The main contributions of this work are summarized as follows.

- This chapter presents REACTOR, a hybrid framework that can effectively extract semantic relations over the low-redundancy enterprise data. Most previous work on relation extraction is for the high-redundancy Web data.
- REACTOR is an unsupervised framework that requires minimal human involvement. It employs a statistical method to automatically generate the training data for the classifier.
- REACTOR can extract inter-sentential relations to significantly boost the recall of the system and the experimental results reveal that information referenced pronominally is very important to inter-sentential relation extraction.
- REACTOR can label each extracted relation with tags that describe the semantic relation accurately. It applies a closed frequent sequence pattern mining algorithm to extract the representative tags.
- The authors extensively evaluate REACTOR over a real-world enterprise data set that contains over three million pages. The experimental results show that REACTOR can achieve significantly higher precision and recall compared with the baseline method.

The rest of this chapter is organized as follows. Section 2 discusses related work and Section 3 introduces the REACTOR framework. Specifically, Section 3.1 gives an overview and Section 3.2 describes how to extract the representative entity pairs. Section 3.3 presents a classifier that is used to detect related entity pairs. Section 3.4 describes how to extract the semantic relations using a clustering algorithm. Relation tagging is introduced in Section 3.5. Section 3.6 introduces the extraction of inter-sentential relations. Section 4 presents the experimental results and Section 5 draws conclusions.

RELATED WORK AND DISCUSSION

Relation extraction was first introduced in the Message Understanding Conference (MUC) (Grishman & Sundheim, 1996), and the Automatic Content Extraction (ACE) program promoted relation extraction as a task of Relation Detection and Characterization (RDC) in 2001, which was renamed to Relation Detection and Recognition (RDR) in the ACE 2004 evaluation.

Following these tasks, many supervised machine learning approaches were proposed such as maximum entropy models (Kambhatla, 2004), kernel methods (Zelenko et al., 2003 ; Giuliano et al., 2006 ; Zhou et al., 2007), Perceptrons (Surdeanu & Ciaramita, 2007) and hidden Markov models (Freitag & Mccallum, 1999 ; Skounakis, Craven, & Ray, 2003). These supervised methods need manually annotated training data to learn an extractor, which makes them difficult to be applied to large-scale relation extraction tasks like relation discovery over the enterprise data, since it is expensive and time consuming to obtain the human-labeled examples. Moreover, these methods usually extract a set of rules from the human tagged training data. The performance of the extracted rules will be very poor when they are applied to data with a different style. Consequently, the researchers have to spend a great deal of time and effort to prepare a set of human tagged examples for each targeting style data when they apply them to the enterprise data that has diverse text styles and genres.

There are also some previous works that adopted weakly supervised learning approaches such as the bootstrapping systems (Agichtein & Gravano, 2000 ; Brin, 1998 ; Zhu et al., 2009 ; Etzioni et al., 2005). These approaches significantly reduce manual labor needed for relation extraction by only needing a small set of seed examples or seed extraction patterns. Beginning with these seeds, bootstrapping methods iteratively discover new extraction patterns and new instances. However, the selection of the seeds requires substantial expertise because the performance of bootstrapping systems heavily depends on the initial seed examples or seed patterns provided to them. It is also unclear how the initial seeds or patterns should be selected and how many seeds are needed, which confuses the non-expert users. Additionally, nontrivial manual effort is also required when shifting to a new relation extraction task since this method demands a set of hand-crafted seeds per relation to launch the training process. What is more, for the bootstrapping systems relations have to be specified in advance for the preparation of the initial seeds. In this setting, however, it is impossible to know the targeting relations beforehand in the enterprise data.

Open Information Extraction (Open IE) was firstly introduced in Banko et al. (2007) as a novel domain-independent relation extraction paradigm that works well on huge and diverse Web corpus. It eliminates the drawbacks of the traditional information extraction paradigm that relies on lots of human involvement in the form of manually tagged training data or hand-craft seed examples. Open IE has been studied in both the Web environment (Banko et al., 2007 ; Banko & Etzioni, 2008 ; Etzioni et al., 2005) and natural language document corpus (Shinyama & Sekine, 2006). Although these Open IE systems are promising and can be suitably applied to extract unknown relations from large scale heterogeneous corpora such as the Web corpus, they have some unsatisfactory aspects in comparison with REAC-TOR. First, the Open IE systems can just label the entity pairs as "trustworthy" or not and are unable to give users more descriptions about the extracted relations. REACTOR can go a further step which can identify the extracted relations with informative lexical descriptions that are very useful and important for extracting unknown relations. Second, although the Open IE systems are self-supervised, they still need a set of human-selected generic, domain independent patterns to create a set of extraction rules. While REACTOR uses a statistical method to select training examples for the classifier automatically. In addition, all Open IE systems rely on the high redundancy of the Web for an abundant supply of simple sentences that are relatively easy to process. When it comes to the enterprise application where the redundancy is much lower than the Web data, this assumption is violated so that the recall of the Open IE system will fall drastically.

Recently, in order to reduce human efforts, another novel paradigm called distant supervision has been developed. These approaches do not require labeled corpora and their training dataset is automatically labeled by aligning an unsupervised corpus with a knowledge base of facts (Hoffmann et al., 2011 ; Madaan et al., 2016 ; Mintz et al., 2009 ; Riedel, Yao, & McCallum, 2010 ; Ritter et al., 2013). They are based on a distant supervision assumption: if a sentence contains a pair of entities that appear in some known fact of a KB, then that sentence is likely to be a positive training example for that KB relation. This allows them to extract features from all the training sentences to learn a relation classifier. These algorithms combine the advantages of supervised approaches and unsupervised approaches. However, these algorithms inevitably need a large-scale KB to provide distant supervision for relation extraction. In this setting, there does not exist a KB containing the relational facts about entities in an enterprise.

There are also some other completely unsupervised approaches for relation extraction (Hassan, Hassan, & Emam, 2006; Hasegawa et al., 2004). The method proposed in Hassan et al. (2006) is to extract patterns from n-gram language model and use an iterative procedure based on graph mutual reinforcement to identify highly confident patterns. In the approach of Hasegawa et al. (2004), clustering techniques are used for unsupervised relation extraction. Context vectors for entity pairs are composed of all words appearing between the entities, and they are clustered using cosine distance. Each generated cluster contains the entity pairs with the same relation type. Overall, these unsupervised methods all depend on the high redundancy level of the large corpora and have the assumption that useful relations will be mentioned frequently. They also assume that the relations mentioned once or twice are not likely to be important. Whereas in this setting of the enterprise application, most relations are mentioned just once or twice due to the data characteristic of low redundancy, accordingly, these unsupervised approaches are not suitable to be applied to the enterprise data.

THE REACTOR FRAMEWORK

Overview

In this subsection, the authors give you a brief introduction to the proposed REACTOR framework. Different modules will be explained in detail in the following subsections.

Given a text corpus, the goal of REACTOR is to extract all semantic relations between any two types of entities. It is assumed that entities of the two corresponding types in this corpus, T_m and T_n, are previously detected like many other relation extraction systems (Agichtein & Gravano, 2000; Zhu et al., 2009 ; Hasegawa et al., 2004) and moreover, the disambiguation process of these entities has been completed. Therefore, each detected entity in the corpus has an identifier that corresponds to a unique real-world entity. As the types and the number of the semantic relations possibly valid between two entities in a pair are unknown, this system aims to extract all related entity pairs with the types of T_m and T_n in the corpus, and select some representative tags to describe the semantic relation for each entity pair. Figure 2 depicts the architecture of REACTOR.

Generally speaking, REACTOR has five modules including Seed Extractor, Relation Detection, Relation Categorization, Relation Tagging, and Anaphora Resolution. The Seed Extractor uses statistics to extract a set of representative entity pairs containing both positive and negative seed examples to train the classifier in the Relation Detection module. Specifically, the Seed Extractor applies a form of *pointwise mutual information* (PMI) between two entities e_i and e_j to assess the probability whether a relationship exists between these two entities. The Relation Detection module classifies each entity pair $\langle e_i, e_j \rangle$ with the targeting types T_m and T_n occurring within the same sentence as related or not. The sentence boundaries in each document are found using the OpenNLP toolkits (n.d.) which can perform sentence detection. Then for each entity pair classified as related, a context vector consisting of words formed from all its occurring sentences can be generated. The third module Relation Categorization employs the hierarchical clustering algorithm to produce several clusters (e.g., $c_1, c_2, \ldots, c_k$) and in each

Figure 2. The REACTOR architecture

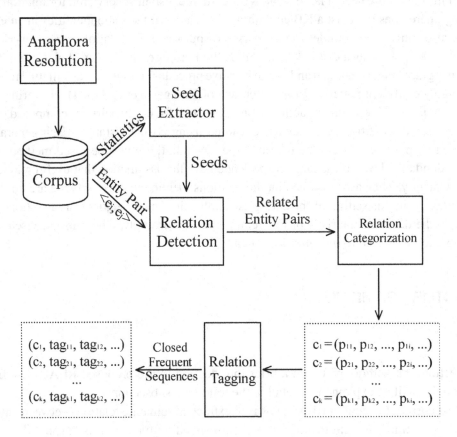

cluster c_i each entity pair $p_{ij} \in c_i$ holds the same semantic relation. To label the extracted relations, the Relation Tagging module employs a closed frequent sequence mining algorithm to identify the closed frequent sequential patterns in all occurring sentences where the entity pairs of each cluster appear. Then the authors use these extracted patterns to label and describe the semantic relation held in each cluster. Finally, in order to extract the inter-sentential relations, the Anaphora Resolution module applies the pronominal anaphora resolution algorithm to the documents and obtains the substitution text where pronominal references are substituted by the noun phrases they refer to. Subsequently, REACTOR could use the other four modules introduced above to process the substitution text to extract the single-sentential and inter-sentential relations together.

Seed Extractor

It is difficult for non-expert users to provide human-selected seeds or manually tagged training examples that are expensive and need significant human effort. The proposed REACTOR adopts a statistical method to extract some representative entity pairs as seeds to train the classifier automatically.

Obviously, to train the classifier, the extracted seeds should contain both positive examples, in which the entity pairs are almost likely to be related and the two entities of each entity pair depend on each other heavily, and negative examples in which the entity pairs are unrelated and the two entities of each entity pair are independent of each other. Therefore, it is needed to define a weighting function that can assign a weight to each entity pair and indicate how strongly the two entities of the entity pair are related. Intuitively, the entity that is strongly related to entity e_i should be the one that frequently co-occurs with entity e_i but infrequently co-occurs with others.

Many weighting functions can be used to measure the dependency between two entities. Previous research on statistical natural language processing has proved that co-occurrence statistics are highly informative and simple when computed over large corpora (Banko & Brill, 2001). Despite that, co-occurrences may not be a good measure for this task whose problem is that co-occurrence statistics have a strong bias towards global common entity pairs in the collection. For example, entity e_j co-occurs with entity e_i many times, but the entity pair $\langle e_i, e_j \rangle$ may still not be a good positive seed if the entity e_j also co-occurs with other entities frequently. Therefore, they should penalize these entities by dividing by their occurrence frequencies, which is like the computation of the *pointwise mutual information* (PMI). The PMI value of an entity pair is computed as:

$$I\left(e_i, e_j\right) = \log_2 \frac{P\left(e_i, e_j\right)}{P\left(e_i\right)P\left(e_j\right)} \tag{1}$$

where $P\left(e_i, e_j\right)$ is the co-occurrence probability of entities e_i and e_j, $P\left(e_i\right)$ and $P\left(e_j\right)$ are the occurrence probabilities of entity e_i and entity e_j respectively in the corpus.

However, the PMI value has a strong bias towards low frequent entity pairs. For example, entities e_i and e_j just appear in the corpus once respectively and moreover, they happen to co-occur within the same sentence. In this situation, the PMI value of this entity pair $\langle e_i, e_j \rangle$ is extremely large so that it is considered as a positive seed. But entities e_i and e_j are likely to be unrelated since they just co-occur by chance.

Therefore, in order to avoid the bias mentioned above, the authors compute the relatedness weight for each entity pair $\langle e_i, e_j \rangle$ as follows:

$$weight\left(e_i, e_j\right) = C\left(e_i, e_j\right)\log_2 \frac{P\left(e_i, e_j\right)}{P\left(e_i\right)P\left(e_j\right)} \tag{2}$$

where $C\left(e_i, e_j\right)$ is the number of co-occurrences of entities e_i and e_j, $P\left(e_i, e_j\right)$ is the co-occurrence probability of entities e_i and e_j, $P\left(e_i\right)$ and $P\left(e_j\right)$ are the occurrence probabilities of entity e_i and entity e_j respectively in the corpus.

For example, they want to compute the relatedness weight for entities "Jane" and "HP Labs China" in PEO-ORG domain. The number of occurrences of entity "Jane" in the corpus is 13, while the number of occurrences of entity "HP Labs China" is 298. And the number of co-occurrences of these two entities is 8. The total number of occurrences of entity pairs in PEO-ORG domain is 12038, while the total numbers of occurrences of entities with types PEO and ORG are 6010021 and 3819621, respectively.

The relatedness weight for this entity pair "Jane" and "HP Labs China" can be computed as

$$8 \times \log_2 \frac{8/12038}{13 \times 298 / (6010021 \times 3819621)} = 175.27.$$ For the entity pair "Owen" and "HP Labs China",

the number of occurrences of entity "Owen" in the corpus is 24 and the number of co-occurrences of these two entities is 1. The relatedness weight for this entity pair "Owen" and "HP Labs China" can be

computed as $1 \times \log_2 \frac{1/12038}{24 \times 298 / (6010021 \times 3819621)} = 18.02.$ The relatedness weight for the entity

pair "Jane" and "HP Labs China" is much larger than it for the entity pair "Owen" and "HP Labs China". Therefore, the entity pair "Jane" and "HP Labs China" is more likely to be related compared with the entity pair "Owen" and "HP Labs China".

Let p_{ij} be an entity pair $\langle e_i, e_j \rangle$ that occurs within one sentence and $P = \{ p_{11}, p_{12}, \ldots, p_{ij}, \ldots \}$ be the set of all such entity pairs in the corpus. According to Equation 2, they can calculate the relatedness weight w_{ij} for each entity pair p_{ij} which can tell us how strongly the entity pair p_{ij} is related. Then, the task of extracting positive seeds is to extract a subset of k entity pairs $P' \subseteq P$, such that $\forall p_{ij} \in P'$ and $\forall p_{sv} \in P - P'$, they have $w_{ij} \geq w_{sv}$. On the contrary, the task of extracting negative seeds is to extract a subset of s entity pairs $P'' \subseteq P$, such that $\forall p_{ij} \in P''$ and $\forall p_{sv} \in P - P''$, they have $w_{ij} \leq w_{sv}$.

With the relatedness weighting function defined in Equation 2, they can compute the relatedness weight $w_{ij} = weight(p_{ij})$ for each entity pair p_{ij}. Then rank $p_{ij} \in P$ with respect to w_{ij} in descending order and select the top k p_{ij}'s as the positive seeds, and in turn rank $p_{ij} \in P$ with respect to w_{ij} in ascending order and select the top s p_{ij}'s as the negative seeds. The two parameters k and s are specified empirically.

Relation Detection

The enterprise data has much lower redundancy in comparison with the Web data, and most of entity pairs only occur a few times in the entire data set shown in Figure 1, which makes the bootstrapping methods (Agichtein & Gravano, 2000 ; Zhu et al., 2009 ; Brin, 1998 ; Etzioni et al., 2005) hard to be applied. Therefore, the authors leverage a classifier to detect the related entity pairs with any occurrence frequency according to the contexts where the entity pairs appear, rather than using a simple frequency threshold to filter the low frequent entity pairs that is used by some relation extraction systems (Banko et al., 2007 ; Hasegawa et al., 2004 ; Gonzàlez & Turmo, 2009 ; Bollegala, Matsuo, & Ishizuka, 2010).

Starting from the seed set $S = \{ s_1, s_2, \ldots, s_{(k+s)} \}$, where $s_i \in S$ is a positive or negative training seed provided by the Seed Extractor, the goal of this stage is to train the classifier and label each entity pair $\langle e_i, e_j \rangle$ with the targeting types T_m and T_n occurring within the same sentence as related or not.

Each occurrence of the seed $s_i \in S$ is considered as a training tuple. Here, they represent each co-occurring sentence $st_i = \langle t_{i1}, t_{i2}, t_{i3}, \ldots \rangle$ as a sequence of tokens t_{iq} in the sentence. The authors also define some domain-independent features that can be used to capture the syntactic information and the entity information for each sentence where the entity pair occurs. They can map each occurrence of the entity pair to a feature vector $\langle x_{i1}, x_{i2}, \ldots \rangle$ where x_{ir} tells the value of the rth feature of the co-occurring sentence st_i. The feature vector can be changed by adding or eliminating some features easily, which gives flexibility to the model in an efficient and simple way. The features used in the experiment are listed as follows:

1. The number of tokens between the entities in the sentence;
2. The type of the entity that appears first in the sentence;
3. The part-of-speech tag sequence between the entities;
4. The part-of-speech tag sequence before the first entity within distance d;
5. The part-of-speech tag sequence after the second entity within distance d;
6. The position and type of the other entities in the sentence.

An example of the feature generation for a certain entity pair with T_m = PEO and T_n = ORG (Here, PEO means PEOPLE and ORG means ORGANIZATION), is shown in Figure 3. In the example, the two considered entities are "Bob" with entity type of PEO and "Sales Group" with entity type of ORG. Firstly, the value of Feature 1 is 1 because the number of tokens between "Bob" and "Sales Group" is 1 and the value of Feature 2 is ORG since the entity "Sales Group" with type of ORG appears first in the sentence compared with the entity "Bob". The Features 3, 4, and 5 are the part-of-speech tag sequences respectively between entities, before "Sales Group" within distance d and after "Bob" within distance d. In the experiments, the performance of the classifier is insensitive to the parameter d and the authors obtain very similar classification results when d is varied from 3 to $+\infty$. In order to reduce the number of features for the SVM classifier for the purpose of efficiency, the authors set d to 5 in the experiments. Finally, as there is an entity "Smith" with type of PEO before the former considered entity "Sales Group" at the fourth position and an entity "Software" with type of ORG after the latter considered entity "Bob" at the fourth position, Feature 6 activates features left_4_PEO and right_4_ORG respectively. As it can be seen, the entities "Bob" and "Sales Group" in this example are unrelated. Those generated features including the syntactic and entity information of the context can support the classifier to label them correctly.

To extract the related entity pairs, firstly, the authors use the feature vectors produced from the seed set S to train the classifier which is *libsvm (2016)* used in the experiment. They use the tool in *libsvm* which does the whole classification procedure including scaling and model selection completely automatically. Then they use OpenNLP toolkits to annotate each sentence in the entire corpus with POS tags. Finally, each occurrence of the entity pair is presented to the trained classifier and the classifier labels each of them as related or unrelated. Since each entity pair may have more than one occurrence, they consider the entity pair as related if and only if the number of occurrences classified as related for this entity pair is larger than or equal to the number of occurrences classified as unrelated.

Figure 3. Example of feature generation (in PEO-ORG domain)

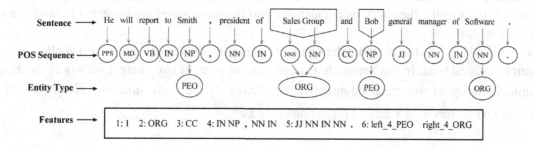

In the process of relation detection, they only use the shallow linguistic processing technique (i.e., part-of-speech tagging). In contrast to deep natural language processing techniques used by many extraction systems (Agichtein & Gravano, 2000 ; Kambhatla, 2004 ; Etzioni et al., 2005 ; Banko et al., 2007 ; Shinyama & Sekine, 2006), shallow NLP techniques are more robust and efficient, which is very important for the relation extraction over the large-scale enterprise data.

It is also noteworthy that differently from some relation extraction systems (Banko et al., 2007 ; Hasegawa et al., 2004 ; Gonzàlez & Turmo, 2009 ; Bollegala et al., 2010) that have a frequency threshold to filter the low frequent entity pairs or a distance threshold to filter the entity pairs with a long distance in the sentence, REACTOR can extract the related entity pair with any frequency and any distance within one sentence, which can significantly improve the performance of relation extraction on the low-redundancy enterprise data.

Relation Categorization

After the classification, the researchers could obtain all related entity pairs. As they do not know any prior knowledge about the number and types of the relations existing in the corpus, therefore, it is extremely useful to identify the semantic relations between entities. To extract the semantic relations, they assume that entity pairs occurring in the similar context likely have the same semantic relation and can be clustered into a group. Entity pairs in each group produced by the clustering algorithm are expected to express the same semantic relation.

They first adopt a vector space model (Salton, Wong, & Yang, 1975) to represent the context of an entity pair. For each entity pair, they firstly obtain all their occurrence sentences and eliminate some non-essential phrases, such as stop words, prepositional phrases and modifiers, from these sentences. Meanwhile, they filter out the other entities appearing in the sentences as well, because these words do not express any semantic relation and would introduce much noise in calculating similarities. In constructing the context vector, they consider not only the bag of words between the entities but also those around the entities in each occurrence sentence within the same distance d as introduced in Section 3.3. These words are stemmed by Porter Stemmer (2006) and are weighted in the context vector by their term frequency empirically (Different term weighting strategies will be discussed in Section 4.2).

For example, for the entity pair "Jane" and "HP Labs China", one of their occurrence sentences is "Michael reports to Jane, who is the project manager of HP Labs China". Before generating the context vector for this occurrence, they eliminate the stop words such as "to", "who", "is", "the" and "of". They also filter out the entity "Michael" because this entity mention does not express any semantic relation between entities "Jane" and "HP Labs China". Therefore, they obtain the context vector {"reports", "project", "manager"} before stemming and weighting.

After generating the context vector for each entity pair, they introduce a similarity function to measure the similarity between any two context vectors and then adopt a clustering algorithm to further group the entity pairs. Finally, the entity pairs clustered into the same group are expected to have the same semantic relation.

Cosine is widely used to compute the similarity between two vectors and is well applied in the information retrieval field. In this approach, they use cosine value of two context vectors to measure the semantic similarity of two corresponding entity pairs. Generally, the cosine similarity $sim\big(c(\alpha),c(\beta)\big)$ of two context vectors $c(\alpha)$ and $c(\beta)$ is computed as:

$$sim(c(\alpha), c(\beta)) = \frac{\sum_{i=1}^{k} a_i \times b_i}{\sqrt{\sum_{i=1}^{k} a_i^2} \times \sqrt{\sum_{i=1}^{k} b_i^2}} \qquad (3)$$

where $c(\alpha) = \langle a_1, a_2, \ldots, a_k \rangle$ and $c(\beta) = \langle b_1, b_2, \ldots, b_k \rangle$.

With cosine similarity, they expect to group the entity pairs such that the similarity within intra-cluster is high and that between inter-clusters is low. As the number of relations is unknown beforehand, they adopt the hierarchical clustering algorithm. This clustering algorithm does not require to pre-define the number of clusters and the result of the clustering is independent of the order of entity pairs. The algorithm iteratively groups two clusters of entity pairs with the maximum similarity, where the similarity between two clusters is defined as the cosine similarity between the furthest entity pairs in the two clusters empirically (Different cluster distance computation strategies will be discussed in Section 4.2). The algorithm terminates when the maximum similarity between any two clusters becomes smaller than a pre-defined threshold γ. The details of the algorithm are shown in Figure 4.

Relation Tagging

Although the entity pairs are clustered into a set of groups each of which represents a type of semantic relation between entities, they do not know the exact semantic relation held in each cluster. For the evaluation and presentation purpose, it is extremely useful and important to label clusters with some representative tags to describe the semantic relations existing in them.

Figure 4. The hierarchical clustering algorithm

Input: A set of n entity pairs: $P = \{p_1, p_2, \ldots, p_n\}$,
           Threshold of similarity: γ.
Output: A set of clusters: $C = \{C_1, C_2, \ldots, C_k\}$.

1:   Initialize n clusters C_i, each as an entity pair p_i
2:   Compute the cosine similarity s_{ij} between entity
      pairs in P
3:   Set the current maximum similarity $s = \max(s_{ij})$
4:   **while** $(s > \gamma)$ **do**
5:      Select s_{lt} where $(l, t) = \arg\max_{i,j} s_{ij}$
6:      Merge clusters C_l and C_t into a new cluster C_u
7:      $s \leftarrow s_{lt}$
8:      **for all** $C_v \neq C_u$ **do**
9:         Compute $s_{uv} = \min(s_{\alpha\beta})$ where $p_\alpha \in C_u$,
           $p_\beta \in C_v$
10:     **end for**
11: **end while**

The authors represent each co-occurring sentence $st_i = \langle t_{i1}, t_{i2}, t_{i3}, \ldots \rangle$ as a sequence of tokens t_{ij} in the sentence. For each co-occurring sentence st_i where the entity pair with types T_m and T_n appears, they replace the two corresponding entities with two variables T_m and T_n respectively to produce $st_i{}'$. The tokens which belong to the entity with the type of T_m are replaced by T_m, whereas the tokens which belong to the entity with the type of T_n are replaced by T_n. Then they construct the sequence database $D = \{st_1{}', st_2{}', \ldots, st_i{}', \ldots\}$ for each cluster.

Let pt_i be a subsequence in D and they denote the set of sequences in which pt_i appears as $D_i = \{st_\alpha{}' \mid pt_i \in st_\alpha{}', st_\alpha{}' \in D\}$. Now, they give out the definition of frequent sequence pattern.

Definition 1 (Frequent Sequence Pattern): A sequence pattern pt_i is *frequent* in a database D, if $\dfrac{|D_i|}{|D|} \geq \sigma$, where σ is a pre-defined threshold and $\dfrac{|D_i|}{|D|}$ is called *relative support* of pt_i.

It is known that the frequent sequence patterns are the subsequences that appear in the data set frequently and moreover, all subsequences of a long frequent sequence pattern must be frequent due to the downward closure property (Agrawal & Srikant, 1994). Thus, the set of frequent sequence patterns has redundancy of sequences caused by the inclusion of both a frequent sequence pattern and its subsequences. Therefore, in this work, they use closed frequent sequence patterns to label the semantic relation. The definition of closed frequent sequence pattern is shown as follows.

Definition 2 (Closed Frequent Sequence Pattern): A frequent sequence pattern pt_i is closed if and only if there exists no super-sequence pt_j of pt_i, s.t. $D_i = D_j$.

To extract the closed frequent sequence pattern, they employ the BIDE algorithm (Wang, Han, & Li, 2007) that can efficiently discover closed frequent sequence patterns without candidate maintenance and test. To express the semantic relation between entities with types T_m and T_n respectively, they only retain the closed frequent sequence patterns that contain both T_m and T_n in their sequences.

Unlike the system proposed in Hasegawa et al. (2004) that just simply selects the most frequent common words to label the extracted relation clusters, they use the closed frequent sequence patterns which can retain the inherent syntactic structure of the sentences where the semantic relations are mentioned and can describe the semantic relation more accurately, which can be seen from the experimental results shown in Section 4.2.

Anaphora Resolution

The analysis in Swampillai and Stevenson (2010) has shown that some inter-sentential relations are commonly asserted using anaphoric expressions. Therefore, it seems reasonable to extract inter-sentential relations by solving pronominal references. The authors use JavaRAP[1] which is a Java-based implementation of the seminal Resolution of Anaphora Procedure (RAP) algorithm (Lappin & Leass, 1994) to resolve the pronominal anaphora. JavaRAP can identify both inter-sentential and intra-sentential antecedents of third person pronouns and lexical anaphors (Qiu, Kan, & Chua, 2004). It takes the parsed sentences as input, and generates a list of anaphora-antecedent pairs as output. Alternately, it can produce an in-place substitution of the anaphors with their antecedents.

For example, given the input sentence "Neal recently had a talk in Austin, TX. He is Senior Vice President of HP Software.", JavaRAP can produce an in-place substitution of the anaphor (i.e., "He") with its antecedent (i.e., "Neal") and output the substitution sentence "Neal recently had a talk in Austin, TX. Neal is Senior Vice President of HP Software.". Hence, they transform the inter-sentential relation between entities "Neal" and "HP Software" in PEO-ORG domain asserted using anaphoric expression into the single-sentential relation via solving the pronominal reference.

In order to extract the inter-sentential relations, they use a module called Anaphora Resolution to apply JavaRAP to the parsed sentences of documents produced by the OpenNLP toolkits and obtain the substitution text where pronominal references are substituted by the noun phrases they refer to. Subsequently, REACTOR leverages the other four modules introduced above to process the substitution text to extract the single-sentential and inter-sentential relations together.

EXPERIMENTS

To evaluate the effectiveness of REACTOR, the authors tested it on a real-world enterprise data set from HP Company whose details are given in Section 4.1. They compared REACTOR with a clustering-based method proposed in Hasegawa et al. (2004). They chose this method as the baseline method because only this existing method can extract different semantic relations appearing in one type of entity pair, which is quite similar to REACTOR. Benefits obtained by applying pronominal anaphora resolution are measured by comparing the system performance with and without taking into account information referenced pronominally. Section 4.2 presents the experimental results, which show that REACTOR achieves significantly higher precision and recall over the enterprise data and can label each extracted semantic relation with tags more accurately compared with the baseline method, meanwhile, pronominal anaphora resolution can improve the system performance greatly.

Data Sets

The experiments were conducted on a large real-world enterprise data set from HP Company in which there are over three million pages including e-mails, internal Web pages, and word processing files. In the data set, about 67% of documents are internal Web pages, about 28% of documents are emails, while the other 5% of documents are word processing files. The average size of these documents is 16.7k and these documents are selected from May 1, 2008 to September 30, 2008 as a subset of all documents within HP. In this data set, there are about 97051 different entities with the type of people, 916 distinct organization entities and 2123 distinct product entities. Moreover, these types of entities have been discovered in advance as the input of the framework.

Methods and Results

This subsection presents the evaluation results of REACTOR. The usual metrics of Precision (P), Recall (R) and F-score (F) on the classification and clustering results are used to evaluate the performance of REACTOR. For evaluation purpose, the authors determined the relation that exists among most entity pairs in one cluster as the major relation of this cluster. The entity pairs having the major relation of this cluster are considered as correct pairs, otherwise, they are considered as incorrect pairs. Furthermore, they only considered the clusters consisting of two or more pairs in the same way as that in Hasegawa et al. (2004). In the experiments, they considered the relations in two different domains. One is the PEOPLE-ORGANIZATION (PEO-ORG) domain and another is the PEOPLE-PRODUCT (PEO-PRO) domain. The authors set k to 100 and s to 70 for PEO-ORG domain and k to 100 and s to 50 for PEO-PRO domain empirically when they selected the seeds in the Seed Extractor module (k represents the number of positive seeds and s represents the number of negative seeds). Meanwhile, the performance of REACTOR is not very sensitive to these two parameters, because these two parameters just affect the training of the classifier. When k is set from 60 to 250, and s is set from 40 to 150 in PEO-ORG domain, and k is set from 60 to 200, and s is set from 30 to 90 in PEO-PRO domain, the classification results are very similar in the experiments they conducted.

Firstly, they evaluated the classification results of the Relation Detection module for both domains. They randomly selected 500 entity pair occurrences in PEO-ORG domain and 250 entity pair occurrences in PEO-PRO domain. The selected occurrences of entity pairs are manually labeled as related or not according to their contexts. There are total 371 occurrences of entity pairs labeled as related in PEO-ORG domain and 203 occurrences of entity pairs labeled as related in PEO-PRO domain. The experimental results of classification are shown in Table 1. From the results it can be seen that the Relation Detection module can achieve significantly high F-score for both domains, which is beneficial for the next module Relation Categorization.

Then, in order to evaluate the clustering results of the Relation Categorization module, the authors created a test data set for clustering and manually labeled semantic relations in this test data set. Since for the large data set, labeling all relations is impractical and it is difficult to quantitatively evaluate REACTOR over the entire data set. To compare REACTOR with the baseline method and give a quantitative analysis, they randomly selected 500 and 250 entity pairs (not entity pair occurrences) classified as related by the Relation Detection module in PEO-ORG domain and PEO-PRO domain respectively as the test data set for clustering, as the Relation Categorization module clusters entity pairs nor entity pair occurrences. They analyzed the test data set and manually labeled the entity pairs into 53 different semantic relations in PEO-ORG domain and 47 different semantic relations in PEO-PRO domain both including a type of "No Relation" which means the two corresponding entities are unrelated. The types of relations and the number of entity pairs in each semantic relation for PEO-ORG domain and PEO-PRO domain are shown in Table 2 and Table 3, respectively. Due to limited space, the authors do not list all semantic relations and put the number of entity pairs of the semantic relations that do not appear in Table 2 and Table 3 into the relation "Others" in the tables for both domains. The relation "Employee of" for PEO-ORG domain in Table 2 means that for each entity pair of the relation "Employee of" there is no context in all its occurrences indicating the concrete semantic relation between the entities, but it can be judged that these two entities are related according their context. For example, for the sentence "Bob of Sales Group talked to …", it can be predicted that "Bob" is an employee of the "Sales Group", but they do not know the concrete role of "Bob" in this organization. Therefore, the authors defined this

Table 1. Experimental results of classification for both domains

Domain	P	R	F
PEO-ORG	0.873	0.960	0.914
PEO-PRO	0.856	0.943	0.897

Table 2. Manually labeled semantic relations in test data set for PEO-ORG domain

Semantic Relation	Leader	Vice President	Director	General Manager
# of pairs	45	26	25	24
Semantic relation	Manager	Technology Consultant	Solution Architect	Program Manager
# of pairs	17	10	9	7
Semantic relation	Project Manager	CTO	Operations Manager	Engineer
# of pairs	7	6	5	5
Semantic relation	Researcher	Product Manager	Developer	Marketing Manager
# of pairs	4	3	2	2
Semantic relation	Presales Manager	Client Manager	Account Manager	Assistant
# of pairs	2	2	2	2
Semantic relation	IT Manager	Employee of	Others	No Relation
# of pairs	2	242	24	27

Table 3. Manually labeled semantic relations in test data set for PEO-PRO domain

Semantic Relation	Change Proposal	Technical Specialist	Manager	Product Manager
# of pairs	48	3	9	8
Semantic relation	Solutions Architect	Technical Consultant	Support	Achieve Certification
# of pairs	7	7	6	6
Semantic relation	Program Manager	Project Manager	Demonstrate	Storage Consultant
# of pairs	4	4	3	2
Semantic relation	Test	Use	Win	Related
# of pairs	11	6	24	25
Semantic relation	Others	No Relation		
# of pairs	55	22		

type of entity relationship as "Employee of". Meanwhile, the relation "Related" for PEO-PRO domain in Table 3 has the similar meaning. From the distribution of semantic relations in Table 2, it can be seen that almost half of the entity pairs in PEO-ORG domain are annotated as "Employee of" that means there is no concrete semantic relation indicated by the context. On the other hand, the number of entity pairs annotated as "Related" for PEO-PRO domain in Table 3 is much less. Since the proposed method aims to extract semantic relations between entities, when the authors evaluated their approach and the baseline method, they did not consider the entity pairs which are annotated as "Employee of" for PEO-ORG domain in Table 2 and "Related" for PEO-PRO domain in Table 3.

The authors evaluated the performance of REACTOR with different term weighting and linkage strategies for clustering in the Relation Categorization module. Table 4 presents the experimental results of REACTOR under different strategy combinations in PEO-ORG domain with the optimal clustering threshold. As hierarchical clustering algorithm needs a pre-defined threshold to terminate the clustering process, the clustering result varies with different pre-defined thresholds. The optimal clustering threshold is the pre-defined threshold generating the best clustering result. Three different cluster distance computation methods (i.e., single linkage, average linkage, and complete linkage) and two different term weighting strategies for generating context vectors (i.e., tf and tf*idf) are compared using all possible combinations. Here tf means the term frequency and idf means the inverse document frequency, both of which are widely used in information retrieval. The results in Table 4 show that when the authors use complete linkage for clustering and tf as term weighting for generating context vectors, they can achieve the best result compared with the other strategy combinations. The tf term weighting is better than tf*idf in relation clustering since the terms retained to generate the context vector are close to the entities in the sentences and most of them indicate the semantic meaning of the relations, meanwhile, those indicating words are relatively frequent in the context vectors compared with other special words existing in each vector. Thus, if tf*idf is used as term weighting, the relative weight of other special words in each context vector will increase and the relative weight of indicating words will decrease because the document frequency of the special words is much smaller than the indicating words. In this case the entity pairs are possible to be merged into one cluster due to the special words consequently, which leads to the dissatisfactory clustering results.

The authors also compared REACTOR with the baseline method under different configurations in the two different domains for clustering over the test data set. The baseline method needs three parameters including maximum context word length, the occurrence frequency threshold of entity pairs, and the norm threshold for context vectors to filter the unreliable pairs. If the authors use the original setting of these thresholds introduced in Hasegawa et al. (2004), all entity pairs in the test data set will be filtered out and no entity pair is retained to start the clustering process, which also strongly reveals the low redundancy of the enterprise data and that the method based on the high redundancy of the Web corpus is not suitable to be applied to the enterprise data set. Thereby, to compare REACTOR with the baseline method, they must change the threshold setting of the baseline method. The simplest way is to directly eliminate those thresholds and all entity pairs are retained for the clustering process which they refer to Baseline. The authors also selected the optimal thresholds for the baseline method which can obtain the best *F*-score. This method is referred to Ba-Optimal. The optimal thresholds are 10 in PEO-ORG domain and 15 in PEO-PRO domain for the maximum context word length, and 0 for both the occurrence frequency threshold and the norm threshold for both domains. Table 5 shows the experimental results of REACTOR and the two baseline methods with the optimal clustering thresholds in two different domains. This proposed approach REACTOR uses complete linkage for clustering and tf for term weighting. It can be seen from the results that the overall Precision, Recall and *F*-score of REACTOR are signifi-

Table 4. Performance of REACTOR with different term weighting and linkage strategies for clustering in PEO-ORG domain

	Threshold	P	R	F
Single+tf*idf	0.0080	0.475	0.569	0.518
Average+tf*idf	0.0016	0.581	0.592	0.586
Complete+tf*idf	0.0007	0.733	0.659	0.694
Single+tf	0.56	0.532	0.613	0.569
Average+tf	0.34	0.771	0.711	0.740
Complete+tf	0.24	**0.795**	**0.819**	**0.807**

Table 5. Experimental results of REACTOR and the baseline methods for clustering in both domains

Domain	Method	Threshold	P	R	F
PEO-ORG	Baseline	0.0001	0.517	0.601	0.556
	Ba-Optimal	0.0003	0.638	0.549	0.590
	REACTOR	0.24	**0.795**	**0.819**	**0.807**
PEO-PRO	Baseline	0.0005	0.608	0.718	0.659
	Ba-Optimal	0.0010	0.696	0.670	0.683
	REACTOR	0.26	**0.846**	**0.729**	**0.783**

cantly better than both Baseline and Ba-Optimal in two different relation extraction tasks. Despite that different clustering thresholds can generate different results, it can be found that if they choose certain linkage strategy and term weighting (e.g., complete linkage+tf), the performance of REACTOR is not very sensitive to the threshold. For PEO-ORG domain, when the pre-defined clustering threshold is set from 0.20 to 0.33, the *F*-score of REACTOR is varied from 0.786 to 0.807, and when the threshold is set to 0.24, REACTOR obtains the best *F*-score (i.e., 0.807). Meanwhile, for PEO-PRO domain, when the pre-defined clustering threshold is set from 0.20 to 0.33, the *F*-score of REACTOR is varied from 0.760 to 0.783, and when the threshold is set to 0.26, REACTOR obtains the best *F*-score (i.e., 0.783).

Then, the authors investigated the performance of the Relation Tagging module, which labels each cluster with tags to describe the semantic relation. To select the representative tags, the model REACTOR firstly replaces the two considered entities in all co-occurring sentences with "PEO" or "ORG" in PEO-ORG domain and "PEO" or "PRO" in PEO-PRO domain respectively according to their entity types. Next, REACTOR runs the BIDE algorithm on the sequence database consisting of all co-occurring sentences for each cluster and sets the relative support threshold to 0.5. Then, REACTOR only retains the closed frequent sequences that contain both "PEO" and "ORG" in PEO-ORG domain or "PEO" and "PRO" in PEO-PRO domain. Table 6 shows a part of clusters for each domain, along with their ratio of the major relation in each cluster following the name of the relation. They also show the tagging results of REACTOR for each cluster and their relative support within the bracket following each selected tag. To compare REACTOR with the baseline method which simply selects the most frequent words between entities in the sentences to label the relation, they also list the labeling results of the baseline method as well as their relative frequency within the bracket following each selected tag in Table 6. The labeling results in PEO-ORG domain are presented on the top of the table and results in PEO-PRO domain are on the bottom of the table. From the tagging results it can be seen that REACTOR can label the clusters more accurately than the baseline method. Specially, when the semantic relation is not mentioned between entities in the sentence, but around the entities such as the relation "Change Proposal" and "Test" in PEO-PRO domain, the baseline method cannot extract the accurate words that express the semantic relation. Furthermore, this framework can retain the inherent syntactic structure of the sentences where the semantic relation is mentioned and describe the targeting semantic relation more concretely than the baseline method.

To measure the benefits obtained by solving pronominal references, the authors compared system performance with and without pronominal anaphora resolution. Due to the impracticalness to give quantitative evaluation over the entire data set, they sampled twenty thousand pages as the test corpus and evaluated the system performance of semantic relation extraction over this corpus in PEO-ORG

Table 6. A part of generated clusters and their relation tagging results for each domain

Major relations	Ratio	REACTOR-Tags (Relative support)	Baseline-Tags (Relative frequency)
Vice President	20/20	PEO vice president ORG (0.772) PEO vice president of ORG (0.557) PEO vice president for ORG (0.5)	vice (0.794), president (0.794) marketing (0.513), senior (0.136)
General Manager	14/14	PEO general manager ORG (0.734) PEO vice president ORG (0.71) PEO vice president general manager ORG (0.69)	president (0.776), vice (0.776) general (0.735), manager (0.735) senior (0.327), workstations (0.204)
Operation Manager	5/6	PEO manager ORG (0.846) PEO operation manager ORG (0.538)	operation (0.846), manager (0.846) solution (0.462), trading (0.462)
Leader	9/9	ORG led by PEO (0.722)	led (0.778), by (0.722), design (0.167)
Director	9/11	PEO director ORG (0.696)	director (0.878), business (0.683)
Technical Consultant	6/6	PEO technical consultant ORG (0.976) PEO senior technical consultant ORG (0.512)	consultant (0.977), technical (0.977) senior (0.512), workstation (0.349)
Program Manager	4/4	PEO program manager ORG (1.0)	manager (1.0), program (1.0)
Project Manager	3/3	PEO project manager ORG (1.0)	project (1.0), manager (1.0)
Researcher	2/3	PEO research analyst ORG (0.576)	research (0.615), analyst (0.576)
CTO	2/2	ORG CTO PEO (0.6)	CTO (0.6), innovation (0.2)
Change Proposal	45/45	proposal was changed by PEO product PRO (0.903) source proposal was changed by PEO PRO (0.875)	product (0.923), using (0.395) source (0.167), proposal (0.0625)
Solutions Architect	5/5	PEO architect PRO (1.0) PEO storage architect PRO (0.929) PEO solutions architect PRO (0.821)	architect (1.0), storage (0.928) solutions (0.821), solution (0.178) senior (0.035), engineer (0.035)
Technical Consultant	4/4	PRO PEO technical consultant (0.933)	regards (0.933), consultant (0.066)
Test	4/4	have already tested the PRO PEO (1.0) have already tested the PRO PEO at the (0.5)	met (1.0), tomas (0.5), martin (0.5)
Use	3/3	employee PEO using an PRO (1.0) taken by employee PEO using an PRO (0.667)	using (1.0), employee (0.333), fort (0.333)
Storage Consultant	2/2	PEO storage PRO (1.0) PEO storage consultant PRO (0.789)	storage (1.0), consultant (0.789)

domain. Currently JavaRAP only considers noun phrases contained within three sentences proceeding the anaphor and those in the sentence where the anaphor resides (Qiu et al., 2004). However, from the analysis in Swampillai and Stevenson (2010) it can be seen that about 76.3% of inter-sentential relations are contained within a window of four sentences. Hence, the limitation of JavaRAP has little impact on the system performance. Table 7 shows the performance of REACTOR with and without pronominal anaphora resolution in PEO-ORG domain over the test corpus. From Table 7 it can be seen that with the same optimal clustering threshold, REACTOR with and without pronominal anaphora resolution get almost the same precision. Despite that, the number of correct entity pairs REACTOR extracts from the two thousand pages increases by 21.2% (i.e., from 435 to 527) after REACTOR makes use of the information referenced pronominally. As the results show, it can be said that solving pronominal references improves REACTOR's performance with high level of recall.

Table 7. System performance with and without pronominal anaphora resolution in PEO-ORG domain

	Threshold	Correct Pairs	Total Pairs	Precision
REACTOR without anaphora resolution	0.21	435	536	0.812
REACTOR with anaphora resolution	0.21	527	650	0.811

CONCLUSION

The existing relation extraction methods, which work on the Web data very well, are not suitable for relation extraction on the low-redundancy enterprise data. This chapter introduces a novel hybrid semantic relation extraction framework called REACTOR, which combines a statistical method, classification, and clustering techniques to extract relations from the enterprise data. A statistical method is introduced to extract a set of representative entity pairs containing both positive and negative examples for the classifier. Then REACTOR employs a classifier to extract all related entity pairs by defining some domain-independent features. A clustering algorithm is used to identify the semantic relation between each pair of entities. To label the extracted semantic relation, REACTOR exploits a closed frequent sequence mining algorithm to extract the representative tags to describe the relationship in each cluster. Meanwhile, REACTOR applies pronominal anaphora resolution to extract more relations expressed across sentence boundaries. Finally, REACTOR was evaluated on a large real-world enterprise corpus from HP and the results show that REACTOR can extract the semantic relation more effectively in comparison with the baseline method, and the extracted tags can describe the semantic relation more accurately. Moreover, as the results show, the application of anaphora resolution improves REACTOR's performance greatly and seems to be very essential for inter-sentential relation extraction.

ACKNOWLEDGMENT

This work was supported in part by National Natural Science Foundation of China under Grant No. 61502253 and 61772079, and the Fundamental Research Funds for the Central Universities.

REFERENCES

Agichtein, E., & Gravano, L. (2000). Snowball: Extracting relations from large plain-text collections. *Proceedings of the fifth ACM Conference on Digital Libraries (DL'00)*, 85-94. 10.1145/336597.336644

Agrawal, R., & Srikant, R. (1994). Fast algorithms for mining association rules in large databases. *Proceedings of the 20th International Conference on Very Large Data Bases (VLDB'94)*, 487-499.

Banko, M., & Brill, E. (2001). Scaling to very very large corpora for natural language disambiguation. *Proceedings of the 39th Annual Meeting on Association for Computational Linguistics (ACL'01)*, 26-33. 10.3115/1073012.1073017

Banko, M., Cafarella, M. J., Soderl, S., Broadhead, M., & Etzioni, O. (2007). Open information extraction from the web. *Proceedings of the 20th International Joint Conference on Artificial Intelligence (IJCAI'07)*, 2670-2676.

Banko, M., & Etzioni, O. (2008). The tradeoffs between open and traditional relation extraction. *Proceedings of the 46th Annual Meeting on Association for Computational Linguistics (ACL'08)*, 28-36.

Bollegala, D. T., Matsuo, Y., & Ishizuka, M. (2010). Relational duality: Unsupervised extraction of semantic relations between entities on the web. *Proceedings of the 19th International Conference on World Wide Web (WWW'10)*, 151-160. 10.1145/1772690.1772707

Brin, S. (1998). Extracting patterns and relations from the world wide web. *Proceedings of the International Workshop on the World Wide Web and Databases (WebDB'98)*, 172-183.

Crowley, C., & Harris, S. (2007). The sedona conference glossary: E-discovery and digital information management. *Proceedings of the Sedona Conference 2007.*

Etzioni, O., Cafarella, M., Downey, D., Popescu, A., Shaked, T., Soderland, S., & Yates, A. et al. (2005). Unsupervised named-entity extraction from the web: An experimental study. *Artificial Intelligence, 165*(1), 91–134. doi:10.1016/j.artint.2005.03.001

Freitag, D., & Mccallum, A. K. (1999). Information extraction with hmms and shrinkage. *Proceedings of the AAAI'99 Workshop on Machine Learning for Information Extraction*, 31–36.

Giuliano, C., Lavelli, A., & Romano, L. (2006). Exploiting shallow linguistic information for relation extraction from biomedical literature. *Proceedings of 11th Conference of the European Chapter of the Association for Computational Linguistics (EACL'06)*, 401-408.

Gonzàlez, E., & Turmo, J. (2009). Unsupervised relation extraction by massive clustering. *Proceedings of the 2009 Ninth IEEE International Conference on Data Mining (ICDM '09)*, 782-787. 10.1109/ICDM.2009.81

Grishman, R., & Sundheim, B. (1996). Message understanding conference-6: A brief history. *Proceedings of 16th Conference on Computational Linguistics (COLING'96)*, 466-471. 10.3115/992628.992709

Hasegawa, T., Sekine, S., & Grishman, R. (2004). Discovering relations among named entities from large corpora. *Proceedings of the 42nd Annual Meeting on Association for Computational Linguistics (ACL'04)*, 415-422. 10.3115/1218955.1219008

Hassan, H., Hassan, A., & Emam, O. (2006). Unsupervised information extraction approach using graph mutual reinforcement. *Proceedings of the 2006 Conference on Empirical Methods in Natural Language Processing (EMNLP'06)*, 501-508. 10.3115/1610075.1610144

Hoffmann, R., Zhang, C., Ling, X., Zettlemoyer, L. S., & Weld, D. S. (2011). Knowledge-based weak supervision for information extraction of overlapping relations. *Proceedings of the 49th Annual Meeting of the Association for Computational Linguistics: Human Language Technologies, 1,* 541-550.

Kambhatla, N. (2004). Combining lexical, syntactic, and semantic features with maximum entropy models for extracting relations. *Proceedings of the ACL 2004 on Interactive poster and demonstration sessions (ACL demo'04).* 10.3115/1219044.1219066

Lappin, S., & Leass, H. J. (1994). An algorithm for pronominal anaphora resolution. *Computational Linguistics, 20*(4), 535–561.

Madaan, A., Mittal, A., Ramakrishnan, G., & Sarawagi, S. (2016). Numerical relation extraction with minimal supervision. *Proceedings of the Thirtieth AAAI Conference on Artificial Intelligence (AAAI'16)*, 2764-2771.

Mintz, M., Bills, S., Snow, R., & Jurafsky, D. (2009). Distant supervision for relation extraction without labeled data. *Proceedings of the Joint Conference of the 47th Annual Meeting of the ACL and the 4th International Joint Conference on Natural Language Processing of the AFNLP, 2*, 1003-1011. 10.3115/1690219.1690287

Qiu, L., Kan, M., & Chua, T. (2004). A public reference implementation of the rap anaphora resolution algorithm. *Proceedings of the Fourth International Conference on Language Resources and Evaluation (LREC'04)*, 291-294.

Riedel, S., Yao, L., & McCallum, A. (2010). Modeling relations and their mentions without labeled text. Modeling Relations and Their Mentions without Labeled Text. In J. L. Balcázar, F. Bonchi, A. Gionis, & M. Sebag (Eds.), *Machine Learning and Knowledge Discovery in Databases. ECML PKDD 2010* (pp. 148–163). Berlin: Springer.

Ritter, A., & Zettlemoyer, L., Mausam, & Etzioni, O. (2013). Modeling missing data in distant supervision for information extraction. *Transactions of the Association for Computational Linguistics, 1*, 367–378.

Salton, G., & McGill, M. J. (1986). *Introduction to modern information retrieval*. New York, NY: McGraw-Hill, Inc.

Salton, G., Wong, A., & Yang, C. S. (1975). A vector space model for automatic indexing. *Communications of the ACM, 18*(11), 613–620. doi:10.1145/361219.361220

Shen, W., Wang, J., Luo, P., & Wang, M. (2012). A graph-based approach for ontology population with named entities. *Proceedings of the 21st ACM International Conference on Information and Knowledge Management (CIKM '12)*, 345–354. 10.1145/2396761.2396807

Shen, W., Wang, J., Luo, P., Wang, M., & Yao, C. (2011). Reactor: A framework for semantic relation extraction and tagging over enterprise data. *Proceedings of the 20th International Conference Companion on World Wide Web (WWW'11)*, 121–122. 10.1145/1963192.1963254

Shinyama, Y., & Sekine, S. (2006). Preemptive information extraction using unrestricted relation discovery. *Proceedings of the main conference on Human Language Technology Conference of the North American Chapter of the Association of Computational Linguistics (HLT-NAACL'06)*, 304–311. 10.3115/1220835.1220874

Skounakis, M., Craven, M., & Ray, S. (2003). Hierarchical hidden markov models for information extraction. *Proceedings of the 18th International Joint Conference on Artificial Intelligence (IJCAI'03)*, 427–433.

Surdeanu, M., & Ciaramita, M. (2007). Robust information extraction with perceptrons. *Proceedings of the NIST 2007 Automatic Content Extraction Workshop (ACE'07)*.

Swampillai, K., & Stevenson, M. (2010). Intersentential relations in information extraction corpora. *Proceedings of the Seventh Conference on International Language Resources and Evaluation (LREC'10)*.

Wang, J., Han, J., & Li, C. (2007). Frequent closed sequence mining without candidate maintenance. *IEEE Transactions on Knowledge and Data Engineering, 19*(8), 1042–1056. doi:10.1109/TKDE.2007.1043

Zelenko, D., Aone, C., & Richardella, A. (2003). Kernel methods for relation extraction. *Journal of Machine Learning Research, 3*, 1083–1106.

Zhou, G., Zhang, M., Ji, D., & Zhu, Q. (2007). Tree kernel-based relation extraction with context-sensitive structured parse tree information. *Proceedings of the 2007 Joint Conference on Empirical Methods in Natural Language Processing and Computational Natural Language Learning (EMNLP-CONLL'07)*, 728-736.

Zhu, J., Nie, Z., Liu, X., Zhang, B., & Wen, J.-R. (2009). StatSnowball: A statistical approach to extracting entity relationships. *Proceedings of the 18th International Conference on World Wide Web (WWW'09)*, 101-110. 10.1145/1526709.1526724

LIBSVM. (2016). LIBSVM – A library for support vector machines. *LIBVSM*. Retrieved from: https://www.csie.ntu.edu.tw/~cjlin/libsvm/

OpenNLP. (n.d.). *Apache OpenNLP*. Retrieved from: http://opennlp.apache.org/

Porter Stemming. (2006). *The Porter Stemming Algorithm*. Retrieved from: http://tartarus.org/martin/PorterStemmer/

ENDNOTE

[1]   http://aye.comp.nus.edu.sg/~qiu/NLPTools/JavaRAP.html

Chapter 4
A Hybrid Concept Learning Approach to Ontology Enrichment

Zenun Kastrati
Norwegian University of Science and Technology (NTNU), Norway

Ali Shariq Imran
Norwegian University of Science and Technology (NTNU), Norway

Sule Yildirim Yayilgan
Norwegian University of Science and Technology (NTNU), Norway

ABSTRACT

The wide use of ontology in different applications has resulted in a plethora of automatic approaches for population and enrichment of an ontology. Ontology enrichment is an iterative process where the existing ontology is continuously updated with new concepts. A key aspect in ontology enrichment process is the concept learning approach. A learning approach can be a linguistic-based, statistical-based, or hybrid-based that employs both linguistic as well as statistical-based learning approaches. This chapter presents a concept enrichment model that combines contextual and semantic information of terms. The proposed model called SEMCON employs a hybrid concept learning approach utilizing functionalities from statistical and linguistic ontology learning techniques. The model introduced for the first time two statistical features that have shown to improve the overall score ranking of highly relevant terms for concept enrichment. The chapter also gives some recommendations and possible future research directions based on the discussion in following sections.

INTRODUCTION

Domain ontologies are a good starting point to model in a formal way the basic vocabulary of a given domain. They provide a broad coverage of concepts and their relationships within a domain. However, in-depth coverage of concepts is often not available, thereby limiting their use in specialized subdomain applications. It is also the business dynamics and changes in the operating environment which require

DOI: 10.4018/978-1-5225-5042-6.ch004

modification to an ontology (McGuinness, 2000). Therefore, the techniques for modifying ontologies, i.e. ontology enrichment, have emerged as an essential prerequisite for ontology-based applications.

An ontology can be enriched with lexical data either by populating the ontology with lexical entries or by adding terms to ontology concepts. The former means updating the existing ontology with new concepts along with their ontological relations and types. This increases the size of the existing ontology which requires more computational resources and more time to compute. Thus, making it less cost effective. The latter means adding new concepts without taking into account the ontological relations and types between concepts. Because of this, the ontology structure will remain the same but its concepts will be enriched with their synonym terms or linguistic variants.

Enrichment of ontology concepts is aiming at improving an existing ontology with new concepts. It is part of the iterative ontology engineering process (Faatz & Steinmetz, 2005). The core of this process is the learning approach which constitute tasks such as identification and acquisition of the relevant terminology through exploring various knowledge resources, and the creation of the concepts.

There is a variety of concept learning approaches that are available to enrich concepts of an ontology. These approaches rely on either linguistic, statistical, or hybrid techniques (Drumond & Girardi, 2008; Hazman, El-Beltagy, & Rafea, 2011). Although, these approaches proved useful for enriching ontologies of many domains, they do have some limitations, especially when it comes to semantic information of terms. The existing approaches use only contextual information without considering the semantic information of terms. Moreover, the contextual information is simply derived by distributional property of terms such as term frequency *tf* or term frequency inverse document frequency *tf*idf*, and co-occurrences of terms.

The focus of this chapter is to enlighten the reader with the ontology concept enrichment process, explore state-of-the-art methods and techniques in this regard, review input data resources, learning approaches and systems build upon them, discuss their limitations and to propose solutions and to give some recommendations accordingly. It also describes the SEMCON model to enriching the domain ontology with new concepts by combining contextual as well as the semantics of terms.

SEMCON uses unstructured data as input for ontology learning process and is composed of two parts - contextual and semantic. Context is defined as the part of a text or statement – passage that surrounds a given term and it determines term meaning. In this work, it is the cosine distance between the feature vectors of any two terms. The feature vectors are composed of values computed by both the frequency of occurrence of terms in corresponding passages, and the statistical features such as font type and font size. The semantics on the other hand is defined by computing a semantic similarity score using lexical database WordNet.

Additionally, this chapter investigates into how much each of contextual and semantic components contributes to the overall task of enriching the domain ontology concepts. Obtained results are compared with *tf*idf*, χ^2, and LSA. Results for several domains including Computer, Software Engineering, C++ Programming, Database, and the Internet are presented in this chapter.

The rest of the chapter is organized as follows. *Background* section presents ontology enrichment pipeline, describes various input data modalities, discusses text-based resources followed by concept learning techniques and applications using them. This section also presents the state-of-the-art systems in the field of ontology enrichment. Section *SEMCON* describes the proposed SEMCON model in detail. In Section, *Experimental Procedures* we describe the experiments including subjective and objective evaluation of SEMCON along with measures used to evaluate the effectiveness of objective methods.

Results obtained by SEMCON and other objective methods and their comparisons are shown in Section *Results and Analysis*. *Recommendation* section highlights some key points for ontology enrichment followed by *Future Research Directions* section. Section *Applications of SEMCON* presents two important fields where SEMCON has successfully been employed. Lastly, section *Conclusion* concludes the paper.

BACKGROUND

This section describes the fundamentals of building an ontology concept enrichment model as shown in Figure 1. Enrichment of ontology concepts aims to improve a given ontology by populating it with new concepts. As part of an ontology engineering process, it involves subtasks from only lower part of ontology learning layer cake model (Cimiano, 2006). Acquisition of the relevant terminology, identification of synonym terms or linguistic variants, and the creation of concepts are the subtasks involved. To accomplish these subtasks, the enrichment process departs from an initial ontology that will be enriched with new concepts. In a simplified view, this initial ontology is constituted by a set of concepts and relations that link these concepts. The next step is the identification and acquiring of the relevant terminology such as synonym terms or linguistic variants. This is achieved by exploring the knowledge input data resources which can be in structured, semi-structured, or unstructured format. Finally, a concept learning approach, which is the core of the entire enrichment process, is employed to the extracted terminology in order to create new concepts for populating the initial ontology.

A vast number of ontology enrichment models are available which rely on a variety of knowledge resources. These resources are primarily used to identify and extract relevant terminology, and their linguistic variants and synonyms. Various concept learning approaches have also been used in litera-

Figure 1. The ontology concept enrichment process

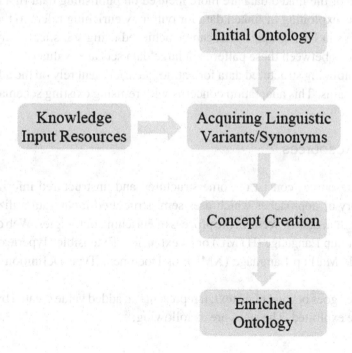

ture to enrich an ontology by populating it with new concepts. Therefore, one way of categorizing the enrichment models is by looking at the approach it takes for ontology enrichment and the kind of data resources it uses. The main aim of this section is to provide an overview of the existing models in light of the learning approach and knowledge resources (input data) it uses, and shed some light on similarities and differences between these approaches.

Modality of Input Resource

Ontology enrichment systems identify and extract their knowledge of interest from the input resources. The input resource encompasses multimedia modalities including but not limited to textual data, audio, images, and videos. The primary focus of this chapter is the text-based resources which can broadly be categorized into structured resources, semi-structured resources, and unstructured resources. These are explained in following subsections.

Structured Resources

The ontology enrichment approaches based on structured input data uses database schemata, existing ontologies, linked data, and lexical semantic databases (e.g. WordNet) to acquire the relevant concepts to enriching an ontology.

Acquiring ontological knowledge using databases is done through the conversion of relational elements into ontological ones. This conversion is achieved using the corresponding E/R model and a set of basic translation rules. These rules enable to identify and extract concepts of the ontology, particularly, they describe what entities and relationships of the E/R model can be modeled as a concept in the ontology. Another resource of structured information to be exploited is linked data. Linked data, in contrast to databases where the data schema is defined formally, have no explicit schema for their dataset due to the fact the publishers of the linked data are more focused on publishing data first rather than creating the schema. Therefore, exploiting of linked data for ontology enriching refers to the process of detecting meaningful patterns in RDF graphs. This can be achieved using statistical analysis where frequent patterns and correlations between these patterns in large data sets are evaluated.

Other approaches utilizing structured data for ontology enrichment rely on the adaptation of existing ontologies to new domains. This adaptation concerns with re-using existing schematic structures of the ontology.

Semi-Structured Resources

The semi-structured resources consist of some structured and unstructured information given by the markups. The category of approaches which uses semi-structured input data utilizes existing markup structure within the textual data to perform the process of enriching ontologies. Web document structures such as Hypertext Markup Language (HTML) or its extension, Extensible Hypertext Markup Language (XHTML), Extensible Markup Language (XML), or Document Type Definition (DTD's) have been exploited.

The semi-structured goes beyond plain text. It represents an added value created by many Web authors which are worth to be exploited. The steps are as following:

1.   The first and foremost step of using semi-structured data is the conversion of web document collection into XHTML web document collection.
2.   Next step is the use of web document markups such as text spans. Text occurring within the text span pairs are used for this purpose.
3.   Next step is the cleaning process. Whitespaces appear in the text span list therefore some cleaning step are needed to remove these whitespaces. Additionally, other cleaning steps such as eliminating punctuation and numbers, and converting all characters to lower case, can be performed.
4.   The final step is the frequency analysis where the frequency of occurrences of the text span is computed. This results in a list of candidate terms ranked by their frequency within the Web document collection. Terms above a specified threshold are considered relevant terms for ontology enrichment.

Another approach which exploits semi-structured data to acquire the terminology for ontology enrichment is presented by Kruschwitz (Kruschwitz, 2001). Kruschwitz initially pre-processes the web document to extract only the text associated to a set of markups such as *<meta>*, *<head>*, *<title>* or emphasizing tags such as *<b>* or *<i>*. Next, the importance of the exploited terms is computed using frequency analysis such as term frequency or term frequency using context where context is defined using co-occurrences of terms within the same unit or block structure, i. e. *title*, *keywords*, *meta*, *headers*, etc. (Manzano-Macho, Gómez-Pérez, & Borrajo, 2008).

Unstructured Resources

Unstructured data, known as free text, is the most difficult input resource to extract the relevant knowledge for enriching ontologies. Approaches that utilize this input data are dependent on natural language processing. They use the interacting constraints on the various language levels to discover and extract concepts and their relationships. Moreover, Hazman et al. (Hazman, El-Beltagy, & Rafea, 2011) showed from the survey performed that Natural Language Processing - NLP is the most common among all the techniques. Hence, they classified all these approaches based on the technique used in addition to NLP. Additionally, they identified three major classes of approaches. The first group of approaches integrates NLP with the statistical techniques. These approaches extract concepts using a shallow parser for identification of noun and noun phrases and frequency of occurrences of these noun and noun phrases. The second category employs pure NLP technique using syntactical dependency and parsers to discover concepts and their relationships. The third category of approaches integrates techniques from different disciplines such as information retrieval, lexical databases, and machine learning, in addition to computational linguistics.

Concept Learning Techniques

The next processing step of ontology enrichment is the acquisition of the terminology and their linguistic variants and synonyms from the knowledge resources. This is carried out via concept learning techniques. There are various concept learning techniques employed by different ontology enrichment approaches which generally can be classified into three major categories: 1) linguistic, 2) statistical, and 3) hybrid.

The linguistic approach also known as symbolic relies on linguistic components, e.g. noun phrases, to identify and acquire relevant concepts for enriching the ontology. The most common linguistic approach is the one which uses NLP technique of lexico-syntactic pattern analysis. Hearst (Hearst, 1992) was the first who introduced and explored some lexico-syntactic patterns in the form of regular expressions to extract ontological knowledge from English texts. The list of Hearst's lexico-syntactic patterns is shown in Table 1.

The Hearst's patterns proved to be successful at identifying and extracting a set of relationships, i.e. hypernym, but this technique of ontology learning is tedious and limited to a small number of patterns. To address this limitation, a machine learning technique has emerged. It tends to replace manually-created patterns with an automatic one and to achieve this it primarily uses a set of known hypernym pairs to automatically identify large numbers of useful lexico-syntactic patterns. More concretely, noun pairs from corpora are collected and a set of hypernym pairs using WordNet is obtained. Next step is collection of sentences in which nouns pairs occur. These sentences are parsed and patterns are extracted automatically from the parsed tree. Finally, a classifier is trained based on these patterns.

Other linguistic approaches rely on the syntactic dependencies analysis. Such approaches follow the idea that syntactic dependencies provide information on the semantic relations between the concepts. Dependencies are found out via a process composed of two phases. In the first phase, the corpus is tagged by a part of speech tagger, while in the second phase the tagged corpus is analyzed in sequences of basic chunks where two consecutive chunks represent a syntactic dependency.

There is another linguistic approach that uses syntactic analysis but with the focus being placed on the syntactic structure of component terms. This approach assumes that a compound/multi-world term, such as *prostate cancer*, is more specific than a single compositional term, i.e. *cancer*, and therefore, it is very likely that a compound term to be a hyponym of a single term.

While linguistic approaches rely on NLP analysis techniques to extract concepts from input data, the statistical approaches rely on the frequency analysis of terms. To identify and extract the relevant knowledge for ontology enrichment, these approaches utilize large corpus of textual data for calculating a distributional property of terms such as term frequency - *tf* or/and term frequency inverse document frequency - *tf*idf*.

Table 1. Hearst's lexico-syntactic patterns

No	Lexico-syntactic patterns
1	$NP_H \ such \ as \ \{NP,\}^* \ \{(or|and)\} \ NP$
2	$such \ as \ NP_H \ as \ \{NP,\}^* \ \{or|and)\} \ NP$
3	$NP\{,NP\}^* \ \{,\} \ (and|or) \ or \ other \ NP_H$
4	$NP\{,NP\}^* \ \{,\} \ (and|or) \ and \ other \ NP_H$
5	$NP_H \ \{,\} \ including \ \{NP,\}^* \ \{(or|and)\} \ NP$
6	$NP_H \ \{,\} \ especially \ \{NP,\}^* \ \{(or|and)\} \ NP$

Other statistical approaches are concerned with batches of terms. These approaches are based on the assumption that identification and extraction of ontological terminology relies not only on the meaning of terms, but also on the basis of their co-occurrences with other terms and the frequencies of the co-occurrences (Maedche, Pekar, & Staab, 2003). Term co-occurrences, also referred to as collocation, defines the context within a discourse which can be either a sentence, paragraph, or an entire document (Heyer, Läuter, Quasthoff, Witting, & Wolff, 2001). A major advantage of these approaches is that they require no prior knowledge of the dataset and their ability to be generalized to other domains. This advantage makes these approaches the most addressed techniques among the statistical concept learning approaches. However, a disadvantage of these techniques is the need of a large corpus of textual data in order to be able to identify and obtain the relevant terminology to enrich ontologies.

Even though both symbolic and statistical approaches have proved useful as concept learning technique for ontology enrichment, they however have some limitations. For example, statistical approaches provide better coverage than symbolic approaches but their results are only probabilities without a conceptual explanation. As a result, a hybrid approach which combines the statistical and the symbolic approaches is introduced. The hybrid approach employs the benefits of both approaches and eliminates their limitations.

Ontology Enrichment Application

This subsection present systems based on the concept learning approaches described in the previous subsection for enriching ontologies. It starts by listing the systems which use linguistic approaches employed as concept learning, continuing with the statistical one, and finalizing with the systems which employ hybrid approaches as concept learning.

Linguistic Approaches

SynDiKATe (Hahn & Romacker, 2001) is an ontology enrichment application which relies on natural language processing analysis. Technical documents in the German language taken from test reports from the information technology domain and medical finding reports are exploited and modelled into a directed graph. The syntactic dependency (sentence level and text level) is then computed using the graph dependency of nodes and edges. The nodes represent terms occurring in documents and edges denote relations between these terms.

medSynDiKATe (Hahn, Romacker & Schulz, 2002) is an extension of SynDiKATe application. It is designed to automatically acquire medical knowledge from medical finding reports. Emphasis was put on the role of various input textual resources required for text understanding with a focus being placed on grammar and domain knowledge. Additionally, a focus is put on alternative ways to support knowledge acquisition to foster the scalability of the system. Two concept learning approaches, automatic and semi-automatic, are employed and fully embedded in the text understanding process.

HASTI (Shamsfard & Barforoush, 2004) is an ontology enrichment application which uses Persian free text as an input. It utilizes a combination of morpho-syntactic and semantic analysis. The enrichment process departs from a seed ontology whose lexicon is nearly empty at the beginning. The new obtained concepts are then inserted on top of the existing ontology.

KnowItAll (Etzioni et al., 2004, 2005) is another system which utilizes natural language processing to identify and acquire the information. It is a domain-independent system. It explores the Web by employing lexico-syntactic patterns analysis to discover relevant information for enriching ontologies.

Relevant concepts are selected by computing a version of pointwise mutual information measure called concept plausibility.

Statistical Approaches

DOODLE II (Yamaguchi, 2001) is an example which uses the statistical approach as a learning technique. A machine-readable dictionary and domain specific texts are used as input to the system to build domain ontologies with both taxonomic (vertical) and non-taxonomic (horizontal) relationships between concepts. The non-taxonomic relationships composed of dependencies between concepts such as synonymy, meronym, antonymy, attribute-of, and possession, are exploited using domain specific texts with the analysis of lexical co-occurrence statistics based on WordSpace. The idea behind the lexical co-occurrence statistics is that terms that appear together may have non-taxanomic relationships between concepts.

EXTREEM-T (Brunzel, 2008) is a system which exploits the semi-structured resources to acquire the relevant terminology to enrich an ontology. It stands for Xhtml TREE Mining and it utilizes statistical technique such as frequency of occurrences of markups.

DL-Learner (Lehmann, 2009) is an ontology enrichment system which uses structured input data and relies on Inductive Logic Programming technique. This technique aims to extract concept via logic learned from examples and prior knowledge.

SYNOPSIS (Duthil et al., 2011) is another system which uses the technique of learning by term collocations and co-occurrences. It automatically builds a lexicon for each specific term called *criterion* by splitting a document into several passages. The correlation between terms and the user criterion is computed using the relative position of these terms and the given criterion. Relative position refers to the number of terms between a term and the user criterion. For each criterion, a lexicon is built in this way.

CoLexIR (Ranwez et al., 2013) is and adaptation of SYNOPSIS. It implements the same learning technique as SYNOPSIS but rather than building lexicon of a term, it builds automatically the lexicon of ontology concepts.

Hybrid Approaches

WEB->KB (Craven et al., 2000) is a system which combines statistical (Bayesian learning) and logical techniques to identify and extract concepts. The system is primarily trained to acquire the relevant terminology and is then allowed to explore semi-structured web documents to locate and extract these concepts. Two inputs are required to train the system; the first is a set of concepts and relations of interest when creating the knowledge base, and the second is a set of training data consisting of labeled regions of hypertext that represent instances of these concepts and relations.

TEXT-TO-ONTO (Cimiano, & Völker, 2005; Maedche et al., 2003) is an ontology learning system which employs learning by term collocations and co-occurrences technique with a basic linguistic processing technique. The input to the system can be a structured, semi-structured, or an unstructured resource. The frequency of term collocations is computed to locate and acquire non-taxonomic relations using background knowledge i.e. a lexicon and a taxonomy.

BOEMIE (Petasis et al., 2011) is an ontology enrichment system which utilizes both symbolic such as shallow syntactic analysis and statistical concept learning technique to identify and extract concept from the input data. It uses large corpora which can be either a text, image, or a video.

Consolidated Overview

A consolidated overview of the approaches for enriching ontologies presented in this chapter is shown in Table 2. It constitutes some of the characteristics of the systems that are presented in this chapter.

The first column of the table contains the reviewed approaches while the following columns denote the characteristics considered and evaluated in this chapter. The entries of the table are values that show which of the evaluated characteristics are supported (denoted with ✓) or not supported (denoted with X) by the approaches. As can be seen from the Table 2, unstructured data are used among all the approaches as input resources to extract the concepts; the structured data is the one supported by only a few approaches (TEXT-to-ONTO and BOEMIE) and semi-structured data are used as input resources by 8 out of 12 approaches presented in this chapter. We also observed that there exists almost an equal use of concept learning techniques among all the approaches shown in this chapter.

Categorizing SEMCON model in one of the categories of approaches of concept enrichment is not an easy task due to differences which exist in many dimensions amongst approaches. Shamsfard and Barforoush (2004) identified six main categories of the major distinguishing factors between ontology learning approaches. Although there exist differences amongst approaches, they however have some dimensions in common. From this perspective, SEMCON can be considered as a hybrid approach that to some extent utilizes both approaches, linguistic and statistical. From the linguistic point of view, SEMCON uses morpho-syntactic analysis to identify and extract noun terms, as part of speech, which represents the most meaningful terms in a document. From the statistical point of view, SEMCON derives the context using cosine similarity between term vectors whose members are frequencies of terms. SEMCON employs, besides term frequency, two new statistical features, i.e. term font size and term font type, to determine the context. In addition to context, SEMCON also incorporates the semantic information of terms using the lexical database WordNet and finally aggregates both contextual and semantic information of this term.

Table 2. A consolidated overview of the evaluated systems

Systems	Input Resource			Learning Technique		
	Structured	Semi-structured	Unstructured	Linguistic	Statisitical	Hybrid
DOODLE II	X	✓	✓	X	✓	X
CoLexIR	X	✓	✓	X	✓	X
HASTI	X	X	✓	X	✓	X
KnowItAll	X	✓	✓	✓	X	X
EXTREEM-T	X	✓	✓	X	✓	X
SynDiKATe	X	X	✓	✓	X	X
MedSynDiKATe	X	X	✓	✓	X	X
SYNOPSIS	X	X	✓	X	✓	X
TEXT-to-ONTO	✓	✓	✓	X	X	✓
WEB->KB	X	✓	✓	X	X	✓
DL-Learner	X	✓	✓	X	✓	X
BOEMIE	✓	✓	✓	X	X	✓

SEMCON

This section describes the proposed SEMCON model to enrich concepts of a domain ontology with new terms which are closely related using the contextual and semantic information. The model, illustrated in Figure 2, consists of four modules, which are explained in the following subsections.

Preprocessing

This module initially collects a document and partitions that into subsets of text known as passages. These passages are text portions which have very strong semantic coherence and are clearly disconnected from adjacent parts (Salton, Singhal, Buckley, & Mitra, 1996). The partitioned passages can either be fixed or variable length. They can also be classified into contextual passages if the partitioning takes into account the context of the document or they can be classified as statistical passages.

Figure 2. Block diagram of SEMCON

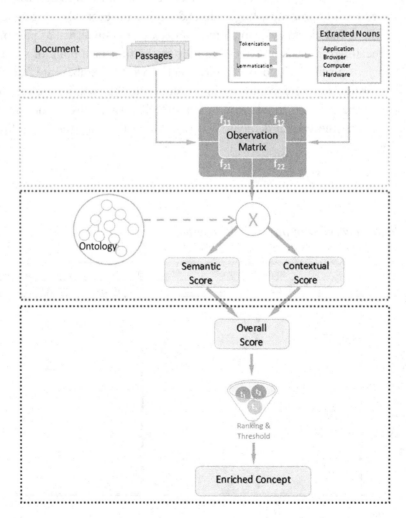

In this model, we take into account the context of a document irrespective of the length of partitioned passages. Partitioned passages are treated as independent documents. A morpho-syntactic analysis using TreeTagger (Schmid, 2013) is performed on the partitioned passages. Passages are later cleaned by removing all punctuation and capitalization followed by a tokenizer step to separate the text into individual terms. The lemmatization is the last step used to find the normalized form of these terms.

The potential terms that are obtained because of this preprocessing step can either be a noun, verb, adverb or adjective. These are different parts-of-speech (POS) of a language. It is a well-established fact that nouns represent the most meaningful terms in a document (Li, Tian, Ye, & Cai, 2010). Thus our focus is on processing only noun terms for further consideration.

Observation Matrix

Computation of the observation matrix is the next step in the proposed model. Observation matrix is a rectangular matrix where the rows represent the extracted passages from a document and columns are the terms extracted from those passages. An example of observation matrix is shown in Table 3.

Each entry of the observation matrix is calculated by accumulating the sum of term frequency, term font size and term font type in each of the extracted passages, as shown in Equation 1. Introducing of term font type and term font size, a very important factors in the information finding process (Halvey & Keane, 2007), is inspired from the representation of tags in the tag cloud (Bateman, Gutwin, & Nacenta, 2008). The effect of these statistical features is discussed in subsection *The Impact of Statistical Features*.

$$E_{i,j} = tf_{i,j} + \sum (ft_{i,j,k} + fs_{i,j,k}) \tag{1}$$

where, $tf_{i,j}$ denotes the frequency of occurrences of a term i in document j. $ft_{i,j,k}$ and $fs_{i,j,k}$ indicate the aggregated values of font types and font sizes computed over all occurrences k of a terms i in a document j.

We adopt a linear increase model for different font types and font sizes. The linear model assumes that the effect of each variable is the same for all values of the other variables. For example, the model assumes that the effect of bold font type terms is the same for every value of underline or italic font type

Table 3. A part of the observation matrix from computer domain

Slide	Computer	Data	Device	Function	Hardware	System	Web
1	6.25	5.25	1.75	0	0	0	0
2	3	0	0	0	0	1.5	8
3	9.25	0	7	1.75	4.75	5.5	0
4	5.5	3.5	8	0	0	0	0
5	5	1.5	1.5	1.5	0	2	0
6	12.25	0	0	1.5	0	6	0
7	2.25	0	0	0	0	6.25	0

terms. The same way, the effect of underlined font type terms is the same for every value of underline bold or italic font type terms, and so on.

Algorithm 1 in Figure 3 describes the computation of observation matrix using three statistical parameters: frequency of term occurrences, bold font type and four different font sizes. More precisely, lines 3-13 of the algorithm show entries of the observation matrix computed using the frequency of occurrences of terms that appear in bold (α) and the frequency of occurrences of these terms with font sizes (β) as, either level 3 (line 4), level 2 (line 6), level 1 (line 8), or title (line 10). In the same fashion, we computed entries of the observation matrix using the terms that appear in a document as either italic, underline, and regular and with font sizes as either level 3, level 2, level 1 or as a title.

The input of the algorithm is a collection of rich documents from which font sizes and font types of terms used to build the observation matrix are derived. In this work, we used the font sizes from the presentations slides where the level 1 font size is set to 28 pt, level 2 is set to 24 pt, and level 3 is set to 20 pt. These parameters can be adjusted for other document types. According to these font size settings, we observed the occurrences of terms among the presentation slides. However, the input of algorithm can be a collection of documents other than ppt as long as font sizes and font types of terms can be computed for all types of rich texts using the HTML tags.

The example illustrated in Figure 4 shows that term *Web* occurred four times in the presentation slides, where two times it appeared as level 1 font size and as bold font type and two times it appeared as level 2 font size.

Computation of Contextual and Semantic Score

The observation matrix is used as an input to compute the term-to-term contextual and semantic score between two terms in order to find a matching term extracted from a passage to a concept in the ontology.

Figure 3. The algorithm for computation of the observation matrix

Algorithm 1 Calculate Observation Matrix
Input: A collection of documents
Output: Entries of the observation matrix
1: **for each** $Doc \in D$ **do**
2:    **for each** $t \in Doc$ **do**
3:       **if** $t \in Doc$ is bold **then**
4:          **if** $t_{size} < 20pt$ **then**
5:            $Compute\ E\ as\ E + tf + 0.75 * \alpha + 0.25 * \beta$
6:          **else if** $20pt \leqslant t_{size} < 24pt$ **then**
7:            $Compute\ E\ as\ E + tf + 0.75 * \alpha + 0.50 * \beta$
8:          **else if** $24pt \leqslant t_{size} < 28pt$ **then**
9:            $Compute\ E\ as\ E + tf + 0.75 * \alpha + 0.75 * \beta$
10:         **else if** $t_{size} \geqslant 28pt$ **then**
11:           $Compute\ E\ as\ E + tf + 0.75 * \alpha + 1.00 * \beta$
12:         **end if**
13:       **end if**
14:    **end for**
15: **end for**

Figure 4. Building of observation matrix using statistical features

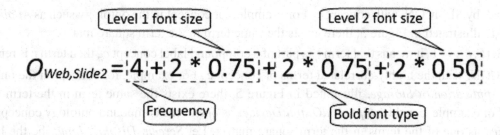

Contextual information score, $S_{con}(t_i, t_j)$, for a pair of terms t_i and t_j is computed using the cosine similarity metric with respect to the passages, as given by Equation 2.

$$S_{con}(t_i, t_j) = \frac{t_i \cdot t_j}{\|t_i\| \cdot \|t_j\|} \qquad (2)$$

where, t_i and t_j represent the term vectors of the observation matrix. The dot product between two term vectors reflects the extent to which two terms are similar in the vector space.

A term square matrix is used to store S_{con} values among all extracted terms. This matrix will later be used in computing an overall correlation between a term occurring in a document and a concept in the ontology, as described in subsection *Overall Score*.

Further, the proposed model maps a term to a concept of ontology via the matching technique. The basic idea behind this technique is to search for the concept labels that occur exactly and/or partially in the observation matrix. The exact and partial matching is defined as the following.

Definition: Let O be the domain ontology and M the observation matrix constituted of a finite set of terms, $M = \{t_1, t_2, t_3, ..., t_i\}$.

The mapping of term $t_i \in M$ into concept $c_j \in O$ is defined as the exact matching $EM(t_i, c_j)$, where,

$$EM(t_i, c_j) = \begin{cases} 1, & if(label(c_j) = t_i) \\ 0, & if(label(c_j) \neq t_i) \end{cases}$$

The mapping of term $t_i \in M$ into concept $c_j \in O$ is defined as the partial matching $PM(t_i, c_j)$ where,

$$PM(t_i, c_j) = \begin{cases} 1, & if(label(c_j) \text{ contains } t_i) \\ 0, & if(label(c_j) \text{ does not contain } t_i) \end{cases}$$

If $EM(t_i, c_j) = 1$, it means that term t_i and single label concept c_j are exactly the same, then term t_i is replaced, by SEMCON, with concept c_j. For example, for concept in the ontology such as *Application* or *Storage,* illustrated in Figure 5, there exists the same term in the term square matrix.

If $PM(t_i, c_j) = 1$, it means that term t_i is part of a compound label concept c_j, then term t_i is replaced, by SEMCON, with the highly-correlated terms of concept c_j. For example, for concept in the ontology such as *Application* or *Storage,* illustrated in Figure 5, there exists the same term in the term square matrix. For example, consider *InputAndOutputDevices* as one of the compound ontology concepts, and the *Device* as one of the terms in the term square matrix. Let *Screen, Display, Input,* be the highly-correlated terms with the term *Device,* and in that case, the *InputAndOutputDevices* will be enriched with the correlation terms of the term *Device* e.g. with *Screen, Display, Input.*

The next step is the computation of the semantic information score. The semantic score is computed using the information found in WordNet database by employing Wu & Palmer similarity measure (Wu & Palmer, 1994). WordNet (Fellbaum, 1998) is a lexical database for the English language that groups terms into sets of synonyms called synsets and defines the semantic relations between these synsets. To find the correct meaning of terms t_i and t_j under consideration, we have tested with two Word Sense Disambiguation techniques, namely, the Predominant sense heuristic, and the Maximizing semantic similarity. The Predominant sense heuristic also known as the First sense heuristic technique relies on the distribution of the senses and it assumes that the most common sense of a word represents the correct meaning of this given word. Maximizing semantic similarity is also a technique used to disambiguate word senses. It follows the idea that the right sense (correct meaning) of a term is the one which maximizes the relatedness between the term and a sense among all possible senses. The empirical analysis shows that both these disambiguation techniques yield almost the same performance in terms of precision but the predominant sense heuristic technique is often used as a baseline (McCarthy, Koeling, Weeds, & Carroll, 2004). Therefore, SEMCON employs the predominant sense heuristic disambiguation technique for finding the correct sense and all the results presented in this chapter are computed based on this technique.

The semantic score, $S_{sem}(t_i, t_j)$, is calculated for all possible pairs t_i and t_j from the observation matrix, where $t_i, t_j \in O$, and O is the observation matrix. As a result, for each term, a hash table is generated where the most similar terms are set as the synonyms for that term. Mathematically, the semantic score is computed using Equation 3.

Figure 5. Ontology sample of the computer domain

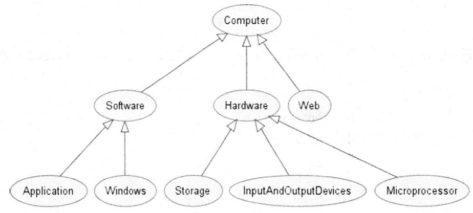

$$S_{sem}(t_i, t_j) = \frac{2 * depth(lcs)}{depth(t_i) + depth(t_j)} \tag{3}$$

where, *depth(lcs)* indicates the least common subsumer of terms t_i and t_j; *depth(t$_i$)* and *depth(t$_j$)* indicate the path's depth of terms t_i and t_j, in the WordNet lexical database.

Overall Score

The overall correlation between two terms, t_i and t_j, is calculated using the contextual and semantic score. Mathematically, the overall score is given in Equation 4.

$$S_{ove}(t_i, t_j) = w * S_{con}(t_i, t_j) + (1 - w) * S_{sem}(t_i, t_j) \tag{4}$$

where, *w* is a parameter with the value set as 0.5 based on the empirical analysis performed on the data set given in Section *Experimental Procedures*. A thorough analysis of the effect of the weight parameter value on the output of the SEMCON is given in subsection *The Effect of Weight Parameter w*. The overall score is in the range (0,1]. The overall score is 1 if two terms are the same and 0 when there is no relationship between them.

Finally, a rank cut-off method is applied using a threshold to obtain terms which are closely related to a given term in the ontology. Terms that are above the specified threshold (top-N) are considered to be the relevant terms for enriching the concepts.

A simple example of the SEMCON output, given in Table 4, shows the top 10 terms obtained as the most relevant terms of *Application* concept. 6 of these terms, namely *Application, Program, Apps, Function, Task* and *Software*, are amongst the top 10 terms selected by the subjects as the closest terms to concept *Application*.

EXPERIMENTAL PROCEDURES

The experiment uses presentation slides dataset from 5 different domains as shown in Table 5. The presentations in the database are from domain of Computer, Database, Internet, C++ Programming and Software Engineering. The dataset was limited to a maximum of 5 presentations with a restricted number of slides due to the subjective nature of the experiment.

Table 4. The Top 10 closely related terms of Application concept

Concept	The Top 10 terms obtained by SEMCON model
Application	Apps, Application, Software, Program, Control, Task, Part, Master, Operation, Function

This section presents two approaches to evaluate the performance of the SEMCON. The first one is the subjective evaluation and the second one is the objective evaluation.

Subjective Evaluation

To evaluate the performance of SEMCON, a subjective survey was carried out by publishing an online questionnaire to 15 subjects. The subjects were all computer science PhD students and Postdocs at the Gjøvik University College. They were asked to select 5 closely related terms from a list of terms for each of the concepts, starting from the most relevant term as their first choice, the second relevant term as the second choice and so on. A screenshot taken from the questionnaire about the computer domain is illustrated in Figure 6.

For each of the concepts given in the subjective survey, we obtained the ranking of the corresponding term and its frequency count. An example of ranking terms and calculating the counts of the corresponding term frequencies is given in Table 6.

'Pos(n)' is the position of the selected term from the term list. It shows how many times a term is selected at the nth position, e.g. the term *Apps* is chosen by two subjects as their *1st* choice for the *Application* concept, by eight subjects as their *2nd* choice and so on. The total number of times a term selected by subjects for the *Application* concept is computed by aggregating all these frequencies together.

For each selected term, a single score is computed using the Borda Count method. Borda Count method is an election method used to determine a winner from a voting where voters rank the candidates in order of preference (Young, 1995). The mathematical formulation of Borda Count is given in Equation 5.

$$BC(t) = \sum_{i=1}^{m} [(m + 1 - i) * freq_i(t)] \tag{5}$$

where *BC(t)* of a given term, *t* is computed by a total sum of the weights of the frequencies $freq_i(t)$. $freq_i(t)$ is the frequency of term *t* chosen at position *i*. *m* is the total number of possible positions, in our case 5.

The scores from the Borda Count are then sorted to obtain the top 'n' terms, giving us the refined list of the highest scoring terms. For our experiment, we set n = 10, and this gives us the top 10 terms as shown in Table 7. This is our ground truth data.

Table 5. Dataset used for experimenting

No	Domain name	# of slides	# of terms	# of concepts
1	Computer	7	79	9
2	Database	9	105	8
3	Internet	7	73	7
4	C++_Programming	9	70	10
5	Software_Engineering	7	42	7

Figure 6. A screenshot taken from the questionnaire

Enrichment of Ontology Concepts

Pick 5 closely related terms from the given list for each of the question word, separated by commas. Choose the most relevant term as the first choice, the second relevant term as second choice and so on. Use the description provided under the question word to consider the context.

Example: for a word 'Assets' closely related terms could be: money, furniture, chair, home, car

List of terms to choose from:

* Required

1. Access	2. Application	3. Apps	4. Asset	5. Basis	6. Browser	7. Circuit
8. Collection	9. Component	10. Computer	11. Computing	12. Concepts	13. Container	14. Control
15. Corporation	16. CPU	17. Data	18. Definitions	19. Device	20. Directory	21. Disk
22. Display	23. Document	24. Domain	25. Drive	26. File	27. Folder	28. Format
29. Function	30. Group	31. Hardware	32. IC	33. Image	34. Information	35. Input
36. Inputting	37. Instruction	38. Internet	39. Interval	40. Intervention	41. IP Address	42. Location
43. Machine	44. Manipulate	45. Master	46. Medium	47. Memory	48. Microchip	49. Microprocessor
50. Microsoft	51. Name	52. Network	53. Operation	54. Operator	55. Output	56. Overwritten
57. Page	58. Part	59. Period	60. Process	61. Program	62. RAM	63. Recording
64. Resource	65. Screen	66. Site	67. Software	68. Storage	69. System	70. Task
71. Time	72. Unit	73. Use	74. User	75. Video	76. Way	77. Windows
78. Web	79. WWW					

Computer *
A machine capable of following instruction to alter data in a desirable way and to perform at least some of these operations without human intervention. A computer is a programmable machine that receives input, stores and manipulates data, and provides output in a useful format.

Software *
Computer software is the intangible part of the computer system. Operating System Software is a master control program for a computer that manages the computer's internal functions and provides you with a means to control the computer's operation.

Hardware *
Computer Hardware is the physical component of computer system which can be installed an operating system and a multitude of software to perform the operator's desired functions.

Objective Evaluation

In addition to the subjective experiment, an objective evaluation is carried out where the results obtained from the SEMCON model are compared with the results obtained from the three state-of-the-art methods namely, Term Frequency Inverse Document Frequency (*tf*idf*) (Sebastiani, 2002), χ^2 (Chi square) (Liu, He, Lim, & Wang, 2013) and Latent Semantic Analysis - LSA (Landauer, Foltz, & Laham, 1998).

tf*idf is a mathematical method which is used to find a key vocabulary that best represents the texts. Mathematically, it is given in Equation 6.

Table 6. Terms selected by subjects for the application concept

Terms	Pos 1	Pos 2	Pos 3	Pos 4	Pos 5	Total
Apps	2	8	2	1	0	13
Software	3	0	4	3	1	11
Program	0	2	3	1	2	8
Application	8	0	0	0	0	8
User	0	1	1	1	3	6
Task	0	0	2	2	1	5
Windows	1	1	0	2	1	5
Browser	0	0	2	2	0	4
Process	0	0	1	1	2	4
Microsoft	1	1	0	0	0	2
System	0	0	0	0	2	2
Computer	0	1	0	0	0	1
Data	0	0	0	0	1	1
Recording	0	0	0	0	1	1

Table 7. Borda Count of subjects responses for the application concept

Rank	Term	Borda Count
1	Apps	50
2	Application	40
3	Software	34
4	Program	21
5	Windows	14
6	Task	11
7	Browser	10
8	Function	9
9	User	9
10	Process	7

$$tf * idf = tf_{i,j} * \log \frac{N}{df_j} \tag{6}$$

where, $tf_{i,j}$ is the term frequency of term j that occurs in a passage i, N is the total number of passages in the corpus and df_j shows the number of passages where the term j occurs.

The traditional $tf*idf$ considers only the term to document relation and thus it is not appropriate for comparison as it is. Therefore, we modified the existing $tf*idf$ in order to take the term to term relation into account. This is achieved using the cosine measure where the dot product between two vectors of the $tf*idf$ matrix shows the extent to which two terms are similar in the vector space.

χ^2 is a statistical method which computes the relationship between two given terms. Mathematically, it is given in Equation 7.

$$\chi^2_{t_a, t_b} = \sum_{i \in \{t_a, \neg t_a\}} \sum_{j \in \{t_b, \neg t_b\}} \frac{(O_{i,j} - E_{i,j})^2}{E_{i,j}} \tag{7}$$

where, $O_{i,j}$ and $E_{i,j}$ show the co-occurrence and the expected co-occurrence frequency between two terms t_a and t_b. More formally, the co-occurrence frequency between two terms t_a and t_b is the observed frequency $O_{i,j}$, where $i \in \{t_a, \neg t_a\}$ and $j \in \{t_b, \neg t_b\}$. Thus, O_{t_a, t_b} is the observed frequency of passages that contains term t_a and term t_b. $O_{t_a, \neg t_b}$ is the observed frequency of passages that contains term t_a but does not contain term t_b. $O_{\neg t_a, t_b}$ is the observed frequency of passages that does not contain term t_a but contains term t_b. $O_{\neg t_a, \neg t_b}$ is the observed frequency of passages that contains neither term t_a nor term t_b.

Latent semantic analysis (LSA), sometimes referred as latent semantic indexing, is a method for extracting and representing the content of a text using the relationships between terms that occur in similar context.

The first step of LSA is representing the text document as a matrix in which each row denotes a unique term and each column denotes a passage. Each cell contains the frequency of occurrence of one term from the passage.

The second step of LSA is applying a Singular Value Decomposition (SVD). SVD decomposes the rectangular matrix into the product of three matrices. One matrix is term vectors, another denotes a diagonal matrix, and the last one denotes passage vectors. More formally, every rectangular matrix M can be decomposed into three matrices T, Σ and P^T, as shown in Equation 8.

$$M = T \Sigma P^T \tag{8}$$

where, T is a term vectors matrix, P^T is a matrix of passage vectors and Σ is a diagonal matrix of decreasing singular values.

The singular values represent the semantic space for terms and passages in a corpus of text. When the matrix Σ contains all the singular values of M, then the original matrix M is reconstructed by multiplying the three matrices T, Σ, and P^T.

The dimensionality of the space of semantic representations can be reduced by deleting some of the singular values, starting with the smallest. The matrix M_k, which is the k dimensional approximation to M, can be built by selecting the k largest singular values. In our case, we set the dimensionality parameter k to 2. The reconstruction of matrix M_k is given in Equation 9.

$$M_k = T \Sigma_k P^T \tag{9}$$

Similarly, the representations of terms and passages by multiplying their corresponding matrix decompositions are obtained. The representations of terms and passages are given in Equation 10.

$$T_k = T \Sigma_k \qquad \qquad P_k^T = \Sigma_k P^T \tag{10}$$

Finally, to calculate the similarity between two terms, we used the cosine measure, where the dot product between two vectors of matrix M_k shows the extent to which two terms are similar in the vector space. Cosine similarity measure is given in Equation 11.

$$Similarity_{LSA}(t_i, t_j) = \frac{t_i \cdot t_j}{\left\| t_i \right\| * \left| t_j \right|} \tag{11}$$

where t_i and t_j are the corresponding latent term space vectors.

Measures of the Effectiveness of the Objective Methods

We employed the standard information retrieval measures such as Precision, Recall and F1 (Sebastiani, 2002) to evaluate the effectiveness of objective methods. The objective methods are evaluated against the subjective ones. The evaluation is conducted by taking the 10 top subjective terms as the ground truth and the top-N terms obtained by the objective methods as a relevance list.

The definition of precision and recall is adjusted in order to evaluate top-N terms obtained by objective methods. The definitions are adopted as follows.

Precision is the ratio of total number of terms which occur simultaneously in the relevance list and in the ground truth list, to the number of terms in the relevance list. Precision is given in Equation 12.

$$Precision = \frac{\left| Relevance \cap Ground\,Truth \right|}{\left| Relevance \right|} * 100 \tag{12}$$

Recall is the ratio of total number of terms which occur simultaneously in the relevance list and in the ground truth list, to the number of terms in the ground truth list. Recall is given in Equation 13.

$$Recall = \frac{|Relevance \cap GroundTruth|}{|GroundTruth|} * 100 \tag{13}$$

Precision and recall are often inversely related to each other, such that if the number of relevant terms increases, then the value of recall increases, while at the same time precision decreases. Thus, we used the standard F1 measure, which is defined as the average of precision and recall and it is given in Equation 16.

$$F1 = \frac{2 * (Precision * Recall)}{Precision + Recall} * 100 \tag{14}$$

RESULTS AND ANALYSIS

The performance of objective methods is evaluated on two criteria. First being how well the objective methods score the top subjective terms. In order to do this, scores for the 10 top terms are taken as the ground truth. The score obtained for these terms using the objective methods are then evaluated. An example for the enrichment of the *Application* concept is observed and the comparison is shown in Table 8. The final score is in the range of [0, 1], where 0 denotes a term with no relatedness, and 1 denotes a highly-related term for enriching the *Application* concept.

The comparison summarized in Table 8, shows that SEMCON generally outperforms the tf*idf, χ^2, and LSA. The red highlighted values show cases when one method performs better than the other. It can be seen from the red highlighted values that the SEMCON model gives much better results for the terms *Windows*, *Browser* and *Process* in contrast to the *tf*idf* and LSA which scores 0 to these three terms and χ^2 which scores close to 0.

This is most likely because these terms did not occur in document/presentation slides that talk contextually about the *Application* concept but they occurred in the WordNet corpus. SEMCON also scores higher for the terms *Program* and *Function*. The term *Task* gets a score of 1.0 by the *tf*idf*, χ^2, and LSA which means that these three methods would rank the term *Task* as its first term to enrich the *Application* concept. The term *Task* however is ranked as the sixth relevant term to enriching the concept *Application* by subjects as shown in Table 7.

The second evaluation criteria is to check if the top terms scored by the objective methods are accurate. For this, we compute the precision, recall and F1 measure on top-15 relevant terms list. Table 9 shows the resulting precision and recall of objective methods on retrieving and ranking of terms as the most relevant term for enriching the *Application* concept in the computer domain. Terms correctly retrieved by the objective methods are highlighted in red in Table 9.

In the following paragraph, we are giving an example to show how the precision and recall, shown in Table 9, are computed. A total number of terms obtained by the intersection of ground truth list (column entitled subjective terms) and relevance list (column entitled *tf*idf*) is equal to 7. Number of terms in ground truth list is 10, while the number of terms in relevance list is 15. Recall is computed as 7/10*100=70.0% and precision as 7/15*100=46.7%. The example illustrated shows computation of

Table 8. The overall objective score for top 10 terms selected by subjects

No	Subjective terms	tf*idf	χ^2	LSA	SEMCON
1	Apps	1.000	1.000	1.000	1.000
2	Application	1.000	1.000	1.000	1.000
3	Software	0.975	0.500	0.981	0.943
4	Program	0.914	0.500	0.894	0.923
5	Windows	0.000	0.028	0.000	0.409
6	Task	1.000	1.000	1.000	0.900
7	Browser	0.000	0.280	0.000	0.479
8	Function	0.569	0.222	0.577	0.701
9	User	0.603	0.417	0.707	0.544
10	Process	0.000	0.067	0.000	0.412

Table 9. Precision and recall of application

Subjective terms	Objective Terms			
	tf*idf	χ^2	LSA	SEMCON
Apps	Apps	Apps	Application	Apps
Application	Application	Application	Control	Application
Software	Control	Control	Apps	Software
Program	Master	Master	Master	Program
Windows	Part	Part	Part	Control
Task	Task	Task	Task	Task
Browser	Software	Program	Web	Part
Function	Program	Software	File	Master
User	Operation	Operation	Page	Operation
Process	Computer	User	Access	Function
	User	Computer	Asset	Computer
	Function	Function	Browser	System
	System	Component	Collection	User
	Component	System	Concept	Browser
	Access	Device	User	Use
Recall	**70.0**	**70.0**	**50.0**	**80.0**
Precision	**46.7**	**46.7**	**33.3**	**53.3**

precision and recall for the *tf*idf* method, in a similar fashion they are also computed for χ^2, LSA, and SEMCON.

Additionally, Table 10 and Table 11 shows precision, recall and F1 results obtained by the SEMCON on retrieving and ranking of terms as the most relevant terms for enriching concepts of computer domain and other domains, respectively.

The performance of SEMCON in terms of F1 measure is compared with the performance of *tf*idf*, χ^2, and LSA. The comparison is performed using results of various domains and it shows that SEMCON achieved better results on finding the highly-related terms to enrich ontology concepts.

Table 12 shows F1 results for computer domain. The results depict that SEMCON achieved the average improvement of 12.2% over the *tf*idf*, 21.8% over the χ^2, and 24.5% over the LSA.

The same comparisons for F1 is also done for other domains. These results are shown in Tables 13-16.

Finally, we evaluated the performance of SEMCON and the three other objective methods by comparing the average results of each domain. The obtained results (precision, recall and F1) illustrated in Figure 7-9 show that SEMCON gives better results than the other three methods for all the domains excepts for the internet domain. This may have happened due to the fact that subjects are making their selections based on the descriptions provided under each concept in the questionnaire, when they were asked to select five closely related terms. In other words, subjects might have used contextual information from the description provided in the questionnaire about each concept rather than their existing prior knowledge. As the ground truth list is composed of terms which carry contextual meaning in a document to describe a particular concept, therefore, this might have served better for *tf*idf* for Internet domain where people choose terms based on the context rather than prior domain knowledge. Nevertheless, there is a significant improvement of results for other domains by SEMCON over other methods.

Table 10. The performance of SEMCON on computer domain

Domain	P(%)	R(%)	F1(%)
Computer	26.7	40.0	32.0
Software	46.7	70.0	56.0
Hardware	33.3	50.0	40.0
Web	46.7	70.0	56.0
Storage	46.7	70.0	56.0
Microprocessor	40.0	60.0	48.0
InputAndOutputDevices	33.3	50.0	40.0
Application	53.3	80.0	64.0
Windows	46.7	70.0	56.0
Average	**41.5**	**62.2**	**49.8**

Table 11. The performance of SEMCON on different domains

Domain	P(%)	R(%)	F1(%)
Computer	41.5	62.2	49.8
Database	34.2	51.3	41.0
Internet	38.1	57.1	45.7
C++_Programming	37.3	56.0	44.8
Software_Engineering	49.5	74.3	59.4

Table 12. The F1 of objective methods performed on computer domain

Domain	tf*idf(%)	χ^2(%)	LSA(%)	SEMCON(%)
Computer	24.0	24.0	32.0	32.0
Software	56.0	48.0	40.0	56.0
Hardware	32.0	40.0	32.0	40.0
Web	32.0	32.0	40.0	56.0
Storage	64.0	56.0	64.0	56.0
Microprocessor	48.0	40.0	56.0	48.0
InputAndOutputDevices	32.0	24.0	8.0	40.0
Application	56.0	56.0	40.0	64.0
Windows	56.0	48.0	48.0	56.0
Average	**44.4**	**40.9**	**40.0**	**49.8**

Table 13. The F1 of objective methods performed on SE domain

Domain	tf*idf(%)	χ^2(%)	LSA(%)	SEMCON(%)
Software	56.0	56.0	40.0	48.0
Cost	40.0	40.0	40.0	48.0
Product	64.0	56.0	48.0	48.0
Attribute	32.0	48.0	32.0	56.0
Process	72.0	48.0	32.0	72.0
Generic	48.0	64.0	64.0	72.0
Hybrid	64.0	56.0	56.0	72.0
Average	**53.7**	**52.6**	**44.6**	**59.4**

Table 14. The F1 of objective methods performed on C++ programming domain

Domain	tf*idf(%)	χ^2(%)	LSA(%)	SEMCON(%)
C++_Programming	24.0	40.0	40.0	40.0
Syntax	56.0	48.0	48.0	48.0
Technique	24.0	16.0	24.0	24.0
Structure	40.0	40.0	32.0	40.0
Expression	48.0	40.0	40.0	48.0
Operator	24.0	24.0	56.0	24.0
Encapsulation	48.0	64.0	64.0	48.0
Inheritance	64.0	56.0	56.0	56.0
Polymorphism	48.0	48.0	40.0	56.0
Platform	56.0	56.0	48.0	64.0
Average	**43.2**	**43.2**	**44.8**	**44.8**

Table 15. The F1 of objective methods performed on database domain

Domain	tf*idf(%)	χ^2(%)	LSA(%)	SEMCON(%)
Database	24.0	16.0	24.0	16.0
Model	48.0	40.0	16.0	48.0
E-R	48.0	48.0	16.0	48.0
User	40.0	16.0	16.0	16.0
SQL	32.0	40.0	16.0	32.0
DDL	64.0	48.0	40.0	64.0
DML	40.0	24.0	32.0	48.0
Administrator	24.0	24.0	16.0	24.0
Average	**40.0**	**32.0**	**22.0**	**41.0**

Table 16. The F1 of objective methods performed on internet domain

Domain	tf*idf(%)	χ^2(%)	LSA(%)	SEMCON(%)
Internet	40.0	24.0	48.0	40.0
Application	40.0	40.0	40.0	32.0
Web	32.0	32.0	40.0	32.0
Access	56.0	48.0	40.0	48.0
Browser	64.0	48.0	48.0	64.0
ISP	72.0	48.0	56.0	64.0
HTML	40.0	48.0	56.0	40.0
Average	**49.1**	**41.4**	**46.9**	**45.7**

Figure 7. Precision for five different domains

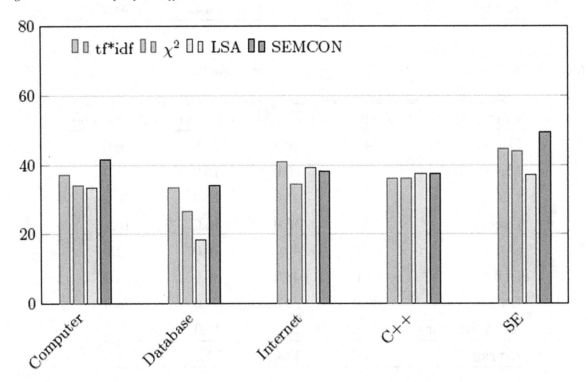

Figure 8. Recall for five different domains

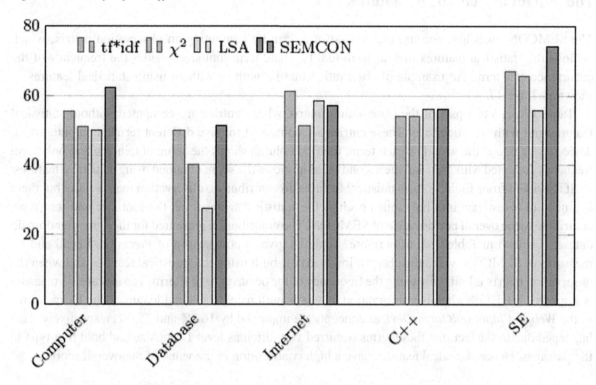

Figure 9. F1 for five different domains

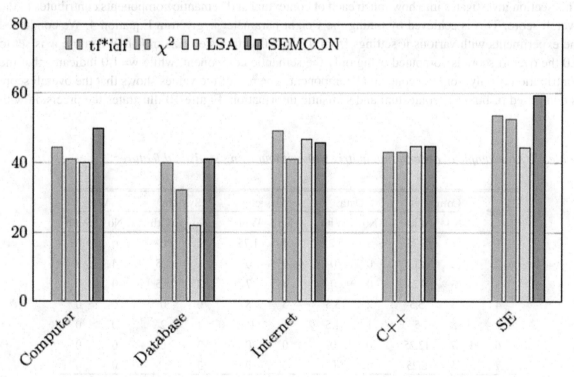

The Impact of Statistical Features

The SEMCON takes into account the context of a term by computing an observation matrix, which exploits the statistical features such as term font type and term font size besides the frequency of the occurrence of a term. An example of observation matrix, with or without using statistical features, is shown in Table 17.

Table 17 depicts a part of the observation matrix whose entries are computed without statistical features and with statistical one. These entries are computed for five different terms: computer, data, device, system, and the web. For each term, the first column shows the score obtained using only term frequency (denoted with No), and the second column shows the score obtained using statistical features.

It is evident from Table 17 that statistical features do contribute to observation matrix score but there is a need to investigate into how much each of the statistical features i.e. the font size and font type, contribute to the overall performance of SEMCON. The contribution presented for the computer domain dataset is shown in Table 18. Furthermore, Table 18 gives a comparison of Precision, Recall and F1 measures of SEMCON, when the observation matrix is built using the statistical features and when the observation matrix is built only using the frequency of the occurrence of a term. The average F1 measure is improved by 3.75% when the observation matrix is built using statistical features. The F1 measures of the *Web* and *InputAndOutputDevices* concepts are improved by 16.7% and 25.0%, respectively. This happened due to the fact that these terms occurred very often as level 1 font size and bold font type in the passages. Hence statistical features have a high contribution in the value of the overall score.

The Effect of Weight Parameter w

This section investigates into how much each of contextual and semantic components contributes to the overall score. This is achieved by tuning the weight parameter w given in Equation 4. We conducted the experiments with various w settings from 0.0 to 1.0 with a step size of 0.1. When the w is set to 0.0 the overall score is computed using only the semantic component, while w=1.0 indicates that the contribution is only from the contextual component. The rest of the values shows that the overall score is composed of both the contextual and semantic information. Figure 10 illustrates the precision with

Table 17. An example of observation matrix with/without using statistical features

Slide	Computer		Data		Device		System		Web	
	No	With	No	With	No	With	No	With	No	With
1	3	6.25	3	5.25	1	1.75	0	0	0	0
2	2	3	0	0	0	0	1	1.5	4	8
3	5	9.25	0	0	4	7	3	5.5	0	0
4	3	5.5	2	3.5	5	8	0	0	0	0
5	3	5	1	1.5	1	1.5	1	2	0	0
6	7	12.25	0	0	0	0	3	6	0	0
7	1	2.25	0	0	0	0	3	6.25	0	0

Table 18. The performance of SEMCON with/without statistical features

Concept	Precision (%)		Recall (%)		F1 (%)	
	No	With	No	With	No	With
Computer	26.7	26.7	40.0	40.0	32.0	32.0
Software	46.7	46.7	70.0	70.0	56.0	56.0
Hardware	33.3	33.3	50.0	50.0	40.0	40.0
Web	40.0	46.7	60.0	70.0	48.0	56.0
Storage	46.7	46.7	70.0	70.0	56.0	56.0
Microprocessor	40.0	40.0	60.0	60.0	48.0	48.0
InputAndOutputDevices	26.7	33.3	40.0	50.0	32.0	40.0
Application	53.3	53.3	80.0	80.0	64.0	64.0
Windows	46.7	46.7	70.0	70.0	56.0	56.0
Average	**40.0**	**41.5**	**60.0**	**62.2**	**48.0**	**49.8**

Figure 10. Precision as a function of weight parameter w

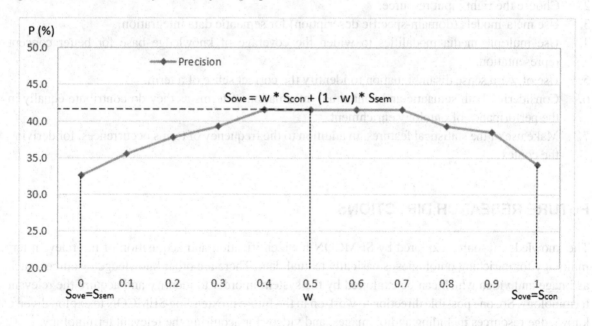

respect to the weight parameter *w*, obtained by experiments carried out on computer domain data set. It can be seen from the chart diagram that the best result in terms of precision is obtained when the value of weighting parameter *w* is set to 0.5. The precision starts declining with an increase or a decrease in the value of *w*. This suggests that both semantic and contextual information should contribute equally to computing the overall score as described in subsection *Overall Score*.

RECOMMENDATIONS

Despite numerous recent developments in ontology engineering, successful integration of ontologies in today's applications, and automatic extraction of semantic concepts are two important problems.

It is important to take advantage of a large number of existing domain-specific ontologies as creating a new ontology is a time-consuming and a laborious process. Using a common ontology is also not feasible in many cases. An ontology can be a source of domain knowledge, therefore, existing ontologies must be capitalized for further populating ontologies with new concepts.

Moreover, updating ontologies with automatically extracted semantic concepts is deemed necessary for speeding up the ontology enrichment process. However, populating ontologies automatically with correct concepts is not a trivial task. One challenging task is the extraction of a relationship between concepts. For domain-specific applications, it is also important to identify the correct sense of a concept.

The success of a many large scale industrial applications and semantic web depends upon the successful integration and automation of ontology enrichment process. NLP and ML techniques can play a vital role in this regard.

Some recommendations are listed below in light of the above discussion.

1. Make use of the existing domain-specific ontologies for extracting relevant concepts.
2. Choose the right input resource.
3. Use meta-models (domain-specific description) for semantic data integration.
4. Use multiple media modalities to widen the coverage of knowledge base for better concept representation.
5. Use of word sense disambiguation to identify the correct sense of a term.
6. Considering both semantic and contextual information of terms as they do contribute equally in the performance of ontology enrichment.
7. Make use of the statistical features, in addition to the frequency of terms occurrences, for deriving the context.

FUTURE RESEARCH DIRECTIONS

The knowledge resource explored by SEMCON for identification and acquisition of the relevant terminology for enriching ontologies is basically textual data. There are other knowledge resources, such as image and video which can be exploited by the system in order to identify and acquire the relevant terminology. So, one possible direction to work on in the future is extending SEMCON to exploit diverse knowledge resources including audio, images, and videos for acquiring the relevant terminology.

The two new statistical features introduced in this chapter for deriving the context proved to be useful in terms of improving the performance of the model. In this regard, the future work may further exploit other features for deriving the context and computing the observation matrix. It might be worth to investigate, in addition to the linear model, other nonlinear models, i.e. exponential, for evaluating the weight of font types and font sizes employed in this chapter.

The size of the dataset used to test the performance of the proposed model was small due to the nature of the subjective experiment. A larger dataset is required to thoroughly evaluate the effectiveness and robustness of the model.

Additionally, deep learning techniques such as embedding can be employed to automatically update ontology with new concepts by learning concepts hierarchy and relationship in existing ontology.

THE APPLICATIONS OF SEMCON

SEMCON can be used in many application areas including but not limited to information systems, eLearning platforms, open educational resources (OER), online social network (OSN) analysis, etc., for building dictionaries, classifying documents, enriching ontologies - among many others. For instance, it can be applied for document classification in information systems where each record can be grouped into different categories automatically utilizing context and semantics.

The two areas where SEMCON has been applied are as follows:

1. The classification of multimedia documents in the web-based eLearning platforms.
2. The analysis of Online Social Networks (OSNs) for identifying criminal activity and possible suspects.

These applications are discussed briefly in this section.

SEMCON for Web-Based eLearning Platforms

Today's eLearning platforms consist of multiple media modalities including presentation slides, lecture videos, transcript files, handouts, and additional documents, delivering thousands of learning objects daily. These media provide a rich source of information that can be utilized for organizing and structuring learning objects.

Structuring and organizing huge amount of learning objects is a labor intensive, prone to errors and a cumbersome task, however. SEMCON on the other hand can prove useful in automatically organizing pedagogical multimedia content using an automatic classification approach based on the ontology described in (Kastrati, Imran, & Yayilgan, 2014). Any new unlabeled learning object can be assigned to a predefined category in an eLearning platform using SEMCON. This is plausible by calculating the similarity between the extracted terms from the learning object and the ontology concepts. The learning object can then be assigned to a category having the highest similarity value with respect to that learning object.

An ontology represents semantic aspects of the learning objects through entities defined within a domain ontology. Therefore, each learning object that uses the ontology is represented as a vector, whose elements indicate the importance of concepts in the ontology.

SEMCON for OSN Analysis for Criminal Activity Detection

Analyzing users' behavior in Online Social Networks (OSNs) for investigating criminal activities is an area of great interest these days. The criminal activity analysis provides a useful source of information for law enforcement and intelligence agencies across the globe. Existing methods monitoring criminal activity normally rely on contextual analysis by computing co-occurrences of terms, which is not much effective.

SEMCON on the other hand can provide useful semantic as well as contextual information in identifying criminal activities by analyzing users' posts and data, and by maintaining a history of recent user activities in the digital platforms. The proposed model (Kastrati, Imran, Yayilgan, & Dalipi, 2015) uses web crawlers suited to retrieve users' data such as posts, feeds, comments from Facebook, and exploits them semantically and contextually using the ontology enhancement objective metric SEMCON. The output of the model is a probability value of a user being a suspect which is computed by finding the similarity between the terms obtained from SEMCON and the concepts of the criminal ontology.

CONCLUSION

This chapter gives an insight into the ontology concept enrichment process, present readers with an overview of state-of-the-art methods and techniques, review existing approaches and their limitations, contains related literature, and propose solutions to address some limitations of the existing systems.

It also presents a new generic model called SEMCON to enriching the domain ontologies with new concepts by combining contextual and semantic information of terms extracted from the domain documents. SEMCON employs a hybrid ontology learning approach to identify and extract new concepts. This approach involves functionalities from both linguistic and statistical ontology learning approaches. From the former approach, SEMCON utilizes morpho-syntactic analysis to identify and extract noun terms, as a part of speech, which represents the most meaningful terms in a document. While from the latter approach, SEMCON derives the context using cosine similarity between term vectors whose members are frequencies of terms occurrences. SEMCON uses, besides term frequency, two new statistical features, i.e. term font size and font type to determine the context of a term. In addition to contextual information, SEMCON also incorporates the semantic information of terms using the lexical database WordNet and finally aggregates both contextual and semantic information of this term.

Several experiments on various small data sets are conducted, where results obtained by SEMCON are compared with results obtained by other objective methods such as $tf*idf$, χ^2, and LSA. The comparison showed that SEMCOM outperforms the three objective methods by 12.2% over the $tf*idf$, 21.8% over the χ^2 and 24.5% over the LSA. The chapter also present experiments about the effect of statistical features on the overall performance of the proposed metric and our findings showed an improved performance. Additionally, we investigated into the amount of contribution made by each of the contextual and semantic components to the overall task of concepts enrichment. The obtained results indicated that a balanced weight between the contextual and semantic components gives the best performance.

REFERENCES

Bateman, S., Gutwin, C., & Nacenta, M. (2008). Seeing Things in the Clouds: The Effect of Visual Features on Tag Cloud Selections. In *Proceedings of the nineteenth ACM conference on Hypertext and hypermedia* (pp. 193-202). ACM. doi:10.1145/1379092.1379130

Brunzel, M. (2008). The XTREEM Methods for Ontology Learning from Web Documents. In *Proceedings of the Conference on Ontology Learning and Population: Bridging the Gap between Text and Knowledge* (pp. 3-26). IOS Press.

Cimiano, P. (2006). *Ontology Learning and Population from Text: Algorithm, Evaluation and Applications*. New York: Springer-Verlag.

Cimiano, P., & Völker, J. (2005). Text2Onto: A Framework for Ontology Learning and Data-Driven Change Discovery. In A. Montoyo, R. Munoz & E. Metais (Ed.), LNCS: Vol. 3513. Natural Language Processing and Information Systems. Springer-Verlag Heidelberg. doi:10.1007/11428817_21

Craven, M., DiPasquo, D., Freitag, D., McCallum, A., Mitchell, T., Nigam, K., & Slattery, S. (2000). Learning to Construct Knowledge Bases from the World Wide Web. *Artificial Intelligence, 118*(1-2), 69–113. doi:10.1016/S0004-3702(00)00004-7

Drumond, L., & Girardi, R. (2008). A Survey of Ontology Learning Procedures. In F. L. G. de Freitas, H. Stuckenschmidt, H. S. Pinto, A. Malucelli, & Ó. Corcho (Eds.), *WONTO. CEUR-WS.org*.

Duthil, B., Trousset, F., Roche, M., Dray, G., Plantie, M., Montmain, J., & Poncelet, P. (2011). Towards an Automatic Characterization of Criteria. In A. Hameurlain, S. Liddle, K-D. Schewe, X.Zhou (Ed.), LNCS: Vol. 6860. Database and Expert Systems Applications (pp. 457-465). Springer-Verlag Heidelberg. doi:10.1007/978-3-642-23088-2_34

Etzioni, O., Kok, S., Soderland, S., Cagarella, M., Popescu, A. M., Weld, D. S., & Yates, A. et al. (2004). Web-Scale Information Extraction in KnowItAll (Preliminary Results). In *Proceedings of the 13th international conference on World Wide Web (WWW '04)*. ACM.

Etzioni, O., Kok, S., Soderland, S., Cagarella, M., Popescu, A. M., Weld, D. S., & Yates, A. et al. (2005). Unsupervised Named-Entity Extraction From the Web: An Experimental Study. *Artificial Intelligence, 165*(1), 91–134. doi:10.1016/j.artint.2005.03.001

Faatz, A., & Steinmetz, R. (2005). An evaluation Framework for Ontology Enrichment. In P. Buitelaar, P. Cimiano, & B. Magnini (Eds.), *Ontology Learning from Text: Methods, Applications and Evaluation* (pp. 77–91). IOS Press.

Fellbaum, C. (1998). *WordNet: An Electronic Lexical Database*. Cambridge, MA: MIT Press.

Hahn, U., & Romacker, M. (2001). The SynDiKATe Text Knowledge Base Generator. In *Proceedings of the 1st International Conference on Human Language Technology Research (HLT'01)*. Association for Computational Linguistics. doi:10.3115/1072133.1072219

Hahn, U., Romacker, M., & Schulz, S. (2002). MEDSYNDIKATE- A Natural Language System for the Extraction of Medical Information from Findings Reports. *International Journal of Medical Informatics, 67*(1-3), 63–74. doi:10.1016/S1386-5056(02)00053-9 PMID:12460632

Halvey, M. J., & Keane, M. T. (2007). An Assessment of Tag Presentation Techniques. In *Proceedings of the 16th International Conference on World Wide Web*. ACM. doi:10.1145/1242572.1242826

Hazman, M., El-Beltagy, S., & Rafea, A. (2011). A survey of Ontology Learning Approaches. *International Journal of Computers and Applications, 22*(8), 36–43. doi:10.5120/2610-3642

Hearst, M. (1992). Automatic Acquisition of Hyponyms from Large Text Corpora. In *Proceedings of the 14th conference on Computational linguistics* (pp. 539-545). ACM. doi:10.3115/992133.992154

Heyer, G., Läuter, M., Quasthoff, U., Wittig, T., & Wolff, C. (2001). Learning Relations Using Collocations. In A. Maedche, S. Staab, C. Nedellec & E. H. Hovy (Ed.), *Workshop on Ontology Learning*. CEUR-WS.org.

Kastrati, Z., Imran, A. S., & Yayilgan, S. (2014). Building Domain Ontologies for Hyperlinked Multimedia Pedagogical Platforms. In C. Stephanidis (Ed.), *HCII 2014 Posters, Part II, CCIS 435* (pp. 95–100). Springer International Publishing. doi:10.1007/978-3-319-07854-0_17

Kastrati, Z., Imran, A. S., Yayilgan, S., & Dalipi, F. (2015). Analysis of Online Social Networks Posts to Investigate Suspects Using SEMCON. In *Proceedings of 17th International Conference on Human-Computer Interaction*. Springer International Publishing. doi:10.1007/978-3-319-20367-6_16

Kruschwitz, U. (2001). Exploiting Structure for Intelligent Web Search. In *Proceedings of the 34th International Conference on System Sciences* (pp. 1-9). IEEE. doi:10.1109/HICSS.2001.926474

Landauer, T. K., Foltz, P. W., & Laham, D. (1998). Introduction to Latent Semantic Analysis. *Discourse Processes*, *25*(2-3), 259–284. doi:10.1080/01638539809545028

Lehmann, J. (2009). DL-Learner: Learning Concepts in Description Logics. *Journal of Machine Learning Research*, *10*, 2639–2642.

Li, H., Tian, Y., Ye, B., & Cai, Q. (2010). Comparison of Current Semantic Similarity Methods in Wordnet. In *Proceedings of International Conference on Computer Application and System Modeling* (vol. 9, pp.408-411). IEEE.

Liu, J., He, Y.-L., Lim, E., & Wang, X.-Z. (2013). A New Method for Knowledge and Information Management Domain Ontology Graph Model. *IEEE Transactions on Systems, Man, and Cybernetics Systems*, *43*(1), 115–127.

Maedche, A., Maedche, E., & Staab, S. (2000). The TEXT-TO-ONTO Ontology Learning Environment. In B. Ganter & G.W. Mineau (Eds.), LNAI: Vol. 1867. Conceptual Structures: Logical, Linguistic, and Computational Issues. Springer-Verlag Heidelberg.

Maedche, A., Pekar, V., & Staab, S. (2003). Ontology Learning Part One - on Discovering Taxonomic Relations from the Web. In N. Zhong, J. Liu, & Y. Yao (Eds.), *Web Intelligence* (pp. 301–320). Springer Berlin Heidelberg. doi:10.1007/978-3-662-05320-1_14

Manzano-Macho, D., Gómez-Pérez, A., & Borrajo, D. (2008). Unsupervised and Domain Independent Ontology Learning: Combining Heterogeneous Sources of Evidence. *Proceedings of sixth International Conference on Language Resources and Evaluation*, 1633-1640.

McCarthy, D., Koeling, R., Weeds, J., & Carroll, J. (2004). Finding Predominant Word Senses in Untagged Text. In *Proceedings of the 42nd Annual Meeting on Association for Computational Linguistics*. Association for Computational Linguistics. doi:10.3115/1218955.1218991

McGuinness, D. (2000). Conceptual Modeling for Distributed Ontology Environments. In B. Ganter & G. W. Mineau (Eds.), *ICCS 2000, LNAI* (Vol. 1867). Springer-Verlag Berlin Heidelberg.

Petasis, G., Karkaletsis, V., Paliouras, G., Krithara, A., & Zavitsanos, E. (2011). Ontology Population and Enrichment: State of the Art. In G. Paliouras, C. D. Spyropoulos, & G. Tsatsaronis (Eds.), *Knowledge-Driven Multimedia Information Extraction and Ontology Evolution. LNCS* (Vol. 6050). Berlin: Springer. doi:10.1007/978-3-642-20795-2_6

Ranwez, S., Duthil, B., Sy, M. F., Montmain, J., Augereau, P., & Ranwez, V. (2013). How Ontology Based Information Retrieval Systems may Benefit From Lexical Text Analysis. In A. Oltramari, P. Vossen, L. Qi, & E. Hovy (Eds.), *Theory and Applications of Natural Language Processing. New Trends of Research in Ontologies and Lexical Resources* (pp. 209–231). Springer-Verlag Heidelberg. doi:10.1007/978-3-642-31782-8_11

Salton, G., Singhal, A., Buckley, C., & Mitra, M. (1996). Automatic Text Decomposition Using Text Segments and Text Themes. In *Proceedings of the seventh ACM conference on Hypertext* (pp. 53-65). ACM. doi:10.1145/234828.234834

Schmid, H. (2013). Probabilistic Part-of-Speech Tagging Using Decision Trees. In D. B. Jones & H. Somers (Eds.), *New Methods in Language Processing* (pp. 154–164). Routledge.

Sebastiani, F. (2002). Machine Learning in Automated Text Categorization. *ACM Computing Surveys*, *34*(1), 1–47. doi:10.1145/505282.505283

Shamsfard, M., & Barforoush, A. A. (2004). Learning Ontologies from Natural Language Texts. *International Journal of Human-Computer Studies*, *69*(1), 17–63. doi:10.1016/j.ijhcs.2003.08.001

Wu, Z., & Palmer, M. (1994). Verb Semantics and Lexical Selection. In *Proceedings of the 32nd Annual Meeting of the Associations for Computational Linguistics* (pp.133-138). Association for Computational Linguistics. doi:10.3115/981732.981751

Yamaguchi, T. (2001). Acquiring Conceptual Relationships from Domain-Specific Texts. In A. Maedche, S. Staab, C. Nedellec & E. H. Hovy (Ed.), *Workshop on Ontology Learning*. CEUR-WS.org.

Young, P. (1995). Optimal Voting Rules. *The Journal of Economic Perspectives*, *9*(1), 51–64. doi:10.1257/jep.9.1.51

Chapter 5
OOPS!
A Pitfall-Based System for Ontology Diagnosis

María Poveda-Villalón
Universidad Politécnica de Madrid, Spain

Asunción Gómez-Pérez
Universidad Politécnica de Madrid, Spain

Mari Carmen Suárez-Figueroa
Universidad Politécnica de Madrid, Spain

ABSTRACT

The first contribution of this paper consists on a live catalogue of pitfalls that extends previous works on modeling errors with pitfalls resulting from an empirical analysis of numerous ontologies. Such a catalogue classifies pitfalls according to the Structural, Functional and Usability-Profiling dimensions. For each pitfall, we include the value of its importance level (critical, important and minor). The second contribution is the description of OntOlogy Pitfall Scanner (OOPS!), a widely used tool for detecting pitfalls in ontologies and targeted at newcomers and domain experts unfamiliar with description logics and ontology implementation languages. The tool operates independently of any ontology development platform and is available through a web application and a web service. The evaluation of the system is provided both through a survey of users' satisfaction and worldwide usage statistics. In addition, the system is also compared with existing ontology evaluation tools in terms of coverage of pitfalls detected.

INTRODUCTION

The Linked Data (LD) effort has become a catalyst for the realization of the vision of the Semantic Web originally proposed by Berners-Lee et al. in (Berners-Lee, Hendler, & Lassila, 2001). In this scenario, a large amount of data, annotated by means of ontologies, is shared on the Web. Such ontologies enrich the published data with semantics and help their integration. In other cases, ontologies are used to model data automatically extracted from web sources, which can be noisy and contain errors. Therefore, ontologies

DOI: 10.4018/978-1-5225-5042-6.ch005

not only must be published according to LD principles[1], but they also must be accurate and of high quality from a knowledge representation perspective in order to avoid inconsistencies or undesired inferences.

The correct application of ontology development methodologies (e.g., METHONTOLOGY (Fernández-López et al., 1999), On-To-Knowledge (Staab et al., 2001), DILIGENT (Pinto, Tempich, & Staab, 2004), or the NeOn Methodology (Suárez-Figueroa et al., 2012)) benefits the quality of the ontology being built. However, such a quality is not totally guaranteed because ontologists face a wide range of difficulties and handicaps when modeling ontologies (Aguado de Cea et al., 2008; Blomqvist, Gangemi, & Presutti, 2009; Rector et al., 2004), and this fact may cause the appearance of anomalies in ontologies. Therefore, in any ontology development project it is vital to perform the ontology evaluation activity since this activity checks the technical quality of an ontology against a frame of reference.

In the last decades a huge amount of research and work on ontology evaluation has been conducted. Some of these attempts define a generic quality evaluation framework (Duque-Ramos et al., 2011; Gangemi et al., 2006; Gómez-Pérez, 2004; Guarino, & Welty, 2009; Strasunskas, & Tomassen, 2008); others propose evaluating an ontology depending on its final (re)use (Suárez-Figueroa, 2010); some others propose quality models based on features, criteria, and metrics (Burton-Jones et al., 2005); whereas others present methods for pattern-based evaluation (Djedidi, & Aufaure, 2010; Presutti et al., 2008).

As a consequence of the emergence of new methods and techniques, a few tools have been proposed. These tools ease the ontology diagnosis by reducing the human intervention. This is the case of XD-Analyzer[2], a plug-in for NeOn Toolkit and Ontocheck[3] (Schober et al., 2012), a plug-in for Protégé. The former checks some structural and architectural ontology features, whereas the latter focuses on metadata aspects. Moki[4] (Pammer, 2010), a wiki-based ontology editor, also provides some evaluation features. Finally, Radon (Ji et al., 2009) is a NeOn Toolkit plug-in that detects and handles logical inconsistencies in ontologies.

This paper presents two main contributions. The first contribution consists of a live and on-line catalogue of pitfalls[5] that extends previous works on modeling errors (Allemang, & Hendler, 2011; Gómez-Pérez, 2004; Noy, & McGuinness, 2001; Rector et al., 2004; Vrandecic 2010) identified in the ontology engineering field including some persistent problems of accessibility emerging in the Linked Data field (Archer, Goedertier, & Loutas, 2012; Heath, & Bizer, 2011; Hogan et al., 2010). The second contribution, OntOlogy Pitfall Scanner (OOPS!) represents a tool for diagnosing (semi-)automatically OWL[6] ontologies. This system aims to help ontology developers to evaluate ontologies and is focused on newcomers and those not familiar with description logics and ontology implementation languages. OOPS! operates independently of any ontology development platform and is available online at http://oops.linkeddata.es/. It should be noted here that the repair of the ontology is out of the scope of OOPS!.

In this paper we first present the catalogue of pitfalls, including a compendium of pitfalls extracted from the literature review and from the manual analysis of ontologies. A classification of such pitfalls according to the Structural, Functional and Usability-Profiling dimensions proposed in (Gangemi et al., 2006) is also provided. Then, for each pitfall, we incorporate its value of importance level (critical, important, and minor) because not all the pitfalls are equally relevant and important. Next, we explain the internal architecture of OOPS! and describe the pitfalls detection methods used within the system. After that, an empirical analysis of the proposed catalogue carried out on 969 ontologies is presented. Then, we present the evaluation of the system based both on a survey of users' satisfaction and on evidence of the real use of the tool worldwide. After that, we review related works about ontology evaluation tools. Finally, we draw the conclusions and provide future lines of work.

COMMON PITFALLS IN ONTOLOGY DEVELOPMENT

One of the most common approaches for evaluating ontologies is to have a checklist of typical errors that other developers have made before. Thus the developer checks the ontology being built against such a list, detects the pitfalls, and corrects them. Our approach does not pretend to create another checklist but to reuse existing works where modeling problems have already been identified and to extend them by incorporating new pitfalls obtained through an empirical evaluation of ontologies already existing.

Catalogue of Common Pitfalls

As our long-term goal is to create and maintain a live and on-line pitfall catalogue, we have followed the process sketched in Figure 1. We started by manually analyzing ontologies and reviewing literature about ontology evaluation and LD.

Regarding works on ontology evaluation, we reviewed, reused, and included in the pitfall catalogue outcomes from (Rector et al., 2004), in which Rector et al. describe a set of common errors made by developers during the ontology modeling activity; from (Gómez-Pérez, 2004), in which Gómez-Pérez provides a classification of errors identified during the evaluation of consistency, completeness, and conciseness of ontology taxonomies; from (Noy, & McGuinness, 2001), where Noy and McGuinness present a methodology for creating ontologies and point out some common errors and how to avoid them; and from (Vrandecic, 2010), in which Vrandecic compiles a number of evaluation methods related to the vocabulary, syntax, structure, semantics, representation and context aspects of ontologies. We have also reused and adapted to the ontology domain some research from the LD area: the main guidelines for LD publication and consumption (Heath, & Bizer, 2011); the problems identified in (Hogan et al., 2010) for accessing RDF[7] on the Web; and the guidelines for creating persistent URIs included in (Archer, Goedertier, & Loutas, 2012).

The catalogue does not pretend to be an exhaustive, rigid and fixed checklist. Besides, in order to keep such a catalogue in continuous evolution we continue working with the manual evaluation of ontologies and aim to discover new pitfalls. We would welcome that OOPS! users and ontology experts propose new pitfalls to introduce them in the catalogue. This evolution of the catalogue is shown in Figure 1 in which the number of pitfall described and the detection methods developed for detecting them are indicated together with chronological information.

The current version of the catalogue[8] consists of a list of 41 pitfalls as well as their descriptions. In each pitfall we include provenance information if the pitfall being described was proposed in a previous work. The list includes the following pitfalls:

- **P01. Creating Polysemous Elements:** An ontology element whose name has different meanings is included in the ontology to represent more than one conceptual idea. For example, the class "Theatre" is used to represent both the artistic discipline and the place in which a play is performed.
- **P02. Creating Synonyms as Classes:** Several classes whose identifiers are synonyms are created and defined as equivalent. For example, the classes "Waterfall" and "Cascade" are defined as equivalents. This pitfall is related to the guidelines presented in (Noy, & McGuinness, 2001), which explain that synonyms for the same concept do not represent different classes.

Figure 1. Workflow for pitfall catalogue maintenance and evolution

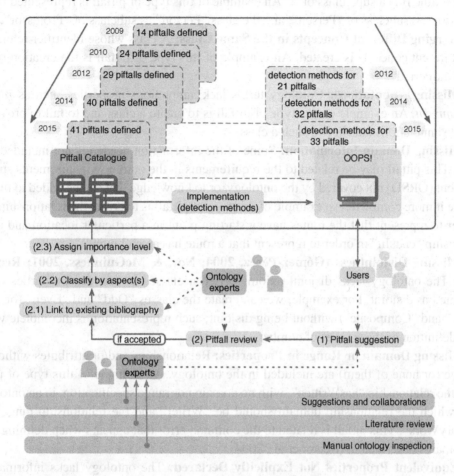

- **P03. Creating the Relationship "is" Instead of Using "rdfs:subClassOf", "rdf:type" or "owl:sameAs":** The "is" relationship is created in the ontology instead of using OWL primitives for representing the subclass relationship ("subclassOf"), the membership to a class ("instanceOf"), or the equality between instances ("sameAs"). An example of this pitfall is to define the class "Actor" in the following way 'Actor ≡ Person ⊓ ∃interprets.Actuation ⊓ ∃is.Man'. This pitfall is related to the guidelines for understanding the "is-a" relation provided in (Noy, & McGuinness, 2001).
- **P04. Creating Unconnected Ontology Elements:** Ontology elements (classes, relationships or attributes) are created with no relation to the rest of the ontology. An example of this type of pitfall is to create the relationship "memberOfTeam" and to miss the class representing teams; thus, the relationship created is isolated in the ontology.
- **P05. Defining Wrong Inverse Relationships:** Two relationships are defined as inverse relations when they are not necessarily inverse. An example of this type of pitfall is to define "isSoldIn" and "isBoughtIn" as inverse relationships.
- **P06. Including Cycles in a Class Hierarchy (Gómez-Pérez, 2004; Noy, & McGuinness, 2001):** A cycle between two classes in the hierarchy is included in the ontology even though the ontology is not intended to have such classes as equivalent. That is, some class A has a subclass B, and at

the same time B is a superclass of A. An example of this type of pitfall is represented by the class "Professor" as subclass of "Person", and the class "Person" as subclass of "Professor".

- **P07. Merging Different Concepts in the Same Class:** A class whose identifier refers to two or more different concepts is created. An example of this type of pitfall is the creation of the class "StyleAndPeriod".

- **P08. Missing Annotations:** Ontology terms lack annotations properties such as *rdfs:label* or *rdfs:comment*. An example of this type of pitfall is to create a class and to fail to provide human readable annotations attached to such a class.

- **P09. Missing Domain Information:** Some of the information needed is not included in the ontology. This pitfall may be related to the requirements in the ontology requirements specification document (ORSD) not covered by the ontology, or to knowledge that can be added to the ontology to make it more complete. An example of this type of pitfall is to create the relationship "startsIn" in order to represent that the routes have a starting point in a particular location and to miss the relationship "endsIn" in order to represent that a route has an end point.

- **P10. Missing Disjointness (Gómez-Pérez, 2004; Noy, & McGuinness, 2001; Rector et al., 2004):** The ontology lacks disjoint axioms between classes or between properties that should be defined as disjoint. For example, we can create the classes "Odd" and "Even" (or the classes "Prime" and "Composite") without being disjoint; such representation is incomplete with regard to the definition of these types of numbers.

- **P11. Missing Domain or Range in Properties:** Relationships and/or attributes without domain or range (or none of them) are included in the ontology. An example of this type of pitfall is to create the relationship "hasWritten", with no domain nor range specification, in an ontology about art in which the relationship domain should be "Writer" and the relationship range should be "LiteraryWork". This pitfall is related to the common error that appears when defining the ranges and domains described in (Rector et al., 2004).

- **P12. Equivalent Properties Not Explicitly Declared:** The ontology lacks information about equivalent properties (owl:equivalentProperty) in the cases of duplicated relationships and/or attributes. An example of this type of pitfalls is to fail to define the relations "hasMember" and "has-Member" as equivalent.

- **P13. Inverse Relationships Not Explicitly Declared:** This pitfall appears when any relationship (except for the symmetric ones) does not have an inverse relationship defined within the ontology. For example, the case in which the ontology developer omits the inverse definition between the relations "hasLanguageCode" and "isCodeOf".

- **P14. Misusing "owl:allValuesFrom" (Rector et al., 2004):** This pitfall consists in using the universal restriction (owl:allValuesFrom) as the default qualifier instead of the existential restriction (owl:someValuesFrom).. An example of this type of pitfall is to define the class "Book" in the following way 'Book ≡ ∃producedBy.Writer ⊓ ∀uses.Paper' thus closing the possibility of adding "Ink" as an element used in the writing.

- **P15. Using "Some Not" in Place of "Not Some" (Rector et al., 2004):** The pitfall consists in using a "some not" structure when a "not some" is required. This is due to the misplacement of the existential quantifier (owl:someValuesFrom) and the negative operator (owl:complementOf).. An example of this type of pitfall is to define a vegetarian pizza as any pizza which has both some topping which is not meat and some topping which is not fish. This example is explained in more detail in (Rector et al., 2004).

- **P16. Using a Primitive Class in Place of a Defined One (Rector et al., 2004):** This pitfall implies creating a primitive class rather than a defined one in case automatic classification of individuals is intended. It is critical to understand that, in general, nothing will be inferred to be subsumed under a primitive class by the classifier (Rector et al., 2004). This pitfall implies that the developer does not understand the open world assumption. An example of this pitfall is to create the primitive class 'CheesyPizza ⊏ Pizza ⊓ ∃hasTopping.Cheese' instead of creating it as a defined class in the following way: 'CheesyPizza ≡ Pizza ⊓ ∃hasTopping.Cheese'. This example is explained in more detail in (Rector et al., 2004).

- **P17. Overspecializing a Hierarchy:** The hierarchy in the ontology is specialized in such a way that the final leaves cannot have instances since they are actually instances and should have been created as such instead of as classes. Authors in (Noy, & McGuinness, 2001) provide guidelines for distinguishing between a class and an instance when modeling hierarchies. An example of this type of pitfall is to create the classes "Madrid", "Barcelona" and "Sevilla", among others, as subclasses of "Place".

- **P18. Overspecializing the Domain or Range (Noy, & McGuinness, 2001; Rector et al., 2004):** This pitfall consists in defining a domain or range not general enough for a property, i.e, no considering all the individuals or datatypes that might be involved in such a domain or range. An example of this type of pitfall is to restrict the domain of the relationship "isOfficialLanguage" to the class "City", instead of allowing the class "Country" or a more general concept such as "GeopoliticalObject" to have an official language.

- **P19. Defining Multiple Domains or Ranges in Properties:** The domain or range (or both) of a property (relationships and attributes) is defined by stating more than one "rdfs:domain" or "rdfs:range" statements.. This pitfall is related both to the common error that appears when defining ranges and domains described in (Rector et al., 2004) and to the guidelines for defining these elements provided in (Noy, & McGuinness, 2001). An example of this type of pitfall is to create the relationship "takesPlaceIn" with one range declaration for the class "City" and other range declaration for the class "Nation", as this implementation represents the intersection of both ranges instead of the union.

- **P20. Misusing Ontology Annotations:** The contents of some annotation properties are swapped or misused. An example of this type of pitfall is to include in the *rdfs:label* annotation of the class "Crossroads" the following sentence 'the place of intersection of two or more roads'; and to include in the *rdfs:comment* annotation the word 'Crossroads'.

- **P21. Using a Miscellaneous Class:** This pitfall refers to the creation of a class with the only goal of classifying the instances that do not belong to any of its sibling classes (classes with which the miscellaneous problematic class shares a common direct ancestor). An example of this type of pitfall is to create the class "HydrographicalResource", and the subclasses "Stream" and "Waterfall", among others, and also the subclass "OtherRiverElement".

- **P22. Using Different Naming Conventions in the Ontology:** Ontology elements are not named following the same convention within the whole ontology. Some notions about naming conventions are provided in (Noy, & McGuinness, 2001). For example, this pitfall appears when a class identifier starts with upper case, e.g. "Ingredient", whereas its subclass identifiers start with lower case, e.g. "flour" and "milk".

- **P23. Duplicating a Datatype Already Provided by the Implementation Language:** A class and its corresponding individuals are created to represent existing datatypes in the implementation language.. A particular case of this pitfall regarding the misuse of classes and property values is addressed in (Noy, & McGuinness, 2001). An example of this type of pitfall is to create the relationship "isEcological" between an instance of "Car" and the instances "Yes" or "No", instead of creating an attribute "isEcological" whose range is Boolean.
- **P24. Using Recursive Definition:** An ontology element is used in its own definition. An example of this type of pitfall is to create the relationship "hasFork" and to establish as its range the following: The set of restaurants that have at least one value for the relationship "hasFork".
- **P25. Defining a Relationship as Inverse to Itself:** A relationship is defined as inverse of itself. In this case, this property could have been defined as "owl:SymmetricProperty" instead. An example of this type of pitfall is to create the relationship "hasBorderWith" and to state that "hasBorderWith" is its inverse relationship.
- **P26. Defining Inverse Relationships for a Symmetric One:** A relationship is defined as "owl:SymmetricProperty", and such a relationship is defined as inverse of another relationship. For example, to create for the symmetric relationship "farFrom" an inverse relationship, e.g. itself, "farFrom".
- **P27. Defining Wrong Equivalent Properties:** Two object properties or two datatype properties are defined as equivalent, using "owl:equivalentProperty", even though they do not have the same semantics.. An example of this type of pitfalls is to mix up common relationships that could hold between several types of entities, as "hasPart" defined in one ontology between human body parts and the relation "hasPart" defined in another ontology between research plans and research projects.
- **P28. Defining Wrong Symmetric Relationships:** A relationship is defined as symmetric when the relationship is not necessarily symmetric. This situation can appear because the domain and range are too specific; for example, if we define the symmetric relationship "hasSpouse" between the concepts "Man" and "Woman" instead of using the concept "Person" both as domain and range of such a relationship.
- **P29. Defining Wrong Transitive Relationships:** A relationship is defined as transitive when the relationship is not necessarily transitive. An example of this type of pitfall is to create the relationship "participatesIn", whose domain is the union of the concepts "Team" and "Individual" and whose range is the concept "Event", and defining the relationship as transitive.
- **P30. Equivalent Classes Not Explicitly Declared:** This pitfall consists in missing the definition of equivalent classes (owl:equivalentClass) in case of duplicated concepts. When an ontology reuses terms from other ontologies, classes that have the same meaning should be defined as equivalent in order to benefit the interoperability between both ontologies. An example of this pitfall is to fail to define the classes 'Trainer' (class in an imported ontology) and 'Coach' (class in the ontology about sports being developed) as equivalent classes.
- **P31. Defining Wrong Equivalent Classes:** Two classes are defined as equivalent when they are not necessarily equivalent. For example, defining "Car" as equivalent to "Vehicle".
- **P32. Several Classes With the Same Label:** Two or more classes have the same content in the *rdfs:label* annotation. For example, to link the label "Theatre" both with the building and the literary discipline, adding no more labels to them.

- **P33. Creating a Property Chain With Just One Property:** There is a property chain that includes only one property in the antecedent part. For example, to create the following property chain: isInChargeOf -> supervises.
- **P34. Untyped Class (Hogan et al., 2010):** A resource is used as a class without having been declared as a Class. An example of this type of pitfall is to create individuals of the class "Person" and to omit that "Person" is a class.
- **P35. Untyped Property (Hogan et al., 2010):** A resource is used as a property without having been declared as a rdf:Property or as some subclass of it. An example of this type of pitfall is to link individual by the relation "hasPart" and to omit that "hasPart" is an object property.
- **P36. URI Contains File Extension (Archer, Goedertier, & Loutas, 2012):** This involves including file extensions as ".owl", ".rdf", ".ttl", ".n3" and ".rdfxml" in an ontology URI. An example of this pitfall is to define an ontology uri as "http://www.biopax.org/release/biopax-level3.owl" containing the extension ".owl" related to the technology used.
- **P37. Ontology Not Available on the Web:** This involves omitting to provide online description or documentation of the ontology when looking up its URI. An example of this pitfall could be the following case: "Ontology Security (ontosec)" (URI: http://www.semanticweb.org/ontologies/2008/11/OntologySecurity.owl) which is not available online as RDF nor as HTML (at the moment of carrying out this work).
- **P38. No OWL Ontology Declaration:** this means failing to declare the *owl:Ontology* tag where the ontology metadata should be provided. An example of this pitfall could be found at the "Creative Commons Rights Expression Language (cc)" ontology (URI: http://creativecommons.org/ns) that does not have any *owl:Ontology* declaration in its RDF file even though it has other OWL elements used as, for example, owl:equivalentProperty (at the moment of carrying out this work).
- **P39. Ambiguous Namespace:** This means failing to define both the ontology URI and the *xml:base* namespace. An example of this pitfall could be found at "Basic Access Control ontology (acl)" (URI: http://www.w3.org/ns/auth/acl) that has no owl:Ontology tag nor xml:base definition.
- **P40. Namespace Hijacking (Heath, & Bizer, 2011):** This means reusing or referring to terms from other namespaces not actually defined in such namespace. This pitfall is related to the Linked Data publishing guidelines provided in (Heath, & Bizer, 2011): "Only define new terms in a namespace that you control." An example of this pitfall is to use "http://www.w3.org/2000/01/rdf-schema#Property" that is not defined in the rdf namespace (http://www.w3.org/2000/01/rdf-schema#) instead of using "http://www.w3.org/1999/02/22-rdf-syntax-ns#Property", that is actually defined in the rdfs namespace (http://www.w3.org/1999/02/22-rdf-syntax-ns#).
- **P41. No License Declared:** The ontology metadata omits information about the license that applies to the ontology.

Pitfalls Classification

Since the list of pitfalls presented refers to different ontology perspectives, it is advisable to classify them according to some evaluation criteria. Users with an interest in a given aspect of ontology evaluation could easily identify the group of pitfalls in which they might be interested. For this reason, we have classified pitfalls according to the dimensions defined in (Gangemi et al., 2006), namely: structural, functional and usability-profiling. Even though these dimensions are enough to classify all the pitfalls in the catalogue, a more fine-grained classification is provided to deal with specific aspects that following and extend the approach described in (Poveda-Villalón, Suárez-Figueroa, & Gómez-Pérez, 2010). Such classification is as follows:

- **Structural Dimension (Gangemi et al., 2006):** It is focused on syntax and formal semantics. For this dimension we consider the following aspects:
  - *Modeling Decisions* **(Poveda-Villalón, Suárez-Figueroa, & Gómez-Pérez, 2010):** This aspect involves evaluating whether developers use the primitives provided by ontology implementation languages in a correct way, and if there are modeling decisions that could be improved.
  - *No Inference* **(Poveda-Villalón, Suárez-Figueroa, & Gómez-Pérez, 2010):** This aspect refers to checking whether desirable or expected knowledge could actually be inferred from the given ontology, but it is not inferred.
  - *Wrong Inference* **(Poveda-Villalón, Suárez-Figueroa, & Gómez-Pérez, 2010):** This aspect refers to the evaluation of the inference of erroneous or invalid knowledge.
  - *Ontology Language*: This aspect refers to checking whether the ontology is compliant both with the ontology language specification and with the syntax in which the ontology is formalized.
- **Functional Dimension (Gangemi et al., 2006):** This is related to the intended use of a given ontology; thus the focus is on the ontology conceptualization. The following aspects are taken into account within this dimension:
  - *Real World Modeling or Common Sense* **(Poveda-Villalón, Suárez-Figueroa, & Gómez-Pérez, 2010):** This aspect deals with the knowledge that domain experts expect to appear in the ontology, but is not represented.
  - *Requirement Completeness* **(Poveda-Villalón, Suárez-Figueroa, & Gómez-Pérez, 2010):** This aspect deals with the coverage of the requirements specified in the ORSD.
  - *Application Context*: This aspect refers to the adequacy of the ontology for a given application or use case.
- **Usability-Profiling Dimension (Gangemi et al., 2006):** It refers to the communication context of an ontology. For this dimension we contemplate the following aspects:
  - *Ontology Understanding* **(Poveda-Villalón, Suárez-Figueroa, & Gómez-Pérez, 2010):** This aspect involves evaluating any kind of information that can help the user to understand the ontology.
  - *Ontology Clarity* **(Poveda-Villalón, Suárez-Figueroa, & Gómez-Pérez, 2010):** This aspect refers to the properties of ontology elements of being easily recognizable and understood by the user.
  - *Ontology Metadata*: This aspect involves evaluating the existence of information that can help to understand the ontology context itself, instead of the conceptualization defined. Some examples of this information are: licensing, provenance, versioning, etc.

Figure 2 represents such classification where each pitfall is classified according to at least one of the abovementioned aspects. Figure 2 also shows the importance level of each pitfall both by attaching a number between brackets to each pitfall title and by using different colors; thus "critical" pitfalls are written in black followed by "(1)", "important" pitfalls are in blue followed by "(2)" and "minor" pitfalls are in brown followed by "(3)".

Figure 2. Pitfall classification

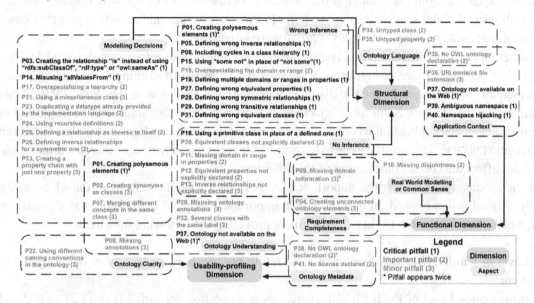

Extension With Pitfalls Importance Levels

It is obvious that not all the pitfalls are equally important; their impact in the ontology will depend on multiple factors. For this reason, the pitfall catalogue has been extended with information about how critical the pitfalls are. We have identified three levels:

- **Critical (1):** It is crucial to correct the pitfall. Otherwise, it could affect the ontology consistency, reasoning and applicability, among others. For example, the consequences of "P19. Defining multiple domains or ranges in properties" could lead to logical inconsistences in the ontology, which represents a critical error when reasoning over the populated ontology.
- **Important (2):** Though not critical for ontology function, it is important to correct this type of pitfall. For example, the logical consequences of "P25. Defining a relationship as inverse to itself" are the same as if such relationship were defined as symmetric. However, the latter option, that is, using the ontology implementation language constructors for the purpose they were conceived, is a sign of good modeling and understanding of the underlying semantics.
- **Minor (3):** It does not represent a problem. However, correcting it makes the ontology better organized and user friendly. For example, the pitfall "P22. Using different naming conventions in the ontology" is about the appearance of the ontology and does not compromise the proper ontology functioning.

These levels do not have clear boundaries in the sense that a particular pitfall in a level could be debatable depending on the modeling styles, ontology requirements, and context of use by an ontology application. For example, in this work we consider an important pitfall not to define domains and ranges for the properties, which is arguable, of course. In some developments, it could be considered a pitfall exactly the opposite (that is, specifying domains and ranges), as developers might be interested in increasing the interoperability of the model obtained instead of its explicit semantics or expressivity. In such a case, it would be enough if the evaluators define the fact of defining domains and ranges as a pitfall instead of doing it as we propose here. In this way, we provide a starting point for ontology evaluation that could be adapted to users' particular requirements.

In other cases, how critical a pitfall is depends on the context of use; for example, in a LD development project (Heath, & Bizer, 2011), an ontology should be published according to the Linked Data rules and principles. In this scenario, the pitfalls "P37. Ontology not available on the Web", "P39. Ambiguous namespace", and "P40. Namespace hijacking" are crucial while they might not be important in the context of an isolated application where the ontology is not designed for sharing. Another pitfall related to LD context is "P36. URI contains file extension". In this case, it may be considered a minor pitfall as it does not affect the correct functioning of the ontology.

At the moment of including the importance levels in the catalogue, 35 out of the 41 pitfalls were already defined and published. In order to attach importance levels to the pitfalls, a study was carried out in which the users had to fill in a questionnaire providing the following information:

- **Level of Confidence:** How confident (s)he felt in the ontology evaluation or ontology modeling domains.
- **Importance Level of Each Pitfall:** There was one question per pitfall (from P01 to P35) where the user had to select the importance level of the given pitfall. The possible values were "Critical", "Important" and "Minor" (see above).
- **Which Pitfalls are Not Important:** A list with all the pitfalls was provided and the users were asked to indicate which pitfall would never represent a problem (not pitfalls that could be a problem only in some cases) for them.
- **Other Comments:** A free text box for providing any comment or suggestions.

Researchers, mainly experts on ontology modeling or evaluation, within the semantic web community[9] and OOPS! users were invited to fill in the questionnaire. We received 55 responses. We have made the questionnaire available on-line at http://goo.gl/SEddMN in order to allow the community to continue with the assessment of the level of importance of the pitfalls. On the other hand, to assign importance levels to pitfalls according to the data gathered through the survey, we have first assigned weight to each response (3 for critical[10], 2 for important, and 1 for minor) and to each expertise level (3 for experts, 2 for medium confidence, and 1 for low confidence). For those pitfalls selected as "not important", we have assigned the weight 0 in the corresponding response. The data generated from the survey responses and the ranking calculations are available at the URL: http://goo.gl/0IkbS2

Then we have ranked the pitfalls according to the well-known "weighted sum" technique and obtained the ranking shown in the first column from the left in Table 1.

Once the pitfalls are ranked, an interval should be defined in order to split the given ranking into 3 parts, one for each importance level. To do this, we have used a method based on the range of the weight values. More precisely, the range (highest weight – lowest weight) is divided into 3. Concretely, the range of the weighted sum ranking is 0.0193 (0.0379 – 0.0186). The division of the range among 3 gives us an interval of 0.0064. Finally, the range of the ranking is split into 3, resulting in the following intervals:

- **Minor:** From 0.0186 to 0.0250 (0.0186 + 0.0064)
- **Important:** From 0.0250 to 0.0314 (0.0250 +0.0064)
- **Critical:** From 0.0314 to 0.0379

In order to demonstrate that the ranking method selected is robust, we compared it with two other ranking methods, namely, the "lexicographic order" (Miettinen, 1999) and the "centroid function" (Barron, & Barrett, 1996). The rankings obtained for these methods are shown in Table 1, more precisely, in the second and third columns from the left respectively. For the case of the "centroid function" we have also calculated the intervals for the "Critical", "Important", and "Minor" categories in the same manner as explained for the "weighted sum". As the "lexicographic order" does not involve weights or ranges, it does not make sense to split the range in this fashion. More precisely, the lexicographic order is calculated as follows: first, the pitfalls are ordered according to the votes that the value "critical (3)" attained. The more votes attained, the higher the pitfall is placed in the ranking. For example, the P06 is first with 46 votes[11]. When two or more pitfalls have the same number of votes in this category, the information about the next importance levels is used to break the tie. For example, P29 and P14 have 37 votes for the value "critical", so the votes for "important (2)" are used, that is, the P14 is placed first with 12 votes, and P14 is next with 9 votes.

Once the rankings were computed, we analyzed the similitudes and differences between them. That is, given two rankings we measure how similar the orders established for the list of pitfalls are. To do so, we calculated the Kendall coefficient (Winkler & Hays, 1985), being the values obtained for each pair of rankings the following[12]:

- **Weighted Sum:** Lexicographic order: 0.882352941
- **Weighted Sum:** Centroid function: 0.905882353
- **Lexicographic Order:** Centroid function: 0.929411765

We can observe that the three values are very high; this fact means that the rankings are very similar and proves that the decision of choosing the weighted sum does not affect significantly the final classification. In fact, there is only one pitfall, "P24. Using recursive definition" that has been attached to different importance levels according to the weighted sum method (classified as "important") and to the centroid function method (classified as "critical").

When a new pitfall is inserted in the catalogue, an importance level has to be assigned to it. This importance level is decided in conjunction with the developers of OOPS!, experienced ontological engineers, and the users (if any) proposing the given pitfall. For the pitfalls P36 to P40, four experts in ontological engineering and vocabulary publication have defined the pitfalls and assigned their importance levels. As a result, the importance levels shown in Table 2 have been attached to each pitfall.

Taking into account the importance levels extracted from the survey and those levels assigned by ontology experts, we have created a final classification of pitfalls as shown in Figure 3.[13]

OOPS! (ONTOLOGY PITFALL SCANNER!)

OOPS! is a web-based tool for diagnosing potential problems in ontologies that could lead to modeling errors. This tool is intended to help ontology developers, mainly newcomers, during the ontology validation activity (Suárez-Figueroa, Aguado-de-Cea, & Gómez-Pérez, 2013). Currently, OOPS! provides mechanisms to (semi-)automatically diagnose 32 pitfalls of the 41 described in the pitfall catalogue as Figure 3 shows.

Table 1. Pitfalls (from P01 to P35) ranked according to the (a) weighted sum, (b) lexicographic order and (c) centroid function techniques

	(a) Weighted Sum		(b) Lexicographic Order	(c) Centroid Function		
	Order	**Weight**	**Order**	**Order**	**Weight**	
Critical (1)	P06. Including cycles in a class hierarchy	0.0379	P06	P06	0.0366	Critical (1)
	P19. Defining multiple domains or ranges in properties	0.0375	P19	P19	0.0359	
	P01. Creating polysemous elements	0.0367	P03	P29	0.0351	
	P03. Creating the relationship "is" instead of using "rdfs:subClassOf", "rdf:type" or "owl:sameAs"	0.0364	P01	P01	0.0346	
	P29. Defining wrong transitive relationships	0.0348	P29	P03	0.0346	
	P28. Defining wrong symmetric relationships	0.0344	P14	P31	0.0343	
	P31. Defining wrong equivalent classes	0.0343	P31	P15	0.0336	
	P05. Defining wrong inverse relationships	0.0342	P16	P14	0.0336	
	P14. Misusing "owl:allValuesFrom"	0.0341	P15	P28	0.0335	
	P27. Defining wrong equivalent properties	0.0340	P27	P16	0.0333	
	P15. Using "some not" in place of "not some"	0.0335	P28	P27	0.0330	
	P16. Using a primitive class in place of a defined one	0.0335	P05	P05	0.0318	
Important (2)	P23. Duplicating a datatype already provided by the implementation language	0.0303	P24	P24	0.0312	Important (2)
	P24. Using recursive definition	0.0303	P12	P23	0.0303	
	P12. Equivalent properties not explicitly declared	0.0301	P10	P12	0.0303	
	P34. Untyped class	0.0284	P23	P10	0.0287	
	P10. Missing disjointness	0.0283	P34	P34	0.0286	
	P35. Untyped property	0.0281	P35	P30	0.0283	
	P25. Defining a relationship as inverse to itself	0.0279	P11	P35	0.0283	
	P30. Equivalent classes not explicitly declared	0.0279	P25	P11	0.0275	
	P18. Overspecializing the domain or range	0.0272	P26	P25	0.0273	
	P26. Defining inverse relationships for a symmetric one	0.0272	P18	P26	0.0270	
	P17. Overspecializing a hierarchy	0.0267	P17	P18	0.0267	
	P11. Missing domain or range in properties	0.0252	P30	P17	0.0261	
Minor (3)	P04. Creating unconnected ontology elements	0.0248	P04	P07	0.0253	Minor (3)
	P09. Missing domain information	0.0245	P07	P04	0.0253	
	P33. Creating a property chain with just one property	0.0240	P02	P09	0.0245	
	P02. Creating synonyms as classes	0.0239	P09	P33	0.0237	
	P07. Merging different concepts in the same class	0.0234	P33	P02	0.0236	
	P21. Using a miscellaneous class	0.0222	P21	P32	0.0226	
	P32. Several classes with the same label	0.0219	P13	P21	0.0226	
	P13. Inverse relationships not explicitly declared	0.0201	P32	P13	0.0215	
	P22. Using different naming conventions in the ontology	0.0189	P20	P20	0.0206	
	P20. Misusing ontology annotations	0.0187	P08	P08	0.0205	
	P08. Missing annotations	0.0186	P22	P22	0.0200	

Table 2. Importance levels for pitfalls assigned by experts

	Pitfalls
Critical (1)	• P37. Ontology not available on the Web • P39. Ambiguous namespace • P40. Namespace hijacking
Important (2)	• P38. No OWL ontology declaration • P41. No license declared
Minor (3)	• P36. URI contains file extension

Figure 3. Classification of pitfalls by level of importance

Critical (1)
P01. Creating polysemous elements
P03. Creating the relationship "is" instead of using "rdfs:subClassOf", "rdf:type" or "owl:sameAs"
P05. Defining wrong inverse relationships
P06. Including cycles in a class hierarchy
P14. Misusing "owl:allValuesFrom"
P15. Using "some not" in place of "not some"
P16. Using a primitive class in place of a defined one
P19. Defining multiple domains or ranges in properties
P27. Defining wrong equivalent properties
P28. Defining wrong symmetric relationships
P29. Defining wrong transitive relationships
P31. Defining wrong equivalent classes
P37. Ontology not available on the Web
P39. Ambiguous namespace
P40. Namespace hijacking

Important (2)
P10. Missing disjointness
P11. Missing domain or range in properties
P12. Equivalent properties not explicitly declared
P17. Overspecializing a hierarchy
P18. Overspecializing the domain or range
P23. Duplicating a datatype already provided by the implementation language
P24. Using recursive definitions
P25. Defining a relationship as inverse to itself
P26. Defining inverse relationships for a symmetric one
P30. Equivalent classes not explicitly declared
P34. Untyped class
P35. Untyped property
P38. No OWL ontology declaration
P41. No license declared

Minor (3)
P02. Creating synonyms as classes
P04. Creating unconnected ontology elements
P07. Merging different concepts in the same class
P08. Missing annotations
P09. Missing domain information
P13. Inverse relationships not explicitly declared
P20. Misusing ontology annotations
P21. Using a miscellaneous class
P22. Using different naming conventions in the ontology
P32. Several classes with the same label
P33. Creating a property chain with just one property
P36. URI contains file extension

This section is divided into two parts: the first subsection explains the internal architecture of OOPS!; and the second subsection describes the detection methods used within the system in order to spot pitfalls in the ontology analyzed.

OOPS! Architecture

Figure 4 presents the underlying architecture of OOPS!. OOPS! is a web application based on Java EE[14], HTML[15], jQuery[16], JSP[17] and CSS[18] technologies. In order to produce a list of evaluation results, OOPS! takes as input an ontology.

The user interface consists of a webpage, in which the user enters either the ontology URI or its OWL code, which describes the ontology to be analyzed. Once the ontology is parsed using the Jena API[19], the "Pitfall Scanner" module inspects the declared ontology[20] looking for pitfalls among those

Figure 4. OOPS! architecture

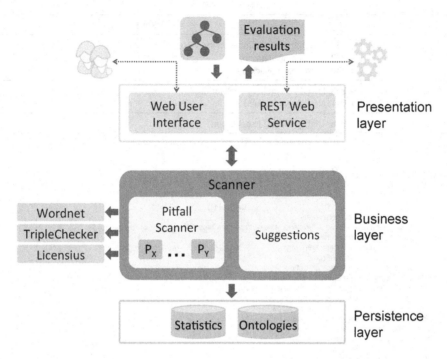

available in the catalogue. More precisely, the 33 pitfalls implemented are those that can be detected (semi-) automatically with the information provided by the ontology OWL code (T-box). Those pitfalls that require an external reference framework (e.g., an ontology requirement document, an A-box or corpora, and/or domain knowledge) or human intervention are not yet automated. During this scanning phase, the ontology elements prone to potential errors are detected, whereas some modeling suggestions are generated by the "Suggestion Scanner" module. Finally, the evaluation results are displayed in the web user interface, which shows the list of pitfalls detected, if any, and the ontology elements affected, as well as explanations describing the findings (Figure 5). The web interface allows not only analyzing all the automated pitfalls, but also choosing specific pitfalls or predefined groups according to the pitfall classification presented in this paper. This "Advanced evaluation" feature is linked from the homepage and available at index http://oops.linkeddata.es/advanced.

Furthermore, to allow other programs and applications to use OOPS! pitfall detection methods, we have developed a web service.[21]

Next subsection describes the different approaches used to implement the methods for detecting pitfalls.

Pitfall Detection Methods

The pitfall catalogue covers many different aspects of ontologies, such as their internal structure, their associated or embedded human-readable documentation, or their availability on the Web. As a consequence, the detection methods implemented to detect pitfalls make use of different techniques and technologies for diagnosing them. More precisely, the detection methods used within OOPS! are based on one (or more) of the following approaches:

Figure 5. OOPS! response example

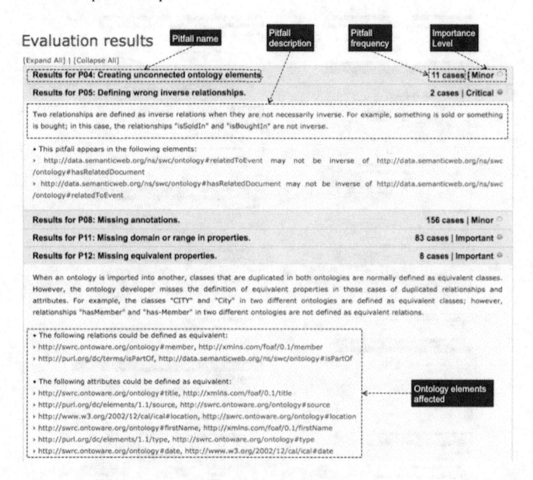

- **Structural Pattern Matching:** The detection methods based on patterns analyze the internal structure of the ontology, seeking specific parts of the model. In these cases, a pitfall is diagnosed when a given structural pattern is spotted. Of the 33 pitfalls, 24 have been implemented using structural patterns. A number of these structural patterns are shown in Figure 6 and Figure 7. In such figures, classes are represented by rectangles, properties by plain arrows, and OWL and RDFS primitives by dotted arrows. Properties can also be represented by diamonds including property characteristics (e.g. transitive). The patterns can also include statements following the OWL functional syntax, mainly to indicate that the pattern checks the lack of such information. It should be noted that some pitfalls are detected by different patterns, for example, "P19. Defining multiple domains or ranges in properties"; in those cases the pitfall is detected when at least one of the patterns is identified in the ontology. In addition, some pitfalls have associated different methods (indicated in Figure 6 and Figure 7 by an "M" and a number) depending on the type of element affected, for example the "P11. Missing domain or range in properties" has two associated methods, one for object properties and other for datatype properties, as shown in Figure 6.

Figure 6. Example of patterns to detect pitfalls (part 1 of 2)

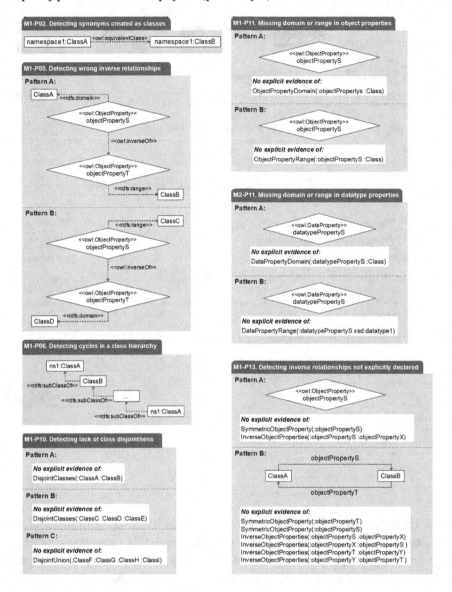

- **Lexical Content Analysis:** The detection methods based on the analysis of lexical entities make use of the content of annotations (e.g., *rdfs:label* or *rdfs:comment*) and identifiers (the ID part of the element URI) for detecting pitfalls. These methods are used in 9 of the 33 implemented pitfalls. For the pitfall "P22. Using different naming conventions in the ontology", the identifiers of the ontology elements are analyzed to check whether all of them use the same naming convection for example, if all the identifiers are formed according to the CamelCase rules.
- **Specific Characteristic Search:** Six detection methods have been automated by checking general characteristics of the ontology not related to the internal structure of the ontology or to the content of the lexical entities. These characteristics could be related, for example, to the name given to the ontology as in the pitfall "P36. URI contains file extension", which is detected when the ontology

Figure 7. Example of patterns to detect pitfalls (part 2 of 2)

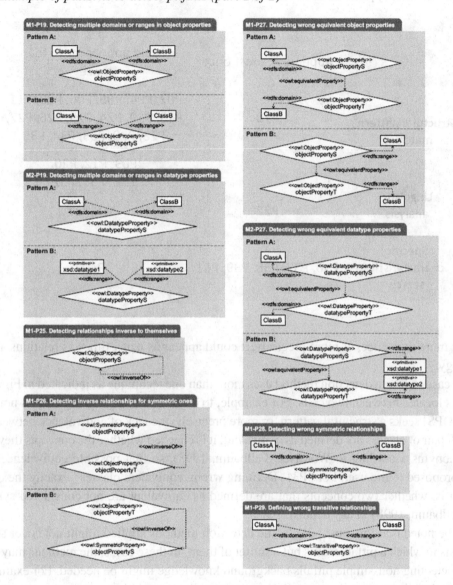

URI refers to the technology or ontology language used during its development as RDF or OWL. Detailed technical information about detection methods for seeking a specific characteristic can be found in (Poveda-Villalón et al., 2013).

In addition, some pitfalls can appear several times in the same ontology while others may appear at most once, since they affect the whole ontology instead of its different elements (classes, properties and axioms, among others).

Figure 8 shows the type of technique(s) used for detecting each pitfall and its cardinality, that is, how many times such a pitfall could be spotted in a given ontology. For example, we can observe that the pitfall "P11. Missing domain or range in properties" is detected by seeking a given pattern and that it

Figure 8. Classification of pitfalls based on the techniques used for their diagnoses

Cardinality / Technique	0..1 Appears at most once	0..N Could appear more than once
Structural pattern matching	P10	P02, P04, P05, P06, P08, P11, P13, P19, P24, P25, P26, P27, P28, P29, P33, P34, P35
Linguistic analysis	P22	P03, P12, P20, P30, P31, P32 P07, P21
Specific characteristic search	P36, P37, P38, P39, P41	P40

could appear more than once, or more precisely, it could appear as many times as relations are defined in the ontology.

There are cases where a detection method uses more than one technique as indicated in Figure 8, with the rectangles located between two cells. For example, to detect "P30. Equivalent classes not explicitly declared", OOPS! seeks a structural pattern, or more precisely, the lack of equivalence between classes. Then for each pair of classes not defined as equivalent, it is checked whether the concepts they represent could be synonyms according to WordNet (Fellbaum, 1998), so that possible equivalences between classed are proposed to the user. For "P31. Defining wrong equivalent classes" exactly the opposite is checked, that is, whether two concepts that are defined as equivalent are not considered synonyms in WordNet (Fellbaum, 1998) in any context.

It should be noted that for some pitfalls, the detection methods applied might not cover all the possible situations in which a pitfall occurs but a subset of them. In these cases, the methods may be indicators, but for detecting non-simple pitfalls background knowledge might be needed. For example, while "P11. Missing domain or range in properties" is detected in all possible cases by the pattern presented in Figure 6, it is not the case for "P05. Defining wrong inverse relationships". In this case, the current pattern will not cover the case of defining, in a math ontology, the relationship "lessThan" as inverse of "greaterThan" instead of "lessThanOrEqual", as some background and common sense knowledge is needed. We plan to improve these methods by incorporating linguistic techniques and resources as proposed in (Suárez-Figueroa, Kamel, & Poveda-Villalón, 2013).

In other cases, a detected pitfall might not represent a factual error, and this might be due to specific modeling decision or requirements. For example, "P02. Creating synonyms as classes" might be implemented in some cases in order to support backwards compatibility between different versions of the same ontology.

MOST COMMON PITFALLS

In order to know which are the most frequent errors in ontology development, we have recorded the number of pitfalls detected in each ontology analyzed with OOPS! To carry out this task we used the 33 pitfalls implemented and 969 ontologies diagnosed up to August 2015.

When analyzing OOPS! execution logs, we could observe that

- Between November 14th, 2011 and August 24th, 2015, 2,753 executions were carried out. During these executions, the ontology being analysed was identified by its URI in 2,532 cases, whereas the ontology was "anonymous" (its URI was not defined or it was "null") in 221 cases.
- From these 2,532 ontologies identified, some URIs indicate that the same ontology has been evaluated several times. We have filtered duplicated URIs, keeping only the first execution per URI. As a result, we counted 852 unique ontologies. Further studies will take into account all the executions per URI and analyse the evolution of the pitfalls appearing.
- With regard to the 221 anonymous ontologies, we have removed executions with equal results, assuming that they belong to the same ontology, thus avoiding duplications. As a result, we counted 117 different anonymous ontologies.
- Overall, OOPS! has analysed 969 ontologies (852 with URI and 117 anonymous). This set of random ontologies submitted by OOPS! users contains upper level ontologies, as well as domain ontologies. These ontologies were developed either by domain experts, students, newcomers or ontology experts.

Finally, Figure 9 shows in how many ontologies each pitfall implemented in OOPS! has been diagnosed. It shows an overview of the pitfalls detected regardless the updates on the number of pitfall implemented. Therefore, the number of pitfalls implemented along the table is not uniform. As already mentioned, pitfalls from P30 to P40 (marked with a * in Figure 9) were added in September 2013 and P41 (marked with ** in Figure 9) was added in March 2015.

Figure 9 reveals that most common pitfalls in ontologies are those related to the lack of explicit human and machine-readable information. However, these pitfalls do not correspond to those defined as critical by ontology practitioners but to those defined as "important" or "minor".

It is worth noting that "P41. No license declared", has been placed 7th in the ranking. This is a very significant fact as it represents one of the most common pitfalls even though it has been the last pitfall added, being evaluated only over 329 ontologies. In a similar way, several of the pitfalls added in September 2013 (namely, P35, P40, P30, P36 and P38) have reached positions in the top half of the ranking.

USER-BASED EVALUATION

OOPS! main goal is to get ontology evaluation closer to ontology developers, mainly newcomers and domain experts who are not familiar with description logics and ontology implementation languages.

In order to have an impression of the users' satisfaction when using OOPS!, a feedback form[22] is available online. Through this form users can express their impressions after using the system. The answers to the questionnaire received so far reveal that (a) the tool clearly shows which is the problem detected; (b) OOPS! is a useful system; and (c) users would use it again and recommend it to their col-

Figure 9. Most frequent pitfalls diagnosed by OOPS! in a set of 969 ontologies

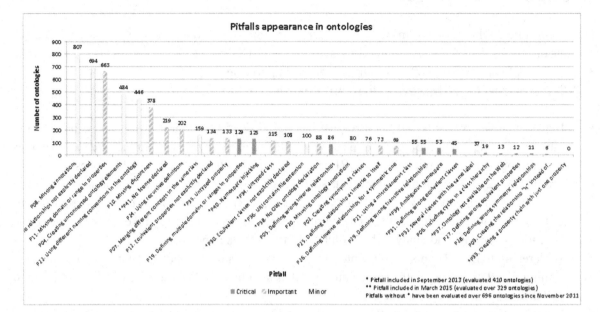

leagues. Some users also pointed out some drawbacks such as (a) only *rdfs:label* and *rdfs:comment* are considered as annotation but not *skos*[23] or *dc*[24] annotations; and (b) OOPS! does not provide suggestions about how to solve a problem.

In that questionnaire, users also indicated how the system effectively improved the ontologies and helped in the process of ontology curation. In this regard, users mainly pointed out that OOPS! was useful for (a) discovering potential missing statements (e.g. human readable annotations, domain and range declarations and property characterization as inverse, among others), (b) detecting incorrect pairs of inverse properties, (c) enriching property definitions (e.g. by adding the symmetric or transitive characteristic). Besides being used to diagnose ontologies, OOPS! has also been useful as part of the ontology assessment process in the context of ontologies for human behavior recognition, as explained in (Rodríguez et al., 2014).

We have also received feedback and suggestions by email in which users show their agreement or disagreement regarding, for example, (a) the pitfall "P13. Inverse relationships not explicitly declared", which is one of the typical debatable modeling decisions; or (b) when any pitfall detected affects ontology elements that belong to an imported ontology. More detailed information about this type of user evaluation can be found at (Poveda-Villalón, Suárez-Figueroa, & Gómez-Pérez, 2012).

Next, we present some evidence of how OOPS! has been used and adopted worldwide up to August 24th, 2015. To do so, we have analyzed the log files from the server and reports from google Analytics service. From these logs we have deduced that OOPS! homepage has been visited over 4000 times from around 90 different countries, and that the system has been executed around 3000 times[25] from 60 countries. It should be noted that the total number of different IP addresses for accessing and executing OOPS! is 1446 and 535, respectively.

Focusing on the ten countries from where OOPS! has been executed most, Figure 10 displays from how many counties OOPS! have been run. It also indicates the top ten countries from where it is used more often, including the number of executions registered.

Figure 10. Map with the top 10 countries executing OOPS!

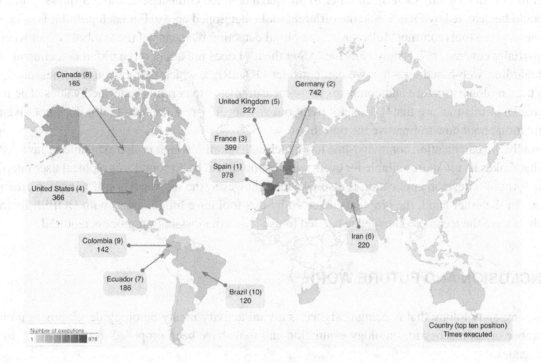

It is worth mentioning that the OOPS! web service[26] has been integrated by third-party software; more precisely, it has been integrated into the LOV[1] and Ontohub[28] repositories. Finally, the system has been distributed for local installation within some private enterprises since their security policies do not allow them to submit the ontologies to an external website.

RELATED WORK

While in the introduction of this work a number of methods and techniques on ontology evaluation have been reviewed, in this section we focus on existing tools. More precisely, we review topology-based tools for ontology evaluation, that is, those tools focused on the internal structure (classes, properties, instances, and the explicit and formal relations between them) of the ontology. Basic systems as syntax validators (e.g., RDF Validation Service[29] or Manchester OWL Validator[30]) are out of scope as they only check whether the ontology is compliant with the given ontology implementation language.

There are systems that depend on an associated ontology editor. This is the case of XD-Analyzer[31], a plug-in for NeOn Toolkit[32], and Ontocheck[33] (Schober et al., 2012), a plug-in for Protégé. The former checks some structural features (such as lack of domain and range definitions, use of intersection in domain and ranges, isolated entities, lack of annotations, and missing types, among others) and architectural features (e.g., unused imported ontologies), whereas the latter focuses on metadata aspects (e.g., annotations and naming conventions). The wiki-based ontology editor Moki[34] (Pammer, 2010) also provides some evaluation features (e.g., lack of annotation and orphaned elements). In addition, even though there is some overlap, the number of problems detected by these tools is lower than the current list of pitfalls detected by OOPS!. In order to provide a detailed comparison, Table 3 shows which pitfall could be detected by OOPS! and the different tools mentioned above. For each pitfall it is indicated whether a given tool (columns) fully covers the pitfall detection by means of the symbol "✓" or whether it is partially covered "≈". Empty cells mean that the tool does not address the pitfall detection at all.

Regarding web-based systems, we can consider OQuaRE[35], which extracts quality measurements from the ontology structure and compares these measurements to certain predefined values. The main drawbacks of this tool are that it does not point out any specific problem and that it does not give any information about how to improve the ontology.

Finally, we can mention command-line tools such as Eyeball[36], which is also available as Java API, a fact that makes its use more suitable for users with technological background. A graphical user interface in the form of a desktop application is also provided; however, the interface is still in an experimental phase. On the other hand, the problems detected by this tool have little overlap with OOPS!. Its main drawbacks are the technical knowledge needed to use it and the installation process required.

CONCLUSION AND FUTURE WORK

Evaluating an ontology that is being designed is a vital activity in any ontology development project. A number of approaches for ontology evaluation and tools have been proposed in the literature in the last decades.

In this work we have focused on a diagnosis method based on a checklist of common errors against which the ontology is compared. Our first contribution, in the form of a live catalogue of pitfalls, represents an extension of previous works about common problems in ontologies.

The automation of the detection process of 33 pitfalls included in the catalogue leads us to our second contribution: OOPS! (OntOlogy Pitfall Scanner!), an online tool for (semi-) automatic ontology diagnosis. This tool aims to help developers, mainly newcomers, during the ontology evaluation activity. OOPS! represents a step forward within ontology evaluation tools since (a) it enlarges the list of errors detected by most recent and available systems, such as MoKi (Pammer, 2010), XD-Analyzer and OntoCheck (Schober et al., 2012); (b) it is fully independent of any ontology development environment; (c) it works with the main web browsers (Firefox, Chrome, Safari, and Internet Explorer); and (d) its modular design facilitates the inclusion or removal of detection methods. In addition, the system could also be used for ontology selection. For example, when an organization wants to publish an existent data set as LD, the publisher has to choose one or more ontologies to model the published data. In this case, OOPS! could be used to compare the candidate ontologies along different quality dimensions.

It can be stated that the approach here presented has been widely accepted by the semantic web community and experts in other areas. Our approach is supported by the following facts:

- OOPS! has been broadly accepted by a high number of users worldwide and has been executed more than 3000 times from 60 different countries.
- It has been continuously used from very different geographical locations.
- It is integrated with third-party software (for example, Linked Open Vocabularies [Vandenbussche et al., 2017] or OntoHub [Mossakowski et al., 2014]) and locally installed in private enterprises (e.g., Semantic Arts[37] and Raytheon[38]).

Table 3. Comparative of pitfall coverage between tools (✓ pitfall covered by the tool, ≈ pitfall partially covered by the tool)

Pitfall	OOPS!	XD-Tools	Moki	Onto-check
P01. Creating polysemous elements				
P02. Creating synonyms as classes	✓			
P03. Creating the relationship "is" instead of using "rdfs:subClassOf", "rdf:type" or "owl:sameAs"	✓			
P04. Creating unconnected ontology elements	≈	✓	≈	≈
P05. Defining wrong inverse relationships	✓			
P06. Including cycles in a class hierarchy	✓			
P07. Merging different concepts in the same class	✓			✓
P08. Missing annotations	✓	✓	✓	✓
P09. Missing domain information				
P10. Missing disjointness	✓			
P11. Missing domain or range in properties	✓	✓	✓	
P12. Equivalent properties not explicitly declared	✓			
P13. Inverse relationships not explicitly declared	✓	✓		
P14. Misusing "owl:allValuesFrom"	☐			
P15. Using "some not" in place of "not some"				
P16. Using a primitive class in place of a defined one				
P17. Overspecializing a hierarchy				
P18. Overspecializing the domain or range				
P19. Defining multiple domains or ranges in properties	✓	✓		
P20. Misusing ontology annotations	✓			

continued in following column

Table 3. Continued

Pitfall	OOPS!	XD-Tools	Moki	Onto-check
P21. Using a miscellaneous class	✓			
P22. Using different naming conventions in the ontology	✓			✓
P23. Duplicating a datatype already provided by the implementation language				
P24. Using recursive definition	≈			
P25. Defining a relationship as inverse to itself	✓			
P26. Defining inverse relationships for a symmetric one	✓			
P27. Defining wrong equivalent properties				
P28. Defining wrong symmetric relationships				
P29. Defining wrong transitive relationships				
P30. Equivalent classes not explicitly declared	✓			
P31. Defining wrong equivalent classes	✓			
P32. Several classes with the same label	✓			
P33. Creating a property chain with just one property	✓			
P34. Untyped class	✓	✓		
P35. Untyped property	✓	✓		
P36. URI contains file extension	✓			
P37. Ontology not available on the Web	✓			
P38. No OWL ontology declaration	✓			
P39. Ambiguous namespace	✓			
P40. Namespace hijacking	✓			
P41. No license declared	✓			

To sum up, it could be stated that the approach proposed in this work has proof of being on the right track since it has become useful for ontology practitioners and for newcomers willing to evaluate their ontologies. All along the paper we have tried to show how both the catalogue and the tool are maintained and evolved according to users' feedback and research results.

Even though there are still several complex issues to address, our immediate future work will concentrate on the automation of the remaining pitfalls and the enhancement of some of the already implemented ones. This extension might require increasing the users' interaction with the system by keeping them on the loop and using natural language processing techniques as proposed in (Suárez-Figueroa, Kamel, & Poveda-Villalón, 2013). Future lines of work should incorporate the repair guidelines proposed in [Poveda-Villalón, 2016] into OOPS! in order to guide users in the ontology repair activity according to the detected pitfalls.

Focusing on the LOD scenario in which a huge amount of data is annotated by making use of ontologies, an immediate line of work is to consider such data during the evaluation with the purpose of enhancing the results. As a first step, mismatches between the model defined and the instantiated data could be detected as well as inconsistencies. An integration of this future work with

Loupe [Mihindukulasooriya et al., 2015], an online system for inspecting datasets, is also planned. This enhancement can also be applied to local knowledge bases.

Another line of work would involve making the system scalable for ontologies that contain a high number of terms. At the moment of writing this paper the system presents important delays with big ontologies, as for example DBpedia ontology[39], being the main bottleneck the number of object properties defined in the ontologies.

More ambitious plans include allowing users to define their own pitfalls or to contextualize existing ones and providing the mechanisms to interpret and process the pitfalls without manual encoding.

Finally, the integration of OOPS! within existing ontology editors, such as Protégé, would be very convenient for the users since they would not need to change platforms to repair their ontologies after the diagnosis phase.

ACKNOWLEDGMENT

We are very grateful to Rosario Plaza for her revisions of the English language; to Antonio Jiménez and Alfonso Mateos for their comments and help on statistics; to Mariano Fernández-López for his revision and suggestions on the ontology part; to Miguel García and Raúl Alcazar for their technical support; to all the anonymous reviewers, and finally, to OOPS! users.

REFERENCES

Aguado de Cea, G., Gómez-Pérez, A., Montiel-Ponsoda, E., & Suárez-Figueroa, M. C. (2008). Natural language-based approach for helping in the reuse of ontology design patterns. In Knowledge Engineering: Practice and Patterns (pp. 32-47). Springer Berlin Heidelberg. doi:10.1007/978-3-540-87696-0_6

Allemang, D., & Hendler, J. (2011). *Semantic web for the working ontologist: effective modeling in RDFS and OWL*. Elsevier.

Archer, P., Goedertier, S., & Loutas, N. (2012). *D7. 1.3–Study on persistent URIs, with identification of best practices and recommendations on the topic for the MSs and the EC*. PwC EU Services.

Barron, F. H., & Barrett, B. E. (1996). Decision quality using ranked attribute weights. *Management Science, 42*(11), 1515–1523. doi:10.1287/mnsc.42.11.1515

Berners-Lee, T., Hendler, J., & Lassila, O. (2001). The semantic web. *Scientific American, 284*(5), 28–37. doi:10.1038/scientificamerican0501-34 PMID:11341160

Blomqvist, E., Gangemi, A., & Presutti, V. (2009). *Experiments on pattern-based ontology design*. In *Proceedings of the fifth international conference on Knowledge capture* (pp. 41-48). ACM. doi:10.1145/1597735.1597743

Burton-Jones, A., Storey, V. C., Sugumaran, V., & Ahluwalia, P. (2005). A semiotic metrics suite for assessing the quality of ontologies. *Data & Knowledge Engineering, 55*(1), 84–102. doi:10.1016/j.datak.2004.11.010

Djedidi, R., & Aufaure, M. A. (2010). ONTO-EVOAL an ontology evolution approach guided by pattern modeling and quality evaluation. In Foundations of Information and Knowledge Systems (pp. 286-305). Springer Berlin Heidelberg.

Duque-Ramos, A., Fernández-Breis, J. T., Stevens, R., & Aussenac-Gilles, N. (2011). OQuaRE: A SQuaRE-based approach for evaluating the quality of ontologies. *Journal of Research and Practice in Information Technology, 43*(2), 159.

Fellbaum, C. (1998). *WordNet: An electronic lexical database*. Retrieved from http://www. cogsci. princeton. edu/wn

Fernández-López, M., Gómez-Pérez, A., Sierra, J. P. & Sierra, A. P. (1999). Building a chemical ontology using methontology and the ontology design environment. *IEEE Intelligent Systems and their Applications, 14*(1), 37-46.

Gangemi, A., Catenacci, C., Ciaramita, M., & Lehmann, J. (2006). *Modelling ontology evaluation and validation*. Springer Berlin Heidelberg.

Gómez-Pérez, A. (2004). Ontology Evaluation. In S. Staab & R. Studer (Eds.), *Handbook on Ontologies* (pp. 251–273). Springer. doi:10.1007/978-3-540-24750-0_13

Guarino, N., & Welty, C. A. (2009). An overview of OntoClean. In *Handbook on ontologies* (pp. 201–220). Springer Berlin Heidelberg. doi:10.1007/978-3-540-92673-3_9

Heath, T., & Bizer, C. (2011). Linked data: Evolving the web into a global data space. *Synthesis Lectures on the Semantic Web: Theory and Technology, 1*(1), 1-136.

Hogan, A., Harth, A., Passant, A., Decker, S., & Polleres, A. (2010). Weaving the pedantic web. *Linked Data on the Web Workshop*.

Ji, Q., Haase, P., Qi, G., Hitzler, P., & Stadtmüller, S. (2009). RaDON—repair and diagnosis in ontology networks. In *The semantic web: research and applications* (pp. 863–867). Springer Berlin Heidelberg. doi:10.1007/978-3-642-02121-3_71

Miettinen, K. (1999). *Non-linear Multiobjective Optimization*. Kluwer Academic Publishers.

Mihindukulasooriya, N., Poveda-Villalón, M., García-Castro, R., & Gómez-Pérez, A. (2015). Loupe - An Online Tool for Inspecting Datasets in the Linked Data Cloud. In *Proceedings of the ISWC 2015 Posters & Demonstrations Track co-located with the 14th International Semantic Web Conference (ISWC-2015)*. CEUR-WS.org. 213

Mossakowski, T., Kutz, O., & Codescu, M. (2014). Ontohub: A semantic repository for heterogeneous ontologies. In *Proc. of the Theory Day in Computer Science (DACS-2014), Satellite workshop of IC-TAC-2014*. University of Bucharest.

Noy, N. F., & McGuinness, D. L. (2001*). Ontology development 101: A guide to creating your first ontology*. Technical Report SMI-2001-0880. Standford Medical Informatics.

Pammer, V. (2010) *PhD Thesis: Automatic Support for Ontology Evaluation Review of Entailed Statements and Assertional Effects for OWL Ontologies*. Engineering Sciences, Graz University of Technology.

Pinto, H. S., Staab, S., & Tempich, C. (2004). DILIGENT: Towards a fine-grained methodology for Distributed, Loosely-controlled and evolvInG. In *ECAI 2004: Proceedings of the 16th European Conference on Artificial Intelligence* (*Vol. 110*, p. 393). IOS Press.

Poveda-Villalón, M. (2016). *Ontology Evaluation: A pitfall-based approach to ontology diagnosis* (Doctoral dissertation). ETSI_Informaticos.

Poveda-Villalón, M., Suárez-Figueroa, M. C., & Gómez-Pérez, A. (2010). A double classification of common pitfalls in ontologies. *Workshop on Ontology Quality at the 17th International Conference on Knowledge Engineering and Knowledge Management*.

Poveda-Villalón, M., Suárez-Figueroa, M. C., & Gómez-Pérez, A. (2012). Validating ontologies with oops! In *Knowledge Engineering and Knowledge Management* (pp. 267–281). Springer Berlin Heidelberg. doi:10.1007/978-3-642-33876-2_24

Poveda-Villalón, M., Vatant, B., Suárez-Figueroa, M. C., & Gómez-Pérez, A. (2013). Detecting Good Practices and Pitfalls when Publishing Vocabularies on the Web. *Workshop on Ontology Patterns at the 12th International Semantic Web Conference*.

Presutti, V., Gangemi, A., David S., Aguado, G., Suárez-Figueroa, M.C., Montiel-Ponsoda, E. & Poveda, M. (2008). *NeOn D2.5.1: A Library of Ontology Design Patterns: reusable solutions for collaborative design of networked ontologies*. NeOn project. (FP6-27595)

Rector, A., Drummond, N., Horridge, M., Rogers, J., Knublauch, H., Stevens, R., & Wroe, C. et al. (2004). OWL pizzas: Practical experience of teaching OWL-DL: Common errors & common patterns. In *Engineering Knowledge in the Age of the Semantic Web* (pp. 63–81). Springer Berlin Heidelberg. doi:10.1007/978-3-540-30202-5_5

Rodríguez, N. D., Cuéllar, M. P., Lilius, J., & Calvo-Flores, M. D. (2014). A survey on ontologies for human behavior recognition. *ACM Computing Surveys*, *46*(4), 43. doi:10.1145/2523819

Schober, D., Tudose, I., Svatek, V. & Boeker, M. (2012). OntoCheck: verifying ontology naming conventions and metadata completeness in Protégé 4. *Journal of Biomedical Semantics, 3*(S2), S4.

Staab, S., Studer, R., Schnurr, H. P., & Sure, Y. (2001). Knowledge processes and ontologies. *IEEE Intelligent Systems*, *16*(1), 26–34. doi:10.1109/5254.912382

Strasunskas, D., & Tomassen, S. L. (2008). The role of ontology in enhancing semantic searches: the EvOQS framework and its initial validation. *International Journal of Knowledge and Learning*, *4*(4), 398-414.

Suárez-Figueroa, M. C. (2010). *NeOn Methodology for Building Ontology Networks: Specification, Scheduling and Reuse* (PhD thesis). Universidad Politécnica de Madrid.

Suárez-Figueroa, M. C., Cea, G. A. D., & Gómez-Pérez, A. (2013). Lights and shadows in creating a glossary about ontology engineering. *Terminology*, *19*(2), 202–236. doi:10.1075/term.19.2.03sua

Suárez-Figueroa, M. C., Gómez-Pérez, A., Motta, E., & Gangemi, A. (Eds.). (2012). *Ontology engineering in a networked world*. Springer. doi:10.1007/978-3-642-24794-1

Suárez-Figueroa, M. C., Kamel, M., & Poveda-Villalón, M. (2013). Benefits of Natural Language Techniques in Ontology Evaluation: the OOPS! Case. *10th International Conference on Terminology and Artificial Intelligence (TIA 2013)*.

Vandenbussche, P. Y., Atemezing, G. A., Poveda-Villalón, M., & Vatant, B. (2017). Linked Open Vocabularies (LOV): A gateway to reusable semantic vocabularies on the Web. *Semantic Web Journal*, *8*(3), 437–452. doi:10.3233/SW-160213

Vrandecic, D. (2010). *Ontology Evaluation* (PhD thesis). KIT.

Winkler, R. L. & Hays, W. (1985). *Statistics: Probability, inference, and decision*. Academic Press.

ENDNOTES

[1] http://www.w3.org/DesignIssues/LinkedData.html

[2] http://neon-toolkit.org/wiki/XDTools

[3] http://protegewiki.stanford.edu/wiki/OntoCheck

[4] https://moki.fbk.eu/website/index.php

[5] It should be observed that the term "pitfall" is used all along this paper for characteristics that often represent a problem or that could lead to errors in ontologies; however, this is not always the case. In other words, depending on the ontology at hand, pitfalls can or cannot represent an actual error.

[6] http://www.w3.org/TR/owl-ref/

[7] http://www.w3.org/TR/rdf-primer/

[8] The online version of the catalogue is available at http://oops.linkeddata.es/catalogue. Previous versions were included in (Poveda-Villalón, Suárez-Figueroa, & Gómez-Pérez, 2010) and (Poveda-Villalón, Suárez-Figueroa, & Gómez-Pérez, 2012).

[9] The call was launched through several mailing list used by the semantic web community and through particular emails sent to known OOPS! users, mainly experts on ontology modeling or evaluation.

[10] It is worth mentioning, since it could seem contradictory, that for processing the data and ranking the pitfalls we have assigned the value 3 for critical pitfalls, so that they appear in the top positions. However, for assigning importance levels within the catalogue we have set the "critical" position in 1, since the critical pitfalls should be corrected in first place.

[11] See file "SurveyImportanceLevelsLexcicographicOrder.pdf" at http://goo.gl/0IkbS2.

[12] The data and calculations for obtaining the coefficients are available at http://goo.gl/QeSyHX

[13] Figure 3 also indicates which pitfalls are currently implemented by OOPS!.

[14] http://www.oracle.com/technetwork/java/javaee/overview/index.html

[15] http://www.w3.org/html/wg/

[16] http://jquery.com/

[17] http://www.oracle.com/technetwork/java/javaee/jsp/index.html

[18] http://www.w3.org/Style/CSS/

[19] http://jena.sourceforge.net/

[20] At the moment of writing this document no inference is used during the evaluation process.

[21] http://oops-ws.oeg-upm.net/

[22] http://goo.gl/9W7bLl

[23] skos is the prefix used for the namespace http://purl.org/linked-data/xkos#

[24] dc is the prefix used for the namespace http://purl.org/dc/terms/

[25] It is worth mentioning that these executions are those registered in the server log since May 2012. This log is different from the OOPS! log of executions that gathers ontologies and results since November 2011.

[26] http://oops-ws.oeg-upm.net/

[27] http://lov.okfn.org/

[28] See http://goo.gl/TKHr5z for more information.

[29] http://www.w3.org/RDF/Validator/

[30] http://owl.cs.manchester.ac.uk/validator/

[31] http://neon-toolkit.org/wiki/XDTools

[32] http://neon-toolkit.org/wiki/Main_Page

[33] http://protegewiki.stanford.edu/wiki/OntoCheck

[34] https://moki.fbk.eu/website/index.php

[35] http://miuras.inf.um.es:9080/oqmodelsliteclient/

[36] http://jena.sourceforge.net/Eyeball/

[37] http://semanticarts.com/

[38] http://www.raytheon.com/

[39] http://wiki.dbpedia.org/Ontology

Chapter 6
Exploring Fuzzy Association Rules in Semantic Network Enrichment Improvement of the Semantic Indexing Process

Souheyl Mallat
Faculty of Science of Monastir, Tunisia

Emna Hkiri
LATICE Laboratory, Tunisia

Mounir Zrigui
Faculty of Science of Monastir, Tunisia

ABSTRACT

In the aim of natural language processing applications improvement, we focus on statistical approach to semantic indexing for multilingual text documents based on conceptual network formalism. We propose to use this formalism as an indexing language to represent the descriptive concepts and their weighting. Our contribution is based on two steps. In the first step, we propose the extraction of index terms using the multilingual lexical resource EuroWordNet (EWN). In the second step, we pass from the representation of index terms to the representation of index concepts through conceptual network formalism. This network is generated using the EWN resource and pass by a classification step based on association rules modelOur proposed indexing approach can be applied to text documents in various languages. Next, we apply the same statistical process regardless of the language in order to extract the significant concepts and their associated weights. We prove that the proposed indexing approach provides encouraging results.

DOI: 10.4018/978-1-5225-5042-6.ch006

1. INTRODUCTION

It is known that ambiguities of natural language, have a detrimental effect on the results of query terms translation in the context of information retrieval by crossing languages. However, research efforts to integrate sense disambiguation techniques in machine translation (MT) have not been successful and get unconvincing results. In addition, our automatic translation system (ATS) (Jianfeng et al., 2001) requires a high precision of disambiguation to achieve an effect on the selection of the best translation in the target language of ambiguous words.

The semantic disambiguation process of the query in the target language is based on a similar document language as the query. This document is a list of relevant sentences (most similar to a user query); these sentences noted List_S are satisfying the query, and they are classified according to their degree of linguistic relevance (semantic, morphological). Building this List_S of words is presented in the work (Mallat et al., 2013) (Mallat et al., 2014). The same lists (of French and English sentences are the result of the multilingual parallel corpus alignment. Both versions of the lists are used as resources for the disambiguation process in the queries translation (Arabic-French) and (Arabic-English). The process is to match the query and the List_S content to find the words of the query in the target language that best fits this List_S. A key feature of the method of disambiguation is that the degree of matching of each translation of an ambiguous word and List_S depends on the highest weight.

Note that this List_S is expressed by singular characteristics of specific themes such as semantic and morphological wealth that is supposed to represent the best the relevant answers to a given query. Indeed, the disambiguation process improvement requires providing an effective method for representing and better analyzing the contents of this list.

In this paper, we focus on the extraction of the concepts (descriptors) or index concepts in order to associate for each document (List_S) a representation of its contents by concepts and their associated weights.

To do this, we focus our work to propose a statistical approach to semantic indexing of multilingual documents (French or English) that are taken only on calculations of the frequency of words. Also, we focus on exploiting taxonomic and non taxonomic relations (contextual) between terms. The proposed indexing approach consists of:

1. Extracting the significant words or index terms associated with the concepts of a document in English or French, based on the two external lexical resource (multilingual thesaurus) EuroWordNet (EWN French and English EWN) (Gonzalo et al., 1998) (Vossen et al., 1997). As we consider that a EWN is composed of a set of lexicons and a set of relations between them designated by concepts.
2. The construction and exploitation of conceptual network formalism of a document that requires the extraction of concept nodes and relations between them extracted from the previous step. In the extraction of relations, we rely on the EWN resource to identify the taxonomic relations, and we add the fuzzy association rules model to identify non taxonomic relations (contextual) between concepts. This model represents an inference mechanism to discover these latent relations, buried in List_S and carried by the semantic context. The goal of this model is to better represent the semantic content of the document. Thus, the novelty of this model involves two aspects: (1) co-occurrence of terms is taken into account during indexing of the List_S. The model's descriptors are no longer words but sets of index terms (term-sets). The term sets capture the intuition that

semantically related terms appear near one another in a List_S. (2) To estimate the importance of the word in the document not only by its frequency of occurrence, but also by semantic proximity and contextual values with the rest of the terms in the List_S.

3. The index concepts are generated with new weights that better represent the content of the List_S by conceptual network formalism.

The paper is organized as follows: section 2 presents the existing problems, namely the disparity of terms and ambiguity faced in the indexing process. In Section 3, we present a bacground and state of the art of the indexing methods. In Section 4 we detail our indexing approach. In Section 5, we present experiments comparison and discussion of the results. Section 6 concludes the paper.

2. PROBLEMATIC

We address in our work three types of problems:

*   The disparity in terms: this problem refers to terms that are lexically different but having related senses (e.g. Cases of synonymy, hyperonymy / hyponymy relations) (Kamal et al., 2015). In classical indexing, the disparity in terms causes the limit restitutions of relevant terms. Hence, this reduces the precision and recall of the indexing method.
*   The semantic ambiguity: this ambiguity relates to the homonyms of words or the multiple meanings of words. Homonym characterizes distinct concepts that are lexically represented by the same word. Polysemy characterizes a word having many senses.
*   The syntactic ambiguity: this ambiguity means that a word appears in various grammatical forms. We find the same word appears as a verb and as a noun, but these two instances do not have the same sense.

3. BACKGROUND AND RELATED WORK

3.1. Extraction of Semantic Relations From Texts

In this section, we present the different semantic relations that can exist between terms, also the different formalisms of knowledge representation. We illustrate two methods of semantic relation acquisition.

3.1.1. Overview of Semantic Relations in Terminology

Terminology are intended to identify the terms of a specific domain, that is to say linguistic units denoting a concept, an object or a process in the given domain (Bourigault, 2000), but also the semantic relations between these terms among themselves. Several types of semantic relations are proposed by terminology resources (Sager, 1990), the choice to include a type of relations is especially dependent on the used resource:

- **The Synsets (Synonym Set):** Represents the sense of the word that defines the set of synonyms and are interconnected by conceptual and semantic-lexical relations (Turenne, 2000). For example the synonymy of person is individual.

- **Taxonomic Relations:** This type structures the terms in a form of tree. Hypernymy relations (is-a) link a general term to a specific term. For example, the hypernym relations between furniture and wardrobe. For example: hyponymy relations (IS-A) is a lexical relation between word senses and more precisely between sets of synonyms synset (Synonym Set). This relation is defined by: X is a hyponym of Y if X is a sort of Y is true. For example a dog is a hyponym of animal and animal is a dog hyperonym. A cat is a hyponym of animal and animal is hypernym of cat. And partitive relations (part-whole or meronymy) are used to define a relation between two terms where one is a part of the other. For example, the hydrogen and oxygen are meronyms of the water (that are the components of the water molecule.

- **The Lexical Semantic Relations:** Combine two types of relations: the first is relations of synonymy or equivalence that connects words with the same meaning for example to defend and to interdict. The second is antonym or opposition relations that connect words with opposite meanings for example free and prisoner.

- Inter-hierarchical relations (transversal) link terms belonging to different branches of one or more hierarchies. These relations are highly variable depending on the domain. For example, the relation ''localized in'' permits linking the words ''cell division'' and ''cell''.

The development of the first systems had been marked by an empirical approach, and the lack of methodology specifying the general principles underlying the construction of these formalisms. Indeed, the set of primitives that underpin these networks is defined a fairly vague, and it becomes too imprecise when it comes to represent a complex field.

Other work later, sought to take advantage of dictionaries for the semantic representation as those of (Richardson, 1997; Grefenstette, 1994). But these are based on classic dictionaries, suffering from lack of conceptual relations. In the following we present the different formalisms of knowledge tacking into account other relations other than synonymy.

3.1.2. Knowledge Representation Formalisms of Semantic Networks

The network theory is considered as a good feature of representation formalism or knowledge structuring. There is different formalism which considered semantic network. The different formalisms are very close in terms of structuring, but the use is different depending on the needs of NLP tasks. There are many types of knowledge representation formalism, like the conceptual graph, ontology, thesauri, and taxonomies. In what follows we describe the characteristics of each type of them.

1. **Conceptual Graph:** A conceptual graph is a labeled graph, composed of nodes representing concepts connected by arcs, as the concept has no meaning without the relations with other related concepts. The relations (arcs) of the graph typically represent binary values between concepts. These concepts can be classes, objects, or some abstract things, and binary relations. Conceptual graphs allow several ways of expressing knowledge such as queries, rules and facts. These graphs are based on a language key of their ease and their similarity to other graphic modeling language

such as UML (Unified Modeling Language) we find the representation of the relations-entities. This representation facilitates users understanding and manipulation of data.

2. **Ontology:** The value of ontology is the organization and structuring of the contents of the voluminous mass of information in all areas. This structure facilitates internal communication to the information system. Ontology is an explicit specification of a conceptualization (Guarino, 2000): the ontology typically contains taxonomic and semantic relations connected to a set of concepts describing a specific domain. According to the definition given by Charlet (2002), the ontology can take many forms such as a relational representation in formal language but essentially contains the notions of a term vocabulary and their meanings. Ontology is considered as the first in the artificial intelligence (AI) domain, used in the construction of logical theories of IA system, called intelligent system.

3. **Taxonomy:** Taxonomy is a semantic resource considered as ontology whose grammar was not formalized, its relations are defined in implicit way, it is only composed by subsumption relations in order to structure controlled vocabularies. It is organized with the terms of the relations of generations or hyperonymy (is-a) and relations of specification or hyponymy (sort-of).

4. **Thesaurus:** The thesaurus is a resource used to represent, annotate, index and classify documents. The main function of the thesaurus is to avoid grouping the terms of the same shape but different in meaning. Note that the thesaurus uses a controlled and hierarchical vocabulary and restricted to one specialty area. Thesauri include tokens or descriptors used to represent the concepts to facilitate the description of the documents in a given domain. These descriptors are defined in different contexts in the thesaurus, the concepts appear uniquely. A thesaurus is structured alphabetically like a dictionary, also it provides semantic relations (synonymy, hyperonymy, hyponymy), and associative relations between terms and the definition of each term. In what follows, we present the strategies proposed to acquire semantic relations.

3.1.3. Strategies of Acquisition of Semantic Relations Based on the Context of the Terms

3.1.3.1. Acquisition Strategy Based on Lexical-Syntactic Patterns

This strategy aims is to define lexical-syntactic patterns characteristics of the target relation (Auger & Barrier, 2008). The patterns are defined from observations corpus and used to extract hypernoymy relations. The use of an automatic identification method of lexical-syntactic patterns corpus allows refining the observations and obtaining better results (Morin, 1999). Transversal relations can also be gained through this strategy (Hamon & al., 2010). The syntactic patterns are then built by supervised learning on syntactic dependence paths between terms. Filter along the length of these paths is then applied. This is also the case when it comes to identify inter-hierarchical relations. The lexical and syntactic patterns are the basis for the learning model definition using SVM (Grouin & al., 2010). In both works, the entities put in relations and their semantic types are known, which is generally the case in conventional approaches to acquire semantic relations between terms. Clues found in corpus in the context can be exploited to infer patterns by Inductive Logic Programming (Claveau & Man, 2004). Hypernymy relations, in the first work, or relations between verbs and nouns in the second, can thus be identified. It is also noted that the lexical-syntactic patterns are rarely used for the acquisition of synonymy relations. However, it seems that some specialty areas, such as biology, are better suited (Weissenbacher, 2004; McCrae, 2008).

3.1.3.2. Strategies of Acquisition Based on the Exploitation of Contextual Distribution Terms

Another use of the context of terms is to provide a distributional analysis (Harris, 1990) in order to group terms sharing contexts (originally syntactic). For example, the terms kidney failure and respiratory distress are semantically close as they share the same contexts care of renal failure and care of respiratory distress, kidney failure and respiratory distress. It is thus possible to identify a semantic relation of proximity between terms (Bourigault & al., 2004) or even synonymy relation (Ferret, 2011). For example, in (Grefenstette, 1994), distributional analysis applied to medical corpus can identify several types of relations: synonymy (large / major / great) meronymy (patient / group) as well as hyperonymy relations patient / woman. This strategy was also used by Resnik (1993) in order to highlight the relations associated with the semantic terms. It is then to replace these terms in the context by their semantic classes, from WordNet. For example, the nurse and doctor terms are replaced by health profession class.

If we summarize a comparison between the various resources used and the two strategies presented above in knowledge representation in a semantic network; we note that these resources provide hierarchical relations (hyperonymy, hyponymy), meronymy relations, synonymies, and associative relations. One of the most frequent criticisms on the work using the formalism of representation, that it does not take into account the contextual relations which are defined implicitly between terms.

3.2. Related Work: The Impact of Different Formalism on the Performance of the Indexing Process

In last decades, many researches in IR have turned to the consideration of the semantics of words in the indexing process by making it capable of dealing with the problems mentioned above. We distinguish the following works:

The work of Kaleta presents a specific issue of semantic analysis of texts in natural language (Kaleta, 2014); text indexing and describes one field of its application (web browsing). The main part of this article describes a computer system assigning a set of semantic indexes (similar to keywords) to a particular text. The indexing algorithm employs a semantic dictionary to find specific words in a text that represent text content. Furthermore, it compares two given sets of semantic indexes to determine similarities between texts (assigning a numerical value). The following section presents one possible approach to the creation of an automatic text indexing system. It uses semantic analysis based on ontology. Semantic indexes are concepts interpreted as in the semantic dictionary. Their roles are the same but they have two main advantages over traditional keywords. The first one is that they are never ambiguous. While a keyword still may have multiple meanings, a semantic index represents only one of those meanings. The second one is that they form a hierarchical structure contained in the semantic dictionary, which allows better automatic processing. The author tested using a corpus of more than fifty thousand short press notes from the Polish Press Agency. The results of this part of the algorithm were also compared to the results of the SVM algorithm using a cosine measure with two different weights: binary and tf-idf. The most important difference is the spread of values. In the case of the semantic algorithm, they range from 0.3 to 0.5, for the SVM with tf-idf from 0.163 to 0.630 and for the SVM with binary weights from 0.211 to 0.9. When searching for texts similar to a given one, a larger spread increases the number of false positives.

In the work of Baziz, authors represent a document by concepts and relations between them (Baziz et al., 2005) (Baziz, 2005). This approach consists of projecting (mapping) the textual content of a document on the WordNet. Extracted terms are then weighted by a new measure CF-IDF (CTF pour

Composite Term Frequency). The value of the weighting is to keep the most representative terms of the document content. Ambiguous terms that belong with several concepts are disambiguated according to this principle: the concept that corresponds to the proper sense of the term is the one that is strongly linked with other words in the document. Finally, the document is represented by a semantic network. This approach was evaluated as part of the CLEF campaign in 2004, using an information retrieval system based on the connectionist model (Boughanem et al., 1998). In addition Baziz propose the DocTree approach that projects the semantic networks from the DocCore method on the "is-a" hierarchy of the WordNet ontology (Baziz et al., 2005). To assess the relevance of document/query, their respective sub trees are compared on the basis of fuzzy operators. These fuzzy operators evaluate to what extent the document deals with the theme described in the query and assign a degree of relevance to the document.

In a different approach, Mallak indexes documents by clustering the most representative concepts of their semantic content (Mallak, 2011). He takes the same mapping technique proposed by Baziz for the detection of key terms. Mallak proposes a new method of disambiguation based on the notion of centrality (Mallak, 2011) (Boughanem et al., 2010). He defines the centrality of concepts-term by the number of semantic relations in WordNet (synonyms, hyperonymy, etc.) that share with the concepts of the other terms in the document. Once all significant terms-concepts of a document are determined, they are grouped into clusters.

Mallak experienced his approach on two collections TREC1 and TREC7. Moreover the proposed disambiguation technique provides more accuracy gain higher than 5% compared to the disambiguation technique of Baziz. Moreover, Malek tested the contribution of its research model and concluded that this model is more efficient than the classical search model

The work of Harrathi offers a multilingual semantic indexing approach in the multilingual information retrieval (Harrathi et al., 2010). This approach begins with the weighting of single and composite words by the CF-IDF measure. The indexing terms whose weight is above a minimum threshold are then projected onto a multilingual semantic ontology in order to get the concepts which define the possible senses of these terms. To find the appropriate sense (or concept) for each ambiguous term, we propose a process of disambiguation. To do this, the context of the target word is first constructed based on the set of all phrases where it appears. Then, a score is assigned to each candidate concept of this term (depending on number of relations in the ontology). The highest score is then selected as the exact meaning.

The authors used two techniques of linguistic and semantic disambiguation. Harrathi evaluated their approach by incorporating it into an information retrieval system based on a language model proposed by Maisonnasse, using the medical resource UMLS (Maisonnasse et al., 2009) and the test collection CLEF 2007. The results showed that this approach provides a gain in precision of 5% compared to a classical indexing.

In biomedical domain, we find Dinh work, which presents an indexing approach based on the concepts of thesaurus MeSh in biomedical IR (Dinh, 2012). Dinh has proposed two techniques of disambiguation (disambiguation of near to near, disambiguation based on improvement). These two techniques assign to each ambiguous concept the proper sense in the context of use. Finally, when applied on medical journals of OHSUMED collection. The results show that information retrieval system results improved with both disambiguation techniques compared to those obtained by classical indexing weighted by Okapi BM25 (a performance gain of 17.35%).

In conclusion, we have reviewed the various approaches of semantic indexing in IR. These approaches have demonstrated that the representation of documents by their concepts is beneficial in the research process. This aids to solve problems of classical approaches. The senses are often identified by disambiguation approaches using external linguistic resources. Based on this same principle, we present in this paper our contribution to the definition of a new method of semantic indexing. This method takes in account the frequency of the term and its taxonomic and non-taxonomic relations with the other terms.

Plus précisement we can also be inspired by the acquisition strategy based on the exploitation of contextual distribution of terms to replace the single compounds by their terms and concepts (represent the nodes in our network) from the lexical database EWNF.

The works presented above reflects the importance of this domain and shows some diversity in formalism representation and strategies to acquire semantic relations between terms. In this paper, we propose first a methodology to represent the List_S by semantic network formalism similar to the work of (Leacock, 1998; Lin, 1998; Agrawal, 1994). Our network is composed essentially of concepts associated to significant terms identified from the List_S. So, we propose in the first step a method of representation of the List_S by a enrichement semantic network formalism (adding other hidden contextual relations) in order to improve the semantic indexing process.

4. PROPOSED INDEXING METHOD

This approach can benefit more by the co-occurrence relations to highlight the terms that may not be frequent but have strong relations of co-occurrences. These last may be discriminatory. Thus, our approach is applied regardless of the language through the existence of multilingual resources. This is performed in two main steps: in a first step, our work focuses on extracting the significant words or index terms from the List_S, based on multilingual thesaurus EuroWordNet (Gonzalo et al., 1998) (Vossen et al., 1997) and calculating statistics. These index terms represent the semantic content of a List-S. In the second step, our work is based on the construction and exploitation of a conceptual network that addresses the semantic and contextual relations between concepts. This step aims to improve the semantic content in terms of indexes generated by the first step. The following figure shows the general architecture of our approach of semantic indexing.

The indexing method consists of two main steps:

4.1. Concept Extraction

The first step in the indexing method is to extract concepts from multilingual List_S. We identify concepts by identifying the index terms that denote in the documents by projecting these words on EWN (mapping). Next, we present these steps in detail: extraction of candidate terms, weightings of word, semantic disambiguation of terms Index and the transformation of terms representation to the concept representation.

4.1.1. Extraction of Candidate Terms

The objective of this step is to extract all the terms from the semantic content of the List_S, by projection on the semantic network EWN. The extraction is to detect simply and composite terms. The identification of composite terms in the list is important for improving the performance of the automatic indexing.

The use of composite terms in the list of sentences greatly reduces the ambiguity of words and improves the precision (reduces the number of senses of a word). The method of identification of simple and

Figure 1. General architecture of our approach to semantic indexing

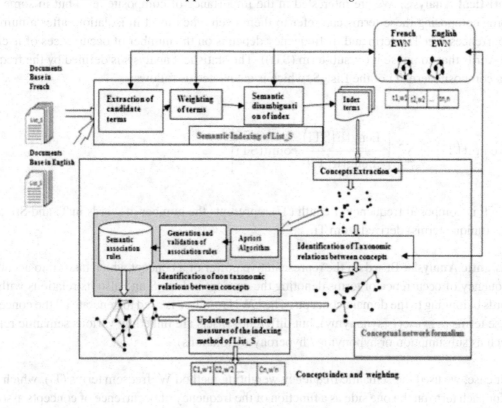

composite terms that we have adopted is based on a symbolic method, which is similar to that presented in (Okita et al., 2010), in their method the authors define patterns to extract noun phrases.

Our proposed method simply requires a morpho-syntactic analysis of the List_S through the TreeTagger tool of Helmut (Schmid, 1997). The analysis provided by TreeTagger, produces a list of tagged words with their grammatical categories. Most of composite terms consist of combinations of nouns, adjectives or prepositions. We produce a list of n-grams ($2 \leq n \leq 3$), whose morphosyntactic structure complies with the following patterns: (Noun + adj, noun + noun, noun + prep + noun).

Noun+adj: Example: "champ sémantique"(engl. "Semantic field"), "définition lexicale" (engl. lexical definition);

Noun+Noun: "roi ban"(engl. "King Ban");

Noun+Prep+Noun: "partie du discours" (engl. "part of speech"), "dictionnaire de langue" (engl. "language dictionary").

4.1.2. Weightings of Candidate Terms

Once simple and composite terms are extracted from the List_S, we do attribute their weight in the List_S. The purpose of this step is to eliminate the least frequent terms in the List_S and keep only the most relevant. To this end, we have proposed a weighting method, which combines statistical and semantic analysis (Huang and Robertson, 2001). The method assigned the terms of the List_S optimally in terms of frequency of each term with their semantic variation.

1. **Statistical Analysis:** We are interested in the importance of composite term but in some cases, words composing these terms can refer to them even when used in isolation, after a number of occurrences. Let Ti a term and its frequency depends on the number of occurrences of itself, and the words that compose it (or sub-term (STi)). The statistical analysis is defined by the frequency of a composite term Ti of the List_S, which is calculated as follows:

$$\text{CF(Ti)} = \text{count}\left(\text{Ti}\right) + \sum_{\text{ST} \in \text{Ti}} \left(\frac{\text{Length}\left(\text{STi}\right)}{\text{Length}\left(\text{Ti}\right)} . \text{count(STi}\right) \tag{1}$$

With CF is composed frequency; Length (Ti) represents the number of words in Ti and Sti, are the sub terms (unique terms) derived from Ti.

2. **Semantic Analysis:** Based on the representative power of a concept which takes into account the frequency of occurrence of terms denoting the concept in List_S and also its relations with other words belonging to the domain concepts. The EWN resource is used to generate all the concepts on these terms as synset1 (synonymy), but different synsets are linked by various semantic relations (such as subsumption or hyponymy / hyperonymy relations).

In our case, we used the semantic frequency weighting method W_freqsem terms (Ti), which is calculated for each term on the one side as a function of the frequency of occurrence of concepts associated with it, on the other side according to the ranks of the sentences which they belong. The coefficients corresponding to each sentence are assigned as follows, if a term belongs to the first sentence its coefficient is 10, 9 for second, and 1 for the tenth and the remaining sentences of List_S.

Suppose a term Ti appears p times in the List_S containing n terms, Mi,j is the coefficient related to sentences containing the conceptual occurrence j of the term Ti. The different senses associated with this term, extracted from a EWN, and for each sense of a term we associate a synset, as well as all semantic relations. The weight of semantic frequency W_freqsem of a term Ti in the List_S is calculated as follows:

$$\text{Wfreq-sem(Ti)} = \frac{\text{P}\left(\text{Ti}\right)}{\max_{p=1\ldots n}\left(\text{P}\left(\text{Tp}\right)\right) * \text{ns}} \tag{2}$$

where:

$$\text{P}\left(\text{Ti}\right) = \sum_{j=1}^{K} \left(\text{Mi, j}\right)$$

$P\left(Ti\right)$ denotes the weight of the term Ti, and ns=k – number (Mi,j=0) (ns:is the number of possible senses of Ti).

W (Ti, List_S) represents the global weight of the term Ti in the List_S, it is defined by the following expression W (Ti, List_S) =Wti= CF (Ti)* Wfreq-sem(Ti). Finally the terms index of the List_S are noted Index (List_S) = (Ti,Wti).

4.1.3. Semantic Disambiguation of Index Terms (SDI)

Semantic disambiguation is a very important task for improving the indexing process. The principle of the disambiguation method is to choose the best concept (sense). In the semantic disambiguation step, we are inspired by the method used by (Baziz et al., 2004) taking into account the representativeness of terms in the context of List_S. So, the best sense for a term Ti in the List_S must be highly correlated with senses associated with other important terms in the List_S. For this reason, we will integrate the weight of the term in the calculation of conceptual scores; it is calculated using the following formula:

$$P\left(C_i^j\right) = \sum_{1 \in [1..m] 1 \neq i} \sum \left(WC_i^j, List\_S\right) * Dist\left(C_i^j, C_l^K\right) \qquad (3)$$

It is based on calculating a weight of symmetrical similarity (P (C)) for each concept associated with a term Ti to the sense j of the indexes list. With m and nl represent respectively the number of terms in Index List_S, and the number of senses of term Ti in EWN, Dist(C_i^j, C_l^k) is the semantic proximity measure between C_i^j and C_l^k concepts. This proximity is calculated by a score based on their mutual minimum distance of (Resnik, 1995) in the network of EWN.

The concept having the highest weight is considered as the best sense for the term Ti. After extraction of terms and calculation of their weights, the List_S will be represented by m words (m <= n) with their respective weights called the set of index terms. These terms form the semantic core noted by N_{sem}(List_S).

4.1.4. Transformation of the Representation of Terms to the Representation of Concepts

The purpose of this step is to extract concepts from multilingual documents. These concepts are denoted in text documents using simple or composite words. These index terms have been extracted during the previous phase. It remains to make the correspondence between the index terms and concepts. To do this, we rely on an external lexical resource: Multilingual EWN thesaurus. As part of our work, we consider that EWN is composed of a set of concepts and a set of taxonomic relations between them.

In our work, we define synonymy relations (is-a) as correspondence between each index term of Nsem (List_S) and a concept C. This concept is represented by (C, Dom (C)), with Dom (c) designate the domain C or the set of synset2 Si of N_{sem} (List_S) with C subsumes Si.

4.2. Construction of Conceptual Network in the Semantic Indexing Method

This network consists essentially of all concepts from Nsem (List_S)) and linked by semantic relations. This network is structured as ((C, Domain (C)), arcs) by using the lexical database EWN. The arcs denote the semantic relations (taxonomic and non taxonomic relations) between the extracted concepts.

4.2.1. Taxonomic Relations Between Nodes (Concepts)

Several types of semantics relations are proposed by the EWNF resource, such as generic-specific relations (hypernym-hyponym (is-a)), composition relations (holonymy-meronymy (part-whole)).

4.2.2. Non Taxonomic (Contextual) Relations Based on the Fuzzy Association Rules Model

We propose to use fuzzy association rules to discover the latent contextual relations between nodes concepts. Association rules are initially introduced in order to generate significant associations between sets of items in a transactional database. In our context, fuzzy association rules (Agrawal et al., 1993) (Agrawal et al., 1994) are used to discover significant relations between the index terms of the List_S. This is first done by the discovery of contextual relations between concepts representing the contents of the List_S. The formalism of association rules is then extended to support associations between concepts. The formal model is defined in the following:

Let Nsem(List_S) = {(X, Dom(X))} the set of concept nodes of List_S. $X, Y \in$ Nsem (List_S).

The association rule s an implication of the form $X \rightarrow Y$, with X, Y $\subset$ I and $X \cap Y = 0$. Generally, X is called the antecedent and Y the consequent. Rule $X \rightarrow Y$ has a support s in the transaction set D if s% of transactions in D contains $X \cup Y$.

The support of a rule is defined as support $(X \cup Y)$. Rule $X \rightarrow Y$ has confidence c if c% of transactions D that contain X also contains Y. The confidence of a rule is defined as support $(X \cup Y)$ / support (X).

We do generate only rules whose support and confidence are respectively higher than thresholds minimum of support (supmin) and confidence (confmin). An itemset whose support is superior to supmin is called frequent itemset. Rule $X \rightarrow Y$ is an interesting rule if $Y \cup X$ is a frequent itemset and the confidence of the rule is higher or equal to confmin. The discovery of association rules is done in two steps:

- Look for the frequent k-itemsets: to do this, the used algorithm is Apriori (Agrawal, 1994).
- Look from these itemsets for the interesting association rules (Agrawal et al., 1993) (Agrawal et al., 1994).

In the context of our work, the transaction database D is the List_S, the transaction is represented by the sentence of List_S, and items are the index terms. Generation of association rules is directly performed from the index terms (ti) of the List_S, we used an implementation of the Apriori algorithm integrated in Weka[3] tool. We detail the integration and implementation of each of these algorithms in the extraction of relations (arcs), which reflect a semantic proximity between nodes (concepts): Generation of frequent itemsets: This step includes three phases:

- Building the set E1 of frequent 1-itemsets that matches the attributes of concepts in List_S, they have a weight greater than the given threshold (supmin);
- From the set E1 frequent -1itemsets calculated in the preceding step, we do generate the set of 2-itemsets candidates to construct E2, which have a greater weight (1-itemset1,1 -itemset2) than supmin. We use the same principle to generate E3 In;
- The stop condition of the algorithm is when there is no new candidate itemsets to generate, in order to return the set E=E1 $\cup$ E2 $\cup$ ...En of all frequent itemsets in the List_S;

Generating semantic association rules: after the construction of the set E that corresponds to important itemsets in List_S, we proceed to the next step of generating the semantic association rules (Agrawal et al., 1994)

A semantic association rule between two concepts C and S (note C → sem (S)) is defined as follows: C → sem (Si) and there exists Ci ∈ Dom (C), and there exists Sj ∈ Dom (S)/ Ci → Sj.

The rule C → sem (S), means if List_S is related by the semantic relation (is-a) to the concept C, it should also be related to the concept S.

Thus, the R rule: Ci → Si: does mean the probability that the semantic content of the List_S relates Si, know that it concerns Ci. This semantic interpretation relies on two basic metrics that are confidence (conf) and the support (sup).

The confidence associated with the rule R: conf (R: Ci → Sj) = P (Ci / Sj) is based on the degree of importance of Sj in List_S, given the degree of importance of Ci in List_S.

Conf (C → sem S) = max, j (conf (R: Ci → Sj)) as Ci ∈ Dom (C), Sj ∈ Dom (S).

The support (Sup) is used to support associations between semantic entities. A support associated with a semantic association rule Sup (C → sem (Sj)) = P (CiSj) (probability of simultaneous occurrence of Ci and Sj) is based on the number of discrete association rules Ci ∈ (Domain (Ci)) and Sj ∈ Domain (Sj), having a support superior or equal to supmin.

$$\text{Conf}\left(R\right) = \frac{\min\left(WCi_{List\_S}, \; WSj_{List\_S}\right)}{WCi_{List\_S}} \tag{4}$$

$$\sup\left(R\right) = \frac{|\{Ci \rightarrow Sj \; / \; \text{conf}\left(Ci \rightarrow Sj\right) \geq \text{confmin}\}|}{|\{Ci \rightarrow Sj, \left(Ci, Sj\right) \in \text{Domaine}\left(C\right) \times \text{Domaine}\left(S\right)\}|} \tag{5}$$

4.3. Illustrative Example

In this example, we apply the Apriori algorithm to extract the contextual relations. We do only keep the concepts having a weight P1-itemsets above the threshold (0.2), for the reasons of reliability and limitation of vocabulary for network construction so the terms with weight ≤ 0.2 will be eliminated. Such as : *"forêt"*, *"réussite"*, *"encadrement"*, *"négociation"*, *"demande"*, *"nombreux"* (*"forest"*, *"success"*, *"leadership"*, *"negotiation"*, *"application"*, *"numerous"*) are the less frequent in the List_S. Other terms are the most frequent 1-itemset in the List_S, which are used to construct the 2-itemset (set of two terms. We calculate subsequently the weight of each 2-itemsets: P2-itemsets ({independence triumph}) = min (0.4, 0.6) = 0.4 ... etc.

Similarly, we only keep 2-itemset that has P2-itemsets a higher of 0.2, which allows us to construct a set of association rules (R: Ci → Sj) We calculate the confidence for each association rule Ri: Conf (Ri: Ci → Sj), we obtain the following Table 2.

Table 1. Generation of association rules from 2-itemset

2-Itemset	Associations Rules:$C_i \rightarrow S_j$	$P_{2\text{-itemsets}}$
{indépendance, triomphe} *(engl.independence, triumph)*	R1: indépendance → triomphe R2: triomphe → indépendance	0.4
{indépendance, acquérir} *(engl.independence, acquire)*	R3: indépendance → acquérir R4: acquérir → indépendance	0.4
{indépendance, région montagneuse} *(engl.independence, mountainous region)*	R5: indépendance→ région montagneuse R6: région montagneuse → indépendance	0.4
{indépendance, opération aérienne} *(engl.independence ; air operation)*	R7: indépendance → opération aérienne R8: opération aérienne → indépendance	0.4
{indépendance, ingérence} *(engl.independence ; interférence)*	R9: indépendance → ingérence R10: ingérence → indépendance	0.4
……….	…………….	………….
{triomphe, acquérir} *(engl. triumph, acquire}*	R: triomphe → acquérir R: acquérir → triomphe	0.5
{acquérir, opération aérienne} *(engl. acquire ; air operation)*	R: acquérir → opération aérienne R: opération aérienne → acquérir	0.5

Table 2. Calculation of confidences for the generated association rules

R_i	R1	R2	R3	R4	R5	R6	R7	R8	R9	R10	…..	R	R	R	R
Conf(R_i)	1	0.8	1	0.8	1	0.8	1	0.66	1	0.57	…..	0.83	1	1	0.83

We retain only the rules that have a confidence ≥ threshold of minConf = 1.These association rules are used to construct the semantic rules that form the basis for the identification of relation between concepts nodes List_S

The next step is the calculation of support for each semantic rule (sup (R_{semk}: $C_i \rightarrow semS_j$)), with k = 1 ..n (number of semantic rules), we obtain the following results:

We retain from the Table 6, the rules of semantic association whose support ≥ 0.5, like R_{sem2} etc. Finally, the selected rules enable the selection of Semantic relations between concepts nodes of the List_S, in order to construct the semantic and contextual network.

Table 3. Calculation of confidence for the semantic association rules

R_{semk}	R_{sem1}	R_{sem2}	R_{sem3}	R_{sem4}	R_{sem5}	…..	R_{sem}	R_{sem}
Sup(R_{sem})	1	0.5	0.5	0.5	0.5	…	1	1/6

4.4. Updating Statistic Measure of Our Semantic Indexing Method and Illustrative Example

Algorithm: Update of statistical measure of the semantic indexing method of each list_S

Data: List of terms index Ti and their weights derived from N_{sem} The list of concepts associated with index terms

Outputs: Generation of list of concepts and their weighting (taking into account the taxonomic and non taxonomic relations): List2(C,W')

```
Begin
N←length of list of concepts
List1(C,W)←∅
List2(C,W)←∅
1.for each concept Ci from 1  to N do
     For eah weight Wi of Ti in synonymy relation  with Ci do
```
$$W(Ci) = \sum W(Ti)$$
```
     List1(C,W)← List1(C,W)(Ci,W(Ci))
   End for
End for
2. for each concept Ci, Cj, Ck,…CN∈  to List1 do
   if (Ci in taxonomic relation with Cj) then
   W'(Ci)= W'(Cj)=W(Ci)+W(Cj)
End if
   if (Ci, Cj in  non taxonomic relation with Ck) then
   W'(Ci)= W'(Cj)=W'(Ck)=W(Ci)+W(Cj) +W(Ck)
End if
else
 W'(Ci)= W(Ci
 W'(Cj)= W(Cj)
 W'(Ck)= W(Ck)
End if
List2(C,W)← List2(C,W) ∪  (Ci,W'(Ci))
End for
End
```

Our indexing approach presented above is illustrated through the following example. Let List_S ((Paris, 0.5), (Toulouse, 0.9), (Center, 0.1), (Studio, 0.4), (Suburbs, 0.7), ...) a list_S described by a given set of weighted concepts which then constitute the nodes concepts List_S.

Considering the taxonomic relation "is-a" of English EWN and assuming we have "Toulouse is-a City" and "Paris is-a City", then Paris and Toulouse belong to the domain of values of the City concept node. Similarly Center and Suburbs belong to the domain of values of the Place concept node, while Studio is associated with the node concept Housing

Hence, we obtain *N(List_ph) = {(City, Dom (City)), (Place, Dom(Place)), (Housing, Dom(Housing))/ Dom(City) = {Toulouse, Paris}, Dom(Place)= {Suburbs, Center} et Dom(Housing) ={Studio}.*

In this example, we aim to discover the non taxonomic relations between Concepts "City, Place and Housing". To do this, we apply both priori and generation of association rules algorithms:

Then, we choose the confidence and support formulas (4 and 5) on the association rules by the Weka tool (configuration $Sup_{min} = 1$ and $Conf_{min} = 1$).

With the configuration ($Conf_{min} = 1$), we obtain the following association rules:

- R2: Studio → Toulouse et R6: Studio → Paris ; =>The rule: **Housing →semCity**
- R4: Suburbs → Toulouse ; => The rule: **Place →semCity**
- R7: Paris → Suburbs ; => The rule: **City →sem Place**
- R9: Studio → Suburbs ;=> The rule: **Housing →sem Place**

Then the extraction of semantic associations rules whose threshold support ($Sup_{min=1}$):

Sup(Housing →sem City)= 1;Sup(Place →sem City)= 0.5

Sup(City →sem Place)= 0.5; Sup(Housing →sem Place)= 1

Table 4. Generation of frequent k-itemsets

	Itemset	Support		Itemset	Support
Frequent 1- itemsets	Toulouse	0.9	2- Itemsets Frequent	Toulouse, Studio	0.4
	Paris	0.5		Toulouse, Suburbs	0.7
	Center	0.1		Paris, Studio	0.4
	Suburbs	0.7		Paris, Suburbs	0.5
	Studio	0.4		Studio, Suburbs	0.4

Table 5. Generated association rules

R1 : Toulouse->Studio	R6:Studio->Paris
R2 : Studio->Toulouse	R7 : Paris->Suburbs
R3 : Toulouse->Suburbs	R8 : Suburbs->Paris
R4 : Suburbs->Toulouse	R9 : Studio->Suburbs
R5 : Paris->Studio	R10 : Suburbs-> Studio

We obviously retain the rules that have a support equal or greater than 1. It is clear that the only selected semantic rules are:

Housing →sem City et Housing →sem Place. Finally, these two rules are conducted under a conceptual network:

Finally, we apply the latest step in our indexing approach with our algorithm, which led to a new conceptual representation:
- Initial conceptual representation: $P(Housing)=0.4$, $W(City)=0.9+0.5=1.4$, $W(Place)=0.1+0.7=0.8$.
-Update the statistical measure: New conceptual representation:

$W'(Housing)=W'(City)=W'(Place)=W(Housing)+W(City)+W(Place)=0.4+1.4+0.8=2.6$.

5. EXPERIMENTATION AND RESULTS

To validate our indexing approach, we used in our experiments the data from the TREC 4(Text Retrieval Evaluation Conference) evaluation campaign of 2001 and 2002 of the ad-hoc5 task. These data consist of a corpus and queries in several languages. During our experimental work, we used 50 List_S in French, and 50 List_S in English respectively corresponding to 50 queries in French and 50 in English. The following table presents a comparison of our indexing method results with classical indexing and indexing method of Baziz. We could not make the comparison with all the work in the state of the art, because these works are similar: works cited in Section 3 propose the semantic indexing that are based on relations of hyperonymy, hyponymy and synonyms for a term co-occurrence. The limit of those works is that they ignore the non taxonomic relations between terms. The difference between them lies in the pretreatment steps and the use of semantic resources. So the results returned by these works are very close (For example the work of Kaleta(2011) provided 63% of accuracy). The only limit of them is that they do not include the appearance of contextual relations in the calculation of co-occurrence for

Figure 2.

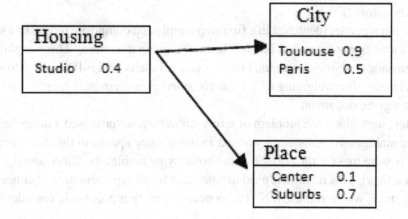

Table 6. Comparison of results of classic indexing methods, Baziz, and our method

50 List_S corresponding of the 50 query of TREC 2001 and 2002	P@5	P@10	P@15	P@20	P@30	P@50	P@90	average precision
Classical Method	38.33	36.26	33.63	28.74	23.08	16.56	10.36	26.7
Semantic indexing of Baziz	49.32	51.52	53.4	56.5	58.37	60.47	62.4	55.99
Our indexing method : (sup$_{min}$=0.5 et conf$_{min}$ =1)	49.36	52.6	55	60.2	65.81	74.24	79.53	62.39

the indexing process. We are based on precision metric on different point x (size of List_S) = 5, 10, 15, 20, 30, 50, 90, the average of precision in %.

The results, presented in the table above, show that our method shows a slight improvement in the first precision points (x = 5 to 20). This can be explained by the fact that the generation of association rules with a configuration of two metrics conf$_{min}$ and sup$_{min}$ (respectively at 1 and 0.5) on a small size List_S leads to validate a small number of rules. The significant improvement is shown for the rest of precision points compared to those obtained by the classic and the method of Baziz. These methods take into account the frequency of occurrence of the term and its taxonomic relations. However the classic indexing method takes into account the frequency of separate terms. This clearly shows both the interest of the proposed weighting of our method: this will allow us in particular to estimate the importance of the term in the List_S not only by its frequency of occurrence, but also by the importance of its taxonomic and non taxonomic (contextual) relations that it has with the rest of the terms in the List_S attributed by the weight W$_{sem}$(Ti). The results also show that these semantic weights provide better precision than those obtained by the classical and Baziz methods.

6. CONCLUSION

We presented in this paper, a statistical approach of semantic indexing of multilingual documents based on the conceptual network formalism. This formalism naturally supports concepts and semantic relations between them (taxonomic and nontaxonomic). Our approach is based on statistical measures and on multilingual thesaurus (EWN).

To extract the concepts, we identified in a first step simple and composite terms. In a second step, we use a weighting formula that is applied on each term of a given document. This weighting is based on statistical and semantic measure. In contrast to the classical measure TF-IDF, our introduced measure allowed us to determine the weighting of a term considering its semantic relations or calculating its co-occurrence in a given document.

In the third step, we address the problem of terms ambiguity, we proposed a disambiguation process by examining the ambiguous terms in the context in which they appear in the document (list_S). Two types of ambiguity were treated: the polysemy and homonymy ambiguity. Subsequently, we defined the synonymy relation (is-a): This relation is used to pass from terms representation to concepts representation. During this stage, we used the EWN. The concept extraction process is considered the first step towards conceptual network construction. In the second step, we identified taxonomic and nontaxonomic relations. Identification of taxonomic relations requires EWN resource; and identification of nontaxonomic relations is based primarily on the use of the same resource, and the integration of a knowledge base consisting of semantic association rules.

Finally, based on this formalism, we apply our algorithm to update the statistical measure of our proposed approach.

Tests and evaluation show the high performance of our approach in the conceptual representation of the documents content against existing works.

Our ongoing works are focused on improving the performance of our method in terms of time response. Indeed, the size of the rule base can be very large, which may increase the time response of the indexing process. Furthermore, the update of the basic rules can also affect this time response. Looking ahead, we plan to find a compromise between the size of the generic basis of rules and the time response provided by our indexing method. Another interesting work research would be to apply this approach to supervised and unsupervised classification on multilingual documents.

REFERENCES

Agrawal, R., Imielinski, T., & Swami, A. (1993). Mining Association rules between sets of items in large databases. SIGMOD93, 207-216. doi:10.1145/170035.170072

Agrawal, R., & Srikant, R. (1994). Fast algorithms for mining association rules in large databases. *Proceedings of 20th International Conference on Very Large Data Bases*, 487-499.

Baziz, M. (2005, Dec.). Indexation Conceptuelle Guidé par Ontolgie pour la Recherche d'Information. *Thèse de Doctorat en Informatique de l'Université Paul Sabatier de Toulouse (Sciences)*.

Baziz, M., Boughane, M., & And Aussenac-Gilles, N. (2005). Conceptual Indexing Based on Document Content Representation. In Lecture Notes in Computer Science: Vol. 3507. *Information Context, Nature, Impact, and Role, 5th International Conference on Conceptions of Library and Information Sciences, CoLIS 2005* (pp. 171–186). Springer.

Baziz, M., & Boughanem, M. (2004). The Use of Ontolmogyfor Semantic Representation of Documents. *The 2nd Semantic Web and Information Retrieval Workshop (SWIR)*, 38-45.

Boughanem, M., Dkaki, T., Mothe, J., & And Soulé-Dupuy, C. (1998). Mercure at TREC7. *TREC, 1998*, 355–360.

Boughanem, M., Mallak, I., & Prade, H. (2010). A new factor for computing the relevance of a document to a query. *IEEE World congress on Computational Intelligence (WCCI 2010)*. doi:10.1109/FUZZY.2010.5584404

Bourigault, D., Aussenac-Gilles, N. & Charlet, J. (2004). Construction de ressources terminologiques ou ontologiques à partir de textes: un cadre unificateur pour trois études de cas. *Revue d'Intelligence Artificielle (RIA) – Techniques Informatiques et structuration de terminologiques, 18*(1), 87–110.

Bourigault, D., & Jacquemin, C. (2000). *Influence des annotations imparfaites sur les systèmes de Traitement Automatique des Langues, un cadre applicatif: la résolution de l'anaphore pronominale*. Academic Press.

Claveau, V., & L'homme, M.-C. (2004). Discoveringe specific semantic relations between nouns and verbs in a specialized french corpus. *Proceedings of the 3rd International Workshop on Computational Terminology, CompuTerm'04*, 39–46.

Dinh, D. (2012). *Accés à l'information biomédicale: vers une approche d'indexation et de recherche d'information conceptuelle basée sur la fusion de ressources termino-ontologiques* (PhD thesis). Université Toulouse 3 Paul Sabatier (UT3 Paul Sabatier).

Ferret, O. (2011). Utiliser l'amorçage pour améliorer une mesure de similarité sémantique. Actes de TALN 2011, 1–6.

Grefenstette, G. (1994). *Explorations in Automatic Thesaurus Discovery*. Dordrecht, The Netherlands: Kluwer. doi:10.1007/978-1-4615-2710-7

Hamon, T., & Nazarenko, A. (2010). Detection of synonymy links between terms: experiment and results. Recent Advances in Computational Terminology, 185–208.

Harris, Z. (1990). La genèse de lanalyse des transformations et de la métalangue. *Langages*, *99*(99), 9–20. doi:10.3406/lgge.1990.1589

Mccrae, J., & Collier, N. (2008). Synonym set extraction from the biomedical literature by lexical pattern discovery. *BMC Bioinformatics*, *9*(1), 159. doi:10.1186/1471-2105-9-159 PMID:18366721

Morin, E. (1999). *Extraction automatique de terminologie à partir de libellés textuels courts* (Doctoral thesis). Université de Nantes, France.

Jianfeng, G., Jian-Yun, N., Endong, X., Jiang, Z., & Ming, H. (2001). *Improving Query Translation for Cross-Language Information Retrieval using Statistical Models*. Paper presented at SIGIR'01, New Orleans, LA.

Grouin, C., Abacha, A. B., Bernhard, D., Cartoni, B., Deléger, L., Grau, B., … Zweigenbaum, P. (2010). Caramba: Concept, assertion, and relation annotation using machine-learning based approaches. *Actes de la conférence conjointe JEP-TALN-RECITAL 2012*.

Hamon, T., & Nazarenko, A. (2010). Detection of synonymy links between terms: experiment and results. Recent Advances in Computational Terminology, 185–208.

Harrathi, R., Roussey, C., Maisonnasse, L., & And Calabretto, S. (2010). *Vers une approche statistique pour l'indexation sémantique des documents multilingue*. Dans: Actes du XXVIII° congrès INFORSID, Marseille.

Huang, X., & Robertson, S. E. (2001). Comparisons of Probabilistic Compound Unit Weighting Methods. *Proc. of the ICDM'01 Workshop on Text Mining*.

Kaleta, Z. (2014). Semantic text indexing. *Journal of Computer Science, 15*(1), 19-34. Retrieved from http://journals.bg.agh.edu.pl/COMPUTER/2014.15.1/csci.2014.15.1.19.pdf

Maisonnasse, L., Gaussier, E., & Chevallet, J. P. (2009). Model Fusion Conceptual Language Modeling. *ECIR, 2009*, 240–250.

Mallak, I. (2011). *De nouveaux facteurs pour l'exploitation de la sémantique d'un texte en recherche d'information* (PhD thesis). Université Toulouse.

Mallat, S., Ben Mohamed, M. A., Hkiri, E., Zouaghi, A., & And Zrigui, M. (2014). Semantic and Contextual Knowledge Representation for Lexical Disambiguation: Case of Arabic-French Query Translation. *Journal of Computing and Information Technology, 22*(3), 191–215. doi:10.2498/cit.1002234

Mallat, S., Zouaghi, A., Hkiri, E., & And Zrigui, M. (2013). Method of lexical enrichment in information retrieval system in Arabic. International Journal of Information Retrieval Research, 3(4), 35-51. doi:10.4018/ijirr.2013100103

Okita, T., Guerra, M., & Graham, A. (2010). Multi-word expression sensitive word alignment. *Proceedings of the 4th International Workshop on Cross Lingual Information Access at COLING 2010*, 26–34.

Resnik, P. (1993). *Selection and Information: A Class-Based Approach to Lexical Relations* (Doctoral thesis). University of Pennsylvania.

Resnik, P. (1995). Disambiguating Noun Groupings with Respect to WordNet Sense. *Proceedings of the Third Workshop on Very Large Corpora*, 54–68.

Richardson, S. (1997). *Determining Similarity and Inferring Relations in a lexical Knowledge Base* (PhD thesis). The City University of New York, New York, NY.

Sager, J. C. (1990). *A Practical Course in Terminology Processing*. Amsterdam: John Benjamins. doi:10.1075/z.44

Sanderson, M. (1994). Word sense disambiguation and information retrieval. In *Proceedings of the 17th Annual International ACM-SIGIR Conference on Research and Development in Information Retrieval*, (pp. 142-151). Springer- Verlag.

Schmid, H. (1997). New Methods in Language Processing. In *Studies Computational Linguistics, chapter Probabilistic part-of-speech tagging using decision trees* (pp. 154–164). London: UCL Press. Retrieved from http://www.ims.uni-stuttgart.de/projekte/corplex/TreeTagger/

Vossen, P., & Peters, W. (1997). The Multilingual design of the EuroWordNet Database. *Lexical Semantic Resources for NLP Applications*. Retrieved from http://citeseer.nj.nec.com/cache/papers/cs/343/http:zSzzSzwww.let.uva.nlz.Sz~ewnzSzdocszSzP013.pdf/vossen97multilingual.pdf

Weissenbacher, D. (2004). La relation de sysnonymie en génomique. In Actes de la conférence RECITAL'2004, Fès, Maroc.

ENDNOTES

[1]   Synset (Synonym Set)
[2]   Synset (Synonym Set):l'ensemble de synonymes
[3]   http://fr.downv.com/software-download/WEKA
[4]   http://trec.nist.gov/
[5]   http://trec.nist.gov/data.html

Chapter 7
Keyword Extraction Based on Selectivity and Generalized Selectivity

Slobodan Beliga
University of Rijeka, Croatia

Ana Meštrović
University of Rijeka, Croatia

Sanda Martinčić-Ipšić
University of Rijeka, Croatia

ABSTRACT

This chapter presents a novel Selectivity-Based Keyword Extraction (SBKE) method, which extracts keywords from the source text represented as a network. The node selectivity value is calculated from a weighted network as the average weight distributed on the links of a single node and is used in the procedure of keyword candidate ranking and extraction. The selectivity slightly outperforms an extraction based on the standard centrality measures. Therefore, the selectivity and its modification – generalized selectivity as the node centrality measures are included in the SBKE method. Selectivity-based extraction does not require linguistic knowledge as it is derived purely from statistical and structural information of the network and it can be easily ported to new languages and used in a multilingual scenario. The true potential of the proposed SBKE method is in its generality, portability and low computation costs, which positions it as a strong candidate for preparing collections which lack human annotations for keyword extraction.

INTRODUCTION

The task of keyword extraction (KE) is to automatically identify a set of terms that best describe the document (Mihalcea & Tarau, 2004). Automatic keyword extraction establishes a foundation for various natural language processing applications: information retrieval, the automatic indexing and classifica-

DOI: 10.4018/978-1-5225-5042-6.ch007

tion of documents, automatic summarization and high-level semantic description (Balaji, Geetha, & Parthasarathi, 2016; Brian & Pradeep, 2010; Cheng & Qu, 2009), etc.

Although the keyword extraction applications usually work on single documents (document-oriented task) (Boudin, 2013; Lahiri, Choudhury, & Caragea, 2014; Palshikar, 2007), keyword extraction is also applicable to a more demanding task, i.e. the keyword extraction from a whole collection of documents (Dostal & Jezek, 2011; Grineva, Grinev, & Lizorkin, 2009; Jones & Paynter, 2002) (collection-oriented task) or from an entire web site (Wu & Agogino, 2003). In the era of big-data, obtaining an effective method for automatic keyword extraction from huge amounts of multi-topic textual sources is a nowadays necessity.

State-of-the-art keyword extraction approaches are based on statistical, linguistic or machine learning methods (Siddiqi & Sharan, 2015; Beliga, Meštrović, & Martinčić-Ipšić, 2015). In the last decade the focus of research has shifted towards unsupervised methods, mainly towards network or graph enabled keyword extraction. In a network enabled keyword extraction the document representation may vary from very simple (words are nodes and their co-occurrence is represented with links), or can incorporate very sophisticated linguistic knowledge like syntactic (Lahiri et al., 2014; Liu & Hu, 2008; Mihalcea & Tarau, 2004) or semantic relations (Grineva et al., 2009; Joorabchi & Mahdi, 2013; Wang, Wang, Senzhang, & Zhoujun, 2014; Bougouin, Boudin, & Daille, 2016; Martinez-Romo, Araujo, & Duque Fernandez, 2016; Rafiei-Asl & Nickabadi, 2017; Ying et al., 2017).

Typically, the source (document, text, data) for keyword extraction is modeled with one network. This way, both the statistical properties (frequencies) as well as the structure of the source text are represented by a unique formal representation, hence a complex network.

A network enabled keyword extraction exploits different measures for the task of identifying and ranking the most representative features of the source – the keywords. The keyword extraction powered by network measures can be on the node, network or subnetwork level (Beliga et al., 2015). Measures on the node level are: degree, strength (Lahiri et al., 2014); on the network level: coreness, clustering coefficient, PageRank motivated ranking score or HITS motivated hub and authority score (Boudin, 2013; Mihalcea & Tarau, 2004); on the subnetwork level: communities (Rafiei-Asl & Nickabadi, 2017; Grineva et al., 2009). Most of the research was motivated by various centrality measures: degree, betweenness, closeness and eigenvector centrality (Ludwig, Thiel, & Nürnberger, 2017; Abilhoa & de Castro, 2014; Lahiri et al., 2014; Boudin, 2013; Matsuo, Ohsawa, & Ishizuka, 2001; Palshikar, 2007; Mihalcea & Tarau, 2004).

This research presents the novel selectivity-based method for the unsupervised keyword extraction from the co-occurrence network of texts. A new network measure – the node selectivity, originally proposed by Masucci and Rodgers (2006, 2009) (that can distinguish an original network from a shuffled one), is applied to automatic keyword extraction. Selectivity is defined as the average weight distributed on the links incident to the single node. Furthermore, we utilize a generalized selectivity measure defined according to the generalized weighted degree originally proposed by Opsahl, Agneessens and Skvoretz (2010). In previous work, the node selectivity measure performed in favor of the differentiation between original and shuffled Croatian texts (Margan, Meštrović, & Martinčić-Ipšić, 2014a; Margan, Martinčić-Ipšić, & Meštrović, 2014b), for the differentiation of text genres (Martinčić-Ipšić, Miličić, & Meštrović, 2016) and for prediction of missing links in networks (Martinčić-Ipšić, Močibob, & Perc, 2017).

The node selectivity measure has been preliminary tested for the keyword extraction task in our early work (Beliga, Meštrović, & Martinčić-Ipšić, 2014), where we explore the potential of the selectivity measure for the keyword extraction in Croatian news articles. The full potential of selectivity was analyzed in (Beliga, Meštrović, & Martinčić-Ipšić, 2016), where we introduce the extension of the proposed Selectivity-Based Keyword Extraction – SBKE method, in a form of generalized selectivity.

The Selectivity-Based Keyword Extraction – SBKE method is architected in two steps: the keyword extraction and the keyword expansion. More precisely, the initial idea of one and two word long sequences (word-pairs) is expanded to three word long sequences (word-triples). Additionally, we examine the potential of the SBKE method for the collection-oriented extraction task. Furthermore, we compare selectivity against other centrality measures (degree, closeness and betweenness) for the keyword candidate selection from English texts. Then, we evaluate the performance of the SBKE method on the English and Croatian datasets comparatively, in a terms of overall inter-indexer scores. Finally, we introduce the generalized selectivity measure, and compare the SBKE results with the different values of the tuning parameter α to other research results reported on the Croatian and English datasets. At the end, we add discussion on possible applications of proposed keyword extraction method in a real-life situation and we discuss the portability of the proposed solution to new languages and domains.

The rest of the article is organized as follows: The following section presents an overview of related work on automatic keyword extraction. In next section, we present the definition of the measures for the network structure analysis. We further present the methodology for the construction of co-occurrence networks from the collection of used text. The centrality motivated keyword extraction approaches are compared afterwards. Next, the architecture of the SBKE method is elaborated upon. We further discuss the application of the SBKE method to the extraction from a collection rather than from individual documents. Possible applications of keyword extraction in real-life scenarios are covered in a separate section. A discussion about achieved results and method properties as well as guidelines for future work is in the last part of the paper respectively.

RELATED WORK

The graph enabled (for simplicity, we interchange the terminology of a graph enabled and network-enabled) keyword extraction has been in the research focus in the last ten years. The overview of reported research results and used measures is organized in reversed chronological order.

Ludwig, Thiel and Nürnberger (2017) present unsupervised graph-based approach for extracting keyphrases from abstracts of scientific articles. The procedure extracts all possible candidates from input text, and then evaluate their quality in order to select the best conceptual keyphrases. They define conceptual keyprases as the ones suitable for describing the topic of a document, which can be used as a conceptualization of the information space. The input text is splitted into sentences and directed links are created for neighboring words in a sentence. A weight represents the co-occurrence frequency of two words in the text. In preprocessing step, they stem all words with Porter stemmer (stemming is the process for reducing inflected, or sometimes derived words, to their word stem, base or root form) and remove stopwords (the most frequent function words, which do not carry strong semantic properties, but are needed for the syntax of language). In the extraction procedure, they utilize closeness and betweenness values of words (nodes) in the graph – and obtain keyword candidates. For keyphrases they combine several keywords by simply summing up the corresponding values of the underlying words in the graph. They remove all keyphrases which contain more than 5 words, and set a threshold for betweenness value on 0.2. Then the candidates are ranked by the combination of calculated closeness values and the average of sums of weights on the closeness paths. They perform only qualitative evaluation by compare obtained results with a results of the Rapid Automatic Keyword Extraction (RAKE) algorithm which indicates that the proposed solution is suitable for the generation of conceptual keyphrases from abstracts of documents.

Abilhoa and de Castro (2014) propose a keyword extraction method representing tweets (microblogs) as graphs and applying centrality measures for finding the relevant keywords. They develop a Twitter Keyword Graph technique where in the preprocessing step they use tokenization, stemming and stopwords removal. They use undirected co-occurrence networks which use simple adjacency relations or exploit the tweets' size which enables adding tweets as cliques into the network and they also examine different weighting principles. Keywords are extracted from the constructed network cascadely, applying centrality measures – closeness and eccentricity. The performance of the algorithm is tested on a single English text (of the literature genre) and compared with the tf-idf (term frequency – inverse document frequency) approach and KEA algorithm. The algorithm is also tested on three sets of Portuguese tweets increasing in size in terms of precision, recall and $F1$ score. The computational time proved to be a robust end efficient to extract keywords from texts, especially from short texts such as microblogs.

Lahiri, Choudhury and Caragea (2014) extract keywords and keyphrases form co-occurrence networks or more precisely from previously extracted noun phrases containing more than five words collocated within a predefined window in an original text. Eleven measures (degree, strength, neighborhood size, coreness, clustering coefficient, structural diversity index, page rank, HITS – hub and authority score, betweenness, closeness and eigenvector centrality) are used for keyword extraction from directed/undirected and weighted networks. The obtained results on four English benchmark datasets (meetings transcriptions ICSI, academic papers NUS and SemEval, abstracts INSPEC) suggest that centrality measures outperform the baseline tf-idf model (measured in terms of precision, recall and $F1$ score). They conclude that simpler measures such as degree and strength outperform computationally more expensive centrality measures such as coreness and betweenness.

Boudin (2013) compares various centrality measures for graph-based keyphrase extraction. Experiments on standard datasets of English (INSPEC and SemEval) and French (DEFT) show that simple degree centrality achieves results comparable to the widely used TextRank algorithm (see below); and that closeness centrality obtains the best results on short documents. Undirected and weighted co-occurrence networks are constructed from syntactically parsed and lemmatized text using a co-occurrence window of size 10. Syntactic parsing filters out only nouns and adjectives according to part-of-speech (POS) tags. Degree, closeness, betweenness and eigenvector centrality are compared to a variation of PageRank – TextRank, originally proposed by Mihalcea and Tarau (2004) as a baseline in terms of precision, recall and $F1$ score. The best results are reported for the degree centrality (on two datasets) and closeness (on one dataset). The authors conclude that degree centrality can successfully replace TextRank derived from PageRank in the keyword extraction task.

Grineva, Grinev and Lizorkin (2009) use community detection techniques for key terms extraction where texts are modeled as a graph of semantic relationships between candidate terms determined from Wikipedia. The results show that the terms related to the main topics of the document tend to form a community, thematically cohesive groups of terms. Community detection allows the effective processing of multiple topics in a document and efficiently filters out noise. The results are reported on weighted and undirected networks from semantically linked, morphologically expanded and disambiguated n-grams from texts linked with the titles of Wikipedia articles. Additionally, for the purpose of noise stability, they repeat the experiment on different multi-topic web pages (news, blogs, forums, social networks, product reviews) confirming that community detection outperforms the tf-idf model on the both tasks in terms of precision, recall and $F1$ measure.

Palshikar (2007) proposes a hybrid structural and statistical approach to extract keywords from a single document. The undirected co-occurrence network, using a dissimilarity measure between two words, calculated from the frequency of their co-occurrence in the preprocessed and lemmatized document, as the link weight, was shown to be appropriate for the centrality measures based approach for keyword extraction.

Mihalcea and Tarau (2004) report on seminal research which introduced a state-of-the-art TextRank model. TextRank is derived from PageRank and introduced to graph-based text processing, keyword and sentence extraction tasks. The English abstracts (INSPEC) are modeled as undirected or directed and weighted co-occurrence networks using a co-occurrence window of variable sizes (2 to 10). Lexical units are preprocessed: stopwords removed, words restricted with POS syntactic filters (filtering out open class words: nouns and adjectives). The PageRank motivated score – the importance of the node – is derived from the importance of the neighboring nodes and used for keyword extraction. The obtained TextRank performance compares favorably with the supervised machine learning n-gram based approach (evaluated in terms of precision, recall and $F1$ score).

Matsuo, Ohsawa and Ishizuka (2001) present an early research where a text document is represented as an undirected and unweighted co-occurrence network. The used text corpora comprise papers published in Journal of AI Research. Based on the network topology, the authors proposed an indexing system called KeyWorld, which extracts important terms (pairs of words) by measuring their contribution to small-world properties. The contribution of the node is based on closeness centrality calculated as the difference in small-world properties of the network with the temporarily elimination of a node combined with inverse document frequency (idf).

The common feature of all these studies is the network enabled keyword extraction technique which utilizes different measures of a network's and node's structural or topological properties. They are mainly tasked with the English language with the exception of French in (Boudin, 2013) and Portuguese in (Abilhoa & de Castro, 2014). Regarding the different strategies in the text preprocessing and in the network construction principles the reported studies vary: *in text preprocessing* (stopwords removal, lemmatization or stemming (Ludwig, Thiel, & Nürnberger, 2017; Abilhoa & de Castro, 2014; Boudin, 2013; Mihalcea & Tarau, 2004)); POS filtering (Boudin, 2013; Lahiri et al., 2014; Mihalcea & Tarau, 2004); *in relations incorporated into network construction* (syntactic (Lahiri et al., 2014; Mihalcea & Tarau, 2004) or semantic (Grineva et al., 2009)); and *in the used types of networks* (3) (undirected (Abilhoa & de Castro, 2014; Boudin, 2013; Grineva et al., 2009; Mihalcea & Tarau, 2004; Palshikar, 2007); directed (Lahiri et al., 2014; Mihalcea & Tarau, 2004); unweighted (Matsuo et al., 2001) and weighted (Abilhoa & de Castro, 2014; Boudin, 2013; Grineva et al., 2009; Palshikar, 2007)). The focus of all these studies is to analyze the potential of different centrality measures for the keyword extraction task by measuring their comparative performance. From the results presented in (Boudin, 2013; Lahiri et al., 2014) the authors suggest that simple centrality measures (degree, strength or closeness) outperform computationally more expensive measures (coreness, betweenness or TextRank). Guided by these findings we focus our work on the examination of the centrality measures as well and we extend the list of standard centrality measures (degree, closeness, betweenness) with the selectivity. Additionally, motivated by the portability of the proposed solution across languages we rely on the co-occurrence networks which incorporate exclusively adjacency relations of words in a text, which can be easily ported across different languages.

Note, that syntax or semantic relations require the incorporation of linguistic knowledge, which is not always available or is dependent on external sources such as Wikipedia or Wordnet.

Still, the incorporation of external semantic information into keyword extraction task has attracted a lot of attention in recently published scientific papers.

Rafiei-Asl and Nickabadi (2017) introduce an unsupervised keyphrase extraction model and implement Topical and Structural Keyphrase Extractor (TSAKE). TSAKE combines the prior knowledge through topical *n*-gram model (built from the Wikipedia's articles) represented as the co-occurrence graph – hence a topical graph. The network analysis is applied to topical graphs to detect sub-topics and extract important words for each sub-topic. Proposed TSAKE model integrates semantic and structural relatedness into several topical graphs and employs a community detection approach and a graph-based ranking in order to extract keyphrases. The directed co-occurrence graph of stemmed words without stopwords is constructed by applying the co-occurrence window of fixed size (five). Weights on the links contain normalized co-occurrence counts. For candidate extraction, noun phrases and phrases with special part-of-speech (POS) patterns are considered. The POS patterns are learned from datasets by converting sets of keyphrases to their POS sequences and selecting the patterns with the highest coverage of the original keyphrases. Next, each keyphrase gets a score from a topical graph according to the value of a network measure. They compare degree, closeness, betweennees, eigenvector, network constraint, clustering coefficient, Page Rank, hub score and authority score measures for the identification of central nodes in the communities (micro topics) of the topical graphs. The closeness exhibits the best performance. The final score of a candidate keyphrase is the weighted sum of its scores in different topics where the weight of each topic's score is the posterior probability of the related topic given the input document. After topical scoring, the extracted candidates are sorted according to final score and the top ranked keyphrases are returned. The results of TSAKE (on three datasets) indicate the superiority of the proposed model over three baseline techniques and six state-of-the-art models.

Ying et al. (2017) propose graph-based method for keyphrase extraction as an improvement of Wan and Xiao's (2008) early work, which does not guarantee that the extracted keyphrases cover all main topics of the document. Ying et al. are combining clustering of semantically similar candidates from Wikipedia according to the values of term relatedness and co-occurrence-based statistics. The term relatedness is calculated twofold as: the co-occurrence-based term relatedness (count of co-occurrences within a window of 2 to 10 words in the whole document) and as Wikipedia-based term relatedness (cosine similarity, Euclidean distance, Point-wise Mutual Information and Normalized Google Similarity Distance for measuring term relatedness from the vectors of Wikipedia concepts). They argue that existing graph-based techniques only consider the co-occurrence between words in a document, disregarding the impact of the sentences. Therefore, they study the advantage of the combining words and sentences by melting three kinds of relationships between them. They construct sentence-to-sentence graph, word-to-word and sentence-to-word graphs, all undirected and weighted. First, in sentence-to-sentence graphs, document is presented as a graph of connected sentences (nodes are sentences). Each link connecting two nodes has a corresponding weight which is decided by the cosine similarity of two sentences (nodes). Second, in word-to-word graph words are modeled as nodes and weights on links are computed as cosine similarity of word embedding vectors. Word embeddings are known to retain syntactic and semantic relations between words and they are obtained from SENNA (pre-trained publicly available word embeddings trained on Wikipedia articles). Third, sentence-to-word graph is constructed between two kinds of nodes words and sentences: there exists a link between sentence and word if the word is contained in the sentence. Weights on the links are calculated according to word frequency in the sentence and inverse sentence frequency. K-means clustering algorithm is used to cluster the candidate keyphrases. The results reported on two datasets outperform the baseline approaches (tf-idf and TextRank).

Bougouin, Boudin and Daille (2016) propose a co-ranking approach TopicCoRank for the tasks of keyphrase extraction (extract words occurring in a document) and keyphrase assignment (provide controlled keyphrases from a domain-specific terminology – i.e. controlled vocabulary) in an integrated and mutual reinforcing manner. TopicCoRank constructs two graphs: one for the document topics and one for keyphrases in a controlled vocabulary. The approach is designed to unify the two graphs and rank both the importance of topics and controlled keyphrases using a co-ranking vote. In a preprocessing step, words are tagged with POS tags. TopicRank algorithm originally construct graphs in which nodes are topics and links are weighted according to the strength of the semantic relation between the connected topics. Next, the topics are ranked using the importance score of the TopicRank formula. Experiments are performed on a French DEFT-2016 benchmark dataset in three domains: linguistics, information science and archeology. TopicCoRank shows statistically significant improvements compared to state-of-the-art methods (TopicRank and KEA++) for both tasks of keyphrase extraction and assignment.

Martinez-Romo, Araujo, and Duque Fernandez (2016) introduce a semantic-graph based approach to develop unsupervised SemGraph algorithm for keyphrase extraction. The main novelty of this algorithm is its ability to identify semantic relationships between words whose presence is statistically significant. The SemGraph constructs a co-occurrence graph in which relations between terms are not based on a simple co-occurrence, but their relationships are established as a result of a significant number of occurrences within a document that represents a semantic unit. Additionally, the graph is enriched with semantic information from WordNet. In the preprocessing step, they clean the text, perform the stemming and carry out an analysis of the logical structure of each document. Then they obtain POS sequences of tags and construct a semantic relationship graph. Undirected graph is constructed from a set of semantic relationships with the words as nodes. The link is established between two words that appear in at least one common document. A co-occurrence weight, above a threshold value is assigned to each link, and measures the deviation of co-occurrence of the two words with respect to the null case. In the next phase, semantic enrichment is performed in order to enhance the semantic relationships between terms with information extracted from WordNet. Finally, in the last step the influence of the threshold value for the co-occurrence weight is used to measure the semantic relationship between two terms in the graph. Evaluation results on standard benchmark dataset SemEval-2010 confirms that SemGraph achieves improvements over the top performing solutions reported on the SemEval-2010 keyphrase extraction task.

All reported methods TSAKE; SemGraph and TopicCoRank are gaining in their performance by the incorporation of the external semantic knowledge either using Wikipedia's entries, WordNet or controlled vocabulary, while Ying et al. (2017) are using pre-trained word embeddings.

In order to illustrate how influential the use of an external semantic source could be, we present some simple Wikipedia statistics (List of Wikipedias, in 2015 and 2017 respectively): the Croatian Wikipedia is only 8.5% (3.2%) of the size of the English Wikipedia quantified by the number of different articles despite the fact that Croatian is ranked in 19th (42nd) place according to the number of articles in years 2015 and 2017 respectively. Additionally, 18.09% (19.8%) of all languages (55/291; 59/298) on Wikipedia contain over 100,000 articles and 54.29% (46.31%) (158/291; 138/298) have less than 10,000 articles which implies that many languages are low-resourced not only in terms of the number of Wikipedia pages but more importantly in terms of the natural language processing tools. Finally, according to Ethnologue (Ethnologue, 2015, 2017) there are over 7,000 living languages, although they are not all equally represented digitally or on the Internet.

All of this motivates us to keep the construction principles as simple as possible, hence to use adjacency relations in co-occurrence networks which assure simple portability across languages. Moreover, we preserve the same construction principles for the document oriented (Boudin, 2013; Lahiri et al., 2014; Palshikar, 2007) and for the collection oriented (Grineva et al., 2009) extraction tasks. Finally, the proposed SBKE method infers the keywords solely on the information captured in the structure of the network, which is beneficial for extraction in the multilingual setup and of high importance for facilitating the portability of the SBKE method to new languages and domains.

COMPLEX NETWORK ANALYSIS

More details about complex networks analysis and the definition of measures can be found in (Newman, 2010). Here we list only the definition of measures needed for keyword extraction task.

In the network, N is the number of nodes and M is the number of links. In weighted language networks, every link connecting two nodes i and j has an associated weight w_{ij} which is a positive integer number.

The node degree k_i is defined as the number of links incident upon a node. In directed networks, the in-degree and out-degree $k_i^{in/out}$ of node i are defined as the number of its *in* neighbors and *out* neighbors respectively.

The degree centrality of the node i is the degree of that node. It can be normalized by dividing it by the maximum possible degree $N - 1$:

$$dc_i = \frac{k_i}{N-1}. \tag{1.1}$$

Analogue, in the directed network, the in/out-degree centralities are defined as in/out-degree of a node. It can be normalized by dividing it by the maximum possible degree $N - 1$:

$$dc_i^{in/out} = \frac{k_i^{in/out}}{N-1}. \tag{1.2}$$

The closeness centrality is defined as the inverse of farness, i.e. the sum of the shortest distances between a node and all the other nodes. Let d_{ij} be the shortest path between nodes i and j. The normalized closeness centrality of a node i is given by:

$$cc_i = \frac{N-1}{\sum_{i \neq j} d_{ij}}. \tag{1.3}$$

The betweenness centrality quantifies the number of times a node acts as a bridge along the shortest path between two other nodes. Let σ_{jk} be the number of the shortest paths from node j to node k and let $\sigma_{jk}(i)$ be the number of those paths that pass through the node i. The normalized betweenness centrality of a node i is given by:

$$bc_i = \frac{\sum_{i \neq j \neq k} \frac{\sigma_{jk}(i)}{\sigma_{jk}}}{(N-1)(N-2)}. \tag{1.4}$$

The strength of the node i is a sum of the weights of all the links incident with the node i:

$$s_i = \sum_j w_{ij}. \tag{1.5}$$

In the directed network, the in/out-strength $s_i^{in/out}$ of the node i is defined as the sum of the weights on its incoming and outgoing links, that is:

$$s_i^{in/out} = \sum_j w_{ji/ij}. \tag{1.6}$$

The selectivity measure as the average strength of a node is initially introduced by Masucci and Rodgers (2006, 2009). For the node i the selectivity is calculated as a fraction of the node's strength and degree:

$$e_i = \frac{s_i}{k_i}. \tag{1.7}$$

In the directed network, the in/out-selectivity of the node i is defined as:

$$e_i^{in/out} = \frac{s_i^{in/out}}{k_i^{in/out}}. \tag{1.8}$$

The generalized selectivity measure is defined according to the originally proposed measure of generalized degree centrality in (Opsahl et al., 2010). The generalized selectivity uses a positive parameter α that can be determined according to the experimental settings and data:

$$ge_i^\alpha = k_i \left(\frac{s_i}{k_i} \right)^\alpha. \tag{1.9}$$

In the directed network, the generalized in/out-selectivity of the node i is defined as:

$$ge_i^{\alpha\ in/out} = k_i^{in/out}\left(\frac{s_i^{in/out}}{k_i^{in/out}}\right)^{\alpha}. \tag{1.10}$$

Generalized selectivity allows a fine tuning of the relative importance between the number of links and weights incident to the node.

METHODOLOGY

The Construction of Co-occurrence Networks

Text can be represented as a complex network of linked words: each individual word is a node and the relations amongst words are links. Co-occurrence networks exploit simple neighbor (adjacency) relation; two words are linked if they are adjacent (Abilhoa & de Castro, 2014; Margan, Martinčić-Ipšić, & Meštrović, 2013). The adjacency relation between words is preserved within the sentence boundaries meaning that punctuation symbols such as [.!?] are boundaries for the construction of co-occurrence links. The weight of the link is equal to the overall co-occurrence frequencies of the corresponding word pairs within a source text. The approach in (Ludwig, Thiel & Nürnberger, 2017; Boudin, 2013; Grineva et al., 2009; Lahiri et al., 2014, Palshikar, 2007) exploits weights as simple frequencies while (Abilhoa & de Castro, 2014) examine different weighting schemas.

Finally, based on our previous findings (Margan et al., 2013, 2014a) and work reported by (Lahiri et al., 2014; Mihalcea & Tarau, 2004) we use directed and weighted networks. More precisely, we construct directed and weighted co-occurrence networks: one from the text in each document (the document oriented extraction task) and an integral one from the texts in all documents (for the collection extraction task).

Figure 1 shows a directed and weighted co-occurrence network construction for two sentences: *"Selectivity-based keyword extraction method is fully unsupervised. It consists of two phases: keyword extraction and keyword expansion."* Node *"keyword"* has the corresponding: in/out-selectivity: $e_{keyword}^{in} = 1$ and $e_{keyword}^{out} = 1.5$; and generalized in/out-selectivity: $ge_{keyword}^{\alpha\ in} = 3$ and $ge_{keyword}^{\alpha\ out} = 4.5$ where $\alpha = 2$.

Network construction and analysis is implemented with the Python programming language using the NetworkX software package developed for the creation, manipulation, and study of the structure, dynamics and functions of complex networks (Hagberg, Swart, & Chult, 2008). The calculation of the selectivity measure is available in LaNCoA: A Python Toolkit for Language Networks Construction and Analysis (Margan & Meštrović, 2015).

Evaluation Methodology

The evaluation of keyword extraction is generally performed in terms of precision, recall and an $F1$ score. When comparing the performance of a machine method with human annotation, precision is calculated as the number of keywords in the intersection of a set of keywords annotated by a human (A) and a set of keywords annotated using machine (B) divided by the number of keywords annotated using machine:

Figure 1. Directed and weighted co-occurrence network

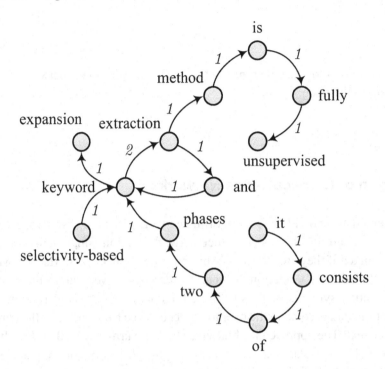

$$P = \frac{|A \cap B|}{|B|}. \tag{2.1}$$

Recall is calculated as the number of keywords in the intersection of a set of keywords annotated by a human and a set of keywords annotated using machine divided by the number of keywords annotated by a human:

$$R = \frac{|A \cap B|}{|A|}. \tag{2.2}$$

$F1$ score is the harmonic mean of precision and recall, calculated as:

$$F1 = \frac{2PR}{P + R}. \tag{2.3}$$

In order to follow the evaluation methodology already used on the HINA dataset we broaden the standard set with an $F2$ score, which gives twice as much importance to the recall than to the precision:

$$F2 = \frac{5PR}{4P + R}.$$ (2.4)

In the general case for measuring the consistency between any two annotators (human and machine, human and human, or machine and machine) the inter-indexer consistency (*IIC*) score is used. The inter-indexer consistency is originally proposed by Rolling (1981) and it is equivalent to the *F*1 score.

Methodologically, all different evaluation approaches compare the obtained results against the gold standard. However, if documents have multiple annotations, it is not clear what the gold standard is. Here we describe two approaches that we apply to the evaluation of experiments in order to enable comparisons with the gold standard.

The first approach merges all keywords from all annotators per document into one set taken as the gold standard (Wang et al., 2014). It is then possible to evaluate machine annotated keywords against human annotated keywords in terms of average precision (P_{avg}), recall (R_{avg}) and *F*1 score ($F1_{avg}$) across all the documents. If N_{doc} is total number of annotated documents and P_i, R_i, $F1_i$, $F2_i$ are P, R, and *F*1 score calculated for the *i*-th (single) document respectively, then P_{avg}, R_{avg} and $F1_{avg}$ are calculated as:

$$P_{avg} = \frac{\sum_{i=1}^{N_{doc}} P_i}{N_{doc}},$$ (2.5)

$$R_{avg} = \frac{\sum_{i=1}^{N_{doc}} R_i}{N_{doc}},$$ (2.6)

$$F1_{avg} = \frac{\sum_{i=1}^{N_{doc}} F1_i}{N_{doc}}.$$ (2.7)

Additionally, the average $F2$ score is calculated using the same principle:

$$F2_{avg} = \frac{\sum_{i=1}^{N_{doc}} F2_i}{N_{doc}}.$$ (2.8)

The second evaluation approach measures the overall inter-indexer consistency score ($IIC_{overall}$ or IIC_o) which is calculated by averaging the inter-indexer consistency with all the other annotators per one document and then averaging these results over all the documents (Joorabchi & Mahdi, 2013):

$$IIC_o = \frac{\sum_{i=1}^{N_{doc}} \sum_{j=1}^{N_{an}} IIC_{ij}}{N_{doc} N_{an}},$$

(2.9)

where IIC_{ij} is $F1$ score over the (single) i-th document per j-th annotator, N_{an} is the total number of annotators and N_{doc} is the total number of annotated documents as in previous equations.

Data

For the network enabled keyword extraction tasks, we use Croatian and English datasets. The HINA dataset contains news articles from the Croatian News Agency (HINA), with manually annotated keywords (keyphrases) by human experts (Mijić, Dalbelo-Bašić, & Šnajder, 2010; HINA, 2010). The documents in the collection are available in XML (*EXtensible Markup Language*) format containing the title, original text and corresponding annotations. In order to enable the evaluation of extracted keywords we use only the test part of the HINA collection – 60 documents. The test part of HINA dataset is annotated by 8 experts independently, where the inter-annotator agreement in terms of $F2$ scores (see Equation 2.4) are on average 46% (between 29.3% and 66.1% reported in (Mijić et al., 2010)) and in terms of average inter-indexer consistency (see Equation 2.9) 39.5%, (in a range between 31.9% and 44.4% - see Table 2). The selected 60 test texts varied in length from very short 59 up to 1,500 tokens (335 on average) and contained 20,125 tokens in total. For all 60 texts, there are 1,473 annotated keywords, all present in the original text. The number of annotated keywords per text varied between 9 and 42 (24 on average). From the documents in the HINA dataset we construct directed and weighted co-occurrence networks: one from the text in each document and an integral one from the texts in all documents; 61 networks in total.

The reported studies on the extraction of Croatian keywords using a HINA dataset are listed in reverse chronological order. The keyphrase extraction for the Croatian language has been addressed in both supervised and unsupervised settings (Ahel, Dalbelo-Bašić, & Šnajder, 2009; Bekavac & Šnajder, 2013; Mijić et al., 2010; Saratlija, Šnajder, & Dalbelo-Bašić, 2011). Ahel et al. (2009) use a Naïve Bayes classifier combined with tf-idf, Mijić et al. (2010) utilize the part-of-speech (POS) and morphosyntactic description (MSD) tags filtering followed by tf-idf ranking. Saratlija et al. (2011) exploit the distributional semantics to build topically related word clusters, from which they extract keywords and expand them into keyphrases. Bekavac and Šnajder (2013) propose a genetic programming approach for the extraction of keywords. The reported results about the extraction of top 15 keyphrases in terms of $F2$ score on HINA dataset are: 56.9% (Ahel et al., 2009) and 52.2% (Mijić et al., 2010) compared with annotators $F2$ scores between 48.5% and 63.2%. The baseline tf-idf (precision 10.5%, recall 18% and $F1$ 13.2%) and minimum description length (MDL) with additional POS filtering (MDL+POS) (precision 13.7%, recall 23.4% and $F1$ 17.2%) results are reported in (Ahel et al., 2009).

The English dataset WIKI-20 consists of 20 technical reports covering different aspects of computer science; each manually annotated by 15 teams of two senior computer science undergraduate students independently (Medelyan, Witten, & Milne, 2008; Medelyan, 2009b). Each team assigned around 5 terms to each report using the titles of Wikipedia articles as the controlled vocabulary. On average 5.7 keyphrases were assigned per document by one team, and the low overlap between the teams is reflected in the average inter-indexer consistency of 30.5%, (between 21.4% and 37.1%). For the WIKI-20 dataset we construct directed and weighted co-occurrence networks: one from the text in each document and an integral one from the texts in all documents; 21 networks in total. The WIKI-20 dataset is used in the studies (Joorabchi & Mahdi, 2013; Wang et al., 2014).

Wang et al. (2014) construct a description graph from candidate phrases in a document according to a predefined controlled vocabulary (English Wikipedia) and determine a mutual semantic related-ness between phrases. Then graph-based ranking methods degree, closeness, betweenness, PageRank, PageRankPrior and tf-idf as baseline are compared for top 5, 10 and 15 candidates extraction achieving the highest $F1$ score of 12% (tf-idf), 17% (PageRankPrior) and 20% (PageRankPrior) respectively. Their results suggest that the incorporation of the description relation into supervised bagging decision trees improves the extraction of the top 5 keyphrases overall inter-indexer consistency to 33.6%. Joorabchi and Mahdi (2013) propose a novel genetic based method for ranking and filtering the most probable keyphrases, where besides positional, statistical and semantical graph measures are also used as features, outperforming the human annotators' gold standard and other methods with 33.5% of the average inter-indexer consistency with human annotators on the top 5 extracted keyphrases. They also incorporate semantic relatedness between topics derived from Wikipedia's structure as the starting point.

Croatian is a highly inflectional Slavic language (words can have seven different cases for singular and seven for plural, genders and numbers). The Croatian word order is mostly free, especially in non-formal writing. These features place Croatian among morphologically rich and mostly free word-order languages. On the other hand, English grammar has minimal inflection compared with most other Indo-European languages, therefore it is considered to be analytic plus English word order is almost exclusively subject-verb-object.

Croatian source text usually requires substantial preprocessing (lemmatization, morphological nor-malization, stopwords removal, part-of-speech (POS) annotation, morphosyntactic description (MSD) tagging, etc.). Although we have designed our approach with light or no linguistic knowledge, some text preprocessing is needed and includes: the conversion of the input text to lowercase, the removal of misspelled symbols and lemmatization. Lemmatization was conducted to circumvent the effects of morphological variations in Croatian. Non-standard word forms such as numbers, dates, acronyms, ab-breviations etc., remain in the text, since the method is preferably resistant to the noise presented in the data source. In the same way we preprocessed the English text: converted to lowercase, removed special symbols and stemmed using Porter stemmer (Bird, Klein, & Loper, 2009).

It is important to note that unlike similar graph-based approaches in (Grineva et al., 2009; Palshikar, 2007) or other supervised and unsupervised approaches for Croatian presented in (Bekavac & Šnajder, 2013; Boudin, 2013; Lahiri et al., 2014; Saratlija et al., 2011), words added to the network in our ap-proach are not restricted to any syntactic or semantic filtering.

CENTRALITY MOTIVATED KEYWORD EXTRACTION

Network enabled keyword extraction methods exploit different measures for the task of the identification and ranking the most representative features of the source – the keywords. The first part of our research compares the performance of different centrality motivated network measures (in/out-degree, closeness and betweenness) with the performance of proposed in/out-selectivity measure on the Croatian and English texts.

The degree (Equations 1.1 and 1.2) of a node (word) is the number of neighboring nodes (different neighboring words). Typically, the nodes with the highest degree in the network are hubs, analogously the words with the highest degree are expectedly stopwords. The closeness (Equation 1.3) of a node (word) is related to the farness of the word from all other words in the text. The betweenness (Equation 1.4) of a node (word) is the measure of how many shortest paths between all other node-pairs are traversing a node. The words with the highest values of the betweenness centrality are considered to be important for the flow of information as well. Selectivity is node level network measure, defined as the ratio of the node strength and the node degree. In weighted and directed co-occurrence networks one can consider the in- and out- links for obtaining in/out-selectivity of the node (Equation 1.8).

The computation of the node's selectivity value is computationally less expensive than the computation of closeness and betweenness. Traditional algorithms for computation of closeness and betweenness have inherently high computational complexities – $O(N^3)$, but the faster variant of algorithm proposed in (Ulrik, 2001) reduced time complexity to $O(NM + N^2 \log N)$. In general, calculating the degree centrality for all nodes in a network has time complexity $O(N^2)$; while for the sparse networks it is $O(M)$ (Zhuge & Zhang, 2010). The same observations hold for the selectivity measure; the algorithm for calculating selectivity values for all nodes in sparse networks have a linear complexity.

Centrality Extraction Results

Comparative performance of centrality measures (closeness, betweenness, in/out-degree and in/out-selectivity) expressed in terms of average P, R and $F1$ score is presented in Table 1. The results are considered for the TOP 5 and the TOP 10 keywords extracted from the WIKI-20 and HINA datasets. The results in terms of $F1$ score are mostly in favor of the in/out-selectivity over other standard centrality network measures regardless of language. Only, for the TOP 10 task for the HINA dataset in/out-degree achieves slightly better $F1$ score. In general, selectivity achieves higher values of $F1$ score for the HINA than for the WIKI-20 dataset. Still, the in/out-selectivity $F1$ scores are only slightly over the lowest results reported in (Wang et al., 2014) on the WIKI-20 dataset (TOP 5 – 3.9% vs. 3.07% and for TOP 10 10.8% vs. 9.74%) and substantially over $F1$ of 13.2% reported for the baseline tf-idf on the HINA (Ahel et al., 2009). However, it is important to notice that (Wang et al., 2014) design their experiment with semantic preprocessing. They use network based centrality measures to extract keyphrases from network of semantic descriptions while we construct networks from the pure texts in documents, which means that we are able to extract only keyword candidates from words that were actually present in documents, without any additional knowledge of the domain or any syntactical preprocessing. Considering the linear computational complexity of selectivity, in/out-selectivity performs satisfactory in terms of P, R and $F1$ scores in comparison with other centrality measures after all.

The obtained results suggest several additional observations. The selectivity can efficiently differentiate between two basic types of nodes (words). The nodes with high strength and high degree values have low selectivity and they are usually closed-class words (e.g. stopwords, conjunctions, prepositions). The nodes with high strength and low degree have high selectivity values. Typically, the highest selectivity value nodes are open-class words which are preferred keyword candidates (nouns, adjectives, verbs) or even part of collocations, names, etc. On the other hand, the highest ranked words with an in/out-degree, closeness and betweenness are stopwords, which are not suitable keyword candidates. For example the TOP 10 ranked words according to in-degree centrality in an integral network constructed from merged texts from the HINA dataset (we show Croatian results translated into English) are: *to be, and, in, on, which, for, but, this, self, of*; according to betweenness they are: *to be, and, in, on, self, this, which, for,*

Croatian, but; according to in/out-selectivity in the same network they are*: Bratislava, area, Tuesday, inland, revolution, verification, decade, Balkan, freedom, Universe*. In short, it seems that selectivity is insensitive to stopwords and therefore can efficiently detect semantically rich open-class words from the network and extract better keyword candidates.

According to the results presented in Table 1, selectivity as the centrality measure has the potential to extract better keyword candidates than other network based centrality measures, mainly because it ranks open-class words higher.

Encouraged by the good performance of the selectivity over other tested graph-based measures (Table 1), we consider the selectivity as the centrality measure incorporated into the proposed SBKE method. Amongst the tested centrality measures, only the selectivity takes into account weights in the network which actually represent the frequencies of word bigrams and captures the importance of the node strength which is crucial for weighted networks. Additionally, since the degree centrality measure also yields optimistic results (Table 1), we decided to combine the degree measure with selectivity. Hence, we include the generalized selectivity measure in the SBKE method, as the extension of our initial experiment based on selectivity. The generalized selectivity measure (Equations 1.9 and 1.10) combines the importance of the node degree and node strength by tuning the parameter α. If the value of α is set between zero and one the generalized selectivity prefers nodes with higher degrees. On the contrary, if the value of α is above one, then it prefers nodes with lower degrees. For $\alpha = 1$ the generalized selectivity is equal to the node strength (Equation 1.5).

Table 1. The TOP 5 (left) and TOP 10 (right) ranked keyword candidates from closeness, betweenness, in/out-degree and in/out-selectivity values obtained from networks of 60 HINA news texts (top) and 20 WIKI-20 documents (bottom) in terms of average Recall (R_{avg}), Precision (P_{avg}) and F1 score ($F1_{avg}$)

DATASET	MEASURE	[%]	TOP 5			TOP 10		
			R_{avg}	P_{avg}	$F1_{avg}$	R_{avg}	P_{avg}	$F1_{avg}$
HINA	Closeness (cc_i)		4.3	39.3	7.2	8.4	42.9	12.8
	Betweenness (bc_i)		3.6	40.8	6.5	9.2	52.8	13.9
	in/out-degree ($dc_i^{in/out}$)		23.0	38.4	17.0	62.1	25.1	**26.6**
	in/out-selectivity ($e_i^{in/out}$)		14.0	35.9	**19.3**	16.8	38.0	22.1
WIKI-20	Closeness (cc_i)		1.6	42.5	3.1	5.3	63.3	9.7
	Betweenness (bc_i)		0.3	10.0	0.5	2.6	55.0	4.9
	in/out-degree ($dc_i^{in/out}$)		0.1	5.0	0.3	2.5	57.5	4.8
	in/out-selectivity ($e_i^{in/out}$)		2.3	17.8	**3.9**	8.6	18.2	**10.8**

Moreover, results in Table 1 suggest that selectivity as a measure is better suited for highly inflectional languages like Croatian than for the inflective ones like English, which is elaborated in detail in the Discussion section. Still, based on these preliminary results we decided to employ the selectivity measure for the further development of the selectivity-based keyword extraction method and later to extend it with the generalized selectivity.

SELECTIVITY-BASED KEYWORD EXTRACTION

The second part of our research develops a Selectivity-Based Keyword Extraction (SBKE) method. The first phase, the construction of all co-occurrence networks is consistent with the principles elaborated in the section above (Methodology). The second phase is the SBKE method itself. SBKE is a fully unsupervised method and consists of two steps: keyword candidate extraction (based on selectivity values) and keyword expansion to longer sequences of keyword candidates.

Keyword Candidate Extraction

For keyword candidate extraction and for the evaluation of the SBKE method with manually annotated keyword sets we use directed and weighted networks all constructed from 60 texts in the HINA and 20 texts in the WIKI-20. From all the constructed networks, we rank the nodes according to the highest $e_i^{in/out}$ selectivity values above a threshold ($e_i^{in/out} > 1$). Preserving the same threshold value in all documents resulted in a different number of nodes (one word long keyword candidates) extracted from each network in SET1, which is the union of the highly-ranked nodes according to the in/out-selectivity values.

Keyword Expansion

Keyword expansion is tasked with the detection of neighboring nodes for already selected keyword candidates (SET1) to two word long sequences of keyword candidates (word-pairs) and to three word long sequences of keyword candidates (word-triples).

The expansion of SET1 to word-pairs (SET2) is obtained from the set of the highest ranked in/out-selectivity value nodes to the neighboring nodes considering the maximum of the in/out weights on the in/out links. More precisely, for nodes that have passed in-selectivity ranking (e_i^{in}), we isolate one neighbor node with the highest outgoing weight ($\max w_i^{out}$) – predecessor. The same procedure is applied to the out-selectivity ranking (e_i^{out}) with a slightly difference - the opposite direction of links; we isolate one neighbor node with the highest ingoing weight ($\max w_i^{in}$) – successor. Therefore, the keyword-two expansion (K2E) presented at the top of Figure 2 results in a SET2 - keyword candidate set of highest ranked word-pairs.

The second part of the expansion is called the keyword-three expansion (K3E) presented at the bottom of Figure 2. The procedure is very similar to K2E. However, the expanding predecessor (the ingoing links of SET2) or the expanding successor (the outgoing links from SET2) is carried out over all the already obtained word-pairs candidates in SET2. The expansion of any predecessor or successor is again for the node with the highest in/out weight value. The result of in/out-selectivity extraction in K3E is a set of word-triples, noted as SET3.

Figure 2. Schematic representation of the SBKE method architecture (keyword extraction – SET1, and expansions to word-pairs – SET2 or word-triples – SET3 for case of in-selectivity at the top and for out-selectivity at the bottom)

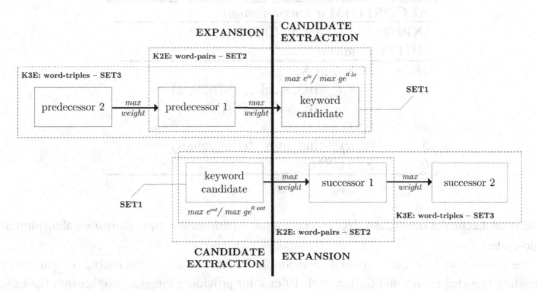

SBKE with Generalized Selectivity

The SBKE method can be easily adjusted by incorporating new measures – hence the generalized selectivity measure. In that case the SBKE method remains the same, except that we replace in/out-selectivity ($e_i^{in/out}$, e in short), with generalized in/out-selectivity ($ge_i^{\alpha\ in/out}$, ge^{α} in short) in the first step of keyword candidates' rankings and extraction (SET1).

Generalized selectivity (ge^{α}), is the node centrality measure that can be tuned with the positive parameter α (Equations 1.9 and 1.10). By changing the value of α it is possible to adjust the relationship between the node degree and strength and accordingly affect the ranking results. For the different values of α, the measure will provide different sets of keywords. For the incorporation of generalized in/out-selectivity into the SBKE method first, we determine the value of the α parameter which best fits the experimental settings according to the IIC_o scores and next we evaluate the performance on both languages (results are in the next section).

In order to determine the value of the tuning parameter α, we extract keywords altering the α values over an interval [0.5, 10] and evelute obtained results with IIC_o as presented in Figure 3. Initially, we test if there is a statistical correlation between the overall inter-indexer consistency scores measured for the TOP 5 and TOP 10 extracted keywords in SET1 of both datasets. The numerical results obtained as Pearson's correlations between IIC_o scores of TOP 5 and TOP 10 extracted keywords (r=0.2281, r^2 =0.0520 for HINA and r=0.2831, r^2 =0.0086 for WIKI-20) indicate weak correlations and they are not statistically significant (at p<0.001, α=0.05).

Therefore, we determine the value of the α parameter based on the IIC_o maximization principle. We propose a simple *α-maximization* algorithm for determining the best α value: for each dataset we calculate IIC_o scores for the TOP 5 and TOP 10 keywords for the different values of $\alpha \in$ [0.5, 10] and

Figure 3. $\alpha-maximization$ algorithm for tuning α values in the generalized selectivity over the highest IIC_o scores

ALGORITHM α-maximization
INPUT: i∈A where A={0.5, 1, ..., 10}
OUTPUT: max α
1:      FOR α in A:
2:           $IIC_o = calc_{IIC}$ (SBKE, α)
3:           IIC_ovalues $\leftarrow$ (IIC_o, α)
4:      END
5:      (x, α) = find_max_x(IIC_ovalues)
6:      RETURN α

choose α that achieves the highest IIC_o score. Figure 3 outlines the α-*maximization* algorithm in the pseudo-code.

In the Figure 4 we report the maximal value for the TOP 5 task in order to enable comparisons with the existing reported results and for the TOP 10 task for providing integral insights into the exposed behavior. It is possible to notice that IIC_o scores behave differently on two different datasets, especially in the case $\alpha = 1$. In the Croatian dataset values of the IIC_o scores initially increase and then steeply decrease, while in the English dataset they steadily increase over the initial interval (α values lower than 2.5).

In the HINA dataset the maximal value of the IIC_o score for the TOP 5 task is obtained at $\alpha = 5.5$ and for the TOP 10 task at $\alpha = 1$. However, an even better TOP 5 IIC_o score for Croatian is achieved with the selectivity measure (note the dots on the y-axis), which is not the case for English. In the WIKI-20 dataset the maximal values of the IIC_o score for the TOP 5 task are obtained at $\alpha = 2.5$ and at $\alpha = 5.5$. Since, the best results of the IIC_o score for the English TOP 10 task are also obtained at $\alpha = 2.5$, we set 2.5 as the final value for the α parameter. Note that unlike Croatian, in the English dataset generalized selectivity yields better results than the selectivity (again represented on the y-axis with dots).

Evaluation of the SBKE Method Results

The evaluation of the SBKE method reported in Table 2 and Table 3 follows the second evaluation principle (see the Evaluation Methodology section) which compares the SBKE method's results with the overall inter-indexer consistency (IIC_o) of human experts on the HINA and WIKI-20 datasets (left parts of Tables 2 and 3 respectively). The average annotators' IIC_o on HINA is 39.5% which is higher than 30.5% reported for WIKI-20. The higher average IIC_o reflects the expertise of annotators vs. teams of students and more importantly; this reflects the fact that the HINA annotations contain keyphrases from original texts while WIKI-20 uses taxonomy of Wikipedia's topics as vocabulary, where the former is more appropriate for the SBKE method.

Figure 4. The performance of the first step (SET1) of the SBKE method in terms of IIC_o scores for the TOP 5 and TOP 10 keywords measured for generalized selectivity ($ge^{\alpha \; in/out}$) with different values of parameter α (plotted as lines) and selectivity ($e^{in/out}$) values (plotted as dots on the y-axis) for the HINA and WIKI-20 datasets

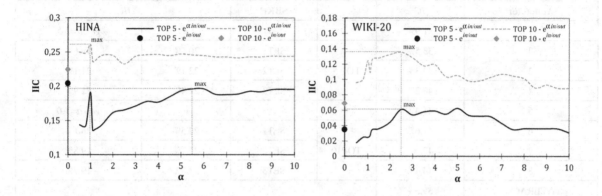

The overall inter-indexer consistency scores for the TOP 5 and TOP 10 keywords extraction task between all human annotators and the SBKE method for the HINA dataset are reported in the right part of Table 2. The expansion of SET1 to SET3 using selectivity slightly improves IIC_o of both tasks, and the highest IIC_o scores are achieved in SET3. This is also the case for the generalized selectivity ($\alpha = 5.5$) at the TOP 5 task, but it is not exhibited at the TOP 10 task.

The IIC_o scores between all human annotators and the SBKE method for the TOP 5 and TOP 10 task for the WIKI-20 dataset for SET1, SET2 and SET3 are reported in the right part of Table 3. In the case of the English language the values of α parameter is set to 2.5, and the IIC_o scores are improved for the generalized selectivity over selectivity. The highest IIC_o scores are achieved for the SET3 regardless of using selectivity or generalized selectivity.

DOCUMENT VS. COLLECTION EXTRACTION

Finally, in order to quantify the performance of selectivity-based keyword extraction in larger and smaller networks, i.e. individual documents and document collection, we construct one integral network from all the documents in the collection using the same construction principle as before and compare it with the average scores of all the individual networks.

Document vs. Collection-Oriented Extraction Results

The evaluation methodology of comparing the document with the collection-oriented extraction task is always against the gold standard – either the union of unique annotated keywords per document (individual task) or the union of all unique annotated keywords from all documents (collection task).

The keyword extraction results in terms of average recall, precision and $F1$ scores for the 60 individual documents (individual networks) are in the left part, while the scores for the complete HINA collection

Table 2. Comparison of overall inter-indexer consistency (IIC_o) scores for the extraction of TOP 5 keywords per 8 human annotators; and for TOP 5 and TOP 10 keywords by SBKE (SET1, SET2 and SET3) over all 60 HINA documents obtained with the selectivity (e) and with the generalized selectivity ($ge^\alpha, \alpha = 5.5, \ \alpha = 1$) measures

Annotator	IIC_o		SBKE	IIC_o	
1	31.9%			*e*	ge^α, α=5.5
2	33.5%	TOP 5	SET1	20.5%	19.6%
3	39.3%		SET2	22.1%	21.1%
4	40.2%		SET3	**22.4%**	**21.9%**
5	41.4%			*e*	ge^α, α=1.0
6	41.6%	TOP10	SET1	22.5%	**26.1%**
7	43.9%		SET2	22.7%	19.8%
8	44.4%		SET3	**23.0%**	19.7%
AVERAGE	**39.5%**				

Table 3. Comparison of the overall inter-indexer consistency (IIC_o) scores for the extraction of TOP 5 keywords per 15 annotating teams; and for TOP 5 and TOP 10 keywords by SBKE (SET1, SET2 and SET3) over all 20 WIKI-20 documents performed with the selectivity (e) and with the generalized selectivity (ge^α, $\alpha = 2.5$) measures

Annotator	IIC_o		SBKE	IIC_o	
1	21.4%			*e*	ge^α, α=2.5
2	24.1%	TOP 5	SET1	3.5%	6.1%
3	26.2%		SET2	7.5%	10.8%
4	28.7%		SET3	**10.3%**	**12.0%**
5	30.2%	TOP10	SET1	6.9%	13.6%
6	30.8%		SET2	11.4%	16.3%
7	31.0%		SET3	**12.5%**	**17.2%**
8	31.2%				
9	31.6%				
10	31.6%				
11	31.6%				
12	32.4%				
13	33.8%				
14	35.5%				
15	37.1%				
AVERAGE	**30.5%**				

are in the right part (integral network) of Table 4. The results of one integral network support the findings of extraction from individual networks: the expansion of keywords to longer sequences (SET2 and SET3) in terms of precision decreases; and in terms of recall increases. The highest average recall of 29.55% in individual networks is obtained with the expansion to SET3. The recall in SET1 (integral) is already at 30.71% and with the expansion to SET3 is almost doubled to 60.47%. The SET2 yields the best results in terms of $F1$ score.

The same experiment is repeated for English (WIKI-20) and the results are listed in Table 5, but with a slight modification applied – the keyword candidates in SET1 are extracted with selectivity values above thresholds of one ($e_i^{in/out} > 1$) and two ($e_i^{in/out} > 2$) respectively. The altered threshold values reduced the number of unique extracted candidates from 1,709 to 462 in SET1. The latter is closer to the total number of annotated keyword by humans in the WIKI-20 (i.e. 428 – calculated in stemmed word form). The higher threshold value filters predecessors/successors with higher weights on the in/out links, which are more frequently co-occurring with the current candidate.

If we compare the average recall of 20 individual networks and integral network (threshold 1) the recall of SET1 is increased by 17.11%. Still, the precision is low, reflecting the greediness of the SBKE method, resulting in moderate $F1$ scores achieved in SET1 (21.48% individual average; 30.5% integral). The increment of the threshold value above 2 is expectedly reflected in the decrease of recall by 43.46% and the increase of precision by 11.22%, resulting in the minor change of $F1$ score by 0.96%. This illustrates the possibility of fine adjustments of the SBKE method to the size of the keyword candidate set. Finally, with the expansion to longer keyword sequences (SET3) the threshold adjustment raises the average $F1$ score of individual networks by 14.02%.

The reported results in both tables (regardless of language) suggest that an expansion to word-pairs (SET2) and word-triples (SET3) using a simple filtering principle and subsequently extracting as many as possible candidates deteriorate the precision of the SBKE method. Furthermore, we show that the adjustment of the filtering threshold can effectively mitigate this effect through the tuning of the number of initial keyword candidates in SET1. Finally, the results of extracting keywords from the whole collection are significantly improved over individual documents extraction (Croatian by 8.95%; English by 12.73% – calculated as the difference between the best $F1$ scores regardless of SET).

From the presented results, it is evident that SBKE yields better results on the whole collection than on an individual document (see Tables 4 and 5). Hence, the recommendation of using a SBKE method is rather on collection-oriented tasks than on document-oriented tasks.

Table 4. Comparison of results for 60 individual networks (left) and one integral network (right) from all HINA news articles in terms of recall (R), precision (P) and F1 score for one word long keywords (SET1), word-pairs (SET2) and word-triples (SET3) (Note, results are reported for all extracted and all annotated keywords)

SET	[%]	60 Individual Networks			Integral Network		
		R_{avg}	P_{avg}	$F1_{avg}$	R	P	$F1$
SET1		18.90	**39.35**	23.60	30.71	**35.80**	33.06
SET2		19.74	39.15	**24.76**	33.46	33.97	**33.71**
SET3		**29.55**	22.96	22.71	**60.47**	19.89	28.89

Table 5. Comparison of results for 20 individual networks (left) and the integral network (right) from the WIKI-20 in terms of recall (R), precision (P) and F1 scores for one word long keywords (SET1) with the selectivity values above thresholds ($e_i^{in/out} > 1$), ($e_i^{in/out} > 2$), word-pairs (SET2) and word-triples (SET3)

SET	[%]	20 Individual Networks ($e_i^{in/out} > 1$)			Integral Network ($e_i^{in/out} > 1$)			Integral Network ($e_i^{in/out} > 2$)		
		R_{avg}	P_{avg}	$F1_{avg}$	R	P	F1	R	P	F1
SET1		59.06	**13.40**	**21.48**	76.17	**19.08**	**30.51**	32.71	30.30	31.46
SET2		60.12	12.33	20.46	76.64	18.87	30.29	36.45	31.97	34.06
SET3		**62.17**	12.05	20.19	**77.50**	15.75	26.18	**36.68**	**32.04**	**34.21**

DISCUSSION

We designed the SBKE method purely from the statistical and structural information encompassed in the source text which is reflected in the structure of the network. Other graph enabled approaches presented in (Grineva et al., 2009; Palshikar, 2007) report high results however they incorporate linguistic knowledge in a form of different syntactic filters (POS tagging, stopwords filtering, noun-phrase parsing, etc.) and therefore, are generally more demanding to implement. Other methods that use supervised approaches on the WIKI-20 dataset (Joorabchi & Mahdi, 2013; Wang et al., 2014) achieve a better overall score. However, on the HINA dataset the SBKE method performs correctly.

In the top left part of Table 6 we report the performance of the SBKE method in parallel with other approaches applied on the HINA dataset: tf-idf, MDL+POS and SBKE (using in/out selectivity) method in terms of the average $F1$ scores over all documents. A comparison is available only with the results reported in terms of the $F1$ score at the TOP 10 extraction task (note that other related results on the HINA are reported in terms of $F2$ and thus not included). The SBKE method outperforms the other two methods especially in the case of SBKE-SET2. In the bottom left part of Table 6 the SBKE using generalized in/out-selectivity is compared with the overall inter-indexer consistency (IIC_o) of human experts. For the WIKI-20 dataset we list the reported results in the related work in terms of the overall inter-indexer consistency in the right part of Table 6. Here, the SBKE method is slightly better than the baseline tf-idf, and all the other supervised methods, as well as the humans, significantly outperform the SBKE method.

Since Croatian is a highly inflectional Slavic language, the source text usually needs substantial preprocessing (lemmatization - morphological normalization, stopwords removal, part-of-speech (POS) annotation, morphosyntactic descriptions (MSD) tagging, etc.), we have showed that a selectivity enabled approach requires little or no linguistic knowledge. The obtained results indicate that a selectivity-based method achieves results which are comparable with reported supervised and unsupervised methods in terms of $F1$, but lag behind human annotators in terms of the overall inter-indexer consistency (Croatian 39.5%). This is a satisfactory result, but on the other hand we should bear in mind that only the statistical and structural properties of the network are used as the extraction information, without any syntactic preprocessing or incorporating lexical and semantical knowledge.

In the extension of presented experiments, we show that the SBKE method can be easily modified with a changed ranking mechanism (e.g. selectivity replaced with generalized selectivity). Tuning the value of α parameter the IIC_o improved the English results in the TOP 5 task: SET1 2.6%; SET2 3.3%;

Table 6. Comparison of the performance of the SBKE method in terms of the F1 and IIC_o score with other approaches (HINA left- TOP10 task, WIKI-20 right – TOP5 task)

HINA			WIKI-20		
Method	**Approach**	*F1**	**Method**	**Approach**	*IIC_o***
tf-idf (Ahel et al., 2009)	unsupervised	13.2%	tf-idf (Medelyan, 2009a)	unsupervised	8.3%
MDL+POS (Ahel et al., 2009)	Supervised	17.2%	SBKE, α=2.5	graph-based	12.0%
SBKE - SET2	graph-based	24.8%	KEA++ (Medelyan, 2009a)	supervised	22.6%
			Humans	gold standard	30.5%
Method	**Approach**	*IIC_o**	Maui (Wang et al., 2014)	supervised	31.6%
SBKE - SET1, α=1.0	graph-based	26.1%	GA (Joorabchi et al., 2013)	supervised	33.5%
Humans	gold standard	39.5%	Maui+ (Wang et al., 2014)	supervised	33.6%
*for TOP 10 KE task			***for TOP 5 KE task*		

SET3 1.7% and in the TOP10 task: SET1 6.7%; SET2 4.9%; SET3 4.7%. At the same time in Croatian the results of generalized selectivity outperform selectivity only in the TOP 10 - SET1 by 3.6%. More precisely, the SBKE with generalized selectivity performance decreases in HINA at the TOP 10 task with the expansion to longer sequences of keyword candidates (from SET1 to SET 2 and to SET3).

For the keyword extraction task the strategy "more is better" can be utilized, since there is no objective judgment on correct keywords (the agreement between human annotators is 39.5% on HINA and 30.5% on WIKI-20). Hence, it is preferable to extract more keywords which make a tradeoff between the precision and recall of the methods. The second polemic issue of keyword extraction task is: shorter keyword sequences are more general vs. longer ones which are more accurate. Motivated by these open arguments, and by the approach of other authors on the same dataset (Ahel et al., 2009; Bekavac & Šnajder, 2013; Mijić et al., 2010; Saratlija et al., 2011), we initially decided to follow the same principle: to extract as many keyword candidates as possible. Thus, the SBKE is designed as "greedy" – to extract as much candidates as possible and this causes the over-generation problem (Boudin, 2015). More precisely, we only apply simple and computationally cheap filtering of the maximal weights in both (in and out) directions of the links ($\max w_i^{in}, \max w_i^{out}$) instead of the fine-tuned ranking. Potentially, this can be overcome with more sophisticated rankings which exploit the structural or topological properties of the network (and are naturally computationally more expensive). Still, this remains an open challenge for future work.

The comparison of the SBKE results for the individual vs. collection-oriented extraction task suggests the significant advantage of the SBKE method on a larger network (document collection) than on smaller networks (isolated documents) in both languages. The results, regardless of the language, suggest that expansion to longer keyword sequences applying a simple filtering principle and subsequently extracting as many as possible candidates deteriorates the precision of the SBKE method, and bursts the recall. Furthermore, the adjustment of the filtering threshold to the expected number of keywords can effectively bypass the effect of over-generation. Finally, the results of extracting keywords from the whole collection are significantly improved over individual documents' extractions (Croatian by 8.95%; English by 12.73%).

Although SBKE performs well in the TOP 5 and TOP 10 Croatian extraction tasks, it still falls short for the English dataset. It seems that selectivity is much more appropriate for the Croatian as a inflectional language than for English as an inflective language, besides the already mentioned characteristic that without any text preprocessing, selectivity successfully differentiates open class words from closed class word (like stopwords), and is therefore resistant to noise present in the text (i.e. numbers, dates, acronyms). It should also be mentioned that when we are comparing across languages, besides the language characteristics, the different nature of annotations also contribute to this difference. Namely, in the Croatian dataset all the annotated keywords were present in the original texts.

For the English language SBKE lags behind other methods especially behind supervised ones which incorporate semantic knowledge. Nevertheless the SBKE with generalized selectivity on average raised the English results by 2.5% at the TOP 5 task and by 5.4% at the TOP10 task. Additionally, the high recall (which can exceed 60% in the individual or 75% in the collection extraction tasks) suggests that SBKE can be applied as a cheap preprocessing method followed by more sophisticated approaches, especially for the extraction of the first initial set of keyword candidates in the new collection which can serve as the first interpolation. We also introduce a thresholding mechanism which can efficiently adapt the number of extracted keywords.

Moreover, we show that the incorporation of the new modified measure of generalized selectivity into SBKE is easy, and allows the fine tuning of SBKE's performance for the dataset and/or for the language. We conclude that SBKE's performance is more applicable to collection extraction than to the document extraction task.

All this can be specifically relevant for keyword extraction tasks in low-resourced languages (regarding the development of language tools), given that the SBKE method is general enough, and can be easily ported to a new language with low computational costs. The proposed SBKE method infers the keywords solely on the information captured in the structure of the network, which is beneficial for extraction in the multilingual setup and of high importance for facilitating the portability of the SBKE method to new languages and domains.

Although there are numerous keyword extraction methods for well-resourced languages (mainly English) with a high reported performance (Rafiei-Asl & Nickabadi, 2017; Ying et al., 2017; Bougouin, Boudin, & Daille, 2016; Martinez-Romo, Araujo, & Duque Fernandez, 2016), in the absence of language tools it is difficult to port them to now language, especially for under-resourced languages. The automatic keyword extraction from texts written in under-resourced languages still remains an open research question. For under-resourced languages there are no reliable tools which can be used for keyword extraction task and text preprocessing, such as: POS and MSD taggers, stemmers, lemmatizers, stopwords lists, lexical resources like WordNet, controlled vocabularies, benchmark or monitoring datasets, and other tools or resources.

In order to support multilingualism, and circumvent poor portability to under resourced languages, we advocate for the use of unsupervised graph- or network-enabled methods. Network structure enables representation of the input text as graph or network, regardless of language, or the domain of interest. The SBKE method use only the knowledge incorporated in the structure of network to extract keywords and therefore circumvent the lack of linguistic tools. Application of the SBKE method instead of developing new tools or resources requires only tuning of various parameters which are inherent for particular implementation (fine tuning of parameters for candidate extraction, setting the filtering thresholds for keyword expansion, setting the value of the α parameter for generalized selectivity, etc.) (Beliga & Martinčić-Ipšić, 2016).

Another open research question in the keyword extraction task is to develop a method that is general enough for keyword extraction in several languages simultaneously, hence in a multilingual setup. The prerequisites needed for this desirable characteristic are that the method does not require deeper linguistic preprocessing are again incorporated into the SBKE method. The work in (Beliga, Kitanović, Ranković, & Martinčić-Ipšić, 2017) examines the potential of SBKE method to extract keywords in a new language (Serbian) and in a bilingual environment of Serbian and English languages. The SBKE is applied on parallel texts (abstracts of scientific publication in the Serbian and English languages) from the domain of geology and mining shows promising results. The new set-up of parallel texts enabled better insights into the performance across different languages simultaneously preserving the nature, size and content of the texts. Usually methods compare unrelated datasets in one language and rarely unrelated datasets in different languages. This set-up provides a controlled and fair environment for the evaluation.

We show that the SBKE method is general enough to be easily ported to another language – Serbian, because it requires only shallow linguistic preprocessing. The applicability of the SBKE method in a new and highly specialized scientific domain – a text collection from the geology and mining domain exposed promising results. Finally, the scientific abstracts are limited in the number of characters, therefore we also test the applicability of SBKE on short texts. To conclude, evaluation results suggest that SBKE can be easily ported to a new language, domain of interest and a type of text in the sense of its structure. Still there are drawbacks, the method can extract only the words that appear in the text. The problem of generating OOV (out of vocabulary) keywords with the SBKE method can be bypassed only by inclusion of the external domain knowledge.

KEYWORD EXTRACTION APPLICATIONS

Nowdays keyword extraction is not an isolated task and is usually incorporated into different NLP or IR applications. It is common to find keyword extraction in document, text or web *classification* (Onan, Korukoğlu, & Bulut, 2016) or *clustering* (Tonella, Ricca, Pianta & Girardi, 2003); document (Ravinuthala & Ch, 2016; Balaji, Geetha & Parthasarathi, 2016) and web content *summarization* (Lynn, Choi & Kim, 2017); document content-based *recommender systems* (Ferrara, Pudota & Tasso, 2011); *e-learning* recommendations (Mbipom, Craw & Massie, 2016); *sentiment analysis and opinion mining* (Berend, 2011); *medical-term extraction* from clinical letters (Liu, Chung, Wang, Ng, & Morlet 2015); *search engines* which support end users in formulating queries (Gong & Liu, 2009); *question-answering* (Moldovan et al., 2000); *advertisements targeting* on web pages (Yih, Goodman & Carvalho, 2006); *topic tracking* in online news (Lee & Kim, 2008); *ontology learning* (El Idrissi, Frikh, & Ouhbi, 2014) and *ontology construction* (Frikh, Djaanfar & Ouhbi, 2011); *social network visualization* (Grineva, Grinev & Lizorkin, 2009); *tag clouds* construction (Dunaiski, Fischer, Greene, Ilvovsky & Kuznetsov, 2015); email *topic detection* (Lahiri, Mihalcea & Lai, 2016), etc. Although we witness extremely diverse applications of keyword extraction in many areas, next, we will focus on some representative examples that have been reported recently.

Onan, Korukoğlu, and Bulut (2016) empirically analyze and evaluate the effectiveness of statistical keyword extraction methods in conjunction with ensemble learning methods for the document classification task. They exploit extracted keywords as the document representation features (ranging from 5 to 100) radically reducing the dimensionality of the document representation model. Empirical analysis of five methods (the most frequent measure based KE, the TF-ISF based KE, the co-occurrence statistical information based KE, the eccentricity-based KE and TextRank algorithm) indicate that bagging ensemble of random forest with the most-frequent based keyword extraction method yields promising result for text classification for the ACM document collection. The highest average predictive performance of 93,80% is obtained. Study indicates that keywords of documents in conjunction with ensemble learning can enhance the predictive performance and scalability of text classification schemes, especially the dimensionality of the vector model, which is of practical importance in the field of text classification.

Mocanu, Tapu and Tapu (2016) present an example of topic modeling for the retrieval of video segments based on the extracted keywords. They propose a novel video retrieval approach based on relevant topics extracted from video subtitles using NLP techniques and combined with the temporal segmentation of the video into scenes. In order to enable efficiently access to the video streams, they from each subtitle extract keyphrases or concepts defined as meaningful and significant expressions of one or more words that contains at least one noun. They structure a list of keyphrases into subjects of interest that corresponds to well-identified and semantically meaningful topics. The keyphrases are extracted based on raw frequencies of words and n-grams in corpus and used to construct a representation graph for each video segment. For each keyword the retrieved concepts are evaluated based on the SemEval-2010 strategy that creates mapping between the topics extracted by human and the output of the system. The results of proposed approach, performed on ten videos with their associated subtitles from France Television broadcast corpus achieves mean average precision (MAP) score of 0.51.

Paramonov, Lagutina, Mamedov and Lagutina (2016) study keyword extraction as the model for the enhancement of web pages in the e-tourism domain, where they propose a construction of a well-connected graph of keywords. They developed a method that exploits a combination of well-known keyphrase extraction algorithms TextRank, topical Page Rank, KEA and Maui with thesaurus-based procedure that improves the text-via-keyphrase graph connectivity. The effectiveness of their approach is demonstrated on the corpus of the Open Karelia tourist information system. As the extracted keyphrases correctly identify the main topics and key terms in the text, they can be useful for improving navigation in websites and information systems. When user explores some text, and clicks on keyphrase, system shows a list of other corresponding keyphrases from which the user can choose a text for further reading. Text linked by common keyphrases forms a well-connected graph, enabling a more convenient navigation for the user. This research is strongly targeted at e-tourism domain – i.e. web sites and information systems containing information about tourist objects and tourist landmarks with their descriptions, photographs, locations, etc. In contrary existing methods for KE are specialized for extraction from news or scientific articles. Therefore, for e-tourism domain, it is important to take into account specificity of the domain as well as requirements of connectivity. It was shown that well-connected text via keyphrases graph could be used as a basis for construction of a domain-specific thesaurus.

The research by Mbipom, Craw, and Massie (2016) point out that the Web content focused on learning is growing incessantly. However, learners can find it hard to retrieve relevant material that is well-aligned with their learning goals and the present stage of their knowledge. In addition, they emphasize the difficulty in assembling effective keyword searches due to both an inherent lack of domain knowledge and the unfamiliarity with the vocabulary used in the domain. Author develop a hybrid approach that allows the background knowledge to influence the retrieval or the recommendation of new learning materials by leveraging the concepts (keywords) extracted according to the controlled vocabulary. In the absence of keywords, they automatically extract *n*-grams from structured collection to provide a set of potential concept labels. Next, they use a domain lexicon to validate the extracted n-grams as in the controlled vocabulary extraction task. The output of this process is a set of extracted concepts, each comprising a label and an associated pseudo-document.

Zimniewicz, Kurowski and Węglarz (2016) are studying keyword extraction techniques from the aspect of operational research. The authors noted that methods can have expensive computational complexity as opposed to the linear complexity of the SBKE method discussed earlier in this paper. They argue that the scalability and performance are crucial in real applications, however they notice a lack of mathematical models helping users to apply scheduling theory for NLP approaches. Moreover, as the number of different approaches for KE is constantly growing, it is difficult to select the best approach, Moreover, it is not trivial to compare and assess the overall performance of different algorithms. Consequently, they propose methods for the evaluation of performance of different KE algorithms, which are based on overall processing time and on the measured quality of obtained keywords. In short, their interdisciplinary research introduces a new scheduling model for keyword extraction and a new evaluation criterion based on the quality of answers given by extraction algorithm- correctness. Finally, they show how to apply the scheduling model to consider a correctness based on scheduled length.

CONCLUSION

In this paper, we propose the Selectivity-Based Keyword Extraction (SBKE) method as a new unsupervised method for network enabled keyword extraction. The node in/out-selectivity and generalized in/out-selectivity values are calculated from a directed weighted network as the average weight distributed on the ingoing/outgoing links of the single node and used in the procedure of keyword candidate ranking and extraction. We proposed keyword expansion to two or three word long keyword sequences determined by the in- or out- weight of the previous or following nodes.

The evaluation of selectivity-based extraction was performed on 60 Croatian documents from HINA and on 20 English documents from WIKI-20 datasets individually. The results (in terms of $F1$ score) are mostly in favor of the in/out-selectivity over the in/out-degree, closeness and betweenness centrality measures regardless of the language.

The performance of the SBKE method is evaluated on the tasks of keyword extraction from individual documents and also on the task of extraction from the whole collections of both datasets. The performance of the SBKE method for individual networks is evaluated against human experts in terms of overall inter-indexer consistency for the TOP 5 and 10 extraction tasks. The obtained Croatian results indicate that the selectivity-based method achieves results which are outperforming reported supervised and unsupervised methods, but lag behind human annotators. The English results show that SBKE outperforms the baseline tf-idf, but lags behind other methods or humans.

The SBKE method can be easily adjusted by incorporating the new ranking mechanism – generalized selectivity measure. In that case the SBKE method remains the same, except that we replace selectivity with a generalized in/out-selectivity measure in the first step of keyword candidates' rankings and extraction. We show that tuning the value of α parameter raised the English results on average by 2.5% at the TOP 5 and by 5.4% at the TOP10 extraction task.

The SBKE method for individual networks and for integral networks is evaluated in terms of average recall, precision and the $F1$ score. The experimental results point out that the selectivity-based keyword extraction has a great potential for extracting keywords from a collection of documents only exploiting the statistics and structure of text reflected in the language network. In terms of $F1$ score, the results of a document collection extraction task far exceed those from individual documents: Croatian by 8.95% and English by 12.73%.

Furthermore, the extraction of keywords from one document is in line with the existing supervised and unsupervised keyphrase extraction methods for the Croatian language. The results are promising especially if we take into account the fact that our approach incorporates no linguistic knowledge, but is derived from pure statistics and the structure of the text is obtained from the network. Moreover, SBKE is general enough and can easily be ported to new languages, while it requires no linguistic preprocessing. We believe that this is especially important for extractions tasks in low-resourced languages that have less developed language tools. Since there are no manual annotations required and preprocessing is minimized, fast computing is also an advantage of our selectivity-based method. Proposed SBKE method infers the keywords solely on the information captured in the structure of the network and disregards any external semantic information, which is beneficial for extraction in the multilingual setup and of high importance for facilitating the portability of the SBKE method to new languages and domains.

Therefore, we conclude that the true potential of the proposed SBKE method, in its generality, portability and low computation costs, which positions it as a strong candidate for preprocessing steps in collections which lack human annotations. In such a scenario, SBKE can be applied as a cheap preprocessing step followed by more sophisticated methods.

In future work we plan to investigate the SBKE method in: (1) different text types – considering the texts of different length, genre and topics, (2) other languages – tests on other English datasets and other languages preferably in a multilingual environment, (3) new filtering strategies – incorporating new network measures into filtering, (4) entity extraction – tests on whether entities can be extracted from complex networks, (5) text summarization – using SBKE in the extraction step in order to identify the most salient elements in a text, (6) twitter messages – large collection of extremely short and noisy texts (microblogs).

ACKNOWLEDGMENT

This work has been supported in part by University of Rijeka under the LangNet project [13.13.2.2.07].

REFERENCES

Abilhoa, W. D., & Castro, L. N. (2014). A keyword extraction method from twitter messages represented as graphs. *Applied Mathematics and Computation*, *240*, 308–325. doi:10.1016/j.amc.2014.04.090

Ahel, R., Dalbelo-Bašić, B., & Šnajder, J. (2009). Automatic keyphrase extraction from Croatian newspaper articles. In *2nd International Conference The Future of Information Sciences, Digital Resources and Knowledge Sharing (INFuture 2009)* (pp. 207-218). Zagreb, Croatia: Faculty of Humanities and Social Sciences.

Balaji, J., Geetha, T., & Parthasarathi, R. (2016). Abstractive Summarization: A Hybrid Approach for the Compression of Semantic Graphs. *International Journal on Semantic Web and Information Systems*, *12*(2), 76–99. doi:10.4018/IJSWIS.2016040104

Bekavac, M., & Šnajder, J. (2013). GPKEX: Genetically Programmed Keyphrase Extraction from Croatian Texts. In *Proceedings of 4th Biennial International Workshop on Balto-Slavic Natural Language Processing* (pp. 43-47). Sofia: ACL.

Beliga, S., Kitanović, O., Stanković, R., & Martinčić-Ipšić, S. (n.d.). *Keyword Extraction from Parallel Abstracts of Scientific Publications.* Paper presented at Semantic Keyword-Based Search on Structured Data Sources: COST Action IC1302 Third International KEYSTONE Conference, Gdańsk, Poland.

Beliga, S., & Martinčić-Ipšić, S. (2017). Network-Enabled Keyword Extraction for Under-Resourced Languages. In *Semantic Keyword-Based Search on Structured Data Sources: COST Action IC1302 Second International KEYSTONE Conference* (pp. 124-135). Cham: Springer International Publishing. doi:10.1007/978-3-319-53640-8_11

Beliga, S., Meštrović, A., & Martinčić-Ipšić, S. (2014). Toward Selectivity Based Keyword Extraction for Croatian News. In *Workshop on Surfacing the Deep and the Social Web* (*Vol. 1310*, pp. 1-14). Riva del Garda, Trentino, Italy: CEUR-WS.org.

Beliga, S., Meštrović, A., & Martinčić-Ipšić, S. (2015). An Overview of Graph-Based Keyword Extraction Methods and Approaches. *Journal of Information and Organizational Sciences*, *39*(1), 1–20.

Beliga, S., Meštrović, A., & Martinčić-Ipšić, S. (2016). Selectivity-Based Keyword Extraction Method. *International Journal on Semantic Web and Information Systems*, *12*(3), 1–26. doi:10.4018/IJSWIS.2016070101

Berend, G. (2011). Opinion expression mining by exploiting keyphrase extraction. *Proc. of the 5th Int. Joint Conf. on NLP*, 1162-1170.

Bird, S., Klein, E., & Loper, E. (2009). *Natural language processing with Python*. Sebastopol, CA: O'Reilly Media, Inc.

Boudin, F. (2013). A comparison of centrality measures for graph-based keyphrase extraction. In *6th International Joint Conference on Natural Language Processing (IJCNLP)* (pp. 834-838). Nagoya, Japan: AFNLP.

Boudin, F. (2015). Reducing Over-generation Errors for Automatic Keyphrase Extraction using Integer Linear Programming. In *ACL 2015 Workshop on Novel Computational Approaches to Keyphrase Extraction* (pp. 19-24). Pékin, China: ACL. doi:10.18653/v1/W15-3605

Bougouin, A., Boudin, F., & Daille, B. (2016). Keyphrase Annotation with Graph Co-Ranking. *Proceedings of COLING 2016, the 26th International Conference on Computational Linguistics: Technical Papers*, 2945-2955.

Brandes, U. (2001). A faster algorithm for betweenness centrality. *The Journal of Mathematical Sociology*, *25*(2), 163–177. doi:10.1080/0022250X.2001.9990249

Cheng, G., & Qu, Y. (2009). Searching Linked Objects with Falcons: Approach, Implementation and Evaluation. *International Journal on Semantic Web and Information Systems*, *5*(3), 49–70. doi:10.4018/jswis.2009081903

Davis, B., Dantuluri, P., Handschuh, S., & Cunningham, H. (2010). Towards Controlled Natural Language for Semantic Annotation. *International Journal on Semantic Web and Information Systems*, 6(4), 64–91. doi:10.4018/jswis.2010100103

Dostal, M., & Jezek, K. (2011). Automatic Keyphrase Extraction based on NLP and Statistical Methods. In *Proceedings of the DATESO 2011: Annual International Workshop on DAtabases, TExts, Specifications and Objects* (Vol. 706, pp. 140-145). Pisek, Czech Republic: CEUR-WS.org.

Dunaiski, M., Fischer, B., Greene, G. J., Ilvovsky, D., & Kuznetsov, S. O. (2015). Browsing Publication Data using Tag Clouds over Concept Lattices Constructed by Key-Phrase Extraction. *Proc. of Russian and South African Workshop on Knowledge Discovery Techniques Based on Formal Concept Analysis (RuZA 2015)*, 10-22.

El Idrissi, O., Frikh, B., & Ouhbi, B. (2014). HCHIRSIMEX: An extended method for domain ontology learning based on conditional mutual information. In *Third IEEE International Colloquium in Information Science and Technology (CIST)*, (pp. 91-95). IEEE. doi:10.1109/CIST.2014.7016600

Ethnologue. (n.d.). Retrieved November 15, 2015 and July 4, 2017, from https://www.ethnologue.com/

Ferrara, F., Pudota, N., & Tasso, C. (2011). A Keyphrase-Based Paper Recommender System. In *Digital Libraries and Archives*. In *Communications in Computer and Information Science* (Vol. 249, pp. 14–25). Springer Berlin Heidelberg.

Frikh, B., Djaanfar, A. S., & Ouhbi, B. (2011). Article. *Int. J. Artif. Intell. Tools*, 20(6), 1157-1170. doi: https://doi.org/10.1142/S0218213011000565

Gong, Z., & Liu, Q. (2009). Improving keyword based web image search with visual feature distribution and term expansion. *Knowledge and Information Systems*, 21(1), 113–132. doi:10.1007/s10115-008-0183-x

Grineva, M., Grinev, M., & Lizorkin, D. (2009). Extracting key terms from noisy and multitheme documents. In *Proceedings of the 18th International Conference on World Wide Web* (pp. 661-670). New York: ACM. doi:10.1145/1526709.1526798

Hagberg, A. A., Schult, D. A., & Swart, P. J. (2008). Exploring Network Structure, Dynamics, and Function using NetworkX. *Proceedings of the 7th Python in Science Conference (SciPy 2008)*, 11-15.

HINA. (2010). Keyphrase Extraction Evaluation Dataset for Croatian (kex.hr) [Data set]. University of Zagreb. Available from Takelab Website: http://takelab.fer.hr/data/kexhr/

Jones, S., & Paynter, G. W. (2002). Automatic extraction of document keyphrases for use in digital libraries: Evaluation and applications. *Journal of the American Society for Information Science and Technology*, 53(8), 653–677. doi:10.1002/asi.10068

Joorabchi, A., & Mahdi, A. E. (2013). Automatic keyphrase annotation of scientific documents using Wikipedia and genetic algorithms. *Journal of Information Science*, 39(3), 410–426. doi:10.1177/0165551512472138

Kim, S. N., Medelyan, O., Kan, M.-Y., & Baldwin, T. (2010). SemEval-2010 task 5: Automatic keyphrase extraction from scientific articles. *SemEval '10 Proceedings of the 5th Int. Workshop on Semantic Evaluation*, 21-26.

Lahiri, S., Choudhury, S. R., & Caragea, C. (2014). *Keyword and Keyphrase Extraction Using Centrality Measures on Collocation Networks.* Retrieved from http://arxiv.org/pdf/1401.6571.pdf

Lahiri, S., Mihalcea, R., & Lai, P. (2017). Keyword extraction from emails. *Natural Language Engineering, 23*(2), 295–317. doi:10.1017/S1351324916000231

Lahiri, S., Mihalcea, R., & Lai, P.-H. (2016). Keyword extraction from emails. *Natural Language Engineering, 23*(2), 295-317. https://doi.org/10.1017/S1351324916000231

Lee, S., & Kim, H. (2008). News Keyword Extraction for Topic Tracking. In *Proceedings of the 2008 4th Int. Conf. on Networked Computing and Advanced Information Management* (vol. 2, pp. 554–559). Washington, DC: IEEE Computer Society. doi:10.1109/NCM.2008.199

List of Wikipedias. (n.d.). Retrieved November 15, 2015 and July 4, 2017 from https://meta.wikimedia.org/wiki/List_of_Wikipedias

Liu, H., & Hu, F. (2008). What role does syntax play in a language network? *Europhysics Letters, 83*(1), 18002. doi:10.1209/0295-5075/83/18002

Liu, W., Chung, B. C., Wang, R., Ng, J., & Morlet, N. (2015). A genetic algorithm enabled ensemble for unsupervised medical term extraction from clinical letters. *Health Information Science and Systems, 3*(5), 1–14. doi:10.1186/s13755-015-0013-y PMID:26664724

Ludwig, P., Thiel, M., & Nürnberger, A. (2017). Unsupervised Extraction of Conceptual Keyphrases from Abstracts. *Semantic Keyword-Based Search on Structured Data Sources: COST Action IC1302 Second International KEYSTONE Conference,* (pp. 37-48). Cham: Springer International Publishing. doi:10.1007/978-3-319-53640-8_4

Lynn, H. M., Choi, C., & Kim, P. (2017). An improved method of automatic text summarization for web contents using lexical chain with semantic-related terms. *Soft Computing.* doi:10.1007/s00500-017-2612-9

Margan, D., Martinčić-Ipšić, S., & Meštrović, A. (2013). Preliminary report on the structure of Croatian linguistic co-occurrence networks. In *5th International Conference on Information Technologies and Information Society* (pp. 89-96). Faculty of Information Studies in Novo mesto.

Margan, D., Martinčić-Ipšić, S., & Meštrović, A. (2014a). Network Diferences Between Normal and Shuffled Texts: Case of Croatian. *Studies in Computational Intelligence, Complex Networks V: Proceedings of the 5th Workshop on Complex Networks CompleNet 2014* (Vol. 549, pp. 275-283). Springer International Publishing. doi:10.1007/978-3-319-05401-8_26

Margan, D., & Meštrović, A. (2015). LaNCoA: A Python Toolkit for Language Networks Construction and Analysis. In *38th International Convention on Information and Communication Technology, Electronics and Microelectronics (MIPRO)* (pp. 1628-1633). Opatija, Croatia: IEEE. doi:10.1109/MIPRO.2015.7160532

Margan, D., Meštrović, A., & Martinčić-Ipšić, S. (2014b). Complex Networks Measures for Differentiation between Normal and Shuffled Croatian Texts. In *37th International Convention on Information and Communication Technology, Electronics and Microelectronics (MIPRO)* (pp. 1598-1602). Opatija, Croatia: IEEE. doi:10.1109/MIPRO.2014.6859820

Martinčić-Ipšić, S., Miličić, T., & Meštrović, A. (2016). Text Type Differentiation Based on the Structural Properties of Language Networks. In G. Dregvaite & R. Damasevicius (Eds.), *Information and Software Technologies. ICIST 2016. Communications in Computer and Information Science* (Vol. 639, pp. 536–548). Cham: Springer International Publishing; doi:10.1007/978-3-319-46254-7_43

Martinčić-Ipšić, S., Močibob, E., & Perc, M. (2017, June). Link Prediction on Twitter. *Plos ONE*.

Martinez-Romo, J., Araujo, L., & Duque Fernandez, A. (2016). SemGraph: Extracting Keyphrases Following a Novel Semantic Graph-Based Approach. *Journal of the Association for Information Science and Technology*, *67*(1), 71–82. doi:10.1002/asi.23365

Masucci, A. P., & Rodgers, G. J. (2006). Network properties of written human language. *Physical Review E: Statistical, Nonlinear, and Soft Matter Physics*, *74*(2), 026102. doi:10.1103/PhysRevE.74.026102 PMID:17025498

Masucci, A. P., & Rodgers, G. J. (2009). Differences between normal and shuffled texts: Structural properties of weighted networks. *Advances in Complex Systems*, *12*(01), 113–129. doi:10.1142/S0219525909002039

Matsuo, Y., Ohsawa, Y., & Ishizuka, M. (2001). *KeyWorld: Extracting keywords from document s small world. In Discovery Science LNAI 2226* (pp. 271–281). Springer Berlin Heidelberg. doi:10.1007/3-540-45650-3_24

Mbipom, B., Craw, S., & Massie, S. (2016). Harnessing background knowledge for e-learning recommendation. In Research and development in intelligent systems XXXIII: incorporating applications and innovations in intelligent systems XXIV. Cham: Springer. doi:10.1007/978-3-319-47175-4_1

Medelyan, O. (2009a). *Human-competitive automatic topic indexing* (Doctoral dissertation). The University of Waikato, Hamilton, New Zealand.

Medelyan, O. (2009b). WIKI-20 dataset [Data set]. University of Waikato. Available from Maui Website: http://maui-indexer.googlecode.com/files/wiki20.tar.gz

Medelyan, O., Witten, I. H., & Milne, D. (2008). Topic indexing with Wikipedia. *Proceedings of Wikipedia and AI workshop at the AAAI-2008 Conference*, 19-24.

Mihalcea, R., & Tarau, P. (2004). TextRank: Bringing order into texts. In *Proceedings of Empirical Methods in Natural Language Processing –EMNLP 2004* (pp. 404–411). Barcelona, Spain: ACL.

Mijić, J., Dalbelo-Bašić, B., & Šnajder, J. (2010). Robust Keyphrase Extraction for a Large-Scale Croatian News Production System. In *Proceedings of the 7th International Conference on Formal Approaches to South Slavic and Balkan Languages* (pp. 59-66). Zagreb, Croatia: Croatian Language Technologies Society.

Mocanu, B., Tapu, R., & Tapu, E. (2016). Video retrieval using relevant topics extraction from movie subtitles. In *12th IEEE International Symposium on Electronics and Telecommunications (ISETC)* (pp. 327-330). IEEE. doi:10.1109/ISETC.2016.7781123

Moldovan, D., Harabagiu, S., Pasca, M., Mihalcea, R., Girju, R., Goodrum, R., & Rus, V. (2000). The structure and performance of an open-domain question answering system. *Proc. of the 38th Annual Meeting on Association for Computational Linguistics*, 563-570. doi:10.3115/1075218.1075289

Newman, M. E. J. (2010). *Networks: An Introduction*. New York: Oxford University Press. doi:10.1093/acprof:oso/9780199206650.001.0001

Onan, A., Korukoğlu, S., & Bulut, H. (2016). Ensemble of keyword extraction methods and classifiers in text classification. *Expert Systems with Applications*, *57*, 232–247. doi:10.1016/j.eswa.2016.03.045

Opsahl, T., Agneessens, F., & Skvoretz, J. (2010). Node centrality in weighted networks: Generalizing degree and shortest paths. *Social Networks*, *32*(3), 245–251. doi:10.1016/j.socnet.2010.03.006

Palshikar, G. K. (2007). Keyword Extraction from a Single Document Using Centrality Measures. *Pattern Recognition and Machine Intelligence (LNCS) Second International Conference, PReMI 2007* (*Vol. 4815*, pp. 503-510). Springer Berlin Heidelberg. doi:10.1007/978-3-540-77046-6_62

Paramonov, I., Lagutina, K., Mamedov, E., & Lagutina, N. (2016). Thesaurus-Based method of Increasing text-via-keyphrase Graph Connectivity During Keyphrase Extraction for e-Tourism Applications. *Proceedings of the Knowledge Engineering and Semantic Web: 7th International Conference, KESW 2016*, 129-141. doi:10.1007/978-3-319-45880-9_11

Rafiei-Asl, J. & Nickabadi, A. (2017). TSAKE: A topical and structural automatic keyphrase extractor. *Applied Soft Computing*, *58*, 620–630. doi: 10.1016/j.asoc.2017.05.014

Ravinuthala, M. K. V., & Ch, S. R. (2016). Thematic Text Graph: A Text Representation Technique for Keyword Weighting in Extractive Summarization System. *International Journal of Information Engineering and Electronic Business*, *8*(4), 18–25. doi:10.5815/ijieeb.2016.04.03

Rolling, L. (1981). Indexing consistency, quality and efficiency. *Information Processing & Management*, *17*(2), 69–76. doi:10.1016/0306-4573(81)90028-5

Saratlija, J., Šnajder, J., & Dalbelo-Bašić, B. (2011). *Unsupervised topic-oriented keyphrase extraction and its application to Croatian. In Text, Speech and Dialogue LNCS* (Vol. 6836, pp. 340–347). Springer Berlin Heidelberg. doi:10.1007/978-3-642-23538-2_43

Siddiqi, S., & Sharan, A. (2015). Keyword and Keyphrase Extraction Techniques: A Literature Review. *International Journal of Computers and Applications*, *109*(2), 18–23. doi:10.5120/19161-0607

Tonella, P., Ricca, F., Pianta, E., & Girardi, C. (2003). Using Keyword Extraction for Web Site Clustering. In *Proceedings of 5th IEEE International Workshop on Web Site Evolution* (pp. 41-48). IEEE. doi:10.1109/WSE.2003.1234007

Wan, X., & Xiao, J. (2008). CollabRank: Towards a Collaborative Approach to Single-Document Keyphrase Extraction. In *Proceedings of the 22nd International Conference on Computational Linguistics (Coling 2008)* (pp. 969-976). Coling 2008 Organizing Committee. doi:10.3115/1599081.1599203

Wang, F., Wang, Z., Senzhang, W., & Zhoujun, L. (2014). Exploiting Description Knowledge for Keyphrase Extraction. In PRICAI 2014: Trends in Artificial Intelligence (LNCS) (Vol. 8862, pp. 130-142). Springer International Publishing. doi:10.1007/978-3-319-13560-1_11

Wu, J.-L., & Agogino, A. M. (2003). Automating Keyphrase Extraction with Multi-Objective Genetic Algorithms, In *Proceedings of the 37th Annual Hawaii International Conference on System Sciences* (pp. 104-111). IEEE.

Yih, W., Goodman, J., & Carvalho, V. R. (2006). Finding Advertising Keywords on Web Pages. In *Proceedings of the 15th Int. Conf. on World Wide Web*, *WWW '06* (pp. 213–222). New York: ACM. doi:10.1145/1135777.1135813

Ying, Y., Qingping, T., Qinzheng, X., Ping, Z., & Panpan, L. (2017). A Graph-Based Approach of Automatic Keyphrase Extraction. *Procedia Computer Science*, *107*, 248–255. doi:10.1016/j.procs.2017.03.087

Zhuge, H., & Zhang, J. (2010). Topological centrality and its e-Science applications. *Journal of the American Society for Information Science and Technology*, *61*(9), 1824–1841. doi:10.1002/asi.21353

Zimniewicz, M., Kurowski, K., & Węglarz, J. (2017). Scheduling aspects in keyword extraction problem. *International Transactions in Operational Research*, *00*, 1–16. doi:10.1111/itor.12368

Chapter 8
Detecting Restriction Class Correspondences in Linked Data:
The Bayes–ReCCE Bayesian Model Approach

Brian Walshe
Barclays, UK

Rob Brennan
Trinity College Dublin, Ireland

Declan O'Sullivan
Trinity College Dublin, Ireland

ABSTRACT

Linked Data consists of many structured data knowledge bases that have been interlinked, often using equivalence statements. These equivalences usually take the form of owl:sameAs statements linking individuals, links between classes are far less common Often, the lack of class links is because their relationships cannot be described as one to one equivalences. Instead, complex correspondences referencing logical combinations of multiple entities are often needed to describe how the classes in an ontology are related to classes in a second ontology. This chapter introduces a novel Bayesian Restriction Class Correspondence Estimation (Bayes-ReCCE) algorithm, an extensional approach to detecting complex correspondences between classes. Bayes-ReCCE operates by analysing features of matched individuals in the knowledge bases, and uses Bayesian inference to search for complex correspondences between the classes these individuals belong to. Bayes-ReCCE is designed to be capable of providing meaningful results even when only small numbers of matched instances are available.

DOI: 10.4018/978-1-5225-5042-6.ch008

INTRODUCTION

Linked Open Data provides access to a wealth of information in standardised and navigable form. It is designed to be combined easily. Bizer (2009) notes however that ... *most Linked Data applications display data from different sources alongside each other but do little to integrate it further. To do so does require mapping of terms from different vocabularies to the applications target schema.* Links usually take the form of owl:sameAs statements linking individuals, but links between classes are far less common (Schmachtenberg, Bizer & Paulheim, 2014). Heterogeneity issues, such as differences in class scope or hierarchy granularity mean that simple one to one correspondences between atomic classes are not always enough to describe the mappings between schemas, or more generally, ontologies. The YAGO2 (Suchanek, Kasneci & Weikum, 2008) knowledge base, for example, contains a rich class hierarchy based on WordNet (Miller,1995), and includes many professions described as classes. An instance of a person in YAGO2 who is a film director, belongs to the class yago:FilmDirector. In contrast, version 3.9 DBpedia (Bizer, Lehmann, Kobilarov, Auer, Becker, Cyganiak & Hellman, 2009) has a shallower class hierarchy, with professions described as attribute-values, not classes. In this version of the DBpedia ontology there is no named class for film directors. If one to one mappings between named classes is the only mechanism available, then we could say that yago:FilmDirector maps to dbpedia:Person with a subsumption relationship; but this does not describe which members of the class Person are film directors. If, instead, complex correspondences between non-atomic classes were used, then it could be asserted that yago:FilmDirector corresponds with the set of instances of Person in DBpedia with the attribute dbpedia-owl:occupation set to dbpedia:Film_director. More formally, correspondences where at least one of the entities described in the correspondence is non-atomic are known as complex correspondences (Ritze, Meilicke, Svab-Zamazal & Stuckenschmidt, 2009).

Research has shown that complex correspondences can be classified into commonly reoccurring Correspondence Patterns (Scharffe, 2009). Extensional methods, which compare the instance sets of classes using some metric such as the Jaccard index, have been shown to be capable of detecting complex correspondences between ontologies used in Linked Open Data (Parundekar, Knoblock & Ambite, 2010; Parundekar, Knoblock & Ambite, 2012). However, extensional approaches have several issues. When only small amounts of instance data are available they can give high scores to spurious matches, and when the amount of data is large, the search space of potential correspondences can grow very quickly. A more subtle problem is that directly comparing the instance sets of two classes to test similarity is not consistent with the Open World Assumption. Furthermore existing extensional approaches have an a priori assumption that all forms of complex correspondences are equally probable, and the approaches do not provide a systematic way for us to specify any prior beliefs we have that certain patterns of correspondences may be more probable than others.

In this chapter we describe Bayes-ReCCE, a scalable complex correspondence detection algorithm which uses Bayesian statistics to estimate the true Jaccard index of the classes being compared, and which provides a method to specify prior beliefs about certain patterns of correspondence being more or less probable than others. Bayes-ReECCE presents the most probable correspondences to a user, combined with a summary of the evidence for each of these correspondences. Using the probability measure for the correspondence and examining the evidence allows a user to make a more informed decision on whether to accept or reject the correspondence.

The objectives of this chapter are to demonstrate:

- A Bayesian method for estimating the probability two classes from separate knowledge bases are equivalent given a sample of their instances. This measure gives us a consistent method of describing how certain we are a given correspondence exists. It can be used in cases where only small amounts of matched data are available.

- Bayes-ReCCE – a generate and test based search strategy which uses the Bayesian similarity estimate to find Class Restriction complex correspondences between ontologies with matched instances.

- A method for presenting to mapping creators the identified complex correspondences along with the evidence that supports their correctness.

The application of Bayes-ReCCE is not only confined to LOD interlinking. For example, it could potentially be used to support: refinement of ontologies (Crotti, Walshe & O'Sullivan, 2015); to improve quality through contributing to type prediction (Paulheim & Bizer, 2014); ontology learning and refinement (Lehmann, Auer, Buhmann & Tramp, 2011; Volker & Niepert, 2011); query rewriting (Gillet, Trojahn, Haemmerle & Pradel, 2013).

BACKGROUND

Complex Correspondence Patterns

Correspondence Patterns are a specific type of Ontology Design Pattern. They serve a similar function to software engineering Design Patterns (Gamma, Helm, Johnson & Vlissides, 1994). The use of patterns provides several benefits. As templates to describe commonly occurring complex relationships between ontologies, it means that the relationships are described in a uniform manner and are easier to interpret. Correspondence patterns provide two layered templates (Scharffe, 2009): an abstract layer which describes the problem being solved expressed in natural language; and a grounding layer, a parameterized template solution expressed in a formal language – typically EDOAL (David, Euzenat, Scharffe & dos Santos, 2011). By specifying values for the parameters in a grounding it is possible to create an instantiated grounding which can be used to perform a task such as query rewriting, instance translation or other automated data mediation tasks (Shvaiko & Euzenat, 2012; Correndo & Shadbolt, 2011).

Since these patterns describe commonly occurring forms of correspondences, they can be used to build a search strategy for complex correspondences between two knowledge bases. The Bayes-ReCCE search strategy, considers three patterns when searching for complex correspondences – Class by Attribute Value (CAV), Class by Attribute Type (CAT) and Class by Attribute Existence (CAE). These patterns are all types of restriction class correspondence pattern and share a similar structure. All specify a target class and a source class and a restriction feature, where the target class corresponds to the source class restricted to those instances which have the restriction feature. The patterns differ in what form the restriction feature takes. We use the notation $C \mid_f$ to denote the restriction of the class C to those instances with feature f.

Class by Attribute Value Correspondences (CAV)

These occur when a named class in one ontology is equivalent to the subclass of a named class in a second ontology of exactly those instances which have a specified property set to a specified value. The restriction feature in this pattern takes the form of a pair, (p,v), where p is a property and v is a value – which could be a literal or a general resource. For example, given two ontologies describing wine, it is possible that one ontology may have a specific class for *BordeauxWine*, but the other does not. If, however, the other ontology has a class for wines in general, *Vin*, and instances of this class have an attribute which describes the region the wine comes from, terroir, then it may be appropriate to say that the target class *BordeauxWine* corresponds with the set of instances of *Vin* with the attribute *terroir* set to the value *Bordelais*.

Class by Attribute Type

Class by Attribute Type Correspondences (CAT) occur when a named class in one ontology is equivalent to the subclass of a named class in a second ontology of exactly those instances which have a specified property set to an object with a specified type. The restriction feature in this pattern takes the form of a pair, (p,t), where p is a property and t is a type. An example of this pattern could be if we said the class EUCitizen corresponds with a restriction on the class Person to the instances which have the property citizenOf set to a country which has type EUMemberState.

The Inverse Class by Attribute Type (CAT^{-1}) correspondence pattern can also occur. This pattern is also specified by a restriction feature of the form (p,t), however in this case, the source class is restricted to those instances, $i,$ which appear as the object of the of a subject, predicate, object relationship $\langle s,p,i \rangle$ where s has type t. For example the class *CarPart* might correspond with the class *MechanicalPart* restricted to the instances which are the object of a *hasPart* relationship for an instance of the class *Car*.

Class by Attribute Existence

Class by Attribute Existence Correspondences (CAE) occur when a named class in one ontology is equivalent to the subclass of a named class in a second ontology of exactly those instances which have a specified property but where the value is unimportant. For example the class Deceased may correspond with the class Person restricted to instances which have the property diedOn set to some value.

Within Bayes-ReCCE, by limiting our search to specific patterns of restriction class correspondence, we are able to employ a "generate and test" approach by creating candidate correspondences fitting the patterns, and then test how well these candidates are supported by the data in the knowledge bases. The method for generating candidates is discussed in detail later. Before we discuss generating candidates we must define what we mean by a "valid" complex correspondence.

Related Work

Research to aid the discovery of complex correspondences for Linked Data has matured in recent years. The COMA Match system was first designed as a framework for combining schema matching approaches and was subsequently extended to match ontologies. The COMA toolset has seen continual development, and as of 2011 included the Enhancement Engine component (Massmann, Raunich, Anmuller,

2011) which can take the one to one mappings produced by the schema matching approaches and use these to create complex correspondences. The search strategy it uses is to first examine possible correspondences involving sets of elements which are close together in the ontology graphs, to determine if any transformation correspondences can be found. It then uses external linguistic oracles to discover additional correspondences using the element names. Qin et al. (2007) has proposed the use of multi relational data mining techniques to detect complex correspondences between ontologies. As was the case with InfoSphere Data Architect, the process begins by generating one to one matches between the classes and between relations in the ontologies. Object reconciliation is then used to find common instances in the ontologies. The system seeks to find as many shared instances as possible. In addition, there is a feedback loop where information about the shared instances discovered at this stage are used to help find more matches between the classes and relations, which in turn are used to find more shared instances. The approach described in (Ritze, Meilicke, Svab-Zamazal & Stuckenschmidt, 2009). uses correspondence patterns to detect complex correspondences. It analyses the structure of the ontologies and uses a series of string manipulation operations to test if the words used in the names classes and properties in one ontology can be re-arranged to form names similar to the ones used in the second ontology. The advantage of this approach is that it does not require any matches instances in order to be able to detect the complex correspondences. Identifying complex (one-to-many or many-to-many) correspondences can be seen as closely related to the problem of determining the semantic relation type of correspondences. For example, a many-to-one situation where several concepts of the first ontology are related to the same concept of the second ontology can indicate is-a or part-of relationships between these concepts. In (Arnold & Rahm, 2014),the authors propose and evaluate a framework two-step enrichment approach to determine semantic ontology mappings that enhances existing match tools.

A rule-learning-based approach for detecting complex correspondences in Linked Data has been proposed in (Hu, Chen, Zhang & Qu, 2011; Janssen, Fallahi, Noessner & Paulheim, 2012). Derived from classical Inductive Logic Programming, the approach in (Hu et al., 2011) uses instance mappings as training data and employs tailoring heuristics to improve the learning efficiency, with initial evaluation showing that the generated Horn-rule mappings are meaningful. They further demonstrate that learning and refinement of non-trivial ontology alignments can be achieved from instances through utilization of inductive rule learning algorithms, by reformulating as problems of association rule mining and separate-and-conquer rule learning, respectively. A novel approach has been proposed to identify complex correspondences based on the unified top-k match graph for top-k matchings (Gal, Sagi, Weidlich, Levy, Shafran, Miklos & Viet Hung, 2012). This uses a clustering problem to group attributes that show ambiguity and are closely related, and for these groups, quality is assessed and, if appropriate, complex correspondences are derived.

DETECTING RESTRICTION CLASS CORRESPONDENCES IN LINKED DATA

Issues, Controversies, Problems

Although detecting complex correspondences is long recognized as important for real-world data integration they remain a relatively unpopular topic in the ontology mapping literature with just one paper devoted to complex correspondences in the 2016 edition of the Ontology Matching workshop (Shvaiko et al. 2016).

A key question for the pursuit of research on complex correspondences is *What is the distribution of complex correspondences in actual Linked Data?* This is important both to provide researchers with guidance on which correspondence patterns should be pursued and to drive interest in complex correspondences as part of the Linked Data ecosystem. Unfortunately there are relatively few sets of published complex correspondences for public linked data, e.g. (Parundekar, et al., 2010; Parundekar, et al., 2012) (Melo, Suchanek & Pease, 2008), and this makes estimation of the frequency and applicability of each correspondence type hard.

Once researchers are convinced to study complex correspondences we must turn to the issue of evaluation techniques. It is the authors' opinion that too much weight is currently put on the Jaccard index as an appropriate measure of class similarity for Linked Data published with an open world assumption. If the extent of a dataset is unknown how confident can we be of similarity measures based on that extent? This is coupled with the additional potential for missing information in a logical model based on mappings (Rousset, Atencia, David, Jouanot, Palombi & Ulliana, 2017) and it is well established that data quality issues are common in Linked Data (Zaveri, Rula, Maurino, Pietrobon, Lehmann, & Auer, 2016). This leads to the question *How can we effectively compute class similarity in the face of these sources of uncertainty?*

Even if we can deal with uncertainty, it will probably be operationalized through a machine learning approach. This means that some form of training data will be required to bootstrap the system. We need new frameworks to evaluate the effect of these inputs on the accuracy of their results and resource requirements. Specifically this means investigating the balance between input matched instance sample size and the accuracy of detected complex correspondences. Given the modern preponderance of machine-generated high recall, low precision techniques (Shvaiko et al. 2016) it is also important to evaluate the additional load these place on second stage (often manual) mapping validation when assessing their utility.

The issue of using the correct predicate to describe the relationship for classes that have been matched is a difficult one. This can be seen in the "sameAs problem" (Halpin, Hayes, Mccusker, Mcguinness, and Thompson, 2011) where *owl:sameAs* is widely used by Linked Data when it is not appropriate. Many of the problems, that apply to incorrect use of owl:sameAs also apply to owl:equivalentClass – such as the relationship being transitive, which has the potential to create "the semantic equivalent of mushy peas", if it is over used (Halpin et al. 2011). Other predicates are available such as *skos:exactMatch* and *skos:closeMatch*. The SKOS reference states that "a *skos:closeMatch* link indicates that two concepts are sufficiently similar that they can be used interchangeably in some information retrieval applications". However, if we were to publish a set of correspondences which we felt represented a close match, and we were to use this predicate, another user on inspecting the link might ask - *are these classes sufficiently similar for my information retrieval task?* The link on its own does not provide enough information to make an informed decision. This problem of explaining matches has been highlighted as one of the ten most pressing challenges in semantic matching (Shvaiko and J. Euzenat, 2008; 2012).

SOLUTIONS AND RECOMMENDATIONS

Prevalence of Complex Correspondences in Linked Data

All the evidence collected to date points at the importance and relevance of CAV as the most frequently occurring pattern in both the data and the published mappings. CAT is the next most frequent pattern observed and the Bayes-ReCCE method also includes support for CAE since this requires no additional implementation beyond CAT. The evidence is summarized here.

Parundekar et al. (2012) show automated discovery of 351 CAV correspondences between DBpedia and Geonames and an additional 5 correspondences with a restriction class on either side of the relation. Geonames publish a set of 32 correspondences between Geonames and DBpedia and all of these fit the CAV pattern. Later an additional 11 CAV mappings between Geonames and DBpedia are described that were discovered as part of this work. Additionally a manual inspection of the relations between LinkedMDB and DBpedia discovered 3 inverse CAT correspondences.

In order to get a better understanding of the distribution of complex correspondences this work analyzed the class restriction correspondences between YAGO (9 Jan 2012 core version) and DBpedia (version 3.7). Both ontologies are large and cover an almost identical domain (the contents of Wikipedia) however both ontologies are stuctured very differently with DBpedia having approximately 170 classes and YAGO 15,000. Hence there is strong reason to believe that it will be a rich source of complex correspondences – but this was chosen to investigate their distribution.

By randomly selecting 50 classes from YAGO that had at least one instance and manually inspecting them it was possible to determine the most appropriate correspondence type with DBpedia classes - equilivence, complex or none. The results were 6 classes with no DBpedia equivalent, 12 direct equivilents, and 32 complex correspondences. 11 of the 32 complex correspondences were CAT and CAE was the next most common type. These results should be treated as necessarily subjective as the selection of the most appropriate complex correspondence type can have many possible criteria and the sample set and scenario is limited. Nonetheless it does provide an additional indicator for the importance of detecting CAV mappings in real-world datasets.

We consider an equivalence correspondence to be valid if the classes described in the correspondence have the same class extension sets. If we knew the exact set associated with the classes, the Jaccard index would provide us a method of measuring their similarity. If A and B are sets then the Jaccard index of A and B is:

$$J(A,B) = \frac{|A \cap B|}{|A \cup B|}$$

With $0 \le J(A,B) \le 1$, and $J(A,B) = 1$ iff the sets of A and B are identical.

However, the extension sets of a given class are not generally known. Often we only know of a few instances in the set. To understand how the Jaccard similarity measure relates to classes in an ontology, we must look at the underlying description logic these classes are described in. Typically the Linked Data KBs have associated OWL TBoxes which describe them. OWL uses an extended form of the $\mathcal{ALC}$ Description Logic. In $\mathcal{ALC}$, N_C is the set of atomic concepts, and N_R is the set of roles with $N_R \cap N_C = \varnothing$. Each atomic concept is a concept, and additional (complex) concepts can be constructed by combining concepts and roles. Each $\mathcal{ALC}$ concept C can be associated with a set by means of an *interpretation,* $\mathcal{I}$, consisting of an interpretation domain " $^{\mathcal{I}}$, and an interpretation function, $\cdot^{\mathcal{I}}$, which maps C to a set $C^{\mathcal{I}} \subset$ " $^{\mathcal{I}}$. In general we, do not know the exact set associated with a given class. The set of all names is denoted N_I, and for $a \in N_I$ and $C \in N_C$ the notation $C(a)$ is used to assert that a is an instance of C.

To allow interpreting ABoxes, Hellmann et al. extend the definition of interpretation. This extended definition (Hellmann, Lehmann & Auer, 2009) states that for the class C and individual a, if $\mathcal{K} = \{\mathcal{T}, \mathcal{A}\}$ is an ontology with TBox $\mathcal{T}$ and ABox $\mathcal{A}$, then a is an instance of C with respect to $\mathcal{K}$, denoted $K \vDash C(a)$ iff for any model $\mathcal{I}$ of $\mathcal{K}$ we have $a^{\mathcal{I}} \in C^{\mathcal{I}}$. The retrieval of class C with respect to $\mathcal{K}$, is defined as: $R_{\mathcal{K}}(C) = \{a | a \in N_I, \mathcal{K} \vDash C(a)\}$, with N_I being the set of all names. More simply, retrieval is the set of all named instances that the knowledgebase $\mathcal{K}$ states are members of class C.

Therefore we can observe that some instances are members of the set, but due to the Open World Assumption, we cannot say that these instances comprise the whole set, unless we have been explicitly told this is the case. In turn this means that if we retrieve the known members of two classes and use the Jaccard to calculate the similarity we cannot be certain that this measure is correct, as instances from the extension set could be missing due to their membership being *unknown*.

When comparing classes between ontologies which have been mapped to one another, there are further difficulties in knowing the extension sets. One cannot, in general, say that all mappings between two ontologies are known, and this introduces a further level of unknowns. Hence for two given classes, in general both all the members of each of the classes' extension sets and all the mappings between the instances in the extension sets are unknown. To explain this difficulty, we extend the concept of retrieval to mapped retrieval.

Suppose $\mathcal{K}_s$ and $\mathcal{K}_t$ are ontologies, our source and target ontologies, C is a class described in $\mathcal{K}_t$, and M is a set of mappings of the things described in $\mathcal{K}_s$ and $\mathcal{K}_t$. Then the mapped retrieval

$$R_{\mathcal{K}_s | \mathcal{K}_t, M}(C) = \{a \mid (a, a') \in M, \mathcal{K}_s \vDash \top (a), \mathcal{K}_t \vDash C(a')\}.$$

That is the set of all things which $\mathcal{K}_s$ states are named things and which are mapped, via M, to a thing which $\mathcal{K}_t$ states is a thing of type C. Using mapped retrieval introduces another step where missing information can become an issue. In order for the individual a to be included in $R_{\mathcal{K}_s | \mathcal{K}_t, M}(C)$, we require that the mapping (a, a') be included in M and that $\mathcal{K}_t \vDash C(a')$. If the mapping is unknown, or $\mathcal{K}_t$ does not tell us that a' is an instance of C, then a will not be included in the mapped retrieval. Note that the set of classes mapped to are the potential restriction classes rather than just those defined in the target ontology itself. Hence if the presence or value of an attribute (property) is an indicator for a suitable restriction class, i.e. a CAT or CAE correspondence, then it will be included in the mapped recall.

One cannot, in general, know the elements of the set associated with a given class. When comparing the elements of the sets associated with classes contained in separate ontologies we are limited to the mapped retrieval, and this is liable to be a much smaller set than the true intersection of the classes' extension sets. We are forced to work with incomplete information, and this introduces an element of uncertainty. It is important to quantify this uncertainty in a manner which can be clearly explained. Bayesian statistics provides a well-established method for doing this (Finetti, 1989). The following section describes how a Bayesian prior probability can be used to estimate the overlap in the sets associated with two classes.

Using a Beta Binomial Distribution to Estimate the Similarity of Two Classes

For classes C and D, we cannot generally calculate the true value of the size of the intersection or union of the sets associated with the classes, which in turn means that we cannot calculate $J(C, D)$ directly. Therefore, we must estimate it. The Jaccard index measures the proportion of instances in the union of two sets which are also in the intersection of the sets. Suppose we name this proportion θ, then for n instances $x_{1..n} \in C \sqcup D$, the probability that k of these instances are also members of $C \sqcap D$ can be calculated using the binomial distribution

$$p(k|\theta, n) = \binom{n}{k} \theta^k (1 - \theta)^{n-k}$$

Using Bayes Theorem, we can say that

$$p(\theta|k, n) = \frac{p(k|\theta, n) P(\theta)}{P(k)}$$

$$\propto p(k|\theta, n) P(\theta)$$

$$= L(\theta \mid k, n)$$

where $L(\theta|k, n)$ is known as the likelihood function. Using (1), one option for estimating θ would be to use the maximum likelihood estimator (MLE). This is the value of θ which maximises $L(\theta \mid k, n)$. Assuming all values of θ are equally probable, then the MLE of $L(\theta \mid k, n)$ is $\hat{\theta} = \dfrac{k}{n}$. Using this MLE we can then decide that C and D are equivalent if $\hat{\theta} > 1 - \varepsilon$.

While easy to implement, this approach does not allow expression about how strongly we believe the results it produces. If we look at a single instance and see that it is a member of both $C \sqcap D$ and $C \sqcup D$, then $n = 1$, $k = 1$, and the MLE is also 1. This MLE is slightly higher than the one obtained from seeing a 1,000 instances of $C \sqcup D$, 999 of which are members $C \sqcap D$. Clearly, the evidence based on a thousand instances should hold much more weight than evidence based on a single instance, but MLE does not give us a clear way of accounting for this difference in weight of evidence.

Instead, the method we employ in this chapter is a Beta Binomial conjugate prior distribution. The following paragraphs give a brief description of how this distribution is derived, and how it can be used. For a thorough explanation of this distribution see (Bishop, 2006)..

Assume that θ is not fixed but that it is a variable drawn from a Beta distribution:

$$\theta \sim Beta(\alpha, \beta)$$

$$p\left(\theta\right) = \frac{\theta^{\alpha-1}\left(1-\theta\right)^{\beta-1}}{B\left(\alpha,\beta\right)}$$

where $B\left(\alpha,\beta\right)$ is Euler's beta function. Then, as $p\left(\theta|k,n\right) \propto p\left(k|\theta,n\right)p\left(\theta\right)$ we have:

$$p\left(\theta|k,n\right) \propto \binom{n}{k}\theta^k\left(1-\theta\right)^{n-k}\theta^{\alpha-1}\left(1-\theta\right)^{\beta-1} \tag{1}$$

$$\propto \theta^{k+\alpha-1}\left(1-\theta\right)^{n-k+\beta-1}$$

Combining equation (2) with the fact that, as it is a probability density function, $\int_0^1 p\left(\theta|k,n\right)d\theta = 1$, shows us that if we observe n instances of $C \sqcup D$, k of which are instances of $C \sqcap D$, then

$$\theta \sim Beta\left(k+\alpha, n-k+\beta\right)$$

The values α and β are known as the prior parameters and allow us to encode or prior belief on what the value of θ should be. Choosing appropriate prior parameters is generally done by intuition, by past experience, or by fitting to experimental data from similar situations (Shultis & Eckhoff, 1979). For example, suppose we wish to test a CAV correspondence between classes A and B with the restriction feature $\left(p,v\right)$. If we do not want to make any strong assumptions, setting $\alpha = \beta = 1$ gives the uninformed prior, which assumes that all values of $\theta \in \left[0,1\right]$ are equally probable. If however, from prior experience we feel that restriction features based on the property p are not common, we might set $\alpha = 1, \beta = 4$ which gives us a prior distribution where low values of θ are more probable. This prior distribution is illustrated in Figure 1 (a). If we then observe 10 instances of class A, 9 of which belong to the restriction class formed by class B and restriction property $\left(p,v\right)$, we can infer the posterior distribution shown in Figure 1 (b). Here the distribution generated using the uniform prior shows higher values of θ to be more probable than the distribution generated using $\alpha = 1, \beta = 4$ as the prior parameters. If we observe 100 instances, 95 of which are in the intersection of the classes, then we can infer the distribution shown in Figure 1 (c).

Treating θ as a random variable with probability density function instead of just a likelihood, allows us to make a much stronger statement about our belief. Instead of simply finding the MLE, and testing if it is higher than the $1 - \varepsilon$ cutoff, we can calculate $P(\theta > 1 - \varepsilon \mid k, n, \alpha, \beta)$. Larger values of k and n will provide a distribution with less variance. Using a conjugate prior means we can understand how the size of our sample of matched instances affects the strength of our belief. It gives us a formal method for balancing our prior beliefs against the extensional evidence we have examined. It is important to note that incompleteness of instance links is not the only possible source of bias in an extensional mapping detection technique such as this – for example there could be cultural, technical or social reasons for the distribution of existent links in the datasets. However it is important to note that there

Figure 1. Prior and posterior distributions with beta parameters $\alpha = 1, \beta = 1$, *and* $\alpha = 1, \beta = 4$

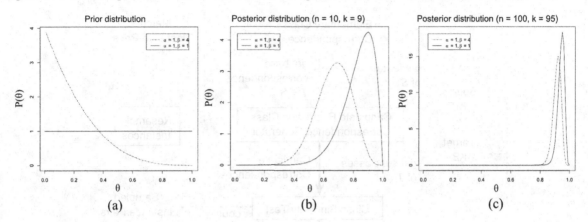

are two mitigating factors in our suggested deployment approach for Bayes-ReCCE (1) since only very small numbers of links are required it is anticipated that it will be a human-supervised process that selects or creates the input links and (2) Bayes-ReCCE only makes ranked recommendations on possible complex correspondences and these will need to be post-processed, in a semi- or fully-supervised tool-chain for the best possible mapping results. Having defined the patterns of correspondence we are searching for, and the criteria which we use to determine if a correspondence is valid, we now describe our search algorithm in detail.

Bayes-ReCCE Complex Correspondence Learning Algorithm

This section describes the steps in the Bayesian Restriction Class Correspondence Estimation (Bayes-ReCCE) algorithm. It detects complex correspondences fitting the CAV, CAT, and CAE patterns described earlier. Bayes-ReCCE uses a generate and test approach to detecting complex correspondences. There are three major steps to this approach, which are illustrated in Figure 2. Bayes-ReCCE requires a set of elementary class correspondences between the ontologies as input. There are many tools and approaches available (Lambrix and Tan, 2006; Hu et al. 2008; Li, Tang, Li, &; Luo, 2009; Seddiqui and Aono, 2009) to assist in this task of finding elementary correspondences, so we assume that creating this input set is a tractable problem. For each elementary correspondence Bayes-ReCCE will create a set of candidate complex correspondences by selecting target classes from the target ontology and restriction features from the source ontology. In the second step, each of the candidate correspondences is tested to estimate the probability that the target and restriction classes in the correspondence are equivalent, rejecting any that do not meet some configurable minimum probability. Finally, in a refinement step the remaining correspondences are examined to remove any that conflict with other correspondences. Each step is described in detail below.

Candidate Restriction Class Correspondence Generation

To detect complex correspondences between a target knowledge base, $\mathcal{K}_t$, and a source, $\mathcal{K}_s$, the Bayes-ReCCE algorithm requires a set of elementary class correspondences between $\mathcal{K}_t$ and $\mathcal{K}_s$, and a set,

Figure 2. Generate and Test approach to detecting complex correspondences

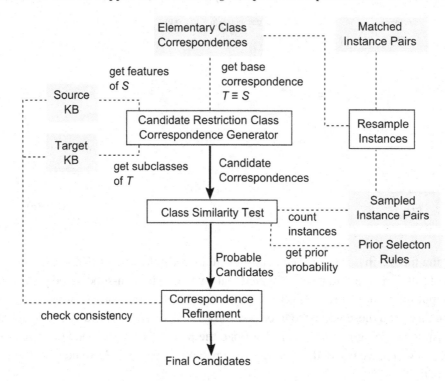

M, of pairs of matched instances from $\mathcal{K}_t$ and $\mathcal{K}_s$. For each input correspondence of the form $T \equiv S$, Bayes-ReCCE will search for correspondences of the form $T_i \equiv S \mid_f$, where T_i is a subclass of T and f is a restriction feature. Let $T_{img} = R_{\mathcal{K}_t \mid \mathcal{K}_s, M}\left(T_i\right)$, be the set of instances of S which match an instance of T_i. Then the features can be generated using the following SPARQL pseudo-queries:

To detect CAV features

```
SELECT DISTINCT ?p ?v
WHERE {
    ?i ?p ?v.
    ?i ∈ T_img .
}
To detect CAT features
SELECT DISTINCT ?p ?t
WHERE {
    ?i ?p ?o.
    ?o rdf:type ?t
    ?i ∈ T_img .
}
To detect CAT⁻¹ features
SELECT DISTINCT ?p ?t
```

```
WHERE {
    ?s ?p ?i.
    ?s rdf:type ?t
    ?i ∈ T_img .
}
To detect CAE features
SELECT DISTINCT ?p
WHERE {
    ?i ?p _.
    ?i ∈ T_img .
}
```

Class Similarity Test

During this step, candidate correspondences of the form $T_i \equiv S \mid_f$ are tested to estimate the probability that T_i really is equivalent to $S \mid_f$. This estimation is performed using the Bayesian method described earlier. This estimates the probability that $\theta = J\left(T_i, S \mid_f\right)$ is greater than $\varepsilon \in [0,1]$. This requires comparison of the sets T_{img} with the set S_M which consists of the instances in the mapped retrieval of S, that is the instances of S which are matched to an instance of T. It is necessary to use S_M because the retreival of S may contain instances of T_i which are not included in T_{img} due to not being included in the mapping set. See Figure 3. Using S_M we calculate $S_f = S_M \mid_f$, the set of matched instances of S which have feature f. We can then use the sizes of the intersection and union of T_{img} and S_f combined with our priors α and β to estimate $P(\theta > \varepsilon)$. If this probability is lower than a specified cut off, p_{MIN}, we reject the correspondence candidate.

Correspondence Refinement Step

Initial implementations of Bayes-ReCCE were observed to over generalise the forms of correspondence detected. For example, detecting that *film directors* correspond with people who had directed any creative work, not just films. A set of heuristic rules are used to remedy this. These rules find the most specific correspondence for each target class. Based on our earlier study of complex correspondences observed in Linked Data, it is assumed that CAV correspondences are the most specific, CAT are less specific, and CAE the least. It is also assumed that if class A is a subclass of B, then a CAT correspondence conditioned on A is more specific than a CAT conditioned on B. These rules are as follows:

1. If $T_i \equiv S \mid_{f_1}$ is a CAE correspondence and there exists a CAV or CAT correspondence $T_i \equiv S \mid_{f_2}$ which uses the same restriction property then $T_i \equiv S \mid_{f_1}$ is removed from the set of candidate correspondences, as $S \mid_{f_2}$ is a more specific class than $S \mid_{f_1}$.

Figure 3. Mapping each of the T_i sets to subsets of S

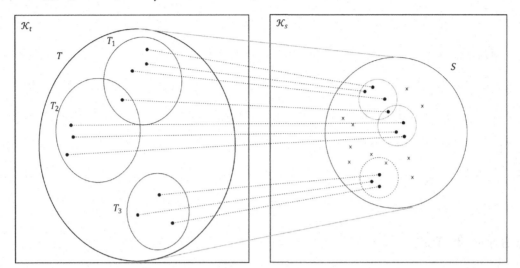

2. If $T_i \equiv S \mid_{f_1}$ is a CAT correspondence and there exists a CAT correspondence $T_i \equiv S \mid_{f_2}$ where the restriction type specified in f_2 is more specific than the restriction type specified in f_1, then $T_i \equiv S \mid_{f_1}$ is removed, as $S \mid_{f_2}$ is a more specific class than $S \mid_{f_1}$.

3. If $T_i \equiv S \mid_{f_1}$ is a CAT correspondence and there exists a CAV correspondence $T_i \equiv S \mid_{f_2}$ where the restriction value specified in f_2 is an instance of the restriction type specified in f_1, then $T_i \equiv S \mid_{f_1}$ is removed, as again, $S \mid_{f_2}$ is a more specific class than $S \mid_{f_1}$.

Once these rules have been applied, it leaves our final set of candidate correspondences.

Resampling the Set of Instance Matches

The number of features examined while searching for the correspondences is a function of the number of instances contained in the knowledge bases. As the size of the ABox increases, the number of features that need to be examined can be very large. If a representative sample of the instances is used instead, it should allow calculation of the class similarity measure to a reasonable degree of accuracy without needing to examine as many features.

Therefore Bayes-ReCCE includes an additional pre-processing step in the search algorithm where the set of matched instances is resampled. For each target class T_i under evaluation, at most N match pairs are selected from M which refer to instances of T_i and add the pairs to the set M'. M' is then used in place of M when evaluating class similarity. The complete Bayes-ReCCE algorithm is listed in Algorithm Listing 1.

Algorithm Listing 1. Bayes-ReCCE

Input:
C, a set of elementary class correspondences
M a set of matched instances,
ε, p_{MIN}, N
prior_rules, a set rules for selecting Bayesian parameters.
Output: RC, a set of restriction correspondences
$RC := \{\}$
M = resample(M, N)
foreach $(T, S) \in C$ **do**
$S_M := instances\, in\, R_{\mathcal{K}_s}(S)\, matched\, to\, T$
foreach $T_i \sqsubset T$ **do**
$T_{img} := R_{\mathcal{K}_t | \mathcal{K}_s, M}(T_i)$
foreach $f \in$ features(T_{img})**do**
$(\alpha, \beta) :=$ selectPrior(f ,prior_rules)
$S_f := S_M \mid_f$
$k := \left| T_{img} \cap S_f \right|$
$n := \left| T_{img} \cup S_f \right|$
if $P(\theta > \varepsilon \mid k, n, \alpha, \beta) > p_{MIN}$ **then**
add $T_i \equiv S \mid_f$ to RC
removeConflicts(RC)
return RC

Empirical Evaluation

This section describes an evaluation of the performance of Bayes-ReCCE on large, real world Linked Data knowledge bases, and assesses the effect of matched instance sample size on its ability to accurately detect complex correspondences. Two sets of gold standard complex correspondences were created for the evaluation: one set with DBpedia as the source ontology and LinkedMDB as the target ontology, and a second set with GeoNames as the source and DBpedia as the target. Bayes-ReCCE was then used to automatically detect complex correspondences between the ontologies, using a range of values of N in the resample step described in Algorithm Listing 1. The correspondences produced each time were compared with the gold standard correspondences to produce an F1 score, and this process was carried out 20 times per value of N to estimate the average F1 score as a function of N, the matched instance sample size. The hypothesis was that:

For some value of N a random sample of N instances per target class will allow Bayes-ReCCE to find a set of complex correspondences with a median F1 score above 0.75 when compared with the gold standard.

If true this would indicate that for this value of N, a sample of instances would have a one in two chance of the mean of the precision and recall scores being above 0.75.

Next the knowledge bases used in the evaluation are described and then the gold standard set of complex correspondences which exist between them. Finally experimental results are discussed.

Datasets

DBpedia is a large, cross-domain knowledge base containing information extracted from Wikipedia. The 2014 releases used in this evaluation contain about 4.5 million things, approximately 4.2m of which are classified in a consistent ontology. This includes details of approximately 1,445,000 persons and 735,000 places. The DBpedia ontology contains 685 classes which form a subsumption hierarchy and 2,795 different properties. DBpedia is one of the central resources in the linked open data cloud, and as such it is highly connected with many other knowledge bases.

GeoNames is a geographical knowledge base which describes over 9 million unique geographical features. The GeoNames class hierarchy is extremely flat, and all features in GeoNames simply have the class *geo:Feature*. Categorisation in GeoNames is achieved using two properties *geo:featureClass* which can take one of 9 values, and geo:featureCode which can take one of 645 values. The combination of *geo:featureClass* and geo:featureCode can be seen as forming a two level hierarchy which is illustrated in Figure 4.

One important distinction between this hierarchy and one provided using classes is that while each individual in general can belong to multiple classes, individuals in GeoNames can only have a maximum of one value each for their geo:featureClass and geo:featureCode properties. In addition GeoNames feature codes and classes use cryptic combinations of letters and it is not immediately obvious what they represent. For example the code "PPLC" refers to the capital of a political entity.

LinkedMDB describes approximately 66,500 instances from the domain of cinema. It has a flat hierarchy of 53 classes.

Figure 4. A partial illustration of the GeoNames classification hierarchy

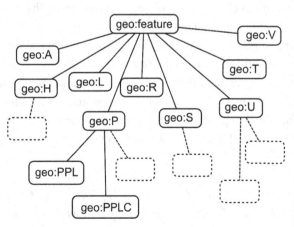

Geoname Feature Classes	
Class	Meaning
A	country, state, region,...
H	stream, lake, ...
L	parks,area, ...
P	city, village,...
R	road, railroad
S	spot, building, farm
T	mountain,hill,rock,...
U	undersea
V	forest,heath,...

Geoname Feature Codes	
Code	Meaning
PPL	populated place
PPLC	capital of a political entity

Relationship Between DBpedia and LinkedMDB

There are 30,354 instance links between DBpedia and LinkedMDB, however there are no published correspondences between the classes used in LinkedMDB and those in the DBpedia ontology. The class *lmdb:film* obviously corresponds with the class *dbpedia-owl:Film*, and in initial inspection it might appear that *lmdb:actor* corresponds with *dbpedia-owl:Actor* and *lmdb:director* corresponds to *dbpedia-owl:MovieDirector*. Further inspection reveals that the correspondences for actors and directors are not so clear cut. There are no individuals in the 2014 release of DBpedia which have type *dbpedia-owl:MovieDirector*, and of the 3838 instances of *lmdb:actor* that are matched to instances in DBpedia, only 49 are identified as having type *dbpdia-owl:Actor*. In addition to this extensional difference, actors in LinkedMDB are specifically film actors, while actors in DBpedia can also include television, theatre and radio actors, so despite having very similar names, the classes are intentionally different.

Instead of using elementary correspondences we can use complex correspondences to provide a more accurate alignment between DBpedia and LinkedMDB. Through manual analysis, we discovered three CAT^{-1} correspondences with DBpedia as the source ontology LinkedMDB as the target ontology. These correspondences are

- *lmdb:actor $\equiv$ dbpedia-owl:Person*|$_{dpbedia-owl:starring}$ of a *dbpedia:Film*
- *lmdb:director $\equiv$ dbpedia-owl:Person*|$_{dpbedia-owl:director}$ of a dbpedia:Film
- *lmdb:producer $\equiv$ dbpedia-owl:Person*|$_{dpbedia-owl:producer}$ of a *dbpedia:Film*

That is LinkedMDB actors correspond to instances of Person in DBpedia who are listed as a star of a film instance, directors in LinkedMDB are listed as the director value of a film in DBpedia, and similarly producers in LinkedMDB are listed as the producer value of a film in DBpedia. The average Jaccard index for the classes in these correspondences is 0.78.

Relationships Between DBpedia and GeoNames

There are approximately 425,000 instance matches between DBpedia and GeoNames (DBpedia Association, 2015). In addition the GeoNames website provides a set of 32 class correspondences from GeoNames to DBpedia classes. Each of these 32 correspondences follows the CAV pattern with GeoNames as the source and DBpedia the target. In each correspondence the target class is a subclass of *dbpedia-owl:Place*, the source class is *geo:Feature*, and the property geo:featureCode is used in the restriction feature. Through manual inspection of the ontologies an additional 11 CAV correspondences were discovered (see Table 1).

The majority of which use *geo:featureCode* in their restriction feature, but in addition we include two correspondences which use geo:featureClass (dbpedia:BodyOfWater, dbpedia:ArchitcturalStructure) and one correspondence using parent feature (dbpedia:Continent). This last correspondence may appear incorrect at first glance, however http://sws.geonames.org/6295630/ refers to the Earth, all continents have this feature as their parent, and they are they are the only features to do so.

Inspecting the extensional similarity of the classes in the correspondences listed on the GeoNames website revealed that some are quite dissimilar. The Jaccard index for each of the target classes and their corresponding restriction classes ranged from 0, for atolls, to 0.9, for hospitals and the mean value was 0.43.

Table 1. New class by attribute value correspondences between DBpedia and GeoNames

Named Class	Restriction Class
dbpedia:Park	rdf:type (X, geo:feature) ∧ geo:featureCode(X, "L.PRK")
dbpedia:Mountain	rdf:type (X, geo:feature) ∧ geo:featureCode(X, "T")
dbpedia:BodyOfWater	rdf:type (X, geo:feature) ∧ geo:featureClass(X, "H")
dbpedia:Country	rdf:type (X, geo:feature) ∧ geo:featureCode(X, "A.PCLI")
dbpedia:Island	rdf:type (X, geo:feature) ∧ geo:featureCode(X, "T.ISL")
dbpedia:Airport	rdf:type (X, geo:feature) ∧ geo:featureCode(X, "S.AIRP")
dbpedia:Hospital	rdf:type (X, geo:feature) ∧ geo:featureCode(X, "S.HSP")
dbpedia:Bridge	rdf:type (X, geo:feature) ∧ geo:featureCode(X, "S.BDG")
dbpedia:Lake	rdf:type (X, geo:feature) ∧ geo:featureCode(X, "H.LK")
dbpedia:River	rdf:type (X, geo:feature) ∧ geo:featureCode(X, "H.STM")

The gold standard set of complex correspondences combined the 32 published correspondences with the 11 discovered manually and listed in Table 1.

Results

This evaluation uses a p_{min} value of 0.5 and an ε value of 0.5 – that is selecting correspondences where there is at least a 50% chance that the classes in the correspondence overlap by 50% or more. This choice of parameters promotes recall over precision. The prior selection rules used in this evaluation were very simple. Any correspondence using owl:sameAs received prior parameters $\alpha = 1, \beta = 9$, and all others used the uninformed prior, $\alpha = \beta = 1$. Applying Bayes-ReCCE to DBpedia and LinkedMDB, the median F1 score very quickly converges to 1 as the number of matched instances is increased. Figure 5 shows the mean F1 score for correspondences found between DBpedia and LinkedMDB as a function of matched instance sample size. The scores are quite variable at first, but this is partially due to the small number of cases in the gold standard. With a sample of 10 matched instances per target class, the interquartile range is above 0.75, and by 30 instances the F1 score has converged to 1.

Figure 6 shows the F1 scores from applying Bayes-ReCCE to GeoNames and DBpedia. Here the F1 score is not as high as with the IMBD to DBPedia mappings. It is important to highlight however, that large amounts of matched instances were not required to achieve reasonable performance. With only 5 instance matches per target class, the 95% confidence interval for the mean F1 score was between 0.58 and 0.62. This compares well with the mean score when using 50 instances, which lies somewhere between 0.63 and 0.65 with 95% confidence. Figure 7 compares the performance of using a Bayesian

Figure 5. Mean F1 scores for correspondences found between DBpedia and LinkedMDB. Boxes show interquartile range, whiskers show the 95% confidence interval, and circles represent outliers

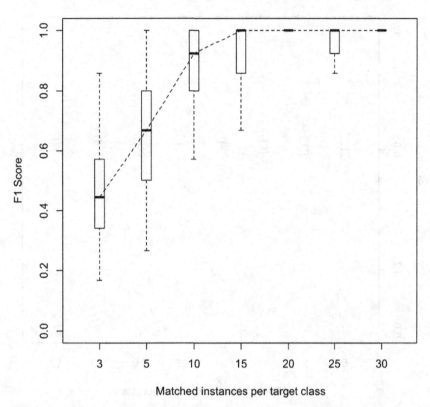

Correspondences with source DBpedia and target LMDB.

Matched instances per target class

estimator of similarity instead the directly observed Jaccard score. Here the same training set was used for each set of training data, and the ReCCE algorithm applied twice – once using the Bayesian Estimator described earlier and once using a direct Jaccard to score class similarity (as is common in other work on instance matching). Here we can see that the using a Bayesian estimator consistently scores a higher F1 score ($F1_{Bayes}$) than using a direct Jaccard ($F1_J$)

Analysis

The Bayes-ReCCE algorithm demonstrated good performance with small samples of matched instances. With only 15 instances per target class the median F1 scores were 1.0 and 0.7 for correspondences between DBpedia and LinkedMDB, and GeoNames and DBpedia respectively. At 30 instances Bayes-ReCCE performed perfectly, detecting correspondences between DBpedia and LinkedMDB, and at 50 instances, the median F1 score for the correspondences detected between GeoNames and DBedia was above 0.63, with a 95% chance that the mean lies between 0.63 and 0.65. Performance for correspondence detection between DBpedia and LinkedMDB was better, and this is most likely as the gold standard correspondences for these ontologies had higher Jaccard indexes for their corresponding classes.

Figure 6. Mean F1 scores for correspondences found between GeoNames and DBpedia. Boxes show interquartile range, whiskers show the 95% confidence interval, and circles represent outliers

Correspondences with source GeoNames and target DBpedia.

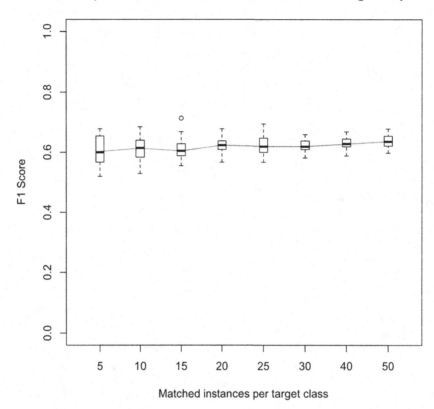

Matched instances per target class

The benefits of using an extensional approach to class similarity are clear. Bayes-ReCCE did not return the false positive dbpedia-owl:Actor ≡ lmdb:actor, or dbpedia-owl:MovieDirector as final candidate correspondences. (Although Bayes-ReCCE does consider these as initial candidate correspondences as they, technically, are a form of CAV which use rdf:type as the restriction property.) See above for a discussion of these false positives. Bayes-ReCCE was also able to find correspondences between DBpedia and GeoNames despite the cryptic codes used in GeoNames.

Correspondence Explanation and Reuse

The problem of explaining matches has been highlighted as one of the ten most pressing challenges in semantic matching (Shvaiko and J. Euzenat, 2008; 2012). The challenge is to provide explanations in a simple yet clear and precise way to facilitate informed decision making. Currently correspondences are described with a specific predicate and an optional confidence value, which can vary between 0 and 1, but which has no commonly agreed meaning.

It is proposed that instead of describing the match with a specific predicate, it includes a summary of the evidence used to select the match and allow the users of the correspondence to decide for themselves if this evidence is sufficient for their particular information retrieval task. This evidence could

Figure 7 Comparing Bayesian estimator with observed Jaccard for class similarity

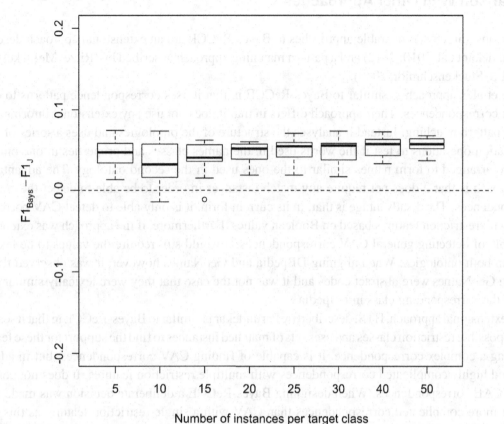

also be included in the metadata of a mapping, that we have motivated and described in separate research (Lambrix and Tan, 2006).With each correspondence, $A \equiv B$, we include the following information

- k, the number of individuals we have observed that are instances of both A, and B.
- n, the number of individuals we have observed that are instances of either A, or B.
- α and β, the parameters of the prior we used when selecting this correspondence.
- j, the minimum Jaccard index we require for a match.
- p, the probability that the true Jaccard index is greater than j.

With this information, a consumer of the correspondence can see how the matcher chose the correspondence, and can calculate for themselves the probability of the correspondence having a different minimum Jaccard index. This would enable reliable, informed decision making about correspondence re-use. For example, if we publish a set of correspondences which we believe to have a minimum Jaccard index of 0.5 or more, but a user requires correspondences which they believe to have a minimum Jaccard of 0.9, they can use the values provided to calculate the probability of the Jaccard being over 0.9 for each of our correspondences, and reject any that do not have a sufficiently high probability.

Comparison With Other Approaches

The two most directly comparable approaches to Bayes-ReCCE are an extensional approach described by (Parundekar et al. 2010; 2012) and a pattern matching approach described by (Ritze, Meilicke, Svab-Zamazal & Stuckenschmidt, 2009).

Ritze et al.'s approach is similar to Bayes-ReCCE in that it uses correspondence patterns to detect complex correspondences. Their approach differs in that it does not use any extensional information to perform pattern matching. Instead it analyses the structure of the ontologies and uses a series of string manipulation operations to test if the words used in the names classes and properties in one ontology can be re-arranged to form names similar to the ones used in the second ontology. The advantage of this approach is that it does not require any match instances in order to be able to detect the complex correspondences. The disadvantage is that, in its current form, it is only able to detect CAV correspondences with restriction features based on Boolean values. Furthermore, if the approach was extended to be capable of detecting general CAV correspondences, it would still require the values to be lexically similar in both ontologies. When aligning DBpedia and GeoNames however, it was observed that the values in GeoNames were abstract codes and it was not the case that they were lexically similar to the name of the corresponding class in DBpedia.

The extensional approach, HTS, described by Parundekar is similar to Bayes-ReCCE in that it searches through possible restriction classes and uses sets of matched instances to find the support for these features describing a complex correspondence. It is capable of finding CAV correspondences, but in addition it can find highly complicated correspondences with multiple restriction features. It does not consider CAT or CAE correspondences. When designing Bayes-ReCCE a deliberate decision was made to not consider more complicated correspondences than CAV with a single restriction feature, as this could produce correspondences that would be difficult to describe to a user, and hence would be difficult for them to evaluate. In addition the ability to have multiple restriction features in a correspondence means that there is a higher chance that the correspondences detected will be over fitting the data, though it is difficult to test if this is a serious problem. In the evaluation of their HTS approach matching DBpedia and GeoNames, Parundekar et al. found 16 complex correspondences, all of which belonged to the CAT pattern. They did not find any complex correspondences with multiple restriction features. Out of the 16 correspondences they detected, 9 were correct compared to the gold standard used in the Bayes-ReCCE evaluation. This would give them a precision score of 0.56, a recall of 0.3 and an F1 score of 0.39.

A comparison of the correspondences detected by Bayes-ReCCE and HTS was conducted by examining the published HTS correspondences discovered between GeoNames and DBpedia. This study focused on CAV correspondences (the only type detected by HTS). Since GeoNames only provides a single class geo:Feature, all CAV correspondences between GeoNames and DBpedia can be expected to consist of a restriction class in GeoNames and a named class in DBpedia. Furthermore as geo:Feature was assumed to be broadly equivalent to dbpedia-owl:Place, this evaluation assumed that all named DBpedia classes in the correspondences will be sub classes of dbpedia-owl:Place. The procedure for evaluation was to first find all CAV correspondences fitting the description above in the set of published correspondences which were discovered using HTS. Then, for each sub class of dbpedia-owl:Place, the Bayes-ReCCE method was used to discover if there was an attribute-value pair in GeoNames which could specify a CAV correspondence between a restriction class in GeoNames and the given sub-class. Twenty instances of each sub-class of dbpedia-owl:Place were used to train the Bayes-ReCCE detector. This number was selected as in the evaluation as it was previously discovered experimentally that no significant improvement in performance was shown after 20 instances. The results of using Bayes-ReCCE are then compared with the CAV correspondences found using HTS. The most important metric is the number of valid correspondences each approach found. In addition, in the case where both methods find a CAV correspondence to a given DBpedia class, a record is made of which method produces a restriction class that more closely resembles the DBpedia class.

Having undertaken the evaluation, the results show that both methods produced similar numbers of acceptable correspondences between GeoNames and DBpedia with each producing 12. Bayes-ReCCE (see Table 2) however, produced only one incorrect correspondence:

- *Stadium ≡ featureCode = L.PRK*

While the HTS method produced four incorrect correspondences:

- *HistoricPlace ≡ inCountry = US*
- *Stadium ≡ parentFeature = 2635167*
- *ProtectedArea ≡ inCountry = CA*
- *Building ≡ inCountry = GB*

This gives a false positive rate of 0.25 for the HTS method versus 0.08 for Bayes-ReCCE.

The nature of these incorrect HTS correspondences is interesting, the attribute-value pairs used in the correspondence restriction class refer to the feature's location and are clearly inappropriate e.g. being located in the country Great Britain is not a defining characteristic of being a building. The mistake produced by Bayes-ReCCE is much less obvious. Stadia are often referred to as parks, it is conceivable that the training data contained many examples of stadia that were mistakenly labelled as a park.

There were three cases where HTS produced correspondences that, while not incorrect, could be improved on. These were:

- *Island ≡ featureClass=T*
- *Hospital ≡ featureClass=S*
- *Skyscraper ≡ featureClass=S*

For all of these cases, Bayes-ReCCE produced the more accurate (narrower) correspondences

- *Island ≡ featureCode = T.ISL*
- *Hospital ≡ featureCode = S.HSP*
- *Skyscraper ≡ featureCode = S.BDG*

There were no cases where HTS produced correspondences that were more specific than Bayes-ReCCE results.

Bayes-ReCCE was shown to be more capable of finding correspondences for classes with very few instances. For example the class Park with 21 instances, which Bayes-ReCCE produced a correct correspondence, and HTS produced no correspondence. Also, two out of the three cases where Bayes-ReCCE produced a more precisely defined correspondence were for classes with few instances – Hospital (23 instances in the training set) and Skyscraper (36 instances).

Table 2. CAV correspondences between DBpedia and Geonames, discovered using Bayes-ReCCE

Named Class	Restriction Class	Restriction Meaning
Park	featureCode = L.PRK	Park: an area, often of forested land, maintained as a place of beauty, or for recreation
ProtectedArea	featureCode = L.PRK	Park:
Mountain	featureCode = T	Mountain, hill, rock, ...
BodyOfWater	featureClass = H	Stream, lake, ...
Country	featureCode = A.PCLI	Independent political entity
Island	featureCode = T.ISL	Island: a tract of land, smaller than a continent, surrounded by water at high water
Airport	featureCode = S.AIRP	Airport: a place where aircraft regularly land and take off, with runways, navigational aids, and major facilities for the commercial handling of passengers and cargo
Hospital	featureCode = S.HSP	Hospital: a building in which sick or injured, especially those confined to bed, are medically treated
Stadium	featureCode = L.PRK	Park:
Skyscraper	featureCode = S.BLDG	Building: a structure built for permanent use, as a house, factory, etc.
Bridge	featureCode = S.BDG	Bridge: a structure erected across an obstacle such as a stream, road, etc., in order to carry roads, railroads, and pedestrians across
Lake	featureClass = H.LK	A large inland body of standing water
River	featureCode = H.STM	A body of running water moving to a lower level in a channel on land

One further observation is that while the HTS detection method is capable of finding complex correspondences with restriction classes defined by multiple properties, no correspondences of this form were found between GeoNames restriction classes and named DBpedia classes.

In summary this evaluation shows that Bayes-ReCCE and HTS were both capable of finding the same number of valid CAV correspondences between DBpedia and GeoNames – 12 each. In one quarter of these cases however, Bayes-ReCCE produced more accurate complex correspondences – that is ones where the restriction class in the correspondence produced by Bayes-ReCCE was more closely related to the named class in the correspondence. Bayes-ReCCE also performed better than HTS when there were less training instances available.

A limitation of this evaluation is that with only 14 CAV correspondences in total found, it is difficult to say with great certainty that Bayes-ReCCE will generally find more accurate CAV correspondences than HTS. A further limitation of this evaluation is that the training sets used for the Bayes-ReCCE detection method were drawn at random, and it is possible that different sampling could produce different results. This is especially true in the case where only a small number of matched instances are available – it is very possible that there is a systematic reason why those particular instances have been matched, which in turn will mean that the available instances are not representative of the population as a whole. The goal of the evaluation was to show that Bayes-ReCCE can outperform HTS while requiring less training data. It is difficult to conclude strongly that this is the case given the evidence provided, but it is clear that both methods produced very similar results and Bayes-ReCCE used less training data.

It **is** relatively safe to conclude that there was nothing gained by using much a larger set of training data. This is an important result. Often when performing ontology mapping the number of matched instances available will be relatively low, and in such cases, the Bayes-ReCCE method is easier to deploy. Furthermore, using smaller training sets places less strain on available storage and computing resources.

FUTURE RESEARCH DIRECTIONS

As part of this investigative work complex correspondences that go beyond the patterns of (Scharffe, 2009) were detected, including the possibility of unions of patterns or the requirement to modify the target ontology (e.g. by adding a new relationship). These topics should be fertile ground for a new generation of complex correspondence methods that can dynamically suggest refinements to both source and target ontologies in order to better integrate them.

It is also an open question as to how best to represent the mapping probability distribution in a mapping language. This could lead to new mapping frameworks that could dynamically re-cast and discard mappings on a per user or use-case basis, potentially making for much more intelligent and responsive data integration systems.

As an extensional approach, Bayes-ReCCE, depends on the presence of (1) equivalent instance data in the ontologies or linked data-sets to be matched and (2) instance equivalence interlines. This limits its applicability to ontologies or linked data where such data exists but this is a probabilistic tool designed deal with the reality of large, public, linked data repositories that usually have plentiful instance data. Intensional approaches in theory have wider applicability but when the details of their current algorithms are investigated, e.g. Ritze et al. (2009), we see serious limitations such as an inability to deal with attributes other than Boolean values whereas Bayes-ReCCE deals with all attribute domains. No doubt there is potential for further work on these methods.

CONCLUSION

Many complex correspondences can be described as commonly re-occurring patterns, containing a small number of features. Our algorithm, Bayes-ReCCE, automates the process of finding complex correspondences which fit these patterns by searching for these features in matched instance data. It was demonstrated that that Bayes-ReCCE was capable of detecting complex correspondences between the DBpedia, LinkedMDB and GeoNames knowledge bases. Since the method requires some set of matched instances as input it is our working assumption that this data will be provided by human supervision of the process, perhaps as part of a wider alignment/mapping tool-chain and we make no claim that the method is suitable for totally unsupervised application to non-overlapping datasets. We demonstrated that Bayes-ReCCE performs well with even small sets of matched data, arguably out-performing the closest competitor approach of Parundekar et al. (2012) with greater accuracy and using less resources.

Bayes-ReCCE advances the state of the art in that it has been demonstrated to be effective when using in the order of tens of instances per class, while other approaches use in the order of thousands. In addition Bayes-ReCCE explains its output in terms of correspondence patterns which can help users interpret the results. This is valuable as interpreting results is seen as one of the leading challenges in ontology mapping.

ACKNOWLEDGMENT

The authors wish to thank Dr. Judie Attard and Prof. Dave Lewis for assistance with the preparation of this manuscript.

This research was supported by Science Foundation Ireland and co-funded by the European Regional Development Fund through the ADAPT Centre for Digital Content Technology [grant number 13/RC/2106]; the CNGL Programme (grant number 12/CE/I2267)]; the FAME Strategic Research Cluster [Grant 08/SRC/I1403]; and the European Union European Union's Horizon 2020 research and innovation programme under ALIGNED [grant agreement number 644055].

REFERENCES

Arnold, P., & Rahm, E. (2014). Enriching ontology mappings with semantic relations. *Data & Knowledge Engineering*, *93*, 1–18. doi:10.1016/j.datak.2014.07.001

Bishop, C. M. (2006). *Pattern Recognition and Machine Learning (Information Science and Statistics)*. Secaucus, NJ: Springer-Verlag New York, Inc.

Bizer, C., Heath, T., & Berners-Lee, T. (2009). Linked Data - The Story So Far. *International Journal on Semantic Web and Information Systems*, *5*(3), 1–22. doi:10.4018/jswis.2009081901

Bizer, C., Lehmann, J., Kobilarov, G., Auer, S., Becker, C., Cyganiak, R., & Hellmann, S. (2009). DBpedia - A Crystallization Point for the Web of Data. *Web Semantics: Science, Services, and Agents on the World Wide Web*, *7*(3), 154–165. doi:10.1016/j.websem.2009.07.002

Correndo, G., & Shadbolt, N. (2011). Translating expressive ontology mappings into rewriting rules to implement query rewriting. OM.

David, J., Euzenat, J., Scharffe, F., & dos Santos, C. (2011). The Alignment API 4.0. *Semantic Web -- Interoperability, Usability. Applicability*, *2*(1), 3–10.

DBpedia Association. (2015). *DBpedia Release 39 - Links to other datasets*. Retrieved July 7, 2017 from http://downloads.dbpedia.org/3.9/links/geonames_links.nt.bz2

De, F. B. (1989). Probabilism: A Critical Essay on the Theory of Probability and on the Value of Science. *Erkenntnis*, *31*(2/3), 169–223.

de Melo, G., Suchanek, F. M., & Pease, A. (2008). Integrating {YAGO} into the Suggested Upper Merged Ontology. In *20th International Conference on Tools with Artificial Intelligence* (vol. 1, pp. 190–193). IEEE.

Gal, A., Sagi, T., Weidlich, M., Levy, E., Shafran, V., Miklós, Z., & Hung, N. Q. V. (2012). Making Sense of Top-k Matchings: A Unified Match Graph for Schema Matching. In *Proceedings of the Ninth International Workshop on Information Integration on the Web* (p. 6:1--6:6). New York: ACM. doi:10.1145/2331801.2331807

Gamma, E., Helm, R., Johnson, R., & Vlissides, J. (1995). *Design Patterns: Elements of Reusable Object-oriented Software*. Boston: Addison-Wesley Longman Publishing Co., Inc.

Gillet, P., Trojahn, C., Haemmerlé, O., & Pradel, C. (2013). Complex Correspondences for Query Patterns Rewriting. In *Proceedings of the 8th International Conference on Ontology Matching* (vol. 1111, pp. 49–60). Aachen, Germany: CEUR-WS.org.

Halpin, H., Hayes, P. J., McCusker, J. P., McGuinness, D. L., & Thompson, H. S. (2010). When owl:sameAs Isn't the Same: An Analysis of Identity in Linked Data. In *The Semantic Web -- ISWC 2010: 9th International Semantic Web Conference, ISWC 2010*, (pp. 305–320). Berlin: Springer Berlin Heidelberg.

Hassanzadeh, O., & Consens, M. (2009). Linked movie data base. *Proceedings of the 2nd Workshop on Linked Data on the Web (LDOW2009)*.

Hellmann, S., Lehmann, J., & Auer, S. (2009). Learning of {OWL} Class Descriptions on Very Large Knowledge Bases. *International Journal on Semantic Web and Information Systems*, 5(2), 25–48. doi:10.4018/jswis.2009040102

Hu, W., Chen, J., Zhang, H., & Qu, Y. (2012). Learning Complex Mappings between Ontologies. *The Semantic Web: Joint International Semantic Technology Conference, JIST 2011*, (pp. 350–357). Berlin: Springer Berlin Heidelberg.

Hu, W., Qu, Y., & Cheng, G. (2008). Matching large ontologies: A divide-and-conquer approach. *Data & Knowledge Engineering*, 67(1), 140–160. doi:10.1016/j.datak.2008.06.003

Janssen, F., Fallahi, F., Noessner, J., & Paulheim, H. (2012). Towards Rule Learning Approaches to Instance-based Ontology Matching. In J. Völker, H. Paulheim, J. Lehmann, & M. Niepert (Eds.), KNOW@ LOD (Vol. 868, pp. 13–18). CEUR-WS.org.

Junior, A. C., Walshe, B., & O'Sullivan, D. (2015). Enhanced Faceted Browsing of a WW1 Dataset Through Ontology Alignment. In *Proceedings of the 17th International Conference on Information Integration and Web-based Applications & Services* (p. 48:1--48:5). New York: ACM. doi:10.1145/2837185.2837259

Lambrix, P., & Tan, H. (2006). SAMBO-A System for Aligning and Merging Biomedical Ontologies. *Web Semantics: Science, Services, and Agents on the World Wide Web*, 4(3), 196–206. doi:10.1016/j.websem.2006.05.003

Lehmann, J., Auer, S., Bühmann, L., & Tramp, S. (2011). Class expression learning for ontology engineering. *Journal of Web Semantics*, 9(1), 71–81. doi:10.1016/j.websem.2011.01.001

Li, J., Tang, J., Li, Y., & Luo, Q. (2009). RiMOM: A Dynamic Multistrategy Ontology Alignment Framework. *IEEE Transactions on Knowledge and Data Engineering*, 21(8), 1218–1232. doi:10.1109/TKDE.2008.202

Mark, W. (2006). *Geonames*. Retrieved May 21, 2015, from www.geonames.org

Miller, G. A. (1995). WordNet: A Lexical Database for English. *Communications of the ACM*, 38(11), 39–41. doi:10.1145/219717.219748

Parundekar, R., Knoblock, C. A., & Ambite, J. L. (2010). Linking and Building Ontologies of Linked Data. In *Proceedings of the 9th International Semantic Web Conference on The Semantic Web - Volume Part I* (pp. 598–614). Berlin: Springer-Verlag. doi:10.1007/978-3-642-17746-0_38

Parundekar, R., Knoblock, C. A., & Ambite, J. L. (2012). Discovering Concept Coverings in Ontologies of Linked Data Sources. In *The Semantic Web -- ISWC 2012: 11th International Semantic Web Conference*, (pp. 427–443). Berlin: Springer Berlin Heidelberg. doi:10.1007/978-3-642-35176-1_27

Paulheim, H., & Bizer, C. (2014). Improving the Quality of Linked Data Using Statistical Distributions. *International Journal on Semantic Web and Information Systems*, *10*(2), 63–86. doi:10.4018/ijswis.2014040104

Pavel, S., & Euzenat, J. (2013). Ontology Matching: State of the Art and Future Challenges. *IEEE Transactions on Knowledge and Data Engineering*, *25*(1), 158–176. doi:10.1109/TKDE.2011.253

Qin, H., Dou, D., & LePendu, P. (2007). Discovering Executable Semantic Mappings Between Ontologies. In *Proceedings of the 2007 OTM Confederated International Conference on On the Move to Meaningful Internet Systems: CoopIS, DOA, ODBASE, GADA, and IS - Volume Part I* (pp. 832–849). Berlin: Springer-Verlag.

Ritze, D., Meilicke, C., Šváb-Zamazal, O., & Stuckenschmidt, H. (2009). A Pattern-based Ontology Matching Approach for Detecting Complex Correspondences. In *Proceedings of the 4th International Conference on Ontology Matching* (vol. 51, pp. 25–36). Aachen, Germany: CEUR-WS.org.

Rousset, M. C., Atencia, M., David, J., Jouanot, F., Palombi, O., & Ulliana, F. (2017). Datalog Revisited for Reasoning in Linked Data. Reasoning Web. *Semantic Interoperability on the Web, 121.*

Scharffe, F. (2009). *Correspondence patterns representation.* University of Innsbruck.

Schmachtenberg, M., Bizer, C., & Paulheim, H. (2014). Adoption of the Linked Data Best Practices in Different Topical Domains. In *Semantic Web Conference* (Vol. 8796, pp. 245–260). Springer. doi:10.1007/978-3-319-11964-9_16

Seddiqui, M. H., & Aono, M. (2009). An efficient and scalable algorithm for segmented alignment of ontologies of arbitrary size. *Web Semantics: Science, Services, and Agents on the World Wide Web*, *7*(4), 344–356. doi:10.1016/j.websem.2009.09.001

Shultis, J., & Eckhoff, N. (1979). Selection of Beta Prior Distribution Parameters from Component Failure Data. *IEEE Transactions on Power Apparatus and Systems, PAS*, *98*(2), 400–407. doi:10.1109/TPAS.1979.319361

Shvaiko, P., & Euzenat, J. (2008). Ten Challenges for Ontology Matching. In *Proceedings of the OTM 2008 Confederated International Conferences, CoopIS, DOA, GADA, IS, and ODBASE 2008. Part II on On the Move to Meaningful Internet Systems* (pp. 1164–1182). Berlin: Springer-Verlag.

Shvaiko, P., Euzenat, J., Jiménez-Ruiz, E., Cheatham, M., Hassanzadeh, O., & Ichise, R. (Eds.). (2016). *Proceedings of the 11th International Workshop on Ontology Matching* (vol. 1766). Academic Press.

Shvaiko, P., Euzenat, J., Shvaiko, P., & Euzenat, J. (2005). A survey of schema-based matching approaches. *Journal on Data Semantics*, *4*, 146–171.

Suchanek, F. M., Kasneci, G., & Weikum, G. (2008). YAGO: A Large Ontology from Wikipedia and WordNet. *Web Semantics: Science, Services, and Agents on the World Wide Web*, *6*(3), 203–217. doi:10.1016/j.websem.2008.06.001

Völker, J., & Niepert, M. (2011). Statistical Schema Induction. In G. Antoniou, M. Grobelnik, E. Simperl, B. Parsia, D. Plexousakis, P. De Leenheer, & J. Pan (Eds.), *The Semantic Web: Research and Applications: 8th Extended Semantic Web Conference, ESWC 2011* (pp. 124–138). Berlin: Springer Berlin Heidelberg.

Zaveri, A., Rula, A., Maurino, A., Pietrobon, R., Lehmann, J., & Auer, S. (2016). Quality assessment for linked data: A survey. *Semantic Web*, *7*(1), 63–93. doi:10.3233/SW-150175

KEY TERMS AND DEFINITIONS

Bayes-ReCCE: A generate and test based search strategy which uses a Bayesian class similarity estimate to find class restriction complex correspondences between ontologies with matched instances.

Complex Correspondence: A relation between entities in two ontologies or knowledge bases where at least one of the entities described in the correspondence is non-atomic.

Correspondence Pattern: Templates to describe commonly occurring complex relationships between ontologies. A type of ontology design pattern.

Extensional Methods: Mapping or correspondence generation methods that depend on the instance data of each class.

Jaccard Index: A set similarity measure based on measuring the intersection over the union of two sets.

Mapped Retrieval: The set of all named things in one ontology which are mapped to a thing which could be defined as a class in a second ontology.

Mapping: A verified, uniquely identified, specification of target and source entities in two ontologies, a relation or correspondence between them and a confidence measure.

APPENDIX 1

The ADAPT Centre for Digital Content Technology

The ADAPT Research Centre focuses on developing next generation digital technologies that transform how people communicate by helping to analyze, transform, personalize and deliver data more effectively. ADAPT (www.adaptcentre.ie) is funded by Science Foundation Ireland (SFI). The Centre is realising an ambitious vision: to become the global reference point for advanced research in Digital Content Technology. The ADAPT Centre uses its scientific expertise to drive collaborative innovation to unlock the potential of digital content, empower and enhance online engagement between people.

ADAPT leverages its research excellence to deliver significant economic and societal impact through innovative research collaboration with industry and through commercialization of results. It undertakes popular education and public engagement initiatives and has international partnerships with academia and industry to attract funding from a range of sources. The ADAPT Centre is led by Trinity College Dublin and is hosted in close collaboration with leading Irish universities: Dublin City University; University College Dublin and Dublin Institute of Technology.

The research described in this chapter took place in the context of ADAPT Theme E – "Managing the Global Conversation". Theme E addresses the integration, management and optimisation of privacy-aware data flows between users and digital content services that are needed to handle the changing usage contexts and a growing variety of data sources that arise from rapid innovation in digital content services. Theme E will apply dynamic, knowledge-driven techniques to ease management decision making across multiple business domains, differing workflow practices and heterogeneous service platforms. Theme E tackles two key challenges to achieve these goals: Content Meta-Data for Privacy Management, and Data Integration Mappings: User interaction and Continuous Management. By addressing issues of data protection, data ethics and data integration together, ADAPT Theme E aims to establish a data governance framework that gives users the confidence to engage with new waves of digital content services while addressing the cost and risk involved in providing those services.

APPENDIX 2

The ALIGNED Project: Aligned, Quality-Centric Software and Data Engineering

ALIGNED (www.aligned-project.eu) allows European data and software engineering industries to exploit new opportunities in web data by developing models, methods and tools for engineering big data information systems. The ALIGNED project is funded by the European Commission as part of the H2020 program and led by Trinity College Dublin. The other partners are: University of Oxford; Universität Leipzig; Semantic Web Company GmbH; Wolters Kluwer Deutschland GmbH; and Adam Mickiewicz University, Poznan.

ALIGNED created a combined software and data engineering meta-model that captures the data lifecycle, domain knowledge, and design intentions. This meta-model allows users to describe their software and data engineering projects. From this meta-model, ALIGNED created tools for software and data engineering of data-intensive systems. The software tools use this model to produce software design models, transformations that generate or configure data-intensive applications. The data tools use the meta-model to produce data development models including data quality and integrity constraints, data test frameworks, data curation workflows and data transformations. In addition, collaboration or process tools help to integrate the outputs of both engineering processes. ALIGNED is developing methods for using these meta-models and tools as part of a software and data engineering process, with an emphasis upon techniques for ensuring data quality and integrity, as well as software security and reliability.

Chapter 9
Graph–Based Abstractive Summarization:
Compression of Semantic Graphs

Balaji Jagan
Anna University, India

Ranjani Parthasarathi
Anna University, India

Geetha T. V.
Anna University, India

ABSTRACT

Customization of information from web documents is an immense job that involves mainly the shortening of original texts. Extractive methods use surface level and statistical features for the selection of important sentences. In contrast, abstractive methods need a formal semantic representation, where the selection of important components and the rephrasing of the selected components are carried out using the semantic features associated with the words as well as the context. In this paper, we propose a semi-supervised bootstrapping approach for the identification of important components for abstractive summarization. The input to the proposed approach is a fully connected semantic graph of a document, where the semantic graphs are constructed for sentences, which are then connected by synonym concepts and co-referring entities to form a complete semantic graph. The direction of the traversal of nodes is determined by a modified spreading activation algorithm, where the importance of the nodes and edges are decided, based on the node and its connected edges under consideration.

1. INTRODUCTION

Text Summarization can be classified as extractive and abstractive methods. An extractive summarization method consists of selecting important sentences, paragraphs etc. from the original document to produce a compressed form of the original text. The importance of the sentences is decided based on the statistical and linguistic features of sentences. In contrast, an abstractive summarization method consists

DOI: 10.4018/978-1-5225-5042-6.ch009

of understanding the original text and rephrasing it into different forms without changing the meaning conveyed in the original text, but in a compressed form of a summary. When compared with an extractive summary, the abstractive summary is a difficult and challenging task, which requires the semantic representation of the text, inference rules and natural language generation (Erkan & Radev 2004).

Extraction involves concatenating extracts taken from the corpus into a summary, whereas abstraction involves generating novel sentences from information extracted from the corpus. It has been observed that in the context of multi-document summarization of news articles, extraction may be inappropriate because it may produce summaries which are overly verbose or biased towards some sources (Barzilay et al., 1999). Extractive summarization (Gupta & Lehal 2010) includes selecting important information, paragraphs etc. from a document and combining it to form a new paragraph called as summery. The choice of the sentences depends upon statistical and linguistic features of the sentences. Extractive summaries are formulated by weighting the sentences as a function of high frequency words. Here, the most frequently occurring or the most favourably positioned text is considered to be the most important.

Abstractive summarization (Khan & Salim 2014) includes understanding the main concepts and relevant information of the main text and then expressing that information in short and clear format. Abstractive summarization techniques can again be classified into two categories- structured based and semantic based methods. Structured based approaches determines the most important information through documents by using templates, extraction rules and other structures such as tree, ontology etc. Semantic based approaches determines the most important information through, conceptual graphs, semantic networks, semantic graphs, etc. Abstractive summarization methods produce more coherent, less redundant and information rich summery. Generating abstract using abstractive summarization methods is a difficult task since it requires more semantic and linguistic analysis.

In general, the text summarization task is performed at various levels, such as the surface, entity and discourse (Hahn & Mani 2000). Surface-level approaches tend to represent information in terms of shallow parsers which can then be selectively combined to yield a selection function used to extract important information. Entity-level approaches (Mani & Maybury 1999) build an internal representation of the text, modeling text entities and their relationships. Text entities are units of texts, such as words, phrases, sentences or even paragraphs. These approaches tend to represent patterns of connectivity in the text to help determine what is salient. Discourse-level approaches (Mann & Thompson 1988) model the structure of the text and its relation to communicate goals.

Summarization is also carried out using graph-based approaches, such as LexRank (Erkan & Radev 2004) and TextRank (Mihalcea & Tarau 2004). LexRank has been applied to multi-document summarization, whereas TextRank has been applied to single document summarization and keyword extraction. Both the approaches apply a random walk in a fully connected undirected graph, to redistribute the node weights where text units (i.e. sentences) are represented as nodes and the similarities between the text units are represented as edges.

Most existing approaches rely on surface information where the important sentences are selected, and are simply added to the summary without understanding the meaning conveyed by the sentences. The disadvantages of these approaches result in summaries with redundant sentences, or less relevant or irrelevant sentences which are not important to the summary. To overcome these difficulties, a semantic interpretation of documents is required. Semantic information can be word level or context level. Word level semantics represents the semantic class associated with the word, such as concepts and attributes. On the other hand, context level semantics represents the semantic relationships existing between two different concepts. One such representation, where both word level and context level semantics are available is the Universal Networking Language (UNL) representation, a directed acyclic graph representation (UNDL 2011).

Limited work on the summarization of documents, represented using UNL has been done; where Sornlertlamvanich et al. (2001) proposed that the removal of non-essential segments in the sentences is performed using the semantic relationships that exist between the concepts in a sentence. The irrelevant sentence units having modifier relationships are removed from the selected sentences. Similarly, Martins & Rino (2002) defines 58 pruning heuristics for the removal of irrelevant sentence segments, where the pruning is carried out based on the semantic relationships. Both the existing UNL document summarizers only consider the intra-sentential dependencies to select the important sentences for summary. However, it fails to capture the connectivity information between the consecutive sentences.

The primary aim of this approach is to compress the document semantic graph into the summary semantic graph. In order to achieve this, we modified the original spreading activation (SA) algorithm by integrating the edge information (where the original SA only focuses on the node information to activate the spreading mechanism). In addition, we propose a semi-supervised pattern based bootstrapping approach, where we learn and assign the graph operations to the nodes and edges of a fully connected semantic graph. The learning of graph operations is decided based on the properties of the nodes and edges. The example patterns are matched with the test data to label appropriate flags. We then introduce the spreading activation algorithm for the traversal of the graph to execute the graph operations. Furthermore, the direction of the traversal of the node is decided during the activation of spreading. The conventional spreading activation algorithm starts the activation with only the node information, and the edges are utilized for the traversal. Finding the strength of the nodes without the edge information may fail to capture the cohesiveness. Thus, we modify the original spreading activation algorithm, by incorporating the edge information to find the strength of the nodes, and to traverse the semantic graph for executing the graph operations.

Here, we use the semantic graphs constructed based on the Universal Networking Language representation (UNDL 2011) for a morphologically rich and a partially free-word order language, Tamil (Balaji et al 2011). UNL semantic graphs are constructed for each sentence in a document. The nodes in the graph represent concepts of a sentence, and the links represent directed semantic relations that exist between two different concepts in a sentence. In addition, to obtain a fully connected semantic graph of document, this approach uses synonym concepts and anaphora resolved sentences (Balaji et al 2012) to connect the sentence level semantic graphs. However, certain concepts in the graph are not connected with any other concepts, but can still be important for summary generation. In the proposed approach, we tackle the dangling nodes using the statistical and semantic features associated with the dangling nodes. Moreover, complex structures of the sentences are tackled and represented, using an identifier (Balaji et al 2012) to find the boundary of the group of nodes conveying a single meaning within the complex structures of the sentences.

The paper is organized as follows. Section 2 discusses the related works on graph based summarization, bootstrapping and spreading activation techniques. Section 3 describes the Universal Networking Language (UNL) and Section 4 describes the building of document level semantic graph. Section 5 presents the semi-supervised learning – bootstrapping of semantic graphs operations in the selection of nodes and sub-graphs. In Section 6, we investigate the performance of our approach and its comparison with the template based and extractive methods. Finally, we conclude this paper with suggestions for future enhancements.

2. RELATED WORK

Although traditional non-graph based approaches are successful in locating salient text units in documents, research based on the graph theory can help people to better understand the relations of the text units (i.e. sentences). Our main aim in this work is to generate a summary from semantic graphs, using a bootstrapping approach where spreading activation takes place for the selection of important components (nodes and links). In this section, we investigate the existing approaches related to graph based summarization, bootstrapping and spreading activation.

2.1 Single-Document Summarization

Hendrickx et al (2008) extended an approach for graph based summarization, where coreference relations are utilized for sentence compression. The relevancy and redundancy are expressed in the links connected with the content units represented as nodes. The sentence compression module outputs full sentences, which are simply added to the summary (Hendrickx et al 2008). Erkan and Radev (2004) presented an extractive summarization procedure, where the salient measures are determined using the graph-based centrality measures of sentences.

Canhasi and Kononenko (2011) presented a frame graph model for extractive summarization where the relation similarity is measured for sentences and are ranked using page rank algorithm iteratively. The existing graph based approaches use node information such as word and its frequency of occurrence, and link information such as in-degree, out-degree connecting each node in a graph. They use semantic role frames where the relation similarity is measured for selecting and ranking the sentences.

Chali and Joty (2008) attempted an unsupervised approach for the query based summary, where the EM algorithm is used for clustering the documents using various lexical, lexico-semantic and cosine similarity features, and ranking the sentences using the K-means algorithm to generate summaries.

Rosner and Camilleri (2008) generated a query based multi-document summary by extracting the frequent items from a clustering of a document set based on the weighted *tfidf*. The irrelevant documents for a query are filtered out and the important sentences are extracted from the selected documents for the summary. Radev et al (2004) proposed a centroid based multi-document summarizer called MEAD, which generates summaries using cluster centroids produced by the topic detection and tracking system.

Another approach to summarization uses a directed document semantic graph, where entities/concepts are represented as nodes and relations between entities/concepts, such as "*is-a*" and "*related*_to" are represented as edges. While entities/concepts are extracted from the parsed sentences, the relations among them are identified, using a set of heuristics (Mohamed and Sanguthevar, 2006). However, while the document centric graphs are merged to form a global graph, the redundant subgraphs are not handled, and this results in the summary containing repetitive information.

Haghighi and Vanderwende (2009) explored various content models for extractive summarization and argued that LDA-style probabilistic topic models produce more structured summary. The important sentences are extracted using bag-of-words approach. Nenkova and Vanderwende (2005) proposed a summarization technique where the probability is computed for each content word by counting the frequency in the document set. Then the words in the sentences with highest scores are selected for summary. Nenkova (2005) discussed various important aspects of summarization techniques. Some of the important aspects of summary relay on the length, text quality such as coherence and cohesion between the sentences.

Yasunaga et al (2017) proposed a neural multi-document summarization (MDS) system where graph convolution network is employed on the sentence relation graphs with sentence embeddings obtained from Recurrent Neural Networks. The salience estimation is computed via multiple layer-wise propagation using high-level hidden sentence features generated using GCN. The sentence level graph is selected based on the personalization features such as the position of a sentence in a document, its length, various coreferent mentions, etc.

Mohammed and Oussalah (2016) proposed an innovative graph-based text summarization model where Semantic Role Labeling (SRL) is used to parse the sentences semantically and grouping semantic arguments while matching semantic roles to Wikipedia concepts. Then the semantic relatedness between the Wikipedia concepts are obtained so that the sentences (nodes) ae linked to build a weighted semantic graph for a document. An iterative ranking algorithm is then applied to the document graphs to extract the most important sentences deemed as the summary.

The above discussed approaches focused on the extractive summary where important sentences are extracted based on the bag-of-words approach, frequency of words, etc. In our approach, the compressed summary semantic graph is a language independent semantic graph where we can generate summary of any target language. Moreover, instead of sentences extraction, we extract important information in terms of concepts and relations (nodes and edges) so as to generate meaningful summary.

2.2 Spreading Activation

Spreading Activation (Anderson 1983) is a graph based algorithm which initially starts with a node with weights in the semantic network, and iteratively spreading that activation out to other nodes connected to the source node in the semantic network (Crestani 1997). In general, Spreading activation algorithms iteratively propagate the activation from the initial set of nodes referred to as the seed, to the other nodes in a network through outward links (Troussov et al 2009).

Spreading activation has been utilized for various NLP tasks; however, we restrict the discussion to summarization alone. Spreading activation has been performed for summarization (Nastase 2008) to select the important nodes for the summary. Thiel & Berthold (2012) proposed two methods for the identification of structural and spatial node similarities through spreading activation. One is the overlap of direct and indirect neighbors, and another is the comparison of distant neighborhood. Since the authors used the cosine similarity measure over directed graphs, they have focused only on node information and not on the link or edge information. The spreading activation algorithm activates the spreading by computing the semantic relatedness measure based on the properties of the terms in the query, the type of rdfs relation associated with instances, and the instances associated in the linked data web. The adaptive threshold has been determined for the activation function to explore the nodes in the linked data (Freitas et al 2011).

With only node information, there is a possibility of losing some important information associated with the edges (representing relationship between the concepts). Thus, instead of considering only node information from the semantic graph, we modified the existing the original spreading activation algorithm by integrating the edge information (semantic relations) while spreading over the entire network of nodes. This helps in identifying the meaningful information in terms of concepts and relations which will be helpful in generating summary.

3. UNIVERSAL NETWORKING LANGUAGE (UNL)

The UNL (UNDL, 2011) is a deep semantic representation, which converts any natural language sentence into an intermediate semantic directed graph structure and vice versa. It consists of Universal words (UWs), attributes and relations. A word or phrase or a sentence is termed as a UW. The purpose of the UNL attributes is to specify the lexical, syntactic and semantic attributes in a sentence. Attributes are used to represent the mood, tense, number, gender etc. A UNL consists of 46 relations and these relations are used to connect two different UWs in a sentence.

The UNL representation is said to be a hyper-graph, when it consist of several interlinked or subordinate sub-graphs. These sub-graphs are represented as hyper-nodes and correspond to the concept of dependent (subordinate) clauses, and a predicate. They are used to define the boundaries between complex semantic entities being represented. A scope is a group of relations between nodes that behave as a single semantic entity in a UNL graph. For instance, in the sentence "*John killed Mary when Peter arrived*", the dependent clause "when Peter arrived" describes the argument of a time relation and, therefore, should be represented as a hyper-node (i.e., as a sub-graph) as represented below:

4. BUILDING DOCUMENT LEVEL UNL SEMANTIC GRAPHS

The input to our single-document summarization is a set of semantic graphs initially constructed for the sentences within a document. The sentence level semantic graphs are constructed using a rule-based approach Balaji et al (2011). Each concept in a sentence is represented as a node, which contains the natural language word, POS tag, semantic constraint, named entity tag, multi-word tag, and frequency of occurrence within a document, sentence identifier and document identifier. The semantic relation that exists between two different concepts in a sentence is represented as an edge. A directed graph based semantic representation is created from the words in the sentences (Balaji et al 2011), where various aspects of the text such as morphological and semantic features associated with words and the context, are represented as nodes and edges respectively. The semantic relations are obtained by the specially designed set of rules, based on the word based morpho-semantic features. Since we built the semantic graph for a Tamil text (Balaji et al 2011), which is a morphologically rich and a relatively free-word

Figure 1. UNL graph representation with nested sub-graphs for "John killed Mary when Peter arrived"

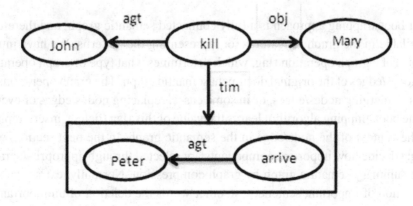

order language, the position of the words in a sentence does not affect the meaning conveyed by the sentence. Moreover, most of the roles played in a sentence are conveyed through morphological suffixes associated with a natural language word. Contrastingly, in fixed-word order languages like English, the roles are conveyed by prepositions, and syntactic parsing is needed to preserve the structure and meaning of the sentence. Therefore, parsing is a difficult process; we used the morpho-semantic features of a morphologically rich language to identify the semantic relations.

In general, coreference information is helpful for the task of automatic summarization (Baldwin & Morton, 1998; Steinberger et al 2007). One of the important aspects of building document semantic graphs is connecting the co-referring entites in a document. Important entities in a text are mentioned multiple times and are spread over the text. Tracking these entities results in identifying what the text is about. Furthermore, the presence of an important entity in a particular sentence may indicate that this might be an important sentence that should be extracted. From a linguistic viewpoint, coreference information can help to maintain the coherence and readability in a text (Bergler et al 2003). Instead of extracting the important sentences based on the occurrence of entities, the proposed approach uses the coreference information for narrowing down the searching and tracking of the important components of the document semantic graph.

In our approach, an anaphora resolution (Balaji et al 2012) has already been performed, and the coreferring entities are connected to form a fully connected document semantic graph (Balaji et al 2013), for each document in a document set.

5. BOOTSTRAPPING FOR LEARNING GRAPH OPERATIONS FOR SUMMARIZATION

In this work, we use bootstrapping for learning the graph operations to be performed on the document semantic graph in order to obtain the summary semantic graph. In the bootstrapping process, we use pattern specification which is important in determining the various graph operations. In order to design this pattern for the purpose of summarization, we need to identify the features that decide which components of the semantic graph are to be selected or modified for building the summary.

Before we explain the bootstrapping procedure, we will explain the graph operations we learn using this procedure, and the context (or features) which decides the learning.

5.1 Graph Operations and Summarization

The input to our bootstrapping approach is a fully connected semantic graph, and therefore, we use the information available in the graph as features for representing the patterns. We have introduced a new feature in the form of a graph operation flag, which determines what type of graph operation we need to execute on the nodes/edges of the original document semantic graph. The graph operations include deleting nodes/edges or merging nodes/edges, or in some cases, replacing nodes/edges or even creating new nodes/edges. The bootstrapping algorithm learns the value of this flag (delete, insert, replace or modify) depending on the context of the node/edge in the semantic graph. In the next section, we will discuss the heuristics that decide how important components are selected through appropriate graph operations, for building the summary semantic graph by graph compression. Normally, extractive summarization involves the selection of important sentences; in other words the deletion of unimportant sentences. In the proposed work, this translates to the deletion of unimportant components of the semantic graph. However, since we are dealing with the construction of abstractive summary, additional operations such as modification, creation and merging of nodes/edges are also carried out. In the reduction of lengthy sentences into a short form without losing its complete meaning, certain components of the semantic graph need modification (i.e. sentences of the summary could be different from their original form); tackling of the dangling nodes in the semantic graph involves the creation of new nodes to connect the dangling nodes, and merging of nodes is performed to obtain a compressed form of summary. Based on the properties discussed above, we present a set of heuristics for each graph operation.

5.1.1 Deletion of Nodes/Edges

Certain components are not important for a summary and thus can be eliminated. The non-essential parts of the semantic graph are removed based on the semantic relations existing between the nodes. Martin and Rino (2002) defined that the non-essential components of the sentences are signaled by the semantic relations "mod" and "*aoj*". Similarly, we define a set of heuristics, where the semantic relations are utilized in the removal of non-essential parts of semantic graph.

The deletion operation can be divided to two: deletion of a node and deletion of an edge.

The heuristics used during the deletion of a node are:

- Deletion of a node C_i independently is based on its POS tag and the frequency of the occurrence of C_i in the document
- Deletion of a node C_i along with the associated edge R is based on the relation labels connecting C_i with the other nodes.

These deletions may lead to several difficulties.

1. If the deletion operation is performed on a leaf node C_i with edge R; then,
    a. if there is no further graph operation associated with edge R
        i. edge R is deleted.
    b. Else
        i. The edge is considered to be a dangling edge and may be used to connect to another node in the graph, which is semantically similar to the deleted node C_i through further graph operations.
2. Else
    a. The edge may be used to connect to another node in the graph, which is semantically similar to the deleted node C_i through further graph operations.
3. The deletion of the node C_i may result in a dangling edge R, that is, the edge R is connected to a single node C_j. Now R has to connect C_j to another new node C_k which is semantically similar to C_i. But, it may be necessary to change the relation label of edge R connecting C_j and C_k.

5.1.2 Insertion of Nodes/Sub-Graphs

The introduction of a new node is carried out, to overcome the dangling node problem, existing in the original semantic graph or as the consequence of a deletion operation. For instance, the terms in a document can occur in a list format, where relations do not occur between them. Such concepts create dangling nodes in the original semantic graph. These dangling nodes may be important for summarization. The dangling nodes are handled by connecting semantically similar concepts with a newly created common node, based on a common upper level concept obtained through semantic abstraction from the UNL Ontology. While inserting a new node C_{new}, it is necessary to introduce an appropriate edge R_{new} between the newly inserted node and the dangling nodes. The edges are labeled with appropriate semantic relations, based on the semantic constraints assigned to the newly inserted node and the semantic constraints of the dangling nodes.

5.1.3 Merging the Components of a Graph

To reduce sentential redundancy, Sornlertlamvanich (2001) has proposed merging nodes with the same UW. In this work, the merging operation replaces edges that connect nodes with different UWs but labeled with the same semantic relation by a single edge, connecting to a subgraph, formed by grouping nodes with edges labeled with the "conjunctive" semantic relation.

Let SG be the semantic graph, and C_i and C_j a pair of its components which forms a relation R. The merging operation is performed based on the following assumptions

Level 1: Node C_i is connected to the nodes C_j and C_k with the same relation R; then the nodes C_j and C_k are grouped and connected with the "and" relation, and node C_i is connected to the group (C_j, C_k) with the same relation R.

Level 2: Node C_i is connected to the node C_a with the relation R; node C_j is connected to node C_b with relation R, and if the nodes C_i and C_j are synonyms, then keep any one node (based on the frequency of occurrence or the strength of the node) C_i or C_j and apply level1.

Level 3: Nodes C_i and C_j are synonyms and are connected to the nodes C_k and C_l with the relations R1 and R2 respectively. If the relations R1 and R2 are dependent relations, then apply level1 and keep the more appropriate relation.

The following section describes the compression of semantic graphs through redundancy elimination with examples. The examples described in section 5.1.4 shows the graph operations performed on the nodes and edges of the semantic graph so as to obtain the summary semantic graph.

5.1.4 Graph Compression Through Redundancy Elimination

Redundant subgraphs are eliminated at two stages. During the first stage, while building a fully connected semantic graph of a document, common nodes/subgraphs across the sentences that overlap with other are merged to avoid redundancy. During stage 2, after the construction of the document graph, the subgraphs of this document graph are assigned a unique label called the canonical label, and the redundant subgraphs having identical canonical labels are eliminated.

Stage 1: Elimination of Overlapping Nodes/Subgraphs

To eliminate the redundant information while grouping the sentence semantic graphs of a document, the following actions take place.

1. If node A is connected to node B with edge R1 and node C with edge R2 in a sentence semantic graph SG_{SENT}, and the node A is connected to node C with edge R2 and node D with edge R5 in another sentence semantic graph SG'_{SENT}, then the subgraph A-R2-C of SG'_{SENT} is merged with the subgraph of SG_{SENT} and the other nodes connected with nodes A and C of SG'_{SENT} are merged with the nodes A and C of SG_{SENT}.

2. If node A is connected to node C with edge R1 in a sentence semantic graph SG_{SENT}, and the node A' (which is a synonym concept of node A) is connected to node C with edge R1 in another document semantic graph SG'_{SENT}, then the subgraph R1-C alone of SG'_{SENT} is merged with the subgraph of SG_{SENT}, and node A' of SG'_{SENT} is connected to node A of SG_{SENT} with "*equ*" semantic relation, only when the nodes A and A' are non-verbal concepts. The semantic relation "*equ*" shows that A and A' are semantically equivalent concepts.

Using the above two conditions, the semantic graphs of multiple documents are grouped together to form a document semantic graph. As already mentioned above, the nodes in the semantic graph contain the word based features and the edges contain the semantic relations that exist between the nodes.

Figure 2. a) subgraph of sentence semantic graph SG_{SENT} b) subgraph of sentence semantic graph SG'_{SENT} c) Merged subgraph of SG_{SENT} and SG'_{SENT}

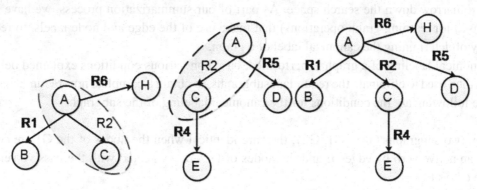

Figure 3. (a) subgraph of sentence semantic graph SG_{SENT} b) subgraph of sentence semantic graph SG'_{SENT} c) Merged subgraph of SG_{SENT} and SG'_{SENT} with synonym concept connected

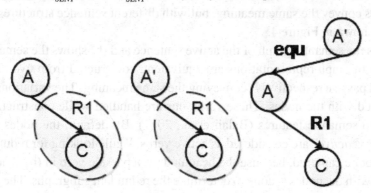

While merging the nodes/subgraphs, various parameters such as term frequency and concept frequency in each document, and sentence identifiers are utilized, to know in which sentences in a document the term/concept occurs. The sentence identifiers are utilized to maintain the sentence ordering at the time of summary generation.

The above two conditions help in identifying and eliminating the redundant subgraphs; however, not all semantically similar subgraphs are captured. For instance, sentences can be represented in the active voice as well as in passive voice. In this case, the sentence structures are different though the meanings conveyed by the sentences are the same. Such redundancies are detected during stage 2, which is performed after the construction of the fully connected semantic graph across documents.

Stage 2: Labeling of Redundant Subgraphs

The elimination of redundant subgraphs requires an operation to check whether two subgraphs are identical or not. One such operation is to perform the graph isomorphism. However, in certain cases where many such checks are required among the same set of subgraphs, a better way of performing this task is to assign a unique label to each subgraph, that is invariant on the ordering of the vertices and edges in the graph. Such a procedure is referred to as the canonical label of the graph $G = (V, E)$ and is denoted by **cl (G)** (Kuramochi & Karypis, 2005). Using canonical labels, the subgraphs having identical canonical labels are identified as redundant subgraphs.

In practice, the complexity of finding a canonical labeling of a graph can be reduced using various heuristics to narrow down the search space. As part of our summarization process, we have used the patterns (used for learning graph operations) that make use of the edge and node labels, to reduce the complexity of determining the canonical label of a graph.

The canonical labeling of a graph is performed, based on various conditions explained below. This labeling is then used to eliminate the redundant subgraphs, to obtain a complete non-redundant semantic graph. The following are the conditions for the canonical labeling of the subgraphs.

1. Given two subgraphs $G = \{G1, G2\}$, they are identical when the nodes of the G1 are connected with an active verb by edges E and the nodes of G2 are connected with the passive verb by the same edges E.

For example:

Active sentence: Raman Ravananai konRaan - Raman killed Ravanan

Passive sentence: Ravanan Ramanaal kollappattaan - Ravanan was killed by Raman

Both the sentences convey the same meaning, but with different sentence structures. The equivalent semantic graphs are shown in Figure 4.

Figure 4 (a) shows the semantic graph of the active sentence and (b) shows the semantic graph of the passive sentences. Both graph representations are equivalent, constructed from two different sentence structures (active and passive respectively) conveying the same meaning. The variations are represented as attributes associated with the nodes. These variations are handled while constructing the semantic graphs, using morpho-semantic features (Balaji et al., 2011). By default, the nodes indicating verbs without the attribute "*@active*" are considered as active verbs. While looking for redundant subgraphs, these graphs could not be captured, because the head node is a passive verb in (b). Therefore, masking the tuples associated with the nodes is done to determine the redundant subgraphs. The masking process

Figure 4. Semantic Graphs of (a) "Raman killed Ravanan" (b) Ravanan was killed by Raman

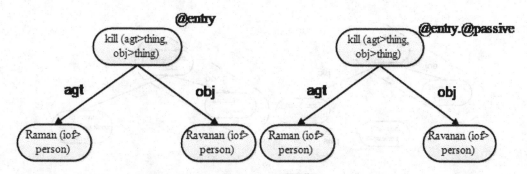

is decided based on the maximum match of the subgraph (b) with the subgraph (a). The canonical label is then assigned to the identical subgraphs.

2. Assume that Graph G1 is constructed for a verbal phrase and Graph G2 is constructed for an adjectival phrase. The subgraphs of G1 and G2 are said to be identical, when the verbal node (N_V) is connected to the node (N_i) with "*aoj*" relation, and the same node (N_V) acts as a modifier (N_M) of the graph G2, which is connected to the node (N_i) with the "*mod*" relation. The canonical label is then assigned to the subgraph (N_M – mod – N_i) of G2. The rest of the nodes connecting N_M are transformed to the verbal node (N_V) of the G1 with their corresponding edges (semantic relations). The example below shows the sentences with the verbal phrase and adjectival phrase, and Figure 5 shows the process of matching identical subgraphs.

Example:
Verbal Phrase: **திருச்சிராப்பள்ளி, இந்தியாவின் தமிழ்நாடு, மாநிலத்தில் அமைந்தள்ளத.**

ThiruchiraapaLLi indiyaavin tamilnadu maanilaththil amainthuLLathu.

Tiruchirapalli is located in Tamil Nadu state of India.

Adjectival Phrase: **காவிரி ஆற்றங்கரையில் அமைந்தள்ள திருச்சிராப்பள்ளி, தமிழகத்தில் உள்ள நான்கு முக்கியமான நகரங்களில் ஒன்றாகும்.**

Kaaviri aaRRangaraiyil amainthuLLa thiruchiraapaLLi, tamilakaththil uLLa naangu mukkiyamaana nakarankaLil ondraagum.

Tiruchirapalli is one of the four most important cities in Tamil Nadu, which is located on the banks of the Cauvery.

In some cases, certain components of the verbal phrases act similar to the components of the adjectival phrases, i.e. the meaning conveyed by the components of the verbal and adjectival phrases are the same. Such identical phrases are identified using the above condition, and each component is assigned a canonical label.

The semantic graphs of the sentences are shown in Figure 5. The subgraphs that are identical are marked inside a circle in Figure 5 (a) and (b). Figure 5 (c) shows the complete graph with the redundant subgraphs removed and the other nodes/subgraphs merged.

Figure 5. Semantic graphs of (a) Verbal phrase (b) Adjectival phrase (c) Embedded Graph

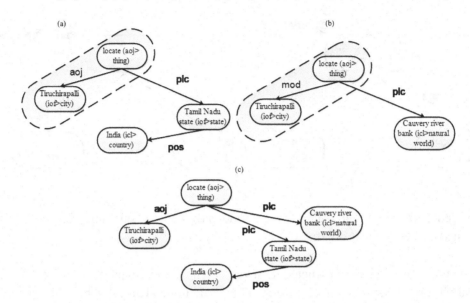

The canonical labels are then processed to remove the redundant subgraphs. After removing the redundancies in the semantic graphs, a complete semantic graph of a document is generated.

The following section explains the features that describe the context which define the above graph operations that need to be performed.

5.2 Identification of Features for Describing Context

While linguistically analyzing the Tamil text, certain features associated with the context are involved in the selection of important nodes for summarization. Feature selection plays an important role in the specification of patterns used in the identification of important components (nodes and edges), from the document semantic graph through appropriate graph operations, necessary for summarization. In the proposed work, these important components are selected, based on the semantic properties, and therefore, we need to identify features of the semantic graph representation, and other contextual and statistical features that decide the graph operations needed to build the summary. The features are classified, based on whether they are associated with the nodes or edges of the semantic graph.

Features associated with the nodes include word based features, such as POS tags, lexical features and semantic constraints associated with a word/ concept, concept based features including the frequency of concepts, and type of relation between an edge and a particular concept. Edge based features consider the relation associated with an edge. In essence, the use of the word based semantic constraints and the edge based semantic relations results in a semantic based rather than a sentence or text unit based graph summarization.

In addition to the node and edge based features, we also have features to represent the boundaries of semantic sub-graphs, and sentence identifiers. In our work, features are used to create a summary semantic graph from the original document semantic graph.

Table 1. Features for learning graph operations

Features Associated With Nodes	Word Based Features	
	POS tag of a word (*POS*) Semantic constraint associated with a word (*SC*) Attributes associated with a word (*Attr*)	Part of Speech information Semantic class feature to obtain the synonyms of the concepts Used to represent number, gender, aspect, mood etc.
	Classical Features	
	Concept identifier Multi-word Expression Identifier	Unique identifier of the semantic concept of a word To identify the word is a multi-word expression
	Statistical Features	
	Frequency of a concept Probabilistic scoring for selection	Frequency of a concept in a document Scoring function for the selection of nodes
Graph Based features	**Context based features**	
	Semantic relations associated with a word (*Relation*) Nested graph identifier (*NG_id*)	Semantic relations of interest while performing spreading activation Identifier to detect the boundary of the sub-graphs
	Flag features	
	Flags (*Create [CF], Delete [DF], Replace [RF], Merge [MF]*)	Graph operation to be performed on the nodes and/or links in the graph

5.3 Bootstrapping for Learning Graph Operations

The first step in this single stage pattern based bootstrapping procedure, is to represent the tuples of the pattern, which describes the context of the semantic graph. During the learning procedure, the patterns with graph operation flags as labels are utilized, to assign the flags in a fully connected semantic graph through matching. The documents of the test corpus have already been tagged with the features identified, except for the graph operation flag which is set as a result of the matching procedure. These labeled examples (where the graph operation flag is set) are then used for the tuple value confidence scoring scheme, to decide which tuple of the pattern is to be masked for partial matching. Again the similarity scoring scheme is also applied to generate new patterns based on partial matching, and the iterations are continued until all the documents have been labeled, or no new patterns are generated. This bootstrapping procedure is similar to the approach proposed by Balaji et al (2014) for learning the semantic relations. In this work, we utilize the procedure to set the graph operation flags associated with nodes/edges of the semantic graph. The bootstrapping flow diagram is shown in Figure 6.

In the following sections, we describe the pattern representation and the scoring methodology used during the bootstrapping procedure.

5.3.1 Pattern Representation

The next step in the bootstrapping procedure is the representation of the pattern using the features identified. In this work, we consider *<concept node – relation – concept node>* as the basic sub-component of the semantic graph, and use this as a basis for the representation of the patterns. The pattern is represented using the context based and classical features; the pattern for learning is defined as follows

Figure 6. Bootstrapping flow diagram

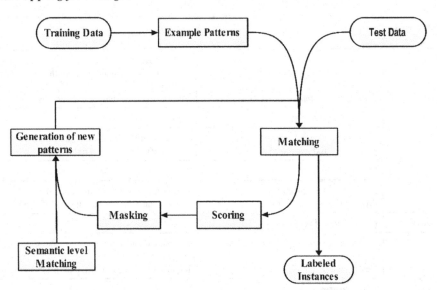

<Component 1 – Relation – Component 2>NG_id+S_id

where components 1 & 2 consist of features, such as the morphological suffix (MS), POS tag (POS), Semantic constraint (SC), Multi-Word tag (MW) and the Flag (*Flag*) representing which operation to perform. These features are tagged for each component in the pattern as ***MS+POS+SC+MW+Flag***. In addition, the pattern may also consider the overall graph features, such as sentence identifiers and/ or sub-graph identifiers. The features used are given in Table 1. The detailed pattern representation is given below.

<MS+POS+SC+MW+Flag - Relation+Flag - MS+POS+SC+MW+Flag>NG_id+S_id

The tuple *MW* and *NG_id* defined in the pattern are optional, while the rest of the tuples are necessary features of the pattern. If the component in the pattern is a multi-word expression, the MW flag is set, and likewise, only if the semantic graph consists of the nested subgraph, which essentially are subgraphs that act as a node, then the *NG_id* is used. Based on the flags, the operations are performed during the spreading activation. The rest of the features listed in Table 1 are used during the selection of nodes and subgraphs.

5.3.2 Matching

In the bootstrapping procedure, matching is carried out through exact matching and partial matching. Here, we make use of two probabilistic scoring schemes (Balaji et al 2014) for the selection of patterns for modification, and the tuples to be considered for masking. The selection of the pattern for modification and the selection of the tuples for masking are carried out, using probabilistic scoring schemes. In the proposed approach, two scoring functions are introduced.

1. Scoring for pattern selection for modification (Balaji et al 2014)
2. Scoring for tuple selection for masking

5.3.2.1 Scoring: Tuple Value Selection for Masking

The pattern for modification is selected based on the pattern selection score discussed above. In order to perform a partial match, the tuples are masked in an iterative manner, to obtain partially matched instances that are then modified to generate new patterns. We use tuple value selection scores, to decide which set of instances would yield patterns for modification. In our approach, the tuple value selection score is determined by the probability of the number of samples, with the tuple value (TV) of all the patterns of a particular flag (F) among all samples with the same tuple value (TV). The tuple value selection score is given in Equation (1).

$$Select\left(TV_i\right) = argmax \sum_{i=1\,j=1}^{mn} P\!\left([TV_i \,/\, P_j, F] \,/\, TV\right)$$

$$Select\left(TV_i\right) = argmax \sum_{i=1\,j=1}^{mn} P\!\left([TV_i \,/\, P_j, F] \,/\, TV\right) \tag{1}$$

The scoring for tuple values selection is based on the occurrence of this tuple value in patterns for setting a particular flag. While the pattern selection score is used to select the pattern for masking, the tuple value selection score selects specific tuple values, which can be abstracted to obtain more generic patterns.

5.3.3 Generation of New Patterns

The node, which is an entity with high frequency in the document, is selected as a starting node to start the bootstrapping process. If the selected node (N_{START}) is a location (which is determined by the semantic constraint associated with N_{START}), then the bootstrapping process starts applying the graph operations based on the following initial conditions.

1. The starting node N_{START} is connected to another node N_i by the semantic relations representing locations (R_{LOC}) such as *plc, plf, plt*, (UNDL, 2011) and then the nodes (N_j) connecting N_{START} either directly or indirectly are marked with the selection flag. R_{MISC} represent the relations of any type other than participant relations.

$$R_{LOC}\left(N_{START},\ N_i\right) \wedge R_{MISC}\left(N_i,\ N_j\right) \Rightarrow Set\ Flag_{SELECT}\left(N_{START},\ R_{LOC},\ N_i, R_{MISC}, N_j\right)$$

$$R_{LOC}\left(N_{START},\ N_i\right) \wedge R_{MISC}\left(N_i,\ N_j\right) \Rightarrow Set\ Flag_{SELECT}\left(N_{START},\ R_{LOC},\ N_i, R_{MISC}, N_j\right) \tag{2}$$

where $i = 1, j > 1$ where $i = 1, j > 1$

2. The starting node N_{START} is connected to another node N_i by the semantic relations representing participants (R_{OBJ}), and then the node (N_j) is connected with node (N_i) by another participant relation (R_{AGT}); then the nodes and edges ($N_{START}, R_{OBJ}, N_i, R_{AGT}, N_j$) are marked with the selection flag.

$$R_{OBJ}\left(N_{START},\ N_i\right)\wedge R_{AGT}\left(N_i,\ N_j\right)\Rightarrow Set\ Flag_{SELECT}\left(N_{START},\ R_{OBJ},\ N_i, R_{AGT}, N_j\right)$$

$$R_{OBJ}\left(N_{START},\ N_i\right)\wedge R_{AGT}\left(N_i,\ N_j\right)\Rightarrow Set\ Flag_{SELECT}\left(N_{START},\ R_{OBJ},\ N_i, R_{AGT}, N_j\right) \quad (3)$$

where $i = 1, j > 1$ *where* $i = 1, j > 1$

3. The starting node N_{START} is connected to another node N_i by the semantic relations representing locations (R_{LOC}) such as *plc, plf,* and *plt,* and then the node (N_j) are connected with N_i by semantic relations representing time (R_{TIME}) such as *tim, tmf,* and *tmt*; then, the nodes and edges (N_{START}, R_{LOC}, N_i, R_{TIME}, N_j) are marked with the selection flag.

$$R_{LOC}\left(N_{START},\ N_i\right)\wedge R_{TIME}\left(N_i,\ N_j\right)\Rightarrow Set\ Flag_{SELECT}\left(N_{START},\ R_{LOC},\ N_i, R_{TIME}, N_j\right)$$

$$R_{LOC}\left(N_{START},\ N_i\right)\wedge R_{TIME}\left(N_i,\ N_j\right)\Rightarrow Set\ Flag_{SELECT}\left(N_{START},\ R_{LOC},\ N_i, R_{TIME}, N_j\right) \quad (4)$$

where $i = 1, j > 1$ *where* $i = 1, j > 1$

4. The starting node N_{START} is connected to another node N_i by the semantic relations representing locations (R_{LOC}) such as *plc, plf, plt*; then the nodes (N_j) connected with N_i by semantic relations representing quantity, and the nodes and edges (N_{START}, R_{LOC}, N_i, R_{QUA}, N_j) are marked with the selection flag. R_{QUA} represent the quantity relation that exist between the nodes N_i and N_j.

$$R_{LOC}\left(N_{START},\ N_i\right)\wedge R_{QUA}\left(N_i,\ N_j\right)\Rightarrow Set\ Flag_{SELECT}\left(N_{START},\ R_{LOC},\ N_i, R_{QUA}, N_j\right)$$

$$R_{LOC}\left(N_{START},\ N_i\right)\wedge R_{QUA}\left(N_i,\ N_j\right)\Rightarrow Set\ Flag_{SELECT}\left(N_{START},\ R_{LOC},\ N_i, R_{QUA}, N_j\right) \quad (5)$$

where $i = 1, j > 1$ *where* $i = 1, j > 1$

If the selected node is a person, then the nodes connected with the participant relations and attributive relations are marked for the selection of the important components. Certain subgraphs are important, where the condition does not depend on the specific property of the starting node.

The node N_i is connected to a set of nodes N_j by the attributive semantic relations (R_{ATTR}) such as *iof* and *nam;* then the nodes (N_j) connected with N_i (N_i, R_{ATTR}, N_j) are marked with the selection flag.

$$R_{ATTR}\left(N_i,\ N_j\right)\Rightarrow Set\ Flag_{SELECT}\left(N_i, R_{ATTR}, N_j\right)\quad where\ i = 1, j > 1$$

$$R_{ATTR}\left(N_i,\ N_j\right)\Rightarrow Set\ Flag_{SELECT}\left(N_i, R_{ATTR}, N_j\right)\quad where\ i = 1, j > 1 \quad (6)$$

Semantic relations such as *man, mod,* and *ben* imply modifier relationships, and removing the nodes having modifier relations would not affect the meaning of the sentence. Therefore, the nodes and edges satisfying these properties are marked for deletion.

The creation of new nodes and edges is performed for the dangling nodes ($N_{D,i}$) which are semantically similar. With the use of the UNL Ontology, the semantic abstraction of the semantically similar concepts is identified and the new node is created. The new node (N_{NEW}) is then connected to the dangling nodes having the same or similar semantic constraints.

5.4 Spreading Activation for Graph Summarization

The existing Spreading Activation search algorithm described by Suchal (2008) has been modified to execute the graph operation flags. The modified spreading activation algorithm is described below.

Modified Spreading activation performs as follows:

- The activation of the starting node is based on the frequency of occurrence and POS information associated with the node.
- The activation of spreading is performed iteratively by considering the strength of the node, which includes the frequency of occurrence, POS tag and the semantic relations (links) connecting the main node (starting node) either directly or indirectly.
- Instead of measuring the distance between the starting node and the current node, the similarity between the starting node and the current node is measured in terms of constraint similarity, attribute similarity and edge similarity.
- Edges labeled with relations are used for the selection of nodes in a graph.
- Instead of checking the termination, we traverse the graph fully for selecting the important nodes.
- Subgraphs are also selected as important components through the nested graph identifier. The nested graph identifier is useful in the identification of the boundary of the components of a graph, so that sub-graphs can be selected easily.
- Graph operations are carried out during the spreading activation of the semantic graphs for the selection of the important nodes/sub-graphs.

The algorithm given below shows the modified spreading activation procedure for the traversal of nodes.

Algorithm: Spread-Activation (v, e, c⇐0, r)
Require: Starting vertex *v*.
Require: Activation energy *e* > 0.
Require: Energy *c* accumulated on graph vertices.
Require: Relation *r* accumulated on graph edges.
Require: Weight *w* assigned on graph edges

1. $c_v \Leftarrow c_v + e + r_w$
2. $e' \Leftarrow e/\text{Vertex-degree }(v)$
3. if $e' > \theta$ then
4. for all vertices t such as, there exists an edge from v to t (represented as a pattern) do

5.   c ⇐Spread-activation (v, e′, c, w)
6.   end for
7.   end if
8.   return c

Input: Completely connected semantic graph which has been tagged. The graph operation flags of the nodes and edges of this tagged document graph have been set, using the bootstrapping learning procedure.

The first step in the spreading activation procedure, is deciding from which node to start. This is done by the energy of the node C_i (concept) or the concept with the maximum frequency of occurrence in the document semantic graph. The graph operation associated with node C_i is first carried out. The details of the graph operations are described by Balaji et al (2013). The direction of the spreading activation, in other words, the edge to follow, has to be decided. The constraint based spread activation model described by Crestani (1997), discussed the distance constraints where the relation strength has been measured based on the relation existing between two nodes, either directly or indirectly. In the same vein, in our approach, we use semantic relations connecting nodes whose strengths are measured based on whether the relations are coordinating or subordinating relations (Balaji et al 2011). The process is continued till the spreading activation cannot continue any further.

The compressed summary semantic graph is obtained using the modified edge integrated spreading activation algorithm from document semantic graph. The important components of the document semantic graph are assigned a set of flags using a pattern based bootstrapping approach. The modified spreading activation procedure is then applied over the flags assigned document semantic graph widely to extract the important components such as nodes and edges.

6. EVALUATION

The evaluation of the summary is carried out from different perspectives. They are

- Human versus machine generated summary
- Extractive versus abstractive summary

There are also automatic methods for summary evaluation, such as ROUGE (Lin 2004), which gives a score based on the similarity in the sequences of words, between a human-written model summary and the machine summary.

ROUGE (Lin 2004) is an automatic evaluation metric that computes an n-gram similarity score between the model summary and the summary to be evaluated. ROUGE stands for Recall-Oriented Understudy for Gisting Evaluation. Several types of ROUGE measures exist, and the one with the highest correlation with manual scores is ROUGE-2 recall – the recall of model summary bigrams. Very high correlations between manual metrics and ROUGE have been observed (Dang & Owczarzak 2009).

The performance of the proposed approach is evaluated by analyzing the compressed graph with the original semantic graph, in terms of the number of nodes before and after compression, the number of newly created nodes and modified nodes, number of nodes before and after merging. We investigated and compared both the original document semantic graph and the compressed summary graph automatically. Furthermore, the summary generated by spreading activation is evaluated, and compared with the human generated summary.

The evaluation of summaries is performed, using intrinsic and extrinsic methods. While the intrinsic method of evaluation is based on user judgments with both precision and ROUGE scores, the extrinsic method is based on the information retrieval task, with queries and evaluation of the FIRE task (FIRE 2010).

We have evaluated our system using the query set of FIRE tasks (FIRE, 2010), and investigated the generated summary, using the guidelines provided by the FIRE evaluation task. Each query is tagged with <title> and <\title>, and the guidelines (for evaluating the summaries) are given in between the tags <narr> and <\narr>. An example of a Tamil query and its equivalent English query is given below.

The FIRE evaluation task consists of 2, 00,000 documents. First, the sentences in each document were converted into a UNL semantic graph (referred to as the sentence semantic graph G_{SENT}) representation, using a rule-based approach proposed by Balaji et al (2011). The common concepts, anaphoric nodes (Balaji et al 2012) and coreference nodes of the sentence semantic graphs are connected, to form a document semantic graph (G_{DOC}). While building the semantic graph, the redundant subgraphs are removed, and the possible graph operations are assigned to the nodes and edges of G_{DOC}. The modified spreading activation algorithm is applied to obtain the summary semantic graph.

To evaluate the precision of the summaries generated, we have compared our system with a template based summary (Subalalitha et al 2011) and extractive summary, using a rule-based approach. The template-based summary proposed by Subalalitha et al (2011) introduced seven templates, specific to the Tourism domain for generating the summary. The concepts of the natural language words matching with the UNL semantic constraints of each template, are considered for the summary. However, while this template based information is language independent, they are domain specific. Adapting these templates to the generic domain requires different or more templates. In fact, we have added new template information to adapt to various domains, such as health, news and sports. For obtaining the extractive summary, we have designed a rule-based extractive summarization approach, which extracts important

Box 1.

```
<top lang='ta'>
<num>202</num>
<title>பிரபல மனிதர்கள் மீது காலணி வீச்சு</title>
<desc>பிரபல மனிதர்கள் மீது நடந்த காலணி வீச்சு நிகழ்வுகள்</desc>
<narr>சமீபத்தில் அமெரிக்க அதிபர் ஜார்ஜ் டபிள்யு புஷ் மீது ஈராக்கிய பத்திரிக்கையாளர் காலணி
வீசிய நிகழ்வு. அது போன்றே இந்திய உள்துறை அமைச்சர் ப.சிதம்பரம் மீது ஜெர்னைல் சிங்
பத்திரிக்கையாளர் காலணி வீசினார். இது போன்ற பிரபல மனிதர்கள் மீது காலணி வீச்சுகள்
நிகழ்ந்தது பற்றிய தகவல்கள் கொண்ட ஆவணங்கள் இடம்பெற வேண்டும்.</narr>
</top>
```

```
<top lang='en'>
<num>202</num>
<title>Shoe throwing at persons of eminence</title>
<desc>Incidents involving throwing of shoes at persons of eminence</desc>
<narr>In the recent past, an Iraqi journalist threw a shoe at the American President George W. Bush. In a similar incident, Jarnail
Singh, a journalist, threw a shoe at the Indian Home Minister, P. Chidambaram. Relevant documents should contain information about
such incidents in which a shoe was thrown at some well-known person. Information about legal steps taken against the offenders is
irrelevant.</narr>
</top>
```

sentences from multiple documents. First, the sentence constituents are identified and extracted, using a set of rules which was designed with the word based morphological features. The semantic constraints of each word are obtained using the UNL list which consists of the root form of the natural language word, its equivalent English translation and the UNL semantic constraint obtained from the UNL Knowledge Base (UNL KB) (UNDL 2010). The important sentences are then extracted, using the term and concept frequencies, and co-occurring concepts in a sentence.

One of the widely used measures for evaluating summaries, is the ROUGE score (Lin 2004). It includes measures to automatically determine the quality of a summary, by comparing it with other (ideal) summaries created by humans. The measures count the number of overlapping units, such as n-gram, word sequences, and word pairs between the computer-generated summary to be evaluated and the ideal summaries created by humans. The proposed summarization approach is evaluated using the ROUGE scores. For each run, four scores, such as ROUGE-1, ROUGE-2, ROUGE-L, and ROUGE-SU4 were computed. In addition, we introduce a new score for graph based summarization called ROUGE-G, to evaluate the summary in terms of nodes and edges. The quality of the summary is investigated and measured, by counting the number of overlapping units (nodes and edges), between a predicted summary graph and the generated summary graph obtained by the proposed approach.

We have also investigated the summaries obtained using different methods, with the reference summaries by ROUGE scores. We have compared the proposed approach with three different methods, such as the summary obtained using term frequency, concept frequency and original spreading activation. From the analysis, the edge integrated spreading activation technique performs better when compared to all other methods. This is because, instead of considering the node information alone for determining the strength, the proposed approach integrated the edge information to find the strength of the nodes for activation, which results in obtaining the good quality of the summary.

Since the evaluation is carried out on the compressed semantic graph, which consists of nodes and edges, it is difficult to evaluate the common subsequence, co-occurring concepts etc. Thus, to evaluate the summary graphs, we introduce a new ROUGE score called **ROUGE-G** (i.e. ROUGE- Graphs). ROUGE-G computes the number of nodes and edges in the candidate summary graph that overlaps those of the reference summary graph.

6.1 Single Document Summarization

6.1.1 Comparison With Template-Based and Extractive Summaries

The summary obtained using these three approaches were given to three experts for the evaluation of precision, and the results given by them are shown in Table 2.

From Table 2, the summaries obtained from the three different methods are compared with a reference summary. When compared to the template based and extractive methods, the proposed graph based approach, generates a summary which covers most information contained in the document. In the template based method, the different sets of templates need not cater to the all the information, and filling the template information need not necessarily explore all the information widely. This may result in a decrease in precision. In rule based extractive summarization, the sentence units are extracted based on the frequency of the occurrence of the concepts and co-occurring concepts in a sentence, which may not extract the important concepts with low frequency. In contrast, the summary obtained using the proposed graph based approach, has information similar to that of the reference summary, and the precision is shown in Table 2.

Table 2. Comparison of the different summarization methods

Methods	Precision		
	User 1	User 2	User 3
Template based Summary	0.48	0.49	0.52
Extractive Summary	0.53	0.51	0.55
Proposed Approach (Abstractive Summary)	0.71	0.67	0.65

6.1.2 Evaluation Using ROUGE Scores

Table 3 shows various ROUGE scores for different summarization methods. Among the methods, the concept based summary (CF) is better than the term based summary (TF). Instead of searching for terms, the CF method searches for concepts, and thus increases the performance. While evaluating the spreading activation, we found that integrating the edge information results in producing a better summary, when compared to the spreading activation proposed by Quillian (1968), because, the original spreading activation starts with a single node, and does not consider the edge information for estimating the signal strength. Instead in the proposed approach, the signal strength is estimated using the information associated with the nodes, and their connected edges of the global semantic graph. Thus the performance increases when compared to other methods. The newly introduced score is ROUGE-G, which can be used to evaluate the semantic summary graphs. The existing ROUGE scores focused on the n-gram, co-occurrence, subsequence etc. The ROUGE scores except 1-gram, investigate the structural information to maintain the coherence and readability of the summary. However, these scores are used to evaluate the extractive summaries. To evaluate the summary graphs, we introduce ROUGE-G where the overlapping nodes and edges of the candidate summary graphs with the reference summary graphs are estimated. Thus, in the proposed graph based approach, the number of nodes and edges of the candidate summary graphs overlapping the reference summary graph gives 65% accuracy.

6.1.3 Evaluation of Edge Integrated Spreading Activation

This section discusses the performance of the proposed edge integrated spreading activation algorithm for obtaining important components for abstractive summarization. We have compared our approach to the original spreading activation theory (Quillian 1968). The spreading activation starts with a node, and spreads over the graph to extract the important components for the summary. The signal strength is

Table 3. ROUGE scores of summary obtained using various methods

Methods	ROUGE-1	ROUGE-2	ROUGE-L	ROUGE –SU4	ROUGE-G
Term Frequency (TF)	0.31717	0. 2432	0.2063	0.1632	0.1505
Concept Frequency (CF)	0.35550	0.3015	0.2635	0.1873	0.2013
Spreading Activation (Quillian, 1968)	0.39810	0.3210	0.2803	0.2235	0.1865
Edge Integrated Spreading Activation [Concepts – Relations (nodes and edges)]	0.7023	0.4861	0.4603	0.3980	0.6593

calculated based on the weight of each node under consideration, and the number of connected edges. Instead, in the proposed graph based approach, the information associated with each node and edge is utilized to calculate the signal strength.

Figure 7 shows the impact of signal decay while performing spreading activation. Similar to the evaluation methods discussed by Nastase (2008), the results shown in Figure 7 – for decay values of 0.1, 0.5, 0.95, 0.99, 0.999, 0.9999, 1 – indicate that faster decay (reflected through a higher decay value) keeps the summary focused initially and slowly spreads out in a wide manner. The ROUGE-G score is computed to evaluate the edge integrated spreading activation theory. When compared to the baseline approach, the proposed approach, which considers the edge information for spreading, produces better results.

7. CONCLUSION

In this paper, a bootstrapping approach for summary generation via spreading activation has been described. While performing the spreading activation, the patterns defined are matched with the components of the semantic graph and the graph operations are applied iteratively to the selection of the important nodes. The tuples for performing each graph operation are defined, and set to each component in the pattern. The original spreading activation algorithm has been modified, by including the link information along with the node information, while the activation starts spreading over the graph. We investigated and evaluated our approach, by comparing the originally generated semantic graph and the compressed graph, in terms of the number of important nodes and links. We have also compared our approach of the modified spreading activation algorithm with the original algorithm. From the results, our approach gives better performance when compared to the original algorithm. The use of word-based semantics and context-based semantics such as semantic relations give better results. To our knowledge, this is the first bootstrapping approach for generating summaries from semantic graphs.

Figure 7. Comparison of original spreading activation and edge integrated spreading activation (Impact of signal decay in spreading activation on summarization performance)

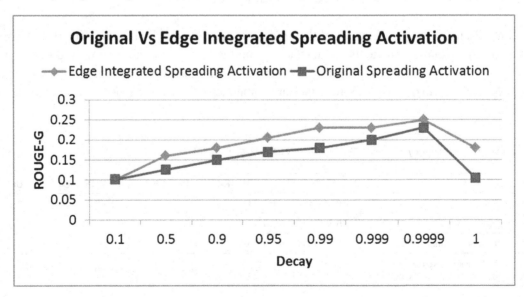

REFERENCES

Anderson, J. R. (1983). A spreading activation theory of memory. *Journal of Verbal Learning and Verbal Behavior, 22*(3), 261–295. doi:10.1016/S0022-5371(83)90201-3

Balaji, J., & Geetha, T. V. (2011). Morpho-Semantic Features for Rule-based Tamil Enconversion. *International Journal of Computers and Applications, 26*(6), 11–18. doi:10.5120/3109-4269

Balaji, J., & Geetha, T. V. (2012a). Two-Stage Bootstrapping for Anaphora Resolution. *24th International Conference on Computational Linguistics COLING 2012*, 507-516.

Balaji, J., & Geetha, T. V. (2012b). Semantic Parsing of Tamil Sentences. *Workshop on Machine Translation and Parsing in Indian Languages (MTPIL) 24th International Conference on Computational Linguistics COLING 2012*, 15-22.

Balaji, J., & Geetha, T. V. (2013a). A Graph Based Query Focused Multi-Document Summarization. *International Journal of Intelligent Information Technologies*.

Balaji, J., & Geetha, T. V. (2013b). Graph based Bootstrapping for Coreference Resolution. *Journal of Intelligent Systems*.

Balaji, J., & Geetha, T. V. (2014). *Semi-Supervised Learning of UNL Semantic Relations of a Morphologically Rich Language*. (Unpublished)

Baldwin, B., & Morton, T. S. (1998). Dynamic coreference-based summarization. *Proceedings of the Third Conference on Empirical Methods in Natural Language Processing*.

Barzilay, McKeown, & Elhadad. (1999). Information fusion in the context of multi-document summarization. *Proc. 37th ACL*, 550–557.

Bergler, S., Witte, R., Khalife, M., Li, Z., & Rudzicz, F. (2003). Using knowledge-poor coreference resolution for text summarization. *DUC, Workshop on Text Summarization*, 85-92.

Canhasi, E., & Kononenko, I. (2011). *Semantic Role Frames Graph-based Multi-document Summarization, Faculty of computer and information science*. University of Ljubljana.

Chali, Y., & Joty, S. R. (2008). Unsupervised approach for selecting sentences in query based summarization. In *FLAIRS Conference*. AAAI Press.

Crestani, F. (1997). Application of spreading activation techniques in information retrieval. *Artificial Intelligence Review, 11*(6), 453–482. doi:10.1023/A:1006569829653

Dang, H. T., & Owczarzak, K. (2009). Overview of the TAC 2009 Summarization Track. In *Proceedings of the Second Text Analysis Conference*. National Institute of Standards and Technology.

Erkan, G., & Radev, D. R. (2004). Lexrank: Graph-based lexical centrality as salience in text summarization. *Journal of Artificial Intelligence Research, 22*(1), 457–479.

FIRE. (2010). Retrieved from www.isical.ac.in/~fire/working-notes.html

Freitas, A., Oliveira, J. G., Curry, E., O'Riain, S., & Silva, J. P. (2011). Treo: Combining Entity-Search, Spreading Activation and Semantic Relatedness for Querying Linked Data. *Proceedings of the 1st Workshop on Question Answering Over Linked Data (QALD-1).*

Gupta, V., & Lehal, G. S. (2010). *A Survey of text summarization of extractive techniques.* University Institute of Engineering and Technology, Computer Science & Engineering, Punjab University, Chandigarh, India.

Haghighi, A., & Vanderwende, L. (2009). Exploring content models for multi-document summarization. In *Proceedings of Human Language Technologies: The 2009 Annual Conference of the North American Chapter of the Association for Computational Linguistics, NAACL '09*, (pp. 362–370). Stroudsburg, PA: Association for Computational Linguistics. doi:10.3115/1620754.1620807

Hahn, U., & Mani, I. (2000). The Challenges of Automatic Summarization. IEEE Computer, 33(11), 29-36.

Hendrickx, I., & Bosma, W. (2008). Using coreference links and sentence compression in graph-based summarization. *Proceedings of the Text Analysis Conference (TAC).*

Khan, A., & Salim, N. (2014). *A Review on Abstractive Summarization Methods.* Faculty of Computing, Universiti Teknologi Malaysia.

Lin, C. Y. (2004). ROUGE: A Package for Automatic Evaluation of Summaries. *Proceedings of Workshop on Text Summarization Branches Out, Post-Conference Workshop of ACL 2004.*

Mani, I., & Maybury, T. M. (1999). *Advances in Automatic Text Summarization.* MIT Press Cambridge.

Mann, W., & Thompson, S. (1988). Rhetorical structure theory. Toward a functional theory of text organization. *Text, 8*(3), 243–281. doi:10.1515/text.1.1988.8.3.243

Martins, C. B., & Rino, L. H. M. (2002). Revisiting UNLSumm Improvement through a case study. *Workshop on Multilingual Information Access and Natural Language Processing, IBERAMIA'2002.*

Mihalcea, R., & Tarau, P. (2004). TextRank: Bringing Order into Texts. *Proceedings of the Conference on Empirical Methods in Natural Language Processing (EMNLP 2004).*

Mohamed, A., & Sanguthevar, R. (2006). Query-based summarization based on document graphs. *Proceedings of the Document Understanding Conference (DUC'06).*

Mohamed, M., & Oussalah, M. (2016). An Iterative Graph-Based Generic Single and Multi-Document Summarization Approach Using Semantic Role Labeling and Wikipedia Concepts. *2016 IEEE Second International Conference on Big Data Computing Service and Applications (BigDataService)*, 117-120. doi:10.1109/BigDataService.2016.31

Nastase, V. (2008). Topic-driven multi-document summarization with encyclopedic knowledge and spreading activation. In *Proceedings of the Conference on Empirical Methods in Natural Language Processing, EMNLP 08.* Stroudsburg, PA: Association for Computational Linguistics.

Nenkova, A. (2005). Automatic text summarization of newswire: Lessons learned from the document understanding conference. In *Proceedings of the 20th National Conference on Artificial Intelligence* (vol. 3, pp. 1436–1441). AAAI Press.

Nenkova, A., & Vanderwende, L. (2005). *The impact of frequency on summarization*. Microsoft Research, Tech. Rep. MSR-TR-2005-101.

Quillian, M. R. (1967). Word Concepts: A Theory and Simulation of Some Basic Semantic Capabilities. *Behavioral Science*, *12*(5), 410–430. doi:10.1002/bs.3830120511 PMID:6059773

Radev, D. R., Jing, H., Stys, M., & Tam, D. (2004). Centroid-based summarization of multiple documents. *Information Processing & Management*, *40*(6), 919–938. doi:10.1016/j.ipm.2003.10.006

Rosner, M., & Camilleri, C. (2008). Multisum: query-based multi-document summarization. In *Proceedings of the Workshop on Multi-source Multilingual Information Extraction and Summarization, MMIES '08*. Stroudsburg, PA: Association for Computational Linguistics. doi:10.3115/1613172.1613180

Sornlertlamvanich, V., Potipiti, T., & Charoenporn, T. (2001). *UNL Document Summarization*. The First International Workshop on MultiMedia Annotation, Tokyo, Japan.

Steinberger, J., Poesio, M., Kabadjov, M. A., & Jeek, K. (2007). Two uses of anaphora resolution in summarization. *Information Processing & Management*, *43*(6), 1663–1680. doi:10.1016/j.ipm.2007.01.010

Subalalitha, C. N., Umamaheswari, E., Geetha, T. V., Ranjani, P., & Karky, M. (2011). Template based multilingual summary generation. *INFITT*.

Suchal, J. (2008). *On Finding Power Method in Spreading Activation Search, SOFSEM 2*. Kosice, Slovakia: Safarik University.

Thiel, K., & Berthold, M. R. (2012). Node Similarities from Spreading Activation. Academic Press.

Troussov, A., Levner, E., Bogdan, C., Judge, J., & Botvich, D. (2009). Spreading Activation Methods. In A. Shawkat & Y. Xiang (Eds.), *Dynamic and Advanced Data Mining for Progressing Technological Development*. IGI Global.

UNDL. (2010). *Universal networking language (unl) knowledge base (UNL KB)*. Retrieved from http://www.unlweb.net/wiki/UNL_Knowledge_Base

UNDL. (2011). *Universal networking language (unl)*. Retrieved from http://www.undl.org/unlsys/unl/unl2005

Yasunaga, M., Zhang, R., Meelu, K., Pareek, A., Srinivasan, K., & Radev, D. (2017). Graph-based Neural Multi-Document Summarization. *CoNLL 2017*.

Chapter 10
Mini–ME Matchmaker and Reasoner for the Semantic Web of Things

Floriano Scioscia
Polytechnic University of Bari, Italy

Michele Ruta
Polytechnic University of Bari, Italy

Giuseppe Loseto
Polytechnic University of Bari, Italy

Filippo Gramegna
Polytechnic University of Bari, Italy

Saverio Ieva
Polytechnic University of Bari, Italy

Agnese Pinto
Polytechnic University of Bari, Italy

Eugenio Di Sciascio
Polytechnic University of Bari, Italy

ABSTRACT

The Semantic Web of Things (SWoT) aims to support smart semantics-enabled applications and services in pervasive contexts. Due to architectural and performance issues, most Semantic Web reasoners are often impractical to be ported: they are resource consuming and are basically designed for standard inference tasks on large ontologies. On the contrary, SWoT use cases generally require quick decision support through semantic matchmaking in resource-constrained environments. This paper describes Mini-ME (the Mini Matchmaking Engine), a mobile inference engine designed from the ground up for the SWoT.

DOI: 10.4018/978-1-5225-5042-6.ch010

It supports Semantic Web technologies and implements both standard (subsumption, satisfiability, classification) and non-standard (abduction, contraction, covering, bonus, difference) inference services for moderately expressive knowledge bases. In addition to an architectural and functional description, usage scenarios and experimental performance evaluation are presented on PC (against other popular Semantic Web reasoners), smartphone and embedded single-board computer testbeds.

INTRODUCTION

Semantic Web technologies have been acknowledged to promote interoperability and intelligent information processing in ubiquitous computing. Scenarios include supply chain management (Giannakis & Louis, 2016), ubiquitous commerce (Liu, 2013; De Virgilio, Di Sciascio, Ruta, Scioscia, & Torlone 2011), peer-to-peer resource discovery (Ruta, Di Sciascio, & Scioscia, 2011; Ruta, Scioscia, Ieva, Capurso & Di Sciascio, 2017) and so on. The ever-increasing computational resources and communications effectiveness of mobile devices enable ubiquitous processing and exchange of rich and structured information for context-aware resource discovery and decision support. The Semantic Web and the Internet of Things paradigms are converging more and more toward the so-called *Semantic Web of Things* (SWoT) (Ruta, Scioscia & Di Sciascio, 2012; Pfisterer *et al.*, 2011). It enables semantic-enhanced pervasive computing by embedding intelligence into ordinary objects and environments through a plethora of heterogeneous micro-devices conveying short information seeds.

Such a vision requires increased flexibility and autonomy of ubiquitous knowledge-based systems in information encoding, management, dissemination and discovery. User agents running on mobile personal devices should be able to discover dynamically the best available resources according to user's profile and preferences, in order to support her current tasks through unobtrusive and context-dependent suggestions. Reasoning and query answering are particularly critical issues, stimulating the need for further specialized inference services in addition to classical ones (like *subsumption* and *satisfiability* check). Furthermore, mobile computing platforms (*e.g.*, smartphones, tablets) are still constrained by hardware/software limitations with respect to typical setups for Semantic Web reasoning engines. In fact, architectural and performance issues affect the porting of current OWL-based reasoners, designed for the Semantic Web, to mobile devices (Bobed, Yus, Bobillo, & Mena, 2015).

This chapter describes *the Mini Matchmaking Engine (Mini-ME)* (Scioscia *et al.*, 2014b), a compact matchmaker and reasoner for the attributed language with unqualified number restrictions (ALN) Description Logic (DL). It is aimed to semantic matchmaking for resource/service discovery in mobile and ubiquitous contexts, although it is also a general-purpose Semantic Web inference engine. Optimized non-standard inference services allow a fine-grained categorization and ranking of matching resources w.r.t. a request, providing both a distance metric and a logic-based explanation of the outcomes. Mini-ME is suitable to a widespread class of applications where large sets of low-complexity component resources can be aggregated to build composed services with growing semantic complexity. This is fit for the computational and power supply limitations of resource providers in ubiquitous contexts and to their short storage availability. An "agile" service discovery architectures able to select, assemble and orchestrate on the fly many elementary components is more manageable and effective in mobile and pervasive applications.

Mini-ME uses the *OWL API* (Horridge & Bechhofer, 2011) to parse and manipulate Knowledge Bases in all supported syntaxes of Web Ontology Language (OWL) version 2 (World Wide Web Consortium [W3C], 2012). It exploits structural inference algorithms on unfolded and CNF (Conjunctive Normal Form) normalized concept expressions for efficient computations also on resource-constrained platforms. Mini-ME implements both standard reasoning tasks for Knowledge Base (KB) management *(subsumption, satisfiability, classification)* and non-standard inference services for semantic-based resource discovery and ranking *(abduction, contraction, covering, bonus, difference)*. The reasoner is developed in Java, with Android as the main target computing platform. Furthermore, reasoner and graphical user interface (GUI) plug-ins have been developed for the Protégé ontology editor (Musen, 2015). Mini-ME has already been employed in prototypical testbeds on mobile and embedded devices for ubiquitous and pervasive computing scenarios.

The chapter is organized as follows. The next section recalls needed theoretical background. Then, a functional and architectural description of the system is given, followed by three usage scenarios, respectively in ontology engineering with Protégé, mobile semantic augmented reality and semantic sensor networks. In the last part of the chapter some experimental evaluation is provided for both standard and non-standard inferences on PC, mobile and embedded computing platforms. Finally, relevant related work and main novel contribution are discussed, before closing remarks.

BACKGROUND

In what follows relevant reasoner background is presented and particularly the logic language it supports is described followed by an overview of the allowed inference services. This should make self-contained the architectural and implementation details given later on.

Description Logics

Description Logics - also known as Terminological languages, Concept languages – are a family of logic formalisms for Knowledge Representation in a decidable fragment of First Order Logic (Baader, Calvanese, McGuinness, Nardi, & Patel-Schneider, 2002). The basic DLs syntax elements are: *concepts* (a.k.a. classes), denoting sets of objects; *roles* (a.k.a. properties), relating pairs of concepts; *individuals* (a.k.a. instances), denoting special named elements in concepts. A *semantic interpretation* is a pair I = $(\Delta, \cdot^I)$, consisting of a *domain* Δ and an *interpretation function* $\cdot^I$ mapping every concept to a subset of Δ, every role to a subset of $\Delta \times \Delta$, and every individual to an element of Δ. Basic elements can be combined using *constructors* to compose concept and role *expressions*. Each DL has a different set of constructors: the conjunction of concepts, usually denoted as $\sqcap$, is used in every DL; some DLs also include disjunction $\sqcup$ and complement $\neg$. Roles can be combined with concepts using *existential* and *universal* quantifications; other constructs may involve counting, such as number restrictions. Semantics of expressions is given by defining the interpretation function over each construct.

In DL-based reasoners, an *ontology* T (a.k.a Terminological Box or TBox) is composed by a set of assertions in the form $A \sqsubseteq D$ (*inclusion* a.k.a. *subsumption*) or $A \equiv D$ (*definition* a.k.a. *equivalence*), with A and D concept expressions. Particularly, a *simple*-TBox is an acyclic TBox such that: (i) A is always an atomic concept; (ii) if A appears in the left-hand side (lhs) of a concept definition assertion, then it cannot appear also in the lhs of any concept inclusion assertion. Mini-ME supports the ALN DL, which has polynomial computational complexity for standard and non-standard inferences in simple-TBoxes, whose depth of concept taxonomy is bounded by the logarithm of the number of axioms in it (see (Ruta *et al.*, 2011) for further explanation). This DL fragment has been selected because it grants good worst-case complexity and memory efficiency of non-standard inference algorithms for semantic matchmaking. Syntax and semantics of ALN DL constructs are summarized in Table 1.

According to the World Wide Web Consortium (W3C) Recommendation for the OWL 2 ontology language, an OWL 2 ontology is basically an RDF (Resource Description Framework) (W3C, 2014) graph referring to the OWL 2 vocabulary (W3C, 2012), serialized in RDF/XML syntax or in one of the other optional syntaxes.

Inference Services

Given a TBox T and a concept expression C, the *unfolding* procedure recursively expands references to axioms in T within the concept expression itself. In this way T is not needed anymore when executing subsequent inferences. On the other hand, *normalization* translates the unfolded concept expression in a canonical (*normal*) form through pre-defined substitution rules preserving its semantics. This makes subsequent inference algorithms applicable to any concept expression. When loading a KB, Mini-ME performs a preprocessing in order to execute unfolding and normalization in *Conjunctive Normal Form* (CNF) (Ruta *et al.*, 2011). Any ALN concept expression C can be reduced to CNF as: $C \equiv C_{CN} \sqcap C_{LT} \sqcap C_{GT} \sqcap C_{\forall}$, where C_{CN} is the conjunction of (possibly negated) atomic concept names, C_{LT} (respectively C_{GT}) is the conjunction of $\leq$ (resp. $\geq$) number restrictions (no more than one per role), and $C_{\forall}$ is the conjunction of universal quantifiers (no more than one per role; fillers are recursively in CNF). Normalization preserves semantic equivalence w.r.t. models induced by the TBox; furthermore, CNF is unique up to commutativity of conjunction operator (Ruta *et al.*, 2011). The normal form of an unsatisfiable concept is simply the bottom concept $\perp$.

Mini-ME was designed as a semantic matchmaker, *i.e.* a tool to find the best resources for a given request, when both resource and request descriptions are satisfiable concept expressions w.r.t. a common ontology. The following standard reasoning services are currently supported:

- **Concept Satisfiability (a.k.a. Consistency) Check:** In a semantic matchmaking framework, given a request R and a supplied resource S as concept expressions w.r.t. a common TBox T, satisfi-

Table 1. Syntax and semantics of ALN constructs and simple TBoxes

Name	Syntax	Semantics
Top	$\top$	Δ^I
Bottom	$\perp$	$\emptyset$
Intersection	$C \sqcap D$	$C^I \cap D^I$
Atomic negation	$\neg A$	$\Delta^I - A^I$
Universal quantification	$\forall R.C$	$\{ d_1 \mid \forall d_2 : (d_1, d_2) \in R^I \rightarrow d_2 \in C^I \}$
Number restriction	$(\geq n\,R)$	$\{ d_1 \mid \# \{ d_2 \mid (d_1, d_2) \in R^I \} \geq n \}$
	$(\leq n\,R)$	$\{ d_1 \mid \# \{ d_2 \mid (d_1, d_2) \in R^I \} \leq n \}$
Inclusion	$A \sqsubseteq D$	$A^I \subseteq D^I$
Definition	$A \equiv D$	$A^I = D^I$

ability allows to determine whether there is a partial (disjoint) match or not, by checking whether $T \models S \sqcap D \sqsubseteq \perp$ holds or not. Due to CNF properties, satisfiability check is trivially performed during normalization.

- **Subsumption Check:** Subsumption determines whether the resource is a full (subsume) match for the request or not, by checking whether $T \models S \sqsubseteq D$ holds or not. The classic structural subsumption algorithm is exploited, reducing the procedure to a set containment test (Baader *et al.*, 2002).

Further non-standard inference services were also implemented, allowing to (i) provide explanation of outcomes beyond the trivial "positive/negative" answer of satisfiability and subsumption tests, (ii) enable a logic-based relevance ranking of a set of available resources w.r.t. a specific query (Ruta *et al.*, 2011) and (iii) aggregate resources in order to satisfy complex requests:

- **Concept Contraction (Colucci *et al.*, 2007):** Given a request R and a supplied resource S, if they are not compatible with each other, Contraction determines which part of R is conflicting with S. If one retracts conflicting requirements G (*Give up*) from R, a concept K (*Keep*) is obtained, representing a contracted version of the original request, such that K ⊓ S is satisfiable w.r.t. T. The solution G to Contraction represents "why" R ⊓ S are not compatible.
- **Concept Abduction (Colucci *et al.*, 2007):** Whenever R and S are compatible, but S does not imply R, Abduction allows to determine what should be hypothesized in S in order to completely satisfy R, also enabling a logic-based relevance ranking of a resource w.r.t. a given request (Ruta *et al.*, 2011). The solution H (*Hypothesis*) to Abduction represents "why" the subsumption relation $T \models S \sqsubseteq R$ does not hold. H can be interpreted as *what is requested in R and not specified in S*.
- **Concept Covering:** Many ubiquitous scenarios require that relatively large number of low-complexity resources are aggregated in order to satisfy an articulated request. To this aim, a further non-standard reasoning task based on the solution of *Concept Covering Problem* (CCoP, formally defined in (Ragone *et al.*, 2007) has been defined. It allows to: (i) cover (*i.e.*, satisfy) features expressed in a request as much as possible, through the conjunction of one or more instances of a KB – seen as elementary building blocks – and (ii) provide explanation of the uncovered part of the request itself. Given a concept expression R (request) and a set of instances $S = \{S_1, S_2, ..., S_n\}$ (available resources), where R and $S_1, S_2, ..., S_n$ are satisfiable in the reference ontology T, *Concept Covering* aims to find a pair (S_c, H) where $S_c \subseteq S$ includes concepts in S covering R w.r.t. T as much as possible and H is the residual part of R not covered by concepts in S_c.
- **Concept Bonus:** A resource S could contain features not requested in R – possibly because the requester did not know or consider them – which could be useful in a query refinement process to improve matchmaking outcome. For this purpose, the Bonus non-standard inference service (Ruta *et al.*, 2011) extracts a concept B from S, which denotes something the resource provides even though the request did not ask for it.
- **Concept Difference:** Finally, advanced multi-agent knowledge sharing and integration scenarios (Scioscia, Ruta & Di Sciascio, 2015) require ways to subtract information in an expression from another one. This is accomplished by means of the Concept Difference reasoning service (Teege, 1994).

Since S is an approximated match of R, it would be useful to evaluate how good the approximation is. Based on the uniqueness of CNF, a *norm* for concept expressions can be computed by "counting" the number of conjuncts in it (Ruta *et al.*, 2011). Hence, numerical *penalty functions* can be defined based on the norm of expressions G and H, which allow to evaluate the goodness of match approximation as well as to rank several resources w.r.t. a request. Also for Difference many valid solutions exist, but a maximality criterion should be adopted in this case (*i.e.*, subtract as much as possible).

In order to use Mini-ME in more general knowledge-based applications, the following reasoning services over ontologies were also implemented:

- **Coherence:** It is a simplified check w.r.t. Satisfiability, because it does not process individuals (the difference is discussed *e.g.* in (Moguillansky *et al.*, 2010)). Since CNF normalization allows to identify unsatisfiable concepts, it is sufficient to normalize every concept during ontology parsing to detect unsatisfiabilities in the ontology.
- **Classification:** Ontology classification computes the overall concept taxonomy induced by the subsumption relation, from ⊤ to ⊥ concept. In order to reduce the subsumption tests, the following optimizations introduced in (Baader, Hollunder, Nebel, Profitlich & Franconi, 1994) were implemented: enhanced traversal top search, enhanced traversal bottom search, exploitation of told subsumers.

MINI-ME: SYSTEM OUTLINE AND FEATURES

Current Mini-ME version is 2.0, available at http://sisinflab.poliba.it/swottools/minime/. In what follows, a description of the matchmaker tool is provided, including architectural and implementation details.

General Architecture

The Mini-ME architecture is sketched as UML diagram in Figure 1. Main components are outlined hereafter:

- **Android Service:** Implements a service (*i.e.*, a background daemon) any Android application can invoke to use the engine;
- **OWL API (Horridge & Bechhofer, 2011):** Provides support for parsing and manipulating the OWL 2 language expressions;
- **MicroReasoner:** Reasoner implementation, exposing fundamental KB operations (load, parse), as well as inference tasks;
- **KB Wrapper:** Implements KB management functions (creation of internal data structures, normalization, unfolding) and inference procedures on ontologies (Classification and Coherence check);
- **Data Structures:** In-memory data structures for concept manipulation and reasoning; the inference procedures on concept expressions (Concept Satisfiability, Subsumption, Abduction, Contraction, Covering, Difference) are implemented at this level.

Figure 1. UML component diagram

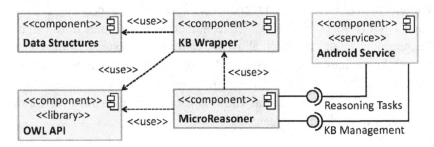

Mini-ME 2.0 was developed in Java using Android SDK Tools, Revision 25, corresponding to Android Platform version 6.0 (API level 23). It was tested with previous version, however, resulting compatible with all devices running Android 2.1 or later. Mini-ME can be used as:

1. *Android Service* by Android applications;
2. Library by calling public methods of the MicroReasoner component directly.

In the last case, it runs unmodified on Java Standard Edition runtime environment (version 6 or later) and supports all OWL 2 syntaxes accepted by the OWL API parser.

Inference Core Framework

Standard Java Collection Framework objects are used to define the low-level data structures package (mentioned before), composed of the following classes:

- **Item:** It represents a named concept expression. When parsing an ontology, the KB Wrapper component builds a Java HashMap object containing all concepts in the TBox as String-Item pairs. Each concept is unfolded, normalized and stored in the HashMap with its name as key and Item instance as value;
- **SemanticDescription:** Models a concept expression in CNF as aggregation of C_{CN}, C_{LT}, C_{GT}, $C_\forall$ components, each one stored in a different Java ArrayList. Methods implement inference services;
- **Concept:** Superclass of all concept types. Subclasses are AtomicConcept, UniversalRestriction and CardinalityRestriction, which is further extended by GreatherThanRestriction and LessThanRestriction. The *equals* method, inherited from java.lang.Object, has been overridden in order to properly implement a logic-based comparison;
- **Abduction and Contraction:** Represent the result returned by Concept Abduction and Concept Contraction, respectively. Abduction contains a SemanticDescription as Hypothesis, while Contraction contains two SemanticDescription objects as Give Up and Keep. Furthermore, they both contain a penalty score induced by the inference procedure;
- **Composition:** Represents the result returned by the Concept Covering service. It contains a vector of Item elements as covering set and a further one as uncovered part of the request.

Mini-ME exploits structural algorithms for standard and non-standard inference services on (unfolded and normalized) concept expressions. The careful optimization of the implementation of both algorithms and data structures enables efficient computations even on resource-constrained systems such as mobile and embedded devices. In particular, the following algorithms can be invoked through the *MicroReasoner* interface:

- **Abduce:** Implements the Concept Abduction service by means of a recursive procedure, reported in Figure 2;
- **Contract:** Performs the Concept Contraction service with a recursive algorithm, detailed in Figure 3;
- **Cover:** Exploits the above Abduction algorithm to solve a CCoP starting from a request and a set of compatible services. The related flow chart is in Figure 4.

USE CASES

Mini-ME provides different tools – such as consistency check and classification tasks-assisting users in knowledge bases engineering in both classical and ubiquitous Semantic Web scenarios. Furthermore, it offers resource discovery capabilities through standard and non-standard inference services to build applications and services for several application scenarios. In particular, by running on mobile and embedded devices, Mini-ME allows leveraging semantics also in pervasive Semantic Web of Things contexts, such as u-commerce, u-learning, u-healthcare, home and building automation, navigation and driving assistance systems, VANETs (Vehicular Ad-hoc NETworks), WSSANs (Wireless Semantic Sensor and Actor Networks), and many more. To focus just on few clear examples, this section illustrates how Mini-ME can be exploited in the following use cases: (i) knowledge engineering with an ontology editor; (ii) a mobile augmented reality explorer to discover points of interest; (iii) a cooperative WSSANs framework.

In the Semantic Web: Protégé Plugins

Mini-ME has been integrated in the *Protégé* ontology editor (Musen, 2015) through the implementation of an OWL reasoner plugin. Standard reasoning tasks are accessible through the Protégé user interface in the *Reasoning* menu. The entry point is the *MinimeReasoner* class, extending *AbstractProtegeOWL-ReasonerInfo*, which manages the synchronization between the knowledge base and the reasoner in case of changes to the currently loaded KB. The class also references the reasoner factory, responsible for the creation of the Mini-ME instance.

Moreover, an additional Protégé plugin was developed to:

- Exploit non-standard inferences through a user-friendly GUI;
- Support users during design and development of ontologies for pervasive and ubiquitous scenarios.

The existing DL Query plugin (http://github.com/protegeproject/dlquery) was adopted as guideline. The proposed plugin is a Tab Widget and it consists of the following components, highlighted in Figure 5:

Figure 2. Concept Abduction algorithm

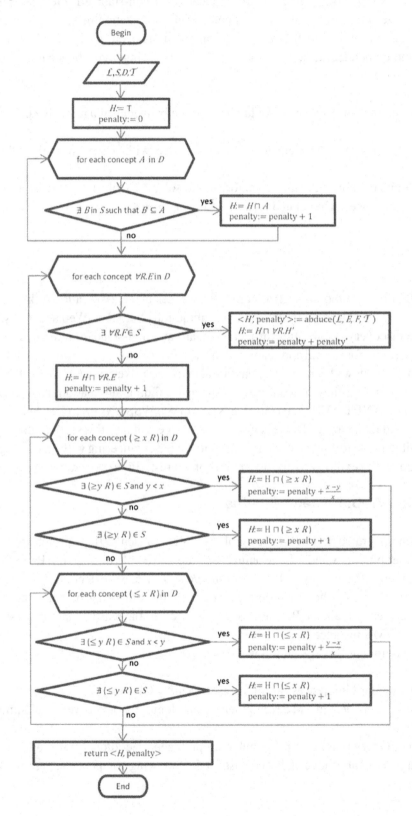

Figure 3. Concept Contraction algorithm

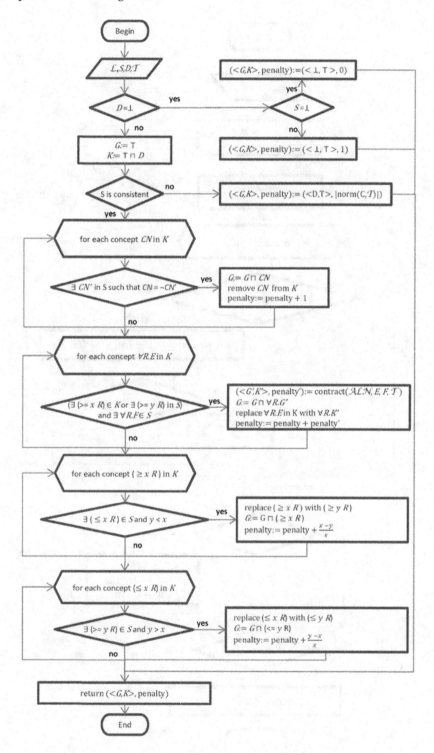

Figure 4. Concept Covering algorithm

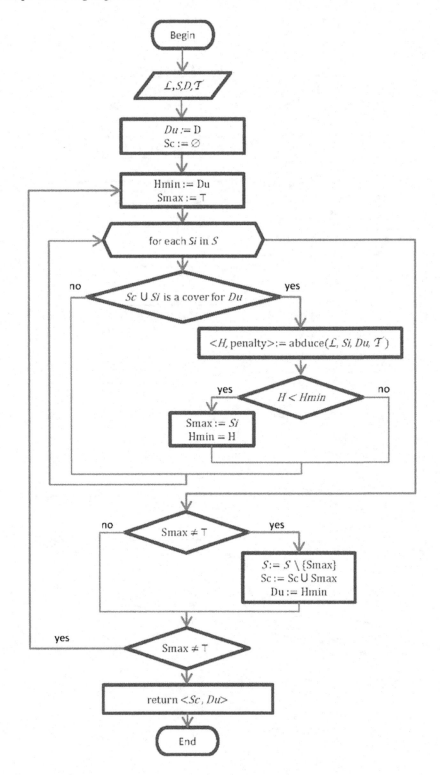

Figure 5. Protégé plugin for non-standard inferences

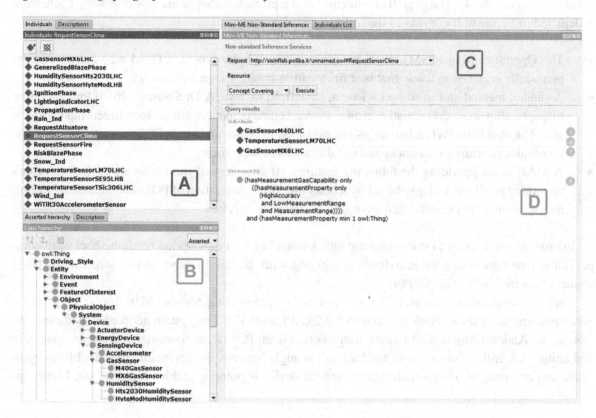

1. *OWLIndividualsList* and *OWLIndividualsTypes* tabs, showing all KB instances with related descriptions;
2. *OWLAssertedClassHierarchy* and *OWLClassDescription* tabs, containing the general taxonomy along with the description of selected classes;
3. An input box used to select the inference task, the request R and –in case of abduction, contraction, bonus and difference– the resource annotation S through a simple list containing the IRI of all individuals defined within the KB. For Concept Covering, a subset of KB individuals can be checked through the Individuals List panel as available resources;
4. The results area shows the output of the chosen inference service. Particularly, Figure 5 shows a CCoP resolution: component individuals and the uncovered part of the request are displayed.

Due to plugin interface changes between Protégé versions 4 and 5, two different versions were developed to be used with Protégé 4.3 and 5.1.

In the Ubiquitous Semantic Web: Mobile Augmented Reality Explorer

Semantic-based technologies can support articulated and meaningful descriptions of locations and Points of Interest (POIs). The use of metadata (annotations) endowed with formal machine-understandable meaning enables advanced location-based resource discovery through proper inferences. The Mini-ME engine powers a novel discovery approach in Mobile Augmented Reality (MAR), implemented for Android (Ruta *et al.*, 2014). The overall architecture of the proposed ubiquitous POI discovery framework is depicted in Figure 6. It consists of the following components:

- The OpenStreetMap (OSM) server working as cartography provider. OSM map entities are semantically enriched in a way that best fits location-based resource discovery.
- A general method and an editor (Scioscia, Binetti, Ruta, Ieva, & Di Sciascio, 2014) for annotating maps, so allowing a collaborative crowd-sourced enhancement of basic OpenStreetMap cartography. The standard OWL 2 languages are exploited to create and share POI annotations, based on ontologies providing the conceptual vocabulary to express them.
- A MAR client providing the following features: (i) discovery of most relevant POIs w.r.t. user's annotated profile, via a logic-based matchmaking; (ii) visualization of POI annotations and examination of discovery results, through a fully visual user interface.

In order to allow users to store semantic annotations in a POI description retaining backward compatibility, new tags have been introduced complying with the basic key-value pair structure of OSM element tags (Scioscia *et al.*, 2014a).

The client application –shown in Figure 7a– was developed using Android SDK Tools, Revision 23, corresponding to Android Platform version 4.2.2 (API level 17). The system adopted a modified version of the Android Augmented Reality framework. Given POI target coordinates (latitude, longitude and altitude), it collects the azimuth and inclination angle between the device and the target from gyroscope and compass, in order to calculate where the device is pointing and its degree of tilt. Using this

Figure 6. Architecture of the MAR System

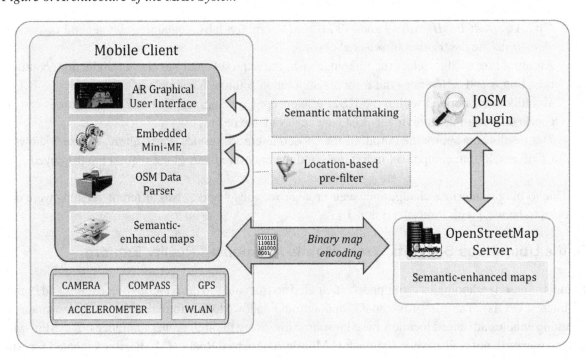

Figure 7. User interface of the semantic MAR explorer: (a) UI, (b) Abduction results, (c) Contraction results

a) User interface

b) Abduction results

c) Contraction results

information, the system decides if and where a POI marker should be displayed within the viewfinder image on the screen.

In the proposed AR POI discovery framework, the user profile plays the role of request R. It consists of a concept expression including personal information like interests and hobbies. The profile can be either composed by browsing visually the ontology modeling the reference domain (Scioscia *et al.*, 2014a), or imported from other applications and services. Available resources are the annotated OSM POIs in the user's area, referred to the same ontology as the user profile. They are extracted from OSM server and cached in the MAR client. Several resource domains (cultural heritage, shopping, accommodation, *etc.*) can be explored by simply switching to the proper reference ontology. Hence the proposed system works as a general-purpose location-based discovery facilitator. Exploiting the embedded Mini-ME engine, the application executes semantic matchmaking between the user profile and the annotations of POIs in her surroundings (enclosed into semantic-enhanced OSM map). Figure 8 sketches the resource discovery process.

The semantic description concerning each POI is stored as an attribute of its marker. A score is finally associated to each POI, estimating the result of the matchmaking between the user profile and the POI annotation. The overall resource score is computed with the utility function:

Figure 8. POI matchmaking process in the MAR system

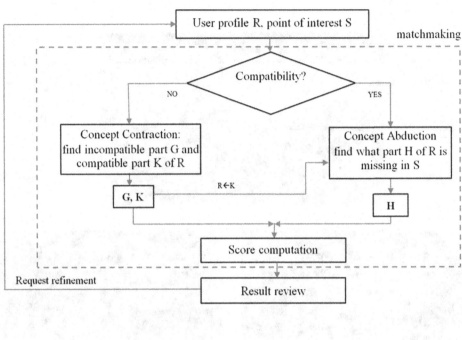

$$f\left(R, POI\right) = 100 * \left[1 - \frac{penalty\left(R, POI\right)}{penalty\left(R, T\right)} * \left(1 + \frac{distance\left(User\_GPS, POI\_GPS\right)}{max\_distance}\right)\right]$$

where penalty (R, POI) is the semantic distance between profile R and POI; this value is normalized dividing by penalty(R,⊤), which is the distance between R and the universal concept and depends only on assertions in the ontology. Geographical distance (normalized by user-specified maximum range) is combined as weighting factor. The purposes of the utility function are: (i) to weight the result of semantic matching according to distance and (ii) to translate the score to a more user-friendly scale. Of course nearer resources are preferred, but in case of a full match penalty (R, POI) = 0 hence f(R, POI) = 100 regardless of distance.

By touching a marker, the user can see its features, which are presented as icons around a wheel shape, in order to provide a clear and concise description, as shown in the central portion (A) of Figure 7b. The View result panel (B) in Figure 7b lists all missing features w.r.t. user profile (C), computed through Concept Abduction. In case of incompatibility, the same left-hand menu shows the Concept Contraction outcome: properties the POI satisfies and incompatible elements (Figure 7c-(D)). Overall, the user can quickly identify what POI resources are most relevant to her needs, by looking at the POI marker color, at the matchmaking result shown in the score panel and – if interested – by exploring POIs features. Simple operations on the device touchscreen allow effortless information acquisition and management.

The proposed AR framework has been integrated in an indoor/outdoor navigation solution for people with motion disabilities, such as wheelchair users (Ruta, Scioscia, Ieva, De Filippis, & Di Sciascio, 2015). Notable features included: annotation of accessibility information in the OSM cartography; a built-in routing engine with support for both outdoor and indoor positioning and navigation in multi-level buildings. A functional prototype was developed for Android mobile devices specifically devoted to assist users with physical disabilities.

In the Semantic Web of Things: Cooperative Semantic Sensor Networks

The Constrained Application Protocol (CoAP) is becoming one of the most widely accepted application-layer protocols for the Web of Things (Bormann, Castellani, & Shelby, 2012). CoAP adopts the CoRE Link Format (Shelby, 2012) specification for resource discovery. This protocol only allows a syntactic string-matching of attributes, lacking any explicit and formal characterization of the resource semantics.

To overcome this limit, the Mini-ME engine has been integrated in a framework for collaborative discovery of sensors and actuators in pervasive contexts. The proposed framework integrates the following components: (i) slight backward-compatible extensions to CoAP and CoRE Link Format resource discovery protocol (Ruta *et al.*, 2013); (ii) high-level event detection and annotation through resource-efficient data mining algorithms on raw data gathered by a Semantic Sensor Network (SSN) using the SSN-XG ontology as reference vocabulary (Compton *et al.*, 2012); (iii) non-standard inferences for semantic matchmaking for resource retrieval and ranking of approximate matches.

The proposed framework architecture is shown in Figure 9. Sensors deployed in an area communicate with a local sink node, which acts as cluster head. Multiple sinks are connected to a gateway, interfacing the micronetwork toward the outside. Each sensor is characterized not only by data-oriented attributes, but also by a semantic annotation describing its features and functionalities. Sinks are able to: (i) register sensors along with their semantic description as CoAP resources; (ii) support logic-based resource discovery on annotated metadata. For these purposes, sink nodes embed CoAP servers. They also gather and process data for event detection. When an event is recognized, it is annotated and a resource record is updated in the server. Beyond the semantic annotation, the record contains further extra-logical context parameters, such as geographic coordinates and a timestamp. The gateway waits

Figure 9. CoAP-based sensor network architecture

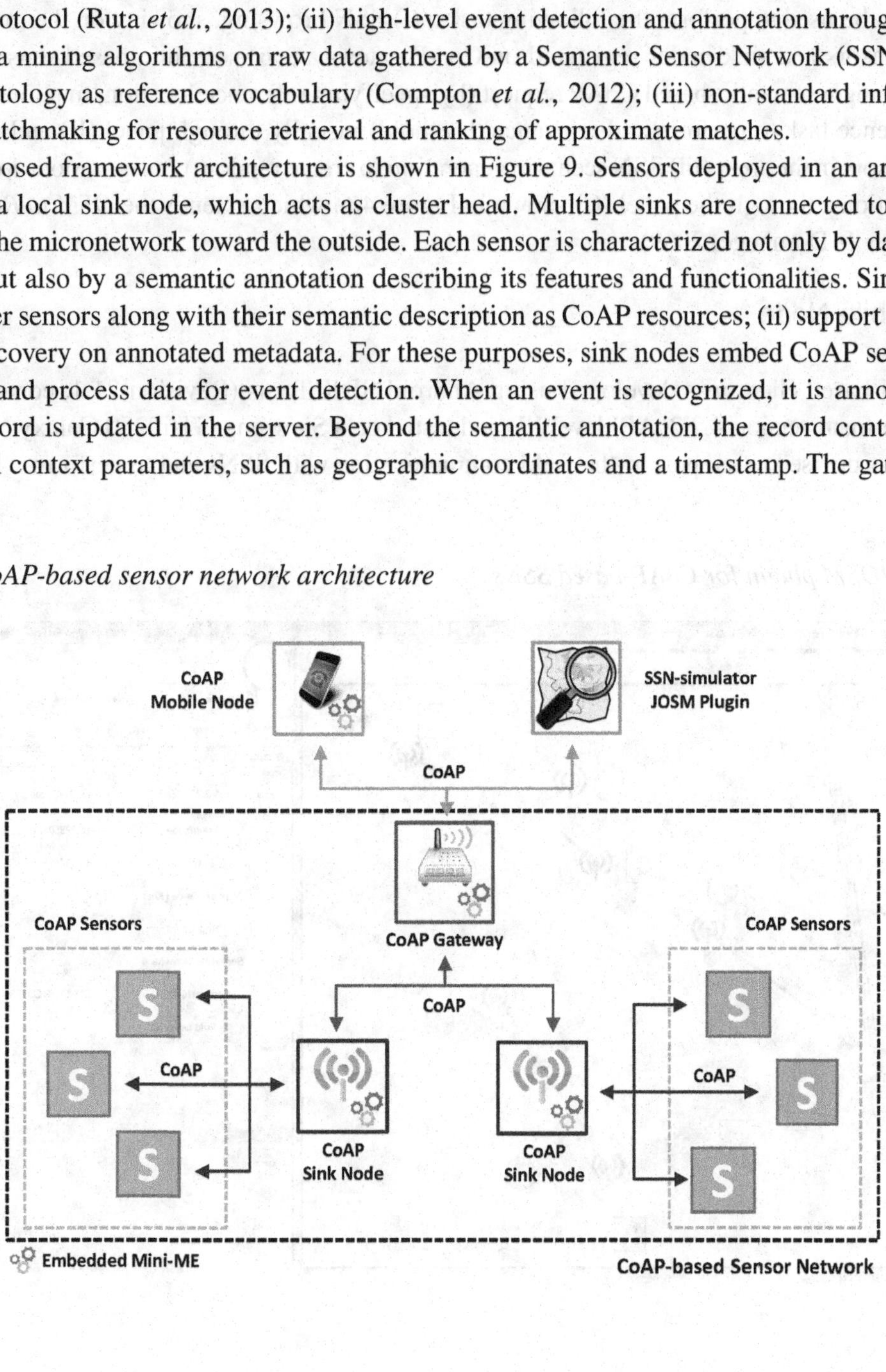

for resource discovery requests from client applications searching for events in the area, and replies on behalf of connected sink nodes.

Modules in the basic framework (Ruta *et al.*, 2013) were improved to support a collaborative sensing process (Ruta *et al.*, 2017b). Communication in SSNs was implemented using a modified version of Californium CoAP library, enabling the semantic-based enhancements of the CoAP protocol.

JOSM SSN Plugin

Figure 10 shows the prototype GUI of the SSN plugin for the Java OpenStreetMap (OSM) open source editor. It can be used to perform the following tasks: (i) SSN browsing, showing on the map in (A) the available sensors and sink nodes registered on CoAP gateways; (ii) semantic-based sensor discovery, for customizing a semantic-based CoAP request (by specifying reference location, maximum discovery range, inference task to perform and relevance threshold) visually through panel (B) and sending it to look for sensors in the area; (iii) SSN scenario generation to create random configurations for large-scale SSN simulations, through the panel (C) shown in Figure 4.6, which extends the *OSM to Rescue plugin* (Gobelbecker & Dornhege, 2009).

CoAP Mobile Node

An Android-based client was developed using Android SDK Tools (Revision 21.1, corresponding to Android Platform version 4.2.2, API level 17) and tested on a Samsung GT-i9250 Galaxy Nexus smartphone. It was devised to support in-the-field communication with SSNs and to perform:

Figure 10. JOSM plugin for CoAP-based SSNs

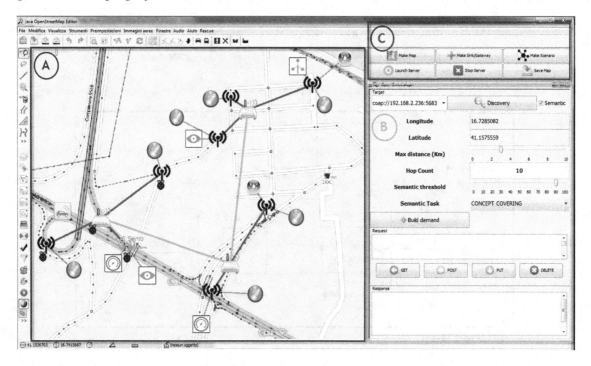

- SSN browsing and sensor discovery, where the user can select a gateway node and view all connected sensors or devices filtered-out by a semantic-based discovery. Each sensor can be also queried to retrieve data it measures;
- Collaborative sensing: when a mobile node (*e.g.*, an Android smartphone) queries a CoAP gateway, it can also act as information source, connected to the gateway temporarily. It can provide data coming from both its embedded micro-devices (e.g., accelerometer, gyroscope) and external sensing peripherals available through wired or wireless connections.

A client application can compose a discovery request and query a SSN gateway to find the set of most suitable sensors having an OWL semantic description referred to a shared ontology. The gateway carries out semantic matchmaking by solving a CCoP, in order to find the set of resources which together satisfy the request to the maximum extent. In case of a partial cover, the response includes both the semantic description of the uncovered part (H) of the request and the percentage of request still not covered. Furthermore, exploiting the proxy support built into CoAP, the gateway has the possibility to forward the uncovered part as a new request towards other SSN nodes in the area of interest, searching for more resources to satisfy missing features. In this way, each semantic-enabled gateway can start a collaborative and multi-hop resource discovery.

PERFORMANCE EVALUATION

An experimental campaign was performed with Mini-ME on PC, mobile and embedded systems, for standard and non-standard inference services. This allows to assess effectiveness of the proposed reasoner, both in comparison with other popular Semantic Web inference engines and w.r.t. requirements of SWoT applications. Followed evaluation criteria and obtained results are outlined hereafter.

Standard inferences on Personal Computers

Mini-ME was compared on PC with: *FaCT++* (Tsarkov & Horrocks, 2006) version 1.6.3, OWL API 3.4 (http://owl.man.ac.uk/factplusplus/); *HermiT* (Glimm, Horrocks, Motik, Stoilos, & Wang, 2014) version 1.3.8 (http://hermit-reasoner.com/); *Pellet* (Sirin, Parsia, Cuenca-Grau, Kalyanpur & Katz, 2007) version 2.3.1 (http://clarkparsia.com/pellet/). All reasoners were tested via the OWL API on a PC testbed (Intel Core i7 CPU 860 at 2.80 GHz –4 cores/8 threads– with 8 GB DDR3 SDRAM (1333 MHz) memory, 1 TB SATA (7200 RPM) hard disk, 64-bit Microsoft Windows 7 Professional and 32-bit Java 7 SE Runtime Environment, build 1.7.0_03-b05). The reference dataset was taken from the 2012 OWL Reasoner Evaluation workshop (http://www.cs.ox.ac.uk/isg/conferences/ORE2012/materials.html): it is composed of 214 OWL ontologies with different size, expressiveness and syntax. For each reasoning task, two tests were performed: (i) correctness of results and turnaround time; (ii) memory usage peak. For turnaround time, each test was repeated four times and the average of the last three runs was taken. For memory tests, the final result was the average value of three runs.

- **Classification:** The input of the classification task was the whole ontology dataset. For each test, one of the following possible outcomes was recorded:

- **Correct:** The computed taxonomy matched with the reference classification (if available in the dataset) or results of all the reasoners were the same. In this case the total time taken to load and classify the ontology was also recorded;
- **Parsing Error:** The ontology could not be parsed by the OWL API due to syntax errors;
- **Failure:** The classification task failed because the ontology contained unsupported logic language constructors;
- **Out of Memory:** The reasoner generated an exception due to memory constraints;
- **Timeout:** The task did not complete within the timeout threshold (set to 60 minutes).

Mini-ME correctly classified 83 out of 214 ontologies; 71 were discarded due to parsing errors, 58 presented unsupported language constructors, and the timeout was reached in 2 cases. Pellet classified correctly 130 ontologies, HermiT 128, FaCT++ 122. The lower "score" of Mini-ME is due to the presence of General Concept Inclusions, cyclic TBoxes or unsupported logic constructors. Parsing errors occurred in the OWL API library and were therefore common to all reasoners.

Performance was measured only for the 73 ontologies correctly classified by all reasoners, dividing them in five categories, according to their number of concepts:

- **Extra Small (XS):** Fewer than 10 concepts; 13 ontologies were in this group;
- **Small (S):** Between 10 and 100 concepts; 9 ontologies;
- **Medium (M):** Between 100 and 1000 concepts; 25 ontologies;
- **Large (L):** Between 1000 and 10000 concepts; 22 ontologies;
- **Extra Large (XL):** More than 10000 concepts; 4 ontologies.

Figure 11 compares the classification times of each reference reasoner w.r.t. the ontology categories. Pellet, HermiT and FaCT++ exhibited a similar trend, with the first two reasoners faster than the other engines for large ontologies. Mini-ME was very competitive for small-medium ontologies (up to about 1200 classes), but less for large ones. This can be considered as an effect of the Mini-ME design, which is optimized to manage elementary TBoxes.

Figure 11. Classification test on PC

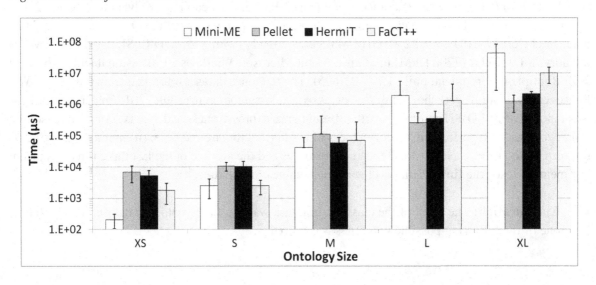

For what concerns the *class satisfiability* test, the adopted dataset consisted of 107 ontologies. Nevertheless, only the 69 ontologies Mini-ME correctly classified in the previous test were considered: for each of them, the dataset specifically indicated one or more classes to be checked. As reported in Figure 12, performances were basically similar, with times differing only for few microseconds and no reasoner consistently faster or slower. Moreover, no correlation between time and ontology size is revisable, whereas time is in direct ratio with the complexity of class description and to its depth in the taxonomy (data not shown).

Figure 13 shows the ontology satisfiability test results. For this task, all reasoners presented performance similar to the ones reported in Figure 11 for classification. In fact, the ontology satisfiability test implies loading, classifying and checking consistency of all concepts in the ontology with the first two steps requiring the larger time. Outcomes of all reasoners were the same, except for ontologies with IDs 199, 200, 202, 203 in the dataset. In contrast to Pellet, HermiT and FaCT++, Mini-ME checks ontology coherence regardless of the ABox. The above ontologies included an unsatisfiable class (GO_0075043) with no instances, therefore the ontology was reported as incoherent by Mini-ME, but as satisfiable by the other reasoners.

Finally, Figure 14 reports on memory usage peak during classification, which was verified as the most intensive task. For small-medium ontologies, used memory was roughly similar for all reasoners. Mini-ME provided good results, with slightly lower memory usage than Pellet and HermiT and on par with FaCT++. Also for large ontologies Mini-ME results were comparable with the other reasoners, but in this case FaCT++ had the best performance.

Standard Inferences on Mobile and Single-Board Computers

Using the same ontology dataset, results obtained on an Android smartphone (Samsung Galaxy Nexus GT-I9250 with dual-core ARM Cortex A9 CPU at 1,2 GHz, 1 GB RAM, 16 GB storage memory, and Android version 4.2.2) and on a Raspberry Pi Model B (equipped with a Broadcom BCM2835 system on a chip, with an ARM1176JZF-S CPU at 700 MHz, 512 MB RAM and Java 7 SE Runtime Environment build 1.7.0_40-b43) were compared to the above outcomes gathered for PC tests.

Results computed by Mini-ME on the mobile platforms were in all cases the same as on the PC. On the mobile and single-board devices, 75 ontologies out of 214 were correctly classified, 55 were dis-

Figure 12. Class Satisfiability on PC

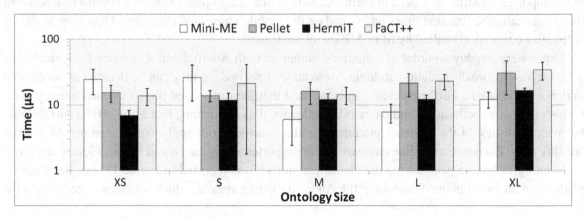

Figure 13. Ontology Satisfiability on PC

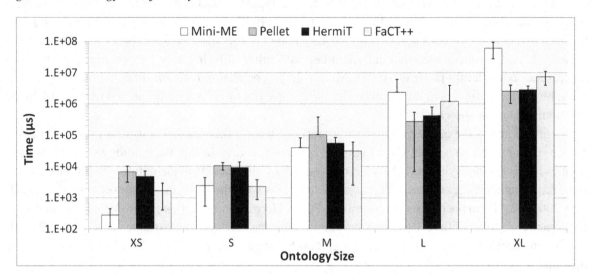

Figure 14. Memory usage test on PC

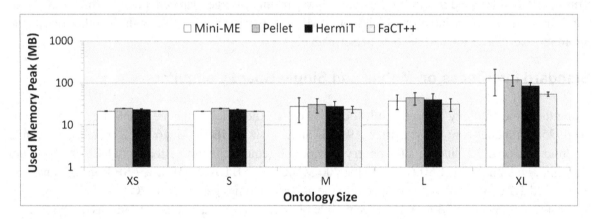

carded due to parsing errors, 56 had unsupported language constructors, 26 generated out-of-memory exceptions (these included ontologies correctly classified on PC or not classified due to parsing errors or unsupported constructors) and 2 of them reached the timeout. Figure 15 shows a comparison between the classification turnaround times on PC and on the mobile/embedded platforms. Data refer to the 73 ontologies correctly classified by Mini-ME on all devices.

Times were roughly an order of magnitude higher on both Android and Raspberry Pi devices. Absolute values for small-medium ontologies were under 1 second, so they can be deemed as acceptable in pervasive contexts. Furthermore, it can be noticed that the turnaround time increased linearly w.r.t. number of classes both on PC and on mobile platforms, thus confirming that Mini-ME has predictable behavior regardless of the reference platform. Similar considerations apply to class and ontology satisfiability tests: the turnaround time comparisons are reported in Figure 16 and Figure 17, respectively.

Memory allocation peak during the classification task was reported in Figure 18. For the Android platform, data were obtained exploiting the Android logging system, which provides a mechanism for

Figure 15. Classification on mobile and single-board computer (PC as baseline)

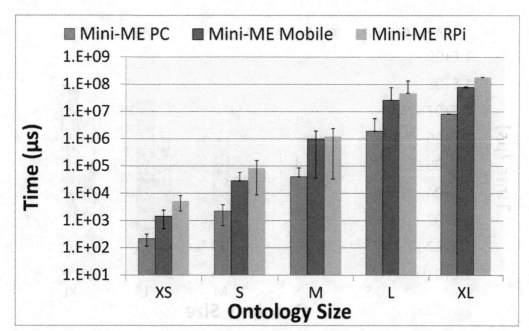

Figure 16. Class Satisfiability on mobile and single-board computer (PC as baseline)

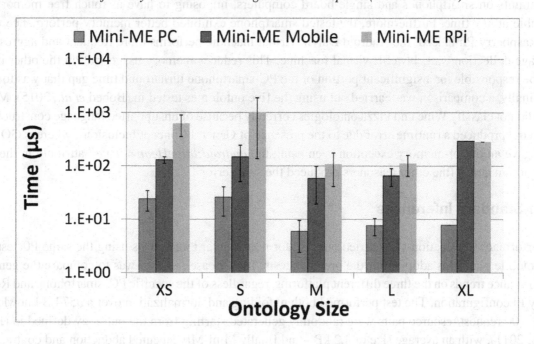

collecting and viewing system debug output, including heap memory data and garbage collector calls. For small-medium ontologies, the required memory was roughly stable. Instead, for large ontologies the used memory increased according to the total number of classes. Moreover, in every test memory usage on Android and Raspberry Pi was significantly lower than on PC. This is due to the harder memory

Figure 17. Ontology Satisfiability on mobile and single-board computer (PC as baseline)

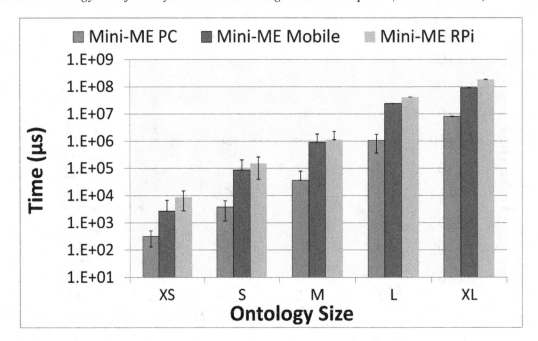

constraints on smartphones and single-board computers, imposing to have as much free memory as possible at any time. Furthermore, the tested smartphone exhibited better memory performance than the Raspberry Pi: indeed, the Android Dalvik virtual machine performs more frequent and aggressive garbage collection w.r.t. Java SE virtual machine. This reduces memory usage, but on the other hand can be responsible for a significant portion of the PC-smartphone turnaround time gap that was found.

Finally, a comparison was carried out using the five ontologies tested in (Bobed *et al.*, 2015). Mini-ME did not classify Wine and Pizza ontologies correctly because of unsupported language constructors, DBpedia produced a runtime error due to the presence of General Concept Inclusions, whereas GO and NCI gave an out-of-memory exception even using the *android:largeHeap="true"* attribute in the application manifest (the other reasoners produced the same error).

Non-Standard Inferences

A performance evaluation was carried out also for non-standard inferences using the same PC testbed and mobile platforms adopted for the previous tests. In this case the goal was to compare the general performance trends on the three different platforms, regardless of the specific PC, smartphone and Raspberry Pi configuration. The test performed both unfolding and normalization over a 557 kB knowledge base. 100 request/resource pairs were randomly generated starting from the ontology defined in (Ruta *et al.*, 2011), with an average size of 4.2 kB - and finally Mini-ME executed abduction and contraction between each pair. Every task was repeated four times and the average turnaround time of the last three runs was taken. Figure 19 reports time results (in microseconds) in case of PC, Android smartphone and Raspberry Pi board testbeds, respectively.

For each request/resource pair, Mini-ME executed a compatibility check; in case, abduction was performed, otherwise contraction was run, followed by abduction with the compatible part of the re-

Figure 18. Memory usage test on mobile and single-board computer (PC as baseline)

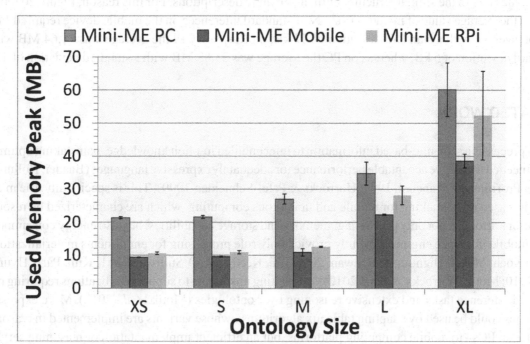

Figure 19. Non-standard inference tests

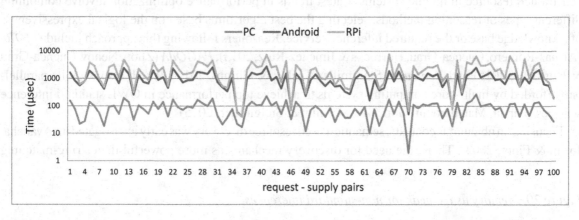

quest. Notice that the computational time basically varies depending on the complexity of the semantic descriptions. Results for mobile and single-board tests were referred to the ones for PC in order to highlight non-standard inferences exhibit similar trends. Processing times are reported in a logarithmic scale: despite the performance gap between PC and mobile platforms, reasoning tasks maintained an acceptable computational load also on the latter. Times were roughly an order of magnitude higher on the mobile devices. This is due not only to their limited computational capabilities, but also – as said above – to the more frequent garbage collection by the Android Dalvik virtual machine. This trend was even more apparent on the Raspberry Pi, which is characterized by lower computational resources than the Android reference platform. On all platforms, all request/resource pairs show slightly variable memory peak values due to the similar structure of their semantic descriptions. For this reason, Figure 20 reports only on the average value of memory peak. Non-standard inferences on the mobile device required 11.32 MB on average with a standard deviation of 27 kB, on Raspberry Pi the average was 11.64 MB with a standard deviation of 5 kB, whereas on PC the average was 23.88 MB with a standard deviation of 4 kB.

RELATED WORK

When processing semantic-based information to infer entailed implicit knowledge, painstaking optimization is needed to achieve acceptable performance for adequately expressive languages (Baader, Hollunder, Nebel, Profitlich, & Franconi, 1994; Horrocks & Patel-Schneider, 1999). This is specifically true in case of logic-based matchmaking for mobile and ubiquitous computing, which are characterized by resource limitations affecting not only processing, memory and storage capabilities, but also energy consumption. Most mobile inference engines currently provide only rule processing for entailments materialization in a KB (Koch, Meyer, Dignum, & Rahwan, 2006; Tai, Keeney, & O'Sullivan, 2011; Kim, Park, Hyun, & Lee, 2010; Motik, Horrocks, & Kim, 2012), so resulting unsuitable to support applications requiring non-standard inference tasks and extensive reasoning over ontologies (Motik *et al.*, 2012). More expressive languages could be used by adapting tableaux algorithms –whose variants are implemented in reasoners running on PCs– to mobile computing platforms, but an efficient implementation of reasoning services is still an open problem. Several techniques (Horrocks & Patel-Schneider, 1999) allow increasing expressiveness or decrease running time at the expense of main memory usage, which is precisely the most constrained resource in mobile systems. Latest trends in performance optimization involve combining different types of reasoning methods, selecting the best algorithms based on the logical expressiveness of a knowledge base or the required inference service. Reasoners following this approach include *MORe* (Armas-Romero, Cuenca-Grau, Horrocks & Jiménez-Ruiz, 2013), *PAGOdA* (Zhou, Nenov, Cuenca-Grau & Horrocks, 2015) and *Konclude* (Steigmiller, Liebig & Glimm, 2014), which also exploits parallelism afforded by multi-core computing systems to achieve top performance in OWL standard inference services (Parsia, Matentzoglu, Gonçalves, Glimm & Steigmiller, 2015).

Focusing on ubiquitous contexts, semantic-based resource discovery was early investigated in (Avancha, Joshi, & Finin, 2002). There, the need for discovery mechanisms more powerful than string-matching

Figure 20. Memory usage peak for non-standard inferences

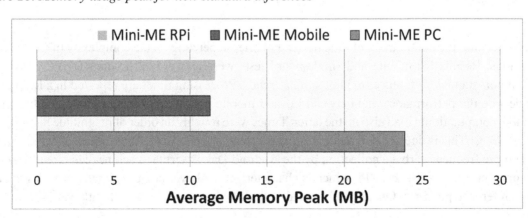

was clearly pointed out for the first time. The issue of approximate matches –lacking exact ones– was discussed, but no formal frameworks were given. In (von Hessling, Kleemann, & Sinner, 2004) semantic user profiles were introduced to increase accuracy in matching services in a mobile environment. If there was no intersection between user interests and service offers, authors concluded the user was not interested in the service; a complete and integrated solution for matching degree calculation was not provided. *Pocket KRHyper* (Sinner & Kleemann, 2005) was the first reasoning engine specifically designed for mobile devices. It supported the ALCHIR+ DL and was built as a Java ME (Micro Edition) library. Pocket KRHyper was exploited in a DL-based matchmaking framework between user profiles and descriptions of mobile resources/services (Kleemann & Sinner, 2005). However, frequent "out of memory" errors strongly limited the size and complexity of manageable logic expressions. To overcome performance constraints, tableaux optimizations to reduce memory consumption were introduced in (Steller & Krishnaswamy, 2008) and implemented in *mTableau*, a modified version of Java Standard Edition Pellet reasoner (Sirin *et al.*, 2007). Comparative performance tests were executed on a PC, showing faster turnaround times than both unmodified Pellet and *Racer* (Haarslev & Müller, 2001) reasoners.

As pointed out by Matentzoglu *et al.* (2015), most reasoners are currently based on the Java programming language. This is not surprising, since the main OWL frameworks, such as the OWL API (Horridge & Bechhofer, 2011) and *Jena* (McBride, 2002), are implemented in Java. Nevertheless, the Java SE technology is not expressly tailored to the current generation of handheld devices. In fact, other relevant inference engines cannot run on common mobile platforms, since they rely on Java class libraries incompatible with most widespread mobile OS (*e.g.*, Android). Bobed *et al.* (2015) recently ported five Semantic Web reasoners to the Android platform (Pellet, *CB* (Kazakov, 2009), Hermit (Glimm *et al.*, 2014) and *JFact*, a Java port of Fact++ (Tsarkov & Horrocks, 2006)), albeit with significant rewriting or restructuring effort in some cases. Similarly, in (Kazakov & Klinov, 2013) the *ELK* reasoner (Kazakov, Krötzsch, & Simancík, 2014) was optimized and evaluated on Android.

Nevertheless, all ported systems were designed mainly for batch jobs over large ontologies and/or expressive languages. This makes mobile device usage less suitable due to computation and memory constraints. The non-standard services of Mini-ME are more useful in ubiquitous scenarios, where mobile agents must provide quick decision support and/or on-the-fly organization in intrinsically unpredictable contexts. Moreover, it can be observed that the above systems, like the matchmaking framework proposed in (Kleemann & Sinner, 2005), only support standard inference services such as satisfiability and subsumption, which provide only binary "yes/no" answers. Consequently, they can only distinguish among *full (subsume)*, *potential (intersection-satisfiable)* and *partial (disjoint)* match types, as defined in (Colucci *et al.*, 2007) and (Li & Horrocks, 2004) respectively. Analogously, in the HTTP-based ubiquitous infrastructure by (Pfisterer *et al.*, 2011), queries allow only exact matches with facts derived from a support knowledge base. Non-standard inferences like abduction and contraction are needed to enable approximate matches, semantic ranking and explanations of outcomes (Colucci *et al.*, 2007). For this reason, initial efforts have been made to port the OWL API to iOS (Ruta, Scioscia, Di Sciascio & Bilenchi, 2016), in order to support cross-platform SWoT applications and services.

In latest years, the bad worst-case complexity of OWL language stimulated a different approach to implement reasoning tools. It was based on simplifying both the underlying logic languages and admitted KB axioms, so that structural algorithms could be adopted, while maintaining sufficient expressiveness for broad application areas. In (Baader, Brandt, & Lutz, 2005), the basic EL DL was extended to EL^{++}, a language deemed suitable for various applications, characterized by very large ontologies with moderate expressiveness. A structural classification algorithm was also devised, which allowed high-performance

EL^{++} ontology classifiers such as *CEL* (Baader, Lutz, & Suntisrivaraporn, 2006), *Snorocket* (Lawley & Bousquet, 2010) and ELK. OWL 2 profiles definition complies with this perspective, focusing on language subsets of practical interest for important application areas rather than on fragments with significant theoretical properties. In a parallel effort motivated by similar principles, in (Ruta, Di Noia, Di Sciascio, Piscitelli, & Scioscia, 2008) an early approach was proposed to adapt non-standard logic-based inferences to pervasive computing contexts. By limiting expressiveness to the AL language, acyclic, structural algorithms were adopted reducing standard and non-standard inference tasks to set-based operations. KB management and reasoning were then executed through a data storage layer, based on a mobile RDBMS (Relational DBMS). Such an approach was further investigated in (Ruta, Scioscia, Di Noia, & Di Sciascio, 2009) and (Ruta *et al.*, 2011), by increasing the expressiveness to ALN DL and allowing larger ontologies and more complex descriptions, through the adoption of both mobile OODBMS (Object-Oriented DBMS) and performance optimized data structures. Finally, in (Ruta, Scioscia, & Di Sciascio, 2010) expressiveness was extended to ALN(D) DL with fuzzy operators. The above tools were designed to run on Java Micro Edition devices and were adopted in several case studies in ubiquitous computing, employing semantic matchmaking over moderately expressive KBs. The reasoning engine presented here recalls lessons learned in those previous efforts, and aims to provide a standards-compliant implementation of most common inferences (both standard and non-standard) for Android, the most widespread mobile platform worldwide.

SUMMARY OF CONTRIBUTIONS

As the chapter pointed out, the theoretical work on the mobile and embedded reasoner named Mini-ME provided several contributions to the state of the art on reasoning for the Semantic Web (of Things). They can be summarized as in what follows:

- Mini-ME was the first mobile reasoner expressly designed and implemented for the Android mobile platform, albeit supporting also Java SE;
- The engine includes both standard reasoning services for KB manipulation and non-standard inference tasks for semantic matchmaking, resource discovery and decision support applications;
- Logical language choice and architectural and implementation optimizations make Mini-ME efficient on both conventional computer architectures and mobile and embedded systems, as demonstrated by an extensive experimental campaign;
- Mini-ME supports a wide range of Semantic Web (of Things) scenarios effectively; this chapter focused particularly on (i) knowledge engineering and KB editing, (ii) mobile resource discovery and (iii) autonomous Wireless Semantic Sensor Networks.

PROJECT DESCRIPTION AND PERSPECTIVES

The chapter presented a prototypical reasoner devised for the ubiquitous computing. It supports Semantic Web technologies through the OWL API and implements both standard and non-standard reasoning tasks. Developed in Java, it targets the Android platform but also runs on Java SE and on embedded devices like Raspberry Pi. Experiments were performed both on PCs and smartphones and evidenced: (i) correctness of implementation, (ii) competitiveness with state of-the-art reasoners in standard inferences, (iii) acceptable performance on target mobile devices.

The work on Mini-ME started in 2011 leveraging both theoretical and practical results reached in 10 years of research on the semantic-based matchmaking and reasoning. This effort produced several publications in international journals, conferences and workshops. In recent years, numerous case studies and prototypes have been developed for different ubiquitous scenarios to prove the feasibility and benefits of non-standard inferences, including ubiquitous commerce (Di Noia *et al.*, 2008), ambient intelligence and infomobility services (Ruta, Scioscia, Di Noia, & Di Sciascio, 2010), home and building automation (Ruta, Scioscia, Loseto, & Di Sciascio, 2014), up to semantic blockchain systems (Ruta *et al.*, 2017a).

A selection of applications can be viewed at http://sisinflab.poliba.it/swottools/. A widespread exploitation of Mini-ME is ongoing in a project funded under the Apulia Region Cluster research program in the healthcare field. Furthermore, some large Italian enterprises have shown their interest for the engine, due to its flexibility and scalability, for an extensive application in their products or services.

The intimate connection between theoretical research, engineering innovation and practical problem-oriented solutions is at the heart of the research activities of the Information Systems Laboratory at Polytechnic University of Bari, and in this perspective Mini-ME is being continuously developed and improved as a key enabling technology. Besides further performance optimization leveraging peculiarities of Android Dalvik (for Android versions up to 4.4) and ART (for versions 5.0 and above) runtimes, ongoing work includes a port to the iOS platform (also compatible with macOS) in the Swift programming language. This is an opportunity to refine architecture and design, as well as to include further optimizations for improving reasoning efficiency, which could be backported to the Java version. Further improvements under investigation include: support for ABox management; implementation of further reasoning tasks; the support for more expressive languages, *e.g.*, with EL^{++} extension of abduction and contraction algorithms.

REFERENCES

Armas-Romero, A., Cuenca-Grau, B., Horrocks, I., & Jiménez-Ruiz, E. (2013). MORe: a Modular OWL Reasoner for Ontology Classification. *Proceedings of the 2nd International Workshop on OWL Reasoner Evaluation (ORE)*, 61-67.

Avancha, S., Joshi, A., & Finin, T. (2002). Enhanced Service Discovery in Bluetooth. *IEEE Computer*, *35*(6), 96–99. doi:10.1109/MC.2002.1009177

Baader, F., Brandt, S., & Lutz, C. (2005). Pushing the EL envelope. *Proceedings of 19th International Joint Conference on Artificial Intelligence*, 364–399.

Baader, F., Calvanese, D., McGuinness, D., Nardi, D., & Patel-Schneider, P. (2002). *The Description Logic Handbook*. Cambridge, UK: Cambridge University Press.

Baader, F., Hollunder, B., Nebel, B., Profitlich, H., & Franconi, E. (1994). An empirical analysis of optimization techniques for terminological representation systems. *Applied Intelligence*, *4*(2), 109–132. doi:10.1007/BF00872105

Baader, F., Lutz, C., & Suntisrivaraporn, B. (2006). CEL – a polynomial-time reasoner for life science ontologies. *Automated Reasoning*, 287–291.

Bobed, C., Yus, R., Bobillo, F., & Mena, E. (2015). Semantic reasoning on mobile devices: Do Androids dream of efficient reasoners? *Web Semantics: Science, Services, and Agents on the World Wide Web*, *35*, 167–183. doi:10.1016/j.websem.2015.09.002

Bormann, C., Castellani, A. P., & Shelby, Z. (2012). CoAP: An Application Protocol for Billions of Tiny Internet Nodes. *IEEE Internet Computing*, *16*(2), 62–67. doi:10.1109/MIC.2012.29

Colucci, S., Di Noia, T., Pinto, A., Ragone, A., Ruta, M., & Tinelli, E. (2007). A Non-Monotonic Approach to Semantic Matchmaking and Request Refinement in E-Marketplaces. *International Journal of Electronic Commerce*, *12*(2), 127–154. doi:10.2753/JEC1086-4415120205

Compton, M., Barnaghi, P., Bermudez, L., Garcìa-Castro, R., Corcho, O., Cox, S., & Taylor, K. et al. (2012). The SSN ontology of the W3C semantic sensor network incubator group. *Web Semantics: Science, Services, and Agents on the World Wide Web*, *17*, 25–32. doi:10.1016/j.websem.2012.05.003

De Virgilio, R., Di Sciascio, E., Ruta, M., Scioscia, F., & Torlone, R. (2011). Semantic-based RFID data management. Unique Radio Innovation for the 21st Century, 111-141. doi:10.1007/978-3-642-03462-6_6

Di Noia, T., Di Sciascio, E., Donini, F. M., Ruta, M., Scioscia, F., & Tinelli, E. (2008). Semantic-based Bluetooth-RFID interaction for advanced resource discovery in pervasive contexts. *International Journal on Semantic Web and Information Systems*, *4*(1), 50–74. doi:10.4018/jswis.2008010104

Giannakis, M., & Louis, M. (2016). A multi-agent based system with big data processing for enhanced supply chain agility. *Journal of Enterprise Information Management*, *29*(5), 706–727. doi:10.1108/JEIM-06-2015-0050

Glimm, B., Horrocks, I., Motik, B., Stoilos, G., & Wang, Z. (2014). HermiT: An OWL 2 reasoner. *Journal of Automated Reasoning*, *53*(3), 245–269. doi:10.1007/s10817-014-9305-1

Gobelbecker, M., & Dornhege, C. (2009). Realistic Cities in Simulated Environments - An OpenStreetMap to Robocup Rescue Converter. *Proceedings of 4th International Workshop on Synthetic Simulation and Robotics to Mitigate Earthquake Disaster (SRMED 2009)*.

Haarslev, V., & Müller, R. (2001). Racer system description. *Automated Reasoning*, 701–705.

Horridge, M., & Bechhofer, S. (2011). The OWL API: A Java API for OWL Ontologies. *Semantic Web*, *2*(1), 11–21.

Horrocks, I., & Patel-Schneider, P. (1999). Optimizing description logic subsumption. *Journal of Logic and Computation*, *9*(3), 267–293. doi:10.1093/logcom/9.3.267

Kazakov, Y. (2009). Consequence-driven reasoning for Horn SHIQ ontologies. *International Joint Conference on Artificial Intelligence*, *9*, 2040–2045.

Kazakov, Y., & Klinov, P. (2013). Experimenting with ELK Reasoner on Android. *Proceedings of 2nd International Workshop on OWL Reasoner Evaluation (ORE)*, 68–74.

Kazakov, Y., Krötzsch, M., & Simancík, F. (2014). The Incredible ELK. *Journal of Automated Reasoning, 53*(1), 1–61. doi:10.1007/s10817-013-9296-3

Kim, T., Park, I., Hyun, S., & Lee, D. (2010). MiRE4OWL: Mobile Rule Engine for OWL. *Proceedings of the 34th IEEE Annual Computer Software and Applications Conference Workshops (CompSACW),* 317–322.

Kleemann, T., & Sinner, A. (2006). User Profiles and Matchmaking on Mobile Phones. In *Proceedings of 16th International Conference on Applications of Declarative Programming and Knowledge Management (INAP 2005)* (pp. 135-147). Springer. doi:10.1007/11963578_11

Koch, F., Meyer, J.-J. C., Dignum, F., & Rahwan, I. (2006). Programming deliberative agents for mobile services: the 3APL-M platform. In Programming multi-agent systems (pp. 222–235). Springer.

Lawley, M. J., & Bousquet, C. (2010). Fast classification in Protégé: Snorocket as an OWL 2 EL reasoner. *Proceedings of 6th Australasian Ontology Workshop (IAOA'10),* 45-49.

Li, L., & Horrocks, I. (2004). A software framework for matchmaking based on Ssemantic Wweb technology. *International Journal of Electronic Commerce, 8*(4), 39–60.

Liu, Q. (2013). U–commerce research: A literature review and classification. *International Journal of Ad Hoc and Ubiquitous Computing, 12*(3), 177–187. doi:10.1504/IJAHUC.2013.052414

Matentzoglu, N., Leo, J., Hudhra, V., Sattler, U., & Parsia, B. (2015). A Survey of Current, Stand-alone OWL Reasoners. *Proceedings of the 4th OWL Reasoner Evaluation (ORE) Workshop,* 68-79.

McBride, B. (2002). Jena: A Semantic Web toolkit. *IEEE Internet Computing, 6*(6), 55–59. doi:10.1109/MIC.2002.1067737

Moguillansky, M., Wassermann, R., & Falappa, M. (2010). An argumentation machinery to reason over inconsistent ontologies. *Advances in Artificial Intelligence–IBERAMIA, 2010,* 100–109.

Motik, B., Horrocks, I., & Kim, S. M. (2012). Delta-reasoner: a semantic web reasoner for an intelligent mobile platform. *Proceedings of the 21st International Conference Companion on World Wide Web,* 63–72. doi:10.1145/2187980.2187988

Musen, M. A. (2015). The Protégé project: a look back and a look forward. *AI Matters, 1*(4), 4-12.

Parsia, B., Matentzoglu, N., Gonçalves, R. S., Glimm, B., & Steigmiller, A. (2015). The OWL reasoner evaluation (ORE) 2015 competition report. *Journal of Automated Reasoning,* 1–28.

Pfisterer, D., Romer, K., Bimschas, D., Hasemann, H., Hauswirth, M., Karnstedt, M., & Truong, C. et al. (2011). SPITFIRE: Toward a Semantic Web of things. *IEEE Communications Magazine, 49*(11), 40–48. doi:10.1109/MCOM.2011.6069708

Ragone, A., Di Noia, T., Di Sciascio, E., Donini, F. M., Colucci, S., & Colasuonno, F. (2007). Fully automated web services discovery and composition through concept covering and concept abduction. *International Journal of Web Services Research, 4*(3), 85–112. doi:10.4018/jwsr.2007070105

Ruta, M., Di Noia, T., Di Sciascio, E., Piscitelli, G., & Scioscia, F. (2008). A semantic-based mobile registry for dynamic RFID-based logistics support. *Proceedings of the 10th International Conference on Electronic Commerce*, 1-9. doi:10.1145/1409540.1409576

Ruta, M., Di Sciascio, E., & Scioscia, F. (2011). Concept abduction and contraction in semantic-based P2P environments. *Web Intelligence and Agent Systems*, *9*(3), 179–207.

Ruta, M., Scioscia, F., De Filippis, D., Ieva, S., Binetti, M., & Di Sciascio, E. (2014). A semantic-enhanced augmented reality tool for OpenStreetMap POI discovery. In *Transportation Research Procedia. 17th Meeting of the EURO Working Group on Transportation* (pp. 479-488). Elsevier.

Ruta, M., Scioscia, F., Di Noia, T., & Di Sciascio, E. (2009). Reasoning in Pervasive Environments: an Implementation of Concept Abduction with Mobile OODBMS. *Proceedings of 2009 IEEE/WIC/ACM International Conference on Web Intelligence*, 145–148. doi:10.1109/WI-IAT.2009.29

Ruta, M., Scioscia, F., Di Noia, T., & Di Sciascio, E. (2010). A hybrid ZigBee/Bluetooth approach to mobile semantic grids. *Computer Systems Science and Engineering*, *25*(3), 235–249.

Ruta, M., Scioscia, F., & Di Sciascio, E. (2010). Mobile Semantic-based Matchmaking: a fuzzy DL approach. *Proceedings of the 7th Extended Semantic Web Conference*, 16–30. doi:10.1007/978-3-642-13486-9_2

Ruta, M., Scioscia, F., & Di Sciascio, E. (2012). Enabling the Semantic Web of Things: framework and architecture. *Proceedings of the Sixth IEEE International Conference on Semantic Computing (ICSC 2012)*, 345-347. doi:10.1109/ICSC.2012.42

Ruta, M., Scioscia, F., Di Sciascio, E., & Bilenchi, I. (2016). OWL API for iOS: early implementation and results. In *Proceedings of the OWL: Experiences and Directions (OWLED) and OWL Reasoner Evaluation Workshop (OWLED-ORE)* (pp. 141-152). Springer.

Ruta, M., Scioscia, F., Ieva, S., Capurso, G., & Di Sciascio, E. (2017). Semantic Blockchain to Improve Scalability in the Internet of Things. *Open Journal of Internet Of Things*, *3*(1), 46-61.

Ruta, M., Scioscia, F., Ieva, S., De Filippis, D., & Di Sciascio, E. (2015). Indoor/outdoor mobile navigation via knowledge-based POI discovery in augmented reality. *Proceedings of the 3rd International Workshop on Data Oriented Constructive Mining and Multi-Agent Simulation and the 7th International Workshop on Emergent Intelligence on Networked Agents (DOCMAS/WEIN-2015)*, 26-30. doi:10.1109/WI-IAT.2015.243

Ruta, M., Scioscia, F., Loseto, G., & Di Sciascio, E. (2014). Semantic-based resource discovery and orchestration in Home and Building Automation: A multi-agent approach. *IEEE Transactions on Industrial Informatics*, *10*(1), 730–741. doi:10.1109/TII.2013.2273433

Ruta, M., Scioscia, F., Pinto, A., Di Sciascio, E., Gramegna, F., Ieva, S., & Loseto, G. (2013). Resource annotation, dissemination and discovery in the Semantic Web of Things: a CoAP-based framework. *Proceedings International Conference on Green Computing and Communication (GreenCom) and Internet of Things (iThings) and Cyber, Physical and Social Computing (CPSCom)*, 527-534. doi:10.1109/GreenCom-iThings-CPSCom.2013.103

Ruta, M., Scioscia, F., Pinto, A., Gramegna, F., Ieva, S., Loseto, G., & Di Sciascio, E. (2017). Cooperative Semantic Sensor Networks for pervasive computing contexts. In *Proceedings of the 7th IEEE International Workshop on Advances in Sensors and Interfaces (IWASI 2017)* (pp. 38-43). New York: IEEE. doi:10.1109/IWASI.2017.7974209

Scioscia, F., Binetti, M., Ruta, M., Ieva, S., & Di Sciascio, E. (2014). A Framework and a Tool for Semantic Annotation of POIs in OpenStreetMap. *Transportation Research Procedia. 16th Meeting of the EURO Working Group on Transportation*, 1092-1101.

Scioscia, F., Ruta, M., & Di Sciascio, E. (2015). A swarm of Mini-MEs: reasoning and information aggregation in ubiquitous multi-agent contexts. *4th OWL Reasoner Evaluation Workshop (ORE 2015), CEUR Workshop Proceedings, 1207*, 15-22.

Scioscia, F., Ruta, M., Loseto, G., Gramegna, F., Ieva, S., Pinto, A., & Di Sciascio, E. (2014). A mobile matchmaker for the Ubiquitous Semantic Web. *International Journal on Semantic Web and Information Systems*, *10*(4), 77–100. doi:10.4018/ijswis.2014100104

Shelby, Z. (2012). *Constrained RESTful Environments (CoRE) Link Format.* Internet Engineering Task Force (IETF) Request For Comments (RFC) 6690. Retrieved June 30th, 2017, from https://tools.ietf.org/html/rfc6690

Sinner, A., & Kleemann, T. (2005, July). KRHyper - In Your Pocket. *Proceedings of 20th International Conference on Automated Deduction (CADE)*, 452-457.

Sirin, E., Parsia, B., Cuenca-Grau, B., Kalyanpur, A., & Katz, Y. (2007). Pellet: A practical OWL-DL reasoner. *Web Semantics: Science, Services, and Agents on the World Wide Web, 5*(2), 51–53. doi:10.1016/j.websem.2007.03.004

Steigmiller, A., Liebig, T., & Glimm, B. (2014). Konclude: System description. *Web Semantics: Science, Services, and Agents on the World Wide Web*, *27*, 78–85. doi:10.1016/j.websem.2014.06.003

Steller, L., & Krishnaswamy, S. (2008). Pervasive Service Discovery: mTableaux Mobile Reasoning. *International Conference on Semantic systems (I-Semantics)*, 93-101.

Tai, W., Keeney, J., & O'Sullivan, D. (2011). COROR: a composable rule-entailment OWL reasoner for resource-constrained devices. *Rule-Based Reasoning, Programming, and Applications*, 212–226.

Teege, G. (1994). Making the Difference: A Subtraction Operation for Description Logics. *Proceedings of the Fourth International Conference on the Principles of Knowledge Representation and Reasoning (KR94)*, 540–550. doi:10.1016/B978-1-4832-1452-8.50145-7

Tsarkov, D., & Horrocks, I. (2006). FaCT++ description logic reasoner: System description. *Automated Reasoning*, 292–297.

von Hessling, A., Kleemann, T., & Sinner, A. (2004). Semantic User Profiles and their Applications in a Mobile Environment. *Workshop on Aartificial Iintelligence in Mmobile Ssystems (AIMS)*, 59-63.

World Wide Web Consortium. (2012). *OWL 2 Web Ontology Language Structural Specification and Functional-Style Syntax* (2nd ed.). W3C Recommendation 11 December 2012. Retrieved June 30th, 2017, from https://www.w3.org/TR/owl2-syntax/

World Wide Web Consortium. (2014). *RDF 1.1 Concepts and Abstract Syntax.* W3C Recommendation 25 February 2014. Retrieved June 30th, 2017, from https://www.w3.org/TR/rdf11-concepts/

Zhou, Y., Nenov, Y., Grau, B. C., & Horrocks, I. (2015). Ontology-based Query Answering with PA-GOdA. *Proceedings of the 4th OWL Reasoner Evaluation (ORE) Workshop*, 1-7.

Chapter 11
Cataloguing the Context of Public SPARQL Endpoints

Ali Hasnain
NUI Galway, Ireland

Qaiser Mehmood
NUI Galway, Ireland

Syeda Sana e Zainab
NUI Galway, Ireland

Aidan Hogan
DCC, University of Chile, Chile

ABSTRACT

Access to hundreds of knowledge bases has been made available on the Web through SPARQL endpoints. Unfortunately, few endpoints publish descriptions of their content. It is thus unclear how agents can learn about the content of a given endpoint. This research investigates the feasibility of a system that gathers information about public endpoints by querying directly about their own content. It would thus be feasible to build a centralised catalogue describing the content indexed by individual endpoints by issuing them SPARQL 1.1 queries; this catalogue could be searched and queried by agents looking for endpoints with content they are interested in. However, the coverage of the catalogue is bounded by the limitations of public endpoints themselves: some may not support SPARQL 1.1, some may return partial responses, some may throw exceptions for expensive aggregate queries, etc. The goal is twofold: 1) using VoID as a bar, to empirically investigate the extent to which endpoints can describe their own content, and 2) to build and analyse the capabilities of an online catalogue.

INTRODUCTION

Linked Data aims at making data available on the Web in an interoperable format so that agents can discover, access, combine and consume content from different sources with higher levels of automation than would otherwise be possible (Heath & Bizer, 2011) . The envisaged result is a "Web of Data": a Web of structured data with rich semantic links where agents can query in a unified manner – across

DOI: 10.4018/978-1-5225-5042-6.ch011

sources – using standard languages and protocols. Over the past few years, hundreds of knowledge bases with billions of facts have been published according to the Semantic Web standards (using RDF as a data model and RDFS and OWL to provide explicit semantics) following the Linked Data principles.

As a convenience for consumer agents, Linked Data publishers often provide a SPARQL endpoint for querying their local content (Jentzsch, Cyganiak, & Bizer, 2011) . SPARQL is a declarative query language for RDF in which graph pattern matching, disjunctive unions, optional clauses, dataset construction, solution modifiers, etc., can be used to query RDF knowledge bases; the recent SPARQL 1.1 release adds features such as aggregates, property paths, sub-queries, federation, and so on (Harris, Seaborne, & Prud'hommeaux, 2013). Hundreds of public endpoints have been published in the past few years for knowledge bases of various sizes and topics (Buil-Aranda, Hogan, Umbrich, & Vandenbussche, 2013; Jentzsch et al., 2011). Using these endpoints, clients can receive direct answers to complex queries using a single request to the server.

However, it is still unclear how clients (be they human users or software agents) should find endpoints relevant for their needs in the first place (Buil-Aranda et al., 2013; Paulheim & Hertling, 2013). A client may have a variety of needs when looking for an endpoint, where they may, for example, seek endpoints with data:

1. About a given resource, e.g., *michael jackson*;
2. About instances of a particular type of class, e.g., *proteins*;
3. About a certain type of relationship between resources, e.g., *directs-movie*;
4. About certain types of values associated with resources, e.g., *rating*;
5. About resources within a given context or with specific values, for example, *crimes with location u.k. in year 1967 or rat genes and disease strains*;
6. A combination of one or more of the above.

Likewise a client may vary in how they are best able to specify these needs: some clients may only have keywords; others may know the specific IRI(s) of the resource, class or property they are interested in; some may be able to specify concrete queries or sub-queries that they wish to answer.

It can be argued that a service offering agents the ability to find relevant public endpoints on the Web would serve as an important part of the SPARQL querying infrastructure, enabling ad-hoc discovery of datasets over the Web. However, realising such a service over the current SPARQL infrastructure on the Web is challenging. Looking at the literature (in particular, works on the related problem of federated querying (Acosta, Vidal, Lampo, Castillo, & Ruckhaus, 2011; Harth et al., 2010; Hasnain et al., 2014, 2017a; Quilitz & Leser, 2008; Schwarte, Haase, Hose, Schenkel, & Schmidt, 2011), authors can find two high-level approaches that have been investigated thus far:

- **Runtime Queries:** The first option is to take an agent's request and query the endpoints directly at runtime to determine if they have relevant metadata or not (Schwarte et al., 2011). For example, if the agent were interested in instances of mo:MusicalWork,[1] one could issue a list of endpoints the following query:

Any endpoint returning true for this query would contain information relevant to the original agent. Likewise, more complex queries could be used depending on the user's need. For example, if a user were interested in endpoints with more than 100 such instances, the service could issue:

Table 1.

```
ASK WHERE { ?s a mo:MusicalWork }
```

Table 2.

```
SELECT (COUNT(DISTINCT ?s) AS ?c)
WHERE { ?s a mo:MusicalWork }
```

Any endpoint returning a result greater than 100 would be relevant.

- **Published Content Descriptions:** The second option is to rely on a static description of the content of each endpoint (Acosta et al., 2011; Harth et al., 2010; Quilitz & Leser, 2008; Schwarte et al., 2011). These works either assume that a description is available in a popular format, such as the Vocabulary of Interlinked Datasets (Alexander, Cyganiak, Hausenblas, & Zhao, 2009), or a custom format (Acosta et al., 2011; Harth et al., 2010; Quilitz & Leser, 2008). For example, the VoID vocabulary allows for defining class partitions that not only state which classes are in a dataset, but how many instances it has, which properties appear, and so forth (Alexander et al., 2009). These descriptions can then be used directly to find endpoints with relevant content.

However, these approaches are themselves problematic.

With respect to the first approach, each user request would require a query to be sent to several hundred public endpoints, which would incur very slow response times and could flood public services with too many requests. Likewise, users would need to know the IRIs of the resources, classes and/or properties they are interested in where supporting keyword search would be cumbersome to support: (i) although SPARQL does support functions such as REGEX that could be used to find relevant terms in literals, these functions are often executed as post-filtering operations, incurring unpredictable performance; (ii) although many SPARQL engines do build and maintain inverted indexes for efficient full-text search with keywords, this support is non-standard, different engines support full-text search in different manners, and determining the engine powering a SPARQL endpoint is non-trivial (Buil-Aranda et al., 2013).

With respect to the second approach, Buil-Aranda et al. (Buil-Aranda et al., 2013) previously observed that only one third of public SPARQL endpoints give static descriptions of their content in a standard location using suitable vocabularies such as VoID, and even where they are provided, it is unclear what level of detail these descriptions contain or indeed how accurate or up-to-date these descriptions are. Over the past several years, at least 159 distinct websites have begun hosting SPARQL endpoints (Buil-Aranda et al., 2013). Putting the burden on publishers to provide static descriptions of their endpoints' content or to otherwise change how they host data would incur a prohibitive technical and social cost.

For these reasons, the feasibility of a third approach is proposed:

- **Computing Content Descriptions:** Rather than relying on publishers to compute and keep content descriptions up to date, authors proposes to compute such descriptions directly from the endpoints themselves. In particular, it is proposed to design a set of queries that can be issued to endpoints to learn about their content, where the results of these queries can then be used to build a catalogue that enables clients to find endpoints with relevant content.

This approach offers a number of useful trade-offs when compared with the previous two approaches discussed earlier.

Comparing the use of computed content descriptions with runtime queries, in the former case, the client will query a centrally indexed catalogue, which incurs a lower cost, both for the client in terms of response time, and also for the remote SPARQL infrastructure in terms of the number of requests generated. However, the client will be restricted to finding endpoints using the metadata collected in the catalogue. For this reason, it is important for the catalogue to capture general descriptions of content.

When compared with using published content descriptions, it is not needed to assume that such descriptions are provided by the publishers of SPARQL endpoints independently of the endpoint itself. Also, by computing the content descriptions, it is ensured that the endpoint is still available (since it needs to answer the queries issued), that the description is at least as recent as the last time the descriptions were computed, and that the statistics have a simple SPARQL query that acts as provenance (rather than using descriptions provided by the publishers themselves that could be produced by tools with, e.g., different interpretations of statistics or that may include manual approximations). However, it is not clear if public endpoints would be able to support the type of complex SPARQL query required to compute detailed content descriptions, and indeed certain types of descriptors (e.g., licence) may not be automatically computed from the endpoint but rather require the perspective of the publisher.

This work explores the feasibility of computing content descriptions directly from SPARQL endpoints. More concretely, SPORTAL (SPARQL PORTAL) is proposed which is a centralised catalogue indexing content descriptions computed from individual SPARQL endpoints (Hasnain et al., 2016a, 2016b). The goal of SPORTAL is to help both human and software agents find public SPARQL endpoints relevant for their needs. The system makes minimal assumptions about how data are hosted: SPORTAL relies only on SPARQL queries to gather information about the content of each endpoint and hence only assumes a working SPARQL interface rather than requiring the publishers hosting endpoints to provide additional descriptions of the datasets. Rather than send a query to each public endpoint at runtime, offline queries were issued to each endpoint to gather metadata about its content, which are later used to find relevant endpoints. Taking a simple example, instead of querying each endpoint every time an agent is looking for a given class, can occasionally query each endpoint (on a fortnightly basis) for an up-to-date list of their classes and use that list to find relevant endpoints for the agent at runtime.

One of the main design questions for SPORTAL then is: what content descriptions should such a system try to compute from endpoints? Ideally the content descriptions should be as general as possible, supporting a variety of different types of clients and searches. With respect to the information collected, SPARQL is a powerful query language that can be used to learn about the underlying knowledge base of the endpoint. With the advent of novel features in SPARQL 1.1 like aggregates, it is now possible to formulate queries that ask, e.g., how many triples the knowledge base contains, which classes or properties are used, how many unique instances of each class appears, which properties are used most frequently with instances of which classes, and so on. In this sense, it can be argued that - at least in theory - SPARQL endpoints can be considered *self-descriptive*: they can describe their own content.

On the other hand, SPORTAL is limited in what it can collect by practical thresholds on the amount of data that a SPARQL endpoint will return. Buil-Aranda et al. (Buil-Aranda et al., 2013) found that many endpoints return a maximum of 10,000 results: given that many endpoints contain millions of resources and text literals, this rules out, for example, building a complete inverted index over the content of an individual endpoint, or indexing all resources that an endpoint mentions. In any case, the goal of SPORTAL is to compute concise content descriptions rather than mirroring remote endpoint content (which would be prohibitively costly for both SPORTAL and the remote endpoints, particularly to keep up-to-date). Thus, the research focuses on computing concise, schema-level descriptions of endpoints. Using such descriptions, one can directly find relevant endpoints given queries of type 2, 3, 4 mentioned earlier, and can indirectly help with other forms of queries (e.g., to find endpoints that contain instances of GENE, though they may not necessary be from a rat). In particular, focus was on computing extended Vocabulary of Interlinked Datasets (VoID) descriptions from endpoints: VoID has become the de-facto standard for describing datasets in RDF (Alexander et al., 2009), and is also used in federated scenarios to find relevant endpoints (Acosta et al., 2011; Akar, Halaç, Ekinci, & Dikenelli, 2012; Basca & Bernstein, 2014; Hasnain et al., 2014, 2017a, 2017b; Quilitz & Leser, 2008; Schwarte et al., 2011).

SPORTAL is further limited by the inability of some endpoints to return answers to complex queries. Buil-Aranda et al. (Buil-Aranda et al., 2013) previously reported that endpoints may exhibit performance and reliability issues, may return partial results, etc. Some endpoints may not support SPARQL 1.1, some may be hosted on underpowered machines, others may index very large and/or diverse datasets over which complex aggregates cannot be successfully executed, and so forth. This again creates a practical limit with respect to how detailed a content description SPORTAL can generate for certain endpoints. For example, in later results it can be seen while 93.8% of operational public endpoints respond successfully when asked for a list of all classes in their dataset, only 40.2% respond successfully when additionally asked how many instances those classes have. Thus, the SPORTAL catalogue would include metadata about the classes that appear in 93.8% of the catalogued endpoints, but only in 40.2% cases would the catalogue have information about how many instances appear in those classes.

Rather than limiting ourselves to building uniform descriptions of each endpoint based on information that can be computed from, say, >90% of endpoints, SPORTAL also considers more complex queries in its scope: while most endpoints cannot return responses to such queries, a non-trivial percentage of endpoints do respond. In the interest of collecting as much data as possible from these latter endpoints, these more complex queries were included. As a result, the descriptive metadata available for an individual endpoint may differ from others depending on its ability to answer increasingly complex queries over its dataset. A core contribution is thus to evaluate the ability of public SPARQL endpoints to answer increasingly complex self-descriptive queries, which reflects the coverage of high-level metadata available to the SPORTAL catalogue (and similar agents) using only the SPARQL interface.

More specifically, the working hypothesis is that -- despite problems with endpoint reliability and performance -- by computing content descriptions using self-descriptive queries issued directly to endpoints, authors can create a catalogue with (i) broader coverage and (ii) more up-to-date information than existing catalogues of SPARQL endpoints that rely on currently-available content descriptions provided by the publishers themselves. Towards investigating the validity of this hypothesis, work is structured as follows:

- *Section* 2 begins with some background on related areas: Linked Data access methods, proposals for describing RDF datasets, proposals for schemes to help find relevant SPARQL endpoints, as well as discussion on how the problem could be viewed from the perspective of Linked Data as a Distributed System.

- In *Section* 3, describes how the content of endpoints can be described in a general-purpose, automated manner. In order to extract a *description* of the content of each endpoint, this research proposes to use a set of 29 self-descriptive SPARQL (1.1) queries that capture a large "computable" subset of a VoID description (Alexander et al., 2009) as well as some additional features.[2]

- In *Section* 4, first investigates, in a controlled environment, how well current SPARQL 1.1 engines can process these self-describing queries, some of which involve aggregation across an entire dataset and thus may require a prohibitive amount of processing, especially for large datasets. Experiments were run over four datasets of increasing size and complexity using four SPARQL engines - 4store (Harris, Lamb, & Shadbolt, 2009), Jena/Fuseki[3], Sesame (Broekstra, Kampman, & van Harmelen, 2002) and Virtuoso (Erling & Mikhailov, 2009) - to see how well the self-descriptive queries perform. These engines are mostly commonly used to power public SPARQL endpoints (Buil-Aranda et al., 2013).

- With an idea of how the queries perform in a local environment for a variety of datasets and engines, in *Section* 5, investigates how effectively public SPARQL endpoints process these queries. A list of 526 public endpoints was considered and investigate the ratio that can answer each of the self-descriptive queries and characterise the typical performance one can expect in a realistic, uncontrolled environment. The results show that, depending on the query, the ratio of operational endpoints[4] returning non-empty (but possibly partial) responses vary from 25 - 94%.

- In *Section* 6, introduces the SPORTAL catalogue based on the results collected from the remote endpoints. This work describes the way it can help both human and software agents to find public endpoints on the Web that may be relevant for their needs. Based on the results of the previous questions, the section discusses the (in)completeness of the catalogue and both the capabilities and limitations of the system. A high-level comparison of the SPORTAL catalogue is also provided with two catalogues based on publisher-provided content descriptions: VoID STORE and DATAHUB.

- *Section* 7 concludes by recapitulating the main results and lessons learnt with respect to the goal of building a central catalogue of public SPARQL endpoints.

BACKGROUND

Before continuing to the core of the work, some brief background is presented on (1) methods for accessing Linked Data, (2) the problem of peer discovery in the area of Distributed Systems, (3) works on finding relevant SPARQL endpoints, and (4) techniques for describing/ summarising RDF datasets.

Linked Data Access Methods

Traditionally there have been three methods provided for consumer agents to access content from knowledge bases published as Linked Data: *DEREFERENCING*, where IRIs of interest are looked up via HTTP; *DUMPS*, where the entire content of a dataset is made available for download; and *SPARQL ENDPOINTS*, where a query interface is provided over the local content. A more recent proposal - *LINKED DATA FRAGMENTS* (Verborgh et al., 2014) - has recently begun to gain attention.

Both dereferencing and dumps are lightweight methods in-tune with current practices on the Web; however, they can be inefficient for agents to use. Consider an agent wishing to retrieve the populations of Asian capitals from DBpedia. An agent has no direct way of finding the correct IRIs to dereference; even if they did, DBpedia specifies a Crawl-delay of 10 seconds: assuming that the *DBpedia* IRIs of 49 Asian capitals needed dereferencing, a polite agent would require 8 minutes to retrieve the respective documents and would ultimately use one triple out of potentially hundreds of thousands in each document. Using a dump would entail downloading an entire dataset to get at 49 triples; hosting a local dump mirror would require constant refreshing.

Hence publishers provide SPARQL endpoints as a convenient alternative to dereferencing or dumps. To get the populations of Asian capitals, an agent could run the following query against the DBpedia SPARQL endpoint[5]:

All going well, the query will return populations in less than a second. Likewise only the data that the client is interested in will be transferred. However, SPARQL endpoints push the burden from data consumers to producers: hosting such a public query service is expensive and as a result, endpoints may not be able to answer all queries for all consumer agents (Buil-Aranda et al., 2013). Despite problems with reliability, SPARQL endpoints still offer an appealing method for consumer agents to interact with remote Linked Data knowledge bases where endpoints such as DBpedia serve millions of queries for clients (Gallego, Fernández, Martínez-Prieto, & de la Fuente, 2011).

As an alternative to SPARQL endpoints, Verborgh et al. (Verborgh et al., 2014), propose methods for providing and organising multiple access methods to a Linked Dataset, including a lightweight "triple pattern fragment", which allows clients to request all triples matching a single pattern, the goal of which is to allow publishers to host highly reliable but greatly simplified query services, thus trying to strike a better balance between the costs on the client and server side. Although their Linked Data Fragments (LDF) proposal offers a valuable compromise between client and server costs, being a recent proposal, SPARQL endpoints still greatly outnumber the number of LDF servers on the Web.

SPARQL Endpoints as a Distributed System

Viewed from the perspective of Distributed Computing, each SPARQL endpoint on the Web involves a client- server architecture, where numerous clients use the SPARQL protocol to interface with a single external server.[6] However, when hundreds of public SPARQL endpoints are viewed collectively, they can be seen as forming a decentralised peer-to-peer (P2P) system. In particular, with the advent of SPARQL 1.1 Federation (Prud'hommeaux & Buil-Aranda, 2013), endpoints can query each other and thus may perform computation on behalf of other peers.

In this light, the goal of finding relevant SPARQL endpoints relates to the core problem of peer discovery in the P2P area, wherein a peer wishes to find another peer with a particular piece of data. To make this task more efficient, *structured P2P systems* impose an overall organisation on the network

Table 3.

```
SELECT ?pop ?city WHERE
{ ?city dct:subject dbc:Capitals_in_Asia ;
dbo:populationTotal ?pop . }
```

overlay to ensure rapid peer discovery; the most common structure is a Distributed Hash Table (DHT), which is effectively a distributed map where keys are hashed to determine on which peer(s) a given set of key - value pairs should be stored (Ratnasamy, Francis, Handley, Karp, & Shenker, 2001; Rowstron & Druschel, 2001; Stoica et al., 2003; Zhao et al., 2004). However, all such structured schemes assume that peers in the network can be assigned data, which is not true of SPARQL endpoints where peers themselves decide which datasets they wish to index.

As such, public SPARQL endpoints collectively form an *unstructured P2P system*, where, since there is no correlation imposed between a peer and the data it indexes, peer discovery would necessarily involve one of two options: a separate search index that records the content at each peer (e.g., trackers in BitTorrent (Qiu & Srikant, 2004), or blindly flooding the network with queries looking for the desired data from peers in a "brute force manner" (e.g., Gnutella (Ripeanu, Iamnitchi, & Foster, 2002)).

Rather than requiring a complete global structure or accepting zero structure, other proposals aim to strike a balance by imposing a limited form of structure over nodes. For example, routing indices (Crespo & Garcia-Molina, 2002) allow nodes to index whatever data they wish, but require that each peer must additionally store pointers to a neighbouring peer that is closer to the desired data; this avoids blind flooding of queries during peer discovery, instead allowing peers to be *routed* to relevant peer(s). Likewise, routing indexes avoid the need for a central index of peer content.

However, the goal is to enable peer discovery of SPARQL endpoints without changing the current infrastructure; therefore, it is important to explore options over the current infrastructure first before proposing that hundreds of stakeholders change how they host their data. For example, it was not presumed that publishers will agree to add and maintain routing indexes towards the endpoints of external publishers. Hence it is assumed that no structure is imposed on the peers, but rather that each SPARQL endpoint indexes its own data. Thus, the scenario is effectively unstructured: there is no guarantees about which data may appear at which endpoint/peer. The hypothesis instead is that the SPARQL query interface can be used to learn about the content at each peer.

Describing/Summarising RDF Datasets

With respect to building a central search service for endpoints based on their content, it would seem infeasible to index all of the data from the endpoint; hence some form of summary or schema overview must be indexed. A variety of works have proposed methods to describe and/or summarise RDF datasets.

In terms of describing metadata about RDF datasets, Cyganiak et al. (Cyganiak, Stenzhorn, Delbru, Decker, & Tummarello, 2008) propose Semantic Sitemaps to mark the locations of different Linked Data access points; however information captured is limited to broad concepts such as change frequency. Alexander et al. (Alexander et al., 2009) later proposed VoID for describing RDF datasets and the links between them. As can be seen that the vocabulary provides terms for describing high-level statistics about a dataset, as well as about the instances of specific classes and the usage of specific properties. A number of works have proposed extensions to the VoID vocabulary. Mountantonakis et al. (Mountantonakis et al., 2014) propose to extend VoID with metrics about the connectivity of pairs of data sources to capture, for example, the number of common RDF terms used in both sources, the increase in average node degree with both sources are combined, etc. Omitola et al. (Omitola et al., 2011) propose to extend VoID to allow publishers to describe in more depth the provenance of their dataset.

With respect to computing dataset descriptions, or profiling datasets, Bohm et al. (Böhm, Lorey, & Naumann, 2011) demonstrated that computing a VoID description for large datasets is feasible using

MapReduce techniques. As part of the LOD Laundromat service -- which aims to clean up and republish existing datasets in a more uniform manner - Beek et al. (Beek, Rietveld, Bazoobandi, Wielemaker, & Schlobach, 2014) compute a VoID description for each dataset indexed. More recently, Fetahu et al. (Fetahu et al., 2014) propose extracting topics from a dataset based on a combination of information retrieval techniques such as PageRank and HITS and Named Entity Recognition applied offline over the dataset. Abejan et al. (Abedjan, Grütze, Jentzsch, & Naumann, 2014) propose ProLOD++: a system to profile Linked Datasets that applies clustering techniques, statistical analysis, and association rules to find semantically related groups of entities, statistical distributions, properties that together uniquely identify resources, as well as suggested changes to the dataset/ontology. Mihindukulasooriya et al. (Mihinduku-lasooriya, Poveda-Villalón, García-Castro, & Gómez-Pérez, 2015) propose Loupe: a system that extracts a schema-level summary of a dataset similar to that captured by VoID (e.g., number of triples, number of instances per class, etc.), with additional information about namespaces, ontological definitions, etc.

Closer to the contribution, various works have proposed using SPARQL to extract high-level information about an RDF dataset. Auer et al. (Auer, Demter, Martin, & Lehmann, 2012) propose LODstats, which applies analytics over a stream of RDF data but which uses SPARQL filters to (reject)/select (ir) relevant triples; use of SPARQL is limited to filters. Langegger & Wöß propose RDFStats (Langegger & Wöß, 2009), which uses a pipeline of SPARQL (1.0) queries to generate a histogram on a per-class basis, representing the predicates and types of values associated with its instances. Holst & Höfig (Holst & Höfig, 2013) propose the use of SPARQL 1.1 queries to discover specific aspects of an RDF dataset, but the VoID is not considered and only run local experiments over three datasets. Mountantonakis et al. (Mountantonakis et al., 2014) propose a set of SPARQL 1.1 queries that can compute the connectivity metrics with which they extend VoID. Mäkelä (Mäkelä, 2014) propose Aether: a system for extracting extended VoID descriptions from a SPARQL 1.1 compliant endpoint; this work is perhaps most similar in spirit to ours, however, the focus is more on getting an overview of a known endpoint rather than building a catalogue that can be used by clients to find endpoints of interest.

The SPARQL 1.1 Service Description (SD) (Williams, 2013), vocabulary was recently recommended by the W3C; however, unlike previously discussed works, which focus on describing the content of datasets, SD describes technical aspects of an endpoint, such as features supported, dataset configurations, etc.

Other works have focused on summarising the content of RDF datasets (rather than describing them using a high-level RDF description). Umbrich et al. (Umbrich, Hose, Karnstedt, Harth, & Polleres, 2011) propose to use an approximate, hash-based indexing structure, called a QTree, to aid in source selection; the QTree allows for determining which sources are likely to contain matches for a given RDF triple pattern but at a fraction of the size of the original dataset. Khatchadourian & Consens (Khatchadourian & Consens, 2010) propose creating bisimulation labels that capture connectivity in an RDF graph on the level of the namespaces of the instance URIs and the schema used. Campinas et al. (Campinas, Delbru, & Tummarello, 2013) propose using existing graph summary algorithms to summarise RDF graphs, where nodes that are equivalent per some relation - e.g., having the same types, or the same attributes - are collapsed into a single node to create a smaller summary graph.

Discovering SPARQL Endpoints

As previously discussed in the introduction, there are two high-level options for discovering SPARQL endpoints with relevant data: (1) flood the endpoints with queries, or (2) build a central search index. For example, federated SPARQL engines employ one or both of these strategies (Acosta et al., 2011;

Akar et al., 2012; Basca & Bernstein, 2014; Quilitz & Leser, 2008; Schwarte et al., 2011). The goal is to build a central catalogue based on data collected from endpoints through their SPARQL interfaces.

Paulheim & Hertling (Paulheim & Hertling, 2013) looked at how to find a SPARQL endpoint containing content about a given Linked Data URI: using VoID descriptions and the DATAHUB catalogue, one could find suitable endpoints for about 15% of the sample of ten thousand URIs considered. Mehdi et al. (Mehdi et al., 2014) looked at the problem of discovering endpoints that may be relevant to a set of domain-specific keywords: their approach involved generating a list of RDF literals from the keywords and flooding queries against endpoints to see if they contained, e.g., case or language-tag variations of the literals.

Buil-Aranda et al. (Buil-Aranda et al., 2013) propose SPARQLES as a catalogue of SPARQL endpoints, but focus on performance and stability metrics rather than cataloguing content; they do however remark that they could only find static descriptions for the content of about one third of the public endpoints surveyed, making endpoint discovery difficult. Likewise, the analysis by Lorey (Lorey, 2014) of public endpoints focused on characterising the performance offered by these services rather than on the problem of discovery.

There are a variety of locations online where lists of public endpoints can be found and searched over. For example, DATAHUB[7] provides a list of hundreds of Linked Datasets, which can be filtered to find those that offer SPARQL endpoint locations. One can, for example, search for datasets relating to UK crime and filter to only show those with SPARQL endpoints. However, the search functionality provided is limited in most cases to keyword search over the dataset title, or to browsing datasets with a given tag, etc. Still, the service often provides links to VoID files that could be used to catalogue the content of endpoints. Unlike SPORTAL however, these VoID files are provided by publishers rather than being computed from the endpoints. Hence, the catalogue will be compared later with that formed by collecting the VoID files that DATAHUB links to for each dataset.

As part of the RKBexplorer infrastructure (Glaser, Millard, & Jaffri, 2008), the VoID STORE allows for performing searches over VoID (2010) files submitted to the system. A service is also provided to find endpoints that index content about a given resource (using the REGEX patterns sometimes provided in VoID). This catalogue could thus be used by clients to find relevant SPARQL endpoints. Currently the store contains information related to 118 endpoints. Like DATAHUB - but unlike SPORTAL - the VoID files indexed by VoID STORE are again computed and uploaded by publishers.

Novelty

This research focuses on the problem of helping clients find relevant SPARQL endpoints. To the best of author's knowledge, there are two online services that clients could use to try to find SPARQL endpoints based on their content: DATAHUB and/or VoID STORE. However, both services rely on static content descriptions provided by publishers themselves. As noted by Buil-Aranda et al. (Buil-Aranda et al., 2013), many of the endpoints listed in the DATAHUB have been offline for years; also, of the endpoints surveyed, VoID descriptions are only available in the DATAHUB for 33.3% and in the VoID STORE for 22.4%. Authors instead propose to compute extended VoID descriptions for public endpoints directly through their SPARQL interface. A high-level comparison between SPORTAL, DATAHUB and VoID STORE is provided in *Section* 6.

SELF-DESCRIPTIVE QUERIES

With respect to describing the content of an endpoint, this section lists the set of SPARQL 1.1 queries that are used to compute a VoID-like description from the content indexed by an endpoint.

Functionality

First, step was to filter unavailable endpoints and to determine those that (partially) support SPARQL 1.1. An endpoint is considered available if it is accessible through the HTTP SPARQL protocol, it responds to a SPARQL-compliant query, and it returns a response in an appropriate SPARQL format; for this, query Q_{A1} (see Table 1) was used, which should be trivial for an endpoint to compute, returning a single binding for any triple. An endpoint is considered SPARQL 1.1 aware if it likewise responds to a query valid only in SPARQL 1.1; for this, query Q_{A2} (see Table 4) was used, which tests two features unique to SPARQL 1.1: sub-queries and the count aggregate function.[8]

Dataset-Level Statistics

Second, a set of queries to capture high-level "dataset-level" statistics is listed that form a core part of VoID. Five queries were issued, as listed in Table 5, to ascertain the number of triples (Q_{B1}), and the number of distinct classes (Q_{B2}), properties (Q_{B3}), subjects (Q_{B4}), and objects (Q_{B5}). These queries require support for SPARQL 1.1 COUNT and sub-query features (as tested in Q_{A2}). The <D> term refers to an IRI constructed from the SPARQL endpoint's URL to indicate the dataset it indexes.

Once these statistics are catalogued for public SPARQL endpoints, agents can use them to find endpoints indexing datasets that fall within a given range of triples in terms of overall size, or, for example, to find the endpoints with the largest datasets. Counts may be particularly useful - in combination with later categories - to order the endpoints; for example, to find the endpoints with a given class (using data from the next category) and order them by the total number of triples they index.

Class-Based Statistics

Third similar statistics about the instances of each class following the notion of *class partitions* in VoID were ascertained: a subset of the data considering only triples where instances of that class are in the subject position. Table 6 lists the six queries used. The first query (Q_{C1}) merely lists all class partitions. The other five queries (Q_{C2-6}) count the triples and distinct classes, predicates, subjects and objects for each class partition; e.g., Q_{C2} retrieves the number of triples where instances of that class are in the subject position. Queries Q_{C2-6} introduce COUNT, sub-queries and also GROUPBY features from SPARQL 1.1.

Table 4. Queries for basic functionalities

No	Query
Q_{A1}	SELECT * WHERE { ?s ?p ?o } LIMIT 1
Q_{A2}	SELECT (COUNT(*) as ?c) WHERE { SELECT * WHERE { ?s ?p ?o } LIMIT 1 }

Table 5. Queries for dataset-level VoID statistics

No	Query
Q_{B1}	CONSTRUCT { <D> v:triples ?x } WHERE { SELECT (COUNT(*) AS ?x) WHERE { ?s ?p ?o } }
Q_{B2}	CONSTRUCT { <D> v:classes ?x } WHERE { SELECT (COUNT(DISTINCT ?o) AS ?x) WHERE { ?s a ?o } }
Q_{B3}	CONSTRUCT { <D> v:properties ?x } WHERE { SELECT (COUNT(DISTINCT ?p) AS ?x) WHERE { ?s ?p ?o } }
Q_{B4}	CONSTRUCT { <D> v:distinctSubjects ?x } WHERE { SELECT (COUNT(DISTINCT ?s) AS ?x) WHERE { ?s ?p ?o } }
Q_{B5}	CONSTRUCT { <D> v:distinctObjects ?x } WHERE { SELECT (COUNT(DISTINCT ?o) AS ?x) WHERE { ?s ?p ?o } }

Table 6. Queries for statistics about classes

No	Query
Q_{C1}	CONSTRUCT { <D> v:classPartition [v:class ?c] } WHERE { ?s a ?c }
Q_{C2}	CONSTRUCT { v:classPartition [v:class ?c ; v:triples ?x] } WHERE { SELECT (COUNT(?p) AS ?x) ?c WHERE { ?s a ?c ; ?p ?o } GROUP BY ?c }
Q_{C3}	CONSTRUCT { v:classPartition [v:class ?c ; v:classes ?x] } WHERE { SELECT (COUNT(DISTINCT ?d) AS ?x) ?c WHERE { ?s a ?c, ?d } GROUP BY ?c }
Q_{C4}	CONSTRUCT { v:classPartition [v:class ?c ; v:properties ?x] } WHERE { SELECT (COUNT(DISTINCT ?p) AS ?x) ?c WHERE { ?s a ?c ; ?p ?o } GROUP BY ?c }
Q_{C5}	CONSTRUCT { v:classPartition [v:class ?c ; v:distinctSubjects ?x] } WHERE { SELECT (COUNT(DISTINCT ?s) AS ?x) ?c WHERE { ?s a ?c } GROUP BY ?c }
Q_{C6}	CONSTRUCT { v:classPartition [v:class ?c ; v:distinctObjects ?x] } WHERE { SELECT (COUNT(DISTINCT ?o) AS ?x) ?c WHERE { ?s a ?c ; ?p ?o } GROUP BY ?c }

Once catalogued, agents can use statistics describing class partitions of the datasets to find endpoints mentioning a given class, where they can additionally (for example) sort results in descending order according to the number of unique instances of that class, or triples used to define such instances, and so forth. Hence the counts computed by (Q_{C2-6}) help agents to distinguish endpoints that may only have one or two instances of a class to those with thousands or millions. Likewise, criteria can be combined arbitrarily for multiple classes, or with the overall statistics computed previously.

Property-Based Statistics

This section looks at property partitions in the dataset, where a property partition refers to the set of triples with that property term in the predicate position. Queries are listed in Table 7. As before, Q_{D1} lists the property partitions. (Q_{D2-4}), count the number of triples, distinct subjects and distinct objects. Classes (which would be '0' for all properties except rdf:type) or properties (which would always be '1') were not.

Using these statistics about property partitions in the catalogue, agents can, for example, retrieve a list of public endpoints using a given property ordered by the number of triples using that specific property.

Table 7. Queries for statistics about properties

No	Query
Q_{D1}	CONSTRUCT { v:propertyPartition [v:property ?p] } WHERE { ?s ?p ?o }
Q_{D2}	CONSTRUCT { v:propertyPartition [v:property ?p ; v:triples ?x] } WHERE { SELECT (COUNT(?o) AS ?x) ?p WHERE { ?s ?p ?o } GROUP BY ?p }
Q_{D3}	CONSTRUCT { v:propertyPartition [v:property ?p ; v:distinctSubjects ?x] } WHERE { SELECT (COUNT(DISTINCT ?s) AS ?x) ?p WHERE { ?s ?p ?o } GROUP BY ?p }
Q_{D4}	CONSTRUCT { v:propertyPartition [v:property ?p ; v:distinctObjects ?x] } WHERE { SELECT (COUNT(DISTINCT ?o) AS ?x) ?p WHERE { ?s ?p ?o } GROUP BY ?p }

Likewise criteria can be combined arbitrarily for multiple properties, or with the dataset- or class-level metadata previously collected; for example, an agent may wish to order endpoints by the ratio of triples using a given property (where the count from Q_{D2} for the property in question can be divided by the total triple count from Q_{B1}), or to find endpoints where all subjects have an rdfs:label value (where the count computed from Q_{D3} for that property should match the count for Q_{B4}).

Nested Class: Property Statistics

Fifth, the focus is to look at how classes and properties are used together in a dataset, gathering statistics on property partitions nested within class partitions: these statistics detail how properties are used for instances of specific classes. Table 8 lists the four queries used. Q_{E1} lists the property partitions nested inside the class partitions, and Q_{E2-4} count the number of triples using a given predicate for instances of that class, as well as the number of distinct subjects and objects those triples have. In terms of technical features, these queries involve GROUP BY over multiple terms. In general, the queries listed in this section are quite complex where one would expect that many endpoints would struggle to return metadata about their content at this detailed level of granularity.

An agent could use the resulting metadata to find endpoints describing instances of specific classes with specific properties, with filtering or sorting criteria based on, e.g., the number of triples. For example, an agent might be specifically interested in images of people, where they would be looking for the class-partition foaf:Person with the nested property-partition foaf:depicts. Using the previous statistics, it would have been possible to find endpoints that have data for the class foaf:Person and triples with

Table 8. Queries for nested property/class statistics

No	Query
Q_{E1}	CONSTRUCT { v:classPartition [v:class ?c ; v:propertyPartition [v:property ?p]] } WHERE { ?s a ?c ; ?p ?o }
Q_{E2}	CONSTRUCT { v:classPartition [v:class ?c v:propertyPartition [v:property ?p ; v:triples ?x]] } WHERE { SELECT (COUNT(?o) AS ?x) ?p WHERE { ?s a ?c ; ?p ?o } GROUP BY ?c ?p }
Q_{E3}	CONSTRUCT { v:classPartition [v:class ?c ; v:propertyPartition [v:distinctSubjects ?x]] } WHERE { SELECT (COUNT(DISTINCT ?s) AS ?x) ?c ?p WHERE { ?s a ?c ; ?p ?o } GROUP BY ?c ?p }
Q_{E4}	CONSTRUCT { v:classPartition [v:class ?c ; v:propertyPartition [v:distinctObjects ?x ; v:property ?p]] } WHERE { SELECT (COUNT(DISTINCT ?o) AS ?x) ?c ?p WHERE { ?s a ?c ; ?p ?o } GROUP BY ?c ?p }

the property foaf:depicts, but not that the images were defined for people. The counts from Q_{E2-E4} again allow an agent to filter or order endpoints by the amount of relevant

Miscellaneous Statistics

In the final set of experiments, the focus is to look at queries that yield statistics not supported by VoID as listed in Table 9. In particular, experiments were designed to see if endpoints can return a subset of statistics from the VoID Extension Vocabulary[9], which include counts of different types of unique RDF terms in different positions: subjects IRIs (Q_{F1}), subject blank nodes (Q_{F2}), objects IRIs (Q_{F3}), literals (Q_{F4}), object blank nodes (Q_{F5}), all blank nodes (Q_{F6}), all IRIs (Q_{F7}), and all terms (Q_{F8}). Inspired by the notion of "schema maps" as proposed by Kinsella et al. (Kinsella, Bojars, Harth, Breslin, & Decker, 2008), queries also count the classes that the subjects and objects of specific properties are instances of (Q_{F9-10}); these are "inverses" of queries (Q_{E3-4}).[10]

The resulting data could serve a number of purposes for agents looking for public endpoints. For example, the agent in question could look for datasets without any blank nodes or for datasets where a given number of the objects of a given property are of a certain type. Likewise, the user can combine these criteria with earlier criteria; for example, to find endpoints with more than ten million triples where at least 30% of the unique object terms are literals.

Table 9. Queries for miscellaneous statistics

No	Query
Q_{F1}	CONSTRUCT { e:distinctIRIReferenceSubjects ?x } WHERE { SELECT (COUNT(DISTINCT ?s) AS ?x) WHERE { ?s ?p ?o FILTER(isIri(?s))} }
Q_{F2}	CONSTRUCT { e:distinctBlankNodeSubjects ?x } WHERE { SELECT (COUNT(DISTINCT ?s) AS ?x) WHERE { ?s ?p ?o FILTER(isBlank(?s))} }
Q_{F3}	CONSTRUCT { e:distinctIRIReferenceObjects ?x } WHERE { SELECT (COUNT(DISTINCT ?o) AS ?x) WHERE { ?s ?p ?o FILTER(isIri(?o))} }
Q_{F4}	CONSTRUCT { e:distinctLiterals ?x } WHERE { SELECT (COUNT(DISTINCT ?o) AS ?x) WHERE { ?s ?p ?o FILTER(isLiteral(?o))} }
Q_{F5}	CONSTRUCT { e:distinctBlankNodeObjects ?x } WHERE { SELECT (COUNT(DISTINCT ?o) AS ?x) WHERE { ?s ?p ?o FILTER(isBlank(?o))} }
Q_{F6}	CONSTRUCT { e:distinctBlankNodes ?x } WHERE { SELECT (COUNT(DISTINCT ?b) AS ?x) WHERE { { ?s ?p ?b } UNION { ?b ?p ?o } FILTER(isBlank(?b)) } }
Q_{F7}	CONSTRUCT { e:distinctIRIReferences ?x } WHERE { SELECT (COUNT(DISTINCT ?u) AS ?x) WHERE { { ?u ?p ?o } UNION { ?s ?u ?o } UNION { ?s ?p ?u } FILTER(isIri(?u) } }
Q_{F8}	CONSTRUCT { e:distinctRDFNodes ?x } WHERE { SELECT (COUNT(DISTINCT ?n) AS ?x) WHERE { { ?n ?p ?o } UNION { ?s ?n ?o } UNION { ?s ?p ?n } } }
Q_{F9}	CONSTRUCT { v:propertyPartition [v:property ?p ; s:subjectTypes [s:subjectClass ?sType ; s:distinctMembers ?x]] } WHERE { SELECT (COUNT(?s) AS ?x) ?p ?sType WHERE { ?s ?p ?o . a ?sType . } GROUP BY ?p ?sType }
Q_{F10}	CONSTRUCT { v:propertyPartition [v:property ?p ; s:objectTypes [s:objectClass ?oType ; s:distinctMembers ?x]] } WHERE { SELECT (COUNT(?o) AS ?x) ?p ?oType WHERE { ?s ?p ?o . ?o a ?oType . } GROUP BY ?p ?oType }

LOCAL EXPERIMENTS

The first set of experiments were designed to test whether the SPARQL implementations can locally answer the queries specified in the previous section. These implementations are used to power individual endpoints and hence would like to see if running these queries is feasible in a locally controlled environment before running remote experiments.

Along these lines, given the 29 self-descriptive queries mentioned previously, four popular SPARQL query engines were tested: *Virtuoso* (07.10.3207), *Fuseki* (1.0.2), *4store* (4s-httpd/v1.1.4) and *Sesame* (2.7.12). Given that the cost of the self-descriptive queries listed previously depends directly on the size and nature of the dataset indexed, for each engine, experiments were performed with respect to the four real-world datasets listed in Table 10, representing a mix of datasets at a variety of scales and with a variety of diversity in predicates and classes used. The experiments are run on a server with *Ubuntu 14*, a *4x Intel Core i5 CPU (M540@2.53 GHz)* processor and 8 GB of *RAM*. A timeout of 10 minutes was set for the first result to return. Result-size thresholds were switched off where applicable.

All the engines passed the functionality tests. Table 11, lists the runtimes for all other queries (spanning Table 4-9), for the four datasets and the four engines. The results were manually inspected to only include runtimes where the correct response was returned. With respect to the (partially) failed queries, in the table, the differentiation is made between:

- **Empty Results (—):** Where zero results are returned, most commonly caused by a 10-minute timeout;
- **Partial Results (~):** Where the stream of results returned is correct but ends prematurely;
- **Incorrect Results (✗):** Where the results returned are false, most commonly caused by counts not considering all results or by query processor bugs.

  In the following, a high-level conclusion from these results is provided.

Datasets

Table 11 shows that while *Fuseki, Sesame* and *Virtuoso* successfully run almost all queries for *DRUG-BANK, JAMENDO* and *KEGG* – datasets around or below a million triples – all engines struggle for the DBpedia dataset, which is two orders of magnitude larger and contains two orders of magnitude more classes, predicates, objects and subjects. This is better illustrated by Figure 1, where the difference between *DBPEDIA* and the other datasets is evident in terms of success rate. Only Virtuoso managed to return correct results for some queries over *DBPEDIA*, including counts for triples, classes, properties, triples per property partition, blank node subjects, blank node objects and blank nodes in any position[11]

Table 10. High-level statistics for datasets used in local experiments

	Triples	Subjects	Predicates	Objects	Classes
DRUGBANK	517,023	19,693	119	276,142	8
JAMENDO	1,049,647	335,925	26	440,686	11
KEGG	1,090,830	34,260	21	939,258	4
DBPEDIA	114,456,676	11,194,893	53,200	27,518,753	447

and object IRIs. With the available memory, queries over the smaller datasets could be processed largely in-memory whereas queries over *DBPEDIA* may have led to a lot of on-disk processing.

Engines

With respect to the success rate of the four implementations, Table 11 and Figure 1, show that 4store struggled the most with the self-descriptive queries specified, returning correct results only for counts of classes, properties and blank nodes. Fuseki was the most reliable engine for the smaller datasets, successfully answering all queries over *DRUGBANK, JAMENDO* and *KEGG*, whereas *Sesame* and *Virtuoso* struggled on queries Q_{D1} and Q_{F10}. From further investigation, it was discovered that for Q_{D1} – list all property partitions – the engines were returning two output triples for every triple indexed, producing a large volume of non-lean data, as opposed to returning two output triples for every unique property. To get around this, a sub-query specifying DISTINCT on ?p could be used at the cost of requiring SPARQL 1.1 support. On the other hand, Q_{F10} would seem on face value to be the most expensive query in the collection, requiring an open join and aggregation step that may naturally fail even for small-to-medium-sized datasets.

Runtimes

Quite a large variance in runtimes between the different engines was observed, varying in orders of magnitude. In order to get a better insight into the differences in performance, Figure 2, shows the ratio of all 116 queries (29 queries × 4 datasets) that ran below a certain runtime, where, for example, it can be seen that *Virtuoso* successfully ran 40% of the queries in less than one second and 72% of the queries in less than ten seconds. The plots end where queries began to fail. Interestingly, although *4store* was the most unreliable engine, it offered the fastest runtimes for the simpler queries it did answer, suggesting some index may have been used for optimisation purposes. Although *Sesame* and *Fuseki* were faster for certain queries, the trend in Figure 2 suggests that overall; *Virtuoso* was fastest for most queries. It was also observed that many queries continued to stream results well in excess of the one-minute connection timeout, with Sesame having some of the slowest successful query executions (the slowest being 44 minutes).

Errors

Although all engines returned empty results, 4store was the only engine that was found to return partial or incorrect answers where, for count queries, the engine seemed to return a partial count of what it had found up to a certain point.[12] Otherwise, the other engines tended to have fail-stop errors, meaning that they either returned full correct results or no results at all. With respect to public SPARQL endpoints, although partial results were expected due to result-size limits (Buil-Aranda et al., 2013), the pattern of errors in Table 11 suggests that *if* one of the latter three engines successfully returns a count result, then that value is likely to be correct.

Figure 1. Ratio of successful queries per dataset/ engine

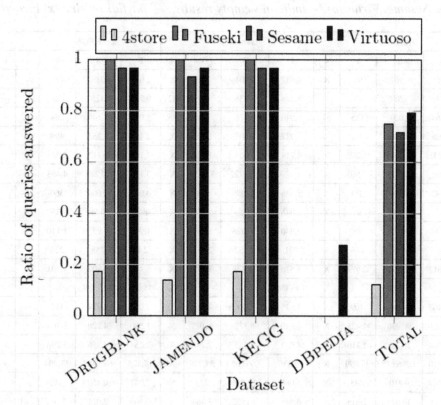

Figure 2. Ratio of queries executed within given runtime

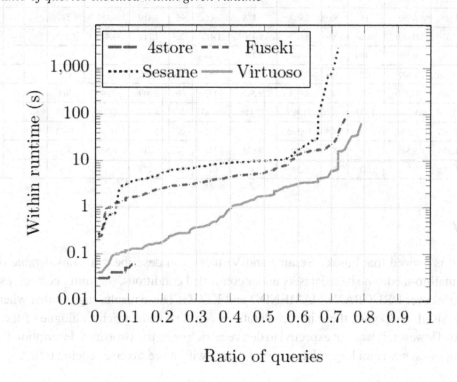

Table 11. Local query runtimes for self-descriptive queries (times in millisecond; engines are keyed as 4store, Fuseki, Sesame, Virtuoso; '-' indicates empty results, '~' partial results, 'x' incorrect results)

No	DrugBank				Jamendo				KEGG				DBpedia			
	4	F	S	V	4	F	S	V	4	F	S	V	4	F	S	V
QB1	X	5,128	6,962	95	X	4,637	6,001	127	X	2,018	3,059	130	-	-	-	6,175
QB2	27	3,140	658	43	X	8,278	2,258	158	42	2,773	325	55	X	-	-	6,260
QB3	29	1,664	7,029	155	34	1,840	6,478	278	35	1,016	3,140	284	-	-	-	25,130
QB4	X	6,029	7,324	252	X	7,987	6,503	1,493	X	2,455	3,263	498	-	-	-	-
QB5	X	17,141	8,764	1,269	X	4,714	6,824	1,736	X	7,174	3,715	2,523	-	-	-	-
QC1	X	4,201	21,845	3,560	X	16,868	166,727	33,559	X	3,125	19,282	4,453	~	-	-l	-
QC2	X	5,342	9,305	374	X	5,336	10,086	291	X	3,097	5,609	360	-	-	-	-
QC3	X	949	758	99	X	2,946	5,153	390	X	801	526	119	-	-	-	-
QC4	X	2,844	9,423	949	X	3,940	10,028	1,135	X	1,990	5,933	1,110	-	-	-	-
QC5	X	227	479	178	X	991	2,952	2,255	X	249	258	226	-	-	-	-
QC6	X	17,612	10,393	2,979	X	5,530	10,339	3,472	X	3,483	6,802	4,301	-	-	-	-
QD1	X	80,119	754,030	-	X	106,486	-	-	X	35,902	323,709	-	-	-	-	-
QD2	X	13,468	8,787	109	X	7,675	740	90	X	5,022	3,917	111	-	-	-	41,188
QD3	X	2,718	90,936	1,425	X	3,870	8,322	3,105	X	1,580	4,120	1,764	-	-	-	-
QD4	X	15,504	10,252	1,710	X	4,983	8,355	2,298	X	2,258	4,356	3,298	-	-	-	-
QE1	X	60,310	1,296,659	17,899	X	39,836	2,663,655	34,926	X	17,825	683,787	37,204	-	-	-	-
QE2	X	13,644	9,410	445	X	5,086	12,886	279	X	2,947	6,469	240	-	-	-	-
QE3	X	4,113	10,029	2,815	X	6,246	10,522	3,464	X	3,505	7,021	2,763	-	-	-	-
QE4	X	20,489	10,603	3,415	X	6,449	10,649	3,448	X	3,359	7,756	4,596	-	-	-	-
QF1	X	2,587	9,990	428	X	4,181	9,131	1,943	X	1,375	4,622	822	-	-	-	-
QF2	30	3,066	8,992	52	36	2,407	8,178	42	45	1,410	4,151	54	-	-	-	378
QF3	X	17,559	11,069	486	X	3,663	9,416	1,467	X	1,711	4,470	1,815	-	-	-	65,398
QF4	X	15,862	9,580	1,100	X	3,061	9,775	644	X	1,761	4,592	1,160	-	-	-	-
QF5	29	14,686	8,877	122	40	3,678	7,755	162	38	1,652	3,880	168	-	-	-	16,192
QF6	52	17,208	17,820	130	58	4,914	15,968	173	60	2,049	7,691	204	-	-	-	16,323
QF7	X	23,360	31,675	1,333	X	11,497	27,428	4,183	X	4,456	13,401	3,131	-	-	-	-
QF8	X	26,517	27,651	1,788	X	10,565	23,549	6,728	X	5,122	11,642	3,615	-	-	-	-
QF9	X	4,725	9,546	414	X	6,746	9,875	315	X	3,210	6,822	271	-	-	-	-
QF10	X	1,272	-	127	X	5,290	-	619	X	1,228	-	149	-	-	-	-

Summary

In general, it is noticed that Fuseki, Sesame and Virtuoso can describe – in considerable detail – the content of small-to-medium-sized datasets under controlled conditions, returning correct results for almost all queries over DRUGBANK, JAMENDO and KEGG. These results suggest that when deployed as public SPARQL endpoints, these implementations could provide a rich catalogue of the content of such datasets. However, it was not expected to derive as rich or as trustworthy a description from 4store-powered endpoints, nor from larger datasets or datasets with more diverse schema terms.

REMOTE EXPERIMENTS

This section looks at how public SPARQL endpoints themselves perform for the list of previously enumerated self-descriptive queries. Along these lines, a list of 540 SPARQL endpoints registered in the DATAHUB (n.d.) was collected in April 2015. Likewise, a list of 137 endpoints from Bio2RDF releases 1-3 was collected. In total, 618 unique endpoints (59 endpoints were present in both lists) were considered. The results are based on experiments performed in April 2015.

Implementations Used

With respect to the previous local experiments, it is interesting to determine which implementations are used by the in-scope endpoints. As per the observations of Buil-Aranda et al. (Buil-Aranda et al., 2013), although there is no generic exact method of determining the engine powering a SPARQL endpoint, the HTTP header may contain some clues in the Server field. Hence the first step was to perform a lookup on the endpoint URLs. Table 12, presents the response codes of this step, where quite a large number of endpoints return error codes 4xx, 5xx, or some other exception. This indicates that a non-trivial fraction of the endpoints from the list are offline.

With respect to the server names returned by those URLs that returned a HTTP response, Table 13 enumerates the main prefixes that were discovered. Although some of the server names denote generic HTTP servers - more specifically *Apache, nginx, Jetty, GlassFish, Restlet* and *lighttpd* - some names that indicate SPARQL implementations - namely *Virtuoso, Fuseki* and *4s-httpd* (4store). Interestingly, two of the engines that performed quite well in the local experiments -*Virtuoso* and *Fuseki* - are quite prevalent amongst SPARQL endpoints[13].

Table 11. HTTP response

Response	No
200 (successful)	307
200(unsuccessful)	43
400	56
404	66
500	4
502	0
503	32
Unknown host	51
Time out	23
Connection refused	18
Not responding	7

Table 12. Server Names

Server-Field	No
Apache	203
Virtuoso	174
nginx	38
Jetty	25
Fuseki	15
Glassfish	3
4s-httpd	2
lighttpd	1
empty	130

Availability and Version

Based on the previous experiment, it was suspected that some of the endpoints in the list may be offline. Hence, the next step was to look at how many endpoints respond to the basic availability query Q_{A1}.

Given that the queries were run in an uncontrolled environment, multiple runs were performed to help mitigate temporary errors and remote server loads: the core idea is that if an endpoint fails at a given moment of time, a catalogue could simply reuse the most recent successful result. Along these lines, three weekly experiments in the month of April 2015 were run. In total, 306 endpoints (49.5%) responded to Q_{A1} at least once in the three weeks; these endpoints were considered to be operational and others to be *offline*. Of the operational endpoints, 7 (1.1%) responded successfully exactly once to Q_{A1}, 28 (4.5%) responded successfully exactly twice, and 272 (44.1%) responded successfully thrice. In the most recent run, 298 endpoints responded to Q_{A1}. Of these, 168 (56.4%) also responded with a single result for Q_{A2}, indicating some support for SPARQL 1.1 in about half of the operational endpoints.

Moving forward, to mitigate the issue of temporary errors, for each endpoint, the most recent non-empty results returned for each endpoint and each query over the three runs were considered.

Success Rates

The focus is on the overall success rates for each query, looking at the ratio of the 307 endpoints that return non-empty results. Figure 3, where shows the success rates varying from 25% for Q_{E3} on the lower end, to 94% for Q_{C1} on the higher end. The three queries with the highest success rates require only SPARQL 1.0 features to run: list all class partitions (Q_{C1}), all property partitions (Q_{D1}), and all nested partitions (Q_{E1}). Hence, only 49% could respond to the SPARQL 1.1 test query Q_{A1} - more endpoints can answer queries not requiring novel SPARQL 1.1 features such as counts or sub-queries. The query with the highest success rate that involved SPARQL 1.1 features was Q_{B1}, where 51% of endpoints responded with a count of triples. In general, queries deriving counts within partitions had the lowest success rates.

Figure 3. Ratio of endpoints returning non-empty results per query

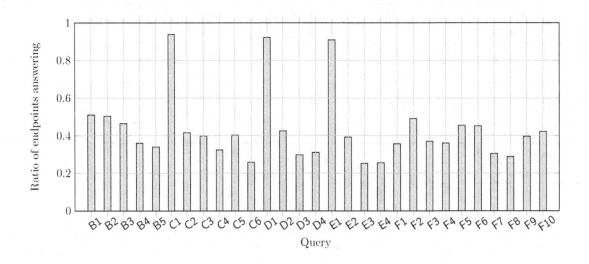

Result Sizes

Figure 4 shows result sizes in log scale for individual queries at various percentiles considering all endpoints that returned a non-empty result. As expected, queries that return a single count triple return one result across all percentiles. For other queries, the result sizes extended into the tens of thousands. One may note that the higher percentiles are quite compressed for certain queries, indicating the presence of result thresholds. For example, for Q_{C1}, a common result-size was precisely 40,000, which would appear to be the effect of a result-size threshold. Hence, unlike the local experiments where result thresholds could be switched off, for public endpoints, partial results are sometimes returned.

Runtimes

Finally, the focus was on runtimes for successfully executed queries, incorporating the total response time for issuing the query and streaming all results. Figure 5, presents the runtimes for each query considering different percentiles across all endpoints returning non-empty results in log scale. A large variance in runtimes is noticed, which is to be expected given that different endpoints host datasets of a variety of sizes and schemata on servers with a variety of computational capacity. In general, the *25th* percentile roughly corresponds with the one second line, but that slower endpoints may take tens or hundreds of seconds. The at max trend seems to be the effect of remote timeout policies, where query runtimes often maxed out at between 100 - 120 seconds, likely returning partial results.

Summary

Although a high success rate is achieved while asking for class and property partitions where it was expected to have such data for over 90% of the endpoints, the success rate for queries using novel SPARQL 1.1 features drops to 25 - 50%. It is also noted that for queries generating larger result sizes, thresholds

Figure 4. Sizes of results for different queries taking 25th, 50th (median), 75th and 100th (max) percentiles, inclusive, across all endpoints returning non-empty results

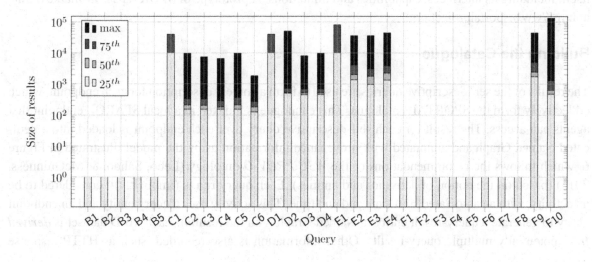

Figure 5. Runtimes for different queries taking 25th, 50th (median), 75th and 100th (max) percentiles inclusive, across all endpoints returning non-empty results

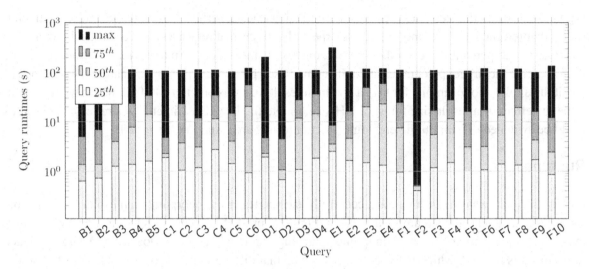

and timeouts would likely lead to only partial results being returned. But based on local experiments and the implementations most prominently used by endpoints, the partial data returned by these endpoints is likely to be accurate even if incomplete.

SPARQL PORTAL

Our primary motivation is to investigate a method for cataloguing the content of public SPARQL endpoints without requiring them to publish separate, static descriptions of their content-or indeed, for publishers to offer any additional infrastructure other than the query interface itself. The previous sections, performed a variety of experiments that characterised the feasibilities and limitations of collecting metadata about the content of endpoints by directly querying them. This section, describes the SPORTAL catalogue itself, including its interfaces, capabilities and limitations. A prototype of SPORTAL is available online at http://www.sportalproject.org.

Building the Catalogue

The results of the self-descriptive queries are used to form a content description for each endpoint, which collectively form the SPORTAL catalogue. This catalogue is indexed in a local SPARQL endpoint that agents can access. The result for each self-descriptive query over each endpoint is loaded into a dedicated Named Graph and annotated with provenance information using the model illustrated in Figure 6, which follows the recommendations of the *W3C PROV-O* ontology (Lebo, Sahoo, & McGuinness, 2013) (based on the notion of activities and entities). Each query run is (implicitly)[14] considered to be an activity, with an associated start time and end time. This activity uses a query entity and an endpoint entity to generate a query-result entity (a Named Graph with the results). Each VoID dataset is *derived from* potentially multiple query-results. Other information is also recorded, such as HTTP response codes, the number of triples generated by the query, whether the query is SPARQL 1.0 or SPARQL 1.1, the text of the query, etc.

Example 1, provides a real-world example output from executing $\mathbf{Q_{B1}}$ over an endpoint, with provenance information following the model previously described.

SPARQL Interface

SPORTAL itself provides a public SPARQL endpoint, where the RDF triples produced by the CONSTRUCT clauses of the self-descriptive queries issued against public endpoints can themselves be queried. This allows users with specific requirements in mind to interrogate the catalogue in a flexible manner.

To take a first example, a client could pose the following query asking for the SPARQL endpoints for which the catalogue has the top 5 largest triple counts.

This will return the answer presented in Table 15.[15]

As another example, referring back to the second client scenario mentioned in the introduction, take a user who is interested in data about proteins and asks for endpoints with at least 50,000 instances of bp:Protein, with results in descending order of number of instances. This user could ask:

This query will return the answer presented in Table 17.

As a final example combining scenarios 2 and 3 in the introduction, consider an agent looking for SPARQL endpoints with at least 50 unique images of people, where this agent may ask.

This returns the result presented in Table 19.

Of course, this is just to briefly highlight three examples of the capabilities of SPORTAL and the kinds of results it can return. One could imagine various other types of queries that a user could be interested in posing over the SPORTAL catalogue, which supports a variety of types of queries referring to high-level dataset statistics as well as schema-level information. However, the catalogue does not support finding endpoints mentioning a specific resource or value, nor does it currently support keyword search on the topic of the dataset.

User Interface

In order to use the SPARQL interface, the agent must first be familiar with SPARQL, and second must know the IRI of the particular classes and/or properties that they are interested in. To help non-expect users, SPORTAL also provides an online user interface with a number of functionalities.

First, users can search for specific endpoints by their URL, by the classes in their datasets, and/or by the properties in their datasets. These features are offered by means of auto-completion on keywords,

Figure 6. SPORTAL provenance data model

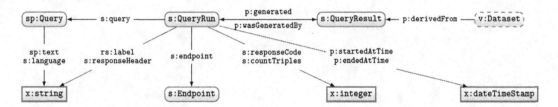

Table 13. Example 1: An example RDF output of QB1 with provenance metadata

```
@prefix ep: <http://www.linklion.org:8890/sparql#> .
@prefix p: <http://www.w3.org/ns/prov#> .

@prefix s: <http://vocab.deri.ie/sad#> .
@prefix sp: <http://spinrdf.org/spin#> .

@prefix rs: <http://www.w3.org/2000/01/rdf-schema#> .
@prefix v: <http://rdfs.org/ns/void#> .
@prefix x: <http://www.w3.org/2001/XMLSchema#> .

## PROVENANCE metadata

# each query run is implicitly a p:Activity ep:totalNumberOfTriplesQueryRun a s:QueryRun ;

  p:generated ep:totalNumberOfTriplesResult ; s:responseCode 200;
  s:countTriples 1 ;

  p:startedAtTime "2015-05-11T21:20:54.065Z"^^x:dateTimeStamp; p:endedAtTime "2015-05-11T21:20:55.511Z"^^x:dateTimeStamp ;

  rs:label "Extracting triple count from 'http://www.linklion.org:8890/sparql' on 2015-05-11T21:20:54.065Z"@en;
  s:resultDataset ep:dataset ;

  s:responseHeader "StatusCode=[HTTP/1.1 200 OK] & Server=[Virtuoso/07.00.3203 (Linux) x86_64-suse-linux-gnu]";
  s:endpoint <http://www.linklion.org:8890/sparql> ; # s:endpoint sub-property of p:used
  s:query ep:totalNumberOfTriplesQuery . # s:query sub-property of p:used

# each query is implicitly a p:Entity
ep:totalNumberOfTriplesQuery a sp:Query ;
  sp:text """PREFIX void: <http://rdfs.org/ns/void#>

        CONSTRUCT { <http://www.linklion.org:8890/sparql#dataset> void:triples ?count }
        WHERE { SELECT (COUNT(*) AS ?count) WHERE { ?s ?p ?o } }""" ;
  s:language "SPARQL1.1" .

# represents the RDF graph returned by the query, implicitly a p:Entity ep:totalNumberOfTriplesResult a s:QueryResult ;
  p:wasGeneratedBy ep:totalNumberOfTriplesQueryRun .

# connects the dataset mentioned in the results and the graph storing the results
ep:dataset p:wasDerivedFrom s:totalNumberOfTriplesResult .

## RDF GENERATED BY THE QUERY

# loaded into the Named Graph ep:totalNumberOfTriplesResult ep:dataset v:triples 77455301 .
```

Table 14.

```
SELECT DISTINCT ?endpoint ?triples
WHERE {? dataset v:triples ?triples ; v:sparqlEndpoint ?endpoint .}
ORDER BY DESC(?triples) LIMIT 5
```

Table 15. SPARQL endpoints with top 5 largest triple counts

?endpoint	?triple
http://commons.dbpedia.org/sparql	1,229,690,546
http://lod.b3kat.de/sparql#dataset	981,672,146
http://www.linklion.org:8890/sparql#dataset	727,421,750
http://live.dbpedia.org/sparql#dataset	560,701,025
http://linked.opendata.cz/sparql#dataset	555,666,667

Table 16.

```
SELECT DISTINCT ?endpoint ?instances
WHERE { ?dataset v:classPartition
[ v:class bp:Protein ; v:distinctSubjects ?instances ] ;
v:sparqlEndpoint ?endpoint . FILTER(?instances > 50000) }
ORDER BY DESC (?instances)
```

Table 17. List of SPARQL endpoints with at least 50,000 instances of "bp:Protein"

?endpoint	?instances
https://www.ebi.ac.uk/rdf/services/reactome/sparql	260,546

Table 18.

```
SELECT DISTINCT ?endpoint ?imgs
WHERE {
?dataset v:classPartition [ v:class f:Person ; v:propertyPartition [
v:property f:depiction; v:distinctObjects ?imgs ] ] ;
v:sparqlEndpoint ?endpoint . FILTER(?imgs > 50) }
ORDER BY DESC (?imgs)
```

Table 19. List of SPARQL endpoints with at least 50 unique images of people

?endpoint	?imgs
http://eu.dbpedia.org/sparql	4,517
http://eudbpedia.deusto.es/sparql	4,517
http://data.open.ac.uk/query	311
http://apps.morelab.deusto.es/labman/sparql	78

meaning that the agent need not know the specific IRIs they are searching for. Taking a simple example, if a user wishes to find endpoints with instances of drugs, they may type *"drug"* into the search bar and then select one of the presented classes matching that search; once a class is selected, the user is presented with a list of public endpoints mentioning that class, ordered by the distinct subjects for that class partition (as available).

If a user clicks on or searches for an endpoint, they can retrieve all the information available about that endpoint as extracted by the queries previously described, providing an overview of how many triples it contains, how many subjects, how many classes, etc. (as available).

The SPORTAL user interface also includes some graphical visualisations of some of the high-level features of the catalogue, such as the most popular classes and properties based on the number of endpoints in which they are found, the most common server headers, and so forth. While this may not be of use to a user with a specific search in mind, it offers a useful overview of the content available across all endpoints on the Web, and the schema-level terms that are most often instantiated.

Updates

An important aspect of the SPORTAL service is to keep up-to-date information about current SPARQL endpoints. Along these lines, the content descriptions were recomputed every 15 days: a backup was taken of the old catalogue and recompute everything from scratch. One shortcoming of this approach is that the catalogue may miss endpoints that were temporarily unavailable during the computation. Currently any special workaround for this issue is not implemented, but this research could in future consider importing data from the previous catalogue for endpoints.

Comparison

Table 22, compares the SPORTAL catalogue with two other publicly available services that could be used to find relevant SPARQL endpoints using VoID descriptions: DataHub and VoID Store. Unlike SPORTAL, both services rely on publisher-contributed VoID descriptions.

In the comparison, all endpoints are included that had an associated VoID description in the given service. For DataHub and VoID Store, it is possible to have multiple VoID descriptions associated with an endpoint, and multiple endpoints associated with a VoID file. A SPARQL endpoint is counted as available if it could respond with a valid SPARQL response to the query (as used, for example, by the SPARQLES system (Buil-Aranda et al., 2013)):

DataHub and VoID are not hosted locally, where links are provided instead. LDspider v1.3 (Isele, Umbrich, Bizer, & Harth, 2010) crawler is used to download the VoID files from these URLs,[16] from which authors extract the availability (number of VoID files successfully downloaded) and the content for later statistics. To give a brief comparison of the coverage of the catalogues, the number of unique

Table 20.

SELECT ?s WHERE { ?s ?p ?o } LIMIT 1

classes and unique properties are displayed that are associated in each catalogue with at least one endpoint; in more detail, the unique classes and unique properties are counted that would be returned for the following queries over the catalogues, respectively:

Although this only partially captures the full wealth of information available in VoID, it gives an overview of the diversity of domain terms indexed from endpoints.

From the results, with respect to endpoints, SPORTAL has the broadest coverage: unlike DataHub and VoID Store, it does not require publishers to compute and submit VoID descriptions but rather computes them automatically. For this reason, SPORTAL indexes twice as many available endpoints as DataHub and more than three times that of VoID Store. The endpoints that SPORTAL indexes have the highest availability ratio: for DataHub and VoID Store, many of the indexed descriptions refer to endpoints that are long dead.

For both SPORTAL and VoID Store, descriptions are hosted locally, meaning that they are always available when the respective catalogue is available; however, for DataHub, 38% of the VoID links provided could not be resolved to RDF content by LDspider.

With respect to the class and property terms mentioned, the SPORTAL catalogue contains orders of magnitude more unique classes and properties than either DataHub or VoID Store.

From these results, it can be concluded that when compared to DataHub and VoID Store, clients using SPORTAL can expect to find a broader range of relevant endpoints for (e.g.) a broader range of classes and properties, and that the endpoints returned are more likely to be available and to still contain the content in question. Thus, there is a benefit of a catalogue based on computing content descriptions rather than relying on those provided by publishers.

Limitations

SPORTAL naturally inherits many of the limitations raised during earlier experiments. For instance, the previous example queries would probably miss endpoints that could not return results for the relevant self-descriptive queries. In general, the catalogue should be considered a best-e ort initiative to collect as much metadata about the content of endpoints as possible, rather than a 100% complete catalogue.

Table 21.

SELECT DISTINCT ?c WHERE { ?s v:class ?c }
SELECT DISTINCT ?p WHERE { ?s v:property ?p }

Table 22. A comparison of the availability and coverage of SPORTAL, DataHub and VoID Store

Service	Endpoints		Descriptions			Classes	Properties
	Total	Available	Total	Available			
SPORTAL	307	231	(75%)	298	298	(100%)	19,216	46,313
DataHub	200	115	(58%)	260	162	(62%)	1,636	829
VoID Store	118	69	(58%)	148	148	(100%)	30	217

Another limitation is that SPORTAL can only help to find endpoints based on the metadata collected from self-describing queries, which mainly centres on the schema terms used. For example, the system cannot help to find endpoints that mention a given literal, or a given subject IRI (which is partially support by VoID Store using REGEX patterns), or to find endpoints based on the text of the description or the tags associated with the relevant dataset (which is supported by DataHub), etc.

It is worth noting that by focusing on the problem of finding relevant SPARQL endpoints, SPORTAL may miss relevant Linked Datasets that do not offer a SPARQL endpoint. According to statistics by Jentzsch et al. (Jentzsch et al., 2011), only 68% of the Linked Datasets surveyed provided a SPARQL endpoint. Hence, in addition to missing out on endpoints that cannot answer the self-descriptive queries that SPORTAL issue, this research also does not cover Linked Datasets without SPARQL endpoints. However, the research focus is specifically on the problem of relevant SPARQL endpoints, which is arguably a significant problem that merits specialised methods such as those proposed here.

CONCLUSION

This research proposed a novel cataloguing scheme for helping agents to find public SPARQL end-points relevant to their needs. Given that the endpoints in question are made available by hundreds of different parties, this research choses to investigate a cataloguing system that works with the existing SPARQL infrastructure and, for each endpoint indexed, only requires a working SPARQL interface The option of flooding runtime requests to public SPARQL endpoints is ruled out for looking the desired content since this would lead to long runtimes and could generate a lot of traffic to public endpoints. Instead, this research proposed to use self-descriptive queries to incrementally generate high-level descriptions of the content of public endpoints. This research experimented with the performance of running these queries for four datasets and four engines, showing that although Fuseki, Sesame and Virtuoso could successfully answer the queries over small-to-medium-sized datasets, only Virtuoso managed to return results to some queries over larger datasets. Later this research looked at what sort of success rate public endpoints had in answering these queries, where out of 306 operational endpoints, the ratio of non-empty responses ranged from 25-94% depending on the query in question. Finally, the details of the SPORTAL prototype are presented that uses the catalogue extracted from public endpoints to help users find interesting datasets on the Web.

Although SPORTAL has its limitations, it has shown that it compares favourably with existing services to help clients find SPARQL endpoints: when compared with DataHub and VoID Store, the SPORTAL catalogue has better coverage of available endpoints and, for example, indexes a much broader range of the class and property terms used in the data of remote endpoints. However, it lacks some of the features of these other services: for example, exploring Linked Datasets (and not just SPARQL endpoints) using tags, keyword search over dataset abstracts, searching by resource IRIs, etc.

Our goal in the immediate future is to build upon the existing prototype by seeking feedback from the Linked Data community on what features they feel might be useful, and to gather feedback on the usability of the system. Authors would also like to investigate fall-back methods of extracting metadata directly from endpoints, such as incremental methods that query, e.g., for statistics about one class/ property partition at a time.[17]

The *SPORTAL prototype* is available online at http://www.sportalproject.org/. *Project Code* is available at https://github.com/SAliHasnain/sparqlautodescription.

ACKNOWLEDGMENT

This chapter is based on the paper "*SPORTAL*: Profiling the content of public sparql endpoints" published at International Journal on Semantic Web and Information Systems (IJSWIS) 2016. This research was supported in part by a research grant from Science Foundation Ireland (SFI) under Grant Number SFI/12/RC/2289, by the Millennium Nucleus Center for Semantic Web Research under Grant NC120004, and by Fondecyt Grant No. 11140900

REFERENCES

Abedjan, Z., Grütze, T., Jentzsch, A., & Naumann, F. (2014). Profiling and mining {RDF} data with {ProLOD++}. *International Conference on Data Engineering ({ICDE})*, 1198–1201. doi:10.1109/ICDE.2014.6816740

Acosta, M., Vidal, M.-E., Lampo, T., Castillo, J., & Ruckhaus, E. (2011). {ANAPSID}: An Adaptive Query Processing Engine for {SPARQL} Endpoints. In *International Semantic Web Conference (ISWC)* (pp. 18–34). Springer. http://doi.org/ doi:10.1007/978-3-642-25073-6_2

Akar, Z., Halaç, T. G., Ekinci, E. E., & Dikenelli, O. (2012). Querying the Web of Interlinked Datasets using VOID Descriptions. In Linked Data On the Web (LDOW). CEUR.

Alexander, K., Cyganiak, R., Hausenblas, M., & Zhao, J. (2009). Describing Linked Datasets. In Linked Data On the Web (LDOW). CEUR.

Auer, S., Demter, J., Martin, M., & Lehmann, J. (2012). {LODStats} -- An Extensible Framework for High-Performance Dataset Analytics. In Knowledge Engineering and Knowledge Management ({EKAW}) (pp. 353–362). Springer.

Basca, C., & Bernstein, A. (2014). Querying a messy web of data with {Avalanche}. *Journal of Web Semantics*, *26*, 1–28. doi:10.1016/j.websem.2014.04.002

Beek, W., Rietveld, L., Bazoobandi, H. R., Wielemaker, J., & Schlobach, S. (2014). {LOD} Laundromat: {A} Uniform Way of Publishing Other People's Dirty Data. In *International Semantic Web Conference (ISWC)* (pp. 213–228). Springer. doi:10.1007/978-3-319-11964-9_14

Böhm, C., Lorey, J., & Naumann, F. (2011). Creating {voiD} descriptions for {Web}-scale data. *Journal of Web Semantics*, *9*(3), 339–345. doi:10.1016/j.websem.2011.06.001

Broekstra, J., Kampman, A., & van Harmelen, F. (2002). Sesame: A Generic Architecture for Storing and Querying {RDF} and {RDF} Schema. In *International Semantic Web Conference (ISWC)* (pp. 54–68). Springer.

Buil-Aranda, C., Hogan, A., Umbrich, J., & Vandenbussche, P.-Y. (2013). SPARQL Web-Querying Infrastructure: Ready for Action? In *International Semantic Web Conference (ISWC)* (pp. 277–293). Springer.

Campinas, S., Delbru, R., & Tummarello, G. (2013). Efficiency and precision trade-offs in graph summary algorithms. *International Database Engineering {&} Applications Symposium (IDEAS)*, 38–47. doi:10.1145/2513591.2513654

Crespo, A., & Garcia-Molina, H. (2002). Routing Indices For Peer-to-Peer Systems. *International Conference on Distributed Computing Systems (ICDCS)*, 23–32. doi:10.1109/ICDCS.2002.1022239

Cyganiak, R., Stenzhorn, H., Delbru, R., Decker, S., & Tummarello, G. (2008). Semantic Sitemaps: Efficient and Flexible Access to Datasets on the Semantic Web. In *European Semantic Web Conference ({ESWC})* (pp. 690–704). Springer. doi:10.1007/978-3-540-68234-9_50

Data Hub. (n.d.). Retrieved from: http://datahub.io/

Erling, O., & Mikhailov, I. (2009). RDF} Support in the {V}irtuoso {DBMS. In *Networked Knowledge -- Networked Media*. Springer. doi:10.1007/978-3-642-02184-8_2

Fetahu, B., Dietze, S., Nunes, B. P., Casanova, M. A., Taibi, D., & Nejdl, W. (2014). A Scalable Approach for Efficiently Generating Structured Dataset Topic Profiles. In *European Semantic Web Conference ({ESWC})* (pp. 519–534). Springer. Retrieved from doi:10.1007/978-3-319-07443-6_35

Gallego, M. A., Fernández, J. D., Martínez-Prieto, M. A., & de la Fuente, P. (2011). *An Empirical Study of Real-World SPARQL Queries*. USEWOD.

Glaser, H., Millard, I., & Jaffri, A. (2008). RKBExplorer.com: {A} Knowledge Driven Infrastructure for {L}inked {D}ata Providers. In *European Semantic Web Conference ({ESWC})* (pp. 797–801). Springer.

Harris, S., Lamb, N., & Shadbolt, N. (2009). 4store: The Design and Implementation of a Clustered {RDF} Store. *Scalable Semantic Web Systems Workshop (SWSS)*.

Harris, S., Seaborne, A., & Prud'hommeaux, E. (2013, March). {SPARQL} 1.1 Query Language.

Harth, A., Hose, K., Karnstedt, M., Polleres, A., Sattler, K.-U., & Umbrich, J. (2010). Data summaries for on-demand queries over linked data. *International Conference on World Wide Web (WWW)*, 411–420. doi:10.1145/1772690.1772733

Harth, A., Umbrich, J., Hogan, A., & Decker, S. (2007). {YARS2:} {A} Federated Repository for Querying Graph Structured Data from the {W}Holst. In *International Semantic Web Conference (ISWC)* (pp. 211–224). Springer. http://doi.org/ doi:<ALIGNMENT.qj></ALIGNMENT>10.1007/978-3-540-76298-0_16

Hasnain, A., Kamdar, M. R., Hasapis, P., Zeginis, D., & Warren, C. N. Jr et al. (2014). Linked Biomedical Dataspace: Lessons Learned integrating Data for Drug Discovery. *International Semantic Web Conference (In-Use Track)*.

Hasnain, A., Mehmood, Q., Zainab, S. S., & Hogan, A. (2016a). SPORTAL: Profiling the Content of Public SPARQL Endpoints. *International Journal on Semantic Web and Information Systems*, *12*(3), 134–163. doi:10.4018/IJSWIS.2016070105

Hasnain, A., Mehmood, Q., Zainab, S. S., & Hogan, A. (2016b). SPORTAL: Searching for Public SPARQL Endpoints. In *International Semantic Web Conference (ISWC) Posters & Demos*. CEUR.

Hasnain, A., Mehmood, Q., e Zainab, S. S., Saleem, M., Warren, C., Zehra, D., ... Rebholz-Schuhmann, D. (2017a). BioFed: federated query processing over life sciences linked open data. *Journal of biomedical Semantics, 8*(1), 13.

Hasnain, A., Zainab, S. S., Zehra, D., Mehmood, Q., Saleem, M., & Rebholz-Schuhmann, D. (2017b). Federated Query Formulation and Processing through BioFed. In *Extended Semantic Web Conference (ESWC)*. CEUR.

Heath, T., & Bizer, C. (2011). *Linked {D}ata: Evolving the {W}eb into a Global Data Space*. Morgan & Claypool.

Holst, T., & Höfig, E. (2013). Investigating the Relevance of {Linked Open Data Sets} with {SPARQL} Queries. COMPSAC Workshops, 230–235.

Isele, R., Umbrich, J., Bizer, C., & Harth, A. (2010). {LDspider}: An Open-source Crawling Framework for the {Web of Linked Data}. In *International Semantic Web Conference (ISWC) Posters & Demos*. CEUR.

Jentzsch, A., Cyganiak, R., & Bizer, C. (2011, September). State of the {LOD Cloud}.

Khatchadourian, S., & Consens, M. P. (2010). ExpLOD: Summary-Based Exploration of Interlinking and {RDF} Usage in the {Linked Open Data Cloud}. In *Extended Semantic Web Conference (ESWC)* (pp. 272–287). Springer. doi:10.1007/978-3-642-13489-0_19

Kinsella, S., Bojars, U., Harth, A., Breslin, J. G., & Decker, S. (2008). An Interactive Map of {Semantic Web} Ontology Usage. In *International Conference on Information Visualisation* (pp. 179–184). doi:10.1109/IV.2008.60

Langegger, A., & Wöß, W. (2009). RDFStats -- An Extensible RDF Statistics Generator and Library. DEXA Workshops, 79–83.

Lebo, T., Sahoo, S., & McGuinness, D. (2013, April). *PROV-O: The PROV Ontology*. Academic Press.

Lorey, J. (2014). Identifying and determining {SPARQL} endpoint characteristics. *IJWIS, 10*(3), 226–244. 10.1108/IJWIS-03-2014-0007

Mäkelä, E. (2014). Aether - Generating and Viewing Extended {VoID} Statistical Descriptions of {RDF} Datasets. In *European Semantic Web Conference ({ESWC})* (pp. 429–433). Springer.

Mehdi, M., Iqbal, A., Hogan, A., Hasnain, A., Khan, Y., Decker, S., & Sahay, R. (2014). Discovering domain-specific public {SPARQL} endpoints: a life-sciences use-case. *International Database Engineering & Applications Symposium (IDEAS)*, 39–45.

Mihindukulasooriya, N., Poveda-Villalón, M., García-Castro, R., & Gómez-Pérez, A. (2015). Loupe -- An Online Tool for Inspecting Datasets in the {Linked Data} Cloud. In *International Semantic Web Conference (ISWC) Posters & Demos*. CEUR.

Mountantonakis, M., Allocca, C., Fafalios, P., Minadakis, N., Marketakis, Y., Lantzaki, C., & Tzitzikas, Y. (2014). Extending {VoID} for Expressing Connectivity Metrics of a Semantic Warehouse. *International Workshop on Dataset PROFIling {&} fEderated Search for Linked Data (PROFILES)*.

Omitola, T., Zuo, L., Gutteridge, C., Millard, I., Glaser, H., Gibbins, N., & Shadbolt, N. (2011). Tracing the provenance of {L}inked {D}ata using {voiD}. *International Conference on Web Intelligence, Mining and Semantics (WIMS)*, 17.

Paulheim, H., & Hertling, S. (2013). Discoverability of SPARQL Endpoints in Linked Open Data. In *International Semantic Web Conference (ISWC) Posters {&} Demos* (pp. 245–248). Springer.

Prud'hommeauxE.Buil-ArandaC. (2013, March). {SPARQL} 1.1 {F}ederated {Q}uery.

Qiu, D., & Srikant, R. (2004). Modeling and performance analysis of {BitTorrent}-like peer-to-peer networks. SIGCOMM, 367–378.

Quilitz, B., & Leser, U. (2008). Querying Distributed {RDF} Data Sources with {SPARQL}. In *European Semantic Web Conference (ESWC)* (pp. 524–538). Springer. doi:10.1007/978-3-540-68234-9_39

Ratnasamy, S., Francis, P., Handley, M., Karp, R. M., & Shenker, S. (2001). *A scalable content-addressable network*. SIGCOMM. doi:10.1145/383059.383072

Ripeanu, M., Iamnitchi, A., & Foster, I. T. (2002). Mapping the {Gnutella Network}. *IEEE Internet Computing, 6*(1), 50–57. <ALIGNMENT.qj></ALIGNMENT>10.1109/4236.978369

Rowstron, A. I. T., & Druschel, P. (2001). Pastry: Scalable, Decentralized Object Location, and Routing for Large-Scale Peer-to-Peer Systems. *IFIP/ACM International Conference on Distributed Systems Platforms (Middleware)*, 329–350.

Schwarte, A., Haase, P., Hose, K., Schenkel, R., & Schmidt, M. (2011). Fed{X}: {A} Federation Layer for Distributed Query Processing on {L}inked {O}pen {D}ata. In *Extended Semantic Web Conference ({ESWC})* (pp. 481–486). Springer.

Stoica, I., Morris, R., Liben-Nowell, D., Karger, D. R., Kaashoek, M. F., Dabek, F., & Balakrishnan, H. (2003). Chord: A scalable peer-to-peer lookup protocol for internet applications. *IEEE/ACM Trans. Netw., 11*(1), 17–32. doi: 10.1109/TNET.2002.808407

Umbrich, J., Hose, K., Karnstedt, M., Harth, A., & Polleres, A. (2011). Comparing data summaries for processing live queries over {L}inked {D}ata. *World Wide Web Journal, 14*(5-6), 495–544. doi:10.1007/s11280-010-0107-z

Verborgh, R., Hartig, O., De Meester, B., Haesendonck, G., De Vocht, L., & Vander Sande, M., … de Walle, R. Van. (2014). Querying Datasets on the {W}eb with High Availability. In *International Semantic Web Conference (ISWC)* (pp. 180–196). Springer. http://doi.org/ doi:<ALIGNMENT.qj></ALIGNMENT>10.1007/978-3-319-11964-9_12

VoID. (2010). *VoID store*. Retrieved from: http://void.rkbexplorer.com/

Williams, G. T. (2013, March). {SPARQL} 1.1 {S}ervice {D}escription.

Zhao, B. Y., Huang, L., Stribling, J., Rhea, S. C., Joseph, A. D., & Kubiatowicz, J. (2004). Tapestry: a resilient global-scale overlay for service deployment. *IEEE Journal on Selected Areas in Communications, 22*(1), 41–53. 10.1109/JSAC.2003.818784

ENDNOTES

[1]   Note that all prefixes used in this chapter are listed in Table 15 of the Appendix.

[2]   Certain aspects of VoID may not be computable directly from a dataset, such as the author(s) of a dataset, how it is licensed, OpenSearch descriptions, etc. Likewise subjective criteria in the computable fragment is not included -- such as the categories of the dataset -- even if candidates could be computed automatically (Fetahu et al., 2014).

[3]   http://jena.apache.org/documentation/fuseki2/; l.a. 2017/3/10

[4]   An endpoint is considered as *operational* if it can be accessed over HTTP through the SPARQL protocol and will return a valid non-empty response to the following query: SELECT * WHERE {?s ?p ?o } LIMIT 1

[5]   http://dbpedia.org/sparql; l.a. 2015/12/10 (42 populations are returned at the time of writing).

[6]   The single server itself of course may be a distributed system, involving multiple replicated or clustered machines (Harris et al., 2009; Harth, Umbrich, Hogan, & Decker, 2007) ; however, this is all transparent from the perspective of the client, who sees one server

[7]   http://datahub.io/, l.a. 2015/12/10.

[8]   This does not imply that the endpoint is fully compliant with SPARQL 1.1; only that it supports a subset of features.

[9]   http://ldf.fi/void-ext#; denoted herein as e: .

[10]   A novel namespace (s:) is created available from http://vocab.deri.ie/sad#.

[11]   In fact, DBPEDIA contained no blank nodes, nor did any of the other datasets.

[12]   Many counts had the value of 1,996 or some other value close to a multiple of a thousand; these results were incorrect where some of the expected values were in the hundreds of thousands.

[13]   These results correspond quite closely with those of Buil-Aranda et al. [10]. It is believed that some Sesame endpoints may be within the Apache category since the default Sesame header is Apache-Coyote/1.1.

[14]   Authors do not explicitly type the entities with PROV-O classes simply to keep the data concise: memberships of the respective classes could be inferred from the domain/range of the PROV-O properties used.

[15]   All such answers were generated from the SPORTAL catalogue in March 2016.

[16]   The exact arguments used were -s seeds.txt -n -o output.nq -b 0 -any23 -bl .xxx, indicating to accept all formats supported by any23, to follow redirects but not links (i.e., download seeds), and to not blacklist any file extensions.

[17]   However, the cost of such an approach would be a prohibitively large number of requests if there are a large number of partitions.

APPENDIX

Prefixes

Table 23, lists all if the prefixes used in the writing

Table 23. IRI prefixes used

Prefix	IRI
bp:	http://www.biopax.org/release/biopax-level3.owl#
dcat:	http://purl.org/dc/terms/
dbo:	http://dbpedia.org/ontology/
e:	http://ldf.fi/void-ext#
f:	http://xmlns.com/foaf/0.1/
mo:	http://purl.org/ontology/mo/
p:	http://www.w3.org/ns/prov#
s:	http://vocab.deri.ie/sad#
sp:	http://spinrdf.org/spin#
rs:	http://www.w3.org/2000/01/rdf-schema#
v:	http://rdfs.org/ns/void#
x:	http://www.w3.org/2001/XMLSchema#

Chapter 12
Semantic Web Search Through Natural Language Dialogues

Dora Melo
Coimbra Business School, Portugal & Laboratory of Informatics, Systems, and Parallelism (LISP), Portugal

Irene Pimenta Rodrigues
University of Évora, Portugal & Laboratory of Informatics, Systems, and Parallelism (LISP), Portugal

Vitor Beires Nogueira
University of Évora, Portugal & Laboratory of Informatics, Systems, and Parallelism (LISP), Portugal

ABSTRACT

The Semantic Web as a knowledge base gives to the Question Answering systems the capabilities needed to go well beyond the usual word matching in the documents and find a more accurate answer, without needing the user intervention to interpret the documents returned. In this chapter, the authors introduce a Dialogue Manager that, throughout the analysis of the question and the type of expected answer, provides accurate answers to the questions posed in Natural Language. The Dialogue Manager not only represents the semantics of the questions but also represents the structure of the discourse, including the user intentions and the questions' context, adding the ability to deal with multiple answers and providing justified answers. The system performance is evaluated by comparing with similar question answering systems. Although the test suite is of small dimension, the results obtained are very promising.

INTRODUCTION

The Semantic Web (SW), presented by Tim Berners-Lee (2001), has been recognized as the next step in the evolution of the World Wide Web. The inclusion of semantic contents on web pages allows machines to process such information and enables users to find, share and combine this information more easily.

Question Answering (QA) systems for Natural Language (NL) on the SW besides establishing the correspondence between words in documents, they must also find a precise answer, without user's help to interpret the documents returned - the use of knowledge and reasoning to interpret and to obtain the answers (Saint-Dizier & Moens, 2011).

DOI: 10.4018/978-1-5225-5042-6.ch012

Consistent with the role of ontologies in structuring and organizing semantic information on the web, QA systems based on ontologies allow exploring the expressive power of ontologies and enriching the queries' interpretation. Ontologies and the SW (Horrocks, 2008) have become formalisms able to represent the conceptual domains of knowledge and promote the capabilities of QA systems based on semantics (Guo & Zhang, 2009).

In this chapter, the authors introduce a Dialogue Manager that, by analysing the NL question (currently, only in English) and the type of expected answer, provides accurate answers. The Dialogue Manager not only represents the semantics of the questions, but also the structure of the discourse that includes the intentions of the user and the questions' context, allowing this way to deal with multiple answers and to justify those answers. The Dialogue Manager makes use of a controlled dialogue with the user for clarifying ambiguous situations. The Dialogue Manager resorts to ontologies, OWL2 descriptions and other web resources such as DBpedia (Auer, Bizer, Kobilarov, & Lehmann, 2007) and WordNet (Fellbaum, 1998). Ontologies are used to define, structure and fit the semantic information of the question and its terms, according to search domain, allowing to associate and contextualize terms, improving the question interpretation. The goal is to provide a tool that is independent of prior knowledge of semantic resources by the user and answer directly and accurately to questions posed in NL.

The remaining chapter is organized as follows. First, the authors present some related work, highlighting the similarities and differences with their proposal. Then, the authors introduce the proposed Dialogue Manager, highlighting its capabilities. Afterwards, the authors present a preliminary evaluation which boils down to an experimental set of tests done to the system. Finally, the authors elaborate about future work and present some conclusions. In addition, a description of the authors' Research Unit LISP - **L**aboratory of **I**nformatics, **S**ystems and **P**arallelism, is presented.

RELATED WORK

Cooperative QA systems are automatic systems of question and answer that automatically collaborate with the users, in order to obtain the information and clarification needed to provide the correct answer. These systems provide the user with additional information, intermediate answers, qualified answers and/ or alternative questions. An approach for processing cooperatives answers over databases is presented in Minker (1998). In McGuinness (2004), the author presents a set of techniques that promote the enhancement, its potential and impact on QA systems. Farah Benamara presents several works in this area: in Benamara (2004b), presents a logic-based model for accurate generation of intentional answers using a Cooperative QA system; in Benamara (2004a), presents a proposal for construction of a Logic-Based QA system, WEBCOOP, that integrates knowledge representation and advanced strategies of reasoning to generate cooperative answers to web queries. More recently, in Bakhtyar, Dang, Inoue, and Wiese (2014), the authors present an implementation of conceptual inductive learning operators in a prototype system for cooperative query answering, which can also be used as a usual concept learning mechanism for concepts described in first-order predicate logic.

The system START (Katz, Lin, & Felshin, 2002b; Katz, Borchardt, Felshin, Shen, & Zaccak, 2007), started in 1993 and evolved throughout the years, is a NLQA system that provides users with appropriate information segments, after parsing the questions, and matches the queries created from the parses trees against its knowledge base. START reformulates user questions into Omnibase (Katz, et al., 2002a) queries, establishing the link between NL and structured databases.

Querix (Kaufmann, Bernstein, & Zumstein, 2006) is an ontology-based QA system that relies on clarification dialogues in the case of ambiguities. NL queries are converted into SPARQL query form and WordNet is used to identify synonyms. Stanford parser is also used in this system to provide a syntax tree for the NL query. Querix does not exploit logic based semantic techniques.

PANTO (Wang, Xiong, Zhou, & Yu, 2007) is a portable NL interface to ontologies that accepts NL as input and outputs SPARQL. It is based on a triple model that constructed a parse tree for the data model using the Stanford parser (Klein & Manning, 2003). PANTO was evaluated with the Mooney geography dataset of 877 questions and they reported precision and recall of 88.05% and 85.86%, respectively.

FREyA (Damljanovic, Agatonovic, & Cunningham, 2010) is a Feedback Refinement and Extended Vocabulary Aggregation system that combines syntactic parsing with ontological knowledge for reducing customization effort. Precision and Recall values for the tested data are equal, reaching 92.4%. FREyA evolved from the previous work QuestIO (Tablan, Damljanovic, & Bontcheva, 2008), a Question-based Interface to Ontologies, which translates the NL a keyword-based question into SPARQL and returns the answer by executing the formal query against an ontology.

PowerAqua (Lopez, Fernández, Motta, & Stieler, 2012) is a multi-ontology based QA system that takes as input queries expressed in NL and is able to return answers drawn from relevant distributed resources on the SW. The system architecture and the reasoning methods are completely domain-independent, relying on the semantics of the ontology and the use of generic lexical resources, such as WordNet. PowerAqua evolved from the earlier AquaLog system (Lopez, Pasin, & Motta, 2005), a portable ontology-based semantic QA system for intranets.

BELA (Walter, Unger, Cimiano, & Bär, 2012) is a NLQA system over linked data, which processes natural language questions in a pipeline consisting of five steps: first, the natural language question parsing is made using syntactic analysis to generate SPARQL query templates also mirroring the semantic interpretation of the question; second, lookup in an inverted index, i.e., all generated queries are sent to the SPARQL endpoint and the highest ranked query that actually returns an answers is selected as final output; third, string similarity computation is used in case that the basic mechanism of index lookup fails; fourth, lookup in a lexical database in order to find synonyms; and fifth, semantic similarity computation is used in case the string similarity and lexical expansion steps do not find sufficiently high ranked hypotheses. This approach uses SPARQL queries to represent the natural question, as well as the corresponding answers and WordNet is used to find synonyms for a given word.

In (Athira, Sreeja, & Reghuraj, 2013), it is presented a NLQA system for a specific domain based on the ontological information, a step towards SWQA. NL processing techniques are used for processing the question and documents and also for answer extraction. Ontology and domain knowledge are used for reformulating queries and identifying the relations. The authors achieved 94% accuracy of NLQA.

Intui3 (Dima, 2014) is a NLQA system over linked data, which accepts as input a question formulated in natural language and uses syntactic and semantic information to construct its interpretation with respect to a given database of RDF triples. The interpretation is mapped to the corresponding SPARQL query, which is then run against a SPARQL endpoint to retrieve the answers to the initial question. The construction of a question interpretation is guided by Frege's Principle of Compositionality, namely the interpretation of a complex expression is determined by the interpretation of its constituent expressions and the rules used to combine them. The system uses an ontology, a predicate index and an entity index to construct the interpretations. Intui3 evolved from their prototype Intui2 (Dima, 2013) that was tested in the QALD-3 DBpedia test set.

QuASE (Sun, et al., 2015) is a three stage open domain approach based on web search and the Freebase knowledge base. First, QuASE uses entity linking, semantic feature construction and candidate ranking on the input question. Then, it selects the documents and according sentences from a web search with a high probability to match the question and presents them as answers to the user. Particularly, to construct answer-type related features is used two novel probabilistic models, which directly evaluate the appropriateness of an answer candidate's types under a given question. Overall, such semantic features turn out to play significant roles in determining the true answers from the large set of answer candidate.

Sina (Shekarpour, Marx, Ngomo, & Auer, 2015) is a scalable keyword search system that answers user queries by transforming user supplied keywords or natural languages queries into conjunctive SPARQL queries over a set of interlinked data sources. The basic idea behind this work was to develop a data-semantics-aware keyword search approach. This approach generates SPARQL queries from both natural language queries and keyword queries, and to achieve maximal flexibility is limited the type of SPARQL queries that can be generated into conjunctive SPARQL queries. A hidden Markov model is used to help in resource disambiguation and determine the most suitable resources for a user-supplied query from different datasets.

In recent years, mechanisms that classify automatically questions have become essential components for QA systems, helping and clarifying the questions types and the expected answers. For instance, in (Song, Wenyin, Gu, Quan, & Hao, 2011) the authors proposed an automatic method for question categorization in a user-interactive QA system, which includes feature space construction, topic-wise words identification and weighting, semantic mapping, and similarity calculation. Manfred Krifka (2011) classified three types of questions, according to the type of the lacking information: constituent questions, polarity questions, and alternative questions. Constituent questions create an open proposition by leaving parts of the description of the proposition unspecified. Languages apply interrogative pro-forms for this purpose. In English, these pro-forms have an initial wh-(pronoun or question).

The authors' proposal, as a Cooperative QA system, exploits a reduced set of NL Processing techniques (like Stanford parser, Discourse Representation Structures, WordNet), inference rules and a controlled dialogue (with the user) when it needs clarification. The main differentiable aspect is the cooperative way to achieve the answers to the NL questions: interacting with the user in order to disambiguate and/or to guide the path to obtaining the correct answer to the query posted. It also uses cooperation to provide more informed answers. The authors' proposal is similar to the ones presented above since it uses semantic interpretation techniques and a syntactic parser to interpret and represent the questions. Finally, it also resorts to reasoning and inference techniques to extract and filter the information needed from the knowledge bases.

DIALOGUE MANAGER

The Dialogue Manager is the main component of the system proposed in (Melo, Rodrigues, & Nogueira, 2012a; Melo, Rodrigues, & Nogueira, 2012b), a Cooperative QA system for Ontologies, and is invoked after the Natural Language question has been transformed into its semantic representation. Essentially, it searches for an answer by looking at the semantic interpretation of the question, the type of the expected answer, the ontology and the information available on the SW, as well as using string similarity matching and generic lexical resources.

Moreover, the Dialogue Manager verifies the question presupposition, chooses the sources of knowledge (Ontologies, WordNet, etc.) to be used; decides when the answer has been achieved or iterates using new sources of knowledge. The decision of when to relax a question in order to justify the answer, when to clarify a question and how to clarify it, is also taken in this module. Thus, the Dialogue Manager represents the intentions and beliefs of the system and the user, the structure of discourse and the context of the question.

The architecture of the Dialogue Manager is presented in Figure 1 and to help understand how it works, a brief discussion of the main components follows.

- Question DRS is the input information for Dialogue Manager and consists of the Discourse Representation Structure (DRS) of the NL question posed by the user and is supported by Discourse Representation Theory (Kamp & Reyle, 1993). The authors considered a DRS as a set of referents, universally quantified variables and a set of conditions (first-order predicates), where the conditions are either atomic (of the type $P(u_1,...,u_n)$ or $u_1 = u_2$) or complex (negation, implication, disjunction, conjunction or generalized quantifiers). The transformation of the NL question into its corresponding DRS is supported by two modules: the Syntactic Analysis and the Semantic Interpretation. The Syntactic Analysis module receives the NL question and uses grammatical interpretation to generate its derivation tree, using the Stanford parser, which is then transformed into its syntactic structure. The Semantic Interpretation module is responsible for rewriting the syntactic structure into its corresponding DRS. This process is based on first-order logic (Hodges, 2001) extended with generalized quantifiers (Barwise & Cooper, 1981). The authors take special care with the discourse entities in order to have the appropriate quantifier introduced by the determinant interpretation. The implementation of this component follows an approach similar to the one for constructing a QA system over document databases proposed in (Quaresma, Rodrigues, Prolo, & Vieira, 2006).

- Ontology Discovery is guided by the Dialogue Manager to obtain the extension of sentence representation along with the reasoning process. The Ontology Discovery is invoked when the Dialogue Manager has to look for knowledge base entities that represent the question's concepts. At this

Figure 1. Dialogue manager architecture

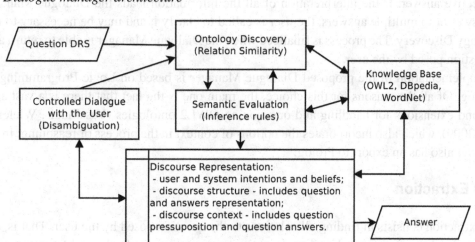

333

stage, the system performs ontology matching, e.g., has to transform the question DRS predicates into their corresponding ontological representation. So, the Ontology Discovery module maps the question's terms into the ontology concepts, in order to define and represent the question in terms of knowledge domain ontology. Essentially, this module searches for similarities between labels according to their string-based similarity, taking into account abbreviations, acronyms, domain and lexical knowledge. To maximize recall, the Ontology Discovery searches for classes, properties, instances and/or data values that have labels matching or contains a search term either exactly or partially. If no entity is found, the question concept is extended with its synonyms, hypernyms and hyponyms obtained from WordNet (Witzig & Center, 2003). Afterwards, a set of semantic resources is extracted and may contain the information requested. If the system did not find any correspondence to a term and its derivatives, e.g., no answer could be found, the user is informed and can clarify the system by reformulating the question or presenting other(s) query(ies).

- The Semantic Evaluation module is responsible for the system pragmatic evaluation, where the question semantics representation is transformed into a constraint satisfaction problem. The Semantic Evaluation must reinterpret the sentence representation, based on the considered ontology, in order to obtain the set of facts that represent the information provided by the question. This step is executed when the Ontology Discovery module finds a representation of the DRS. Afterwards, the system has to find the resources/entities of the knowledge base that are the solution to the ontological representation of the DRS. The solution will be added to the solutions set and the ontology representation of the DRS will be added to the discourse representation associated with the question. The Semantic Evaluation uses ontologies, SPARQL queries, and logic based semantic techniques.

In outline, the Dialogue Manager is invoked after transforming the NL question into its semantic representation and controls all the steps until the end, e.g., until the system can return an answer to the user. More specifically, the Ontology Discovery is invoked in order to provide the extension of sentence's representation. When the extension of the sentence's representation is complete, the Dialogue Manager adds to its knowledge a set of semantic resources. Afterwards, the Semantic Evaluation is invoked. At this step, the question semantics is transformed into a constraint satisfaction problem, by adding conditions to the discourse entities. This extra information can help the Dialogue Manager to formulate a more objective answer. If the interpretation of all the information leads the Dialogue Manager to an empty answer or to multiple answers, the user is called to clarify it and may be necessary to re-invoke the Ontology Discovery. The process is finalized when the Dialogue Manager is able to return an answer to the question posed by the user.

The implementation of the proposed Dialogue Manager is based on Logic Programming, specifically Prolog. Of all the reasons for this choice, the main one is the fact that there is a vast amount of libraries and extensions for handling and questioning OWL2 ontologies (Vassiliadis, Wielemaker, & Mungall, 2009), which also incorporates the notions of context in the process of reasoning. In addition, the WordNet also has an export to Prolog.

Answer Extraction

Answer extraction consists in finding all solutions to the question posed by the user. That is, when the NL question has been transformed into its semantic representation, the Dialogue Manager resorts to the ontology structure and the information available on the SW, as well as string similarity matching and generic lexical resources, in order to obtain the set of entities that are solutions to the question. The Dialogue Manager must supervise the search (made in the Ontology Discovery step) and validation (made by the Semantic Interpretation module) of the entities among the knowledge base and when a solution is found, it will be added to the discourse representation associated to the initial question.

Consider the question "Where is the Taj Mahal?", presented in (Burger, et al., 2001), and its semantic representation:

$$drs \begin{bmatrix} 'PLACE/LOCATION', \\ [where\text{-}X, exist\text{-}Y, exist\text{-}Z], [name(Y, 'Taj\,Mahal'), location(Y, Z), place(X)], [is(X, Z)] \end{bmatrix}$$

where the discourse referents are $where - X$, $exist - Y$ and $exist - Z$, with X an entity of the discourse universally quantified and Y and Z existentially quantified discourse entities, the predicate main question is $is(X, Z)$ and the presuppositions predicates are $name(Y, 'Taj\ Mahal')$, $location(Y, Z)$ and $place(X)$.

For this query, there are entities in DBpedia, which are related to the name "Taj Mahal". So, there is possible to obtain facts about the entities through a non-taxonomic relation that verifies the question. For instance, one entity that is related to the term "Taj Mahal" is the resource http://dbpedia.org/resource/Taj_Mahal_Palace and to state that this entity has its location in Bhopal and that Bhopal is a place, the DBpedia contains the following statements, i.e., triples RDF:

$dbpedia : Taj\_Mahal\_Palace\ \ dbpedia\text{-}owl : location\ \ dbpedia : Bhopal.$

$dbpedia : Bhopal\ \ rdf : type\ \ dbpedia\text{-}owl : Place.$

where:

$dbpedia :$ matches $< http : // dbpedia.org >;$
$dbpedia\text{-}owl :$ matches $< http : // dbpedia.org / ontology/ >;$ and
$rdf :$ matches $< http : // www.w3.org / 1999 / 02 / 22\text{-}rdf\text{-}syntax\text{-}ns\# >.$

That is, these statements validate the mappings of the questions terms in the ontology, namely: location is mapped into http://dbpedia.org/ontology/location and place is mapped into http://dbpedia.org/ontology/Place, and determine a solution to the semantic representation of the question.

$X = http : // dbpedia.org / resource / Bhopal$
$Y = http : // dbpedia.org / resource / Taj\_Mahal\_Palace$
$Z = http : // dbpedia.org / resource / Bhopal$

The solution, the RDF triples that generate the solution and the mappings of the question's terms in the ontology, which validate the semantic representation of the question, are added to the knowledge base of the question, the discourse's representation.

Answer Processing

Answer processing consists in determining the final representation of the answer returned to the user, which is interpreted in the knowledge base with the facts that were extracted. At this stage, the Dialogue Manager analyses the facts obtained (questions solutions) and gives the user an appropriate answer, taking into account the type of the question and the type of the expected answer:

- If the solutions set is empty, the answer has to inform that fact and the user can re-write the initial question, or make a new one, or simply stop the process.
- If the solutions set has only one solution, the answer presented to the user, besides direct and objective, also informs about the entities that support this, allowing a better communication between the system and the user.
- If the solutions set has multiple solutions, various interpretations can be made. If there is not enough information to decide which one is the correct, a controlled dialogue with the user is initiated. So, a set of alternatives is presented and the user's answer to those alternatives will clarify or restrict the subject is referring to. The set of alternatives is based on attributes that can distinguish the solutions. The Algorithm 1 shows how the system clarifies the ambiguity of multiple solutions. For each solution is constructed a set of alternatives based on the attributes of the best property that distinguish them. The set of alternatives is presented to the user. When the user's choice clarifies the ambiguity, the system can provide the answer to the initial question.

Algorithm 1. Multiple Solution's Clarification

Require: $S = \{s \mid s \text{ is a solution of the question}\}$
Ensure: Set an answer to the question
1: *while* $\#S > 1$ *do*
2:        For each referent collect their properties
3:        Choose the best property to differentiate the referents
4:
$A =$ values of the best property for each solution (where the property is defined)
5:        Show the clarification's alternatives based on the set A
6:        Receive the user's choice
7:        Restrict the set of solutions S to the user's choice
8: *end while*
9: Show solution S to the user

The Semantic Evaluation may induce the system to determine multiple results, reflecting ambiguities in question. In situations where the system does not have sufficient information to clarify the ambiguities, it needs to clarify the user intentions. For that, the system initiates a controlled dialogue, by activating the clarification mechanism presented in Algorithm 1. The reformulation of this algorithm follows the idea presented in (Quintano & Rodrigues, 2006) and to help understand how it works, a brief discussion of the main steps follows.

Evaluation of the Properties

The clarification alternatives must fulfill two important aspects: report the user intentions and supply the information that the user most likely knows. Regarding the latter, for instance, if the clarification concerns to a person characteristics, the authors can assume that it is more likely that the user knows its country than its birth date.

Regarding user intentions, the choice of alternatives to be presented to the user tries to compact the information by selecting properties more informative, achieved by resorting to the model of Decision Tree Learning (Quinlan, 1986). More precisely, the ID3 (Inductive Decision Tree) algorithm is used as a classification method in the construction of decision trees. The main reason for this choice is that decision trees can be applied to large data sets and make possible a real view of the nature of the decision process. In addition, decision trees are among the most practical and commonly method used in inductive inference.

Generally, in a decision tree, each node contains a test on a property; and each descending branch corresponds to a possible value of this property, their combination corresponds to the alternatives that will be presented to the user.

The ID3 algorithm was the first algorithm to be used for induction of decision trees. It is a recursive algorithm, which searches the set of properties that best divide the examples at the moment of choice, generating sub-trees. The ID3 algorithm uses Entropy and Information Gain to build the decision tree. However, the classification of properties by maximizing the information gain gives preference to properties with many values. For that reason, the authors also introduced the Information Gain Ratio as evaluation criteria, promoting properties with small Entropy and therefore promoting properties with fewer values. The concepts Entropy, Information Gain and Information Gain Ratio were originally presented in (Quinlan, 1986).

The Entropy of a set can be defined as the purity (certainty, accuracy) of that set. This concept borrowed from Information Theory defines the measure of "lack of information", namely the number of bits needed, on average, to represent the missing information, using optimal coding. If the set is completely uniform, the Entropy value is zero, and if the set is divided equitably, the Entropy value is equal to 1. Formally, the Entropy of a set is defined as follows:

Definition 1: *Given a set T , with instances of the class i , with probability $p_i \neq 0$. The Entropy of the set T is obtained by the following expression*

$$Entropy\left(T\right) = -\sum p_i \times log_2\left(p_i\right).$$

The Entropy of a set T verifies the property $0 < Entropy\left(T\right) < log_2\left(n\right)$, where n is the total of classes i .

Back to the example, the question posed by the user refers to the location of "Taj Mahal". When the Dialogue Manager analyses the solutions set and detects multiple solutions (i.e., there are several entities that represent the term "Taj Mahal", see Table 1), Algorithm 1 is performed.

DBpedia properties are expressed by RDF triples which impose the proprieties of each question's referents. In the example, the referent X associated to the question adverb is excluded, because it is semantically related to what the user wants to know. By analogy, the referent Z is also excluded, because the condition $is(X,Z)$ makes it semantically equal to the referent X. Thus, only remains the referent Y, which is associated with the name "Taj Mahal". Consequently, the set T contains only RDF triples (in the form Y $Property$ $Value$) associated to the referent Y.

Table 1 presents the different values of the solutions found by the system associated to the referent Y. To these values, corresponding to the classes where instances of T belong, are added the set of all RDF triples which are related with them. For instance, the class related to the term "Taj Mahal" has 81 RDF triples. The set T has 225 RDF triples. Thus, according to Definition 1 and the values presented in Table 2, the Entropy value of the set is:

$$Entropy(T) = \Sigma\left(-p_i \log_2(p_i)\right) =$$
$$= 0.5306152278 + 0.5041618283 + 0.4282672424 + 0.4789088711 =$$
$$= 1.9419531697$$

Table 1. Resources of the knowledge base, solutions' entities of the question "Where is the Taj Mahal?", that generate ambiguity

Name	Ontology's Resources
Taj Mahal	http://dbpedia.org/resource/Taj_Mahal
Taj Mahal Palace & Tower	http://dbpedia.org/resource/Taj_Mahal_Palace_&_Tower
Taj Mahal Palace	http://dbpedia.org/resource/Taj_Mahal_Palace
Taj Mahal Hotel (Delhi)	http://dbpedia.org/resource/Taj_Mahal_Hotel_(Delhi)

Table 2. Calculus of the parts for each class, to obtain the entropy value of the set T

Class i	$\#(Class\ i)$	$p_i = \dfrac{\#(Class\ i)}{\#T}$	$-p_i \times \log_2(p_i)$
Taj Mahal	81	$81 / 225 = 0.36$	0.5306152278
Taj Mahal Palace & Tower	58	$58 / 225 = 0.2577777778$	0.5041618283
Taj Mahal Palace	37	$37 / 225 = 0.1644444444$	0.4282672424
Taj Mahal Hotel (Delhi)	49	$49 / 225 = 0.2177777778$	0.4789088711

and has $0 < Entropia\left(T\right) = 1.9419531697 < log_2\left(n\right) = log_2\left(4\right) = 2$.

A derivation tree construction is guided by the goal of reducing the Entropy, the difficulty of predicting the variable that defines the classes. Thus,

Definition 2: *The Information Gain is the expected reduction in Entropy caused by partitioning the data, according to the property testing P. The Information Gain value for the property P is obtained by the expression:*

$$Gain\left(T,P\right) = Entropy\left(T\right) - \sum_{v \in values(P)} \left(\frac{|T_v|}{|T|} \times Entropy\left(T_v\right) \right).$$

Back to the example, it is necessary to calculate the Information Gain for each distinct property value and add it proportionally to obtain the final Entropy value of the property. The set T has 74 distinct properties (parameter *Property* in RDF triples) and the Definition 2 is applied on each property, used to clarify the multiplicity of solutions, the Table 3 presents the results of the Entropy and Information Gain values for some of the properties. 66 of the 74 properties have Entropy value equal to zero, which means that such properties generate just one alternative clarification and will result in an unnecessary step.

Choose the Best Property

The Information Gain criterion of a property selects the one that maximizes the Information Gain. However, this criterion gives preference to attributes with many possible values (which corresponds to the number of edges of the decision tree). In these cases, it could choose an irrelevant attribute, where

Table 3. Values of the entropy, information gain and the information gain ratio of the properties used to clarify the solutions' multiplicity of the question "Where is the Taj Mahal?"

Properties	Entropy	Information Gain	Gain Ratio
http://purl.org/dc/terms/subject	0.0869565	1.855	21.3325053331
http://dbpedia.org/property/location	0.333333	1.60862	4.8258648259
http://dbpedia.org/ontology/location	0.333333	1.60862	4.8258648259
http://dbpedia.org/property/wikiPageUsesTemplate	0.5	1.44195	2.8839
http://dbpedia.org/property/latns	1	0.941953	0.941953
http://dbpedia.org/property/longd	1	0.941953	0.941953
http://dbpedia.org/property/longew	1	0.941953	0.941953
http://www.w3.org/1999/02/22-rdf-syntax-ns	1.19356	0.748398	0.6270300613
http://dbpedia.org/property/architecture	0	1.94195	NA
...	...	...	...
http://dbpedia.org/property/longitude	0	1.94195	NA

there is only one alternative for each possible value. Therefore, the number of alternatives would be equal to the number of identifiers and the Entropy value would be minimal, because, in each property, all samples (if only one) belong to the same class, which would generate a maximum gain, although totally useless. When this problem occurs, e.g., when the property P to the set T has $Entropy(T, P) = 0$, which corresponds to the Information Gain maximum value, the Information Gain Ratio is used as evaluation criteria to choose the best property.

The concept Information Gain Ratio is the weight of Information Gain of the property relative to the Entropy of the property, e.g.,

Definition 3: *Consider the property P of the set T, the Information Gain Ratio value of the property P in the set T is obtain using the following expression:*

$$GainRatio(T,P) = \frac{Gain(T,P)}{Entropy(T,P)}.$$

The Information Gain Ratio is not defined when $Entropy(T,P) = 0$.

Table 3 also presents the values of the Information Gain Ratio to each property for the example considered.

However, even with these criteria, it is possible to have as best property, a property that presents information less known by the user. For example, if the best property represents numeric values (such as birth dates, the number of citizen card, etc.), it is more likely that the user may not know such information. So, by presenting such alternatives to the user could result in unnecessary step. In these cases, the authors define as a priority the properties containing information (value) that is non-numeric.

Definition 4: *Consider the property P to the set T. P is the best property when the Information Gain Ratio value is the highest and its values are non-numeric.*

Back to the example, and according to the Table 3, the property with the highest value of the Information Gain Ratio is http://purl.org/dc/terms/subject. Since this property has text values, it will be the chosen one. If the values of this property were numerical, the next property to be chosen would be the one with the best value of the Information Gain Ratio with a non-numerical domain.

Controlled Dialogue With the User

After defining how the evaluation of the properties is made - through the use of Entropy, Information Gain and information Gain Ratio; after defining how to choose the best property to present their values to the user as an alternative to the controlled dialogue - using the higher value of the Information Gain Ratio and the property that the information should be non-numeric; according to Algorithm 1, it remains to construct the set A, whose elements are the values of the best property, and then present them to the user, so that he can clarify the system on his intentions.

In the controlled dialogue with the user, besides specifying the alternatives presented by the system, the user also has three possibilities to interact with the system, namely: the symbol ?, meaning "I do not know"; the symbol !, meaning "show all answers"; and the term *quit*, that ends the process. In the first case, the system displays a new set of alternatives according to the current evaluation of properties. In the second case, the system displays all solutions and the process is finished. In the third case, the system simply ends the process.

Continuing the example and according to the evaluation, the best property is http://purl.org/dc/terms/subject, e.g., the one that satisfies the Definition 4. Consider T_1 the set of events of the set T where the best property occurs. The set of alternatives A is formed by the different values of the best property in the set T_1. Afterwards, the system starts a controlled dialogue with the user and presents the alternatives A:

$USER$: "*Where is Taj Mahal?*"
$SYSTEM$: "*Taj Mahal*" *refers to a* :
1 − *Buildings and structures completed in* 1654
2 − *Buildings and structures in Agra*
3 − *Mausoleums in India*
4 − *Mughal architecture*
...
$USER$: 3

The user choice (option 3) enables the system to clarify the subject that was questioned. In the example, the alternative chosen by the user leads the system to one solution. So the ambiguity is solved and the Dialogue Manager is able to process the answer and present it to the user.

$LOCATION / PLACE$:
  Agra, India
$RESOURCE$:
  $http://dbpedia.org/resource/Taj\_Mahal$
  The Taj Mahal is a mausoleum located in Agra, India.

If the user chooses one alternative with multiple solutions, the system has to execute the Algorithm 1 to clarify the ambiguity and a similar mechanism occurs with the difference that now the knowledge base has a richer question context.

The interaction with the user is used to help the system to reach the right path to the answer. Thus, this cooperation between the user and the system puts the user closer to the answer that meets its intentions. In many cases, the user is the only one who can help the system in the deduction and interpretation of the sentence information.

EXPERIMENTAL RESULTS

In the Dialogue Manager evaluation, the authors used the DBpedia ontology OWL2 (Bizer, et al., 2009), that covers about 359 classes forming a subsumption hierarchy, the classes are described by 1,775 different properties. The DBpedia knowledge base contained about 2,350,000 instances. The authors also used SPARQL endpoints, to query DBpedia database, and the DBpedia Lookup Service to look up DBpedia URIs by related keywords.

The evaluation test was performed using a set of 84 questions, randomly selected from the questions' set presented in TREC 9 (The Ninth Text REtrieval Conference (Voorhees, 2001), the main reason for this choice was the considerable amount of legitimate direct and simple "wh" questions with answers on the web). The set under analysis contains only direct "wh" questions, which comprises the following questions:

222. *Who is Anubis?*

232. *Who invented television?*

390. *Where was John Adams born?*

459. *When was John D. Rockefeller born?*

534. *Where is Windsor Castle?*

759. *What is the collective noun for geese?*

Comparison With Other Similar Systems

The set of questions was used to evaluate the proposed system performance on answering questions and also to compare its performance to that of two other similar systems: START and PowerAqua (version with DBpedia (Lopez, Fernández, Motta, & Stieler, 2012)). The main reason for this choice was that both systems provide a web interface for the question-answering mechanism. Although START is quite old, over the last decade, it evolved into a powerful tool, enclosing a very efficient syntactic and semantic techniques for answering questions posed in NL. None of these systems has a dialogue mechanism, but PowerAqua in the answer's interface allows the user to restrict and to interpret the results obtained. The tests were performed manually by the authors and the answers were validated one by one. Table 4 presents the performance of the current proposal and of the other two systems, providing the numbers of no-answers, correct answers, and wrong answers. It shows, that the authors can consider, that their proposal has good results compared to the other systems in terms of correct answers. The authors have detected that when their system does not find any solution, if it is applied constraint relaxation techniques to the referent predicates, the system can obtain more solutions, e.g., if the authors build a new set of questions related to the initial question, by combining the exclusion of the terms which restrict the initial question, then the system is able to find solutions to those new questions that might be solutions to the initial question. So, in order to improve the results of empty answers and wrong answer, in the future, the authors intend to apply constraint relaxation techniques when the system is searching through the ontology and thus the authors can increase the range of possible solutions. The authors also intend to implement other reasoning techniques with the goal to obtain better results.

Test Results of the Current Proposal

In Table 5, the authors can observe that their system has not obtained any answer to 10 questions (12% of the questions). That is, the system did not find, in the knowledge base, the resources that correspond to the questions terms or the entities that are solutions to these questions. For instance, in the question 759, the system did not find resources to enabling it to relate the terms "collective noun" and "geese". By starting a dialogue with the user, it is possible to rewrite the question, clarify the terms or place a new question. This way, and when the knowledge base has an answer, clearly the system will be able to increase the results. Analyzing the remaining corpus, reduced to 74 questions, the system obtained 68 correct answers (81% of the questions). Within these, 48 questions were multiple answers (57% of the questions) that, with the user clarification, the system returned the expected answer. The authors found that, for each question with multiple-solution, the system achieved an average of 3-4 (3.6167) solutions. Clearly, a reduced set of alternatives, highlighting the potential of the system in searching for the correct answer. In the remaining 6 questions (7% of the questions), the system did not get the correct answer.

The failures result from some factors that lead to incorrect interpretations, namely: semantic representation of the question; incomplete or badly formulated questions; dimension of the knowledge base,

Table 4. Information results of performance test applied to authors' proposal with the two systems, START and PowerAqua-DBpedia

System	No Answer	Correct Answer	Wrong Answer
Authors' Proposal	10	68	6
START	8	67	9
PowerAqua-DBpedia	3	66	15

Table 5. Information results of evaluation test applied to authors' proposal, a cooperative questions answering system for semantic web

	Total	Ratio
No Answer	10	12%
Correct Answer	68	81%
Simple Correct Answer	20	24%
Multiple Correct Answer	48	57%
Wrong Answer	6	7%
Simple Wrong Answer	2	2%
Multiple Wrong Answer	4	5%

or incomplete information and non-uniform ontology resources. For instance, in question "222. Who is Anubis?" the entity that represents "Anubis" is semantically related to the fact of being a person, which determines the answer to achieve. That is, the system has to find the entities in the knowledge base that are persons and whose name is "Anubis". However, the entity that gives the correct answer http://dbpedia.org/resource/Anubis bears no relation to the condition of being a person. Therefore the system is influenced in the path that will lead the system to achieve an incorrect answer, motivated both by the semantic representation of the question, as by the incomplete information resource, the knowledge base.

This is still a preliminary evaluation, summarizing just a first set of tests, whose results have produced satisfactorily, allowing the authors to verify the effectiveness of the proposed QA system and to identify the weaknesses that will enable the authors to improve its performance. In the future, the authors intend to present a more complete evaluation, tests with average users, extend the set of questions to others questions' types and to include the execution time in the evaluation. However, the results encouraged the authors to proceed.

FUTURE RESEARCH DIRECTIONS

As future work, the authors plan to improve the search ontology techniques and the inference rules, by adding constraint relaxation techniques and heuristic techniques, aiming to enhance the results of correctness and the execution time. The authors also plan to increase the number of tests, covering the remaining questions types (including more complex questions) and to define a more complete quantitative, qualitative and comparative evaluation of the system performance. In addition, the authors intend to extend the system to the Portuguese language. For this purpose, it is necessary to enrich the knowledge domain with Portuguese DBpedia ontology and Portuguese WordNet, enabling to support the concept of open domain and to take advantage of the large amount of heterogeneous semantic information provided by the SW.

CONCLUSION

The authors presented a Dialogue Manager that, throughout the analysis of the question and the type of the expected answer, allows to provide accurate answers to questions in NL. The Dialogue Manager not only represents the question semantics but also represents the structure of the discourse that includes the user intentions and the question's context, giving to the system the ability to deal with multiple answers and to provide justified answers.

The experiments made on a set of simple and direct "wh" questions showed that the proposed system has promising results. The authors also tested some complex questions and the system behaved as expected, returning the desired answers. Adding a tool, like Dialogue Manager, to the QA system improves substantially its performance. Resorting to a controlled dialogue, in order to clarify ambiguities, helps the system to better interpret the user intentions. These dialogues increase the results obtained by the system and help it to generate an answer that is more objective and with the information desired by the user. Since one of the authors' goals is to generate answers expressed in NL, their experiments showed the success of their approach. Therefore, the authors consider that their proposal is closer to one that helps to bridge the gap between the SW and real world users.

THE LISP RESEARCH UNIT

The LISP, Laboratory of Informatics, Systems and Parallelism (http://www.en.iifa.uevora.pt/sobre/estrutura_do_iifa/(centro_investigacao)/64191), research unit was funded in 2015 and builds on the strengths of its individual researchers, providing a framework for collaborative work. LISP core topics include high-performance declarative computing, natural language understanding, information retrieval and legal reasoning, formal methods for code integrity, security and cloud computing. Application-wise, LISP projects target resource planning and optimisation in health informatics, natural resources and transportation, also business intelligence and computer forensics.

Besides the Universities of Évora, Beira Interior and the Algarve, LISP also integrates the Beja Polytechnic Institute, further extending its regional coverage and researcher pool.

All three universities promote PhD programmes in Computer Science, for which the collaboration among members of the laboratory is paramount. These benefit from student mobility in Erasmus Mundus and Erasmus Plus networks.

REFERENCES

Athira, P. M., Sreeja, M., & Reghuraj, P. (2013). Architecture of an Ontology-Based Domain-Specific Natural Language Question Answering System. *International Journal of Web & Semantic Technology*, *4*. doi:10.5121/ijwest.2013.4403

Auer, S., Bizer, C., Kobilarov, G., Lehmann, J., Cyganiak, R., & Ives, Z. (2007). Dbpedia: A nucleus for a web of open data. *The Semantic Web*, *4825*, 722–735. doi:10.1007/978-3-540-76298-0_52

Bakhtyar, M., Dang, N., Inoue, K., & Wiese, L. (2014). Implementing Inductive Concept Learning For Cooperative Query Answering. *Data Analysis, Machine Learning and Knowledge Discovery*, 127-134. doi:10.1007/978-3-319-01595-8_14

Barwise, J., & Cooper, R. (1981). Generalized quantifiers and natural language. *Linguistics and Philosophy*, *4*(2), 159–219. doi:10.1007/BF00350139

Benamara, F. (2004a). Cooperative Question Answering in Restricted Domains: the WEBCOOP Experiment. In D. M. Aliod, & J. L. Vicedo (Eds.), ACL Worshop on Question Answering in Restricted Domains (pp. 31-38). Barcelona, Spain: Association for Computational Linguistics.

Benamara, F. (2004b). Generating Intensional Answers in Intelligent Question Answering Systems. In A. Belz, R. Evans, & P. Piwek (Eds.), Lecture Notes in Computer Science: Vol. 3123. Natural Language Generation (pp. 11-20). Springer Berlin Heidelberg. doi:10.1007/978-3-540-27823-8_2

Berners-Lee, T., Hendler, J., & Lassila, O. (2001). The semantic web. *Scientific American*, *284*(5), 34–43. doi:10.1038/scientificamerican0501-34 PMID:11396337

Bizer, C., Lehmann, J., Kobilarov, G., Auer, S., Becker, C., Cyganiak, R., & Hellmann, S. (2009). DBpedia-A crystallization point for the Web of Data. *Web Semantics: Science, Services, and Agents on the World Wide Web*, *7*(3), 154–165. doi:10.1016/j.websem.2009.07.002

Burger, J., Cardie, C., Chaudhri, V., Gaizauskas, R., Harabagiu, S., Israel, D., . . . Miller, G. (2001). Issues, tasks and program structures to roadmap research in question & answering (Q&A). *Document Understanding Conferences Roadmapping Documents*, 1-35.

Damljanovic, D., Agatonovic, M., & Cunningham, H. (2010). *Natural language interfaces to ontologies: combining syntactic analysis and ontology-based lookup through the user interaction.* Heraklion, Crete, Greece: Springer-Verlag. doi:10.1007/978-3-642-13486-9_8

Dima, C. (2013). Intui2: A prototype system for question answering over linked data. *Proceedings of the Question Answering over Linked Data lab (QALD-3) at CLEF*.

Dima, C. (2014, September). Answering Natural Language Questions with Intui3. Working Notes for CLEF 2014 Conference, 1180, 1201-1211.

Fellbaum, C. (1998, May). *WordNet: An Electronic Lexical Database (Language, Speech, and Communication*. The MIT Press.

Guo, Q., & Zhang, M. (2009). Question answering based on pervasive agent ontology and Semantic Web. Knowledge-Based Systems, 22, 443-448. doi:10.1016/j.knosys.2009.06.003

Hodges, W. (2001). Classical logic I: first-order logic. *The Blackwell guide to philosophical logic*, 9-32.

Horrocks, I. (2008, December). Ontologies and the semantic web. *Communications of the ACM*, *51*(12), 58–67. doi:10.1145/1409360.1409377

Kamp, H., & Reyle, U. (1993). *From Discourse to Logic*. Dordrecht, The Netherlands: Kluwer Academic Publishers.

Katz, B., Borchardt, G., Felshin, S., Shen, Y., & Zaccak, G. (2007). Answering English Questions using Foreign-Language, Semi-Structured Sources. *First IEEE International Conference on Semantic Computing (ICSC 2007)*, 439-445. doi:10.1109/ICSC.2007.59

Katz, B., Felshin, S., Yuret, D., Ibrahim, A., Lin, J. J., Marton, G., & Temelkuran, B. et al. (2002a). Omnibase: Uniform Access to Heterogeneous Data for Question Answering. *6th International Conference on Applications of Natural Language to Information Systems* (pp. 230-234). London, UK: Springer-Verlag. doi:10.1007/3-540-36271-1_23

Katz, B., Lin, J. J., & Felshin, S. (2002b). The START Multimedia Information System: Current Technology and Future Directions. *MIS 2002, International Workshop on Multimedia Information Systems* (pp. 117-123). Tempe, AZ: Arizona State University.

Kaufmann, E., Bernstein, A., & Zumstein, R. (2006). Querix: A Natural Language Interface to Query Ontologies Based on Clarification Dialogs. In *5th International Semantic Web Conference (ISWC 2006)* (pp. 980-981). Athens, GA: Springer. doi:10.1007/11926078_78

Klein, D., & Manning, C. D. (2003). Accurate unlexicalized parsing. *41st Annual Meeting on Association for Computational Linguistics* (vol. 1, pp. 423-430). Sapporo, Japan: Association for Computational Linguistics. doi:10.3115/1075096.1075150

Krifka, M. (2011). Questions. In K. v. Heusinger, C. Maienborn, & P. Portner (Eds.), Semantics: An international handbook of Natural Language Meaning (pp. 1742-1785). Berlin: Mouton de Gruyter.

Lopez, V., Fernández, M., Motta, E., & Stieler, N. (2012). PowerAqua: Supporting users in querying and exploring the Semantic Web. *Semantic Web, 3,* 249–265. doi:10.3233/SW-2011-0030

Lopez, V., Pasin, M., & Motta, E. (2005). AquaLog: An Ontology-Portable Question Answering System. *Lecture Notes in Computer Science, 3532,* 546–562. doi:10.1007/11431053_37

McGuinness, D. L. (2004). Question Answering on the Semantic Web. *IEEE Intelligent Systems, 19*(1), 82–85. doi:10.1109/MIS.2004.1265890

Melo, D., Rodrigues, I. P., & Nogueira, V. B. (2012a). Puzzle Out the Semantic Web Search. International Journal of Computational Linguistics and Applications, 3, 91-106.

Melo, D., Rodrigues, I. P., & Nogueira, V. B. (2012b). Work Out the Semantic Web Search: The Cooperative Way. *Advances in Artificial Intelligence, 2012,* 867831:1-867831:9. doi:10.1155/2012/867831

Minker, J. (1998). An overview of cooperative answering in databases. In T. Andreasen, H. Christiansen, & H. Larsen (Eds.), Lecture Notes in Computer Science: Vol. 1495. Flexible Query Answering Systems (pp. 282-285). Springer Berlin Heidelberg. doi:10.1007/BFb0056009

Quaresma, P., Rodrigues, I., Prolo, C., & Vieira, R. (2006). Um sistema de Pergunta-Resposta para uma base de Documentos. *Letras de Hoje,* 43-63.

Quinlan, J. R. (1986). Induction of Decision Trees. *Machine Learning, 1*(1), 81–106. doi:10.1007/BF00116251

Quintano, L., & Rodrigues, I. (2006). Using a logic programming framework to control database query dialogues in natural language. In *22nd international conference on Logic Programming* (pp. 406-420). Seattle, WA: Springer-Verlag. doi:10.1007/11799573_30

Saint-Dizier, P., & Moens, M.-F. (2011). Knowledge and reasoning for question answering: Research perspectives. *Information Processing & Management, 47,* 899 - 906.

Shekarpour, S., Marx, E., Ngomo, N. A., & Auer, S. (2015). SINA: Semantic interpretation of user queries for question answering on interlinked data. *Web Semantics: Science, Services, and Agents on the World Wide Web, 30,* 39–51. doi:10.1016/j.websem.2014.06.002

Song, W., Wenyin, L., Gu, N., Quan, X., & Hao, T. (2011). Automatic categorization of questions for user-interactive question answering. *Information Processing & Management, 47*(2), 147–156. doi:10.1016/j.ipm.2010.03.002

Sun, H., Ma, H., Yih, W., Tsai, C., Liu, J., & Chang, M. (2015). Open Domain Question Answering via Semantic Enrichment. *Proceedings of the 24th International Conference on World Wide Web,* 1045-1055. doi:10.1145/2736277.2741651

Tablan, V., Damljanovic, D., & Bontcheva, K. (2008). A natural language query interface to structured information. In *5th European semantic web conference on The semantic web: research and applications* (pp. 361-375). Tenerife, Canary Islands, Spain: Springer-Verlag.

Vassiliadis, V., Wielemaker, J., & Mungall, C. (2009). Processing OWL2 Ontologies using Thea: An Application of Logic Programming. *6th International Workshop on OWl: Experiences and Direction, OWLD 2009.*

Voorhees, E. M. (2001). Overview of the TREC-9 Question Answering Track. In *Ninth Text REtrieval Conference (TREC-9)* (pp. 71-80). Gaithersburg, MD: National Institute of Standards and Technology (NIST).

Walter, S., Unger, C., Cimiano, P., & Bär, D. (2012). Evaluation of a Layered Approach to Question Answering over Linked Data. *The Semantic Web -- ISWC 2012: 11th International Semantic Web Conference, 7650,* 362-374. doi:10.1007/978-3-642-35173-0_25

Wang, C., Xiong, M., Zhou, Q., & Yu, Y. (2007). PANTO: A Portable Natural Language Interface to Ontologies. *4th European conference on The Semantic Web: Research and Applications* (pp. 473-487). Innsbruck, Austria: Springer-Verlag. doi:10.1007/978-3-540-72667-8_34

Witzig, S., & Center, A. (2003). Accessing wordnet from prolog. Artificial Intelligence Centre, University of Georgia.

KEY TERMS AND DEFINITIONS

Answer Extraction: The process of finding all solutions to the question posed by the user.

Answer Processing: The process of determining the final representation of the answer returned to the user, which is interpreted in the knowledge base with the facts that were extracted.

Best Property of a Set: A property of a set that has the highest Information Gain Ratio value among all properties of the set and its information values are non-numeric.

Controlled Dialogue: A clarification mechanism that presents to the user a set of alternatives, based on the multiple solutions found to the question posed by the user, and guides the system in clarifying the ambiguities and the user intentions about the question posed.

Dialogue Manager: The main component of the Natural Language Cooperative Question Answering system for Ontologies. The Dialogue Manager is invoked after the Natural Language question has been transformed into its semantic representation. Essentially, it searches for an answer by looking at the semantic interpretation of the question, the type of the expected answer, the ontology and the information available on the Semantic Web, as well as using string similarity matching and generic lexical resources.

Discourse Representation Structure (DRS): A set of referents, universally quantified variables and a set of conditions (first-order predicates), where the conditions are either atomic (of the $P\left(u_1,...,u_n\right)$ type or $u_1 = u_2$) or complex (negation, implication, disjunction, conjunction or generalized quantifiers).

Entropy of a Set: The purity (certainty, accuracy) of the set. The Entropy concept borrowed from Information Theory defines the measure of "lack of information", namely the number of bits needed, on average, to represent the missing information, using optimal coding. If the set is completely uniform, the Entropy value is zero, and if the set is divided equitably, the Entropy value is 1.

Information Gain: The expected reduction in Entropy caused by partitioning the data set, according to some property testing.

Information Gain Ratio: The weight of Information Gain of some property relative to the Entropy of that property. The Information Gain Ratio is not defined when the Entropy of that property is equal to zero.

Question DRS: A Discourse Representation Structure (DRS) of the Natural Language question posed by the user. The Question DRS is the input information for Dialogue Manager.

Chapter 13
Ontology Maintenance Through Semantic Text Mining:
An Application for IT Governance Domain

Andrea Ko
Corvinus University of Budapest, Hungary

Saira Gillani
Saudi Electronic University, Saudi Arabia

ABSTRACT

Manual ontology population and enrichment is a complex task that require professional experience involving a lot of efforts. The authors' paper deals with the challenges and possible solutions for semi-automatic ontology enrichment and population. ProMine has two main contributions; one is the semantic-based text mining approach for automatically identifying domain-specific knowledge elements; the other is the automatic categorization of these extracted knowledge elements by using Wiktionary. ProMine ontology enrichment solution was applied in IT audit domain of an e-learning system. After seven cycles of the application ProMine, the number of automatically identified new concepts are significantly increased and ProMine categorized new concepts with high precision and recall.

INTRODUCTION

Intelligent systems are all around us, we use them in cars, mobiles, smart meters and in several other places. These systems are context-sensitive and require domain-specific knowledge to operate. In a case of complex domains, ontologies are widely used to provide the underlying knowledge structure. We followed this ontology based approach in several research projects related to intelligent systems development. The ProKEX research (Gábor & Kő, 2016) aimed to develop a complex application to extract, organize and preserve knowledge embedded in organizational processes in order to (1) enrich the organizational knowledge base in a systematic and controlled way. ProKEX IT solution integrates (a) an organizational process management tool, (b) a learning management tool, (c) a monitoring and feedback tool and (d) data and text mining tools for developing a knowledge base (domain ontology)

DOI: 10.4018/978-1-5225-5042-6.ch013

and the interfaces which are responsible for the communication between these components. The text mining solution, which we applied in ProKEX called ProMine was used for ontology enrichment based on the extraction of deep representations from business processes. ProMine extracts new domain-related concepts using a new filtering mechanism to filter the most relevant concepts, based on a novel hybrid similarity measure (Gillani & Kő, 2016).

SAKE (Semantic-enabled agile knowledge-based e-Government) solution (Kő, Kovács, & Gábor, 2011) was utilized in several other fields and projects; especially in the investigation of job market needs, educational system supply and managing information overload gained benefit from it (Kő et al., 2011; Matas, 2012; "UbiPOL ", 2009). In SAKE project ontology development was one of the most complex and time-consuming tasks that required professional experience involving a lot of expert discussions and efforts. Ubipol (Ubiquitous Participation Platform for Policy Making) solution ("UbiPOL ", 2009) is a ubiquitous platform that allows citizens to become involved in policy-making processes (PMPs) regardless of their current location and time. It performs private semantic information retrieval based on an ontology outlined in policies; and ubiquitous data-mining at the device level, along with privacy-preserving data-mining at the server level (Husaini, Ko, Tapucu, & Saygın, 2012; Kő, 2012). In all projects mentioned above, the authors struggled with ontology maintenance and enrichment, because the domain knowledge and the regulatory environment become outdated fast.

Ontologies have been studied for a long time in the fields of semantic technologies, artificial intelligence and knowledge management. Current state-of-the art research in ontologies has focused on the development methods and possible applications of ontologies (Khondoker & Mueller, 2010; López, Pérez, & Amaya, 2000; Pan, Staab, Aßmann, Ebert, & Zhao, 2012). However, there remain many obstacles for the management and enrichment of ontologies (Gasevic, Zouaq, Torniai, Jovanovic, & Hatala, 2011; Miranda, Isaias, & Costa, 2014). Ontology learning, enrichment and maintenance is an ongoing and complex process, with several challenges (Shamsfard & Abdollahzadeh Barforoush, 2003; Wong, Liu, & Bennamoun, 2012; Zouaq, Gasevic, & Hatala, 2011). It has a key role in ontology management; it tackles the issues to turn facts and patterns from the content into shareable high-level constructs or ontologies.

Any ontology update or maintenance can have several consequences. Deleting or adding an ontology object have effect to other objects, it can modify relations, objects and axioms. In a case of the huge number of ontology objects, regular update requires standard process.

This paper aims to discuss an ontology enrichment and maintenance method, using an innovative text mining solution, namely ProMine. We describe the ontology learning environment based on a semantic text mining method, which is applied to populate, enrich and renew IT governance domain ontology. The method can be used for ontology maintenance and as well as for validation purposes in another domain. Domain experts, in our case IT audit professionals (Certified Information Systems Auditors (CISAs)) prepared the first version of IT governance/IT audit domain ontology, which was populated and enriched with ProMine solution.

IT is a strategic asset and important contributor to economic success (ISACA, 2011). Today in our technology-enabled world, where organizations are faced with digital transformation, the digital presence and protect IT resources are vital to be competitive. IT governance field has a key importance for IT professionals especially for managers. It helps to ensure that the investments in IT generate value and mitigate IT-associated risks, avoiding failure. IT governance has several definitions, like in ISACA glossary: the responsibility of executives and the board of directors; consists of the leadership, organizational structures and processes that ensure that the enterprise's IT sustains and extends the enterprise's strategies and objectives. (ISACA, 2017). Governance of Enterprise IT (GEIT) deals with organizing the IT resources of an enterprise for the purpose of satisfying stakeholders' needs. It includes the following three key elements: evaluate, direct and monitor on the general management of IT resources (ISACA, 2016b).

IT governance and IT audit domain are very complex areas, they have to renew systematically because of the frequent changes in IT technology and because of the new IT security risks, which arise every day. Additionally this field is strictly regulated and regulations, standards are updated from time to time.

The security risks are mitigated by controls. These controls (their planning, operation and monitoring) are in the focus of IT audit and IT governance as well (ISACA, 2015), (ISACA, 2016a). Legal and regulatory risks were identified as a major area of risks in the internal audit survey 2014 (Michael Cowan, 2014). COBIT as the most decisive IT audit standard, was recently renewed. According to these modifications, companies have to update their IT security and audit related policies as well. Because of the frequent changes in the field, there is a regular need for renewal IT governance domain ontology too.

The main contributions of our approach are:

- Combining semantic relatedness measures and pattern acquisition techniques for information extraction.
- Populating and enriching large-scale domain ontologies that can facilitate the time-consuming and costly manual enrichment process of ontologies.

The novel aspect of our proposed framework is semi-automatically semantic concept categorization with semantic interpretation with easy implementation/low computation work. The contributions of this paper are twofold. First, an automatic semantic concept extraction approach is presented that extracts semantic knowledge elements by using domain corpus and lexical semantic resources. This concept extraction approach extracts new concepts automatically without human interaction. Second, the proposed semi-automatic (at one level domain expert opinion is required) concept categorization approach exploits ontology hierarchical structure and relations to provide a more accurate assessment of the similarity between terms. Moreover, using Wiktionary-based concepts make this model easy to interpret, as it is illustrated with a number of examples.

This paper is structured as follows: First, ontology enrichment challenges are outlined and ontology learning related state of the art is discussed. ProMine Ontology Learning Framework is presented afterwards, followed by the application of ProMine for IT governance domain ontology population and enrichment. Assessment of the ProMine application is detailed in datasets and evaluation procedure part. Finally, results and conclusion is presented.

RELATED WORK

The review of related work concerns achievements in the concept extraction and semantic concept categorization for ontology learning and state of the art of ontology enrichment.

Ontology learning refers to the process of integration of a set of methods and techniques used for ontology engineering from scratch, enriching, or adapting an existing ontology in a semi-automatic fashion using several sources(Meyer & Gurevych, 2012). Ontology learning is a research area, which deals with the challenges to turn facts and patterns from the content into shareable high-level constructs or ontologies(Wong et al., 2012). For ontology learning, there are different approaches presented in literature, these approaches can group into three main categories; manual approaches, semi-automatic and automatic approaches. In manual approaches, domain experts play an essential role in every task such as concept extraction, defining classes, hierarchies and generating instances (Noy&Mc2001). Such type of ontologies have high level of accuracy because these are executed and verified by humans. However, it requires a lot of time and human efforts and for large scale ontologies it also becomes impossible to manage such ontologies (Nguyen & Yang, 2012). In contrast, automatic approaches try to perform all tasks automatically without human involvement (Blaschke & Valencia, 2002; Dahab, Hassan, & Rafea, 2008; C.-S. Lee, Kao, Kuo, & Wang, 2007). However, if these methods are analyzed in detail, then will come to know, that all these systems are performing some tasks of ontology construction automatically and for others human participation is required as in (Dahab et al., 2008) system at semantic patterns construction phase, ontology engineers select the text and enables the editor to generate the correspondence semantic pattern. Episode-based Chinese domain ontology construction system (C.-S. Lee et al., 2007) also needs domain experts for validate the attributes, operations, and associations. Therefore, this is not fully automated system. Many researchers believe that ontology learning as a whole process cannot be, by its very nature, fully automatic (Buitelaar & Cimiano, 2008; Nguyen & Yang, 2012; Völker, 2009). In some tasks such as mapping and evaluation of ontology, a significant degree of user involvement is unavoidable, because some qualitative aspects related to these tasks directly relate to human perception. Therefore, a semi-automatic ontology construction approach is required in which at some stage of the ontology learning process a user is asked to judge the correctness of the results. These semi-automatic approaches require expert knowledge to verify the obtained information and decide which information should be included in the ontology. Similarly, this presented system is also using a semi-automatic approach of ontology learning in which new concepts are extracted automatically while for the evaluation of categorization process, domain expert's opinion is needed.

ISOLDE (Weber & Buitelaar, 2006) is a system to populate a base domain ontology with new concepts and relations by combining a domain corpus, a general purpose NER and web resources like Wikipedia, Wiktionary and a German online dictionary (DWDS). In the first place, this system extracts instances from a base ontology with the help of NER system. New concepts are generated by applying lexico-syntactic patterns from base ontology class candidates. For filtration of these concepts, web resources are exploited and to determine the relevance between these concepts, a statistical measure x^2 x^2 of are used. Their results showed that semi-structured data resources seems worthwhile. This approach is basically aims at a taxonomy rather than a complete ontology. Generally, there are more error chances in automatic taxonomy construction.

In (Meyer & Gurevych, 2012), authors used Wiktionary for the construction of an upper level ontology. They highlighted the limitations of Wikipedia to use it as a knowledge base. They described a two stepped approach "OntoWiktionary", one is harvesting knowledge to extract knowledge from Wiktionary and other step is ontologizing knowledge for formation of concepts and relations. in first phase, they developed a new adapter, Wikokit, which allows to extract data from Wiktionary. In ontologizing phase, this system defines concepts of OntOWiktiOnary with the help of ontoWordNet. This two phase approach automatically enriched the extracted data and this data can be used to improve NLP solutions. our work is different in that we have seed ontology and want to enrich this seed ontology with new domain concepts. it means taxonomy or categories are already defined in the seed ontology and want to enrich these categories with new domain concepts. Although, ProMine is also used Wiktionary as a part with other resources for concept extraction and categorization. However, focus of our work is different from OntoWiktionary.

Literature showed that Wikipedia became an important resource for ontology learning (Janik & Kochut, 2008; Suchanek, Kasneci, & Weikum, 2008). Although, Wikipedia yields a densely connected taxonomy of concepts, Ponzetto and Strube (Ponzetto & Strube, 2007) point out that the Wikipedia categories "do not form a taxonomy with a fully-fledged subsumption hierarchy." but represents the domain the concept is used in. Another problem of a Wikipedia-based ontology lies in the lexicalizations of concepts. In order to reduce redundancy, each concept is encoded only once within Wikipedia and thus described within the article with the most common lexicalization of the concept. Another problem with Wikipedia is that it is a very huge, rich database so, there are chances that any two entities have more than one relations with different strengths. To assign weights according to their strength is a quite tricky task and a heuristic algorithm with a lot of computation is required.

To overcome these literature gaps, ProMine framework uses Wiktionary as an external resource for the semantic concept categorization module. It takes categories from the seed ontology with some basic concepts and enrich these categories with the help of Wiktionary. The objective of our framework is to facilitate ontology learning from texts in real-world settings through two main basic tasks; one is concept extraction from text and the other is semantic concept categorization.

PROMINE ONTOLOGY LEARNING FRAMEWORK

This section proposes a flexible framework called ProMine for ontology learning from text. This system involves the successive application of various NLP techniques and learning algorithms for concept extraction and ontology enrichment. ProMine development is part of PROKEX project (EUREKA_HU_12-1-2012-0039) to build ontologies semi-automatically by processing a collection of texts of different domains. ProMine uses several text mining and data mining techniques for ontology learning which led to the development and enrichment of a domain ontology. Therefore, with the help of this framework an ontology can be built rather to enrich and populate an existing ontology .

We have developed a prototype workbench that performs two basic tasks; one is knowledge element extraction from the domain document corpus and other sources, and the other task is semantic concept categorizer that will help the enrichment and population of domain ontology with these extracted knowledge elements. Initial work of ProMine concept extraction is presented in (Gillani & Kő, 2014). This prototype will show our proposed framework's efficacy as a workbench for testing and evaluating semantic concept categorization.

This section embodies ProMine as a framework to extract knowledge elements from the context data as illustrated in Figure1. The workflow of our ontology framework proceeds through the phases of (i) Preliminary Phase for text preprocessing; (ii) Concept Enrichment Phase to extract concepts from domain corpus and other sources; (iii) Similarity Matching between candidate concepts by using a similarity measure that is the combination of a statistical measure and a semantic measure; (iv) The last phase or module of ProMine framework is a semantic concept categorization that is used to refine extracted knowledge elements in the form of categories for ontology enrichment. Below we provide detailed descriptions of these phases.

Figure 1. ProMine: A text mining framework of ontology population and enrichment (Source: Gillani, 2015)

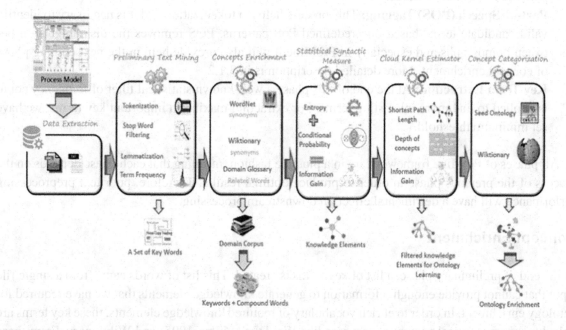

Preliminary Phase: Preprocessing of Data

A major difference between existing ontology learning frameworks and ProMine is the data extraction that starts from a small sized input file. This file can be an output file of a process model in the form of XML file (semi structured data) or any text file (unstructured data). At the first step of this framework(data extraction phase), the pertinent information from these input files is extracted automatically by ProMine. After extracting specific text from the input files, this text is saved in a text file.

After text extraction, the most crucial part, cleaning of extracted text starts. Preprocessing portrays any sort of transformation performed on unstructured text to set it up in such format that it will be easily and efficiently processed. This preprocessing module ensures that data are prepared for subsequent activities, which are discussed later in the description. Text preprocessing is an integral part of natural language processing (NLP) system. Text preprocessing includes in general different NLP and text mining techniques such as tokenization, stop word removal, part-of-speech (POS) tagging, stemming or lemmatization and frequency count.

By applying these techniques, the input text is transformed into term vector and the weight of each term is based on the frequency of the term in an input file. For multivariate text analysis, in ProMine, the following preprocessing techniques have been implemented.

- **Tokenization:** In this process unstructured text is segmented into tokens or words and these words are our processing unit. Word boundaries are defined and this process is totally domain dependent. This is also called sentence segmentation.
- **Stop Words Filtering:** To reduce the dimensionality of tokenized data, stop word filter is applied. In this process most frequent but unimportant words that have no semantic content relative to a

specific domain are removed from the data. This list of words is user defined so modification is possible in this list of words.

- **Part-of-Speech (POS) Tagging:** This process helps in tokenization and it is necessary to identify valid candidate terms based on predefined PoS patterns. POS removes the disambiguation between homographs and especially in ProMine it will also provide help in the next coming phase of concept enrichment. More detailed description is in 3.1.2.
- **Key Term Extraction:** At the end of this phase a well-known statistical filter of frequency count is applied to find more interesting terms. For extracting maximum important key terms, we have set minimum threshold.

All phases of ProMine framework are in a pipeline fashion, meaning that each phase depends on the success of the previous phase in order to produce optimal results. Therefore, poor text preprocessing performance will have a detrimental effect on downstream processing.

Concept Enrichment

At the end of preliminary phase, a list of key terms is created. This list of words came from a single file input that cannot provide enough information to generate knowledge elements that we have required for ontology enrichment. In order to enrich vocabulary of required knowledge elements, these key terms are linked to external lexical semantic resources like WordNet (Miller, 1995) and Wiktionary. From these lexicons, we extract similar words (synonyms). WordNet is a semantic database that provides a synset of a given key-word and words in this synset are linked by semantic relations (Luong, Gauch, & Wang, 2012). As of the current version 3.0, WordNet contains 82,115 synsets for 117,798 unique nouns. Using WordNet without further considerations limits the performance of a system, since each resource has its own advantages. Wiktionary is larger in size as compared to WordNet. Like Wikipedia, any web user can edit it that causes to grow its content very quickly. However, semantic relations in parsed Wiktionary are less than WordNet. Therefore, we have used both WordNet & Wiktionary as external sources to expand a concept's vocabulary for extracting useful knowledge elements. For every key term, we get a set of synonyms from WordNet. Additionally Wiktionary generate a combine synset of unique words that is a list of candidate words related to a key term.

WordNet has different senses of a word so; many irrelevant words (have semantically same meaning, but can not a part of specific domain) are also generated. We have to filter out such candidate words. For this purpose, a domain corpus is required that may include domain glossaries or legal documents or any type of domain related documents. To overcome such ambiguity, we apply a procedure of few steps that will filter out such ambiguous words and as well as automatically extracts a set of domain-specific key-concepts in the form of compound words from the domain corpus. WordNet database does not provide all compound words/multiword terms. Concepts can be more informative in compound or multi-word terms as compared to single words. Therefore, at this step, multiword terms are also extracted from the given corpus because these multiword terms represent concepts that are more important to get meaningful knowledge elements. For example for "governance" keyword, the multiword terms can be: "enterprise governance", "corporate governance" and "IT Governance". These multiword terms have different meanings: "Corporate governance broadly refers to the mechanisms, processes and relations by which corporations are controlled and directed" (Shailer, 2004), while "enterprise governance is the set of responsibilities and practices exercised by the board and executive management with the goal of

Figure 2. ProMine: Data extraction and word expansion

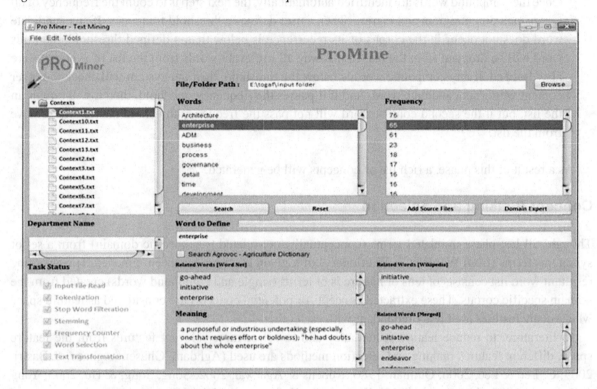

providing strategic direction, ensuring that objectives are achieved, ascertaining that risks are managed appropriately and verifying that the enterprise's resources are used responsibly" (Selig, 2008) and "IT governance" is the responsibility of executives and the board of directors, and consists of the leadership, organizational structures and processes that ensure that the enterprise's IT sustains and extends the organization's strategies and objectives (ITGI, 2007). All these words have different meanings and all multiword concepts are important in IT service management.

Therefore, to make compound words, all candidate words will pass through the following described procedure.

1. The first step in making compound words is the pre-processing (as described in the first phase of ProMine framework) of the domain corpus. Here, we applied both Stanford POS tagger and Stanford lemmatizer that provides lemmas of English words. As a result of this step, our corpus contains stem or base words with POS tagging. By applying lemmatizer we have saved memory space.
2. The noun - noun compound is a common type of multiword expression in English. On the second step, we extract two-word noun compounds (bigram) via the POS tags. From these two-word noun compound, one word is our candidate word from a candidate list of words and other word is from the corpus. We pass every candidate word in the corpus and if a noun is found either its right or left, it is joined to the candidate word and make a compound word. If no noun word is found on the right side or left side of the candidate word, it keeps it as a single word (unigram).

3. Once the compound words are identified automatically, the next step is to count the frequency of all words including unigram and bigram. Then a user defines a threshold frequency. If any candidate word does not occur in the corpus or its recurrence is below than a defined threshold, then this word will be dropped from the list. In this way all irrelevant words from the list of synonyms are also dropped. If any compound word is below the threshold, then our system will check the other content word (not candidate word) and if it passes the frequency threshold, then it will remain in the list, but if the second content word will not pass the frequency threshold then it will remove from the list.

As a result of this phase, a rich list of concepts will be generated.

Concept Ranking and Selection

Though, till last phase unrelated terms (conceptually, not related to a specific domain) from a set of synonyms terms (from WordNet & Wiktionary) of a given key term has been removed. However, the resultant word list consists of tens or hundreds of terms (single and compound words) created from the domain specific corpus. These extracted concepts or potential concepts are considered as feature space where many features are highly redundant with each other.

In literature, to reduce feature redundancy and to select more relevant features from the feature space, different features ranking and selection methods are used (Aghdam, Ghasem-Aghaee, & Basiri, 2009; C. Lee & Lee, 2006; Quinlan, 1986; Rubens & Agarwal, 2002; Song, Song, & Hu, 2003; Yang & Pedersen, 1997; Zouaq et al., 2011). We are using Information Gain (IG) for term ranking, Yang and Pederson (Yang & Pedersen, 1997) also used IG as a term goodness criterion for reducing feature space by selecting more informative concepts from concept lists. Yang and Pederson found information gain (IG) is the most effective in aggressive term removal without losing important information (Yang & Pedersen, 1997).

ProMine extracts a list of words against each "keyword". This list may contain hundreds or thousands words. To choose the most relevant concept to the keyword, we are applying our own proposed hybrid similarity measure. By using this measure, ProMine removes all those terms that have low similarity than a predetermined threshold and only the highest-ranked features are kept.

As we mentioned earlier, every keyword has a list of concepts which we are calling search space. We take a concept from search space and try to find the relevancy of this concept with the keyword and its synonyms. For this purpose, we are using a novel hybrid similarity measure (Gillani & Kő, 2016) that consists of two measures; one is statistical measure and the other one is semantic similarity measure. Statistical measure is based on information gain. At first place we calculate information gain of every concept against the keyword. Here, we are considering the keyword and its synonyms as a target space. The purpose of this method to rank the list concept with the relevance of the keyword.

First, we calculate entropy, which is the measure of unpredictability and provide the foundation of IG. Entropy is defined as

$$Entropy = -\sum_{i=1}^{m} P_r(c_i) log Pr(c_i)$$ (1)

where $\left\{c_i\right\}_{i=1}^{m}$ is the set of words in the target space (synonym set of a key word). This target space has an array of m size (where m may be up to tens), and we need to measure the goodness of a potential term globally with respect to all target space on average. For example for a word "governance" all these synonyms (administration, governing body, establishment, brass, organization, organization including governance) will be considered the target space i.e $\left\{c_i\right\}_{i=1}^{m}$. In this way, the candidate concept will be checked with respect to key word as well as with set of synonyms of this key word.

After calculating entropy, we have to find out probability with respect to candidate concept ($P_r(t)$) by following equation

$$P_r\left(t\right) = \sum_{i=1}^{m} P_r\left(c_i|t\right) log P_r\left(c_i|t\right) \tag{2}$$

where $P_r\left(t\right)$ represents candidate concept; for example "corporate governance" is the candidate concept and its probability will be calculated with respect to "governance" and synonym set of "governance".

$$G\left(t\right) = -\sum_{i=1}^{m} P_r(c_i) log P_r\left(c_i\right) + \sum_{i=1}^{m} P_r\left(c_i|t\right) log P_r\left(c_i|t\right) \tag{3}$$

Now with the help of equation 1 and equation 2 information gain (IG) will be found out. In the second phase of this measure, the similarity between the two concepts $c1$ and $c2$ is measured by three attributes path length, depth and information gain (IG). This measure can be computed as follows:

$$Similarity\left(c1,c2\right) = f\left(len, depth, IG\right) \tag{4}$$

where the conceptual distance between the two nodes is represented by the term len, this is also known as the shortest path length between the two concepts $c1$ and $c2$. The depth of the concept nodes is represented by depth (Gillani & Ko, 2016) and IG is the information gain of $c1$ and $c2$. The depth and the path length is calculated from the lexical database WordNet, While IG is derived from the domain corpus.

The above formula measures the goodness of a candidate concept globally with respect to the key word and it's all synonyms on average. On the basis of this similarity measure all candidate concepts are ranked and concepts with lowest information gain will be removed by defining a threshold value. At the end of this step, we have a final list of concepts that are more similar to the key-word. In this way, at the end, all key terms have their own lists of concepts that at the end of this phase are called knowledge elements for ontology enrichment.

Semantic Concept Categorization

ProMine architecture performs basically two main tasks; one is concept extraction and the second is semantic concept categorization. At the end of third phase, we have a refined list of domain specific concepts against each key term that was selected in the second phase. These extracted concepts are semantically similar to the key term. Now, we want to categorize these concepts in such a manner that ontology to be enriched. For this purpose, it is necessary to find out concept relationships between these words and existing (seed) domain ontology. We proposed a novel semantic concept categorization method to enrich an existing ontology. This method will classify new domain-specific concepts according to the existing taxonomy of the seed ontology. For concept categorization, this method will use the knowledge of existing concept categories (taxonomy of classes) of the ontology with the help of external knowledge resources such as Wiktionary.

The proposed approach tries to find a semantic similarity between extracted concepts using some fragment of the ontology that describes a certain category. The outline of our approach is presented below:

1. Select the target categories that are defined in the ontology represented as "CATi". Where CAT represents category and i is an iterator. We know that every category "CATi" hold an arbitrary number of concepts denoted as CNij where CN represents concepts, "i" is category iterator and "j" is concept iterator. Some of these concepts may belong to more than one category (as a member of the hierarchy). For example, "Risk" is a concept that falls under the category of "IT Audit Process", "IT Governance" and "System Acquisition". Such an overlapping begets another challenge of the underlying problem.

2. For each concept of every category, a set of related terms that will include synonyms and derived terms will be realized using Wiktionary. We denote these terms as TR_CNijk where k is iterator of every term in the set. This set represents semantically similar words of the selected concepts. For example, if one category contains ten concepts, then 10 sets of semantically similar words will be prepared at the end of this step.

3. The third step of ProMine is concerned with matching. The system takes every potential candidate from the given set of concepts say PCNx where "x" represents the counter of every Potential CoNcept (PCN). This step checks its relevance or semantic relationship to each concept CNij in every category CATi. Here one essential aspect is the decidability of inclusion of potential concept PCNx in more than one category CATi. Although, it is arguable either to use a strict threshold based criteria or restricting it to the highest relevant category. We justify that the potential candidate can be put into more than one category.

4. It can be noticed that one every single pass of the algorithm, each potential candidate PCNx is put into one or more category. For the next step, this "fresh" concept (like other peer concepts) will also be expanded into its relevant synonyms.

5. If there is any concept observed with no match in either of the categories, then it will be subjected to "Miscellaneous" category. As the whole process is exhausted, domain expert will manually identify their respective categories.

The five functional steps ensure that the proposed ontology enrichment algorithm will populate the given taxonomy with new concepts that are extracted from domain corpus and other external sources.

Application of ProMine for IT Governance Ontology Enrichment

ProMine ontology enrichment capability was tested in a knowledge management solution (ProKEX) and in an ontology-based e-learning environment applied for IT auditors' training in CISA preparation courses (Gillani & Ko, 2015). With a growing demand for individuals possessing IT audit, control and security

Figure 3. A proposed semantic concept categorization algorithm

```
Let us have a relation "R" that associates every CONCEPT to its related
CATEGORY:
R = {con : CONCEPT; cat : CATEGORY| con ↦ cat}
Let Miscellaneous = {c : CONCEPT| c has unknown category}
Let W = { set of new words } ← process(document)
For all i ∈W{%% Repeat for every new word i
    For all j ∈range(R) { %% Repeat for every category j
        K_match = φ
        N_match =φ
        For all k ∈ domain ({con ↦ cat : R|cat == j}{
        %% Repeat for every concept k in category j
            M = { set of Synonyms and Related words of k }
            %% Obtained from Wikipedia
            IF (i == k)
              K_match = k_match ∪{ j }
            ELSEIF (i ∈M)
              M_match = M_match∪{ j }
}
}
  IF (|k_match| ≥ 1)
    do nothing
  ELSEIF (|M_match| == 1)
    R = R∪{i ↦ j} where j ∈M_match
    ELSEIF (|M_match| > 1)
    Apply Similarity measure and ADD in category with most match
ELSE
    Miscellaneous = Miscellaneous ∪{ i }
}
```

skills, CISA has become a preferred certification program by individuals and organizations around the world (the certification program is accredited under ISO/IEC 17024:2003 by ANSI). This certifications have been recognized by government entities, major industry publications, standard bodies and major consulting groups. Hungarian legislation recognize CISA for internal auditor job role (Rendelet, 2012). In our previous paper, we presented a method to enrich IT audit domain with ProMine, while in this work we focus on the IT governance subdomain of IT audit domain. We improved the ontology enrichment method (in terms of semantic similarity) and we tested it in the IT governance field.

Datasets and Evaluation Procedure

In order to apply our proposed ontology based categorization method for ontology enrichment, we have taken two types of datasets. As we mentioned above, our focus domain is IT governance. Therefore, a domain text corpus had to be prepared as well as the relevant domain seed ontology with some sample concepts.

Text Corpus Description

The text corpus examined is taken from the ISACA latest literature about IT Governance. From standardisation aspects, the corpus included COBIT 5 (ISACA, 2012), Val IT (ISACA, 2008) and Risk IT (ISACA, 2009). These standards are available at www.isaca.org. ISACA was incorporated in 1969 by a small group of individuals to provide a centralized source of information and guidance in the growing

Figure 4. ProMine: Semantic concept categorization procedure

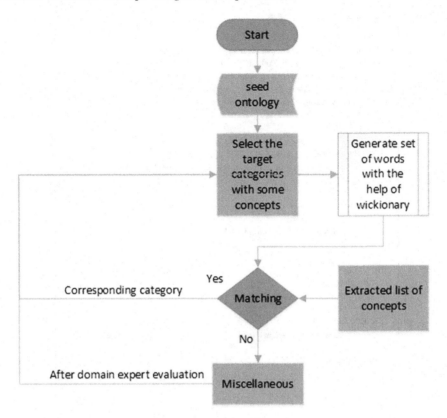

field of auditing controls for computer systems. ISACA provides practical guidance, benchmarks and disseminate best practices in IT governance domain. We collected the latest IT governance related literature from ISACA Journal and web sources (Tiwana, 2013), (ISACA, 2016). Today's de facto standard for IT governance is COBIT, therefore COBIT 5 has been included in this corpus. Text preprocessing techniques including NLP techniques are applied to this corpus as detailed in Preprocessing of Data section.

Seed Ontology

We developed an IT audit seed ontology with IT governance subdomain using the suggestion of ISACA IT audit sample curriculum (Gillani & Ko, 2015). ISACA divides the IT audit field for five main areas. The "process of auditing information systems" area deals with risk-based audit planning; audit project management techniques, control objectives and controls related to information systems, ISACA IT audit and assurance standards, guidelines, and tools and techniques. "Governance and management of IT" area has ten subtopics, each that focuses on the management of process IT areas such as human resources (HR), IT organizational structure legal issues, and standards and monitoring of assurance practices. "Information systems acquisition, development and implementation" area has six topic areas that focus on business case development, information systems implementation and migration, project management and controls. "Information systems operation, maintenance and support" area have ten subtopics, namely service level management, maintenance of information systems, problem and incident management, change and configuration management, and backup and restoration of systems. "Protection of information assets" area has five subareas; design and implementation of system and security controls, data classification, physical access, and the process of retrieving and disposing of information assets. Based on ISACA suggested categorization five main knowledge areas/category are distinguished in the seed ontology as shown in Figure 5. Some of the main concepts of the main knowledge areas are also given in Figure 5.

Empirical Evaluation

In order to test the ProMine system for ontology enrichment, we described our empirical evaluation procedure in an incremental iterative process with four essential steps as illustrated in Figure 6. The focus of the evaluation was to define an experiment to enrich a domain seed ontology by using a domain-specific corpus and some other external resources such as WordNet and Wiktionary as discussed in section 3.

Aforementioned domain corpus is used to extract lists of concepts with the help of WordNet and Wiktionary. After extraction of these concepts, concepts relatedness with domain is also checked by statistical and semantic measures. We find a number of domain related concepts at the end of ProMine Concept extraction step. Point-by-point description of the ProMine concept extraction procedure is given in section 3.

Once a set of key-concepts has been extracted from a domain corpus, the next empirical step is the categorization of these concepts according to ontology categories. For this purpose, we have taken a seed ontology of IT Audit that has five main categories and each category contains few concepts. To enrich these categories with new domain concepts, the proposed algorithm is used as in Figure 4. According

Figure 5. IT Audit Seed Ontology used in our categorization experiments

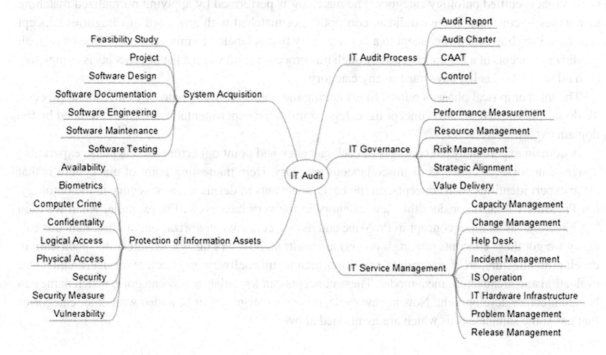

Figure 6. Empirical evaluation process

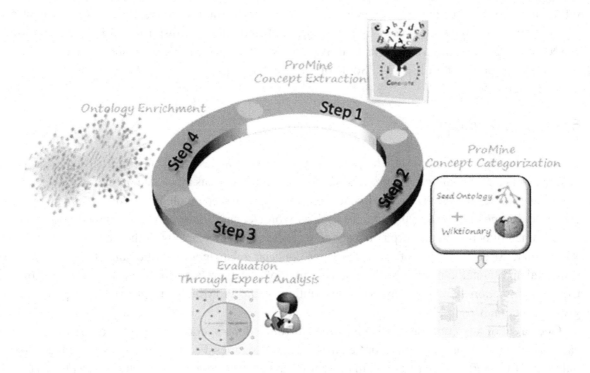

to this algorithm, a set of related concepts against each category's concept is made and then each candidate concept from concept list and is matched against the concept sets of all ontology categories. If the concept is matched with any word of these concept sets, then the system puts that candidate concept to into that specified ontology category. The matching is performed by applying normalized matching techniques to concepts. If the candidate concept is not matched with any word of categories concept sets, then ProMine puts this concept to a new category that is labeled as miscellaneous. One by one, all candidate concepts of a list are checked through this procedure and when a list of concepts is completed, then all words of this list have must in any category.

The third empirical phase is related to evaluating the precision of the ontology enrichment process. To do this, at the end of each concept list categorization, the experimental results are evaluated by the domain expert.

A domain expert analyzed concepts of each category and point out errors. In this phase expert also assigns categories to concepts of miscellaneous category. Here interesting point of our system is that if the expert identifies such concepts, on the basis, she wants to define a new category in the ontology, our ProMine will also consider this new category in the very next cycle. For example, when we used "architecture" as an input concept in ProMine and during concept categorization, in miscellaneous category we got these concepts (amongst others) as result: architecture design, architecture specification, baseline architecture, architecture decomposition, architecture delivery, architecture service, architecture evaluation and architecture meta model. These concepts can formulate a new category, which name can be: architecture development. Now in new cycle, this new category will be added with other categories that has some sample words which are mentioned above.

The results of this step are shown in Table 2. We used precision and recall measures to demonstrate the effectiveness of our proposed semantic concept categorization technique. After this phase, numerous new concepts are ready for ontology maintenance. It is important to mention that after completing first cycle, ProMine starts step one again with new concept list and repeat whole empirical procedure until all extracted concept lists are categorized. As shown in Table 2, we are able to obtain promising precision results in general for most of the categories. Since our system showed good precision for ontology maintenance at the end of the first cycle, but results showed that every next cycle gave more precisions in the categorization process. The reason is as categories gradually have more concepts, chance to match candidate concept with any category is increased. Therefore, in after coming cycles, in the miscellaneous category contained less false negatives(that should be categorized by the system) as compared to earlier cycles.

Results and Discussion

Results are shown in Figure 7 and 8. To find results we used following contingency Table 1. In this table; TP are those concepts which are fit into our ontology and our system has put them in their corresponding categories, FP are those concepts that are wrongly categorized. FN are those concepts which are incorrectly categorized by our system ProMine, while these concepts should be in miscellaneous category (a new category that system generates itself in each cycle). TN describes a situation in concept categorization when ProMine correctly categories a negative test case into the miscellaneous category. We used this table to find precision and recall indicators to measure the performance of our system.

TP represents situation in concept categorization when ProMine correctly categories a positive test case into the positive category. Results shows our system perform correctly and puts a new concept in its right category and otherwise puts in the miscellaneous category. As the number of cycles increases false positives, further decrease as we can see at sixth and seventh cycle, false positives are zero.

We have evaluated our results by applying two major measures that are precision and recall. First we have calculated true-positive rate that is:

$$\text{TP rate} = \frac{\text{TP}}{\text{TP} + \text{FN}} \tag{5}$$

The true-positive rate, which is also known as sensitivity or recall measures the proportion of actual positives which are correctly identified. If we see in Figure 7, the trend of the line will show that the proportion of positives is gradually increasing and this high recall relates to a low false negative rate that indicates our proposed technique is returning a majority of all positive results (high recall). However, this will happen gradually by increasing number of cycles as categories will be enriched with new concepts. Recall is a measure to determine that how many truly relevant results are returned.

Table 1. Contingency table

	Categorized	Non Categorized
Categorized	True Positives (TP)	False Positives (FP)
Non categorized	False Negatives (FN)	True Negatives (TN)

Table 2. Contingency table for concept categorization

No. of Cycles	No. of Concepts	TP	FP	FN
1	159	79	33	47
2	113	59	13	41
3	97	65	13	19
4	133	93	9	31
5	50	35	4	11
6	152	120	0	32
7	31	26	0	5

Figure 7. Recall of semantic concept categorization

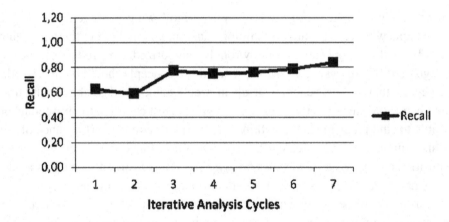

We have also used the precision indicator in order to measure the quality of our results as shown in Figure 8. Precision is the fraction of correctly matched concepts (true positives) over the total number of extracted concepts (true positives and false positives). In this context, correctly enriched entities are the concepts and instances that are in the correct category. We used precision to measure the correctness of our proposed technique.

$$Precision = TP / (TP + FP) \qquad (6)$$

Figure 8 shows the precision of the proposed categorization method. An ideal system with high precision and high recall will return many results, with all results labeled correctly. As the number of cycles passed, our system showed good precision in enriching the ontology, a perspective of the work is to extend the number of cycles. If we see precision and recall both then we will come to know that both are increasing gradually. High scores for both showed that the proposed categorization method is returning accurate results (high precision), as well as returning a majority of all positive results (high recall). Our experimental evaluation using precision and recall measures as well as human judgments showed that our method categorized new concepts with high precision and recall.

Figure 8. The precision of semantic concept categorization

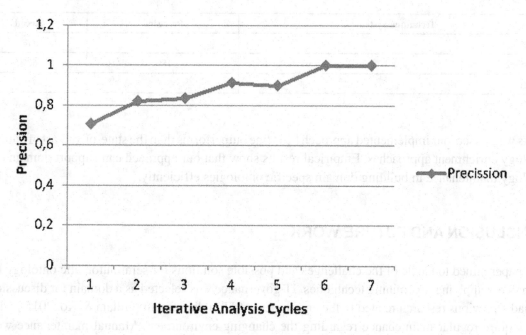

Table 3. Evaluation of the overall semantic concept categorization method

Cycle	Total Observation	Wrong Categorized	Retrieval Measure	
			Precision(%)	Recall(%)
1	159	33	70.54	0.63
2	113	13	81.94	0.59
3	97	13	83.33	0.77
4	133	9	91.18	0.75
5	50	4	89.74	0.76
6	172	0	100	0.70
7	31	0	100	0.84

We have also compared our results with the results of two other ontology enrichment techniques. The authors in (Navigli & Velardi, 2006) proposed a technique to enrich an existing ontology using on-line glossaries. They are also using seed ontology as we are doing, however the authors used manual extraction patterns. The other state of the art ontology enrichment technique that we used for comparison analysis is Astrakhantsv's approach (Astrakhantsev, Turdakov, & Fedorenko, 2014). This approach is not using existing ontologies. We have chosen these two techniques because our technique is using seed ontology so we want to show the clear results difference between techniques that are using seed ontology and that are not using seed ontology.

Table 4. Evaluation results for ontology enrichment

Technique/System	Precision	Recall
Baseline1	78%	77%
Baseline2	18%	62%
ProMine	88%	72%

As we can see, our implemented approach ProMine outperforms than the state-of-the-art of automatic ontology enrichment approaches. Empirical results show that our approach can support domain expert ontology maintenance in building domain specific ontologies efficiently.

CONCLUSION AND FUTURE WORK

This paper aimed to tackle of the challenges and possible solutions for semi-automatic ontology learning process applying text mining techniques. IT governance was selected as a domain for discussion, as we had a previous research related to the enrichment of IT audit domain (Gillani & Ko, 2015). Ontologies require regular maintenance regarding the changing environment. Manual maintenance work is error-prone and time consuming; a possible even semi-automatic support has a high added value. We applied ProMine, a framework for ontology learning and enrichment that uses lexical resources such as WorldNet and Wiktionary in combination with a domain Corpus. The paper provided a review of ontology learning related literature and discussed the deficiencies of the approaches in the context of ProMine. There are two major contributions of this paper. One is that we presented a semantic-based text mining approach for identifying domain-specific knowledge elements; the other is the categorization method of these extracted knowledge elements by using Wiktionary. Compared with our previous research the value added is a new semantic similarity measure, the different domain (IT governance) for testing and the context (ProKEX intelligent system development). We evaluated our system in a cyclic way with the help of domain expert analysis. From our evaluation, we conclude that ProMine generates a large number of concepts and at the same time categorize these concepts according to given ontology categories or classes. This categorization is good quality and with the passage of time its precision and recall increases. The experiments proved the applicability of automatic concept extraction and automatic concepts categorization. We intend to conduct additional testing of our proposed system, especially test the relevancy of extracted concepts to other domains because more relevant concepts would be more accurately categorized. A detailed comparison analysis is also required to validate our technique.

REFERENCES

Aghdam, M. H., Ghasem-Aghaee, N., & Basiri, M. E. (2009). Text feature selection using ant colony optimization. *Expert Systems with Applications*, *36*(3), 6843–6853. doi:10.1016/j.eswa.2008.08.022

Astrakhantsev, N., Turdakov, D. Y., & Fedorenko, D. G. (2014). *Automatic Enrichment of Informal Ontology by Analyzing a Domain-Specific Text Collection*. Paper presented at the Computational Linguistics and Intellectual Technologies: Papers from the Annual International Conference "Dialogue".

Blaschke, C., & Valencia, A. (2002). Automatic ontology construction from the literature. *Genome Informatics, 13*, 201-213.

Buitelaar, P., & Cimiano, P. (2008). *Ontology learning and population: bridging the gap between text and knowledge* (Vol. 167). Ios Press.

Dahab, M. Y., Hassan, H. A., & Rafea, A. (2008). TextOntoEx: Automatic ontology construction from natural English text. *Expert Systems with Applications, 34*(2), 1474–1480. doi:10.1016/j.eswa.2007.01.043

Gábor, A., & Kő, A. (Eds.). (2016). *Corporate Knowledge Discovery and Organizational Learning*. Springer International Publishing. doi:10.1007/978-3-319-28917-5

Gasevic, D., Zouaq, A., Torniai, C., Jovanovic, J., & Hatala, M. (2011). An approach to folksonomy-based ontology maintenance for learning environments. *Learning Technologies. IEEE Transactions on, 4*(4), 301–314.

Gillani, S., & Ko, A. (2015). Incremental ontology population and enrichment through semantic-based text mining: An application for it audit domain. *International Journal on Semantic Web and Information Systems, 11*(3), 44–66. doi:10.4018/IJSWIS.2015070103

Gillani, S., & Ko, A. (2016). ProMine: a text mining solution for concept extraction and filtering. In Corporate Knowledge Discovery and Organizational Learning (pp. 59-82). Springer International Publishing. doi:10.1007/978-3-319-28917-5_3

Gillani, S. A., & Kő, A. (2014). *Process-based knowledge extraction in a public authority: A text mining approach. In Electronic Government and the Information Systems Perspective* (pp. 91–103). Springer.

Gillani Andleeb, S. (2015). *From text mining to knowledge mining: An integrated framework of concept extraction and categorization for domain ontology* (Doctoral dissertation). Budapesti Corvinus Egyetem.

Husaini, M. a., Ko, A., Tapucu, D., & Saygın, Y. (2012). *Ontology Supported Policy Modeling in Opinion Mining Process*. Paper presented at the On the Move to Meaningful Internet Systems: OTM 2012 Workshops. doi:10.1007/978-3-642-33618-8_34

ISACA. (2008). *The Val IT Framework 2.0*. ISACA.

ISACA. (2009). *The Risk It Framework 2009*. ISACA.

ISACA. (2011). *Global Status Report on the Governance of Enterprise IT (Geit) - 2011*. ISACA.

ISACA. (2012). *COBIT 5 2012*. ISACA.

ISACA. (2015). CISA Review Manual 2015. ISACA, CISA.

ISACA. (2016a). *Governance, Risk and Compliance* (Vol. 6). ISACA Journal.

ISACA. (2016b). *Getting Started With GEIT: A Primer for Implementing Governance of Enterprise IT*. ISACA.

Janik, M., & Kochut, K. J. (2008). *Wikipedia in action: Ontological knowledge in text categorization*. Paper presented at the Semantic Computing, 2008 IEEE International Conference on. doi:10.1109/ICSC.2008.53

Khondoker, M. R., & Mueller, P. (2010). *Comparing ontology development tools based on an online survey*. Academic Press.

Kő, A. (Ed.). (2012). eParticipation and Policy-making Support in Ubipol Approach. Academic Press.

Kő, A., Kovács, B., & Gábor, A. (2011). Agile Knowledge-Based E-Government Supported By SAKE System. *Journal of Cases on Information Technology*, *13*(3), 1–20. doi:10.4018/jcit.2011070101

Lee, C., & Lee, G. G. (2006). Information gain and divergence-based feature selection for machine learning-based text categorization. *Information Processing & Management*, *42*(1), 155–165. doi:10.1016/j.ipm.2004.08.006

Lee, C.-S., Kao, Y.-F., Kuo, Y.-H., & Wang, M.-H. (2007). Automated ontology construction for unstructured text documents. *Data & Knowledge Engineering*, *60*(3), 547–566. doi:10.1016/j.datak.2006.04.001

López, M. F., Pérez, A. G., & Amaya, M. D. R. (2000). *Ontology's crossed life cycles. In Knowledge Engineering and Knowledge Management Methods, Models, and Tools* (pp. 65–79). Springer. doi:10.1007/3-540-39967-4_6

Luong, H., Gauch, S., & Wang, Q. (2012). *Ontology Learning Using Word Net Lexical Expansion and Text Mining*. Academic Press.

Matas, P. M. (2012). *SMART (Supporting dynamic MAtching for Regional developmenT) Leonardo da Vinci Transfer of Innovation Project*. European Commission.

Meyer, C. M., & Gurevych, I. (2012). OntoWiktionary: Constructing an Ontology from the. *Semi-Automatic Ontology Development: Processes and Resources: Processes and Resources*, 131.

Michael Cowan, H. C., English, S., & Hammond, S. (2014). *State of Internal Audit Survey 2014 – Adapting to Complex Challenges?* Retrieved from http://accelus.thomsonreuters.com/sites/default/files/GRC01260.pdf

Miller, G. A. (1995). WordNet: A lexical database for English. *Communications of the ACM*, *38*(11), 39–41. doi:10.1145/219717.219748

Miranda, P., Isaias, P., & Costa, C. J. (2014). *From Information Systems to e-Learning 3.0 Systems's Critical Success Factors: A Framework Proposal. In Learning and Collaboration Technologies. Designing and Developing Novel Learning Experiences* (pp. 180–191). Springer.

Navigli, R., & Velardi, P. (2006). *Ontology enrichment through automatic semantic annotation of on-line glossaries. In Managing Knowledge in a World of Networks* (pp. 126–140). Springer.

Nguyen, B.-A., & Yang, D.-L. (2012). A semi-automatic approach to construct Vietnamese ontology from online text. *The International Review of Research in Open and Distributed Learning*, *13*(5), 148–172. doi:10.19173/irrodl.v13i5.1250

Pan, J. Z., Staab, S., Aßmann, U., Ebert, J., & Zhao, Y. (2012). *Ontology-Driven Software Development*. Springer Science & Business Media.

Ponzetto, S. P., & Strube, M. (2007). *Deriving a large scale taxonomy from Wikipedia*. Paper presented at the AAAI.

Quinlan, J. R. (1986). Induction of decision trees. *Machine Learning*, *1*(1), 81–106. doi:10.1007/BF00116251

Rendelet, K. (2012). *a közszolgálati tisztviselők képesítési előírásairól*. Retrieved from http://www.complex.hu/jr/gen/hjegy_doc.cgi?docid=A1200029.KOR

Rubens, M., & Agarwal, P. (2002). *Information Extraction from Online Automotive Classifieds*. Academic Press.

Selig, G. J. (2008). *Implementing IT Governance-A Practical Guide to Global Best Practices in IT Management*. Van Haren.

Shailer, G. E. (2004). *Introduction to Corporate Governance in Australia*. Pearson Education Australia.

Shamsfard, M., & Abdollahzadeh Barforoush, A. (2003). The state of the art in ontology learning: A framework for comparison. *The Knowledge Engineering Review*, *18*(04), 293–316. doi:10.1017/S0269888903000687

Song, M., Song, I.-Y., & Hu, X. (2003). KPSpotter: a flexible information gain-based keyphrase extraction system. *Proceedings of the 5th ACM international workshop on Web information and data management*. doi:10.1145/956699.956710

Suchanek, F. M., Kasneci, G., & Weikum, G. (2008). Yago: A large ontology from wikipedia and wordnet. *Web Semantics: Science, Services, and Agents on the World Wide Web*, *6*(3), 203–217. doi:10.1016/j.websem.2008.06.001

Tiwana, A., Konsynski, B., & Venkatraman, N. (2013). Special issue: Information technology and organizational governance: The IT governance cube. *Journal of Management Information Systems*, *30*(3), 7–12. doi:10.2753/MIS0742-1222300301

UbiPOL. (2009). *Ubiquitous Participation Platform for Policy-making*. ICT for Governance and Policy Modelling.

Völker, J. (2009). *Learning expressive ontologies* (Vol. 2). IOS Press.

Weber, N., & Buitelaar, P. (2006). Web-based ontology learning with isolde. *Proc. of the ISWC Workshop on Web Content Mining with Human Language Technologies*.

Wong, W., Liu, W., & Bennamoun, M. (2012). Ontology learning from text: A look back and into the future. *ACM Computing Surveys*, *44*(4), 20. doi:10.1145/2333112.2333115

Yang, Y., & Pedersen, J. O. (1997). *A comparative study on feature selection in text categorization*. Paper presented at the ICML.

Zouaq, A., Gasevic, D., & Hatala, M. (2011). Towards open ontology learning and filtering. *Information Systems*, *36*(7), 1064–1081. doi:10.1016/j.is.2011.03.005

Chapter 14
Geocoding Tweets Based on Semantic Web and Ontologies

Imelda Escamilla
Instituto Politécnico Nacional, Mexico

Miguel Torres Ruíz
Instituto Politécnico Nacional, Mexico

Marco Moreno Ibarra
Instituto Politécnico Nacional, Mexico

Vladimir Luna Soto
Instituto Politécnico Nacional, Mexico

Rolando Quintero
Instituto Politécnico Nacional, Mexico

Giovanni Guzmán
Instituto Politécnico Nacional, Mexico

ABSTRACT

Human ability to understand approximate references to locations, disambiguated by means of context and reasoning about spatial relationships, is the key to describe spatial environments and to share information about them. In this paper, we propose an approach for geocoding that takes advantage of the spatial relationships contained in the text of tweets, using semantic web, ontologies and spatial analyses. Microblog text has special characteristics (e.g. slang, abbreviations, acronyms, etc.) and thus represents a special variation of natural language. The main objective of this work is to associate spatial relationships found in text with a spatial footprint, to determine the location of the event described in the tweet. The feasibility of the proposal is demonstrated using a corpus of 200,000 tweets posted in Spanish related with traffic events in Mexico City.

DOI: 10.4018/978-1-5225-5042-6.ch014

INTRODUCTION

In recent years the amount of data available on the social web has grown massively. Therefore, researchers have developed approaches that leverage this social web data to tackle interesting challenges of the semantic web. Among these are methods for learning ontologies from social media or crowdsourcing, extracting semantics from data collected by citizen science and participatory sensing initiatives, or for better understanding and describing user activities. The rich data provided by the social web can be used to build the semantic web. This task includes learning basic semantic relationships, e.g., between entities, or by employing more sophisticated methods to construct a complete knowledge graph or ontology. There are additional synergies between the social web and the semantic web. For example, content from the social web could be enriched and linked to the semantic web using named entity recognition and linking, as well as sentiment analysis (Hotho, A., Jäschke, R., & Lerman, K., 2017).

Currently Every second, on average, around 6,000 tweets are tweeted on Twitter which corresponds to over 350,000 tweets sent per minute, 500 million tweets per day and around 200 billion tweets per year according to twitter-statistics (Internet Live Stats, n.d.) making it a tool that can help significantly in the semantic web due to its agile reading (no more than 140 characters), dynamic (information available in real time), accessible (for almost any device connected to Internet), functional (allows you to embed pictures, videos and links to other content), organized (with hashtags that represent subjects and ordered by date of publication), interactive (can view posts from other people, follow them, respond, share your posts by retweet or save them to mark them as favorites), non-invasive (no chat Instant Messaging) and with the possibility of anonymity (using nicknames or impersonal nicknames) (Pérez et al., 2012; Duque et al., 2012; Gómez et al., 2012; Kassens, 2012; Wakefield et al., 2011; Welch & Bonnan, 2012).

This has led many research efforts on various topics to exploit this information such as event detection (Atefeh & Khreich, 2015; Tonon et al., 2017), health monitoring (Nielsen et al., 2015), emergency detection (Seol et al., 2013), and among others. Many of these applications can be benefited with information about the location, where the events occur, but unfortunately, this information is very poor, because only 1% of tweets contain geo-tags (Takhteyev et al., 2012).

The extraction of information from tweets presents some challenges, i.e., information is completely unstructured and its limited to 140 characters, tweets can contain grammatical errors, and abbreviations and each user has its own writing style, so information can be incomplete, false or not credible (Ritter, 2012).

However, Gutierrez et al. (2015) and Oussalah et al. (2013) established that the use of information content in tweets, provides geographic information, because the texts commonly refers to further locations. The tweet analysis allows us to know and evaluate social and natural events. Nevertheless, geocoding methods are used to translate geographic locations represented in the text (*e.g.* detection and location of events in a geographic area). They have focused on point feature type (Iversen et al., 2014; Hart & Zandbergen, 2013; Krumm & Horvitz, 2015) and there are not approaches oriented towards polygon representation.

Every day millions of tweets related to road events are published, both by private users and by public or private institutions. Each tweet describes events such as accidents, roadblocks, traffic reports, among others, and their particular location. Recovering this location from raw text is not a simple task, because the natural language does not follow a format or standard and to be useful, the location of this type of event should be estimated with the highest possible accuracy.

Thus, in this paper, a methodology focused on geocoding events appearing in tweets about traffic events of the Mexico City is proposed. The work consists of identifying events, geographic features and their spatial relationships, supported by conceptual representations, Natural Language Processing techniques and classification algorithms. Unlike other works, the detection of trending topics is not supported in this paper.

This paper is organized as follows: Section 2 describes the related work in the fields of geocoding based on short texts. The proposed methodology is presented in Section 3. In Section 4 the evaluation and comparison of the proposed method with other approaches are presented. Section 5 outlines the conclusions and future work.

RELATED WORK

Gutierrez et al. (2015) and Oussalah et al. (2013) state that the use of information contained in tweets, provides a significant amount of geographic information, because texts commonly refer to places. The analysis of these tweets allows to know and evaluate social and natural events.

The topic of event detection on Twitter has generated much interest in the field of research, focusing on analyzing events of all kinds (Atefeh & Khreich, 2015).

For example in the work of Nielsen et al. (2015) performs a detailed analysis of information flowing from Twitter to perform health monitoring, in particular, focuses its efforts on the analysis of the behavior of influenza. Proposing an approach based on Machine Learning, to obtain the locations.

Another highly studied approach is the detection of road events. The work proposed by Gutierrez et al. (2015), proposes a method to obtain traffic information, using an approach based on Vector Support Machines (SVM) and a closter algorithm to follow the evolution of events. On the other hand Albuquerque et al. (2015) presents a domain ontology related to road events, called TEDO and describes a tool to identify the location of the events in the tweets using the metadata of the events.

Finally, we have the works that focus on recovering and disambiguating the places mentioned in the tweets, such as Lee et al. (2015), which describes a method based on Machine Learning to extract and disambiguate the locations in the message. Another approach is that of Roller et al. (2012) that combines techniques of Named Entity Recognition and Wikipedia on a corpus that twitter and gets a list with terms that represent locations.

On the other hand, in (Graham et al., 2014), the techniques of Named Entity Recognition with a gazetteers are combined to assign labels as the names are recognized in the text. Zhang and Gelernter (2014) describe a model to determine which location presents a correct match with the location found in the tweet, using the metadata and information extracted from the city, state and country, obtaining an F-measure of 85.22. The authors suggest that the errors they present are mainly due to misspellings or lack of information.

Regarding this work, it proposes a method for geocoding traffic events described in tweets published in an urban area, by using ontologies to locate and define the spatial relationships between the features (*e.g.* road infrastructure, POI´s, and among others) involved in the traffic events (like traffic jams, accidents, demonstrations, road works).

THE PROPOSED METHODOLOGY

The methodology is a general framework that consists of detecting and locating traffic events, geographic entities and their spatial relationships in particular tweets. This approach consists of four main stages that are depicted in Figure 1.

1. **Collection and Reliability:** In this stage, the published tweets were collected and the reliability of the source of the tweets was evaluated, discarding the publications that do not come from a trusted source. The remaining tweets are stored in our database. Moreover, the traffic events dictionaries were generated (Demonstrations, Traffic Jam, Traffic Accidents and Road works) and in the same way, the Frequent Terms Dictionaries (Abbreviations, Nicknames, Acronyms and Hashtags).
2. **Preprocessing and Classification:** At this stage, the Frequent Terms Dictionaries were used to replace the words in tweets by those contained in our Dictionaries; thereby the database was standardized. Thus, by using the traffic events Dictionaries, the classification was performed in which some classes were defined as follows: Demonstrations, Traffic Accidents, Traffic Jam and Roadwork.
3. **Semantic Geocoding:** This stage consists of two main tasks: the first one is to identify the elements related to the event, and by using the proposed road infrastructure ontology, a geographic feature to each of them is assigned. The second task consists of generating a syntactic dependencies tree for each tweet and retrieving the words that describe the spatial relationships between the event features. These words are searched in the ontology with the defined spatial relationships, in order to retrieve the related spatial operations. Finally, when these spatial operations are applied to the retrieved geographic entities, the objects that represents geographically traffic events were obtained. At the same time, an evaluation of the geographic objects was performed to verify that the described event in the tweet is spatially valid.
4. **Mapping and Assessment:** This stage is in charged of visualizing the obtained geographic object of traffic events on a mapping application. The comparison of the geocode events with a geocoding sample, was made by a user. Thus, it serves as a baseline, and the obtained results were also compared against Google. Finally, they are evaluated by applying the *precision*, *recall* and *F* measures.

Collection and Reliability

This stage is composed of three tasks: the first one consists of receiving and storing the tweets that are recently posted in a temporal database, along with the user data linked to the publication. The second task computes the *User Reliability (UR),* taking into account the user information previously stored. The *Tweet Reliability (TR)* is evaluated by discarding the publications that do not come from a trusted source. The remaining tweets are stored in a database.

User Reliability

To compute the tweet reliability, it is necessary to obtain the posted user reliability. So, the characteristics such as the number of users that an account is following, the number of followers that an account currently has, the average of retweets and others are considered for the computation. Therefore, this

Figure 1. Stages that composed the proposed methodology

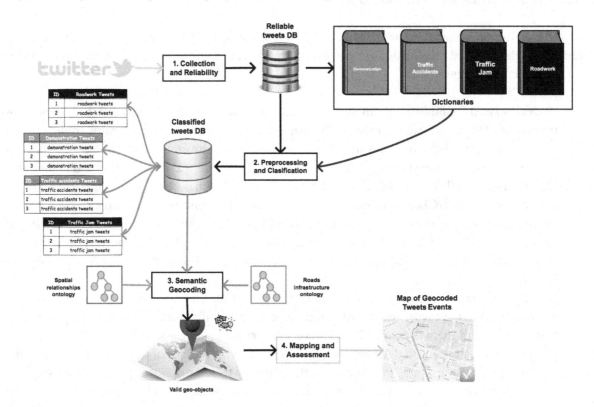

computation is based on the formula defined in (Moriya & Ryoke, 2013) and considered the previous characteristics. The User Reliability is computed by applying Equation 1.

$$UR\big(u\big) = AvgRT\big(u,t\big) \times UMention\big(u,t\big) \ UR\big(u\big) = AvgRT\big(u,t\big) \times UMention\big(u,t\big) \qquad (1)$$

where:

$$AvgRT\big(u,t\big)$$

$AvgRT\big(u,t\big)$ represents the average number of retweets that mentioned target users.
$UMention\big(u,t\big) \ UMention\big(u,t\big)$ describes the tweets rate that mentioned target user.

This value is placed for each single user and stored in the temporary database created in the collection task.

Tweet Reliability

This equation computes the tweet reliability, considering the value of the user reliability and some features like the tweet length, total number of words in the tweet, number of common terms, number of hashtags, and the number of retweets. This computation is defined by Equation 2.

$$TR(t) = \sum_{i=1}^{i=n} F_i + UR(u_j) \quad TR(t) = \sum_{i=1}^{i=n} F_i + UR(u_j) \tag{2}$$

where F_i F_i represents the value obtained for each tweet feature.

$UR(u_j)$ $UR(u_j)$ determines the user reliability associated with the publication.

Finally, the tweet reliability for each tweet in the collection is obtained and stored in the temporary database, which is sorted by descending order. Publications with the lowest values are discarded. The remaining tweets are stored in the database.

The third task uses the tweet dataset to create a Frequent Terms Dictionaries (FTD). The common words are obtained from the tweets collection by applying Equation 3, in order to obtain the weight of the local term. Equation 4 is applied to obtain the weight of the global term. In addition, Equation 5 provides an analysis of the term in all the tweets of the dataset.

$$tf(t, tw) = \frac{f(t, tw)}{\max\{f(w, tw) : \epsilon \, tw\}} \quad tf(t, tw) = \frac{f(t, tw)}{\max\{f(w, tw) : \epsilon \, tw\}} \tag{3}$$

where:

$tf(t, tw)$ $tf(t, tw)$ represents the occurrence frequency of the term (t) (t) along the tweet (tw) (tw)

$f(t, tw)$ $f(t, tw)$ determines the number of occurrences of the term (t) (t) in the tweet (tw) (tw)

$\max\{f(w, tw) : \epsilon \, tw\}$ $\max\{f(w, tw) : \epsilon \, tw\}$ provides the total number of words (w) (w) in the tweet (tw) (tw).

$$idf(t, Tw) = log \frac{|Tw|}{1 + |tw \epsilon \, Tw : t \epsilon \, tw|} \quad idf(t, Tw) = log \frac{|Tw|}{1 + |tw \epsilon \, Tw : t \epsilon \, tw|} \tag{4}$$

where:

$idf\left(t, Tw\right) idf\left(t, Tw\right)$ represents the coefficient that determines the discriminatory capacity of the term $\left(t\right)\left(t\right)$ in the tweet in relation to the tweets collection $\left(Tw\right)\left(Tw\right)$.

$\left|Tw\right| \left|Tw\right|$ determines the number of tweets in the collection.

$1 + \left|tw\epsilon\ Tw : t\epsilon\ tw\right| 1 + \left|tw\epsilon\ Tw : t\epsilon\ tw\right|$ provides the number of tweets $\left(tw\right)\left(tw\right)$ where the term $\left(t\right)$ $\left(t\right)$ occurs.

$$tfidf\left(t, tw, Tw\right) = tf\left(t, tw\right) \times idf\left(t, Tw\right)\ tfidf\left(t, tw, Tw\right) = tf\left(t, tw\right) \times idf\left(t, Tw\right) \qquad 5)$$

where:

$tfidf\left(t, tw, Tw\right) tfidf\left(t, tw, Tw\right)$ represents the weight of term $\left(t\right)\left(t\right)$ related to the tweet $\left(tw\right)\left(tw\right)$, in which occurs and its relationship with the tweets collection $\left(Tw\right)\left(Tw\right)$.

$tf\left(t, tw\right) tf\left(t, tw\right)$ provides the weight of the local term $\left(t\right)\left(t\right)$ in the tweet $\left(tw\right)\left(tw\right)$.

$idf\left(t, Tw\right) idf\left(t, Tw\right)$ determines the weight of the global term $\left(t\right)\left(t\right)$ in the tweets collection $\left(Tw\right)$ $\left(Tw\right)$.

The generated script analyzes all the tweets of the collection by applying the last equation. A list with the most frequent terms is obtained by the script. For the experiments, over three hundred thousand tweets in Spanish in one month approximately were collected.

From the most frequent terms, 45 common abbreviations, 79 common nicknames, 65 common acronyms, 142 common hashtags, 129 common demonstrations terms, 147 common traffic accidents terms, 89 traffic jam terms, and 63 roadwork terms have been identified. This information was divided into the results of the frequency term script in four traffic event dictionaries (Demonstration, Traffic accident, Traffic Jam and Roadwork) and four frequent terms dictionaries (Abbreviations, Nicknames, Acronyms and Hashtags), which are presented in Figure 2.

Preprocessing and Classification

This stage is based on two processes. The first one consists of preprocessing dataset of tweets. This process changes each tweet to lowercase and removes accent marks (e.g. CUAUHTÉMOC AV. – cuauhtémoc av.).

Moreover, a dictionary of abbreviations and acronyms is used. They are replaced with the complete word (cuauhtemoc av. – cuauhtemoc avenue and ipn av. – instituto politecnico nacional avenue). Moreover, the dictionaries of hashtags and nicknames to replace mentions to other accounts, nicknames, misspellings and hashtags are considered (i.e. @OVIALCDMX, 'Revolution, '#mazarikstreet') with the official name (e.g. 'The eje' – 'revolution monument' and '#mazarikstreet' – 'mazarik street').

In addition, stop words have to be filtered out (e.g. articles and pronouns), in this case, the list of stop words has been defined by the Natural Language Toolkit Library (n.d.). The second task consists of classifying tweets by event type and using the traffic-related events Dictionaries, in order to define the classes: Demonstrations, Traffic Accidents, Traffic Jam and Roadwork.

Figure 2. The collected information from the most frequent terms in tweets collection

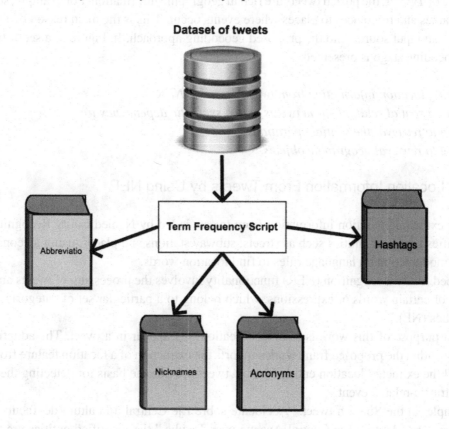

Tweets Classification

Given a tweets collection (Tw) (Tw), and a set denoted by $C = \{C_1, C_2, ..., C_L\}$ $C = \{C_1, C_2, ..., C_L\}$ of L L classes with their respective labels, a binary function of text classification $F : Tw \times C \rightarrow \{0,1\}$ $F : Tw \times C \rightarrow \{0,1\}$ is proposed. For example, a function that assigns the value 0 or 1 to the tuple $[tw_j, C_p]$ $[tw_j, C_p]$, such that $tw_j \epsilon Tw$ $tw_j \epsilon Tw$ and $c_p \epsilon C$ $c_p \epsilon C$. If the assigned value is 1, then the tweet tw_j tw_j is a member of the c_p c_p class. If the assigned value is 0, it means that tweet tw_j tw_j is not a member of the c_p c_p class. Finally, each tweet collection is placed in a corresponding event type label that was classified and stored in a table into the database.

Semantic Geocoding

The local addresses consist of multiple components of elements (*e.g.* house number, street name, street direction, city, state, and postal code), which are used to express a location on the Earth's surface. In a Geographic Information System (GIS), the addresses are converted to features on a map by means of geocoding process. It involves a set of steps, whereby the geographic coordinates are assigned to an address, comparing the address elements to those in reference data (Hart & Zandbergen, 2013).

In the case of Twitter, the posted tweets are rich in geographic information. For example, street names, landmarks names and references to places where events occur. This is the main reason that tweets have been taken as an input source into the proposed geocoding approach. In Figure 3, a set of tasks for the semantic geocoding stage is presented.

1. *Extracting location information from tweets by using NER.*
2. *Extracting spatial relations from tweets with a syntactic dependency tree.*
3. *Quering to retrieval the spatial operations.*
4. *Quering to retrieval geographic objects.*

Extracting Location Information From Tweets by Using NER

The task for extracting location information from tweets is led by Named Entity Recognition (NER), which identifies names of entities such as streets, subway stations and places, using a geonames gazetteer and the model based on language rules to find location words.

The Named Entity Recognition (NER) functionality involves the processing of tweets and identifies occurrences of certain words or expressions, which belong to a particular set of categories referred as Named Entities (NE).

The main purpose of this work is to detect location that appear in a tweet. The adoption of NER functionality within the proposed framework supports the extraction of a location feature from the tweet message. All the extracted location entities from a tweet provide the basis for detecting the location of a particular traffic-related event.

For example, in the Spanish tweet: "Accidente sobre Eje Central a la altura de Tacuba." or in the English tweet: "Accident on Eje Central Avenue near Tacuba." the identified entities are the follows: "Eje Central" and "Tacuba". These locations are subsequently used as a parameter in the query to the road infrastructure ontology.

Figure 3. Tasks of the semantic geocoding stage

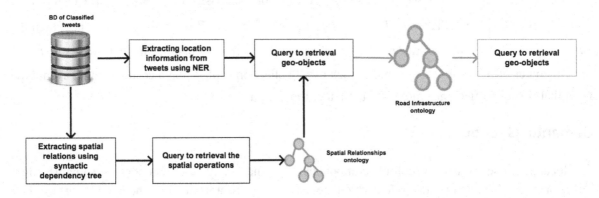

Extracting Spatial Relations From Tweets With a Syntactic Dependency Tree

This task extracts spatial relations from tweets by means of the syntactic dependency tree. The process is defined by the following steps:

1. Generate a syntactic dependency tree of the tweet in order to identify the spatial relations, *e.g.* in the Spanish tweet: "Accidente sobre Eje Central a la altura de Tacuba." or in the English tweet: "Accident on Eje Central Avenue near Tacuba."
2. Use the dependency tree leaves in order to identify the relationship, discarding words that represent locations or traffic-related events located in dictionaries (*e.g.* in the Spanish tweet: "Accidente sobre Eje Central a la altura de Tacuba."– "sobre" and "a la altura" or in the English tweet: "Accident on Eje Central Avenue near Tacuba." – "on" and "near"). These relations are subsequently used in the query to the road infrastructure ontology. The syntactic dependency tree is depicted in Figure 4.

Although both images represent the same information, the language changes completely the way of processing information. For example, in the case of streets names, buildings and toponyms imply to find the location. For spatial relations, it means to interpret properly the relationship or behavior.

Quering to Retrieval the Spatial Operations

According to Yecheng (2011), The next concepts are considererd the fundamental classes in the design of the ontology (see Figure 5).

The spatial relations implemented into the ontology were obtained from the terms of the last task. Thus, a query to the retrieve the class to which belongs this terms as well as the related spatial operations was built.

For example, in the Spanish tweet: "Accidente sobre Eje Central a la altura de Tacuba." or in the English tweet: "Accident on Eje Central Avenue near Tacuba." the query is built as follows:

PREFIX afn: <http://jena.hpl.hp.com/ARQ/function#>
PREFIX fn: <http://www.w3.org/2005/xpath-functions#>
PREFIX geo: <http://www.opengis.net/ont/geosparql#>
PREFIX geof: <http://www.opengis.net/def/function/geosparql/>
PREFIX gml: <http://www.opengis.net/ont/gml#>
PREFIX owl: <http://www.w3.org/2002/07/owl#>

Figure 4. The syntactic dependency tree tweet

```
1 accidente    accidente    NCMS000  NC  pos=noun|type=common|gen=masculine|num=singular
2 sobre        sobre        SP       SP  pos=adposition|type=preposition
3 Eje_Central  eje_central  NP00SP0  NP  pos=noun|type=proper|neclass=person
4 a            a            SP       SP  pos=adposition|type=preposition
5 la           el           DA0FS0   DA  pos=determiner|type=article|gen=feminine|num=singular
6 altura       altura       NCFS000  NC  pos=noun|type=common|gen=feminine|num=singular
7 de           de           SP       SP  pos=adposition|type=preposition
8 Tacuba       tacuba       NP00G00  NP  pos=noun|type=proper|neclass=location
```

Figure 5. Concepts of the ontology

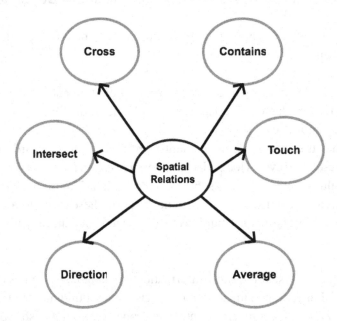

```
PREFIX par: <http://parliament.semwebcentral.org/parliament#>
PREFIX rdf: <http://www.w3.org/1999/02/22-rdf-syntax-ns#>
PREFIX rdfs: <http://www.w3.org/2000/01/rdf-schema#>
PREFIX sf: <http://www.opengis.net/ont/sf#>
PREFIX time: <http://www.w3.org/2006/time#>
PREFIX units: <http://www.opengis.net/def/uom/OGC/1.0/>
PREFIX xsd: <http://www.w3.org/2001/XMLSchema#>
PREFIX onto: <http://datos.relacionesEspaciales.mx/ontology/>
PREFIX recurso: <_>
SELECT * WHERE{
?s rdfs:label "a la altura"@es.
?s ?o ?p.
?p ?q owl:Class.
filter(?p != onto:spatialrelationships).
}
```

The last query retrieves the term related spatial operation that in this case it corresponds to "Intersect".

Quering to Retrieval Geographic Objects

A gazetteer with the road infrastructure of the Mexico City was built. It used the plugin developed by Rivera et al, (2015) for transforming all road infrastructure into the RDF file for generating individuals in order to semi-automatically populate the ontology.

When the population process has finished, the queries are generated according to the number of spatial objects involved in the event. A query that uses as parameters the spatial operations and the retrieved locations is built. The result is a set of valid geographic objects, that represents the traffic-related events.

For example, for the Spanish tweet: "Accidente sobre Eje Central a la altura de Tacuba.", the query is built as follows:

```
PREFIX afn: <http://jena.hpl.hp.com/ARQ/function#>
PREFIX fn: <http://www.w3.org/2005/xpath-functions#>
PREFIX geo: <http://www.opengis.net/ont/geosparql#>
PREFIX geof: <http://www.opengis.net/def/function/geosparql/>
PREFIX gml: <http://www.opengis.net/ont/gml#>
PREFIX owl: <http://www.w3.org/2002/07/owl#>
PREFIX par: <http://parliament.semwebcentral.org/parliament#>
PREFIX rdf: <http://www.w3.org/1999/02/22-rdf-syntax-ns#>
PREFIX rdfs: <http://www.w3.org/2000/01/rdf-schema#>
PREFIX sf: <http://www.opengis.net/ont/sf#>
PREFIX time: <http://www.w3.org/2006/time#>
PREFIX units: <http://www.opengis.net/def/uom/OGC/1.0/>
PREFIX xsd: <http://www.w3.org/2001/XMLSchema#>
PREFIX onto: <http://datos.roadInfrastructure.mx/ontology/>
PREFIX geometria: <http://datos.roadInfrastructure.mx/recurso/geometry/>
PREFIX recurso: <http://datos.roadInfrastructure.mx/recurso/>
SELECT DISTINCT ?obj1 ?obj2 WHERE{
?obj1 geometria:hasGeometry ?aGeom.
?obj1 rdfs:label "EJE CENTRAL"@es.
?aGeom geo:asWKT ?pos1.

?obj2 geometria:hasGeometry ?aGeom2.
?obj2 rdfs:label "TACUBA"@es.
?aGeom2 geo:asWKT ?pos2.

FILTER(geof:sfIntersects(?pos1,?pos2)).
}
```

If the result of this query is empty, then the traffic event is not valid or it is probably that locations do not have spatial relationships.

Mapping and Assessment

This stage is composed of two processes: In the first one, the geographic objects that were retrieved from tweets are mapped in the digital cartography, and they represent traffic-related events described in each tweet. Figure 6 and Figure 7 depict two examples of tweets.

The set of valid geographic objects, which represent the traffic-related events, could be:

- A unique geometry.
- A multiple geometry.
- A collection of geometries.

In the first Spanish tweet: "Accidente sobre Eje Central a la altura de Tacuba." or the English tweet: "Accident on Eje Central Avenue near Tacuba." (see Figure 6).

For the second Spanish tweet in Spanish: "Largos asentamientos en Viaducto Tlalpan desde Anillo Periferico hasta Avenida Insurgentes". The same tweet in English: "Long settlements in Viaducto Tlalpan from Anillo Periferico to Insurgentes Avenue". First the Figure 7 shows the syntactic dependency tree and Figure 8 show a map.

```
PREFIX afn: <http://jena.hpl.hp.com/ARQ/function#>
PREFIX fn: <http://www.w3.org/2005/xpath-functions#>
PREFIX geo: <http://www.opengis.net/ont/geosparql#>
PREFIX geof: <http://www.opengis.net/def/function/geosparql/>
PREFIX gml: <http://www.opengis.net/ont/gml#>
PREFIX owl: <http://www.w3.org/2002/07/owl#>
PREFIX par: <http://parliament.semwebcentral.org/parliament#>
PREFIX rdf: <http://www.w3.org/1999/02/22-rdf-syntax-ns#>
PREFIX rdfs: <http://www.w3.org/2000/01/rdf-schema#>
PREFIX sf: <http://www.opengis.net/ont/sf#>
PREFIX time: <http://www.w3.org/2006/time#>
PREFIX units: <http://www.opengis.net/def/uom/OGC/1.0/>
```

Figure 6. A map that contains a point event type generated for the first tweet

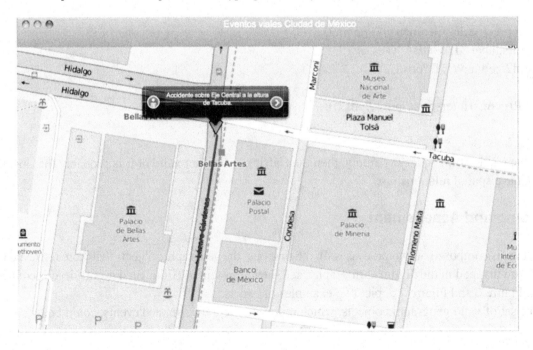

```
PREFIX xsd:
PREFIX onto: <http://datos.callesmexico.mx/ontologia/>
PREFIX geometria: <http://datos.callesmexico.mx/recurso/geometry/>
PREFIX recurso: <http://datos.callesmexico.mx/recurso/>

SELECT DISTINCT ?p1 ?p2 ?p3 WHERE{
?p1 rdfs:label " VIADUCTO TLALPAN "@es.
?p1 geometria:hasGeometry ?aGeom.
?aGeom geo:asWKT ?pos1.
?p2 rdfs:label " ANILLO PERIFERICO "@es.
?p2 geometria:hasGeometry ?aGeom.
?aGeom geo:asWKT ?pos2.
?p3 rdfs:label " AVENIDA INSURGENTES "@es.
?p3 geometria:hasGeometry ?aGeom.
?aGeom geo:asWKT ?pos3.
geof:sfIntersects(?pos1,?pos2)AS ?punto1)
geof:sfIntersects(?pos1,?pos3)AS ?punto2)
FILTER(geof:sfIntersects(?punto1,?punto2))
}
```

The second process consists of assessing the transformation, which is described as follows:

1. The selected collection of tweets for the experiments is geocoded by a user. For this work, the geocoded dataset is considered the gold standard metric.
2. The selected set of tweets for the experiments is compared to the results of the geocoding method provided for Google Maps.
3. The results are evaluated by applying the *precision*, *recall* and *F* measures (Paradesi, 2011).

EXPERIMENTS AND RESULTS

For the development, an API to collect tweets was used. In addition, PostgresSQL with the spatial extension PostGIS as the server of the spatial database has been considered. For the classification the WEKA framework was chosen. Moreover, the Web Mapping Service Interface Standard (WMS), as well as the

Figure 7. The syntactic dependency tree tweet

```
1 transito            transitar            VMIP1S0  VMI
2 lento               lento                AQ0MS00  AQ
3 sobre               sobre                SP       SP
4 Viaducto_Tlalpan    viaducto_tlalpan     NP00SP0  NP
5 desde               desde                SP       SP
6 Anillo_Periferico   anillo_periferico    NP00G00  NP
7 hasta               hasta                SP       SP
8 Avenida_Insurgentes avenida_insurgentes  NP00G00  NP
```

Figure 8. A map that contains a line event type generated for the second tweet

GeoServer and OpenLayers as a base component with the own digital cartography of road infrastructure of the Mexico City were used. In addition, the Triple Stored (Parliament) for implementing a SPARQL Endpoint and the ontology editor Protégé for developing the ontologies, in conjunction with the plugin developed by Rivera et al, (2015) were employed.

Dataset

From November 2014 to November 2016, tweets in Spanish of traffic-related events in the Mexico City were collected by using the Twitter Streaming API and eliminating repeated tweets. The final dataset contains 660,480 tweets generated by 4,258 users. From these tweets, 100,000 messages for our evaluation were extracted.

The Gold Standard for Geo-Tags of Tweets

A manually gold standard for traffic-related events that appear in the Mexico City was defined, in order to score the method; each participant was given the same set of tweets. In addition, a digital map for locating the event and a blank table with columns for the street, building, abbreviations and event type were provided to the participants. Thus, each participant was also given the same instructions that constitute a location in a tweet and some examples of how include in each category. They completed their locations coding independently and their results were assembled into a table for tweet-by-tweet comparison. Finally, a list of places described in tweets, are considered as the gold standard.

Classification Algorithms

The implementations provided by the Weka framework (Watanabe et al., 2011) were used. Thus, with a pruned C45 decision tree, the precision of 0.858 and a recall of 0.856 were achieved (see Table 1), its *kappa* statistics was 0.79. These values imply that the best results were obtained with a pruned C45 decision tree with respect to other classification algorithms. All classifiers outperform a ZeroR baseline

Table 1. Precision, recall and F measures for different classification algorithms

Algorithm	Precision	Recall	F
Prunned C45 decision tree	0.858	0.856	0.857
Multiplayer perceptron	0.829	0.837	0.833
Naïve Bayes	0.783	0.871	0.825
ZeroR	0.319	1.000	0.484

that classifies each instance as an event. For these experiments, a 10-fold cross-validation approach was used. Thus, Table 1 provides the results from our evaluation with three different classification algorithms.

Textual and User Features

According to the obtained results, the features that analyze the textual content of the tweets deliver a slightly higher precision, recall, and F scores than user features. However, an improvement is evident when all textual and user features are used together. Thus, in Table 2, the obtained values combining the methods are presented.

Moreover, Figure 9 depicts when the textual and user features are independently used, the results were not good. In contrast, when all the features are considered, the classification improves significantly the results (see the thick continuous black line).

Results of the Semantic Geocoding Methodology

The results obtained by applying our semantic geocoding methodology are presented in Table 3. These consist of a set of tweets collected in the Mexico City. The approach attained an F measure of 0.872 for streets, an F measure of 0.829 for POIs, and an F measure of 0.960 for traffic-related events.

Comparison Between the Proposed Algorithm With the Geocoding Service of Google

Google provides a geocoding service that gives location tags words in text. The same dataset of tweets through this service was executed, in order to compare it with the obtained results of our methodology (see Table 4). This experiment showed that the Google geocoding service was not able to geographically locate the tweets and in most of the cases, the information was incorrect.

Table 2. Precision, recall and F measures

Featured Used	Precision	Recall	F
Textual features	0.827	0.765	0.795
User features	0.799	0.749	0.773
All features	**0.858**	**0.856**	**0.857**

Figure 9. Curves for classifier with all features, only textual features, and only user features. The areas under the curve are 0.908, 0.893 and 0.873, respectively

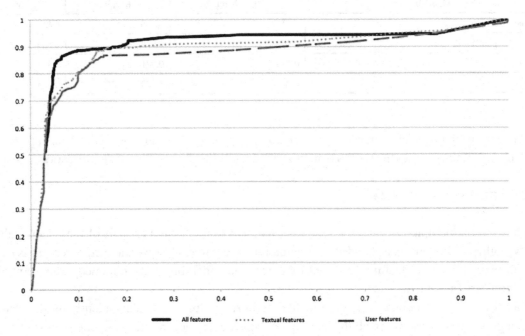

Table 3. Precision, recall and F measures for geocoding methodology

Feature	Precision	Recall	F
Street	0.878	0.870	0.872
POIs	0.880	0.784	0.829
Public transport stations	0.845	0.734	0.785
Traffic-related events	0.945	0.956	0.960

Table 4. Precision, recall and F measures for geocoding service of Google

Feature	Precision		Recall		F	
	Google	Our Method	Google	Our Method	Google	Our Method
Street	0.820	0.874	0.560	0.866	0.665	0.872
POIs	0.720	0.889	0.615	0.784	0.663	0.829
Public transport stations	0.730	0.890	0.527	0.734	0.612	0.785
Eventos	0.10	0.945	0.02	0.956	0.039	0.960

CONCLUSION AND FUTURE WORK

In this paper, a novel methodology to detect geospatial real world traffic-related events by analyzing the Twitter streaming, by using the ontology and user features is proposed. This work has shown that the methodology can reliably detect whether clusters of tweets issued spatially close to each other, describing a real world traffic-related event. The proposed geocoding approach is fully automatic, from the collection of tweets to visualization of the geographic objects that represent the traffic events.

It is important to highlight that our work generates an important contribution for semantic web using existing natural language conversations and conceptual representations like ontologies, in order to make the geocoding process and interpret spatial relationships contained into the tweets, as well as the use of syntactic dependency trees for the detection of those relationships inside the text.

With respect to the results, the use of textual and user features has improved the classification scores. Thus, this ontology-driven approach implies to obtain a better geographic location, because the conceptual representation disambiguates the terms and the relationships.

Open questions that have not been yet evaluated are the follows. How many events are happening in a specific geographic area? is it possible to detect these events with the proposed methodology? Future works are oriented towards planning the way to detect events in real-time directly from the Twitter stream. The methodology to identify locations in other languages requires some adjustments for its application with diverse languages. Even though, differences in naming of streets and addressing among cultures must be respected and treated carefully.

ACKNOWLEDGMENT

This work was partially sponsored by the Instituto Politécnico Nacional (IPN), and the Secretaría de Investigación y Posgrado (SIP) under grants 20162006, 20161899, 20161869, and 20161611. Additionally, we are thankful to the reviewers for their invaluable and constructive feedback that helped improve the quality of the paper. We are thankful to the reviewers for their invaluable and constructive feedback that helped improve the quality of the paper.

REFERENCES

Agarwal, P., Vaithiyanathan, R., Sharma, S., & Shroff, G. (2012). Catching the Long-Tail: Extracting Local News Events from Twitter. ICWSM.

Albuquerque, F. C., Casanova, M. A., Lopes, H., Redlich, L. R., de Macedo, J. A. F., Lemos, M., & Renso, C. et al. (2015). A methodology for traffic-related Twitter messages interpretation. *Computers in Industry*.

Atefeh, F., & Khreich, W. (2015). A survey of techniques for event detection in twitter. *Computational Intelligence*, *31*(1), 132–164. doi:10.1111/coin.12017

Blanco, R., Ottaviano, G., & Meij, E. (2015, February). Fast and space-efficient entity linking for queries. In *Proceedings of the Eighth ACM International Conference on Web Search and Data Mining* (pp. 179-188). ACM. doi:10.1145/2684822.2685317

Bouillot, F., Poncelet, P., & Roche, M. (2012). How and why exploit tweet's location information? *AGILE'2012: 15th International Conference on Geographic Information Science.*

Chenji, H., Zhang, W., Stoleru, R., & Arnett, C. (2013). DistressNet: A disaster response system providing constant availability cloud-like services. *Ad Hoc Networks*, *11*(8), 2440–2460. doi:10.1016/j.adhoc.2013.06.008

Crooks, A. T., & Wise, S. (2013). GIS and agent-based models for humanitarian assistance. *Computers, Environment and Urban Systems*, *41*, 100–111. doi:10.1016/j.compenvurbsys.2013.05.003

Daly, E. M., Lecue, F., & Bicer, V. (2013). Westland row why so slow?: fusing social media and linked data sources for understanding real-time traffic conditions. In *Proceedings of the 2013 international conference on Intelligent user interfaces* (pp. 203-212). ACM. doi:10.1145/2449396.2449423

Duque, A. P. G., Pérez, M. E. D. M., & de Guevara, F. G. L. (2012). Usos de Twitter en las universidades iberoamericanas. *Revista Latinoamericana de Tecnología Educativa-RELATEC*, *11*(1), 27–39.

Eisenstein, J., O'Connor, B., Smith, N. A., & Xing, E. P. (2010). A latent variable model for geographic lexical variation. In *Proceedings of the 2010 Conference on Empirical Methods in Natural Language Processing* (pp. 1277-1287). Association for Computational Linguistics.

Gelernter, J., & Balaji, S. (2013). An algorithm for local geoparsing of microtext. *GeoInformatica*, *17*(4), 635–667. doi:10.1007/s10707-012-0173-8

Gómez, A. B., Martínez, A. C., Sánchez, Á. C., & Rus, T. I. (2012). El uso de Twitter como herramienta de formación del profesorado en la Facultad de Educación de la Universidad de Murcia. *I Congreso Nacional de Investigación e Innovación en Educación Infantil y Primaria.*

Graham, M., Hale, S. A., & Gaffney, D. (2014). Where in the world are you? Geolocation and language identification in Twitter. *The Professional Geographer*, *66*(4), 568–578. doi:10.1080/00330124.2014.907699

Gutierrez, C., Figuerias, P., Oliveira, P., Costa, R., & Jardim-Goncalves, R. (2015, July). Twitter mining for traffic events detection. In *Science and Information Conference (SAI)*, 2015 (pp. 371-378). IEEE.

Hart, T. C., & Zandbergen, P. A. (2013). Reference data and geocoding quality: Examining completeness and positional accuracy of street geocoded crime incidents. *Policing: An International Journal of Police Strategies & Management*, *36*(2), 263–294. doi:10.1108/13639511311329705

Hotho, A., Jäschke, R., & Lerman, K. (2017). Mining social semantics on the social web. *Semantic Web*, *8*(5), 623–624. doi:10.3233/SW-170272

Internet Live Stats. (n.d.) Twitter Statistics. *Internet Live Stats.* Retrieved from: http:// www.internetlivestats.com/twitter-statistics

Iversen, G. H. (2014). *U.S. Patent No. 8,806,322*. Washington, DC: U.S. Patent and Trademark Office.

Krumm, J., & Horvitz, E. (2015). *Eyewitness: Identifying Local Events via Space-Time Signals in Twitter Feeds*. Academic Press.

Lee, R., & Sumiya, K. (2010). Measuring geographical regularities of crowd behaviors for Twitter-based geo-social event detection. In *Proceedings of the 2nd ACM SIGSPATIAL international workshop on location based social networks* (pp. 1-10). ACM. doi:10.1145/1867699.1867701

Lee, S., Farag, M., Kanan, T., & Fox, E. A. (2015, June). Read between the lines: A Machine Learning Approach for Disambiguating the Geo-location of Tweets. In *Proceedings of the 15th ACM/IEEE-CS Joint Conference on Digital Libraries* (pp. 273-274). ACM. doi:10.1145/2756406.2756971

Meij, E., Weerkamp, W., & de Rijke, M. (2012). Adding semantics to microblog posts. In *Proceedings of the fifth ACM international conference on Web search and data mining* (pp. 563-572). ACM. doi:10.1145/2124295.2124364

Moriya, M., & Ryoke, M. (2013). Information Balance between Transmitters and Receivers Based on the Twitter after Great East Japan Earthquake. *International Journal of Knowledge and Systems Science*, *4*(2), 66–76. doi:10.4018/jkss.2013040107

Moro, A., Raganato, A., & Navigli, R. (2014). Entity linking meets word sense disambiguation: A unified approach. *Transactions of the Association for Computational Linguistics*, *2*, 231–244.

Natural Languauge Toolkit Library. (n.d.). Retrieved from: http://www.nltk.org/

Nielsen, S. S., Nielsen, G. B., Denwood, M. J., Haugegaard, J., & Houe, H. (2015). Comparison of recording of pericarditis and lung disorders at routine meat inspection with findings at systematic health monitoring in Danish finisher pigs. *Acta Veterinaria Scandinavica*, *57*(1), 1. doi:10.1186/s13028-015-0109-z PMID:25887329

Oussalah, M., Bhat, F., Challis, K., & Schnier, T. (2013). A software architecture for Twitter collection, search and geolocation services. *Knowledge-Based Systems*, *37*, 105–120. doi:10.1016/j.knosys.2012.07.017

Paradesi, S. M. (2011). Geotagging Tweets Using Their Content. *FLAIRS Conference*.

Pérez, P. A., Maeso, S. C., Ezkerro, A. M., & Otaduy, M. P. (2012). Twitter en la Universidad. *Revista del Congrés Internacional de Docència Universitària i Innovació*, *1*(1).

Qin, X., Parker, S., Liu, Y., Graettinger, A. J., & Forde, S. (2013). Intelligent geocoding system to locate traffic crashes. *Accident; Analysis and Prevention*, *50*, 1034–1041. doi:10.1016/j.aap.2012.08.007 PMID:22921783

Ritter, A., Etzioni, O., & Clark, S. (2012). Open domain event extraction from twitter. In *Proceedings of the 18th ACM SIGKDD international conference on Knowledge discovery and data mining* (pp. 1104-1112). ACM. doi:10.1145/2339530.2339704

Rivera, L. C., Vilches-Blázquez, L. M., Torres-Ruiz, M., & Ibarra, M. A. M. (2015). Semantic Recommender System for Touristic Context Based on Linked Data. In Information Fusion and Geographic Information Systems (IF&GIS'2015) (pp. 77-89). Springer International Publishing.

Roller, S., Speriosu, M., Rallapalli, S., Wing, B., & Baldridge, J. (2012, July). Supervised text-based geolocation using language models on an adaptive grid. In *Proceedings of the 2012 Joint Conference on Empirical Methods in Natural Language Processing and Computational Natural Language Learning* (pp. 1500-1510). Association for Computational Linguistics.

Seol, J. W., Jeong, K. Y., & Lee, K. S. (2013). Follower classification through social network analysis in twitter. In *Grid and Pervasive Computing* (pp. 926–931). Springer Berlin Heidelberg. doi:10.1007/978-3-642-38027-3_108

Takhteyev, Y., Gruzd, A., & Wellman, B. (2012). Geography of Twitter networks. *Social Networks*, *34*(1), 73–81. doi:10.1016/j.socnet.2011.05.006

Tonon, A., Cudré-Mauroux, P., Blarer, A., Lenders, V., & Motik, B. (2017, May). ArmaTweet: Detecting Events by Semantic Tweet Analysis. In *European Semantic Web Conference* (pp. 138-153). Springer. doi:10.1007/978-3-319-58451-5_10

Wakefield, J. S., Warren, S. J., & Alsobrook, M. (2011). Learning and teaching as communicative actions: A mixed-methods Twitter study. *Knowledge Management & E-Learning: An International Journal, 3*(4), 563-584.

Watanabe, K., Ochi, M., Okabe, M., & Onai, R. (2011). Jasmine: a real-time local-event detection system based on geolocation information propagated to microblogs. In *Proceedings of the 20th ACM international conference on Information and knowledge management* (pp. 2541-2544). ACM. doi:10.1145/2063576.2064014

Welch, B. K., & Bonnan-White, J. (2012). Twittering to increase student engagement in the university classroom. *Knowledge Management & E-Learning: An International Journal, 4*(3), 325-345.

Yuan, Y. (2011, June). Extracting spatial relations from document for geographic information retrieval. In *Geoinformatics, 2011 19th International Conference on* (pp. 1-5). IEEE. doi:10.1109/GeoInformatics.2011.5980797

Zhang, W., & Gelernter, J. (2014). Geocoding location expressions in Twitter messages: A preference learning method. *Journal of Spatial Information Science, 2014*(9), 37-70.

Zhao, K., Meng, X., Li, H., & Wang, Z. (2015, October). Using encyclopedic knowledge to understand queries. In *Proceedings of the First International Workshop on Novel Web Search Interfaces and Systems* (pp. 17-22). ACM. doi:10.1145/2810355.2810358

Chapter 15
Semantic–Based Geospatial Data Integration With Unique Features

Ying Zhang
North China Electric Power University, China

Chaopeng Li
North China Electric Power University, China

Na Chen
Hebei Vocational College of Rail Transportation, China

Shaowen Liu
North China Electric Power University, China

Liming Du
North China Electric Power University, China

Zhuxiao Wang
North China Electric Power University, China

Miaomiao Ma
North China Electric Power University, China

ABSTRACT

Since large amount of geospatial data are produced by various sources, geospatial data integration is difficult because of the shortage of semantics. Despite standardised data format and data access protocols, such as Web Feature Service (WFS), can enable end-users with access to heterogeneous data stored in different formats from various sources, it is still time-consuming and ineffective due to the lack of semantics. To solve this problem, a prototype to implement the geospatial data integration is proposed by addressing the following four problems, i.e., geospatial data retrieving, modeling, linking and integrating. We mainly adopt four kinds of geospatial data sources to evaluate the performance of the proposed approach. The experimental results illustrate that the proposed linking method can get high

DOI: 10.4018/978-1-5225-5042-6.ch015

performance in generating the matched candidate record pairs in terms of Reduction Ratio(RR), Pairs Completeness(PC), Pairs Quality(PQ) and F-score. The integrating results denote that each data source can get much Complementary Completeness(CC) and Increased Completeness(IC).

1. INTRODUCTION

Geospatial data integration can be used to improve data quality, to reduce costs, and to make data more useful to the public(Auer et al.,2009; Bittner et al.,2009; Brodt et al.,2010; Kuhn,2002; Su et al.,2012; De Carvalho et al.,2012; Su & Lochovsky,2010; Ballatore et al.,2014; Buccella et al.,2010; Fonseca, Egenhofer et al.,2002; Malik et al.,2010;Vaccari et al.,2009). However, the large amount of data is produced by a variety of sources, stored in incompatible formats, and accessible through different GIS applications. Thus, geospatial data integration is difficult and becoming an increasingly important subject.

To implement the geospatial data integration, four problems need to be addressed: geospatial data retrieving, modeling, linking and integrating This paper proposes corresponding approach for each issue. Besides, our work takes advantage of Karma (Szekely et al.,2011; Knoblock et al.,2012; Taheriyan et al.,2012; Tuchinda et al.,2011; Knoblock et al.,2011), which is a general information integration tool. It supports importing data from a variety of sources including relational databases, spreadsheet, KML and semi-structured Web pages, and publishing data in a variety of formats such as RDF. The source modeling work is based on these functions.

1. **Data Retrieval:** This problem concerns data extraction from Web APIs, which provide users with access to the corresponding databases. Diverse APIs have different input requirements. It is hard for users without adequate background knowledge to exploit the growing amount of heterogeneous geospatial data. The objective of our retrieval approach is to enable both API providers and API users to semi-automatically model Web API and invoke the related services to extract the geospatial data.
2. **Source Modeling:** The retrieved geospatial data from various sources are often described according to multiple perceptions, different terms and with different level of detail (Witten et al.,1999; Baeza-Yates & Ribeiro-Neto,1999; Li & Fonseca,2014). To overcome the diverse nature of geospatial data and to represent them in a uniform way, recent research has applied the concepts of the Semantic Web to geospatial data integration (Janowicz et al.,2011; Peng,2005; Arpinar et al.,2006; Oussalah et al.,2013). Semantic Web (Berners-Lee et al.,2001) introduces the ontology languages such as Resource Description Framework (RDF) and Web Ontology Language (OWL) to provide benefits of semantic annotation. By providing a semantic interpretation of the data, RDF and OWL allows software programs to understand structures and meanings of different information sources. In this paper, we align the extracted data in a semantic way. We build a generic geospatial ontology and take advantage of Karma to map and align the extracted geospatial data based on the generic geospatial ontology.
3. **Record Linking:** This problem is about recognizing the same entity from different sources. The task of record linkage is commonly used for improving data quality and integrity by reducing costs and efforts in data acquisition. Our main contribution focuses on addressing this problem. In the previous work, the record linking process has been done by defining a set of semantic rules. These methods missed the unique characteristics of geospatial data such as geospatial relationships

directly, which are significant for linking and whose functions cannot be expressed by semantic techniques. We make the best of such unique features and semantic techniques in geospatial data linking. Features refer to characteristics in this work. Further, in addition to the basic functions, the geospatial relationships endow the geospatial data linking with translation function, which can save the translating cost among all the geospatial sources with different languages.

4. **Data Integration:** The problem of data integration is to combine data of different sources and provide users a unified view of the data (Lenzerini,2002; Hastings,2008). Assuming that the same records from different sources are linked together, we can treat the problem of combining the data from multiple sources similar to the way we union the attributes of the same geospatial entity from multiple sources and provide a consolidated view of the integrated data.

The rest of the paper is organized as follows. Section 2 discusses a motivating example that we use throughout paper to explain our approach. Section 3 presents the data retrieval approach. Section 4 presents an overview of related work. Section 5 describes the modeling work of geospatial data. In Section 6, the linking process is discussed in more detail. The integration is then presented in Section 7, followed by the experimental evaluation and discussion in Section 8. The paper is concluded in Section 9 with an outlook to future challenges and work in this area.

2. MOTIVATIONAL EXAMPLE

In order to motivate the problem context, we utilise the following example scenario using real-world geospatial data sources to illustrate the proposed solution throughout the paper. From end-user's perspective, autonomous driving, for instance, would take advantage of the comprehensive geospatial data. In the example scenario, users might access to various geospatial data sources such as OpenStreetMap, Wikimapia, USGS and EPA's data set. Thus, the general problem that we need to address is how to dynamically combine a set of geospatial data sources and generate fusion algorithms to produce the needed integrated results.

In recent years, a web phenomenon known as Volunteered Geographic Information (VGI) has produced a large number of geographic data sets. OSM is a leading VGI project, aims at building an open-content world map through user contributions (Ballatore et al.,2013). In the OSM dataset, objects are encoded as nodes, ways and relations. Nodes denote the centroids of places or points of interest. Ways include lines and polygons. Lines are used to represent the roads, while places are usually described by polygons. Relations denote the groups of objects. The world data set currently contains 2 billion nodes, 200 million ways and 1 million relations. To data, the OSM community has over 453,000 contributors.

Wikimapia is another open-content collaborative mapping project that aims to mark and describe all geographical objects in the world. In October, 2013 the project's website claimed that the registered users and guests have already marked over 22,000,000 objects. In Wikimapia, places are described by polygon.

USGS (The United States Geological Survey) is a scientific agency of the United States government. The scientists of the USGS study the landscape of the United States, its natural resources, and the natural hazards that threaten it. The organization has four major science disciplines, concerning biology, geography, gology, and hydrology. Our experiments take advantage of geographic data of USGS.

To improve public health and the environment, the United States Environmental Protection Agency (EPA) collects information about facilities sites subject to environmental regulation. The EPA Geospatial Data Access Project provides downloadable files of these sites in the following formats: Extensible Markup Language (XML), Keyhole Markup Language (KML) and Comma Separated Value (CSV).

Since different sources provide diverse types of data and have different coverage, the first specific instance of the given general problem that we will focus on is how to extract geospatial data from diverse sources. In general, different sources possess disparate retrieval method. For example, in our motivating example, Wikimapia allows users to extract geospatial data from Wikimapia maps with some specific APIs. In contrast, OpenStreetMap has an editing API for extracting geospatial data from OpenStreetMap database. Different API requires distinct input parameters. It is not convenient for end-users without adequate background knowledge to take advantage of these distinct APIs to retrieve geospatial data.

After retrieving process, the next instance of the general problem is how to align the extracted geospatial data, since they are heterogenous and difficult for users to understand and use. For instance, OpenStreetMap uses "name" to describe entity, USGS adopts "feature_name" to describe it, and EPA uses "primary_name" to represent entity. Different data sets describe the same thing with diverse format and content. For example, both Wikimapia and OpenStreetMap employ "coordinate_system" to describe coordinate systems, EPA uses "HDatum_Desc" to identify it, but USGS uses "srid" to denote that. In addition, different data sources introduce diverse geospatial data types to describe the same kind of entities. For instance, USGS and EPA take advantage of "latitude" and "longitude" to describe the location, while Wikimapia use "polygon" and "point" to represent it. Because of the heterogeneity of the extracted geospatial data, users still can't use them primely. It needs a proper method to solve the problem of alignment.

The third instance of the given problem is record linkage, which can be used for improving data quality by reducing costs in data acquisition. In our motivating example, we take a building entity as an example. The entity is named "Music practice rooms" by Wikimapia with coordinate "Point(-118.2847599,34.0226275)". In contrast, the same entity is described by "Mrs Willis H Booth Ferris Memorial Hall" in OpenStreetMap, and its coordinate is "Polygon((-118.28469 34.022675, -118.284744 34.02265, ..., -118.28469 34.022675))". The previous research work developed various indexing techniques to link the same record from different sources. However, most of them transferred the record linkage problem to keyword matching problem. For instance, in order to link the given building entity from Wikimapia and OpenStreetMap, the conventional methods would take indexing to act on "name" values. As we can see, it is not a good choice because the names of the same entity are totally different in various sources. In addition, the indexing techniques used for record linkage need to preprocess the extracted data with translation function if the geospatial data sources are in different languages. Thus, how to address this problem is the main contribution of our work.

Finally, users need a unified view to observe the integrated data from various sources. In the example scenario, Wikimapia provides names, latitudes, longitudes and polygon outlines for building entities, OpenStreetMap gives elevation and address information, such as state and county name, and EPA presents state_code, county_code and postal_code. Thus, it is necessary to combine complementary properties and eliminate data redundancy from the linked data to give users a neat and complete view.

3. RELATED RESEARCH

This paper is related to four three areas of work. For the data retrieval problem, earlier work focuses on (1) automatic extraction of lists and table (Crescenzi & Mecca,2004; Gatterbauer et al.,2007) or (2) using machine learning to capture the retrieval models or rules from users' labeled examples (Muslea et al.,2003; Cohen et al.,2002), or (3) exploiting Semantic Web technologies to facilitate extraction process (Shyu et al.,2007; Wiegand & García,2007; Ballatore et al.,2013; Yue et al.,2011). Automatic extraction only works on the condition that lists and tables can be identified. Machine learning techniques require users to provide more examples to alleviate the complicated structure of Web sources. With Semantic Web techniques such as ontology, reasoning can be done to infer various types of information that can meet specific criteria for use in the data retrieval process. However, there are a large number of comparisons in the reasoning process. In addition, the extraction of geospatial data is typically hindered by domain-related terminology mismatches, Fugazza (Fugazza,2011) set up a knowledge base that served as groundwork for harmonising domain knowledge from distinct areas. In this work, we build the generic geospatial ontology to get specific geospatial data, but we don't need to do many comparisons since we take advantage of Karma to map and align the retrieved heterogenous data according to the provided generic ontology. Because the extracting process happened before the semantic mapping process, the presented geospatial data extraction will not be hindered by the domain-related terminology mismatches.

The second area of related work is on modeling geospatial data. Google Refine (Huynh & Mazzoc-chi,2011) provides users with an interface to import data from various sources and allows users to model sources by aligning columns to Freebase schema types. It also provides capabilities to integrate data from sources but does not use Semantic Web techniques. Di et al.(2006) present a study on ontology-driven automatic creation and execution of geospatial processing models to produce user-specific products by wrapping data and processes with Web services. Each geospatial process transforms geospatial data from one state to another. As geospatial data are often described according to multiple perceptions, the interoperability standards, such as Geography Markup Language, have been put forward to address the syntactical heterogeneity. Nevertheless, the semantic heterogeneity is the most hard-facing problem. Lima et al.(2011) presents an approach and an implemented tool, named GeoMap, for automatically building a geospatial peer ontology as a semantic view of data stored in the geographic database to solve the semantic heterogeneity problem. However, it just can generate ontologies from a few of databases such as Oracle. In contrast, our Karma-based modeling approach mapped the geospatial data based on worksheets which can be obtained from any kind of DBMSs, such as PostGis and other data sources such as GML.

The third research area related to this paper includes work on record linking. As many businesses, government agencies and research projects collect increasingly large amount of geospatial data, techniques that allow efficient processing and integrating of such massive sources have attracted interest from both academia and industry. One task that has been recognized to be of increasing importance in many applications is the record linkage, which is commonly used for improving data quality and integrity. Christen (2012) presents a survey of 12 variations of 6 linking techniques. An indexing technique commonly called blocking (Winkler,2006; Fellegi & Sunter,1969; Baxter,2003) has been employed in all the record linkage approaches, and the blocking key, which is based on a single field or the concatenation of values from several fields, is often used for reducing the large number of potential comparisons by grouping similar values into the same block. The experimental results highlight that the definition of suitable blocking keys is one of the most crucial components for record linkage, but not the actual linking techniques employed. In our work, we utilise the spatial relationships to do linking work instead of trying to select the perfect blocking keys, which can badly affect the linking results. Our approach prevents the effect on the record linkage from blocking keys. Some work such as Safe Software's FME (n.d.) and Talend Open Studio with spatial extension (Talend, n.d.) used geospatial relationships to do the linking work, but their purpose focused on transforming data, analysing data or migrating data, and not providing a comprehensive dataset for users. Silk framework (Volz,2009) is based on the Linked Data paradigm, which is built on two simple ideas: First, RDF provides an expressive data model for representing structured information. Second, RDF links are set between entities in different data sources. Compared with Silk framework, our method would not require such conditions. Any data source can be included for linking in our work. Dey et al. (2011) put forward that the existing techniques cannot be directly applied when the matching records reside at a remote site, because they would pose a tremendous communication bottleneck in a distributed environment while transferring the entire remote data. They developed a matching tree for attribute acquisition and proposed three different schemes of using this tree to reduce the communication overhead significantly. Our approach is designed to transfer common attribute values of all the remote records to the local site. The communication overhead will be significantly large when the geospatial sources have huge amounts of records. So, in the next step, we will extend our work to implement the record linkage in an online, distributed environment.

4. GEOSPATIAL DATA RETRIEVING

As Web APIs provide users with access to the related databases, users can use these services to fetch and save raw data from/to the associated sources. The objective of our retrieving approach is to enable both API providers and API users to semi-automatically model Web API and invoke the corresponding services to extract the geospatial data. The retrieving approach presented in this paper builds upon and extends Karma (Taheriyan,2012).

There are two steps in this process. Firstly, we encapsulate the various retrieval algorithms as different Web Services for Web APIs and import them to the Web Server of Karma. With these services, users can fetch and save the data with various formats such as XML and JSON. In the second step, we semi-automatically model Web API and invoke the related services to extract data.

We use an example API to show the steps of retrieving geospatial data. Since we encapsulate Web APIs as Web Services, both inputs and outputs of Web API are included in that of the corresponding Web Service. For instance, the inputs to the API are a group of bounding box values, namely, minimum longitude, minimum latitude, maximum longitude and maximum latitude. The output values are building name, place id, coordinate system, geographic polygon and the Spatial Reference System Identifier (SRID). An invocation URL of the corresponding Web Service is shown in Figure 1a. It consists of service name, the required bounding box values and the needed geospatial data type. After uploading this URL, we can invoke corresponding Web Service by Karma. The generated ouputs with JSON format are illustrated in Figure 1b. The result worksheet contains both inputs and outputs for users as shown in Figure 1c.

5. GEOSPATIAL DATA MODELING

As the extracted geospatial data from different sources are heterogenous, namely, the formats and content of various sources are different from each other, and there is no semantic meaning in the extracted data, it is difficult for users to understand and use the data. Thus, in this section, we align the extracted data with a semantic way using Karma, which can map structured data to RDF according to the given

Figure 1. The process of building service model: (a) Service Invocation URL, (b) JSON response, (c) Web API inputs and outputs, (d) Geospatial modeling

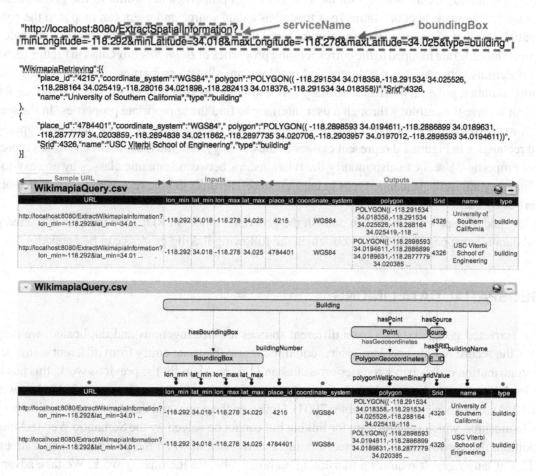

ontology. In this work, we build a generic geospatial ontology and take advantage of Karma to map and align the extracted geospatial data based on the generic geospatial ontology.

Figure 2 shows the structure of the generated generic geospatial ontology. The round rectangles represent classes, the solid arrows denote the object properties (the relationship between classes), the dashed arrows describe the data properties, and the rectangles represent the data property values. We can see that the Layer class includes RoadLayer and BuildingLayer subclasses. The subclasses and properties of RoadLayer class are used to model geospatial data of road type. Similarly, the building type of geospatial data is represented by the subclasses and properties of BuildingLayer class. The PointFeature class and PolygonFeature class are exploited to model the Building entity, while PolylineFeature class is used to describe the Road entity. SpatialReferenceSystem class is used to define a specific map projection for sources. The data properties such as polylineWellKnownBinary, polylineWellKnownText, polygonWellKnownBinary and polygonWellKnownText are specified geospatial data types used for describing Polyline and Polygon. In contrast, data properties like Latitude and Longitude are used to describe Point.

The approach of Karma to mapping data to ontology involves two steps: characterizing the type of data by assigning a semantic type to each column and identifying the relationships between the inferred semantic types in the ontology. For the first step, the data columns (obtained through the invocation URL given by Figure 1a) are all linked with the ranges of data properties according to the given ontology. For example, the worksheet of Figure 1c is treated as a data source and users can map it to the generic geospatial ontology. Service inputs (minimum longitude, minimum latitude, maximum longitude and maximum latitude) are mapped to the corresponding properties of *BoundingBox* Class in Figure 1d, while the connections between output columns and ontology are all data properties such as building_name, building_number, polygonWellKnownBinary and sridValue. Karma provides a visual interface where users can browse the ontology through a user interface to find the appropriate properties. In the second step, Karma uses paths of object properties to specify the relationships between semantic types. The round rectangles in Figure 1 d represent classes in the ontology, and the links between classes represent Object properties. Users can also modify the relationships between semantic classes by an easy-to-use GUI like they adjust the semantic types in the first step. The links in blue represent the modified object properties by user.

After modeling process, users can publish the generated model in RDF, and then the extracted geospatial data are mapped to RDF data, on which the following linking process can be applied.

6. GEOSPATIAL DATA LINKING

As the extracted geospatial data from different sources are heterogenous and duplicated, we need to address the record linking problem, which could recognise the same entity from different sources. The main contribution of this paper focuses on addressing this problem. In the previous work, this has been done by defining a set of semantic rules for performing the linking process (Janowicz,2012; Janowicz et al.,2010; Andrea Rodriguez & Egenhofer,2004). However, the geospatial data has some specific geospatial relationships, which is significant for linking but cannot be solved by the Semantic Web techniques. In addition, the previous work will meet a complicated problem when the geospatial data sources are in different languages. It requires a translating preprocess before the linking work. We take advantage of geospatial relationships to obtain the record linkages from various sources with different languages, which can avoid the translating cost of the previous work. In this section, we draw upon the research in the area of record linking with geospatial relationships.

6.1 Basic Notation

We consider a set of attributes $Y=\{y_1,y_2,..., y_k, G_1,G_2,G_3\}$ common to dataset A and B. The y_k-value of a record r is denoted by $r(y_k)$. G_1, G_2 and G_3 represent three attributes with geospatial data types supported by PostGis. $r(G_1)=$Point(*latitude, longitude*) denote the Point attribute with latitude and longitude values, $r(G_2)=$Polyline(P_1,P_2, ..., P_n) represent the Polyline attribute with a sequence of Points, and $r(G_3)=$Polygon(P_1,P_2, ..., P_n, P_1) represent the Polygon attribute with a close sequence of Points.

Compared with other data, there is something unique about geospatial data such as geospatial relationships, which are more important than semantic rules to recognise the same entity from different sources. In our presented approach, we take advantage of three geospatial functions ("contain", "overlap" and "distance") supported by PostGIS to do linking work. They are expressed as following:

Figure 2. The generic geospatial ontology

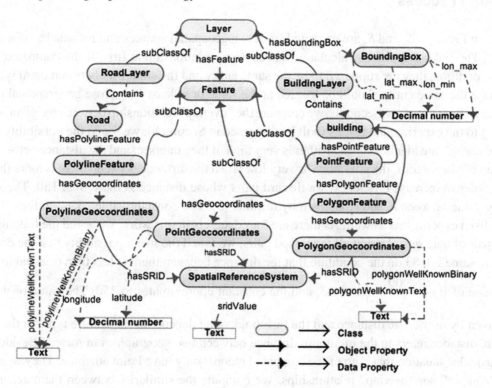

$$
isContained(r_1(G_i), r_2(G_j)) = \begin{cases} True, & \text{if and only if no points of } r_2(G_j) \\ & \text{lie in the exterior of } r_1(G_i), \text{ and} \\ & \text{at least one point of the interior} \\ & \text{of } r_2(G_j) \text{ lies in the interior of } r_1(G_i), \\ False, & \text{otherwise.} \end{cases} \tag{1}
$$

$$
isOverlap(r_1(G_i), r_2(G_j)) = \begin{cases} True, & \text{if } r_1(G_i) \text{ and } r_2(G_j) \text{ intersect,} \\ & \text{but one does not completely} \\ & \text{contain another,} \\ False, & \text{otherwise.} \end{cases} \tag{2}
$$

$$
distance(r_1(G_i), r_2(G_j)) = (float) \text{ value } \quad (i, j \in \{1, 2, 3\}) \tag{3}
$$

For geography type, *distance(r_1(G_i), r_2(G_j))* defaults to return the minimum distance between two geographics in meters.

6.2 Linking Process

As shown in Figure 3, S_1 and S_2 are extracted from two geospatial sources and modeled as discussed in Section 5. The linking approach calculates the "contain" relationship at first. If the compared records meet this condition, they are supposed to be the same entity and the similarity between them is equal to 1.0, because the same entity should be located at the same or at least very close geographical position even in the different sources. Secondly, we compare the "overlap" relationship between the given records. According to the experimental results (will be discussed in Section 8), we found the possibility that the compared records are identical to each other is very high, if they intersect and the distance between them is less than 60. In contrast, the possibility is very low when the distance between them is more than 150. Thus, in order to increase efficiency, we discard pairs whose distance is more than 150. The specific similarity value between r_1 and r_2 is given by formula (5). The constant value "350" in the formula is obtained from experiments as well. As there are four data sets in this work, we tested the linking results for each pair of data sets. Among all the linked pairs, we found the mean possibility that the compared records are same is 0.83 on the condition that the distance between them is less than or equal to 60. We set the value of $\left| 1 - \dfrac{60}{constant} \right|$ to 0.83, and the constant approximates to 350. The value of *threshold* can be given by users. The distance and the threshold value depend on the feature type. In the linking algorithm, distance refers to the minimum distance between two geographies in meters. Besides, there is one particular situation that both of the compared records only have Point attribute. They would have neither "contain" nor "overlap" relationships. We compute the similarity between them according to formula (5).

$$similarity(r_1, r_2) = \left| 1 - \frac{distance(r_1(G_i), r_2(G_j))}{350} \right| (i, j \in \{1, 2, 3\}) \tag{5}$$

6.3 Curating the Links

We create a Web interface depicted in Figure 4a to make it easy for users to review and curate the linking results. Each row represents a link. The first cell shows the geospatial type of records being linked. For instance, the type of the linked records is Building in the given example. The next columns show the record values that were used to create the link. The top part shows information about one geospatial source, while the bottom part shows a record in another source. The "Comment" column provides the foundation for the corresponding link. That is in accordance with the linking algorithms. For example, although two buildings from diverse sources have different names and coordinates, they are the same one if the geospatial relationship between them is "contain". They are exactly matched and the similarity between them is set to "1.0". Otherwise, if the geospatial relationship between them is "overlap", and the distance between them is short and the similarity value is less than the threshold, we will consider these two buildings are same. The last column gives a recommended result like "Match" on the condition that the similarity degree is higher than the threshold given by users. It also shows buttons to enable users to revise links and provide comments. Users can use this interface to curate all links.

Figure 3. The main idea of the Linking Algorithm

```
Input:    RDF file: S1, S2;
Output:  matchedPairList;
for all r1 in S1 and r2 in S2 do
    if(isContained(r1(Gi), r2(Gj))=true or
                        isContained(r2(Gi), r1(Gj))=true){
        similarity(r1, r2) ← 1.0;
        matchedPairList.add(r1, r2);
    }else if(isOverlap(r1(Gi), r2(Gj))=true and
                        distance(r1(Gi), r2(Gj))<150){
```

$$similarity(r_1, r_2) \leftarrow \left| 1 - \frac{distance(r_1(G_i), r_2(G_j))}{350} \right|$$

```
        if(similarity(r1, r2)>threshold){
            matchedPairList.add(r1, r2);
        }
    }else if(Ur1(G1)=1 and Ur2(G1)=1 and
                        distance(r1(G1), r2(G1))<150){
```

$$similarity(r_1, r_2) \leftarrow \left| 1 - \frac{distance(r_1(G_1), r_2(G_1))}{350} \right|$$

```
        if(similarity(r1, r2)>threshold){
            matchedPairList.add(r1, r2);
        }
    }
}
```

In addition to supporting the user interface for human verification of links, the linking process affords other benefits. We use SPARQL statements to construct a dataset of owl:sameAs triples containing all links with a matching score above the given threshold value and those links that have been verified by a user. The generated triples are illustrated in Figure 4b. Due to space limitations, we removed namespaces. These triples will be stored in the repository and used for integration across sources in the following section.

7. GEOSPATIAL DATA INTEGRATION

Since the retrieved geospatial data varies from source to source, some of them are duplicated, while others are complementary to each other. Our goal in data integration is to provide users an easy way to get complete and integrated geospatial data by eliminating the data redundancy and combining the complementary properties from the linked data. However, it is very difficult when the geospatial data sources are in different languages. It requires integrating process to have extra translating function. Fortunately, the linking process takes advantage of to obtain the record linkages, which avoids the translating process of the conventional methods. That is to say, we use the geospatial relationships to link the same entity, with the result that the geospatial data integration was endowed with translation function.

7.1 The Integrating Process

Based on the linking results, i.e., the generated owl:sameAs triple store, we utilise SPARQL to do the union work. As shown in Figure 5, we select each pair of the linked records according to the owl:sameAs property, and then combine all the attributes of them. For example, Entity_A has six attributes such as name, state, county, city, latitude and longitude, while Entity_B has just two attributes like name and polygon. Cause they are the same entity (linked by owl:sameAs), we will combine all the attributes for this entity by SPARQL statements. The details are expressed as following:

(1) *Statement 1:* Extract the linked subjects from different sources;
Select distinct **?subject1, ?subject2**
Where{
?subject1 owl:sameAs ?subject2.
?subject1 a GeoOnt:Building
}
(2) *Statement 2:* Retrieve attributes from one source;
Select ?subject1, ?name, ?state, ?county, ?city, ?longitude,
?latitude
Where{
?subject1 GeoOnt:hasName ?name.
?subject1 GeoOnt:hasPoint ?p.
?p GeoOnt:hasGeocoordinates ?g.
?g GeoOnt:xInDecimalLongitude ?longitude.
?g GeoOnt:yInDecimalLatitude ?latitude.
?subject1 GeoOnt:hasAddress ?a.

Figure 4. The Interface enables users: (a) to review the linking results (b) to generate the Owl:sameAs triples

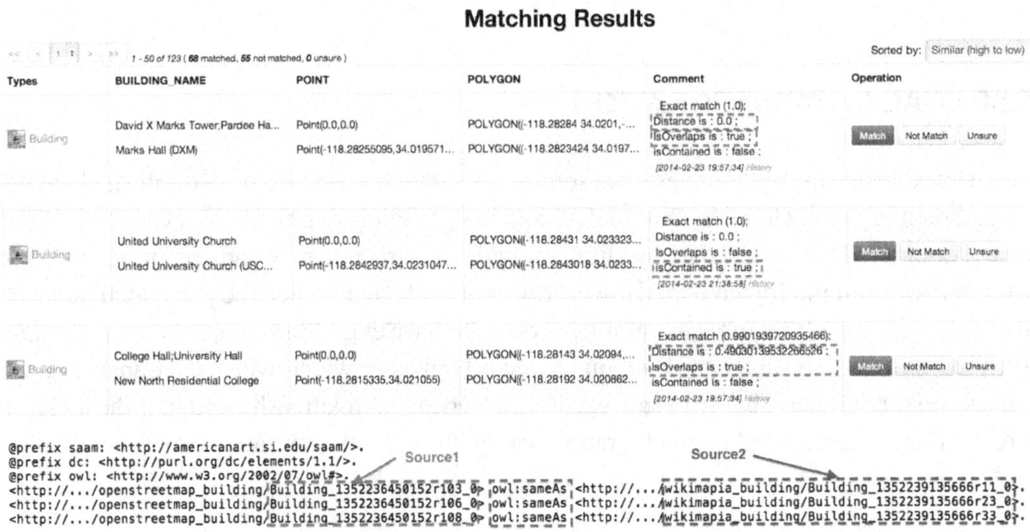

?a GeoOnt:hasState ?state.
?a GeoOnt:hasCounty ?county.
?a GeoOnt:hasCity ?city.
}

(3) *Statement 3:* Retrieve attributes from the linked sources with subjet1;

Select ?subject2,?name,?polygon
Where{
?subject2 GeoOnt:hasName ?name.
?subject2 GeoOnt:hasPolygon ?pg.
?pg GeoOnt:hasGeocoordinates ?g.
?g GeoOnt:polygonWellKnownText ?polygon
}

7.2 Display Integration Results With Translation Function

Figure 5 provides users a unified view of the integrated results. Each row denotes a matched pair of entities. Some columns have two parts: the top part shows the attribute values coming from one source and the bottom part shows the values coming from the linked sources. The other columns have only one part that means the linked sources share the same values of the given attributes.

Figure 5. The union work

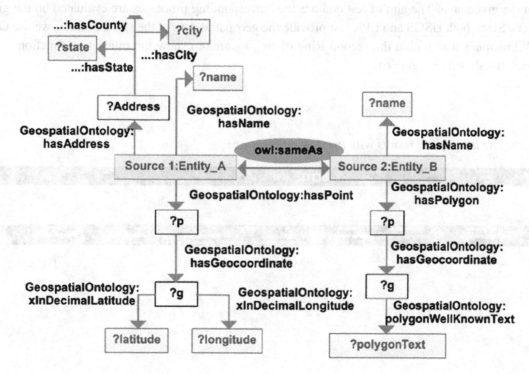

As shown in Figure 6, it's easy to see that the integration process is endowed with the translation function. For instance, the data in one source is in Chinese, while the data in the linked source is in English. We can see that both Chinese and English information are combined together after integration work. The integration process saves the translating cost among all the geospatial sources with different languages because we take advantage of geospatial relationships to get the linking records instead of using string matching.

8. TESTING AND VALIDATION

In order to study the actual performance of the presented approaches, we evaluate them on four real-world data sets. All experiments were conducted on a computer with a 2.3 GHz Intel Core i7 processor and 16 Gigabytes of main memory. For all tables and databases within the experiments, PostgreSQL(Obe & Hsu,2014) with the PostGIS(Obe & Hsu,2015) extension is used.

Figure 7 shows the component model of the whole system. In this section, we evaluate the main contribution of this paper, namely, the linking and the integrating processes.

8.1 Test Data Sets

In our experiment, we mainly adopt four kinds of geospatial data sources, namely, OpenStreetMap(OSM), Wikmapia, USGS and EPA.

Table 1 illustrates the data sets used in our experiments. Each data set uses a bounding box to describe the geographic area. In our experiments, we take geospatial data type "building" as an example to explicate the presented approaches. So, the number of records denotes the quantity of buildings within the given area. The aim of test denotes the corresponding processes are evaluated on the given data sets. Since both USGS and EPA just provide the geospatial data of the United States, we use OSM and Wikimapia's data within the second Ring of Beijing area to show the translation function of our approach (as shown in Figure 6).

Figure 6. The integration results with translation function

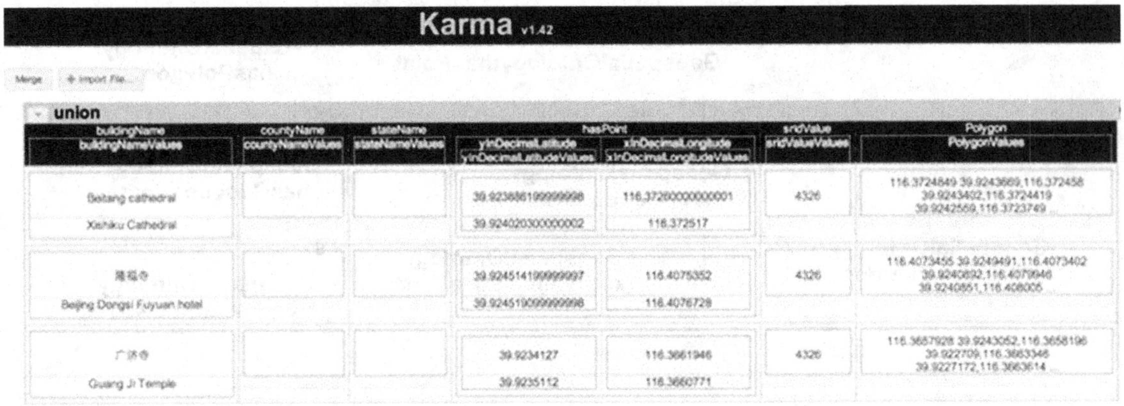

Figure 7. The component model of the experimental system

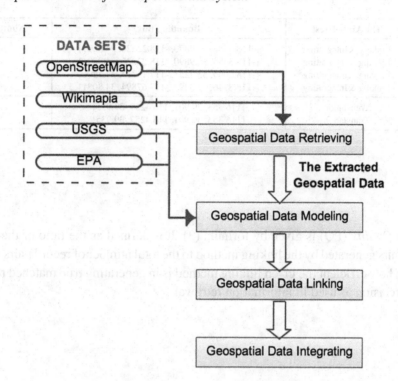

8.2 Geospatial Data Linking Evaluation

Four measures are used to assess the complexity of the linking step and the quality of the resulting candidate record pairs (Christen & Goiser,2007; Elfeky et al.,2002; Christen,2012). The following notation will be used in this evaluation: $n_A=|A|$ and $n_B=|B|$ are the number of records in databases A and B, respectively. The total number of true matched and true nonmatched record pairs in the ground truth are denoted with n_M and n_N, separately. The number of true matched and true nonmatched record pairs generated by the linking process is denoted with s_M and s_N, respectively, with $s_M+s_N \leq n_M+n_N$. In addition, r_M denotes the number of matched record pairs generated by the linking process.

We take the following formula as the *Reduction Ratio* (RR) to measure the reduction of the comparison space, i.e., the fraction of record pairs that are removed by the linking approach.

$$RR = 1.0 - \frac{s_M + s_N}{n_M + n_N} \tag{1}$$

The higher the RR value, the less candidate record pairs are being generated.

Pairs Completeness (PC) is the number of true matched record pairs produced by the linking technique divided by the total number of true matched pairs as explicated in formula (2). PC corresponds to recall as utilised in information retrieval [41].

Table 1. Data sets used in experiments

Data Set Name	The Aim of Test	Bounding Box	Number of Records
OSM	Linking &Integrating	[-118.3385, 33.9890, -118.22326, 34.0891]	1821
Wikimapia	Linking &Integrating	[-118.3385, 33.9890, -118.22326, 34.0891]	2718
EPA's Data	Linking &Integrating	[-118.6009, 33.7251, -117.75214, 34.4206]	5218
USGS	Linking &Integrating	[-118.8946, 33.3392, -117.67894, 34.8081]	1998
OSM	Translation	[116.353, 39.901, 116.4257, 39.935]	1228
Wikimapia	Translation	[116.353, 39.901, 116.4257, 39.935]	484

$$PC = \frac{s_M}{n_M} \qquad (2)$$

Thirdly, *Pairs Quality* (PQ) is given by formula (3). It is defined as the ratio of the number of true matched record pairs generated by the linking method to the total number of record pairs generated. Pairs Quality measures how efficient the given linking method is in generating true matched record pairs, and corresponds to precision as used in information retrieval.

$$PQ = \frac{s_M}{r_M} \qquad (3)$$

Finally, we evaluate the harmonic mean of PC and PQ, i.e., *F-score* (Andrea Rodriguez & Egenhofer,2004; Muslea et al.,2003). It is calculated by formula (4). F-score will have a high value only when both PC and PQ have high values, and can be seen as a way to find the best compromise between PC and PQ.

$$\text{F-score} = 2\left(\frac{PC \times PQ}{PC + PQ}\right) \qquad (4)$$

As shown in Table 1, there are four data sets in total in our experiments. We evaluate the linking results for each pair of data sets, so the total number of linking tests equals to $C_4^2 = 6$. We take "Building" type as an example to do linking work. In the test, we examined the quality of linking approach in the situation of varying Maximum Distance Values (MDV), such as 20,40,60 and 80, between building entities from each pair of linked data sets. It means we will consider that the compared entities are not same when the distance between them is more than MDV. Correspondingly, the threshold values of similarity are set to 0.943, 0.886, 0.830 and 0.771 according to formula (5). We evaluate the quality of each pair of the linked data sets four times with four different similarity threshold values.

According to Figure 8, we can see that in all of the six linking tests, the lower threshold value of similarity, i.e., the larger MDV, gets the lower *Reduction Ratio*. As the threshold value of similarity decreases, i.e., the MDV increases, the *Pairs Completeness* value increases, while the *Pairs Quality* value goes down. According to Figure 8a, the larger number of the compared records can get the better effect of the reduction. In contrast, as the number of the compared records grows, the PC values become scattered along with the varying maximum distance values from Figure 8b. From Figure 8c, we can

Figure 8. The experimental results

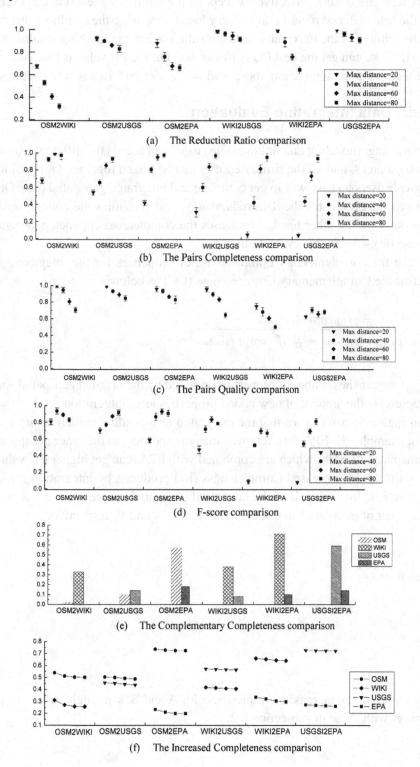

(a)　The Reduction Ratio comparison

(b)　The Pairs Completeness comparison

(c)　The Pairs Quality comparison

(d)　F-score comparison

(e)　The Complementary Completeness comparison

(f)　The Increased Completeness comparison

see that our linking method works effectively except on the last linking test (i.e. USGS2EPA), of which the number of the true matched record pairs is very low. Comparing the results of the six tests, we can conclude that the settings of the maximum distance values affect the lingking results. When we set the small value to MDV, we can get the best PQ performance, but the PC value is low. According to Figure 8d, F-score values are not monotonic any more, and MDV=60 performs best in most tests.

8.3 Geospatial Data Integrating Evaluation

Based on the extracting, modeling and linking steps, users can access the different extracted geospatial data from various sources, and all the similar entities can be linked together. Our goal in the data integration is to provide users an easy way to get complete and integrated geospatial data. On the one hand, the integration process eliminates the data redundancy, and combines the complementary properties from the linked data. On the other hand, it increases the completeness of each geospatial data source. We estimate these two sides in this evaluation.

In order to test the complementary completeness of properties for the integrated geospatial data sources, we define the Complementary Completeness (CC) as below:

$$CC = 1 - \frac{\# \, of \, properties_{source}}{\# \, of \, properties_{source} + \# \, of \, properties_{new}} \tag{5}$$

$\# of\, properties_{source}$ means the number of properties provided by the original geospatial source, while $\# of\, properties_{new}$ represents the amount of new added properties after integration.

As shown in Figure 8e, we can see that the integrated results add complementary completeness for each source. For example, the EPA data set owns many properties, so the other geospatial sources such as OSM, Wikimapia and USGS, which are combined with EPA, can get higher CC values.

In order to estimate the Increased Completeness (IC) produced by integration for each geospatial source. We calculate IC for each pair of the integrated geospatial sources by the following definitions. We suppose each pair of geospatial sources are denoted by A and B, respectively.

$$IC_A = 1 - \frac{n_A}{n_A + n_B - s_M} \tag{6}$$

$$IC_B = 1 - \frac{n_B}{n_A + n_B - s_M} \tag{7}$$

IC_A and IC_B represent the increased completeness for A and B, separately, while n_A, n_B and s_M share the same meanings with those in subsection 8.2.

Figure 8f illustrates the Increased Completeness for each pair of integrated sources. The number of records in EPA's data set is the largest among four testing data sets, thus the increased completeness values of geospatial sources integrated with EPA get high. In addition, as the MDV increases, the s_M value grows slowly, so there is a slow decline in Increased Completeness of each testing group.

Finally, GIS researchers have worked on different approaches and ontologies to integrate geospatial sources. Yue et al. (2007, 2011) present a method to add semantics into current geospatial catalogue services for geospatial data discovery and processing. They created three types of ontologies to define data and service semantics that enable dynamic and automatic composition of geospatial Web service chains to achieve a complex geospatial goal. Zhou (2008) designed a prototype to provide a demonstration of using recent advancement in GIScience and other fields to achieve semantic-based GIS applications over cyberinfrastructure. The prototype develops a work flow linking multiple ontologies to achieve semantic-based geospatial analysis. It also employs several semantic integration algorithms for the work of semantic integration. Past efforts to enable sharing have produced standardised data format such as GML and data access protocols like Web Feature Service (WFS) . These standards help enabling users to have access to heterogeneous data stored in different formats from diverse sources, but the usability of the access is limited to the lack of data semantics. Zhao (2008) presents a method to enable ontology query on spatial data available from WFS services and on data stored in databases directly. Users do not need to create ontology instances explicitly and thus avoid the problems of data replication. Instead, users queries are rewritten to WFS getFeature requests and SQL queries to databases. Since some of the key challenges in supporting large-scale geospatial data integration are computing the quality of the data and providing high quality answers to the user queries based on a quality criteria given by the users (Thakkar et al. 2007), Snehal Thakklar described a framework called the Quality-driven Geospatial Mdeiator (QGM) to support quality-driven large-scale geospatial data integration. All researches above take advantage of semantic techniques, however, none of them consider the useful spatial characteristics of geospatial data. In contrast, our approach makes use of both semantic techniques and the spatial relationships, which are significant in the respect of geospatial data, to do linking and integrating work.

9. CONCLUSION AND FUTURE WORK

Four problems are related to geospatial data integration: data extracting, source modeling, record linking and data integrating. This paper gave an overview of data integration. The main contribution of this work focused on the recording linking. We make the best of the unique characteristics of geospatial data such as geospatial relationships, which are significant for linking. In addition to the basic functions, the geospatial relationships endow the geospatial data linking with translation function, which can save the translating cost among all the geospatial sources with different languages. In the experiment, we measured the quality of the presented linking algorithms in terms of RR, PC, PQ and F-score. Besides, we assessed the final integrating results using complementary completeness (CC) and the increased completeness (IC). The results denote that each source gets much Complementary Completeness and Increased Completeness in the integration.

As future work, we plan to implement a more general framework to enable users to extract geospatial data automatically and improve the efficiency of retrieving process. Moreover, we plan to investigate the estimation of the data quality provided by sources and extract the geospatial data with the required quality. For the problem of linking entities across sources, in addition to using spatial characteristics, we are working to use other common attributes, such as the entity name, to optimize the geospatial data linking process and to improve the integration results. Besides, our approach has been designed to transfer common attribute values of all the remote records to the local site for integration. The communication overhead will be significantly large when the geospatial sources have huge amounts of records. Next, we will extend our work to implement record linkage and integration in an online, distributed environment. Finally, we will extend the Web application for final users to approve links by providing a visual interface where users can browse the matched pair of records on the maps.

ACKNOWLEDGMENT

This work was jointly supported by the National Natural Science Foundation of China (No.61305056, No.61300132, No. 61403137), Beijing Higher Education Young Elite Teacher Project (No.YETP0702, No.YETP0706), Overseas Expertise Introduction Program for Disciplines Innovation in Universities(Project 111) (No. B13009), and the Fundamental Research Funds for the Central Universities (No.2015MS35, No. 2015MS28).

REFERENCES

Andrea Rodriguez, M., & Egenhofer, M. J. (2004). Comparing geospatial entity classes: An asymmetric and context-dependent similarity measure. *International Journal of Geographical Information Science*, *18*(3), 229–256. doi:10.1080/13658810310001629592

Arpinar, I., Sheth, A., & Ramakrishnan, C. (2006). Geospatial Ontology Development and Semantic Analytics. *Transactions in GIS*, *10*(4), 551–575. doi:10.1111/j.1467-9671.2006.01012.x

Auer, S., Lehmann, J., & Hellmann, S. (2009). *Linkedgeodata: Adding a spatial dimension to the web of data*. Springer Berlin Heidelberg.

Baeza-Yates, R., & Ribeiro-Neto, B. (1999). *Modern information retrieval* (Vol. 463). New York: ACM press.

Bai, H., Ge, Y., Wang, J., Li, D., Liao, Y., & Zheng, X. (2014). A method for extracting rules from spatial data based on rough fuzzy sets. *Knowledge-Based Systems*, *57*, 28–40. doi:10.1016/j.knosys.2013.12.008

Ballatore, A., Bertolotto, M., & Wilson, D. C. (2013). Geographic knowledge extraction and semantic similarity in OpenStreetMap. *Knowledge and Information Systems*, *37*(1), 61–81. doi:10.1007/s10115-012-0571-0

Ballatore, A., Bertolotto, M., & Wilson, D. C. (2014). Linking geographic vocabularies through WordNet. *Annals of GIS*, *20*(2), 73–84. doi:10.1080/19475683.2014.904440

Baxter, R., Christen, P., & Churches, T. (2003, August). A comparison of fast blocking methods for record linkage. *ACM SIGKDD*, 3, 25-27.

Berners-Lee, T., Hendler, J., & Lassila, O. (2001). The semantic web. *Scientific American*, 284(5), 28–37. doi:10.1038/scientificamerican0501-34 PMID:11341160

Bittner, T., Donnelly, M., & Smith, B. (2009). A spatio-temporal ontology for geographic information integration. *International Journal of Geographical Information Science*, 23(6), 765–798. doi:10.1080/13658810701776767

Brodt, A., Nicklas, D., & Mitschang, B. (2010, November). Deep integration of spatial query processing into native RDF triple stores. In *Proceedings of the 18th SIGSPATIAL International Conference on Advances in Geographic Information Systems* (pp. 33-42). ACM. doi:10.1145/1869790.1869799

Buccella, A., Cechich, A., Gendarmi, D., Lanubile, F., Semeraro, G., & Colagrossi, A. (2010). GeoMergeP: Geographic information integration through enriched ontology matching. *New Generation Computing*, 28(1), 41–71. doi:10.1007/s00354-008-0074-4

Christen, P. (2012). A survey of indexing techniques for scalable record linkage and deduplication. *Knowledge and Data Engineering. IEEE Transactions on*, 24(9), 1537–1555.

Christen, P., & Goiser, K. (2007). Quality and complexity measures for data linkage and deduplication. In *Quality Measures in Data Mining* (pp. 127–151). Springer Berlin Heidelberg. doi:10.1007/978-3-540-44918-8_6

Cohen, W. W., Hurst, M., & Jensen, L. S. (2002, May). A flexible learning system for wrapping tables and lists in HTML documents. In *Proceedings of the 11th international conference on World Wide Web* (pp. 232-241). ACM. doi:10.1145/511446.511477

Crescenzi, V., & Mecca, G. (2004). Automatic information extraction from large websites. *Journal of the ACM*, 51(5), 731–779. doi:10.1145/1017460.1017462

De Carvalho, M. G., Laender, A. H., Gonçalves, M. A., & Da Silva, A. S. (2012). A genetic programming approach to record deduplication. *Knowledge and Data Engineering. IEEE Transactions on*, 24(3), 399–412.

Dey, D., Mookerjee, V. S., & Liu, D. (2011). Efficient techniques for online record linkage. *Knowledge and Data Engineering. IEEE Transactions on*, 23(3), 373–387.

Di, L., Zhao, P., Yang, W., & Yue, P. (2006, June). Ontology-driven automatic geospatial-processing modeling based on web-service chaining. *Proceedings of the sixth annual NASA earth science technology conference*, 27-29.

Elfeky, M. G., Verykios, V. S., & Elmagarmid, A. K. (2002). TAILOR: A record linkage toolbox. In *Data Engineering, 2002. Proceedings. 18th International Conference on* (pp. 17-28). IEEE. doi:10.1109/ICDE.2002.994694

Fellegi, I. P., & Sunter, A. B. (1969). A theory for record linkage. *Journal of the American Statistical Association*, 64(328), 1183–1210. doi:10.1080/01621459.1969.10501049

Fonseca, F. T., Egenhofer, M. J., Agouris, P., & Câmara, G. (2002). Using ontologies for integrated geographic information systems. *Transactions in GIS, 6*(3), 231–257. doi:10.1111/1467-9671.00109

Fugazza, C. (2011). Toward semantics-aware annotation and retrieval of spatial data. *Earth Science Informatics, 4*(4), 225–239. doi:10.1007/s12145-011-0088-1

Gatterbauer, W., Bohunsky, P., Herzog, M., Krüpl, B., & Pollak, B. (2007, May). Towards domain-independent information extraction from web tables. In *Proceedings of the 16th international conference on World Wide Web* (pp. 71-80). ACM. doi:10.1145/1242572.1242583

Hastings, J. T. (2008). Automated conflation of digital gazetteer data. *International Journal of Geographical Information Science, 22*(10), 1109–1127. doi:10.1080/13658810701851453

Huynh, D., & Mazzocchi, S. (2011). *Google refine*. Academic Press.

Janowicz, K., Raubal, M., & Kuhn, W. (2011). The semantics of similarity in geographic information retrieval. *Journal of Spatial Information Science, 2011*(2), 29-57.

Janowicz, K., Schade, S., Bröring, A., Keßler, C., Maué, P., & Stasch, C. (2010). Semantic enablement for spatial data infrastructures. *Transactions in GIS, 14*(2), 111–129. doi:10.1111/j.1467-9671.2010.01186.x

Janowicz, K., Scheider, S., Pehle, T., & Hart, G. (2012). Geospatial semantics and linked spatiotemporal data–Past, present, and future. *Semantic Web, 3*(4), 321–332.

Knoblock, C. A., Szekely, P., Ambite, J. L., Goel, A., Gupta, S., Lerman, K., . . . Mallick, P. (2012). Semi-automatically mapping structured sources into the semantic web. In The Semantic Web: Research and Applications (pp. 375-390). Springer Berlin Heidelberg. doi:10.1007/978-3-642-30284-8_32

Knoblock, C. A., Szekely, P., Ambite, J. L., Goel, A., Gupta, S., Lerman, K., . . . Mallick, P. (2012). Semi-automatically mapping structured sources into the semantic web. In The Semantic Web: Research and Applications (pp. 375-390). Springer Berlin Heidelberg. doi:10.1007/978-3-642-30284-8_32

Knoblock, C. A., Szekely, P. A., Ambite, J. L., Gupta, S., Goel, A., Muslea, M., ... & Mallick, P. (2011). Interactively Mapping Data Sources into the Semantic Web. *LISC, 783*.

Kuhn, W. (2002). Modeling the semantics of geographic categories through conceptual integration. In *Geographic Information Science* (pp. 108–118). Springer Berlin Heidelberg. doi:10.1007/3-540-45799-2_8

Lenzerini, M. (2002, June). Data integration: A theoretical perspective. In *Proceedings of the twenty-first ACM SIGMOD-SIGACT-SIGART symposium on Principles of database systems* (pp. 233-246). ACM. doi:10.1145/543613.543644

Li, B., & Fonseca, F. (2006). TDD: A comprehensive model for qualitative spatial similarity assessment. *Spatial Cognition and Computation, 6*(1), 31–62. doi:10.1207/s15427633scc0601_2

Lima, D., Mendonça, A., Salgado, A. C., & Souza, D. (2011). Building Geospatial Ontologies From Geographic Database Schemas. In *Peer Data Management Systems* (pp. 1–12). GeoInfo.

Malik, Z., Rezgui, A., Medjahed, B., Ouzzani, M., & Krishna Sinha, A. (2010). Semantic integration in geosciences. *International Journal of Semantic Computing, 4*(03), 301–330. doi:10.1142/S1793351X10001036

Muslea, I., Minton, S., & Knoblock, C. A. (2003, August). *Active learning with strong and weak views: a case study on wrapper induction* (Vol. 3). IJCAI.

Obe, R. O., & Hsu, L. S. (2014). *PostgreSQL: Up and Running: A Practical Introduction to the Advanced Open Source Database*. O'Reilly Media, Inc.

Obe, R. O., & Hsu, L. S. (2015). *PostGIS in action*. Manning Publications Co.

Oussalah, M., Bhat, F., Challis, K., & Schnier, T. (2013). A software architecture for Twitter collection, search and geolocation services. *Knowledge-Based Systems*, *37*, 105–120. doi:10.1016/j.knosys.2012.07.017

Peng, Z. (2005). A proposed framework for featurelevel geospatial data sharing: A case study for transportation network data. *International Journal of Geographical Information Science*, *19*(4), 459–481. doi:10.1080/13658810512331319127

Shyu, C. R., Klaric, M., Scott, G. J., Barb, A. S., Davis, C. H., & Palaniappan, K. (2007). GeoIRIS: Geospatial information retrieval and indexing system—Content mining, semantics modeling, and complex queries. *Geoscience and Remote Sensing. IEEE Transactions on*, *45*(4), 839–852.

Su, W., Wang, J., Lochovsky, F., & Liu, Y. (2012). Combining Tag and Value Similarity for Data Extraction and Alignment. *IEEE Transactions on Knowledge and Data Engineering*, *24*(7), 1186–1200. doi:10.1109/TKDE.2011.66

Su, W., Wang, J., & Lochovsky, F. H. (2010). Record matching over query results from multiple web databases. *Knowledge and Data Engineering. IEEE Transactions on*, *22*(4), 578–589.

Szekely, P., Knoblock, C. A., Gupta, S., Taheriyan, M., & Wu, B. (2011, November). Exploiting semantics of web services for geospatial data fusion. In *Proceedings of the 1st ACM SIGSPATIAL International Workshop on Spatial Semantics and Ontologies* (pp. 32-39). ACM. doi:10.1145/2068976.2068981

Taheriyan, M., Knoblock, C. A., Szekely, P., & Ambite, J. L. (2012, May). Semi-automatically modeling web apis to create linked apis. *Proceedings of the ESWC 2012 Workshop on Linked APIs*.

Taheriyan, M., Knoblock, C. A., Szekely, P., & Ambite, J. L. (2012). Rapidly integrating services into the linked data cloud. In *The Semantic Web–ISWC 2012* (pp. 559–574). Springer Berlin Heidelberg. doi:10.1007/978-3-642-35176-1_35

Thakkar, S., Knoblock, C. A., & Ambite, J. L. (2007, November). Quality-driven geospatial data integration. In *Proceedings of the 15th annual ACM international symposium on Advances in geographic information systems* (p. 16). ACM.

Tuchinda, R., Knoblock, C. A., & Szekely, P. (2011). Building mashups by demonstration. *ACM Transactions on the Web*, *5*(3), 16. doi:10.1145/1993053.1993058

Vaccari, L., Shvaiko, P., & Marchese, M. (2009). A geo-service semantic integration in spatial data infrastructures. *International Journal of Spatial Data Infrastructures Research*, *4*, 24–51.

Volz, J., Bizer, C., Gaedke, M., & Kobilarov, G. (2009). Silk-A Link Discovery Framework for the Web of Data. *LDOW, 538*.

Wiegand, N., & García, C. (2007). A Task-Based Ontology Approach to Automate Geospatial Data Retrieval. *Transactions in GIS, 11*(3), 355–376. doi:10.1111/j.1467-9671.2007.01050.x

Winkler, W. E. (2006). *Overview of record linkage and current research directions*. Bureau of the Census.

Witten, I. H., Moffat, A., & Bell, T. C. (1999). *Managing gigabytes: compressing and indexing documents and images*. Morgan Kaufmann.

Yue, P., Di, L., Yang, W., Yu, G., & Zhao, P. (2007). Semantics-based automatic composition of geospatial Web service chains. *Computers & Geosciences, 33*(5), 649–665. doi:10.1016/j.cageo.2006.09.003

Yue, P., Gong, J., Di, L., He, L., & Wei, Y. (2011). Integrating semantic web technologies and geospatial catalog services for geospatial information discovery and processing in cyberinfrastructure. *GeoInformatica, 15*(2), 273–303. doi:10.1007/s10707-009-0096-1

Zhao, T., Zhang, C., Wei, M., & Peng, Z. R. (2008). Ontology-based geospatial data query and integration. In *Geographic Information Science* (pp. 370–392). Springer Berlin Heidelberg. doi:10.1007/978-3-540-87473-7_24

Zhou, N. (2008). Geospatial Semantic Integration. In Encyclopedia of GIS (pp. 386-388). Springer US. doi:10.1007/978-0-387-35973-1_511

Compilation of References

Abedjan, Z., Grütze, T., Jentzsch, A., & Naumann, F. (2014). Profiling and mining {RDF} data with {ProLOD++}. *International Conference on Data Engineering ({ICDE})*, 1198–1201. doi:10.1109/ICDE.2014.6816740

Abilhoa, W. D., & Castro, L. N. (2014). A keyword extraction method from twitter messages represented as graphs. *Applied Mathematics and Computation, 240*, 308–325. doi:10.1016/j.amc.2014.04.090

Acosta, M., Vidal, M.-E., Lampo, T., Castillo, J., & Ruckhaus, E. (2011). {ANAPSID}: An Adaptive Query Processing Engine for {SPARQL} Endpoints. In *International Semantic Web Conference (ISWC)* (pp. 18–34). Springer. http://doi.org/ doi:10.1007/978-3-642-25073-6_2

Agarwal, P., Vaithiyanathan, R., Sharma, S., & Shroff, G. (2012). Catching the Long-Tail: Extracting Local News Events from Twitter. ICWSM.

Aghdam, M. H., Ghasem-Aghaee, N., & Basiri, M. E. (2009). Text feature selection using ant colony optimization. *Expert Systems with Applications, 36*(3), 6843–6853. doi:10.1016/j.eswa.2008.08.022

Agichtein, E., & Gravano, L. (2000). Snowball: Extracting relations from large plain-text collections. *Proceedings of the fifth ACM Conference on Digital Libraries (DL'00)*, 85-94. 10.1145/336597.336644

Agrawal, R., & Srikant, R. (1994). Fast algorithms for mining association rules in large databases. *Proceedings of 20th International Conference on Very Large Data Bases*, 487-499.

Agrawal, R., Imielinski, T., & Swami, A. (1993). Mining Association rules between sets of items in large databases. SIGMOD93, 207-216. doi:10.1145/170035.170072

Agrawal, R., & Srikant, R. (1994). Fast algorithms for mining association rules in large databases. *Proceedings of the 20th International Conference on Very Large Data Bases (VLDB'94)*, 487-499.

Aguado de Cea, G., Gómez-Pérez, A., Montiel-Ponsoda, E., & Suárez-Figueroa, M. C. (2008). Natural language-based approach for helping in the reuse of ontology design patterns. In Knowledge Engineering: Practice and Patterns (pp. 32-47). Springer Berlin Heidelberg. doi:10.1007/978-3-540-87696-0_6

Ahel, R., Dalbelo-Bašić, B., & Šnajder, J. (2009). Automatic keyphrase extraction from Croatian newspaper articles. In *2nd International Conference The Future of Information Sciences, Digital Resources and Knowledge Sharing (INFuture 2009)* (pp. 207-218). Zagreb, Croatia: Faculty of Humanities and Social Sciences.

Akar, Z., Halaç, T. G., Ekinci, E. E., & Dikenelli, O. (2012). Querying the Web of Interlinked Datasets using VOID Descriptions. In Linked Data On the Web (LDOW). CEUR.

Albuquerque, F. C., Casanova, M. A., Lopes, H., Redlich, L. R., de Macedo, J. A. F., Lemos, M., & Renso, C. et al. (2015). A methodology for traffic-related Twitter messages interpretation. *Computers in Industry*.

Alexander, K., Cyganiak, R., Hausenblas, M., & Zhao, J. (2009). Describing Linked Datasets. In Linked Data On the Web (LDOW). CEUR.

Allemang, D., & Hendler, J. (2011). *Semantic web for the working ontologist: effective modeling in RDFS and OWL.* Elsevier.

Anderson, J. R. (1983). A spreading activation theory of memory. *Journal of Verbal Learning and Verbal Behavior*, *22*(3), 261–295. doi:10.1016/S0022-5371(83)90201-3

Andrea Rodriguez, M., & Egenhofer, M. J. (2004). Comparing geospatial entity classes: An asymmetric and context-dependent similarity measure. *International Journal of Geographical Information Science*, *18*(3), 229–256. doi:10.10 80/13658810310001629592

Archer, P., Goedertier, S., & Loutas, N. (2012). *D7. 1.3–Study on persistent URIs, with identification of best practices and recommendations on the topic for the MSs and the EC.* PwC EU Services.

Armas-Romero, A., Cuenca-Grau, B., Horrocks, I., & Jiménez-Ruiz, E. (2013). MORe: a Modular OWL Reasoner for Ontology Classification. *Proceedings of the 2nd International Workshop on OWL Reasoner Evaluation (ORE)*, 61-67.

Arnold, P., & Rahm, E. (2014). Enriching ontology mappings with semantic relations. *Data & Knowledge Engineering*, *93*, 1–18. doi:10.1016/j.datak.2014.07.001

Arpinar, I., Sheth, A., & Ramakrishnan, C. (2006). Geospatial Ontology Development and Semantic Analytics. *Transactions in GIS*, *10*(4), 551–575. doi:10.1111/j.1467-9671.2006.01012.x

Astrakhantsev, N., Turdakov, D. Y., & Fedorenko, D. G. (2014). *Automatic Enrichment of Informal Ontology by Analyzing a Domain-Specific Text Collection.* Paper presented at the Computational Linguistics and Intellectual Technologies: Papers from the Annual International Conference "Dialogue".

Atefeh, F., & Khreich, W. (2015). A survey of techniques for event detection in twitter. *Computational Intelligence*, *31*(1), 132–164. doi:10.1111/coin.12017

Athira, P. M., Sreeja, M., & Reghuraj, P. (2013). Architecture of an Ontology-Based Domain-Specific Natural Language Question Answering System. *International Journal of Web & Semantic Technology*, *4*. doi:10.5121/ijwest.2013.4403

Auer, S., Demter, J., Martin, M., & Lehmann, J. (2012). {LODStats} -- An Extensible Framework for High-Performance Dataset Analytics. In Knowledge Engineering and Knowledge Management ({EKAW}) (pp. 353–362). Springer.

Auer, S., Bizer, C., Kobilarov, G., Lehmann, J., Cyganiak, R., & Ives, Z. (2007). Dbpedia: A nucleus for a web of open data. *The Semantic Web*, *4825*, 722–735. doi:10.1007/978-3-540-76298-0_52

Auer, S., Jan, D., Martin, M., & Lehmann, J. (2012). *LODStats - an Extensible Framework for High-Performance Dataset Analytics.* Berlin: Springer. doi:10.1007/978-3-642-33876-2_31

Auer, S., Lehmann, J., & Hellmann, S. (2009). *Linkedgeodata: Adding a spatial dimension to the web of data.* Springer Berlin Heidelberg.

Avancha, S., Joshi, A., & Finin, T. (2002). Enhanced Service Discovery in Bluetooth. *IEEE Computer*, *35*(6), 96–99. doi:10.1109/MC.2002.1009177

Baader, F., Lutz, C., & Suntisrivaraporn, B. (2006). CEL – a polynomial-time reasoner for life science ontologies. *Automated Reasoning*, 287–291.

Baader, F., Brandt, S., & Lutz, C. (2005). Pushing the EL envelope. *Proceedings of 19th International Joint Conference on Artificial Intelligence*, 364–399.

Baader, F., Calvanese, D., McGuinness, D., Nardi, D., & Patel-Schneider, P. (2002). *The Description Logic Handbook.* Cambridge, UK: Cambridge University Press.

Baader, F., Hollunder, B., Nebel, B., Profitlich, H., & Franconi, E. (1994). An empirical analysis of optimization techniques for terminological representation systems. *Applied Intelligence, 4*(2), 109–132. doi:10.1007/BF00872105

Baeza-Yates, R., & Ribeiro-Neto, B. (1999). *Modern information retrieval* (Vol. 463). New York: ACM press.

Bai, H., Ge, Y., Wang, J., Li, D., Liao, Y., & Zheng, X. (2014). A method for extracting rules from spatial data based on rough fuzzy sets. *Knowledge-Based Systems, 57,* 28–40. doi:10.1016/j.knosys.2013.12.008

Bakhtyar, M., Dang, N., Inoue, K., & Wiese, L. (2014). Implementing Inductive Concept Learning For Cooperative Query Answering. *Data Analysis, Machine Learning and Knowledge Discovery,* 127-134. doi:10.1007/978-3-319-01595-8_14

Balaji, J., & Geetha, T. V. (2012a). Two-Stage Bootstrapping for Anaphora Resolution. *24th International Conference on Computational Linguistics COLING 2012,* 507-516.

Balaji, J., & Geetha, T. V. (2012b). Semantic Parsing of Tamil Sentences. *Workshop on Machine Translation and Parsing in Indian Languages (MTPIL) 24th International Conference on Computational Linguistics COLING 2012,* 15-22.

Balaji, J., & Geetha, T. V. (2013a). A Graph Based Query Focused Multi-Document Summarization. *International Journal of Intelligent Information Technologies.*

Balaji, J., & Geetha, T. V. (2013b). Graph based Bootstrapping for Coreference Resolution. *Journal of Intelligent Systems.*

Balaji, J., & Geetha, T. V. (2014). *Semi-Supervised Learning of UNL Semantic Relations of a Morphologically Rich Language.* (Unpublished)

Balaji, J., & Geetha, T. V. (2011). Morpho-Semantic Features for Rule-based Tamil Enconversion. *International Journal of Computers and Applications, 26*(6), 11–18. doi:10.5120/3109-4269

Balaji, J., Geetha, T., & Parthasarathi, R. (2016). Abstractive Summarization: A Hybrid Approach for the Compression of Semantic Graphs. *International Journal on Semantic Web and Information Systems, 12*(2), 76–99. doi:10.4018/IJSWIS.2016040104

Baldwin, B., & Morton, T. S. (1998). Dynamic coreference-based summarization. *Proceedings of the Third Conference on Empirical Methods in Natural Language Processing.*

Ballatore, A., Bertolotto, M., & Wilson, D. C. (2013). Geographic knowledge extraction and semantic similarity in OpenStreetMap. *Knowledge and Information Systems, 37*(1), 61–81. doi:10.1007/s10115-012-0571-0

Ballatore, A., Bertolotto, M., & Wilson, D. C. (2014). Linking geographic vocabularies through WordNet. *Annals of GIS, 20*(2), 73–84. doi:10.1080/19475683.2014.904440

Ballou, D., & Tayi, G. (1999). Enhancing data quality in data warehouse environments. *Communications of the ACM, 42*(1), 73–78. doi:10.1145/291469.291471

Bang, M., & Eriksson, H. (2006). Towards document repositories based on semantic documents. In *Proceedings of 6th International Conference on Knowledge Management and Knowledge Technologies (I-KNOW'06).* Springer.

Banko, M., & Brill, E. (2001). Scaling to very very large corpora for natural language disambiguation. *Proceedings of the 39th Annual Meeting on Association for Computational Linguistics (ACL'01),* 26-33. 10.3115/1073012.1073017

Banko, M., Cafarella, M. J., Soderl, S., Broadhead, M., & Etzioni, O. (2007). Open information extraction from the web. *Proceedings of the 20th International Joint Conference on Artificial Intelligence (IJCAI'07),* 2670-2676.

Banko, M., & Etzioni, O. (2008). The tradeoffs between open and traditional relation extraction. *Proceedings of the 46th Annual Meeting on Association for Computational Linguistics (ACL'08)*, 28-36.

Barron, F. H., & Barrett, B. E. (1996). Decision quality using ranked attribute weights. *Management Science, 42*(11), 1515–1523. doi:10.1287/mnsc.42.11.1515

Barwise, J., & Cooper, R. (1981). Generalized quantifiers and natural language. *Linguistics and Philosophy, 4*(2), 159–219. doi:10.1007/BF00350139

Barzilay, McKeown, & Elhadad. (1999). Information fusion in the context of multi-document summarization. *Proc. 37th ACL*, 550–557.

Basca, C., & Bernstein, A. (2014). Querying a messy web of data with {Avalanche}. *Journal of Web Semantics, 26*, 1–28. doi:10.1016/j.websem.2014.04.002

Bateman, S., Gutwin, C., & Nacenta, M. (2008). Seeing Things in the Clouds: The Effect of Visual Features on Tag Cloud Selections. In *Proceedings of the nineteenth ACM conference on Hypertext and hypermedia* (pp. 193-202). ACM. doi:10.1145/1379092.1379130

Baxter, R., Christen, P., & Churches, T. (2003, August). A comparison of fast blocking methods for record linkage. ACM SIGKDD, 3, 25-27.

Baziz, M. (2005, Dec.). Indexation Conceptuelle Guidé par Ontolgie pour la Recherche d'Information. *Thèse de Doctorat en Informatique de l'Université Paul Sabatier de Toulouse (Sciences).*

Baziz, M., & Boughanem, M. (2004). The Use of Ontolmogyfor Semantic Representation of Documents. *The 2nd Semantic Web and Information Retrieval Workshop (SWIR)*, 38-45.

Baziz, M., Boughane, M., & And Aussenac-Gilles, N. (2005). Conceptual Indexing Based on Document Content Representation. In Lecture Notes in Computer Science: Vol. 3507. *Information Context, Nature, Impact, and Role, 5th International Conference on Conceptions of Library and Information Sciences, CoLIS 2005* (pp. 171–186). Springer.

Beckett, D. (2004). *RDF/XML syntax specification (revised)* (Recommendation). W3C.

Beek, W., Rietveld, L., Bazoobandi, H. R., Wielemaker, J., & Schlobach, S. (2014). {LOD} Laundromat: {A} Uniform Way of Publishing Other People's Dirty Data. In *International Semantic Web Conference (ISWC)* (pp. 213–228). Springer. doi:10.1007/978-3-319-11964-9_14

Bekavac, M., & Šnajder, J. (2013). GPKEX: Genetically Programmed Keyphrase Extraction from Croatian Texts. In *Proceedings of 4th Biennial International Workshop on Balto-Slavic Natural Language Processing* (pp. 43-47). Sofia: ACL.

Beliga, S., & Martinčić-Ipšić, S. (2017). Network-Enabled Keyword Extraction for Under-Resourced Languages. In *Semantic Keyword-Based Search on Structured Data Sources: COST Action IC1302 Second International KEYSTONE Conference* (pp. 124-135). Cham: Springer International Publishing. doi:10.1007/978-3-319-53640-8_11

Beliga, S., Kitanović, O., Stanković, R., & Martinčić-Ipšić, S. (n.d.). *Keyword Extraction from Parallel Abstracts of Scientific Publications.* Paper presented at Semantic Keyword-Based Search on Structured Data Sources: COST Action IC1302 Third International KEYSTONE Conference, Gdańsk, Poland.

Beliga, S., Meštrović, A., & Martinčić-Ipšić, S. (2014). Toward Selectivity Based Keyword Extraction for Croatian News. In *Workshop on Surfacing the Deep and the Social Web* (Vol. 1310, pp. 1-14). Riva del Garda, Trentino, Italy: CEUR-WS.org.

Beliga, S., Meštrović, A., & Martinčić-Ipšić, S. (2015). An Overview of Graph-Based Keyword Extraction Methods and Approaches. *Journal of Information and Organizational Sciences, 39*(1), 1–20.

Beliga, S., Meštrović, A., & Martinčić-Ipšić, S. (2016). Selectivity-Based Keyword Extraction Method. *International Journal on Semantic Web and Information Systems, 12*(3), 1–26. doi:10.4018/IJSWIS.2016070101

Benamara, F. (2004a). Cooperative Question Answering in Restricted Domains: the WEBCOOP Experiment. In D. M. Aliod, & J. L. Vicedo (Eds.), ACL Worshop on Question Answering in Restricted Domains (pp. 31-38). Barcelona, Spain: Association for Computational Linguistics.

Benamara, F. (2004b). Generating Intensional Answers in Intelligent Question Answering Systems. In A. Belz, R. Evans, & P. Piwek (Eds.), Lecture Notes in Computer Science: Vol. 3123. Natural Language Generation (pp. 11-20). Springer Berlin Heidelberg. doi:10.1007/978-3-540-27823-8_2

Berend, G. (2011). Opinion expression mining by exploiting keyphrase extraction. *Proc. of the 5th Int. Joint Conf. on NLP*, 1162-1170.

Bergler, S., Witte, R., Khalife, M., Li, Z., & Rudzicz, F. (2003). Using knowledge-poor coreference resolution for text summarization. *DUC, Workshop on Text Summarization*, 85-92.

Berners-Lee, T., Hendler, J., & Lassila, O. (2001). The semantic web. *Scientific American, 284*(5), 28–37. doi:10.1038/scientificamerican0501-34 PMID:11341160

Bird, S., Klein, E., & Loper, E. (2009). *Natural language processing with Python*. Sebastopol, CA: O'Reilly Media, Inc.

Bishop, C. M. (2006). *Pattern Recognition and Machine Learning (Information Science and Statistics)*. Secaucus, NJ: Springer-Verlag New York, Inc.

Bittner, T., Donnelly, M., & Smith, B. (2009). A spatio-temporal ontology for geographic information integration. *International Journal of Geographical Information Science, 23*(6), 765–798. doi:10.1080/13658810701776767

Bizer, C. (2007). *Quality-Driven Information Filtering in the Context of Web-Based Information Systems*. Berlin: Freie Universität.

Bizer, C., Heath, T., & Berners-Lee, T. (2009). Linked Data - The Story So Far. *International Journal on Semantic Web and Information Systems, 5*(3), 1–22. doi:10.4018/jswis.2009081901

Bizer, C., Lehmann, J., Kobilarov, G., Auer, S., Becker, C. C., & Hellmann, S. (2009). DBpedia-A crystallization point for the Web of Data. *Web Semantics: Science, Services, and Agents on the World Wide Web, 7*(3), 154–165. doi:10.1016/j.websem.2009.07.002

Blanco, R., Ottaviano, G., & Meij, E. (2015, February). Fast and space-efficient entity linking for queries. In *Proceedings of the Eighth ACM International Conference on Web Search and Data Mining* (pp. 179-188). ACM. doi:10.1145/2684822.2685317

Blaschke, C., & Valencia, A. (2002). Automatic ontology construction from the literature. *Genome Informatics, 13*, 201-213.

Blomqvist, E., Gangemi, A., & Presutti, V. (2009). *Experiments on pattern-based ontology design*. In *Proceedings of the fifth international conference on Knowledge capture* (pp. 41-48). ACM. doi:10.1145/1597735.1597743

Bobed, C., Yus, R., Bobillo, F., & Mena, E. (2015). Semantic reasoning on mobile devices: Do Androids dream of efficient reasoners? *Web Semantics: Science, Services, and Agents on the World Wide Web, 35*, 167–183. doi:10.1016/j.websem.2015.09.002

Böhm, C., Lorey, J., & Naumann, F. (2011). Creating {voiD} descriptions for {Web}-scale data. *Journal of Web Semantics, 9*(3), 339–345. doi:10.1016/j.websem.2011.06.001

Bollegala, D. T., Matsuo, Y., & Ishizuka, M. (2010). Relational duality: Unsupervised extraction of semantic relations between entities on the web. *Proceedings of the 19th International Conference on World Wide Web (WWW'10)*, 151-160. 10.1145/1772690.1772707

Boncz, P., & Pham, M. D. (2013). *BSBM V3.1 Results (April 2013)*. Retrieved on June 24, 2017 from http://wifo5-03.informatik.uni-mannheim.de/bizer/berlinsparqlbenchmark/results/V7/

Bormann, C., Castellani, A. P., & Shelby, Z. (2012). CoAP: An Application Protocol for Billions of Tiny Internet Nodes. *IEEE Internet Computing, 16*(2), 62–67. doi:10.1109/MIC.2012.29

Boudin, F. (2015). Reducing Over-generation Errors for Automatic Keyphrase Extraction using Integer Linear Programming. In *ACL 2015 Workshop on Novel Computational Approaches to Keyphrase Extraction* (pp. 19-24). Pékin, China: ACL. doi:10.18653/v1/W15-3605

Boudin, F. (2013). A comparison of centrality measures for graph-based keyphrase extraction. In *6th International Joint Conference on Natural Language Processing (IJCNLP)* (pp. 834-838). Nagoya, Japan: AFNLP.

Boughanem, M., Mallak, I., & Prade, H. (2010). A new factor for computing the relevance of a document to a query. *IEEE World congress on Computational Intelligence (WCCI 2010)*. doi:10.1109/FUZZY.2010.5584404

Boughanem, M., Dkaki, T., Mothe, J., & And Soulé-Dupuy, C. (1998). Mercure at TREC7. *TREC, 1998*, 355–360.

Bougouin, A., Boudin, F., & Daille, B. (2016). Keyphrase Annotation with Graph Co-Ranking. *Proceedings of COLING 2016, the 26th International Conference on Computational Linguistics: Technical Papers*, 2945-2955.

Bouillot, F., Poncelet, P., & Roche, M. (2012). How and why exploit tweet's location information? *AGILE'2012: 15th International Conference on Geographic Information Science*.

Bourigault, D., & Jacquemin, C. (2000). *Influence des annotations imparfaites sur les systèmes de Traitement Automatique des Langues, un cadre applicatif: la résolution de l'anaphore pronominale*. Academic Press.

Bourigault, D., Aussenac-Gilles, N. & Charlet, J. (2004). Construction de ressources terminologiques ou ontologiques à partir de textes: un cadre unificateur pour trois études de cas. *Revue d'Intelligence Artificielle (RIA) – Techniques Informatiques et structuration de terminologiques, 18*(1), 87–110.

Brandes, U. (2001). A faster algorithm for betweenness centrality. *The Journal of Mathematical Sociology, 25*(2), 163–177. doi:10.1080/0022250X.2001.9990249

Brin, S. (1998). Extracting patterns and relations from the world wide web. *Proceedings of the International Workshop on the World Wide Web and Databases (WebDB'98)*, 172-183.

Brodt, A., Nicklas, D., & Mitschang, B. (2010, November). Deep integration of spatial query processing into native RDF triple stores. In *Proceedings of the 18th SIGSPATIAL International Conference on Advances in Geographic Information Systems* (pp. 33-42). ACM. doi:10.1145/1869790.1869799

Broekstra, J., Kampman, A., & van Harmelen, F. (2002). Sesame: A Generic Architecture for Storing and Querying {RDF} and {RDF} Schema. In *International Semantic Web Conference (ISWC)* (pp. 54–68). Springer.

Brunzel, M. (2008). The XTREEM Methods for Ontology Learning from Web Documents. In *Proceedings of the Conference on Ontology Learning and Population: Bridging the Gap between Text and Knowledge* (pp. 3-26). IOS Press.

Buccella, A., Cechich, A., Gendarmi, D., Lanubile, F., Semeraro, G., & Colagrossi, A. (2010). GeoMergeP: Geographic information integration through enriched ontology matching. *New Generation Computing*, *28*(1), 41–71. doi:10.1007/s00354-008-0074-4

Buil-Aranda, C., Hogan, A., Umbrich, J., & Vandenbussche, P.-Y. (2013). SPARQL Web-Querying Infrastructure: Ready for Action? In *International Semantic Web Conference (ISWC)* (pp. 277–293). Springer.

Buitelaar, P., & Cimiano, P. (2008). *Ontology learning and population: bridging the gap between text and knowledge* (Vol. 167). Ios Press.

Burger, J., Cardie, C., Chaudhri, V., Gaizauskas, R., Harabagiu, S., Israel, D., . . . Miller, G. (2001). Issues, tasks and program structures to roadmap research in question & answering (Q&A). *Document Understanding Conferences Roadmapping Documents*, 1-35.

Burton-Jones, A., Storey, V. C., Sugumaran, V., & Ahluwalia, P. (2005). A semiotic metrics suite for assessing the quality of ontologies. *Data & Knowledge Engineering*, *55*(1), 84–102. doi:10.1016/j.datak.2004.11.010

Campinas, S., Delbru, R., & Tummarello, G. (2013). Efficiency and precision trade-offs in graph summary algorithms. *International Database Engineering {&} Applications Symposium (IDEAS)*, 38–47. doi:10.1145/2513591.2513654

Candela, L., Castelli, D., & Pagano, P. (2010). Making Virtual Research Environments in the Cloud a Reality: the gCube Approach. *ERCIM News, 2010*(83), 32.

Canhasi, E., & Kononenko, I. (2011). *Semantic Role Frames Graph-based Multi-document Summarization, Faculty of computer and information science*. University of Ljubljana.

Cattoni, R., Corcoglioniti, F., Girardi, C., Magnini, B., Serafini, L., & Zanoli, R. (2012). The KnowledgeStore: An entity-based storage system. In *Proceedings of the 8th International Conference on Language Resources and Evaluation (LREC'12)*. European Language Resources Association (ELRA).

Cattoni, R., Corcoglioniti, F., Girardi, C., Magnini, B., Serafini, L., & Zanoli, R. (2013). Anchoring Background Knowledge to Rich Multimedia Contexts in the KnowledgeStore. New Trends of Research in Ontologies and Lexical Resources, 91-112. doi:10.1007/978-3-642-31782-8_6

Chali, Y., & Joty, S. R. (2008). Unsupervised approach for selecting sentences in query based summarization. In *FLAIRS Conference*. AAAI Press.

Cheng, G., & Qu, Y. (2009). Searching Linked Objects with Falcons: Approach, Implementation and Evaluation. *International Journal on Semantic Web and Information Systems*, *5*(3), 49–70. doi:10.4018/jswis.2009081903

Chenji, H., Zhang, W., Stoleru, R., & Arnett, C. (2013). DistressNet: A disaster response system providing constant availability cloud-like services. *Ad Hoc Networks*, *11*(8), 2440–2460. doi:10.1016/j.adhoc.2013.06.008

Christen, P. (2012). A survey of indexing techniques for scalable record linkage and deduplication. *Knowledge and Data Engineering. IEEE Transactions on*, *24*(9), 1537–1555.

Christen, P., & Goiser, K. (2007). Quality and complexity measures for data linkage and deduplication. In *Quality Measures in Data Mining* (pp. 127–151). Springer Berlin Heidelberg. doi:10.1007/978-3-540-44918-8_6

Cimiano, P., & Völker, J. (2005). Text2Onto: A Framework for Ontology Learning and Data-Driven Change Discovery. In A. Montoyo, R. Munoz & E. Metais (Ed.), LNCS: Vol. 3513. Natural Language Processing and Information Systems. Springer-Verlag Heidelberg. doi:10.1007/11428817_21

Cimiano, P. (2006). *Ontology Learning and Population from Text: Algorithm, Evaluation and Applications*. New York: Springer-Verlag.

Claveau, V., & L'homme, M.-C. (2004). Discoveringe specific semantic relations between nouns and verbs in a specialized french corpus. *Proceedings of the 3rd International Workshop on Computational Terminology, CompuTerm'04*, 39–46.

Cohen, W. W., Hurst, M., & Jensen, L. S. (2002, May). A flexible learning system for wrapping tables and lists in HTML documents. In *Proceedings of the 11th international conference on World Wide Web* (pp. 232-241). ACM. doi:10.1145/511446.511477

Colucci, S., Di Noia, T., Pinto, A., Ragone, A., Ruta, M., & Tinelli, E. (2007). A Non-Monotonic Approach to Semantic Matchmaking and Request Refinement in E-Marketplaces. *International Journal of Electronic Commerce, 12*(2), 127–154. doi:10.2753/JEC1086-4415120205

Compton, M., Barnaghi, P., Bermudez, L., Garcìa-Castro, R., Corcho, O., Cox, S., & Taylor, K. et al. (2012). The SSN ontology of the W3C semantic sensor network incubator group. *Web Semantics: Science, Services, and Agents on the World Wide Web, 17*, 25–32. doi:10.1016/j.websem.2012.05.003

Corcoglioniti, F., Rospocher, M., Cattoni, R., Magnini, B., & Serafini, L. (2013). Interlinking unstructured and structured knowledge in an integrated framework. In *IEEE 7th International Conference on Semantic Computing* (pp. 40–47). IEEE Computer Society. doi:10.1109/ICSC.2013.17

Corcoglioniti, F., Rospocher, M., Mostarda, M., & Amadori, M. (2015). Processing billions of RDF triples on a single machine using streaming and sorting. In *Symposium on Applied Computing, SAC 2015*. ACM. Retrieved from http://rdfpro.fbk.eu

Corcoglioniti, F., Dragoni, M., Rospocher, M., & Palmero Aprosio, A. (2016). Knowledge Extraction for Information Retrieval. In H. Sack, E. Blomqvist, M. d'Aquin, C. Ghidini, S. Ponzetto, & C. Lange (Eds.), Lecture Notes in Computer Science: Vol. 9678. *The Semantic Web. Latest Advances and New Domains. ESWC 2016*. Springer.

Corcoglioniti, F., Rospocher, M., Cattoni, R., Magnini, B., & Serafini, L. (2015). The KnowledgeStore: A Storage Framework for Interlinking Unstructured and Structured Knowledge. *International Journal on Semantic Web and Information Systems, 11*(2), 1–35. doi:10.4018/IJSWIS.2015040101

Corcoglioniti, F., Rospocher, M., & Palmero Aprosio, A. (2016, December 1). Frame-Based Ontology Population with PIKES. *IEEE Transactions on Knowledge and Data Engineering, 28*(12), 3261–3275. doi:10.1109/TKDE.2016.2602206

Corcoglioniti, F., Rospocher, M., Palmero Aprosio, A., & Tonelli, S. (2016). PreMOn: a Lemon Extension for Exposing Predicate Models as Linked Data. In *Proceedings of Language Resources and Evaluation*. LREC.

Correndo, G., & Shadbolt, N. (2011). Translating expressive ontology mappings into rewriting rules to implement query rewriting. OM.

Craven, M., DiPasquo, D., Freitag, D., McCallum, A., Mitchell, T., Nigam, K., & Slattery, S. (2000). Learning to Construct Knowledge Bases from the World Wide Web. *Artificial Intelligence, 118*(1-2), 69–113. doi:10.1016/S0004-3702(00)00004-7

Crescenzi, V., & Mecca, G. (2004). Automatic information extraction from large websites. *Journal of the ACM, 51*(5), 731–779. doi:10.1145/1017460.1017462

Crespo, A., & Garcia-Molina, H. (2002). Routing Indices For Peer-to-Peer Systems. *International Conference on Distributed Computing Systems (ICDCS)*, 23–32. doi:10.1109/ICDCS.2002.1022239

Crestani, F. (1997). Application of spreading activation techniques in information retrieval. *Artificial Intelligence Review*, *11*(6), 453–482. doi:10.1023/A:1006569829653

Crooks, A. T., & Wise, S. (2013). GIS and agent-based models for humanitarian assistance. *Computers, Environment and Urban Systems*, *41*, 100–111. doi:10.1016/j.compenvurbsys.2013.05.003

Croset, S., Grabmüller, C., Li, C., Kavaliauskas, S., & Rebholz-Schuhmann, D. (2010). The CALBC RDF triple store: Retrieval over large literature content. In *Proceedings of the Workshop on Semantic Web Applications and Tools for Life Sciences (SWAT4LS), (Vol. 698)*. CEUR-WS.org. doi:10.1038/npre.2010.5383.1

Crowley, C., & Harris, S. (2007). The sedona conference glossary: E-discovery and digital information management. *Proceedings of the Sedona Conference 2007*.

Cybulska, A., & Vossen, P. (2014). Using a sledgehammer to crack a nut? Lexical diversity and event coreference resolution. In *Proceedings of the 9th International Conference on Language Resources and Evaluation (LREC'14)*. European Language Resources Association (ELRA).

Cyganiak, R., Field, S., Gregory, A., Halb, W., & Tennison, J. (2010). Semantic Statistics: Bringing Together SDMX and SCOVO. *WWW Workshop on Linked Data on the web*.

Cyganiak, R., Stenzhorn, H., Delbru, R., Decker, S., & Tummarello, G. (2008). Semantic Sitemaps: Efficient and Flexible Access to Datasets on the Semantic Web. In *European Semantic Web Conference ({ESWC})* (pp. 690–704). Springer. doi:10.1007/978-3-540-68234-9_50

Dahab, M. Y., Hassan, H. A., & Rafea, A. (2008). TextOntoEx: Automatic ontology construction from natural English text. *Expert Systems with Applications*, *34*(2), 1474–1480. doi:10.1016/j.eswa.2007.01.043

Daly, E. M., Lecue, F., & Bicer, V. (2013). Westland row why so slow?: fusing social media and linked data sources for understanding real-time traffic conditions. In *Proceedings of the 2013 international conference on Intelligent user interfaces* (pp. 203-212). ACM. doi:10.1145/2449396.2449423

Damljanovic, D., Agatonovic, M., & Cunningham, H. (2010). *Natural language interfaces to ontologies: combining syntactic analysis and ontology-based lookup through the user interaction*. Heraklion, Crete, Greece: Springer-Verlag. doi:10.1007/978-3-642-13486-9_8

Damova, M., Kiryakov, A., Simov, K., & Petrov, S. (2010). *Mapping the central LOD ontologies to PROTON upper-level ontology*. Ontology Mapping Workshop at ISWC 2010, Shanghai, China. Retrieved from http://proton.semanticweb.org/

Dang, H. T., & Owczarzak, K. (2009). Overview of the TAC 2009 Summarization Track. In *Proceedings of the Second Text Analysis Conference*. National Institute of Standards and Technology.

Darari, F., Nutt, W., Pirrò, G., & Razniewski, S. (2013). *Completeness statements about RDF data sources and their use for query answering. In The Semantic Web--ISWC 2013* (pp. 66–83). Berlin: Springer.

Data Hub. (n.d.). Retrieved from: http://datahub.io/

David, J., Euzenat, J., Scharffe, F., & dos Santos, C. (2011). The Alignment API 4.0. *Semantic Web -- Interoperability, Usability. Applicability*, *2*(1), 3–10.

Davis, B., Dantuluri, P., Handschuh, S., & Cunningham, H. (2010). Towards Controlled Natural Language for Semantic Annotation. *International Journal on Semantic Web and Information Systems*, *6*(4), 64–91. doi:10.4018/jswis.2010100103

DBpedia Association. (2015). *DBpedia Release 39 - Links to other datasets*. Retrieved July 7, 2017 from http://downloads.dbpedia.org/3.9/links/geonames_links.nt.bz2

De Carvalho, M. G., Laender, A. H., Gonçalves, M. A., & Da Silva, A. S. (2012). A genetic programming approach to record deduplication. *Knowledge and Data Engineering. IEEE Transactions on, 24*(3), 399–412.

de Melo, G., Suchanek, F. M., & Pease, A. (2008). Integrating {YAGO} into the Suggested Upper Merged Ontology. In *20th International Conference on Tools with Artificial Intelligence* (vol. 1, pp. 190–193). IEEE.

De Virgilio, R., Di Sciascio, E., Ruta, M., Scioscia, F., & Torlone, R. (2011). Semantic-based RFID data management. Unique Radio Innovation for the 21st Century, 111-141. doi:10.1007/978-3-642-03462-6_6

Debattista, J., Lange, C., & Auer, S. (2015). *Luzzu Quality Metric Language--A DSL for Linked Data Quality Assessment.* arXiv preprint arXiv:1412.3750

De, F. B. (1989). Probabilism: A Critical Essay on the Theory of Probability and on the Value of Science. *Erkenntnis, 31*(2/3), 169–223.

Dey, D., Mookerjee, V. S., & Liu, D. (2011). Efficient techniques for online record linkage. *Knowledge and Data Engineering. IEEE Transactions on, 23*(3), 373–387.

Di Noia, T., Di Sciascio, E., Donini, F. M., Ruta, M., Scioscia, F., & Tinelli, E. (2008). Semantic-based Bluetooth-RFID interaction for advanced resource discovery in pervasive contexts. *International Journal on Semantic Web and Information Systems, 4*(1), 50–74. doi:10.4018/jswis.2008010104

Di, L., Zhao, P., Yang, W., & Yue, P. (2006, June). Ontology-driven automatic geospatial-processing modeling based on web-service chaining. *Proceedings of the sixth annual NASA earth science technology conference,* 27-29.

Dima, C. (2013). Intui2: A prototype system for question answering over linked data. *Proceedings of the Question Answering over Linked Data lab (QALD-3) at CLEF.*

Dima, C. (2014, September). Answering Natural Language Questions with Intui3. Working Notes for CLEF 2014 Conference, 1180, 1201-1211.

Dinh, D. (2012). *Accés à l'information biomédicale: vers une approche d'indexation et de recherche d'information conceptuelle basée sur la fusion de ressources termino-ontologiques* (PhD thesis). Université Toulouse 3 Paul Sabatier (UT3 Paul Sabatier).

Dividino, R. Q., Gottron, T., Scherp, A., & Gröner, G. (2014). From Changes to Dynamics: Dynamics Analysis of Linked Open Data Sources. *1st International Workshop on Dataset Profiling & Federated Search for Linked Data (PROFILES'14).*

Djedidi, R., & Aufaure, M. A. (2010). ONTO-EVOAL an ontology evolution approach guided by pattern modeling and quality evaluation. In Foundations of Information and Knowledge Systems (pp. 286-305). Springer Berlin Heidelberg.

Dostal, M., & Jezek, K. (2011). Automatic Keyphrase Extraction based on NLP and Statistical Methods. In *Proceedings of the DATESO 2011: Annual International Workshop on DAtabases, TExts, Specifications and Objects (Vol. 706,* pp. 140-145). Pisek, Czech Republic: CEUR-WS.org.

Drumond, L., & Girardi, R. (2008). A Survey of Ontology Learning Procedures. In F. L. G. de Freitas, H. Stuckenschmidt, H. S. Pinto, A. Malucelli, & Ó. Corcho (Eds.), *WONTO. CEUR-WS.org.*

Dunaiski, M., Fischer, B., Greene, G. J., Ilvovsky, D., & Kuznetsov, S. O. (2015). Browsing Publication Data using Tag Clouds over Concept Lattices Constructed by Key-Phrase Extraction. *Proc. of Russian and South African Workshop on Knowledge Discovery Techniques Based on Formal Concept Analysis (RuZA 2015),* 10-22.

Duque, A. P. G., Pérez, M. E. D. M., & de Guevara, F. G. L. (2012). Usos de Twitter en las universidades iberoamericanas. *Revista Latinoamericana de Tecnología Educativa-RELATEC, 11*(1), 27–39.

Duque-Ramos, A., Fernández-Breis, J. T., Stevens, R., & Aussenac-Gilles, N. (2011). OQuaRE: A SQuaRE-based approach for evaluating the quality of ontologies. *Journal of Research and Practice in Information Technology, 43*(2), 159.

Duthil, B., Trousset, F., Roche, M., Dray, G., Plantie, M., Montmain, J., & Poncelet, P. (2011). Towards an Automatic Characterization of Criteria. In A. Hameurlain, S. Liddle, K-D. Schewe, X.Zhou (Ed.), LNCS: Vol. 6860. Database and Expert Systems Applications (pp. 457-465). Springer-Verlag Heidelberg. doi:10.1007/978-3-642-23088-2_34

Eisenstein, J., O'Connor, B., Smith, N. A., & Xing, E. P. (2010). A latent variable model for geographic lexical variation. In *Proceedings of the 2010 Conference on Empirical Methods in Natural Language Processing* (pp. 1277-1287). Association for Computational Linguistics.

El Idrissi, O., Frikh, B., & Ouhbi, B. (2014). HCHIRSIMEX: An extended method for domain ontology learning based on conditional mutual information. In *Third IEEE International Colloquium in Information Science and Technology (CIST)*, (pp. 91-95). IEEE. doi:10.1109/CIST.2014.7016600

Elfeky, M. G., Verykios, V. S., & Elmagarmid, A. K. (2002). TAILOR: A record linkage toolbox. In *Data Engineering, 2002. Proceedings. 18th International Conference on* (pp. 17-28). IEEE. doi:10.1109/ICDE.2002.994694

Eriksson, H. (2007, July). The semantic-document approach to combining documents and ontologies. *International Journal of Human-Computer Studies, 65*(7), 624–639. doi:10.1016/j.ijhcs.2007.03.008

Erkan, G., & Radev, D. R. (2004). Lexrank: Graph-based lexical centrality as salience in text summarization. *Journal of Artificial Intelligence Research, 22*(1), 457–479.

Erling, O., & Mikhailov, I. (2009). RDF} Support in the {V}irtuoso {DBMS. In *Networked Knowledge -- Networked Media*. Springer. doi:10.1007/978-3-642-02184-8_2

Ethnologue. (n.d.). Retrieved November 15, 2015 and July 4, 2017, from https://www.ethnologue.com/

Etzioni, O., Cafarella, M., Downey, D., Popescu, A., Shaked, T., Soderland, S., & Yates, A. et al. (2005). Unsupervised named-entity extraction from the web: An experimental study. *Artificial Intelligence, 165*(1), 91–134. doi:10.1016/j.artint.2005.03.001

Etzioni, O., Kok, S., Soderland, S., Cagarella, M., Popescu, A. M., Weld, D. S., & Yates, A. et al. (2004). Web-Scale Information Extraction in KnowItAll (Preliminary Results). In *Proceedings of the 13th international conference on World Wide Web (WWW '04)*. ACM.

Faatz, A., & Steinmetz, R. (2005). An evaluation Framework for Ontology Enrichment. In P. Buitelaar, P. Cimiano, & B. Magnini (Eds.), *Ontology Learning from Text: Methods, Applications and Evaluation* (pp. 77–91). IOS Press.

Fafalios, P., & Tzitzikas, Y. (2013, July). X-ENS: semantic enrichment of web search results at real-time. In *Proceedings of the 36th international ACM SIGIR conference on Research and development in information retrieval* (pp. 1089-1090). ACM. doi:10.1145/2484028.2484200

Fafalios, P., & Tzitzikas, Y. (2014). Exploratory Professional Search through Semantic Post-Analysis of Search Results. In *Professional Search in the Modern World*. Lecture Notes in Computer Science. Springer. doi:10.1007/978-3-319-12511-4_9

Fellbaum, C. (1998). *WordNet: An electronic lexical database*. Retrieved from http://www. cogsci. princeton. edu/wn

Fellbaum, C. (1998, May). *WordNet: An Electronic Lexical Database (Language, Speech, and Communication*. The MIT Press.

Fellbaum, C. (1998). *WordNet: An Electronic Lexical Database*. Cambridge, MA: MIT Press.

Fellegi, I. P., & Sunter, A. B. (1969). A theory for record linkage. *Journal of the American Statistical Association*, *64*(328), 1183–1210. doi:10.1080/01621459.1969.10501049

Fernández-López, M., Gómez-Pérez, A., Sierra, J. P. & Sierra, A. P. (1999). Building a chemical ontology using methontology and the ontology design environment. *IEEE Intelligent Systems and their Applications, 14*(1), 37-46.

Ferrara, F., Pudota, N., & Tasso, C. (2011). A Keyphrase-Based Paper Recommender System. In *Digital Libraries and Archives*. In *Communications in Computer and Information Science* (Vol. 249, pp. 14–25). Springer Berlin Heidelberg.

Ferret, O. (2011). Utiliser l'amorçage pour améliorer une mesure de similarité sémantique. Actes de TALN 2011, 1–6.

Fetahu, B., Dietze, S., Nunes, B. P., Casanova, M. A., Taibi, D., & Nejdl, W. (2014). A Scalable Approach for Efficiently Generating Structured Dataset Topic Profiles. In *European Semantic Web Conference ({ESWC})* (pp. 519–534). Springer. Retrieved from doi:10.1007/978-3-319-07443-6_35

FIRE. (2010). Retrieved from www.isical.ac.in/~fire/working-notes.html

Fokkens, A., Soroa, A., Beloki, Z., Ockeloen, N., Rigau, G., van Hage, W. R., & Vossen, P. (2014). NAF and GAF: Linking linguistic annotations. In *Proceedings of 10th Joint ISO-ACL SIGSEM Workshop on Interoperable Semantic Annotation* (pp. 9–16). Association for Computational Linguistics. See also http://groundedannotationframework.org/

Fonseca, F. T., Egenhofer, M. J., Agouris, P., & Câmara, G. (2002). Using ontologies for integrated geographic information systems. *Transactions in GIS, 6*(3), 231–257. doi:10.1111/1467-9671.00109

Frege, G. (2000). Ueber sinn und bedeutunq [On sense and reference]. *Perspectives in the Philosophy of Language: A Concise Anthology*, 45. Retrieved from http://en.wikipedia.org/wiki/Sense_and_reference

Freitag, D., & Mccallum, A. K. (1999). Information extraction with hmms and shrinkage. *Proceedings of the AAAI'99 Workshop on Machine Learning for Information Extraction*, 31–36.

Freitas, A., Oliveira, J. G., Curry, E., O'Riain, S., & Silva, J. P. (2011). Treo: Combining Entity-Search, Spreading Activation and Semantic Relatedness for Querying Linked Data. *Proceedings of the 1st Workshop on Question Answering Over Linked Data (QALD-1)*.

Frikh, B., Djaanfar, A. S., & Ouhbi, B. (2011). Article. *Int. J. Artif. Intell. Tools, 20*(6), 1157-1170. doi: https://doi.org/10.1142/S0218213011000565

Fugazza, C. (2011). Toward semantics-aware annotation and retrieval of spatial data. *Earth Science Informatics, 4*(4), 225–239. doi:10.1007/s12145-011-0088-1

Fürber, C., & Hepp, M. (2010, May). *Using sparql and spin for data quality management on the semantic web*. Berlin: Springer.

Fürber, C., & Hepp, M. (2011). *Swiqa-a semantic web information quality assessment framework* (Vol. 15). ECIS.

Gábor, A., & Kő, A. (Eds.). (2016). *Corporate Knowledge Discovery and Organizational Learning*. Springer International Publishing. doi:10.1007/978-3-319-28917-5

Gal, A., Sagi, T., Weidlich, M., Levy, E., Shafran, V., Miklós, Z., & Hung, N. Q. V. (2012). Making Sense of Top-k Matchings: A Unified Match Graph for Schema Matching. In *Proceedings of the Ninth International Workshop on Information Integration on the Web* (p. 6:1--6:6). New York: ACM. doi:10.1145/2331801.2331807

Gallego, M. A., Fernández, J. D., Martínez-Prieto, M. A., & de la Fuente, P. (2011). *An Empirical Study of Real-World SPARQL Queries*. USEWOD.

Gamma, E., Helm, R., Johnson, R., & Vlissides, J. (1995). *Design Patterns: Elements of Reusable Object-oriented Software*. Boston: Addison-Wesley Longman Publishing Co., Inc.

Gangemi, A., Catenacci, C., Ciaramita, M., & Lehmann, J. (2006). *Modelling ontology evaluation and validation*. Springer Berlin Heidelberg.

Gantz, J., & Reinsel, D. (2011). *Extracting Value from Chaos (Tech. Rep.)*. IDC Iview.

Gasevic, D., Zouaq, A., Torniai, C., Jovanovic, J., & Hatala, M. (2011). An approach to folksonomy-based ontology maintenance for learning environments. *Learning Technologies. IEEE Transactions on, 4*(4), 301–314.

Gatterbauer, W., Bohunsky, P., Herzog, M., Krüpl, B., & Pollak, B. (2007, May). Towards domain-independent information extraction from web tables. In *Proceedings of the 16th international conference on World Wide Web* (pp. 71-80). ACM. doi:10.1145/1242572.1242583

Gelernter, J., & Balajì, S. (2013). An algorithm for local geoparsing of microtext. *GeoInformatica, 17*(4), 635–667. doi:10.1007/s10707-012-0173-8

Georgiev, G., Popov, B., Osenova, P., & Dimitrov, M. (2013). Adaptive semantic publishing. In *Proceedings of the Workshop on Semantic Web Enterprise Adoption and Best Practice co-located with 12th International Semantic Web Conference (ISWC 2013), (Vol. 1106)*. CEUR-WS.org.

Giannakis, M., & Louis, M. (2016). A multi-agent based system with big data processing for enhanced supply chain agility. *Journal of Enterprise Information Management, 29*(5), 706–727. doi:10.1108/JEIM-06-2015-0050

Gillani Andleeb, S. (2015). *From text mining to knowledge mining: An integrated framework of concept extraction and categorization for domain ontology* (Doctoral dissertation). Budapesti Corvinus Egyetem.

Gillani, S., & Ko, A. (2016). ProMine: a text mining solution for concept extraction and filtering. In Corporate Knowledge Discovery and Organizational Learning (pp. 59-82). Springer International Publishing. doi:10.1007/978-3-319-28917-5_3

Gillani, S. A., & Kő, A. (2014). *Process-based knowledge extraction in a public authority: A text mining approach. In Electronic Government and the Information Systems Perspective* (pp. 91–103). Springer.

Gillani, S., & Ko, A. (2015). Incremental ontology population and enrichment through semantic-based text mining: An application for it audit domain. *International Journal on Semantic Web and Information Systems, 11*(3), 44–66. doi:10.4018/IJSWIS.2015070103

Gillet, P., Trojahn, C., Haemmerlé, O., & Pradel, C. (2013). Complex Correspondences for Query Patterns Rewriting. In *Proceedings of the 8th International Conference on Ontology Matching* (vol. 1111, pp. 49–60). Aachen, Germany: CEUR-WS.org.

Gimenez-Garcia, J., Thakkar, H., & Zimmermann, A. (2016). Assessing trust with PageRank in the Web of Data. In *International Semantic Web Conference* (pp. 293-307). Springer. doi:10.1007/978-3-319-47602-5_45

Giuliano, C., Lavelli, A., & Romano, L. (2006). Exploiting shallow linguistic information for relation extraction from biomedical literature. *Proceedings of 11th Conference of the European Chapter of the Association for Computational Linguistics (EACL'06)*, 401-408.

Glaser, H., Millard, I., & Jaffri, A. (2008). RKBExplorer.com: {A} Knowledge Driven Infrastructure for {L}inked {D}ata Providers. In *European Semantic Web Conference ({ESWC})* (pp. 797–801). Springer.

Glimm, B., Horrocks, I., Motik, B., Stoilos, G., & Wang, Z. (2014). HermiT: An OWL 2 reasoner. *Journal of Automated Reasoning, 53*(3), 245–269. doi:10.1007/s10817-014-9305-1

Göbelbecker, M., & Dornhege, C. (2009). Realistic Cities in Simulated Environments - An OpenStreetMap to Robocup Rescue Converter. *Proceedings of 4th International Workshop on Synthetic Simulation and Robotics to Mitigate Earthquake Disaster (SRMED 2009)*.

Gómez, A. B., Martínez, A. C., Sánchez, Á. C., & Rus, T. I. (2012). El uso de Twitter como herramienta de formación del profesorado en la Facultad de Educación de la Universidad de Murcia. *I Congreso Nacional de Investigación e Innovación en Educación Infantil y Primaria*.

Gómez-Pérez, A. (2004). Ontology Evaluation. In S. Staab & R. Studer (Eds.), *Handbook on Ontologies* (pp. 251–273). Springer. doi:10.1007/978-3-540-24750-0_13

Gong, Z., & Liu, Q. (2009). Improving keyword based web image search with visual feature distribution and term expansion. *Knowledge and Information Systems*, *21*(1), 113–132. doi:10.1007/s10115-008-0183-x

Gönül, S., & Sinaci, A. A. (2012). Semantic content management and integration with JCR/CMIS compliant content repositories. In *Proceedings of the 8th International Conference on Semantic Systems (I-SEMANTICS'12)* (pp. 181–184). ACM. Retrieved from http://stanbol.apache.org/

Gonzàlez, E., & Turmo, J. (2009). Unsupervised relation extraction by massive clustering. *Proceedings of the 2009 Ninth IEEE International Conference on Data Mining (ICDM '09)*, 782-787. 10.1109/ICDM.2009.81

Graham, M., Hale, S. A., & Gaffney, D. (2014). Where in the world are you? Geolocation and language identification in Twitter. *The Professional Geographer*, *66*(4), 568–578. doi:10.1080/00330124.2014.907699

Grefenstette, G. (1994). *Explorations in Automatic Thesaurus Discovery*. Dordrecht, The Netherlands: Kluwer. doi:10.1007/978-1-4615-2710-7

Grineva, M., Grinev, M., & Lizorkin, D. (2009). Extracting key terms from noisy and multitheme documents. In *Proceedings of the 18th International Conference on World Wide Web* (pp. 661-670). New York: ACM. doi:10.1145/1526709.1526798

Grishman, R. (2010). Information Extraction. In The Handbook of Computational Linguistics and Natural Language Processing (pp. 515–530). Wiley-Blackwell. doi:10.1002/9781444324044.ch18

Grishman, R., & Sundheim, B. (1996). Message understanding conference-6: A brief history. *Proceedings of 16th Conference on Computational Linguistics (COLING'96)*, 466-471. 10.3115/992628.992709

Grouin, C., Abacha, A. B., Bernhard, D., Cartoni, B., Deléger, L., Grau, B., … Zweigenbaum, P. (2010). Caramba: Concept, assertion, and relation annotation using machine-learning based approaches. *Actes de la conférence conjointe JEP-TALN-RECITAL 2012*.

Groza, T., Handschuh, S., Möller, K., Grimnes, G., Sauermann, L., Minack, E., & Gudjónsdottir, R. et al. (2007). The NEPOMUK Project – On the way to the Social Semantic Desktop. In *Proceedings of I-SEMANTICS 2007*. Retrieved from http://nepomuk.semanticdesktop.org/

Guarino, N., & Welty, C. A. (2009). An overview of OntoClean. In *Handbook on ontologies* (pp. 201–220). Springer Berlin Heidelberg. doi:10.1007/978-3-540-92673-3_9

Guéret, C., Groth, P., Stadler, C., & Lehmann, J. (2012). Assessing linked data mappings using network measures. In *The Semantic Web: Research and Applications* (pp. 87–102). Berlin: Springer. doi:10.1007/978-3-642-30284-8_13

Guo, Q., & Zhang, M. (2009). Question answering based on pervasive agent ontology and Semantic Web. Knowledge-Based Systems, 22, 443-448. doi:10.1016/j.knosys.2009.06.003

Gupta, V., & Lehal, G. S. (2010). *A Survey of text summarization of extractive techniques*. University Institute of Engineering and Technology, Computer Science & Engineering, Punjab University, Chandigarh, India.

Gutierrez, C., Figuerias, P., Oliveira, P., Costa, R., & Jardim-Goncalves, R. (2015, July). Twitter mining for traffic events detection. In *Science and Information Conference (SAI)*, 2015 (pp. 371-378). IEEE.

Haarslev, V., & Müller, R. (2001). Racer system description. *Automated Reasoning*, 701–705.

Hagberg, A. A., Schult, D. A., & Swart, P. J. (2008). Exploring Network Structure, Dynamics, and Function using NetworkX. *Proceedings of the 7th Python in Science Conference (SciPy 2008)*, 11-15.

Haghighi, A., & Vanderwende, L. (2009). Exploring content models for multi-document summarization. In *Proceedings of Human Language Technologies: The 2009 Annual Conference of the North American Chapter of the Association for Computational Linguistics, NAACL '09*, (pp. 362–370). Stroudsburg, PA: Association for Computational Linguistics. doi:10.3115/1620754.1620807

Hahn, U., & Mani, I. (2000). The Challenges of Automatic Summarization. IEEE Computer, 33(11), 29-36.

Hahn, U., & Romacker, M. (2001). The SynDiKATe Text Knowledge Base Generator. In *Proceedings of the 1st International Conference on Human Language Technology Research (HLT'01)*. Association for Computational Linguistics. doi:10.3115/1072133.1072219

Hahn, U., Romacker, M., & Schulz, S. (2002). MEDSYNDIKATE- A Natural Language System for the Extraction of Medical Information from Findings Reports. *International Journal of Medical Informatics*, 67(1-3), 63–74. doi:10.1016/S1386-5056(02)00053-9 PMID:12460632

Halpin, H., Hayes, P. J., McCusker, J. P., McGuinness, D. L., & Thompson, H. S. (2010). When owl:sameAs Isn't the Same: An Analysis of Identity in Linked Data. In *The Semantic Web -- ISWC 2010: 9th International Semantic Web Conference, ISWC 2010*, (pp. 305–320). Berlin: Springer Berlin Heidelberg.

Halvey, M. J., & Keane, M. T. (2007). An Assessment of Tag Presentation Techniques. In *Proceedings of the 16th International Conference on World Wide Web*. ACM. doi:10.1145/1242572.1242826

Hamon, T., & Nazarenko, A. (2010). Detection of synonymy links between terms: experiment and results. Recent Advances in Computational Terminology, 185–208.

Harrathi, R., Roussey, C., Maisonnasse, L., & And Calabretto, S. (2010). *Vers une approche statistique pour l'indexation sémantique des documents multilingue*. Dans: Actes du XXVIII° congrès INFORSID, Marseille.

Harris, S., & Seaborne, A. (2013). *SPARQL 1.1 Query Language*. W3C Recommendation. Retrieved June 24, 2017 from http://www.w3.org/TR/2013/REC-sparql11-query-20130321/

Harris, S., Seaborne, A., & Prud'hommeaux, E. (2013, March). {SPARQL} 1.1 Query Language.

Harris, S., Lamb, N., & Shadbolt, N. (2009). 4store: The Design and Implementation of a Clustered {RDF} Store. *Scalable Semantic Web Systems Workshop (SWSS)*.

Harris, Z. (1990). La genèse de lanalyse des transformations et de la métalangue. *Langages*, 99(99), 9–20. doi:10.3406/lgge.1990.1589

Harth, A., Hose, K., Karnstedt, M., Polleres, A., Sattler, K.-U., & Umbrich, J. (2010). Data summaries for on-demand queries over linked data. *International Conference on World Wide Web (WWW)*, 411–420. doi:10.1145/1772690.1772733

Harth, A., & Speiser, S. (2012, July). *On Completeness Classes for Query Evaluation on Linked Data*. AAAI.

Harth, A., Umbrich, J., Hogan, A., & Decker, S. (2007). {YARS2:} {A} Federated Repository for Querying Graph Structured Data from the {W}Holst. In *International Semantic Web Conference (ISWC)* (pp. 211–224). Springer. http://doi.org/ doi:<ALIGNMENT.qj></ALIGNMENT>10.1007/978-3-540-76298-0_16

Hartig, O. (2009). Provenance Information in the Web of Data. *LDOW, 538.*

Hartig, O., & Zhao, J. (2009). Using web data provenance for quality assessment. *CEUR Workshop.*

Hartig, O., & Zhao, J. (2010). Publishing and consuming provenance metadata on the web of linked data. In *Provenance and annotation of data and processes* (pp. 78–90). Berlin: Springer. doi:10.1007/978-3-642-17819-1_10

Hart, T. C., & Zandbergen, P. A. (2013). Reference data and geocoding quality: Examining completeness and positional accuracy of street geocoded crime incidents. *Policing: An International Journal of Police Strategies & Management, 36*(2), 263–294. doi:10.1108/13639511311329705

Hasegawa, T., Sekine, S., & Grishman, R. (2004). Discovering relations among named entities from large corpora. *Proceedings of the 42nd Annual Meeting on Association for Computational Linguistics (ACL'04)*, 415-422. 10.3115/1218955.1219008

Hasnain, A., Mehmood, Q., e Zainab, S. S., Saleem, M., Warren, C., Zehra, D., ... Rebholz-Schuhmann, D. (2017a). BioFed: federated query processing over life sciences linked open data. *Journal of biomedical Semantics, 8*(1), 13.

Hasnain, A., Kamdar, M. R., Hasapis, P., Zeginis, D., & Warren, C. N. Jr et al. (2014). Linked Biomedical Dataspace: Lessons Learned integrating Data for Drug Discovery. *International Semantic Web Conference (In-Use Track).*

Hasnain, A., Mehmood, Q., Zainab, S. S., & Hogan, A. (2016a). SPORTAL: Profiling the Content of Public SPARQL Endpoints. *International Journal on Semantic Web and Information Systems, 12*(3), 134–163. doi:10.4018/IJSWIS.2016070105

Hasnain, A., Mehmood, Q., Zainab, S. S., & Hogan, A. (2016b). SPORTAL: Searching for Public SPARQL Endpoints. In *International Semantic Web Conference (ISWC) Posters & Demos.* CEUR.

Hasnain, A., Zainab, S. S., Zehra, D., Mehmood, Q., Saleem, M., & Rebholz-Schuhmann, D. (2017b). Federated Query Formulation and Processing through BioFed. In *Extended Semantic Web Conference (ESWC).* CEUR.

Hassan, H., Hassan, A., & Emam, O. (2006). Unsupervised information extraction approach using graph mutual reinforcement. *Proceedings of the 2006 Conference on Empirical Methods in Natural Language Processing (EMNLP'06)*, 501-508. 10.3115/1610075.1610144

Hassanzadeh, O., & Consens, M. (2009). Linked movie data base. *Proceedings of the 2nd Workshop on Linked Data on the Web (LDOW2009).*

Hastings, J. T. (2008). Automated conflation of digital gazetteer data. *International Journal of Geographical Information Science, 22*(10), 1109–1127. doi:10.1080/13658810701851453

Hazman, M., El-Beltagy, S., & Rafea, A. (2011). A survey of Ontology Learning Approaches. *International Journal of Computers and Applications, 22*(8), 36–43. doi:10.5120/2610-3642

Hearst, M. (1992). Automatic Acquisition of Hyponyms from Large Text Corpora. In *Proceedings of the 14th conference on Computational linguistics* (pp. 539-545). ACM. doi:10.3115/992133.992154

Heath, T., & Bizer, C. (2011). *Linked {D}ata: Evolving the {W}eb into a Global Data Space.* Morgan & Claypool.

Heath, T., & Bizer, C. (2011). Linked data: Evolving the web into a global data space. *Synthesis Lectures on the Semantic Web: Theory and Technology, 1*(1), 1-136.

Hellmann, S., Lehmann, J., Auer, S., & Brümmer, M. (2013). Integrating NLP using Linked Data. In *Proceedings of 12th International Semantic Web Conference (ISWC)* (pp. 98–113). Springer. Retrieved from http://persistence.uni-leipzig.org/nlp2rdf/

Hellmann, S., Lehmann, J., & Auer, S. (2009). Learning of {OWL} Class Descriptions on Very Large Knowledge Bases. *International Journal on Semantic Web and Information Systems, 5*(2), 25–48. doi:10.4018/jswis.2009040102

Hendrickx, I., & Bosma, W. (2008). Using coreference links and sentence compression in graph-based summarization. *Proceedings of the Text Analysis Conference (TAC)*.

Heyer, G., Läuter, M., Quasthoff, U., Wittig, T., & Wolff, C. (2001). Learning Relations Using Collocations. In A. Maedche, S. Staab, C. Nedellec & E. H. Hovy (Ed.), *Workshop on Ontology Learning*. CEUR-WS.org.

HINA. (2010). Keyphrase Extraction Evaluation Dataset for Croatian (kex.hr) [Data set]. University of Zagreb. Available from Takelab Website: http://takelab.fer.hr/data/kexhr/

Hodges, W. (2001). Classical logic I: first-order logic. *The Blackwell guide to philosophical logic*, 9-32.

Hoffart, J., Suchanek, F. M., Berberich, K., & Weikum, G. (2013). YAGO2: A spatially and temporally enhanced knowledge base from Wikipedia. *Artificial Intelligence, 194*, 28–61. doi:10.1016/j.artint.2012.06.001

Hoffmann, R., Zhang, C., Ling, X., Zettlemoyer, L. S., & Weld, D. S. (2011). Knowledge-based weak supervision for information extraction of overlapping relations. *Proceedings of the 49th Annual Meeting of the Association for Computational Linguistics: Human Language Technologies, 1*, 541-550.

Hogan, A., Harth, A., Passant, A., Decker, S., & Polleres, A. (2010). Weaving the pedantic web. *Linked Data on the Web Workshop*.

Hogan, A., Harth, A., Umbrich, J., Kinsella, S., Polleres, A., & Decker, S. (2011). Searching and browsing linked data with swse: The semantic web search engine. *Web Semantics: Science, Services, and Agents on the World Wide Web, 9*(4), 365–401. doi:10.1016/j.websem.2011.06.004

Hogan, A., Umbrich, J., Harth, A., Cyganiak, R., Polleres, A., & Decker, S. (2012). An empirical survey of linked data conformance. *Web Semantics: Science, Services, and Agents on the World Wide Web, 14*, 14–44. doi:10.1016/j.websem.2012.02.001

Holst, T., & Höfig, E. (2013). Investigating the Relevance of {Linked Open Data Sets} with {SPARQL} Queries. COMPSAC Workshops, 230–235.

Hopkinson, I., Maude, S., & Rospocher, M. (2014). A simple API to the KnowledgeStore. In *Proceedings of the ISWC Developers Workshop 2014, co-located with the 13th International Semantic Web Conference (ISWC'2014)* (Vol. 1268, pp. 7–12). CEUR-WS.org.

Horridge, M., & Bechhofer, S. (2011). The OWL API: A Java API for OWL Ontologies. *Semantic Web, 2*(1), 11–21.

Horrocks, I. (2008, December). Ontologies and the semantic web. *Communications of the ACM, 51*(12), 58–67. doi:10.1145/1409360.1409377

Horrocks, I., & Patel-Schneider, P. (1999). Optimizing description logic subsumption. *Journal of Logic and Computation, 9*(3), 267–293. doi:10.1093/logcom/9.3.267

Hotho, A., Jäschke, R., & Lerman, K. (2017). Mining social semantics on the social web. *Semantic Web, 8*(5), 623–624. doi:10.3233/SW-170272

Hu, W., Chen, J., Zhang, H., & Qu, Y. (2012). Learning Complex Mappings between Ontologies. *The Semantic Web: Joint International Semantic Technology Conference, JIST 2011*, (pp. 350–357). Berlin: Springer Berlin Heidelberg.

Huang, X., & Robertson, S. E. (2001). Comparisons of Probabilistic Compound Unit Weighting Methods. *Proc. of the ICDM'01 Workshop on Text Mining*.

Husaini, M. a., Ko, A., Tapucu, D., & Saygın, Y. (2012). *Ontology Supported Policy Modeling in Opinion Mining Process*. Paper presented at the On the Move to Meaningful Internet Systems: OTM 2012 Workshops. doi:10.1007/978-3-642-33618-8_34

Hu, W., Qu, Y., & Cheng, G. (2008). Matching large ontologies: A divide-and-conquer approach. *Data & Knowledge Engineering, 67*(1), 140–160. doi:10.1016/j.datak.2008.06.003

Huynh, D., & Mazzocchi, S. (2011). *Google refine*. Academic Press.

Internet Live Stats. (n.d.) Twitter Statistics. *Internet Live Stats*. Retrieved from: http:// www.internetlivestats.com/twitter-statistics

ISACA. (2008). *The Val IT Framework 2.0*. ISACA.

ISACA. (2009). *The Risk It Framework 2009*. ISACA.

ISACA. (2011). *Global Status Report on the Governance of Enterprise IT (Geit) - 2011*. ISACA.

ISACA. (2012). *COBIT 5 2012*. ISACA.

ISACA. (2015). CISA Review Manual 2015. ISACA, CISA.

ISACA. (2016a). *Governance, Risk and Compliance* (Vol. 6). ISACA Journal.

ISACA. (2016b). *Getting Started With GEIT: A Primer for Implementing Governance of Enterprise IT*. ISACA.

Isele, R., Umbrich, J., Bizer, C., & Harth, A. (2010). {LDspider}: An Open-source Crawling Framework for the {Web of Linked Data}. In *International Semantic Web Conference (ISWC) Posters & Demos*. CEUR.

Iversen, G. H. (2014). *U.S. Patent No. 8,806,322*. Washington, DC: U.S. Patent and Trademark Office.

Janik, M., & Kochut, K. J. (2008). *Wikipedia in action: Ontological knowledge in text categorization*. Paper presented at the Semantic Computing, 2008 IEEE International Conference on. doi:10.1109/ICSC.2008.53

Janowicz, K., Raubal, M., & Kuhn, W. (2011). The semantics of similarity in geographic information retrieval. *Journal of Spatial Information Science, 2011*(2), 29-57.

Janowicz, K., Schade, S., Bröring, A., Keßler, C., Maué, P., & Stasch, C. (2010). Semantic enablement for spatial data infrastructures. *Transactions in GIS, 14*(2), 111–129. doi:10.1111/j.1467-9671.2010.01186.x

Janowicz, K., Scheider, S., Pehle, T., & Hart, G. (2012). Geospatial semantics and linked spatiotemporal data–Past, present, and future. *Semantic Web, 3*(4), 321–332.

Janssen, F., Fallahi, F., Noessner, J., & Paulheim, H. (2012). Towards Rule Learning Approaches to Instance-based Ontology Matching. In J. Völker, H. Paulheim, J. Lehmann, & M. Niepert (Eds.), KNOW@LOD (Vol. 868, pp. 13–18). CEUR-WS.org.

Jentzsch, A., Cyganiak, R., & Bizer, C. (2011, September). State of the {LOD Cloud}.

Jianfeng, G., Jian-Yun, N., Endong, X., Jiang, Z., & Ming, H. (2001). *Improving Query Translation for Cross-Language Information Retrieval using Statistical Models.* Paper presented at SIGIR'01, New Orleans, LA.

Ji, Q., Haase, P., Qi, G., Hitzler, P., & Stadtmüller, S. (2009). RaDON—repair and diagnosis in ontology networks. In *The semantic web: research and applications* (pp. 863–867). Springer Berlin Heidelberg. doi:10.1007/978-3-642-02121-3_71

Jones, S., & Paynter, G. W. (2002). Automatic extraction of document keyphrases for use in digital libraries: Evaluation and applications. *Journal of the American Society for Information Science and Technology, 53*(8), 653–677. doi:10.1002/asi.10068

Jonnalagadda, S., Del Fiol, G., Medlin, R. R., Weir, C., Fiszman, M., Mostafa, J., & Liu, H. (2012). Automatically extracting sentences from Medline citations to support clinicians' information needs. In *IEEE 2nd International Conference on Healthcare Informatics, Imaging and Systems Biology, HISB 2012,* (pp. 72–72). IEEE Computer Society.

Joorabchi, A., & Mahdi, A. E. (2013). Automatic keyphrase annotation of scientific documents using Wikipedia and genetic algorithms. *Journal of Information Science, 39*(3), 410–426. doi:10.1177/0165551512472138

Junior, A. C., Walshe, B., & O'Sullivan, D. (2015). Enhanced Faceted Browsing of a WW1 Dataset Through Ontology Alignment. In *Proceedings of the 17th International Conference on Information Integration and Web-based Applications & Services* (p. 48:1--48:5). New York: ACM. doi:10.1145/2837185.2837259

Kaleta, Z. (2014). Semantic text indexing. *Journal of Computer Science, 15*(1), 19-34. Retrieved from http://journals.bg.agh.edu.pl/COMPUTER/2014.15.1/csci.2014.15.1.19.pdf

Kambhatla, N. (2004). Combining lexical, syntactic, and semantic features with maximum entropy models for extracting relations. *Proceedings of the ACL 2004 on Interactive poster and demonstration sessions (ACL demo'04).* 10.3115/1219044.1219066

Kamp, H., & Reyle, U. (1993). *From Discourse to Logic.* Dordrecht, The Netherlands: Kluwer Academic Publishers.

Kastrati, Z., Imran, A. S., & Yayilgan, S. (2014). Building Domain Ontologies for Hyperlinked Multimedia Pedagogical Platforms. In C. Stephanidis (Ed.), *HCII 2014 Posters, Part II, CCIS 435* (pp. 95–100). Springer International Publishing. doi:10.1007/978-3-319-07854-0_17

Kastrati, Z., Imran, A. S., Yayilgan, S., & Dalipi, F. (2015). Analysis of Online Social Networks Posts to Investigate Suspects Using SEMCON. In *Proceedings of 17th International Conference on Human-Computer Interaction.* Springer International Publishing. doi:10.1007/978-3-319-20367-6_16

Katz, B., Borchardt, G., Felshin, S., Shen, Y., & Zaccak, G. (2007). Answering English Questions using Foreign-Language, Semi-Structured Sources. *First IEEE International Conference on Semantic Computing (ICSC 2007),* 439-445. doi:10.1109/ICSC.2007.59

Katz, B., Felshin, S., Yuret, D., Ibrahim, A., Lin, J. J., Marton, G., & Temelkuran, B. et al. (2002a). Omnibase: Uniform Access to Heterogeneous Data for Question Answering. *6th International Conference on Applications of Natural Language to Information Systems* (pp. 230-234). London, UK: Springer-Verlag. doi:10.1007/3-540-36271-1_23

Katz, B., Lin, J. J., & Felshin, S. (2002b). The START Multimedia Information System: Current Technology and Future Directions. *MIS 2002, International Workshop on Multimedia Information Systems* (pp. 117-123). Tempe, AZ: Arizona State University.

Kaufmann, E., Bernstein, A., & Zumstein, R. (2006). Querix: A Natural Language Interface to Query Ontologies Based on Clarification Dialogs. In *5th International Semantic Web Conference (ISWC 2006)* (pp. 980-981). Athens, GA: Springer. doi:10.1007/11926078_78

Kazakov, Y., & Klinov, P. (2013). Experimenting with ELK Reasoner on Android. *Proceedings of 2nd International Workshop on OWL Reasoner Evaluation (ORE)*, 68–74.

Kazakov, Y. (2009). Consequence-driven reasoning for Horn SHIQ ontologies. *International Joint Conference on Artificial Intelligence*, 9, 2040–2045.

Kazakov, Y., Krötzsch, M., & Simancík, F. (2014). The Incredible ELK. *Journal of Automated Reasoning, 53*(1), 1–61. doi:10.1007/s10817-013-9296-3

Keith Alexander, M., Cyganiak, R., Hausenblas, M., & Zhao, J. (2011). *Describing linked datasets with the void vocabulary*. Academic Press.

Khan, A., & Salim, N. (2014). *A Review on Abstractive Summarization Methods*. Faculty of Computing, Universiti Teknologi Malaysia.

Khatchadourian, S., & Consens, M. P. (2010). ExpLOD: Summary-Based Exploration of Interlinking and {RDF} Usage in the {Linked Open Data Cloud}. In *Extended Semantic Web Conference (ESWC)* (pp. 272–287). Springer. doi:10.1007/978-3-642-13489-0_19

Khondoker, M. R., & Mueller, P. (2010). *Comparing ontology development tools based on an online survey*. Academic Press.

Kim, S. N., Medelyan, O., Kan, M.-Y., & Baldwin, T. (2010). SemEval-2010 task 5: Automatic keyphrase extraction from scientific articles. *SemEval '10 Proceedings of the 5th Int. Workshop on Semantic Evaluation*, 21-26.

Kim, T., Park, I., Hyun, S., & Lee, D. (2010). MiRE4OWL: Mobile Rule Engine for OWL. *Proceedings of the 34th IEEE Annual Computer Software and Applications Conference Workshops (CompSACW)*, 317–322.

Kinsella, S., Bojars, U., Harth, A., Breslin, J. G., & Decker, S. (2008). An Interactive Map of {Semantic Web} Ontology Usage. In *International Conference on Information Visualisation* (pp. 179–184). doi:10.1109/IV.2008.60

Kleemann, T., & Sinner, A. (2006). User Profiles and Matchmaking on Mobile Phones. In *Proceedings of 16th International Conference on Applications of Declarative Programming and Knowledge Management (INAP 2005)* (pp. 135-147). Springer. doi:10.1007/11963578_11

Klein, D., & Manning, C. D. (2003). Accurate unlexicalized parsing. *41st Annual Meeting on Association for Computational Linguistics* (vol. 1, pp. 423-430). Sapporo, Japan: Association for Computational Linguistics. doi:10.3115/1075096.1075150

Knap, T., & Michelfeit, J. (2012). *Linked Data Aggregation Algorithm: Increasing Completeness and Consistency of Data*. Charles University.

Knap, T., Michelfeit, J., Daniel, J., Jerman, P., Rychnovský, D., Soukup, T., & Nečaský, M. (2012). ODCleanStore: a framework for managing and providing integrated linked data on the web. In *Web Information Systems Engineering-WISE* (pp. 815–816). Berlin: Springer. doi:10.1007/978-3-642-35063-4_74

Knight, S. A., & Burn, J. M. (2005). Developing a framework for assessing information quality on the World Wide Web. *Informing Science: International Journal of an Emerging Transdiscipline, 8*(5), 159–172.

Knoblock, C. A., Szekely, P. A., Ambite, J. L., Gupta, S., Goel, A., Muslea, M., ... & Mallick, P. (2011). Interactively Mapping Data Sources into the Semantic Web. *LISC, 783*.

Knoblock, C. A., Szekely, P., Ambite, J. L., Goel, A., Gupta, S., Lerman, K., . . . Mallick, P. (2012). Semi-automatically mapping structured sources into the semantic web. In The Semantic Web: Research and Applications (pp. 375-390). Springer Berlin Heidelberg. doi:10.1007/978-3-642-30284-8_32

Kő, A. (Ed.). (2012). eParticipation and Policy-making Support in Ubipol Approach. Academic Press.

Kő, A., Kovács, B., & Gábor, A. (2011). Agile Knowledge-Based E-Government Supported By SAKE System. *Journal of Cases on Information Technology, 13*(3), 1–20. doi:10.4018/jcit.2011070101

Koch, F., Meyer, J.-J. C., Dignum, F., & Rahwan, I. (2006). Programming deliberative agents for mobile services: the 3APL-M platform. In Programming multi-agent systems (pp. 222–235). Springer.

Kontokostas, D., Westphal, P., Auer, S., Hellmann, S., Lehmann, J., Cornelissen, R., & Zaveri, A. (2014, April). Test-driven evaluation of linked data quality. In *Proceedings of the 23rd international conference on World Wide Web* (pp. 747-758). ACM.

Krifka, M. (2011). Questions. In K. v. Heusinger, C. Maienborn, & P. Portner (Eds.), Semantics: An international hand-book of Natural Language Meaning (pp. 1742-1785). Berlin: Mouton de Gruyter.

Krumm, J., & Horvitz, E. (2015). *Eyewitness: Identifying Local Events via Space-Time Signals in Twitter Feeds*. Academic Press.

Kruschwitz, U. (2001). Exploiting Structure for Intelligent Web Search. In *Proceedings of the 34th International Conference on System Sciences* (pp. 1-9). IEEE. doi:10.1109/HICSS.2001.926474

Kuhn, W. (2002). Modeling the semantics of geographic categories through conceptual integration. In *Geographic Information Science* (pp. 108–118). Springer Berlin Heidelberg. doi:10.1007/3-540-45799-2_8

Kurz, T., Güntner, G., Damjanovic, V., Schaffert, S., & Fernandez, M. (2014). Semantic enhancement for media asset management systems. *Multimedia Tools and Applications, 70*(2), 949–975. doi:10.1007/s11042-012-1197-7

Lahiri, S., Choudhury, S. R., & Caragea, C. (2014). *Keyword and Keyphrase Extraction Using Centrality Measures on Collocation Networks*. Retrieved from http://arxiv.org/pdf/1401.6571.pdf

Lahiri, S., Mihalcea, R., & Lai, P.-H. (2016). Keyword extraction from emails. *Natural Language Engineering, 23*(2), 295-317. https://doi.org/10.1017/S1351324916000231

Lahiri, S., Mihalcea, R., & Lai, P. (2017). Keyword extraction from emails. *Natural Language Engineering, 23*(2), 295–317. doi:10.1017/S1351324916000231

Lambrix, P., & Tan, H. (2006). SAMBO-A System for Aligning and Merging Biomedical Ontologies. *Web Semantics: Science, Services, and Agents on the World Wide Web, 4*(3), 196–206. doi:10.1016/j.websem.2006.05.003

Landauer, T. K., Foltz, P. W., & Laham, D. (1998). Introduction to Latent Semantic Analysis. *Discourse Processes, 25*(2-3), 259–284. doi:10.1080/01638539809545028

Langegger, A., & Wöß, W. (2009). RDFStats -- An Extensible RDF Statistics Generator and Library. DEXA Workshops, 79–83.

Lappin, S., & Leass, H. J. (1994). An algorithm for pronominal anaphora resolution. *Computational Linguistics, 20*(4), 535–561.

Lawley, M. J., & Bousquet, C. (2010). Fast classification in Protégé: Snorocket as an OWL 2 EL reasoner. *Proceedings of 6th Australasian Ontology Workshop (IAOA'10)*, 45-49.

Lebo, T., Sahoo, S., & McGuinness, D. (2013, April). *PROV-O: The PROV Ontology*. Academic Press.

Lee, C., & Lee, G. G. (2006). Information gain and divergence-based feature selection for machine learning-based text categorization. *Information Processing & Management, 42*(1), 155–165. doi:10.1016/j.ipm.2004.08.006

Lee, C.-S., Kao, Y.-F., Kuo, Y.-H., & Wang, M.-H. (2007). Automated ontology construction for unstructured text documents. *Data & Knowledge Engineering*, *60*(3), 547–566. doi:10.1016/j.datak.2006.04.001

Lee, R., & Sumiya, K. (2010). Measuring geographical regularities of crowd behaviors for Twitter-based geo-social event detection. In *Proceedings of the 2nd ACM SIGSPATIAL international workshop on location based social networks* (pp. 1-10). ACM. doi:10.1145/1867699.1867701

Lee, S., Farag, M., Kanan, T., & Fox, E. A. (2015, June). Read between the lines: A Machine Learning Approach for Disambiguating the Geo-location of Tweets. In *Proceedings of the 15th ACM/IEEE-CS Joint Conference on Digital Libraries* (pp. 273-274). ACM. doi:10.1145/2756406.2756971

Lee, S., & Kim, H. (2008). News Keyword Extraction for Topic Tracking. In *Proceedings of the 2008 4th Int. Conf. on Networked Computing and Advanced Information Management* (vol. 2, pp. 554–559). Washington, DC: IEEE Computer Society. doi:10.1109/NCM.2008.199

Lehmann, J., Isele, R., Jakob, M., Jentzsch, A., Kontokostas, D., Mendes, P. N., . . . Bizer, C. (2015). DBpedia - A large-scale, multilingual knowledge base extracted from Wikipedia. *Semantic Web, 6*(2), 167–195. Retrieved from http://dbpedia.org/

Lehmann, J. (2009). DL-Learner: Learning Concepts in Description Logics. *Journal of Machine Learning Research*, *10*, 2639–2642.

Lehmann, J., Auer, S., Bühmann, L., & Tramp, S. (2011). Class expression learning for ontology engineering. *Journal of Web Semantics*, *9*(1), 71–81. doi:10.1016/j.websem.2011.01.001

Lenzerini, M. (2002, June). Data integration: A theoretical perspective. In *Proceedings of the twenty-first ACM SIGMOD-SIGACT-SIGART symposium on Principles of database systems* (pp. 233-246). ACM. doi:10.1145/543613.543644

Li, B., & Fonseca, F. (2006). TDD: A comprehensive model for qualitative spatial similarity assessment. *Spatial Cognition and Computation, 6*(1), 31–62. doi:10.1207/s15427633scc0601_2

LIBSVM. (2016). LIBSVM – A library for support vector machines. *LIBVSM*. Retrieved from: https://www.csie.ntu.edu.tw/~cjlin/libsvm/

Li, H., Tian, Y., Ye, B., & Cai, Q. (2010). Comparison of Current Semantic Similarity Methods in Wordnet. In *Proceedings of International Conference on Computer Application and System Modeling* (vol. 9, pp.408-411). IEEE.

Li, J., Tang, J., Li, Y., & Luo, Q. (2009). RiMOM: A Dynamic Multistrategy Ontology Alignment Framework. *IEEE Transactions on Knowledge and Data Engineering*, *21*(8), 1218–1232. doi:10.1109/TKDE.2008.202

Li, L., & Horrocks, I. (2004). A software framework for matchmaking based on Ssemantic Wweb technology. *International Journal of Electronic Commerce*, *8*(4), 39–60.

Lima, D., Mendonça, A., Salgado, A. C., & Souza, D. (2011). Building Geospatial Ontologies From Geographic Database Schemas. In *Peer Data Management Systems* (pp. 1–12). GeoInfo.

Lin, C. Y. (2004). ROUGE: A Package for Automatic Evaluation of Summaries. *Proceedings of Workshop on Text Summarization Branches Out, Post-Conference Workshop of ACL 2004*.

List of Wikipedias. (n.d.). Retrieved November 15, 2015 and July 4, 2017 from https://meta.wikimedia.org/wiki/List_of_Wikipedias

Liu, H., & Hu, F. (2008). What role does syntax play in a language network? *Europhysics Letters*, *83*(1), 18002. doi:10.1209/0295-5075/83/18002

Liu, J., He, Y.-L., Lim, E., & Wang, X.-Z. (2013). A New Method for Knowledge and Information Management Domain Ontology Graph Model. *IEEE Transactions on Systems, Man, and Cybernetics Systems*, *43*(1), 115–127.

Liu, Q. (2013). U–commerce research: A literature review and classification. *International Journal of Ad Hoc and Ubiquitous Computing*, *12*(3), 177–187. doi:10.1504/IJAHUC.2013.052414

Liu, W., Chung, B. C., Wang, R., Ng, J., & Morlet, N. (2015). A genetic algorithm enabled ensemble for unsupervised medical term extraction from clinical letters. *Health Information Science and Systems*, *3*(5), 1–14. doi:10.1186/s13755-015-0013-y PMID:26664724

Liu, W., Liu, J., Duan, H., Hu, W., & Wei, B. (2017). *Exploiting Source-Object Networks to Resolve Object Conflicts in Linked Data*. Springer. doi:10.1007/978-3-319-58068-5_4

LODsyndesis. (n.d.). *LODsyndesis: Connectivity of LOD datasets*. Retrieved from: http://www.ics.forth.gr/isl/LODsyndesis

López, M. F., Pérez, A. G., & Amaya, M. D. R. (2000). *Ontology's crossed life cycles. In Knowledge Engineering and Knowledge Management Methods, Models, and Tools* (pp. 65–79). Springer. doi:10.1007/3-540-39967-4_6

Lopez, V., Fernández, M., Motta, E., & Stieler, N. (2012). PowerAqua: Supporting users in querying and exploring the Semantic Web. *Semantic Web*, *3*, 249–265. doi:10.3233/SW-2011-0030

Lopez, V., Pasin, M., & Motta, E. (2005). AquaLog: An Ontology-Portable Question Answering System. *Lecture Notes in Computer Science*, *3532*, 546–562. doi:10.1007/11431053_37

Lorey, J. (2014). Identifying and determining {SPARQL} endpoint characteristics. *IJWIS*, *10*(3), 226–244. 10.1108/IJWIS-03-2014-0007

Ludwig, P., Thiel, M., & Nürnberger, A. (2017). Unsupervised Extraction of Conceptual Keyphrases from Abstracts. *Semantic Keyword-Based Search on Structured Data Sources: COST Action IC1302 Second International KEYSTONE Conference*, (pp. 37-48). Cham: Springer International Publishing. doi:10.1007/978-3-319-53640-8_4

Luong, H., Gauch, S., & Wang, Q. (2012). *Ontology Learning Using Word Net Lexical Expansion and Text Mining*. Academic Press.

Lynn, H. M., Choi, C., & Kim, P. (2017). An improved method of automatic text summarization for web contents using lexical chain with semantic-related terms. *Soft Computing*. doi:10.1007/s00500-017-2612-9

Madaan, A., Mittal, A., Ramakrishnan, G., & Sarawagi, S. (2016). Numerical relation extraction with minimal supervision. *Proceedings of the Thirtieth AAAI Conference on Artificial Intelligence (AAAI'16)*, 2764-2771.

Maedche, A., Maedche, E., & Staab, S. (2000). The TEXT-TO-ONTO Ontology Learning Environment. In B. Ganter & G.W. Mineau (Eds.), LNAI: Vol. 1867. Conceptual Structures: Logical, Linguistic, and Computational Issues. Springer-Verlag Heidelberg.

Maedche, A., Pekar, V., & Staab, S. (2003). Ontology Learning Part One - on Discovering Taxonomic Relations from the Web. In N. Zhong, J. Liu, & Y. Yao (Eds.), *Web Intelligence* (pp. 301–320). Springer Berlin Heidelberg. doi:10.1007/978-3-662-05320-1_14

Maisonnasse, L., Gaussier, E., & Chevallet, J. P. (2009). Model Fusion Conceptual Language Modeling. *ECIR*, *2009*, 240–250.

Mäkelä, E. (2014). Aether - Generating and Viewing Extended {VoID} Statistical Descriptions of {RDF} Datasets. In *European Semantic Web Conference ({ESWC})* (pp. 429–433). Springer.

Malik, Z., Rezgui, A., Medjahed, B., Ouzzani, M., & Krishna Sinha, A. (2010). Semantic integration in geosciences. *International Journal of Semantic Computing*, *4*(03), 301–330. doi:10.1142/S1793351X10001036

Mallak, I. (2011). *De nouveaux facteurs pour l'exploitation de la sémantique d'un texte en recherche d'information* (PhD thesis). Université Toulouse.

Mallat, S., Zouaghi, A., Hkiri, E., & And Zrigui, M. (2013). Method of lexical enrichment in information retrieval system in Arabic. International Journal of Information Retrieval Research, 3(4), 35-51. doi:10.4018/ijirr.2013100103

Mallat, S., Ben Mohamed, M. A., Hkiri, E., Zouaghi, A., & And Zrigui, M. (2014). Semantic and Contextual Knowledge Representation for Lexical Disambiguation: Case of Arabic-French Query Translation. *Journal of Computing and Information Technology*, *22*(3), 191–215. doi:10.2498/cit.1002234

Mani, I., & Maybury, T. M. (1999). *Advances in Automatic Text Summarization*. MIT Press Cambridge.

Mann, W., & Thompson, S. (1988). Rhetorical structure theory. Toward a functional theory of text organization. *Text*, *8*(3), 243–281. doi:10.1515/text.1.1988.8.3.243

Manzano-Macho, D., Gómez-Pérez, A., & Borrajo, D. (2008). Unsupervised and Domain Independent Ontology Learning: Combining Heterogeneous Sources of Evidence. *Proceedings of sixth International Conference on Language Resources and Evaluation*, 1633-1640.

Margan, D., Martinčić-Ipšić, S., & Meštrović, A. (2013). Preliminary report on the structure of Croatian linguistic co-occurrence networks. In *5th International Conference on Information Technologies and Information Society* (pp. 89-96). Faculty of Information Studies in Novo mesto.

Margan, D., Martinčić-Ipšić, S., & Meštrović, A. (2014a). Network Diferences Between Normal and Shuffled Texts: Case of Croatian. *Studies in Computational Intelligence, Complex Networks V: Proceedings of the 5th Workshop on Complex Networks CompleNet 2014* (Vol. 549, pp. 275-283). Springer International Publishing. doi:10.1007/978-3-319-05401-8_26

Margan, D., & Meštrović, A. (2015). LaNCoA: A Python Toolkit for Language Networks Construction and Analysis. In *38th International Convention on Information and Communication Technology, Electronics and Microelectronics (MIPRO)* (pp. 1628-1633). Opatija, Croatia: IEEE. doi:10.1109/MIPRO.2015.7160532

Margan, D., Meštrović, A., & Martinčić-Ipšić, S. (2014b). Complex Networks Measures for Differentiation between Normal and Shuffled Croatian Texts. In *37th International Convention on Information and Communication Technology, Electronics and Microelectronics (MIPRO)* (pp. 1598-1602). Opatija, Croatia: IEEE. doi:10.1109/MIPRO.2014.6859820

Mark, W. (2006). *Geonames*. Retrieved May 21, 2015, from www.geonames.org

Marketakis, Y., Minadakis, N., Kondylakis, H., Konsolaki, K., Samaritakis, G., Theodoridou, M., & Doerr, M. et al. (2016). X3ML Mapping Framework for Information Integration in Cultural Heritage and beyond. *International Journal on Digital Libraries*, 1–19.

Martinčić-Ipšić, S., Močibob, E., & Perc, M. (2017, June). Link Prediction on Twitter. *Plos ONE*.

Martinčić-Ipšić, S., Miličić, T., & Meštrović, A. (2016). Text Type Differentiation Based on the Structural Properties of Language Networks. In G. Dregvaite & R. Damasevicius (Eds.), *Information and Software Technologies. ICIST 2016. Communications in Computer and Information Science* (Vol. 639, pp. 536–548). Cham: Springer International Publishing; doi:10.1007/978-3-319-46254-7_43

Martinez-Romo, J., Araujo, L., & Duque Fernandez, A. (2016). SemGraph: Extracting Keyphrases Following a Novel Semantic Graph-Based Approach. *Journal of the Association for Information Science and Technology*, *67*(1), 71–82. doi:10.1002/asi.23365

Martins, C. B., & Rino, L. H. M. (2002). Revisiting UNLSumm Improvement through a case study. *Workshop on Multilingual Information Access and Natural Language Processing, IBERAMIA'2002.*

Masucci, A. P., & Rodgers, G. J. (2006). Network properties of written human language. *Physical Review E: Statistical, Nonlinear, and Soft Matter Physics*, 74(2), 026102. doi:10.1103/PhysRevE.74.026102 PMID:17025498

Masucci, A. P., & Rodgers, G. J. (2009). Differences between normal and shuffled texts: Structural properties of weighted networks. *Advances in Complex Systems*, 12(01), 113–129. doi:10.1142/S0219525909002039

Matas, P. M. (2012). *SMART (Supporting dynamic MAtching for Regional developmenT) Leonardo da Vinci Transfer of Innovation Project.* European Commission.

Matentzoglu, N., Leo, J., Hudhra, V., Sattler, U., & Parsia, B. (2015). A Survey of Current, Stand-alone OWL Reasoners. *Proceedings of the 4th OWL Reasoner Evaluation (ORE) Workshop*, 68-79.

Matsuo, Y., Ohsawa, Y., & Ishizuka, M. (2001). *KeyWorld: Extracting keywords from document s small world. In Discovery Science LNAI 2226* (pp. 271–281). Springer Berlin Heidelberg. doi:10.1007/3-540-45650-3_24

Mbipom, B., Craw, S., & Massie, S. (2016). Harnessing background knowledge for e-learning recommendation. In Research and development in intelligent systems XXXIII: incorporating applications and innovations in intelligent systems XXIV. Cham: Springer. doi:10.1007/978-3-319-47175-4_1

McBride, B. (2002). Jena: A Semantic Web toolkit. *IEEE Internet Computing*, 6(6), 55–59. doi:10.1109/MIC.2002.1067737

McCarthy, D., Koeling, R., Weeds, J., & Carroll, J. (2004). Finding Predominant Word Senses in Untagged Text. In *Proceedings of the 42nd Annual Meeting on Association for Computational Linguistics*. Association for Computational Linguistics. doi:10.3115/1218955.1218991

Mccrae, J., & Collier, N. (2008). Synonym set extraction from the biomedical literature by lexical pattern discovery. *BMC Bioinformatics*, 9(1), 159. doi:10.1186/1471-2105-9-159 PMID:18366721

McGuinness, D. (2000). Conceptual Modeling for Distributed Ontology Environments. In B. Ganter & G. W. Mineau (Eds.), *ICCS 2000, LNAI* (Vol. 1867). Springer-Verlag Berlin Heidelberg.

McGuinness, D. L. (2004). Question Answering on the Semantic Web. *IEEE Intelligent Systems*, 19(1), 82–85. doi:10.1109/MIS.2004.1265890

Medelyan, O. (2009a). *Human-competitive automatic topic indexing* (Doctoral dissertation). The University of Waikato, Hamilton, New Zealand.

Medelyan, O. (2009b). WIKI-20 dataset [Data set]. University of Waikato. Available from Maui Website: http://maui-indexer.googlecode.com/files/wiki20.tar.gz

Medelyan, O., Witten, I. H., & Milne, D. (2008). Topic indexing with Wikipedia. *Proceedings of Wikipedia and AI workshop at the AAAI-2008 Conference*, 19-24.

Mehdi, M., Iqbal, A., Hogan, A., Hasnain, A., Khan, Y., Decker, S., & Sahay, R. (2014). Discovering domain-specific public {SPARQL} endpoints: a life-sciences use-case. *International Database Engineering & Applications Symposium (IDEAS)*, 39–45.

Meij, E., Weerkamp, W., & de Rijke, M. (2012). Adding semantics to microblog posts. In *Proceedings of the fifth ACM international conference on Web search and data mining* (pp. 563-572). ACM. doi:10.1145/2124295.2124364

Melo, D., Rodrigues, I. P., & Nogueira, V. B. (2012a). Puzzle Out the Semantic Web Search. International Journal of Computational Linguistics and Applications, 3, 91-106.

Melo, D., Rodrigues, I. P., & Nogueira, V. B. (2012b). Work Out the Semantic Web Search: The Cooperative Way. *Advances in Artificial Intelligence, 2012*, 867831:1-867831:9. doi:10.1155/2012/867831

Mendes, P. N., Mühleisen, H., & Bizer, C. (2012, March). Sieve: linked data quality assessment and fusion. In *Proceedings of the 2012 Joint EDBT/ICDT Workshops* (pp. 116-123). ACM. doi:10.1145/2320765.2320803

Meyer, C. M., & Gurevych, I. (2012). OntoWiktionary: Constructing an Ontology from the. *Semi-Automatic Ontology Development: Processes and Resources: Processes and Resources*, 131.

Michael Cowan, H. C., English, S., & Hammond, S. (2014). *State of Internal Audit Survey 2014 –Adapting to Complex Challenges?* Retrieved from http://accelus.thomsonreuters.com/sites/default/files/GRC01260.pdf

Michelfeit, J., & Knap, T. (2012). Linked Data Fusion in ODCleanStore★. *11th International Semantic Web Conference ISWC*, 45.

Miettinen, K. (1999). *Non-linear Multiobjective Optimization*. Kluwer Academic Publishers.

Mihalcea, R., & Tarau, P. (2004). TextRank: Bringing order into texts. In *Proceedings of Empirical Methods in Natural Language Processing –EMNLP 2004* (pp. 404–411). Barcelona, Spain: ACL.

Mihalcea, R., & Tarau, P. (2004). TextRank: Bringing Order into Texts. *Proceedings of the Conference on Empirical Methods in Natural Language Processing (EMNLP 2004)*.

Mihindukulasooriya, N., Poveda-Villalón, M., García-Castro, R., & Gómez-Pérez, A. (2015). Loupe - An Online Tool for Inspecting Datasets in the Linked Data Cloud. In *Proceedings of the ISWC 2015 Posters & Demonstrations Track co-located with the 14th International Semantic Web Conference (ISWC-2015)*. CEUR-WS.org. 213

Mihindukulasooriya, N., Poveda-Villalón, M., García-Castro, R., & Gómez-Pérez, A. (2015). Loupe -- An Online Tool for Inspecting Datasets in the {Linked Data} Cloud. In *International Semantic Web Conference (ISWC) Posters & Demos*. CEUR.

Mijić, J., Dalbelo-Bašić, B., & Šnajder, J. (2010). Robust Keyphrase Extraction for a Large-Scale Croatian News Production System. In *Proceedings of the 7th International Conference on Formal Approaches to South Slavic and Balkan Languages* (pp. 59-66). Zagreb, Croatia: Croatian Language Technologies Society.

Miller, G. A. (1995). WordNet: A Lexical Database for English. *Communications of the ACM, 38*(11), 39–41. doi:10.1145/219717.219748

Minard, A.-L., Speranza, M., Urizar, R., Altuna, B., van Erp, M., Schoen, A., & van Son, C. (2016). MEANTIME, the NewsReader Multilingual Event and Time Corpus. In N. Calzolari, K. Choukri, T. Declerck, S. Goggi, M. Grobelnik, B. Maegaard, & S. Piperidis (Eds.), *LREC: European Language Resources Association*. ELRA.

Minker, J. (1998). An overview of cooperative answering in databases. In T. Andreasen, H. Christiansen, & H. Larsen (Eds.), Lecture Notes in Computer Science: Vol. 1495. Flexible Query Answering Systems (pp. 282-285). Springer Berlin Heidelberg. doi:10.1007/BFb0056009

Mintz, M., Bills, S., Snow, R., & Jurafsky, D. (2009). Distant supervision for relation extraction without labeled data. *Proceedings of the Joint Conference of the 47th Annual Meeting of the ACL and the 4th International Joint Conference on Natural Language Processing of the AFNLP, 2*, 1003-1011. 10.3115/1690219.1690287

Miranda, P., Isaias, P., & Costa, C. J. (2014). *From Information Systems to e-Learning 3.0 Systems's Critical Success Factors: A Framework Proposal. In Learning and Collaboration Technologies. Designing and Developing Novel Learning Experiences* (pp. 180–191). Springer.

Missier, P., Belhajjame, K., & Cheney, J. (2013, March). The W3C PROV family of specifications for modelling provenance metadata. In *Proceedings of the 16th International Conference on Extending Database Technology* (pp. 773-776). ACM. doi:10.1145/2452376.2452478

Mocanu, B., Tapu, R., & Tapu, E. (2016). Video retrieval using relevant topics extraction from movie subtitles. In *12th IEEE International Symposium on Electronics and Telecommunications (ISETC)* (pp. 327-330). IEEE. doi:10.1109/ISETC.2016.7781123

Moguillansky, M., Wassermann, R., & Falappa, M. (2010). An argumentation machinery to reason over inconsistent ontologies. *Advances in Artificial Intelligence–IBERAMIA*, *2010*, 100–109.

Mohamed, A., & Sanguthevar, R. (2006). Query-based summarization based on document graphs. *Proceedings of the Document Understanding Conference (DUC'06)*.

Mohamed, M., & Oussalah, M. (2016). An Iterative Graph-Based Generic Single and Multi-Document Summarization Approach Using Semantic Role Labeling and Wikipedia Concepts. *2016 IEEE Second International Conference on Big Data Computing Service and Applications (BigDataService)*, 117-120. doi:10.1109/BigDataService.2016.31

Moldovan, D., Harabagiu, S., Pasca, M., Mihalcea, R., Girju, R., Goodrum, R., & Rus, V. (2000). The structure and performance of an open-domain question answering system. *Proc. of the 38th Annual Meeting on Association for Computational Linguistics*, 563-570. doi:10.3115/1075218.1075289

Morin, E. (1999). *Extraction automatique de terminologie à partir de libellés textuels courts* (Doctoral thesis). Université de Nantes, France.

Moriya, M., & Ryoke, M. (2013). Information Balance between Transmitters and Receivers Based on the Twitter after Great East Japan Earthquake. *International Journal of Knowledge and Systems Science*, *4*(2), 66–76. doi:10.4018/jkss.2013040107

Moro, A., Raganato, A., & Navigli, R. (2014). Entity linking meets word sense disambiguation: A unified approach. *Transactions of the Association for Computational Linguistics*, *2*, 231–244.

Mossakowski, T., Kutz, O., & Codescu, M. (2014). Ontohub: A semantic repository for heterogeneous ontologies. In *Proc. of the Theory Day in Computer Science (DACS-2014), Satellite workshop of ICTAC-2014*. University of Bucharest.

Motik, B., Parsia, B., & Patel-Schneider, P. F. (2009). *OWL 2 Web Ontology Language structural specification and functional-style syntax* (Recommendation). W3C.

Motik, B., Horrocks, I., & Kim, S. M. (2012). Delta-reasoner: a semantic web reasoner for an intelligent mobile platform. *Proceedings of the 21st International Conference Companion on World Wide Web*, 63–72. doi:10.1145/2187980.2187988

Motik, B., Nenov, Y., Piro, R., Horrocks, I., & Olteanu, D. (2014). Parallel materialisation of Datalog programs in centralised, main-memory RDF systems. In *Proceedings of the 28th AAAI Conference on Artificial Intelligence*, (pp. 129–137). AAAI Press.

Mountantonakis, M., Allocca, C., Fafalios, P., Minadakis, N., Marketakis, Y., Lantzaki, C., & Tzitzikas, Y. (2014). Extending {VoID} for Expressing Connectivity Metrics of a Semantic Warehouse. *International Workshop on Dataset PROFIling {&} fEderated Search for Linked Data (PROFILES)*.

Mountantonakis, M., Minadakis, N., Marketakis, Y., Fafalios, P., & Tzitzikas, Y. (2016). Quantifying the connectivity of a semantic warehouse and understanding its evolution over time. *International Journal on Semantic Web and Information Systems*, *12*(3), 27–78. doi:10.4018/IJSWIS.2016070102

Mountantonakis, M., & Tzitzikas, Y. (2016). On measuring the lattice of commonalities among several linked datasets. *Proceedings of the VLDB Endowment*, 1101-1112. doi:10.14778/2994509.2994527

Musen, M. A. (2015). The Protégé project: a look back and a look forward. *AI Matters*, *1*(4), 4-12.

Muslea, I., Minton, S., & Knoblock, C. A. (2003, August). *Active learning with strong and weak views: a case study on wrapper induction* (Vol. 3). IJCAI.

Mylka, A., Sauermann, L., Sintek, M., & van Elst, L. (2013a). *NIE - Nepomuk Information Element Ontology*. Retrieved June 24, 2017, from http://oscaf.sourceforge.net/nie.html

Mylka, A., Sauermann, L., Sintek, M., & van Elst, L. (2013b). *NFO - Nepomuk File Ontology*. Retrieved June 24, 2017, from http://oscaf.sourceforge.net/nfo.html

Nastase, V. (2008). Topic-driven multi-document summarization with encyclopedic knowledge and spreading activation. In *Proceedings of the Conference on Empirical Methods in Natural Language Processing, EMNLP 08*. Stroudsburg, PA: Association for Computational Linguistics.

Natural Languauge Toolkit Library. (n.d.). Retrieved from: http://www.nltk.org/

Navigli, R., & Velardi, P. (2006). *Ontology enrichment through automatic semantic annotation of on-line glossaries. In Managing Knowledge in a World of Networks* (pp. 126–140). Springer.

Nenkova, A. (2005). Automatic text summarization of newswire: Lessons learned from the document understanding conference. In *Proceedings of the 20th National Conference on Artificial Intelligence* (vol. 3, pp. 1436–1441). AAAI Press.

Nenkova, A., & Vanderwende, L. (2005). *The impact of frequency on summarization*. Microsoft Research, Tech. Rep. MSR-TR-2005-101.

Nentwig, M., Soru, T., Ngomo, A.-C. N., & Rahm, E. (2014). Linklion: A link repository for the web of data. In *European Semantic Web Conference* (pp. 439-443). Springer. doi:10.1007/978-3-319-11955-7_63

Newman, M. E. J. (2010). *Networks: An Introduction*. New York: Oxford University Press. doi:10.1093/acprof:oso/9780199206650.001.0001

Nguyen, B.-A., & Yang, D.-L. (2012). A semi-automatic approach to construct Vietnamese ontology from online text. *The International Review of Research in Open and Distributed Learning*, *13*(5), 148–172. doi:10.19173/irrodl.v13i5.1250

Nielsen, S. S., Nielsen, G. B., Denwood, M. J., Haugegaard, J., & Houe, H. (2015). Comparison of recording of pericarditis and lung disorders at routine meat inspection with findings at systematic health monitoring in Danish finisher pigs. *Acta Veterinaria Scandinavica*, *57*(1), 1. doi:10.1186/s13028-015-0109-z PMID:25887329

Noy, N. F., & McGuinness, D. L. (2001*). Ontology development 101: A guide to creating your first ontology*. Technical Report SMI-2001-0880. Standford Medical Informatics.

Obe, R. O., & Hsu, L. S. (2014). *PostgreSQL: Up and Running: A Practical Introduction to the Advanced Open Source Database*. O'Reilly Media, Inc.

Obe, R. O., & Hsu, L. S. (2015). *PostGIS in action*. Manning Publications Co.

Okita, T., Guerra, M., & Graham, A. (2010). Multi-word expression sensitive word alignment. *Proceedings of the 4th International Workshop on Cross Lingual Information Access at COLING 2010*, 26–34.

Omitola, T., Zuo, L., Gutteridge, C., Millard, I., Glaser, H., Gibbins, N., & Shadbolt, N. (2011). Tracing the provenance of {L}inked {D}ata using {voiD}. *International Conference on Web Intelligence, Mining and Semantics (WIMS)*, 17.

Onan, A., Korukoğlu, S., & Bulut, H. (2016). Ensemble of keyword extraction methods and classifiers in text classification. *Expert Systems with Applications*, *57*, 232–247. doi:10.1016/j.eswa.2016.03.045

OpenNLP. (n.d.). *Apache OpenNLP*. Retrieved from: http://opennlp.apache.org/

Opsahl, T., Agneessens, F., & Skvoretz, J. (2010). Node centrality in weighted networks: Generalizing degree and shortest paths. *Social Networks*, *32*(3), 245–251. doi:10.1016/j.socnet.2010.03.006

Oren, E., Delbru, R., Catasta, M., Cyganiak, R., Stenzhorn, H., & Tummarello, G. (2008). Sindice. com: A document-oriented lookup index for open linked data. *International Journal of Metadata, Semantics and Ontologies*, *3*(1), 37–52. doi:10.1504/IJMSO.2008.021204

Oussalah, M., Bhat, F., Challis, K., & Schnier, T. (2013). A software architecture for Twitter collection, search and geolocation services. *Knowledge-Based Systems*, *37*, 105–120. doi:10.1016/j.knosys.2012.07.017

Palmero Aprosio, A., Corcoglioniti, F., Dragoni, M., & Rospocher, M. (2015). Supervised Opinion Frames Detection with RAID. Semantic Web Evaluation Challenges, 251-263. doi:10.1007/978-3-319-25518-7_22

Palshikar, G. K. (2007). Keyword Extraction from a Single Document Using Centrality Measures. *Pattern Recognition and Machine Intelligence (LNCS) Second International Conference, PReMI 2007* (Vol. *4815*, pp. 503-510). Springer Berlin Heidelberg. doi:10.1007/978-3-540-77046-6_62

Pammer, V. (2010) *PhD Thesis: Automatic Support for Ontology Evaluation Review of Entailed Statements and Assertional Effects for OWL Ontologies*. Engineering Sciences, Graz University of Technology.

Pan, J. Z., Staab, S., Aßmann, U., Ebert, J., & Zhao, Y. (2012). *Ontology-Driven Software Development*. Springer Science & Business Media.

Paradesi, S. M. (2011). Geotagging Tweets Using Their Content. *FLAIRS Conference*.

Paramonov, I., Lagutina, K., Mamedov, E., & Lagutina, N. (2016). Thesaurus-Based method of Increasing text-via-keyphrase Graph Connectivity During Keyphrase Extraction for e-Tourism Applications. *Proceedings of the Knowledge Engineering and Semantic Web: 7th International Conference, KESW 2016*, 129-141. doi:10.1007/978-3-319-45880-9_11

Parsia, B., Matentzoglu, N., Gonçalves, R. S., Glimm, B., & Steigmiller, A. (2015). The OWL reasoner evaluation (ORE) 2015 competition report. *Journal of Automated Reasoning*, 1–28.

Parundekar, R., Knoblock, C. A., & Ambite, J. L. (2012). Discovering Concept Coverings in Ontologies of Linked Data Sources. In *The Semantic Web -- ISWC 2012: 11th International Semantic Web Conference*, (pp. 427–443). Berlin: Springer Berlin Heidelberg. doi:10.1007/978-3-642-35176-1_27

Parundekar, R., Knoblock, C. A., & Ambite, J. L. (2010). Linking and Building Ontologies of Linked Data. In *Proceedings of the 9th International Semantic Web Conference on The Semantic Web - Volume Part I* (pp. 598–614). Berlin: Springer-Verlag. doi:10.1007/978-3-642-17746-0_38

Patel-Schneider, P. F., & Franconi, E. (2012). Ontology constraints in incomplete and complete data. In *Proceedings of the 11th International Conference on the Semantic Web (ISWC'12)* (pp. 444–459). Springer-Verlag. doi:10.1007/978-3-642-35176-1_28

Paulheim, H., & Bizer, C. (2014). Improving the Quality of Linked Data Using Statistical Distributions. *International Journal on Semantic Web and Information Systems*, *10*(2), 63–86. doi:10.4018/ijswis.2014040104

Paulheim, H., & Hertling, S. (2013). Discoverability of SPARQL Endpoints in Linked Open Data. In *International Semantic Web Conference (ISWC) Posters {&} Demos* (pp. 245–248). Springer.

Pavel, S., & Euzenat, J. (2013). Ontology Matching: State of the Art and Future Challenges. *IEEE Transactions on Knowledge and Data Engineering, 25*(1), 158–176. doi:10.1109/TKDE.2011.253

Peng, Z. (2005). A proposed framework for featurelevel geospatial data sharing: A case study for transportation network data. *International Journal of Geographical Information Science, 19*(4), 459–481. doi:10.1080/13658810512331319127

Pérez, P. A., Maeso, S. C., Ezkerro, A. M., & Otaduy, M. P. (2012). Twitter en la Universidad. *Revista del Congrés Internacional de Docència Universitària i Innovació, 1*(1).

Petasis, G., Karkaletsis, V., Paliouras, G., Krithara, A., & Zavitsanos, E. (2011). Ontology population and enrichment: State of the art. In *Knowledge-driven Multimedia Information Extraction and Ontology Evolution* (pp. 134–166). Springer. doi:10.1007/978-3-642-20795-2_6

Pfisterer, D., Romer, K., Bimschas, D., Hasemann, H., Hauswirth, M., Karnstedt, M., & Truong, C. et al. (2011). SPITFIRE: Toward a Semantic Web of things. *IEEE Communications Magazine, 49*(11), 40–48. doi:10.1109/MCOM.2011.6069708

Pinto, H. S., Staab, S., & Tempich, C. (2004). DILIGENT: Towards a fine-grained methodology for Distributed, Loosely-controlled and evolvInG. In *ECAI 2004: Proceedings of the 16th European Conference on Artificial Intelligence (Vol. 110*, p. 393). IOS Press.

Ponzetto, S. P., & Strube, M. (2007). *Deriving a large scale taxonomy from Wikipedia.* Paper presented at the AAAI.

Popov, B., Kiryakov, A., Kirilov, A., Manov, D., & Goranov, M. (2003). Kim – Semantic Annotation Platform. In *Proceedings of the 2nd International Conference on the Semantic Web (ISWC'03)* (pp. 834–849). Springer Berlin Heidelberg.

Porter Stemming. (2006). *The Porter Stemming Algorithm.* Retrieved from: http://tartarus.org/martin/PorterStemmer/

Poveda-Villalón, M. (2016). *Ontology Evaluation: A pitfall-based approach to ontology diagnosis* (Doctoral dissertation). ETSI_Informaticos.

Poveda-Villalón, M., Suárez-Figueroa, M. C., & Gómez-Pérez, A. (2010). A double classification of common pitfalls in ontologies. *Workshop on Ontology Quality at the 17th International Conference on Knowledge Engineering and Knowledge Management.*

Poveda-Villalón, M., Vatant, B., Suárez-Figueroa, M. C., & Gómez-Pérez, A. (2013). Detecting Good Practices and Pitfalls when Publishing Vocabularies on the Web. *Workshop on Ontology Patterns at the 12th International Semantic Web Conference.*

Poveda-Villalón, M., Suárez-Figueroa, M. C., & Gómez-Pérez, A. (2012). Validating ontologies with oops! In *Knowledge Engineering and Knowledge Management* (pp. 267–281). Springer Berlin Heidelberg. doi:10.1007/978-3-642-33876-2_24

Presutti, V., Gangemi, A., David S., Aguado, G., Suárez-Figueroa, M.C., Montiel-Ponsoda, E. & Poveda, M. (2008). *NeOn D2.5.1: A Library of Ontology Design Patterns: reusable solutions for collaborative design of networked ontologies.* NeOn project. (FP6-27595)

Presutti, V., Draicchio, F., & Gangemi, A. (2012). Knowledge extraction based on discourse representation theory and linguistic frames. In *Proceedings of International Conference on Knowledge Engineering and Knowledge Management (EKAW),* (pp. 114–129). Springer. doi:10.1007/978-3-642-33876-2_12

Prud'hommeauxE.Buil-ArandaC. (2013, March). {SPARQL} 1.1 {F}ederated {Q}uery.

Pustejovsky, J., Lee, K., Bunt, H., & Romary, L. (2010). ISO-TimeML: An international standard for semantic annotation. In *Proceedings of the 7th International Conference on Language Resources and Evaluation (LREC'10).* European Language Resources Association (ELRA).

Qin, H., Dou, D., & LePendu, P. (2007). Discovering Executable Semantic Mappings Between Ontologies. In *Proceedings of the 2007 OTM Confederated International Conference on On the Move to Meaningful Internet Systems: CoopIS, DOA, ODBASE, GADA, and IS - Volume Part I* (pp. 832–849). Berlin: Springer-Verlag.

Qin, X., Parker, S., Liu, Y., Graettinger, A. J., & Forde, S. (2013). Intelligent geocoding system to locate traffic crashes. *Accident; Analysis and Prevention*, *50*, 1034–1041. doi:10.1016/j.aap.2012.08.007 PMID:22921783

Qiu, D., & Srikant, R. (2004). Modeling and performance analysis of {BitTorrent}-like peer-to-peer networks. SIG-COMM, 367–378.

Qiu, L., Kan, M., & Chua, T. (2004). A public reference implementation of the rap anaphora resolution algorithm. *Proceedings of the Fourth International Conference on Language Resources and Evaluation (LREC'04)*, 291-294.

Quaresma, P., Rodrigues, I., Prolo, C., & Vieira, R. (2006). Um sistema de Pergunta-Resposta para uma base de Documentos. *Letras de Hoje*, 43-63.

Quilitz, B., & Leser, U. (2008). Querying Distributed {RDF} Data Sources with {SPARQL}. In *European Semantic Web Conference (ESWC)* (pp. 524–538). Springer. doi:10.1007/978-3-540-68234-9_39

Quillian, M. R. (1967). Word Concepts: A Theory and Simulation of Some Basic Semantic Capabilities. *Behavioral Science*, *12*(5), 410–430. doi:10.1002/bs.3830120511 PMID:6059773

Quinlan, J. R. (1986). Induction of Decision Trees. *Machine Learning*, *1*(1), 81–106. doi:10.1007/BF00116251

Quintano, L., & Rodrigues, I. (2006). Using a logic programming framework to control database query dialogues in natural language. In *22nd international conference on Logic Programming* (pp. 406-420). Seattle, WA: Springer-Verlag. doi:10.1007/11799573_30

Radev, D. R., Jing, H., Stys, M., & Tam, D. (2004). Centroid-based summarization of multiple documents. *Information Processing & Management*, *40*(6), 919–938. doi:10.1016/j.ipm.2003.10.006

Rafiei-Asl, J. & Nickabadi, A. (2017). TSAKE: A topical and structural automatic keyphrase extractor. *Applied Soft Computing*, *58*, 620–630. doi: 10.1016/j.asoc.2017.05.014

Ragone, A., Di Noia, T., Di Sciascio, E., Donini, F. M., Colucci, S., & Colasuonno, F. (2007). Fully automated web services discovery and composition through concept covering and concept abduction. *International Journal of Web Services Research*, *4*(3), 85–112. doi:10.4018/jwsr.2007070105

Ranwez, S., Duthil, B., Sy, M. F., Montmain, J., Augereau, P., & Ranwez, V. (2013). How Ontology Based Information Retrieval Systems may Benefit From Lexical Text Analysis. In A. Oltramari, P. Vossen, L. Qi, & E. Hovy (Eds.), *Theory and Applications of Natural Language Processing. New Trends of Research in Ontologies and Lexical Resources* (pp. 209–231). Springer-Verlag Heidelberg. doi:10.1007/978-3-642-31782-8_11

Ratnasamy, S., Francis, P., Handley, M., Karp, R. M., & Shenker, S. (2001). *A scalable content-addressable network*. SIGCOMM. doi:10.1145/383059.383072

Ravinuthala, M. K. V., & Ch, S. R. (2016). Thematic Text Graph: A Text Representation Technique for Keyword Weighting in Extractive Summarization System. *International Journal of Information Engineering and Electronic Business*, *8*(4), 18–25. doi:10.5815/ijieeb.2016.04.03

Rector, A., Drummond, N., Horridge, M., Rogers, J., Knublauch, H., Stevens, R., & Wroe, C. et al. (2004). OWL pizzas: Practical experience of teaching OWL-DL: Common errors & common patterns. In *Engineering Knowledge in the Age of the Semantic Web* (pp. 63–81). Springer Berlin Heidelberg. doi:10.1007/978-3-540-30202-5_5

Rendelet, K. (2012). *a közszolgálati tisztviselők képesítési előírásairól*. Retrieved from http://www.complex.hu/jr/gen/hjegy_doc.cgi?docid=A1200029.KOR

Resnik, P. (1993). *Selection and Information: A Class-Based Approach to Lexical Relations* (Doctoral thesis). University of Pennsylvania.

Resnik, P. (1995). Disambiguating Noun Groupings with Respect to WordNet Sense. *Proceedings of the Third Workshop on Very Large Corpora*, 54–68.

Richardson, S. (1997). *Determining Similarity and Inferring Relations in a lexical Knowledge Base* (PhD thesis). The City University of New York, New York, NY.

Riedel, S., Yao, L., & McCallum, A. (2010). Modeling relations and their mentions without labeled text. Modeling Relations and Their Mentions without Labeled Text. In J. L. Balcázar, F. Bonchi, A. Gionis, & M. Sebag (Eds.), *Machine Learning and Knowledge Discovery in Databases. ECML PKDD 2010* (pp. 148–163). Berlin: Springer.

Ripeanu, M., Iamnitchi, A., & Foster, I. T. (2002). Mapping the {Gnutella Network}. *IEEE Internet Computing, 6*(1), 50–57. <ALIGNMENT.qj></ALIGNMENT>10.1109/4236.978369

Ritter, A., Etzioni, O., & Clark, S. (2012). Open domain event extraction from twitter. In *Proceedings of the 18th ACM SIGKDD international conference on Knowledge discovery and data mining* (pp. 1104-1112). ACM. doi:10.1145/2339530.2339704

Ritter, A., & Zettlemoyer, L., Mausam, & Etzioni, O. (2013). Modeling missing data in distant supervision for information extraction. *Transactions of the Association for Computational Linguistics, 1*, 367–378.

Ritze, D., Meilicke, C., Šváb-Zamazal, O., & Stuckenschmidt, H. (2009). A Pattern-based Ontology Matching Approach for Detecting Complex Correspondences. In *Proceedings of the 4th International Conference on Ontology Matching* (vol. 51, pp. 25–36). Aachen, Germany: CEUR-WS.org.

Rivera, L. C., Vilches-Blázquez, L. M., Torres-Ruiz, M., & Ibarra, M. A. M. (2015). Semantic Recommender System for Touristic Context Based on Linked Data. In Information Fusion and Geographic Information Systems (IF&GIS'2015) (pp. 77-89). Springer International Publishing.

Rodríguez, N. D., Cuéllar, M. P., Lilius, J., & Calvo-Flores, M. D. (2014). A survey on ontologies for human behavior recognition. *ACM Computing Surveys, 46*(4), 43. doi:10.1145/2523819

Roller, S., Speriosu, M., Rallapalli, S., Wing, B., & Baldridge, J. (2012, July). Supervised text-based geolocation using language models on an adaptive grid. In *Proceedings of the 2012 Joint Conference on Empirical Methods in Natural Language Processing and Computational Natural Language Learning* (pp. 1500-1510). Association for Computational Linguistics.

Rolling, L. (1981). Indexing consistency, quality and efficiency. *Information Processing & Management, 17*(2), 69–76. doi:10.1016/0306-4573(81)90028-5

Rosner, M., & Camilleri, C. (2008). Multisum: query-based multi-document summarization. In *Proceedings of the Workshop on Multi-source Multilingual Information Extraction and Summarization, MMIES '08*. Stroudsburg, PA: Association for Computational Linguistics. doi:10.3115/1613172.1613180

Rospocher, M., van Erp, M., Vossen, P., Fokkens, A., Aldabe, I., Rigau, G., & Bogaard, T. et al. (2016). Building event-centric knowledge graphs from news. *Journal of Web Semantics, 37-38*, 132–151. doi:10.1016/j.websem.2015.12.004

Rousset, M. C., Atencia, M., David, J., Jouanot, F., Palombi, O., & Ulliana, F. (2017). Datalog Revisited for Reasoning in Linked Data. Reasoning Web. *Semantic Interoperability on the Web, 121*.

Rowstron, A. I. T., & Druschel, P. (2001). Pastry: Scalable, Decentralized Object Location, and Routing for Large-Scale Peer-to-Peer Systems. *IFIP/ACM International Conference on Distributed Systems Platforms (Middleware)*, 329–350.

Rubens, M., & Agarwal, P. (2002). *Information Extraction from Online Automotive Classifieds*. Academic Press.

Ruta, M., Scioscia, F., De Filippis, D., Ieva, S., Binetti, M., & Di Sciascio, E. (2014). A semantic-enhanced augmented reality tool for OpenStreetMap POI discovery. In *Transportation Research Procedia. 17th Meeting of the EURO Working Group on Transportation* (pp. 479-488). Elsevier.

Ruta, M., Scioscia, F., Di Sciascio, E., & Bilenchi, I. (2016). OWL API for iOS: early implementation and results. In *Proceedings of the OWL: Experiences and Directions (OWLED) and OWL Reasoner Evaluation Workshop (OWLED-ORE)* (pp. 141-152). Springer.

Ruta, M., Scioscia, F., Ieva, S., Capurso, G., & Di Sciascio, E. (2017). Semantic Blockchain to Improve Scalability in the Internet of Things. *Open Journal of Internet Of Things*, *3*(1), 46-61.

Ruta, M., Di Noia, T., Di Sciascio, E., Piscitelli, G., & Scioscia, F. (2008). A semantic-based mobile registry for dynamic RFID-based logistics support. *Proceedings of the 10th International Conference on Electronic Commerce*, 1-9. doi:10.1145/1409540.1409576

Ruta, M., Di Sciascio, E., & Scioscia, F. (2011). Concept abduction and contraction in semantic-based P2P environments. *Web Intelligence and Agent Systems*, *9*(3), 179–207.

Ruta, M., Scioscia, F., Di Noia, T., & Di Sciascio, E. (2009). Reasoning in Pervasive Environments: an Implementation of Concept Abduction with Mobile OODBMS. *Proceedings of 2009 IEEE/WIC/ACM International Conference on Web Intelligence*, 145–148. doi:10.1109/WI-IAT.2009.29

Ruta, M., Scioscia, F., Di Noia, T., & Di Sciascio, E. (2010). A hybrid ZigBee/Bluetooth approach to mobile semantic grids. *Computer Systems Science and Engineering*, *25*(3), 235–249.

Ruta, M., Scioscia, F., & Di Sciascio, E. (2010). Mobile Semantic-based Matchmaking: a fuzzy DL approach. *Proceedings of the 7th Extended Semantic Web Conference*, 16–30. doi:10.1007/978-3-642-13486-9_2

Ruta, M., Scioscia, F., & Di Sciascio, E. (2012). Enabling the Semantic Web of Things: framework and architecture. *Proceedings of the Sixth IEEE International Conference on Semantic Computing (ICSC 2012)*, 345-347. doi:10.1109/ICSC.2012.42

Ruta, M., Scioscia, F., Ieva, S., De Filippis, D., & Di Sciascio, E. (2015). Indoor/outdoor mobile navigation via knowledge-based POI discovery in augmented reality. *Proceedings of the 3rd International Workshop on Data Oriented Constructive Mining and Multi-Agent Simulation and the 7th International Workshop on Emergent Intelligence on Networked Agents (DOCMAS/WEIN-2015)*, 26-30. doi:10.1109/WI-IAT.2015.243

Ruta, M., Scioscia, F., Loseto, G., & Di Sciascio, E. (2014). Semantic-based resource discovery and orchestration in Home and Building Automation: A multi-agent approach. *IEEE Transactions on Industrial Informatics*, *10*(1), 730–741. doi:10.1109/TII.2013.2273433

Ruta, M., Scioscia, F., Pinto, A., Di Sciascio, E., Gramegna, F., Ieva, S., & Loseto, G. (2013). Resource annotation, dissemination and discovery in the Semantic Web of Things: a CoAP-based framework. *Proceedings International Conference on Green Computing and Communication (GreenCom) and Internet of Things (iThings) and Cyber, Physical and Social Computing (CPSCom)*, 527-534. doi:10.1109/GreenCom-iThings-CPSCom.2013.103

Ruta, M., Scioscia, F., Pinto, A., Gramegna, F., Ieva, S., Loseto, G., & Di Sciascio, E. (2017). Cooperative Semantic Sensor Networks for pervasive computing contexts. In *Proceedings of the 7th IEEE International Workshop on Advances in Sensors and Interfaces (IWASI 2017)* (pp. 38-43). New York: IEEE. doi:10.1109/IWASI.2017.7974209

Sager, J. C. (1990). *A Practical Course in Terminology Processing*. Amsterdam: John Benjamins. doi:10.1075/z.44

Saint-Dizier, P., & Moens, M.-F. (2011). Knowledge and reasoning for question answering: Research perspectives. *Information Processing & Management, 47*, 899 - 906.

Salton, G., & McGill, M. J. (1986). *Introduction to modern information retrieval*. New York, NY: McGraw-Hill, Inc.

Salton, G., Singhal, A., Buckley, C., & Mitra, M. (1996). Automatic Text Decomposition Using Text Segments and Text Themes. In *Proceedings of the seventh ACM conference on Hypertext* (pp. 53-65). ACM. doi:10.1145/234828.234834

Salton, G., Wong, A., & Yang, C. S. (1975). A vector space model for automatic indexing. *Communications of the ACM, 18*(11), 613–620. doi:10.1145/361219.361220

Sanderson, M. (1994). Word sense disambiguation and information retrieval. In *Proceedings of the 17th Annual International ACM-SIGIR Conference on Research and Development in Information Retrieval*, (pp. 142-151). Springer- Verlag.

Sarasua, C., Staab, S., & Thimm, M. (n.d.). Methods for Intrinsic Evaluation of Links in the Web of Data. In *European Semantic Web Conference* (pp. 68-84). Springer.

Saratlija, J., Šnajder, J., & Dalbelo-Bašić, B. (2011). *Unsupervised topic-oriented keyphrase extraction and its application to Croatian. In Text, Speech and Dialogue LNCS* (Vol. 6836, pp. 340–347). Springer Berlin Heidelberg. doi:10.1007/978-3-642-23538-2_43

Scharffe, F. (2009). *Correspondence patterns representation*. University of Innsbruck.

Schmachtenberg, M., Bizer, C., & Paulheim, H. (2014). Adoption of the Linked Data Best Practices in Different Topical Domains. In *Semantic Web Conference* (Vol. 8796, pp. 245–260). Springer. doi:10.1007/978-3-319-11964-9_16

Schmid, H. (1997). New Methods in Language Processing. In *Studies Computational Linguistics, chapter Probabilistic part-of-speech tagging using decision trees* (pp. 154–164). London: UCL Press. Retrieved from http://www.ims.uni-stuttgart.de/projekte/corplex/TreeTagger/

Schmid, H. (2013). Probabilistic Part-of-Speech Tagging Using Decision Trees. In D. B. Jones & H. Somers (Eds.), *New Methods in Language Processing* (pp. 154–164). Routledge.

Schober, D., Tudose, I., Svatek, V. & Boeker, M. (2012). OntoCheck: verifying ontology naming conventions and metadata completeness in Protégé 4. *Journal of Biomedical Semantics, 3*(S2), S4.

Schwarte, A., Haase, P., Hose, K., Schenkel, R., & Schmidt, M. (2011). Fed{X}: {A} Federation Layer for Distributed Query Processing on {L}inked {O}pen {D}ata. In *Extended Semantic Web Conference ({ESWC})* (pp. 481–486). Springer.

Scioscia, F., Binetti, M., Ruta, M., Ieva, S., & Di Sciascio, E. (2014). A Framework and a Tool for Semantic Annotation of POIs in OpenStreetMap. *Transportation Research Procedia. 16th Meeting of the EURO Working Group on Transportation*, 1092-1101.

Scioscia, F., Ruta, M., & Di Sciascio, E. (2015). A swarm of Mini-MEs: reasoning and information aggregation in ubiquitous multi-agent contexts. *4th OWL Reasoner Evaluation Workshop (ORE 2015), CEUR Workshop Proceedings, 1207*, 15-22.

Scioscia, F., Ruta, M., Loseto, G., Gramegna, F., Ieva, S., Pinto, A., & Di Sciascio, E. (2014). A mobile matchmaker for the Ubiquitous Semantic Web. *International Journal on Semantic Web and Information Systems*, *10*(4), 77–100. doi:10.4018/ijswis.2014100104

Sebastiani, F. (2002). Machine Learning in Automated Text Categorization. *ACM Computing Surveys*, *34*(1), 1–47. doi:10.1145/505282.505283

Seddiqui, M. H., & Aono, M. (2009). An efficient and scalable algorithm for segmented alignment of ontologies of arbitrary size. *Web Semantics: Science, Services, and Agents on the World Wide Web*, *7*(4), 344–356. doi:10.1016/j.websem.2009.09.001

Segers, R. H., Vossen, P. T. J. M., Rospocher, M., Serafini, L., Laparra, E. L., & Rigau, G. (2015). ESO: a Frame based Ontology for Events and Implied Situations. *Maplex 2015 Workshop*.

Selig, G. J. (2008). *Implementing IT Governance-A Practical Guide to Global Best Practices in IT Management*. Van Haren.

Seol, J. W., Jeong, K. Y., & Lee, K. S. (2013). Follower classification through social network analysis in twitter. In *Grid and Pervasive Computing* (pp. 926–931). Springer Berlin Heidelberg. doi:10.1007/978-3-642-38027-3_108

Shailer, G. E. (2004). *Introduction to Corporate Governance in Australia*. Pearson Education Australia.

Shamsfard, M., & Abdollahzadeh Barforoush, A. (2003). The state of the art in ontology learning: A framework for comparison. *The Knowledge Engineering Review*, *18*(04), 293–316. doi:10.1017/S0269888903000687

Shamsfard, M., & Barforoush, A. A. (2004). Learning Ontologies from Natural Language Texts. *International Journal of Human-Computer Studies*, *69*(1), 17–63. doi:10.1016/j.ijhcs.2003.08.001

Shanks, G. G., & Darke, P. (1998). Understanding Data Quality and Data Warehousing: A Semiotic Approach. In IQ (pp. 292-309). Academic Press.

Shekarpour, S., Marx, E., Ngomo, N. A., & Auer, S. (2015). SINA: Semantic interpretation of user queries for question answering on interlinked data. *Web Semantics: Science, Services, and Agents on the World Wide Web*, *30*, 39–51. doi:10.1016/j.websem.2014.06.002

Shelby, Z. (2012). *Constrained RESTful Environments (CoRE) Link Format*. Internet Engineering Task Force (IETF) Request For Comments (RFC) 6690. Retrieved June 30th, 2017, from https://tools.ietf.org/html/rfc6690

Shen, W., Wang, J., Luo, P., & Wang, M. (2012). A graph-based approach for ontology population with named entities. *Proceedings of the 21st ACM International Conference on Information and Knowledge Management (CIKM '12)*, 345–354. 10.1145/2396761.2396807

Shen, W., Wang, J., Luo, P., Wang, M., & Yao, C. (2011). Reactor: A framework for semantic relation extraction and tagging over enterprise data. *Proceedings of the 20th International Conference Companion on World Wide Web (WWW'11)*, 121–122. 10.1145/1963192.1963254

Shinyama, Y., & Sekine, S. (2006). Preemptive information extraction using unrestricted relation discovery. *Proceedings of the main conference on Human Language Technology Conference of the North American Chapter of the Association of Computational Linguistics (HLT-NAACL'06)*, 304–311. 10.3115/1220835.1220874

Shultis, J., & Eckhoff, N. (1979). Selection of Beta Prior Distribution Parameters from Component Failure Data. *IEEE Transactions on Power Apparatus and Systems, PAS*, *98*(2), 400–407. doi:10.1109/TPAS.1979.319361

Shvaiko, P., Euzenat, J., Jiménez-Ruiz, E., Cheatham, M., Hassanzadeh, O., & Ichise, R. (Eds.). (2016). *Proceedings of the 11th International Workshop on Ontology Matching* (vol. 1766). Academic Press.

Shvaiko, P., & Euzenat, J. (2008). Ten Challenges for Ontology Matching. In *Proceedings of the OTM 2008 Confederated International Conferences, CoopIS, DOA, GADA, IS, and ODBASE 2008. Part II on On the Move to Meaningful Internet Systems* (pp. 1164–1182). Berlin: Springer-Verlag.

Shvaiko, P., Euzenat, J., Shvaiko, P., & Euzenat, J. (2005). A survey of schema-based matching approaches. *Journal on Data Semantics, 4*, 146–171.

Shyu, C. R., Klaric, M., Scott, G. J., Barb, A. S., Davis, C. H., & Palaniappan, K. (2007). GeoIRIS: Geospatial information retrieval and indexing system—Content mining, semantics modeling, and complex queries. *Geoscience and Remote Sensing. IEEE Transactions on, 45*(4), 839–852.

Siddiqi, S., & Sharan, A. (2015). Keyword and Keyphrase Extraction Techniques: A Literature Review. *International Journal of Computers and Applications, 109*(2), 18–23. doi:10.5120/19161-0607

Sinner, A., & Kleemann, T. (2005, July). KRHyper - In Your Pocket. *Proceedings of 20th International Conference on Automated Deduction (CADE)*, 452-457.

Sirin, E., Parsia, B., Cuenca-Grau, B., Kalyanpur, A., & Katz, Y. (2007). Pellet: A practical OWL-DL reasoner. *Web Semantics: Science, Services, and Agents on the World Wide Web, 5*(2), 51–53. doi:10.1016/j.websem.2007.03.004

Skounakis, M., Craven, M., & Ray, S. (2003). Hierarchical hidden markov models for information extraction. *Proceedings of the 18th International Joint Conference on Artificial Intelligence (IJCAI'03)*, 427–433.

Song, M., Song, I.-Y., & Hu, X. (2003). KPSpotter: a flexible information gain-based keyphrase extraction system. *Proceedings of the 5th ACM international workshop on Web information and data management.* doi:10.1145/956699.956710

Song, W., Wenyin, L., Gu, N., Quan, X., & Hao, T. (2011). Automatic categorization of questions for user-interactive question answering. *Information Processing & Management, 47*(2), 147–156. doi:10.1016/j.ipm.2010.03.002

Sornlertlamvanich, V., Potipiti, T., & Charoenporn, T. (2001). *UNL Document Summarization.* The First International Workshop on MultiMedia Annotation, Tokyo, Japan.

Staab, S., Studer, R., Schnurr, H. P., & Sure, Y. (2001). Knowledge processes and ontologies. *IEEE Intelligent Systems, 16*(1), 26–34. doi:10.1109/5254.912382

Steigmiller, A., Liebig, T., & Glimm, B. (2014). Konclude: System description. *Web Semantics: Science, Services, and Agents on the World Wide Web, 27*, 78–85. doi:10.1016/j.websem.2014.06.003

Steinberger, J., Poesio, M., Kabadjov, M. A., & Jeek, K. (2007). Two uses of anaphora resolution in summarization. *Information Processing & Management, 43*(6), 1663–1680. doi:10.1016/j.ipm.2007.01.010

Steller, L., & Krishnaswamy, S. (2008). Pervasive Service Discovery: mTableaux Mobile Reasoning. *International Conference on Semantic systems (I-Semantics)*, 93-101.

Stoica, I., Morris, R., Liben-Nowell, D., Karger, D. R., Kaashoek, M. F., Dabek, F., & Balakrishnan, H. (2003). Chord: A scalable peer-to-peer lookup protocol for internet applications. *IEEE/ACM Trans. Netw., 11*(1), 17–32. doi:10.1109/TNET.2002.808407

Strasunskas, D., & Tomassen, S. L. (2008). The role of ontology in enhancing semantic searches: the EvOQS framework and its initial validation. *International Journal of Knowledge and Learning, 4*(4), 398-414.

Suárez-Figueroa, M. C. (2010). *NeOn Methodology for Building Ontology Networks: Specification, Scheduling and Reuse* (PhD thesis). Universidad Politécnica de Madrid.

Suárez-Figueroa, M. C., Cea, G. A. D., & Gómez-Pérez, A. (2013). Lights and shadows in creating a glossary about ontology engineering. *Terminology, 19*(2), 202–236. doi:10.1075/term.19.2.03sua

Suárez-Figueroa, M. C., Gómez-Pérez, A., Motta, E., & Gangemi, A. (Eds.). (2012). *Ontology engineering in a networked world*. Springer. doi:10.1007/978-3-642-24794-1

Suárez-Figueroa, M. C., Kamel, M., & Poveda-Villalón, M. (2013). Benefits of Natural Language Techniques in Ontology Evaluation: the OOPS! Case. *10th International Conference on Terminology and Artificial Intelligence (TIA 2013)*.

Subalalitha, C. N., Umamaheswari, E., Geetha, T. V., Ranjani, P., & Karky, M. (2011). Template based multilingual summary generation. *INFITT*.

Suchal, J. (2008). *On Finding Power Method in Spreading Activation Search, SOFSEM 2*. Kosice, Slovakia: Safarik University.

Suchanek, F. M., Kasneci, G., & Weikum, G. (2008). YAGO: A Large Ontology from Wikipedia and WordNet. *Web Semantics: Science, Services, and Agents on the World Wide Web, 6*(3), 203–217. doi:10.1016/j.websem.2008.06.001

Sun, H., Ma, H., Yih, W., Tsai, C., Liu, J., & Chang, M. (2015). Open Domain Question Answering via Semantic Enrichment. *Proceedings of the 24th International Conference on World Wide Web*, 1045-1055. doi:10.1145/2736277.2741651

Surdeanu, M., & Ciaramita, M. (2007). Robust information extraction with perceptrons. *Proceedings of the NIST 2007 Automatic Content Extraction Workshop (ACE'07)*.

Su, W., Wang, J., & Lochovsky, F. H. (2010). Record matching over query results from multiple web databases. *Knowledge and Data Engineering. IEEE Transactions on, 22*(4), 578–589.

Su, W., Wang, J., Lochovsky, F., & Liu, Y. (2012). Combining Tag and Value Similarity for Data Extraction and Alignment. *IEEE Transactions on Knowledge and Data Engineering, 24*(7), 1186–1200. doi:10.1109/TKDE.2011.66

Swampillai, K., & Stevenson, M. (2010). Intersentential relations in information extraction corpora. *Proceedings of the Seventh Conference on International Language Resources and Evaluation (LREC'10)*.

Szekely, P., Knoblock, C. A., Gupta, S., Taheriyan, M., & Wu, B. (2011, November). Exploiting semantics of web services for geospatial data fusion. In *Proceedings of the 1st ACM SIGSPATIAL International Workshop on Spatial Semantics and Ontologies* (pp. 32-39). ACM. doi:10.1145/2068976.2068981

Tablan, V., Damljanovic, D., & Bontcheva, K. (2008). A natural language query interface to structured information. In *5th European semantic web conference on The semantic web: research and applications* (pp. 361-375). Tenerife, Canary Islands, Spain: Springer-Verlag.

Taheriyan, M., Knoblock, C. A., Szekely, P., & Ambite, J. L. (2012). Rapidly integrating services into the linked data cloud. In *The Semantic Web–ISWC 2012* (pp. 559–574). Springer Berlin Heidelberg. doi:10.1007/978-3-642-35176-1_35

Taheriyan, M., Knoblock, C. A., Szekely, P., & Ambite, J. L. (2012, May). Semi-automatically modeling web apis to create linked apis. *Proceedings of the ESWC 2012 Workshop on Linked APIs*.

Tai, W., Keeney, J., & O'Sullivan, D. (2011). COROR: a composable rule-entailment OWL reasoner for resource-constrained devices. *Rule-Based Reasoning, Programming, and Applications*, 212–226.

Takhteyev, Y., Gruzd, A., & Wellman, B. (2012). Geography of Twitter networks. *Social Networks, 34*(1), 73–81. doi:10.1016/j.socnet.2011.05.006

Tao, J., Sirin, E., Bao, J., & McGuinness, D. L. (2010). Integrity constraints in OWL. In *Proceedings of the 24th AAAI Conference on Artificial Intelligence, AAAI 2010*, (p. 1443-1448). AAAI Press.

TaxonConcept. (n.d.). Retrieved from: http://www.taxonconcept.org/

Teege, G. (1994). Making the Difference: A Subtraction Operation for Description Logics. *Proceedings of the Fourth International Conference on the Principles of Knowledge Representation and Reasoning (KR94)*, 540–550. doi:10.1016/B978-1-4832-1452-8.50145-7

Thakkar, S., Knoblock, C. A., & Ambite, J. L. (2007, November). Quality-driven geospatial data integration. In *Proceedings of the 15th annual ACM international symposium on Advances in geographic information systems* (p. 16). ACM.

Thiel, K., & Berthold, M. R. (2012). Node Similarities from Spreading Activation. Academic Press.

Tiwana, A., Konsynski, B., & Venkatraman, N. (2013). Special issue: Information technology and organizational governance: The IT governance cube. *Journal of Management Information Systems*, *30*(3), 7–12. doi:10.2753/MIS0742-1222300301

Tonella, P., Ricca, F., Pianta, E., & Girardi, C. (2003). Using Keyword Extraction for Web Site Clustering. In *Proceedings of 5th IEEE International Workshop on Web Site Evolution* (pp. 41-48). IEEE. doi:10.1109/WSE.2003.1234007

Tonon, A., Cudré-Mauroux, P., Blarer, A., Lenders, V., & Motik, B. (2017, May). ArmaTweet: Detecting Events by Semantic Tweet Analysis. In *European Semantic Web Conference* (pp. 138-153). Springer. doi:10.1007/978-3-319-58451-5_10

Troussov, A., Levner, E., Bogdan, C., Judge, J., & Botvich, D. (2009). Spreading Activation Methods. In A. Shawkat & Y. Xiang (Eds.), *Dynamic and Advanced Data Mining for Progressing Technological Development*. IGI Global.

Tsarkov, D., & Horrocks, I. (2006). FaCT++ description logic reasoner: System description. *Automated Reasoning*, 292–297.

Tsiflidou, E., & Manouselis, N. (2013). Tools and Techniques for Assessing Metadata Quality. In *Metadata and Semantics Research* (pp. 99–110). Springer. doi:10.1007/978-3-319-03437-9_11

Tuchinda, R., Knoblock, C. A., & Szekely, P. (2011). Building mashups by demonstration. *ACM Transactions on the Web*, *5*(3), 16. doi:10.1145/1993053.1993058

Tzitzikas, Y., Kampouraki, M., & Analyti, A. (2014). Curating the Specificity of Ontological. *Journal on Data Semantics, 3*(2), 75-106.

Tzitzikas, Y., Minadakis, N., Marketakis, Y., Fafalios, P., Allocca, C., Mountantonakis, M., & Zidianaki, I. (2014, May). Matware: Constructing and exploiting domain specific warehouses by aggregating semantic data. In The Semantic Web: Trends and Challenges (pp. 721-736). Springer.

Tzitzikas, Y., Allocca, C., Bekiari, C., Marketakis, Y., Fafalios, P., Doerr, M., & Candela, L. (2013, November). Integrating heterogeneous and distributed information about marine species through a top level ontology. In *Metadata and Semantics Research* (pp. 289–301). Springer. doi:10.1007/978-3-319-03437-9_29

Tzitzikas, Y., Minadakis, N., Marketakis, Y., Fafalios, P., Allocca, C., & Mountantonakis, M. (2014, March). *Quantifying the Connectivity of a Semantic Warehouse*. EDBT/ICDT Workshops.

UbiPOL. (2009). *Ubiquitous Participation Platform for Policy-making*. ICT for Governance and Policy Modelling.

Umbrich, J., Hose, K., Karnstedt, M., Harth, A., & Polleres, A. (2011). Comparing data summaries for processing live queries over {L}inked {D}ata. *World Wide Web Journal*, *14*(5-6), 495–544. doi:10.1007/s11280-010-0107-z

UNDL. (2010). *Universal networking language (unl) knowledge base (UNL KB)*. Retrieved from http://www.unlweb.net/wiki/UNL_Knowledge_Base

UNDL. (2011). *Universal networking language (unl)*. Retrieved from http://www.undl.org/unlsys/unl/unl2005

Vaccari, L., Shvaiko, P., & Marchese, M. (2009). A geo-service semantic integration in spatial data infrastructures. *International Journal of Spatial Data Infrastructures Research, 4*, 24–51.

van Hage, W. R., & Ploeger, T. (2014). *Deliverable D7.3.1.* Retrieved from http://www.newsreader-project.eu/publications/deliverables/

van Hage, W. R., Malaisé, V., Segers, R., Hollink, L., & Schreiber, G. (2011). Design and use of the Simple Event Model (SEM). *Web Semantics: Science, Services, and Agents on the World Wide Web, 9*(2), 128–136. doi:10.1016/j.websem.2011.03.003

Vandenbussche, P. Y., Atemezing, G. A., Poveda-Villalón, M., & Vatant, B. (2017). Linked Open Vocabularies (LOV): A gateway to reusable semantic vocabularies on the Web. *Semantic Web Journal, 8*(3), 437–452. doi:10.3233/SW-160213

Vassiliadis, V., Wielemaker, J., & Mungall, C. (2009). Processing OWL2 Ontologies using Thea: An Application of Logic Programming. *6th International Workshop on OWl: Experiences and Direction, OWLD 2009.*

Verborgh, R., Hartig, O., De Meester, B., Haesendonck, G., De Vocht, L., & Vander Sande, M., … de Walle, R. Van. (2014). Querying Datasets on the {W}eb with High Availability. In *International Semantic Web Conference (ISWC)* (pp. 180–196). Springer. http://doi.org/ doi:<ALIGNMENT.qj></ALIGNMENT>10.1007/978-3-319-11964-9_12

VoID. (2010). *VoID store.* Retrieved from: http://void.rkbexplorer.com/

Völker, J., & Niepert, M. (2011). Statistical Schema Induction. In G. Antoniou, M. Grobelnik, E. Simperl, B. Parsia, D. Plexousakis, P. De Leenheer, & J. Pan (Eds.), *The Semantic Web: Research and Applications: 8th Extended Semantic Web Conference, ESWC 2011* (pp. 124–138). Berlin: Springer Berlin Heidelberg.

Völker, J. (2009). *Learning expressive ontologies* (Vol. 2). IOS Press.

Volz, J., Bizer, C., Gaedke, M., & Kobilarov, G. (2009). Silk-A Link Discovery Framework for the Web of Data. *LDOW, 538.*

Volz, J., Bizer, C., Gaedke, M., & Kobilarov, G. (2009). Silk-A Link Discovery Framework for the Web of Data. *Proceedings of the WWW'09 Workshop on Linked Data on the Web.*

von Hessling, A., Kleemann, T., & Sinner, A. (2004). Semantic User Profiles and their Applications in a Mobile Environment. *Workshop on Aartificial Iintelligence in Mmobile Ssystems (AIMS)*, 59-63.

Voorhees, E. M. (2001). Overview of the TREC-9 Question Answering Track. In *Ninth Text REtrieval Conference (TREC-9)* (pp. 71-80). Gaithersburg, MD: National Institute of Standards and Technology (NIST).

Vossen, P., & Peters, W. (1997). The Multilingual design of the EuroWordNet Database. *Lexical Semantic Resources for NLP Applications.* Retrieved from http://citeseer.nj.nec.com/cache/papers/cs/343/http:zSzzSzwww.let.uva.nlz.Sz~ewnzSzdocszSzP013.pdf/vossen97multilingual.pdf

Vossen, P., Agerri, R., Aldabe, I., Cybulska, A., van Erp, M., Fokkens, A., . . . Segers, R. (2016) NewsReader: Using knowledge resources in a cross-lingual reading machine to generate more knowledge from massive streams of news. *Knowledge-Based Systems, 110.* https://doi.org/10.1016/j.knosys.2016.07.013

Vrandecic, D. (2010). *Ontology Evaluation* (PhD thesis). KIT.

W3C. (2013a). *PROV Model Primer.* W3C Working Group Note. Retrieved from: https://www.w3.org/TR/2013/NOTE-prov-primer-20130430/

W3C. (2013b). *PROV-Overview: An Overview of the PROV Family of Documents.* W3C Working Group Note. Retrieved from: https://www.w3.org/TR/prov-overview/

W3C. (2013c). *The RDF Data Cube Vocabulary: W3C Proposed Recommendation.* Retrieved from: https://www.w3.org/TR/2013/PR-vocab-data-cube-20131217/

Wakefield, J. S., Warren, S. J., & Alsobrook, M. (2011). Learning and teaching as communicative actions: A mixed-methods Twitter study. *Knowledge Management & E-Learning: An International Journal, 3*(4), 563-584.

Walter, S., Unger, C., Cimiano, P., & Bär, D. (2012). Evaluation of a Layered Approach to Question Answering over Linked Data. *The Semantic Web -- ISWC 2012: 11th International Semantic Web Conference, 7650*, 362-374. doi:10.1007/978-3-642-35173-0_25

Wan, X., & Xiao, J. (2008). CollabRank: Towards a Collaborative Approach to Single-Document Keyphrase Extraction. In *Proceedings of the 22nd International Conference on Computational Linguistics (Coling 2008)* (pp. 969-976). Coling 2008 Organizing Committee. doi:10.3115/1599081.1599203

Wang, F., Wang, Z., Senzhang, W., & Zhoujun, L. (2014). Exploiting Description Knowledge for Keyphrase Extraction. In PRICAI 2014: Trends in Artificial Intelligence (LNCS) (Vol. 8862, pp. 130-142). Springer International Publishing. doi:10.1007/978-3-319-13560-1_11

Wang, C., Xiong, M., Zhou, Q., & Yu, Y. (2007). PANTO: A Portable Natural Language Interface to Ontologies. *4th European conference on The Semantic Web: Research and Applications* (pp. 473-487). Innsbruck, Austria: Springer-Verlag. doi:10.1007/978-3-540-72667-8_34

Wang, J., Han, J., & Li, C. (2007). Frequent closed sequence mining without candidate maintenance. *IEEE Transactions on Knowledge and Data Engineering, 19*(8), 1042–1056. doi:10.1109/TKDE.2007.1043

Wang, R. Y., & Strong, D. M. (1996). Beyond accuracy: What data quality means to data. *Journal of Management Information Systems, 12*(4), 5–33. doi:10.1080/07421222.1996.11518099

Watanabe, K., Ochi, M., Okabe, M., & Onai, R. (2011). Jasmine: a real-time local-event detection system based on geo-location information propagated to microblogs. In *Proceedings of the 20th ACM international conference on Information and knowledge management* (pp. 2541-2544). ACM. doi:10.1145/2063576.2064014

Weber, N., & Buitelaar, P. (2006). Web-based ontology learning with isolde. *Proc. of the ISWC Workshop on Web Content Mining with Human Language Technologies.*

Weikum, G., & Theobald, M. (2010). From information to knowledge: Harvesting entities and relationships from Web sources. In *Proceedings of the 29th ACM SIGMOD-SIGACT-SIGART Symposium on Principles of Database Systems (PODS'10)* (pp. 65–76). ACM. doi:10.1145/1807085.1807097

Weissenbacher, D. (2004). La relation de sysnonymie en génomique. In Actes de la conférence RECITAL'2004, Fès, Maroc.

Welch, B. K., & Bonnan-White, J. (2012). Twittering to increase student engagement in the university classroom. *Knowledge Management & E-Learning: An International Journal, 4*(3), 325-345.

Wiegand, N., & García, C. (2007). A Task-Based Ontology Approach to Automate Geospatial Data Retrieval. *Transactions in GIS, 11*(3), 355–376. doi:10.1111/j.1467-9671.2007.01050.x

Williams, G. T. (2013, March). {SPARQL} 1.1 {S}ervice {D}escription.

Winkler, R. L. & Hays, W. (1985). *Statistics: Probability, inference, and decision.* Academic Press.

Winkler, W. E. (2006). *Overview of record linkage and current research directions.* Bureau of the Census.

Witten, I. H., Moffat, A., & Bell, T. C. (1999). *Managing gigabytes: compressing and indexing documents and images.* Morgan Kaufmann.

Witzig, S., & Center, A. (2003). Accessing wordnet from prolog. Artificial Intelligence Centre, University of Georgia.

Wong, W., Liu, W., & Bennamoun, M. (2012). Ontology learning from text: A look back and into the future. *ACM Computing Surveys*, *44*(4), 20. doi:10.1145/2333112.2333115

World Wide Web Consortium. (2012). *OWL 2 Web Ontology Language Structural Specification and Functional-Style Syntax* (2nd ed.). W3C Recommendation 11 December 2012. Retrieved June 30th, 2017, from https://www.w3.org/TR/owl2-syntax/

World Wide Web Consortium. (2014). *RDF 1.1 Concepts and Abstract Syntax*. W3C Recommendation 25 February 2014. Retrieved June 30th, 2017, from https://www.w3.org/TR/rdf11-concepts/

Wu, J.-L., & Agogino, A. M. (2003). Automating Keyphrase Extraction with Multi-Objective Genetic Algorithms, In *Proceedings of the 37th Annual Hawaii International Conference on System Sciences* (pp. 104-111). IEEE.

Wu, Z., & Palmer, M. (1994). Verb Semantics and Lexical Selection. In *Proceedings of the 32nd Annual Meeting of the Associations for Computational Linguistics* (pp.133-138). Association for Computational Linguistics. doi:10.3115/981732.981751

Xiao, H., & Cruz, I. F. (2006). Application design and interoperability for managing personal information in the Semantic Desktop. In *Proceedings of the Semantic Desktop and Social Semantic Collaboration Workshop (SemDesk'06) co-located at the 5th International Semantic Web Conference ISWC 2006, (Vol. 202)*. CEUR-WS.org.

Yamaguchi, T. (2001). Acquiring Conceptual Relationships from Domain-Specific Texts. In A. Maedche, S. Staab, C. Nedellec & E. H. Hovy (Ed.), *Workshop on Ontology Learning*. CEUR-WS.org.

Yang, Y., & Pedersen, J. O. (1997). *A comparative study on feature selection in text categorization*. Paper presented at the ICML.

Yasunaga, M., Zhang, R., Meelu, K., Pareek, A., Srinivasan, K., & Radev, D. (2017). Graph-based Neural Multi-Document Summarization. *CoNLL 2017*.

Yih, W., Goodman, J., & Carvalho, V. R. (2006). Finding Advertising Keywords on Web Pages. In *Proceedings of the 15th Int. Conf. on World Wide Web, WWW '06* (pp. 213–222). New York: ACM. doi:10.1145/1135777.1135813

Ying, Y., Qingping, T., Qinzheng, X., Ping, Z., & Panpan, L. (2017). A Graph-Based Approach of Automatic Keyphrase Extraction. *Procedia Computer Science*, *107*, 248–255. doi:10.1016/j.procs.2017.03.087

Young, P. (1995). Optimal Voting Rules. *The Journal of Economic Perspectives*, *9*(1), 51–64. doi:10.1257/jep.9.1.51

Yuan, Y. (2011, June). Extracting spatial relations from document for geographic information retrieval. In *Geoinformatics, 2011 19th International Conference on* (pp. 1-5). IEEE. doi:10.1109/GeoInformatics.2011.5980797

Yue, P., Di, L., Yang, W., Yu, G., & Zhao, P. (2007). Semantics-based automatic composition of geospatial Web service chains. *Computers & Geosciences*, *33*(5), 649–665. doi:10.1016/j.cageo.2006.09.003

Yue, P., Gong, J., Di, L., He, L., & Wei, Y. (2011). Integrating semantic web technologies and geospatial catalog services for geospatial information discovery and processing in cyberinfrastructure. *GeoInformatica*, *15*(2), 273–303. doi:10.1007/s10707-009-0096-1

Zanoli, R., Corcoglioniti, F., & Girardi, C. (2011). Exploiting Background Knowledge for Clustering Person Names. EVALITA 2011, 135-145.

Zaveri, A., Kontokostas, D., Sherif, M. A., Bühmann, L., Morsey, M., Auer, S., & Lehmann, J. (2013, September). User-driven quality evaluation of dbpedia. In *Proceedings of the 9th International Conference on Semantic Systems* (pp. 97-104). ACM. doi:10.1145/2506182.2506195

Zaveri, A., Rula, A., Maurino, A., Pietrobon, R., Lehmann, J., & Auer, S. (2016). Quality assessment for linked data: A survey. *Semantic Web*, 7(1), 63–93. doi:10.3233/SW-150175

Zaveri, A., Rula, A., Maurino, A., Pietrobon, R., Lehmann, J., Auer, S., & Hitzler, P. (2016). *Quality assessment for linked data: A survey*. Semantic Web.

Zelenko, D., Aone, C., & Richardella, A. (2003). Kernel methods for relation extraction. *Journal of Machine Learning Research*, 3, 1083–1106.

Zhang, W., & Gelernter, J. (2014). Geocoding location expressions in Twitter messages: A preference learning method. *Journal of Spatial Information Science, 2014*(9), 37-70.

Zhao, B. Y., Huang, L., Stribling, J., Rhea, S. C., Joseph, A. D., & Kubiatowicz, J. (2004). Tapestry: a resilient global-scale overlay for service deployment. *IEEE Journal on Selected Areas in Communications, 22*(1), 41–53. 10.1109/JSAC.2003.818784

Zhao, K., Meng, X., Li, H., & Wang, Z. (2015, October). Using encyclopedic knowledge to understand queries. In *Proceedings of the First International Workshop on Novel Web Search Interfaces and Systems* (pp. 17-22). ACM. doi:10.1145/2810355.2810358

Zhao, T., Zhang, C., Wei, M., & Peng, Z. R. (2008). Ontology-based geospatial data query and integration. In *Geographic Information Science* (pp. 370–392). Springer Berlin Heidelberg. doi:10.1007/978-3-540-87473-7_24

Zhou, N. (2008). Geospatial Semantic Integration. In Encyclopedia of GIS (pp. 386-388). Springer US. doi:10.1007/978-0-387-35973-1_511

Zhou, G., Zhang, M., Ji, D., & Zhu, Q. (2007). Tree kernel-based relation extraction with context-sensitive structured parse tree information. *Proceedings of the 2007 Joint Conference on Empirical Methods in Natural Language Processing and Computational Natural Language Learning (EMNLP-CONLL'07)*, 728-736.

Zhou, Y., Nenov, Y., Grau, B. C., & Horrocks, I. (2015). Ontology-based Query Answering with PAGOdA. *Proceedings of the 4th OWL Reasoner Evaluation (ORE) Workshop*, 1-7.

Zhu, J., Nie, Z., Liu, X., Zhang, B., & Wen, J.-R. (2009). StatSnowball: A statistical approach to extracting entity relationships. *Proceedings of the 18th International Conference on World Wide Web (WWW'09)*, 101-110. 10.1145/1526709.1526724

Zhuge, H., & Zhang, J. (2010). Topological centrality and its e-Science applications. *Journal of the American Society for Information Science and Technology, 61*(9), 1824–1841. doi:10.1002/asi.21353

Zimniewicz, M., Kurowski, K., & Węglarz, J. (2017). Scheduling aspects in keyword extraction problem. *International Transactions in Operational Research*, 00, 1–16. doi:10.1111/itor.12368

Zouaq, A., Gasevic, D., & Hatala, M. (2011). Towards open ontology learning and filtering. *Information Systems, 36*(7), 1064–1081. doi:10.1016/j.is.2011.03.005

About the Contributors

Miltiadis D. Lytras is a Research Professor at The American College of Greece—Deree College—with a research focus on semantic web, knowledge management, smart cities research, technology-enabled innovation, cognitive computing and e-learning, with more than 150 publications. He has co-edited more than 45 special issues in International Journals (IEEE Transaction on Knowledge and Data Engineering, IEEE Internet Computing, IEEE Transactions on Education, Computers in Human Behaviour, Telematics and Informatics, Journal of Knowledge Management, WWW Journal) and has authored/(co-)edited 45 books (e.g. Open Source for Knowledge and Learning Management, Ubiquitous and Pervasive Knowledge Management, Intelligent Learning Infrastructures for Knowledge Intensive Organizations, Semantic Web Based Information Systems, China Information Technology Handbook, Real World Applications of Semantic Web and Ontologies, Web 2.0: The Business Model, etc.). He (has) serves(ed) as the (Co) Editor in Chief of 8 international journals (e.g. International Journal on Semantic Web and Information Systems, International Journal of Knowledge Society Research, International Journal of Knowledge and Learning, International Journal of Technology Enhanced Learning).

Naif R. Aljohani is Assistant Professor and Head of Department of Information System at the Faculty of Computing and Information Technology in King Abdul Aziz University, Jeddah, Saudi Arabia. He holds a PhD in Computer Science from the University of Southampton, UK. He received the Bachelor's degree in Computer Education from King Abdul Aziz University, 2005. In 2009, he received the Master degree in Computer Networks from La Trobe University, Australia. His research interests are in the areas of mobile and ubiquitous computing, mobile and ubiquitous learning, learning and knowledge analytic, semantic web, Web Science, technology enhanced learning and human computer interaction. He has more than 40 research publications.

Ernesto Damiani is a Full Professor at the Universita degli Studi di Milano, where he leads the SESAR research lab, and the leader of the Big Data Initiative at the EBTIC/Khalifa University in Abu Dhabi, UAE. Ernesto holds/has held visiting positions at a number of international institutions, including George Mason University in Virginia, US, Tokyo Denki University, Japan, LaTrobe University in Melbourne, Australia, and the Institut National des Sciences Appliquées (INSA) at Lyon, France. He is a Fellow of the Japanese Society for the Progress of Science. He is the Principal Investigator of the H2020 TOREADOR project. He was a recipient of the Chester-Sall Award from the IEEE IES Society (2007). He was named ACM Distinguished Scientist (2008) and received the IFIP TC2 Outstanding Contributions Award (2012). Ernesto serves in the editorial board of several international journals; among others, he is the EiC of the International Journal on Big Data and of the International Journal of

Knowledge and Learning. He is Associate Editor of IEEE Transactions on Service-oriented Computing and of the IEEE Transactions on Fuzzy Systems. Ernesto is a senior member of the IEEE and served as Vice-Chair of the IEEE Technical Committee on Industrial Informatics. In 2008, Ernesto was nominated ACM Distinguished Scientist and received the Chester Sall Award from the IEEE Industrial Electronics Society. Ernesto has co-authored over 350 scientific papers and many books, including "Open Source Systems Security Certification" (Springer 2009).

Kwok Tai Chui received the B.Eng. degree in Electronic and Communication Engineering – Business Intelligence Minor, with first-class honor, from City University of Hong Kong in 2013, where he is a Ph.D. candidate and is fully completed at the winter in 2017. He was the recipient of international awards in several IEEE events. For instance, he received the 2nd Prize Award (Postgraduate Category) of 2014 IEEE Region 10 Student Paper Contest, and Best Paper Award in IEEE The International Conference on Consumer Electronics-China, in both 2014 and 2015. He has been serving as Guest Editors in Journal of Internet Technology, Managing Editor in International Journal on Semantic Web and Information Systems, International Advisory Board in International Journal of Healthcare Information Systems and Informatics, Editorial Advisory Board in Journal of Science and Technology Policy Management, Associate Editor in International Journal of User-Driven Healthcare and International Journal of Public Health Management and Ethics, Editorial Review Board of 6 journals, Technical Program Committee in The International Conference on Biomedical Engineering and Biotechnology (since 2015), The International Conference on Electronics, Communications and Networks (since 2016) and Wireless Telecommunications Symposium (since 2016).

* * *

Slobodan Beliga gained his master's degree in informatics in the field of Text Mining and Machine Learning from the University of Rijeka, Department of Informatics in 2013. In the same year, he also gained a master's degree as a specialist in the Education of Informatics. He currently works as a teaching and research assistant at the University of Rijeka, Department of Informatics where he has also enrolled in doctoral studies in informatics. His research interests are natural language processing, information retrieval and complex networks analysis.

Rob Brennan is a senior research fellow in the Knowledge and Data Engineering group, in the ADAPT Centre at Trinity College Dublin. He has over 12 years' experience in leveraging semantic web technologies for data quality, curation, integration and network management. He has previously worked in the Ericsson Network Management Research centre, several internet and web start-ups and as a researcher in Dublin City University where he completed his PhD in 2004. He was the coordinator of the ALIGNED H2020 European project and his current research interests are in data value driven data governance.

Roldano Cattoni was born in 1964 in Trento (Italy). In 1989 received degree in computer science with honours. Universita' di Milano (thesis on Knowledge Representation). In 1990 joined the Computer Vision Group at ITC-IRST working for 5 years on planning and control of mobile robots. Since 1997 interested in probabilistic reasoning, in particular Bayesian Belief Networks, applied for visual based monitoring and user profiling. In late 1998 joined the Software Engineering Group at IRST, working in the field of Software Agents and Distributed Computing. In early 2000 joined the Speech Recognition Group, doing research on multi-language translation. After working on Interlingua-based Machine Translation, in 2003 moved to Statistical Machine Translation. In 2007, when ITC-irst changed into FBK, joined the Human Language Technology research unit.

Na Chen received her master degree from Beijing Jiaotong University, in 2007. At present, she is an associate professor in Hebei Vocational College of Rail Transportation. Her research direction is data mining and digital information processing.

Francesco Corcoglioniti is a postdoc researcher at Fondazione Bruno Kessler (FBK), where he previously carried out his PhD activities. His research interests cross the areas of Semantic Web, Data Management and Natural Language Processing, with applications to Knowledge Extraction from text and Social Media Analytics.

Eugenio Di Sciascio received the master's degree with honours from University of Bari, and the Ph.D. from Polytechnic University of Bari. He is currently full professor of Information Systems at the same university, where he is serving as Rector. He leads the research group of the Information Systems Laboratory. Formerly, he has been an assistant professor at University of Lecce and associate professor at Polytechnic University of Bari. His research interests include multimedia information retrieval, knowledge representation and e-commerce. He is involved in several national and European research projects related to his research interests. He co-authored papers that received best paper awards at the ICEC- 2004, IEEE CEC-EEE-2006, ICEC-2007, SEMAPRO-2010 and ICWE-2010 Conferences.

Liming Du got her bachelor degree from Tangshan Normal University in 2014. At present, she is working on the master degree in North China Electric Power University. Her research interests include Information integration, Data mining and Machine learning.

Imelda Escamilla got a PhD degree in Computer Science at the National Polytechnic Institute. She is specialist in Geographic Information Systems. Her areas of interest are Semantic Geocoding, Ontology development, Geographic datamining, Disaster Management. She obtained a Master Science Degree with honorific mention with the work "Spatial analysis to define areas of interest using conceptual representations" and won a Honorable Mention in the Mexican National Civil Protection Prize in 2014 with the work "Automatic system for evaluating emergency vulnerabilities". Recently she did a research stay at Universidade Federal de Minas Gerais in Brazil, working with brazilian researchers in the field of semantic geocoding.

Pavlos Fafalios obtained his PhD at the Computer Science Department of University of Crete (Greece) in 2016. During his graduate studies, he was also research assistant at the Information Systems Laboratory of FORTH-ICS. He recently moved to L3S Research Center (University of Hannover, Germany) as a postdoctoral researcher, where he works on methods for the semantic exploration of Web Archives. His research interests fall in the following areas: Exploratory and Semantic Search, Semantic Data Management, Entity Linking, Data Integration, Linked Data.

Saira Gillani received her Phd degree in Information Systems from Corvinus University of Budapest, Hungary. She is an assistant professor in the college of computing and informatics, Saudi Electronic University, Jeddah, Saudi Arabia. Her current research activities include Text Mining, information extraction, ontology learning and internet of things.

Asunción Gómez-Pérez is Vice-Rector for Research, Innovation and Doctoral Studies and Full Professor at Universidad Politécnica de Madrid (UPM). She is the Director of the Ontology Engineering Group (OEG) (since 1995), Academic Director of the Master's Degree in Artificial Intelligence and Coordinator of the PhD Programme in Artificial Intelligence at the same University. She holds a PhD in Computer Science (1993) and a Master on Business Administration (1992). Before joining UPM, she was visiting as a postdoc the Knowledge Systems Laboratory at Stanford University. She has supervised 18 Ph.D thesis, she has coordinated 4 EU projects SEALS, SemSorGrid4Env and Ontogrid and now she is coordinating LIDER. She has participated 21 EU projects as main researchers, and in more than 40 national projects funded by Spanish research agencies and companies. Her main research interests are ontologies, semantic technologies, linked data and the semantic Web. She has published more than 150 papers and two books on Ontological Engineering. She has been co-director of the summer school on Ontological Engineering and the Semantic Web since 2003 up to 2011. She acts as reviewers in journals and conferences related with semantic technologies.

Filippo Gramegna received the M.S. degree in information technology engineering from the Polytechnic University of Bari, Bari, Italy in 2009. He is currently a Research Assistant at the Polytechnic University of Bari, Bari, Italy. His research interests include semantic matchmaking for ubiquitous contexts, Vehicular Ad-hoc Networks and automated driving assistance. On these topics, he has coauthored papers in international journals and conferences.

Ali Hasnain is a Post Doctoral Researcher and Adjunct Lecturer at Insight Centre for Data Analytics (NUIG), (formerly: Digital Enterprise Research Institute (DERI), Galway Ireland). Before joining DERI, Hasnain completed a Master Degree in "Engineering and Management of Information Systems" from Royal Institute of Technology, KTH, Stockholm Sweden. He received another Master Degree from the same University in "Project Management and Operational Development". Along with the research activities he was been involved in Teaching and Research and Development activities at KTH as well as couple of years of industrial experience as Consultant and as Project Manager. Ali Hasnain is the Program Committee Member of different international workshops, e.g., VOILA at ISWC and conferences e.g, KESW. Moreover he has been involved in organising different workshops and tutorial e.g. at SeWeBMeDA-2017, K-Cap 2015 and SWAT4LS 2015 for international audiences. His current research interests include: Linked Open Data Big Data, Semantic Models, Data Cataloguing and Linking, Semantic Matching and Relatedness, Link Discovery, Visual Query Formulation, Data Provenance and Data Integration.

Aidan Hogan received his PhD from the National University of Ireland Galway in 2011, associated with the DERI Galway (now called INSIGHT Galway). He continued as a Postdoctoral Researcher at DERI until 2013. Currently he is an Assistant Professor in the Department of Computer Science, at the University of Chile. He is also an Associate Researcher of the Chilean Center for Semantic Web Researcher. His research interests centre on the Semantic Web and Linked Data.

Saverio Ieva received the master's degree in Information Technology Engineering from Polytechnic University of Bari in 2007. He is currently a research assistant at the Information Systems Laboratory (SisInfLab) in the same university. His research interests include pervasive computing and the Internet of Things, knowledge representation systems and applications for navigation systems. On these topics, he has co-authored papers in international journals and conferences.

Ali Shariq Imran obtained his Ph.D. from University of Oslo (UiO), Norway in Computer Science and a Masters in Software Engineering and Computing from National University of Science & Technology, Pakistan. His current research interests lie in the areas of signal processing, semantic web, eLearning, and online social network analysis. He is currently associated with the signal processing group at the department of electronic systems in NTNU as a postdoc. He is a member of IEEE, Norway section and has co-authored more than 40 peer-reviewed international journal and conference papers.

Balaji Jagan is working as a Lead Consultant in Wipro Technologies, Bangalore. His major responsibilities are building Machine Learning algorithms for various applications of Natural Language Processing. He completed his research (Ph.D) in the Department of Computer Science and Engineering, Anna University, Chennai, India, in the Semantic Interpretation. He is expertise in Information retrieval, Information Extraction, Semantic text processing, Graph based algorithms and Machine learning approaches, and published research papers in various international journals and in the conference proceedings. He has extensive research and IT experience in the area of NLP and Machine Learning.

Zenun Kastrati is currently a PhD candidate at the Faculty of Information Technology and Electrical Engineering at Norwegian University of Science and Technology, Norway. His PhD project focuses on text mining and semantic web. He did a Research Master (MSc) in Computer Science at the University of Prishtina, Kosovo. From 2009, he has been working as a teaching assistant at the Department of Computer Engineering within the Faculty of Electrical and Computer Engineering at the University of Prishtina. He has published several papers on international journals and conferences related to the semantic web.

Andrea Kő, PhD, Habil, CISA is a Professor of Corvinus University of Budapest, Department of Information Systems. She has MSc in Mathematics and Physics from Eötvös Lóránd University of Budapest, Hungary (1988), a University Doctoral degree in Computer Science (1992) from Corvinus University of Budapest, Hungary and a PhD degree in Management and Business Administration (2005) from Corvinus University of Budapest, Hungary. She participated in several international and national research projects in the areas of: intelligent systems, knowledge management; semantic technologies and e-government. She has published more than 100 papers in international scientific journals and conferences. Her research interests include knowledge management, semantic technologies; business intelligence, intelligent systems and IT audit.

Na Li got his bachelor degree from Shandong Agriculture University in 2014. At present, he is working on the master degree in North China Electric Power University. His research interests include Information integration, Data mining and Machine learning.

Shaowen Liu received the B.Eng. degree in water resources and hydropower engineering from North China Electric Power University in 2013. Since 2015, he has been a graduate student in the school of control and computer engineering, North China Electric Power University, China. His current research interests include semantic web services, information integration, etc.

Giuseppe Loseto received the master's degree in Information Technology Engineering from Polytechnic University of Bari in 2009, and the Ph.D. in Information Engineering in 2013 from the same institution. He is currently a post-doc research fellow at the Information Systems Laboratory (SisInfLab) in the same University. His research interests include pervasive computing and the Internet of Things, knowledge representation systems and applications for home and building automation and ubiquitous smart environments. On these topics, he has coauthored papers in international journals and conferences and received the best poster paper award at the ESWC-2011 Conference.

Vladimir Luna got a PhD degree in Computer Science at the National Polytechnic Institute. He is a specialist in Geographic Information Systems. His research is focused on the flow of information from its conceptualization in human minds to its implementation is computer applications. Currently he is studying the process surrounding the conceptualization, design, and instantiation of user profiling.

Ping Luo is currently an Associate Professor at Institute of Computing Technology, Chinese Academy of Sciences. Before joining ICT, he worked as Senior Research Scientist at the Hewlett-Packard Labs. His general area of research is knowledge discovery and machine learning. He has published 30+ papers in some prestigious refereed journals and conference proceedings, such as IEEE Transactions on Information Theory, IEEE Transactions on Knowledge and Data Engineering, Journal of Parallel and Distributed Computing, ACM SIGKDD, ACM CIKM, IJCAI. He is the recipient of the Doctoral Dissertation Award, China Computer Federation (2009), the ACM CIKM Best Student Paper Award (2012).

Miaomiao Ma received her MS and PhD degrees in Control Theory and Engineering from Jilin University in 2006 and 2009, respectively. In autumn 2006, she was a visiting scholar at the Institute for Systems Theory in Engineering, the University of Stuttgart, Germany. In the winter of 2007, she was again with the University of Stuttgart as a visiting scholar. In July 2009, she joined the North China Electric Power University in China. She is currently an associate professor in the School of Control and Computer Engineering. Her current research interests include model predictive control, optimal and robust control, and applications in power systems.

Bernardo Magnini is senior researcher at Fondazione Bruno Kessler (FBK), where he is responsible of the Research Unit on Natural Language Processing and scientific coordinator of the Cognitive Computing Research Line. His interests are in Computational Linguistics, particularly lexical semantics, lexical resources, question answering and textual entailment, areas where he has published more than 170 papers. He coordinated several international research projects, including QALL-ME, LIVEMEMORIES and EXCITEMENT, launched the Italian EVALITA evaluation campaign, and co-chaired CLIC-it, the first Italian conference on Computational Linguistics. He has been contract professor at the University of Trento and Bolzano and staff member and lecturer at the ICT International Doctoral School of the University of Trento. He is member of the Scientific Committee of Know Center (Graz) and of the Institute for Applied Linguistics at Eurac Research (Bolzano), president of the Italian Association for Computational Linguistics and manager of the W3C Italian Office.

Souheyl Mallat is a PhD student in Computer Sciences at the Faculty of Economics and Management of Sfax, under the guidance of Dr. Mounir Zrigui since 2011. His main research interests are in Information retrieval in multilingual context (Arabic, French, English).

Yannis Marketakis is an R&D Engineer in the Information Systems Laboratory at FORTH-ICS. His main research interests include: information systems, digital preservation, knowledge representation using semantic web technologies, linked data, data integration using semantic web technologies and conceptual modeling. He has participated in several EU projects and in more than 30 scientific publications.

Sanda Martinčić-Ipšić obtained her B.Sc. degree in Computer Science in 1994 from the University of Ljubljana Faculty of Computer Science and Informatics, and her M.Sc. degree in informatics from the University of Ljubljana, Faculty of Economy in 1999. In 2007 she obtained a Ph.D degree in Computer Science from the University of Zagreb, Faculty of Electrical Engineering and Computing. Dr. Martinčić-Ipšić currently works as an associate professor of Computer Science at the University of Rijeka, Department of Informatics. Her research interests include speech and language technologies, natural language processing, complex networks, automatic speech recognition, speech synthesis, corpora development, with a special focus on the Croatian language. She has published more than 60 scientific papers and books.

Qaiser Mehmood holds the MSc degree in computer engineering from Mid Sweden University, Sweden. He is a PhD student at Insight Centre for Data Analytics (formerly: Digital Enterpirse Research Insititute DERI), National University Of Ireland Galway Ireland. His research interests include Semantic Web, Query Federation, Data Cataloguing Linking and Path Queries.

Dora Melo is Associate Professor at Iscac - Coimbra Business School, Polytechnic Institute of Coimbra and Researcher at LISP- Laboratory of Informatics, Systems and Parallelism, Portugal. She got her Ph.D. in Computer Sciences in 2014, at University of Évora, Portugal. Her areas of interest include knowledge representation and reasoning, ontologies, linguistics, natural languages, knowledge-based systems, question-answer systems, logic programming, semantic web, object-oriented programming.

Ana Meštrović gained her B.Sc. degree in mathematics and informatics from the Faculty of Arts and Sciences, University of Rijeka in 2001. She gained an M.Sc. degree in informatics in 2005 and Ph.D degree in informatics in 2009 from the Faculty of Organization and Informatics Varaždin, University of Zagreb. Since 2001 she has been working at the Department of Informatics, University of Rijeka. Dr. Meštrović is currently an associate professor. Her research interests are in knowledge epresentation, semantic technologies, natural language processing and complex networks.

Marco Moreno-Ibarra is a full-time research professor at the Centre for Computing Research (CIC) of the Instituto Politécnico Nacional (IPN), PhD in Computer Science (2007) and member of the National Research System level 2. Former Director of the National Calculus Centre (CENAC), former Director of Systems, Informatics and Telecommunications of National Council of Research, Science and Technology (CONACYT) and former head of the Laboratory of Intelligent Processing of Geospatial Information. He has over 100 articles in journals, national and international conferences as well as being a reviewer for publications such as the International Journal of Geographical Information Science, Computers and

Geosciences and Computers in Human Behavior, among others. He teaches the courses of Foundations of Geographic Information Science and Tools for the design and implementation of GIS within the master and doctorate programs in computer science at CIC-IPN. His research areas include GIS design, automatic generalization, volunteered geographic information and geospatial semantic similarity.

Michalis Mountantonakis is a PhD candidate in the Computer Science Department of University of Crete (Greece) and is also a research assistant at the Information System Laboratory at FORTH-ICS (Greece). His main research interests include: linked data, data integration of large in number linked datasets, connectivity and semantic data management and knowledge representation using semantic web technologies. The results of his research have been published in several refereed international conferences and journals while he has been involved in several EU projects, including the FP7 project iMarine and the H2020 project BlueBRIDGE and has been participated in several scientific publications.

Minadakis Nikos is Research and Development Engineer at Foundation of Research and Technology of Hellas (FORTH). He graduate from the Computer Engineering and Informatics Department of the University of Patras and holds a Master Degree in Computer Science and Technology. He works mainly on Designing, Developing and Managing semantic information systems. He has been involved in more than 10 research European and National Projects and more than 20 research publications in scientific journals and conferences.

Vitor Beires Nogueira is Assistant Professor at the Informatics Department of University of Évora and Researcher at LISP - Laboratory of Informatics, Systems and Parallelism of Universty of Évora, Portugal. He got his Ph.D. in Informatics in 2009, at University of Évora, Portugal. His areas of interests include logic programming, semantic web, knowledge representation and ontologies.

Declan O'Sullivan's primary research focus is on developing techniques for the agile, managed and sustainable integration and publication of data/information. Given the dynamic nature and ever rising volumes of data/information that needs to be coped with, current integration solutions are increasingly found to be too static, too brittle and lacking a proper lifecycle approach. Advancing the research in both the semantic web and linked data communities, this research agenda was inspired by the nature of the problems he observed in his 13 years in industry, IONA Technologies and Broadcom Eireann – a joint venture of Ericsson and Telecom Ireland. Within the Science Foundation Ireland ADAPT Centre for Digital Content Technology, he is a principal investigator. Professor O'Sullivan's research interests also include how ethical and privacy considerations should be built into the technologies being developed by ADAPT, both in the development processes themselves but also within the technologies deployed. He leads the Ethics and Privacy group within the centre that drives and coordinates this research agenda. He is the author of over 170 peer-reviewed publications, and has received significant funding from national and European agencies as a Principal Investigator and Co-Principal Investigator.

Irene Pimenta Rodrigues is Associate Professor at the Informatics Department of University of Évora and Researcher at LISP - Laboratory of Informatics, Systems and Parallelism of Universty of Évora, Portugal. She got her Ph.D. in Computer Sciences in 1995, at Universidade Nova de Lisboa, Portugal. Her areas of interests include assembly language programming, Prolog, data structures, text mining and advanced machine learning.

Agnese Pinto received the M.S. degree in Management Engineering and Ph.D. degree in Electrical and Information Engineering from the Polytechnic University of Bari, Bari, Italy, in 2004 and 2015, respectively. She is currently a Postdoctoral Research Fellow with the same institution. Research activity of Agnese Pinto started in 2004 soon after graduation. Her research interests include Description Logics, semantic matchmaking, ubiquitous knowledge management and storage, machine learning for data mining in pervasive environments. She coauthored papers about her research interests in international journals and conferences.

María Poveda-Villalón is a postdoctoral researcher at Ontology Engineering Group of the Universidad Politécnica de Madrid. Her research activities focus on Ontological Engineering, Ontology Evaluation, Knowledge Representation and the Semantic Web. Previously she finished her studies in Computer Science (2009) by Universidad Politécnica de Madrid, and then she moved to study the Artificial Intelligence Research Master finished in 2010 in the same university. She has collaborated during research stays with Mondeca (París, France) in 2013, the Free University of Berlin in 2012 and the University of Liverpool in 2011. She has worked in the context of Spanish research projects as well as in European projects. She has attended international conferences and co-organized the "4th Linked Data in Architecture and Construction Workshop (LDAC2016)", the "13th OWL: Experiences and Directions Workshop and 5th OWL reasoner evaluation workshop" and the "Linked Energy Data Vocamp".

Rolando Quintero was born in Mexico City in 1975, he obtained a Ph.D. in Computer Science from the National Polytechnic Institute of Mexico. He is a researcher at the Center for Computing Research of the IPN. Author of more than 100 scientific papers in conferences and journals. He is a member of the National System of Researchers, SNI Level 1, from the Mexican Council of Science and Technology (CONACyT). He has conducted basic research projects and technological development with national institutions. He has directed about twenty graduate thesis in his areas of interest that include knowledge representation and processing of semantic information.

Marco Rospocher is a tenured research scientist at Fondazione Bruno Kessler (FBK), within the Data and Knowledge Management (DKM) research unit. He received his PhD in Information and Communication Technologies from the University of Trento in 2006. His current research interests are in the area of Semantic Web and Knowledge Representation, focusing in particular on ontologies, formalisms for Knowledge Representation and Reasoning, and methodologies and tools for Knowledge Acquisition and Information Extraction. He has been involved in a number of international research projects, including the EU-funded projects APOSDLE (FP6), PESCaDO (FP7), and NewsReader (FP7). He coauthored more than 70 scientific publications in international journals, conferences and workshops. He usually serves in the programme committees of relevant international conferences and workshops, and regularly reviews submissions for top-ranked international journals. He co-chaired the Cognitive Computing track at ACM SAC 2017 and the Posters and Demos track at ISWC 2014. He regularly supervises Master and Ph.D. students.

Michele Ruta received the master's degree in Electronics Engineering from the Polytechnic University of Bari in 2002 and the Ph.D. in Computer Science from the same university in 2007. He is currently associate professor at Polytechnic University of Bari and local representative of the Smart City lab federation of the Italian University Consortium for Information Technology. Michele Ruta's research interests include pervasive computing and ubiquitous web, mobile e-commerce applications, knowledge representation systems and applications for wireless ad-hoc contexts. On these topics, he has co-authored more than 100 papers in international journals and conferences. He is involved in various research projects and has been Program Committee member of several international conferences and workshops in areas related to his research interest. He co-authored papers that received the best paper award at the ICEC-2007 and SEMAPRO-2010 Conferences.

Syeda Sana E Zainab is a Research Assistant at the Insight Centre for Data Analytics, National University of Ireland, Galway. In 2010, she was awarded a Bachelors in Software Engineering from one of the most prestigious Engineering University in Pakistan (University of Engineering and Technology). Syeda started her research at the National University of Ireland in 2014 and completed her Master of Applied Science in 2016. In her research, she investigated the use of semantic web and related technologies for Datasets Integration, Query Federation and Software/Application development for Data Visualization. She was also involved in cataloging and linking of Datasets.

Floriano Scioscia received the master's degree in Information Technology Engineering from Polytechnic University of Bari in 2006, and the Ph.D. in Information Engineering in 2010 from the same institution. He is currently a post-doc research fellow at the Information Systems Laboratory (SisInfLab) in the same University. His research interests include knowledge representation systems and applications for pervasive computing and the Internet of Things. He co-authored about 70 papers in international journals, edited books and conferences and received the best paper award at the ICEC-2007 and SEMAPRO-2010 Conferences.

Luciano Serafini is an experienced researcher in knowledge representation and reasoning, semantic web, statistical relational learning and ontologies. Since 1989 he worked as a researcher at the Fondazione Bruno Kessler, leading the data and knowledge management research unit since 2007. Hi is the main inventor a logic called multi-context systems and a logic based ontology matching algorithms. In the last years he is interested in studying approaches for integrating logical reasoning and machine learning. He teaches at University of Trento and Bolzano courses in database and knowledge representation and reasoning; he regularly supervises Ms. and PhD students; he served as a PC member in the main conferences in Artificial Intelligence, Ontologies, and Semantic Web; he organizes main scientific events, He contributed to many industrial and research projects.

Wei Shen received the BS degree from Beihang University, China, in 2009 and the PhD degree in computer science from Tsinghua University, China, in 2014. He is an assistant professor in the College of Computer and Control Engineering, Nankai University, China. His research interests include entity linking, knowledge base population, and text mining. He is a recipient of the Google PhD fellowship.

Mari Carmen Suárez-Figueroa, PhD, is a lecturer at the Escuela Técnica Superior de Ingenieros Informáticos, Universidad Politécnica de Madrid (UPM) and a senior researcher at the Ontology Engineering Group. She graduated in Computer Science in 2001 and got the PhD in Artificial Intelligence in 2010. She has received an Outstanding Award granted by the UPM PhD Commission. Her research lines include ontology development methodologies, ontology development in different domains, ontology evaluation, ontology design patterns, and linked data. In these areas, she has participated in several

European and Spanish projects. She has been research visitor at University of Liverpool in 2004, at KMi (Open University) in 2007, and at IRIT (Toulouse) in 2012. She is co-editor of the book "Ontology Engineering in a Networked World" (Springer 2012). She co-organized sessions, conferences, workshops, and tutorials in international events such as EKAW 2016, ESWC 2014, TKE 2012, ISWC 2012, EKAW 2012, EKAW 2008, ESWC 2008, and WWW 2006.

Yannis Tzitzikas is Associate Professor of Information Systems in the Computer Science Dep. at University of Crete and Affiliated Researcher of the Information Systems Laboratory at FORTH-ICS (Greece). He has published more than 100 papers in refereed international conferences and journals, including prestigious journals and venues (e.g., ACM Transactions on the Web, VLDB Journal, IEEE Transactions on Knowledge and Data Engineering, JIIS, JDAPD, ISWC), and he has received two best paper awards.

Brian Walshe was awarded a PhD for his thesis "Detecting Restriction Class Correspondences in Linked Open Data" from University of Dublin, Trinity College in 2014.

Jianyong Wang is currently a professor in the Department of Computer Science and Technology, Tsinghua University, Beijing, China. He received his PhD degree in Computer Science in 1999 from the Institute of Computing Technology, Chinese Academy of Sciences. He was an assistant professor at Peking University, and visited Simon Fraser University, University of Illinois at Urbana-Champaign, and University of Minnesota at Twin Cities before joining Tsinghua University in December 2004. His research interests mainly include data mining and Web information management. He has co-authored over 60 papers in some leading international conferences and some top international journals. He is serving or ever served as a PC member for some leading international conferences, such as SIGKDD, VLDB, ICDE, WWW, and an associate editor of IEEE TKDE and ACM TKDD. He is a Fellow of the IEEE, a member of the ACM.

Min Wang joined Visa as the Senior Vice President and head of Visa Research in May 2015. In her role, Wang leads the research on data analytics, security and the future of payments. Prior to Visa, Wang was part of Google Research where she was a Senior Staff Research Scientist and research manager focused on knowledge integration and inferencing at Google's headquarters in Mountain View, California. Before Google, Wang was Director of HP Labs China in Beijing, China, where she was also named an HP Distinguished Technologist. Wang also held a senior research role as the manager of the Unified Data Analytics Department at IBM's Thomas J. Watson Research Center in Hawthorne, New York. Wang has received several distinguished research awards for her work on data management. In 2009, Wang received the ACM SIGMOD Test of Time Award for her 1999 SIGMOD paper, "Approximate Computation of Multidimensional Aggregates of Sparse Data Using Wavelets." Wang received her PhD in Computer Science from Duke University and BS and MS degrees, both in Computer Science, from Tsinghua University, Beijing, China.

Zhuxiao Wang got his Ph.D. degree from the Institute of Computing Technology, the Chinese Academy of Sciences in 2010. Since 2010, he has been a faculty member in the School of Control and Computer Engineering, North China Electric Power University, China. His current research interests include knowledge representation and reasoning, self-healing systems, distributed computing. He is a member of Chinese Society for Electrical Engineering.

Sule Yildirim-Yayilgan worked as the head of the computer science department between 2006 and 2009 at Hedmark University College (HIHM) and at Gjøvik University College (GUC) between 2009 and 2015 before her current position at NTNU. She has recently been coordinating a project funded by the Ministry of Foreign Affairs, Norway. She has been participating in projects funded by the Research Council of Norway, Regional Research Council of Norway and the EU Eurostars Programme. She belongs to the Norwegian Information Laboratory, Center for Cyber Information Security and the Norwegian Biometrics Laboratory. Her main fields of interests are artificial intelligence, application of machine learning in various fields, biometrics, and image processing. She has been supervising tens of students in computer science, and currently supervises three PhD students and several postdocs, and acts as PC member in conferences of her research fields.

Ying Zhang received the B.Eng. degree in computer science from Beijing Jiaotong University, China, in 2004, and the PhD degree in computer science technology from Beijing Jiaotong University, China, in July 2009.She has been an associate professor at the North China Electric Power University. Her research interests include semantic web services, geospatial data integration, distributed service discovery and distributed computing.

Index

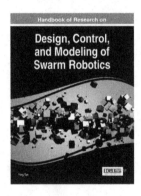

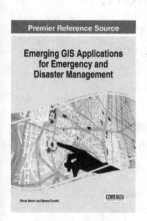

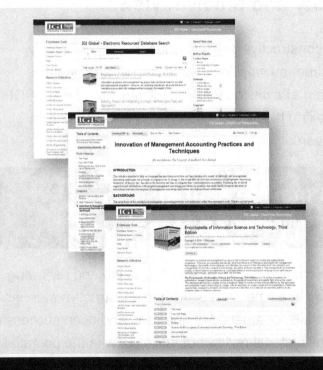

Information Resources Management Association

Advancing the Concepts & Practices of Information Resources
Management in Modern Organizations

Become an IRMA Member

Members of the **Information Resources Management Association (IRMA)** understand the importance of community within their field of study. The Information Resources Management Association is an ideal venue through which professionals, students, and academicians can convene and share the latest industry innovations and scholarly research that is changing the field of information science and technology. Become a member today and enjoy the benefits of membership as well as the opportunity to collaborate and network with fellow experts in the field.

IRMA Membership Benefits:

- **One FREE Journal Subscription**

- **30% Off Additional Journal Subscriptions**

- **20% Off Book Purchases**

- Updates on the latest events and research on Information Resources Management through the IRMA-L listserv.

- Updates on new open access and downloadable content added to Research IRM.

- A copy of the Information Technology Management Newsletter twice a year.

- A certificate of membership.

IRMA Membership $195

Scan code or visit **irma-international.org** and begin by selecting your free journal subscription.

Membership is good for one full year.

www.irma-international.org

Printed in the United States
By Bookmasters